MW01502961

Not For Tourists™ Guide to **CHICAGO**

2006

Not For Tourists Inc

published and designed by
Not For Tourists Inc
NFT™- Not For Tourists™- Guide to CHICAGO 2006
www.notfortourists.com

Publisher & Editor
Jane Pirone

Information Design
Jane Pirone
Rob Tallia
Scot Covey
Diana Pizzari

Managing Editors
Rob Tallia
Diana Pizzari

City Editor
Kathie Bergquist

Writing and Editing
Kathie Bergquist
Cathleen Cueto
Annie Karni
Diana Pizzari
Rob Tallia

Research
Ben Bray
Naomi Hanson
Katie Lewis

Research Interns
Niki Shelley

Database Design
Scot Covey

Graphic Design/Production
Ran Lee
Christopher Salyers

Graphic Design/Production Intern
Juri Imamura

Sales and Marketing
Alli Hirschman
Annie Holt
Iya C. Perry

Contributors-Chicago
Caren Beilin
Craig Berman
Robert Biedrzycki
Lisa Boyle
Ira Brooker
David R. Chapa
Jeff Fleischer
Richard Fox
Darwyn Jones
David Kodeski
Dana Kaye Litoff
Jeff Moyers
JT Newman
Marie-Jo Proulx
Jeffery T. Ramone
Taryn Rejholic
Tiffany Roget
Felicia Swanson
Patty Templeton
Katharine Whisler

All rights reserved. No portion of this book may be reproduced without written permission from the publisher.

Printed in China
ISBN# 0-9758664-9-4 $16.95
Copyright © 2005 by Not For Tourists, Inc.

Every effort has been made to ensure that the information in this book is as up-to-date as possible at press time. However, many details are liable to change—as we have learned. The publishers cannot accept responsibility for any consequences arising from use of this book.

Not For Tourists does not solicit individuals, organizations, or businesses for listings inclusion in our guides, nor do we accept payment for inclusion into the editorial portion of our book; the advertising sections, however, are exempt from this policy. We always welcome communications from anyone regarding ANYTHING having to do with our books; please visit us on our website at www.notfortourists.com for appropriate contact information.

Dear NFT User,

The lakefront, the skyscrapers, the Cubs and The Sox and (who woulda thunk it) The Bulls, The Southside St. Patty's Day Parade, Oprah Winfrey, Roger Ebert, Steppenwolf and Second City, The Mag Mile, The U of C, The Kennedy Expressway and O'Hare... Aldermen and silver shovels, Trump Hotel and Casino, Pilsen Murals, the giant Jellybean and Gehry Bandshell, Trucks for Hire, The "L", Da Mare, Bud Billiken, Von Freeman and The New Apartment Lounge, Charlie Trotter and Superdawg and Thillens Field... Wind chill factors and record highs, Jesse Jackson, Studs Terkel, V.I. Warshawsky, and Dorothy Tillman's hats. Whether you think it's the City That Works, or the City That Works Your Nerves, these are the things that make Chicago the great, vibrant, boisterous, smelly, entirely American city that it is—and that is why we love it.

If this is your first time using the NFT Chicago guide, we are sure you will find it practical, enlightening, and entertaining, whether you're new to Chicago, a frequent business traveler, interested in exploring new neighborhoods, or taking a closer look at your own.

Whether you need a 24-hour plumber, a bite to eat in Jefferson Park, directions to a lecture at U of C, or help navigating Chicago's independent theater scene, NFT Chicago is the only resource you need.

If you're already a devoted NFT fan, we hope you'll be pleased with this newly revised edition. Besides the excellent neighborhood-by-neighborhood coverage, and the practical and general information you've come to rely on from NFT, we've also added new sections on **Six Flags Great America**, the **Chicago Botanic Gardens and Ravinia Festival**, and the **Brookfield Zoo**. We've also revamped the nightlife section and enlisted more neighborhood contributors than ever before to make NFT Chicago as thorough and up-to-date as humanly possible.

And of course, we rely on your input as well. If you see room for improvement, know of any essential places that we somehow missed, or you just want to say howdy and keep up the good work, we encourage you to log on to our website, **www.notfortourists.com**, and tell us what's on your mind.

Cordially Yours,
Kathie, Jane, Rob, and Diana

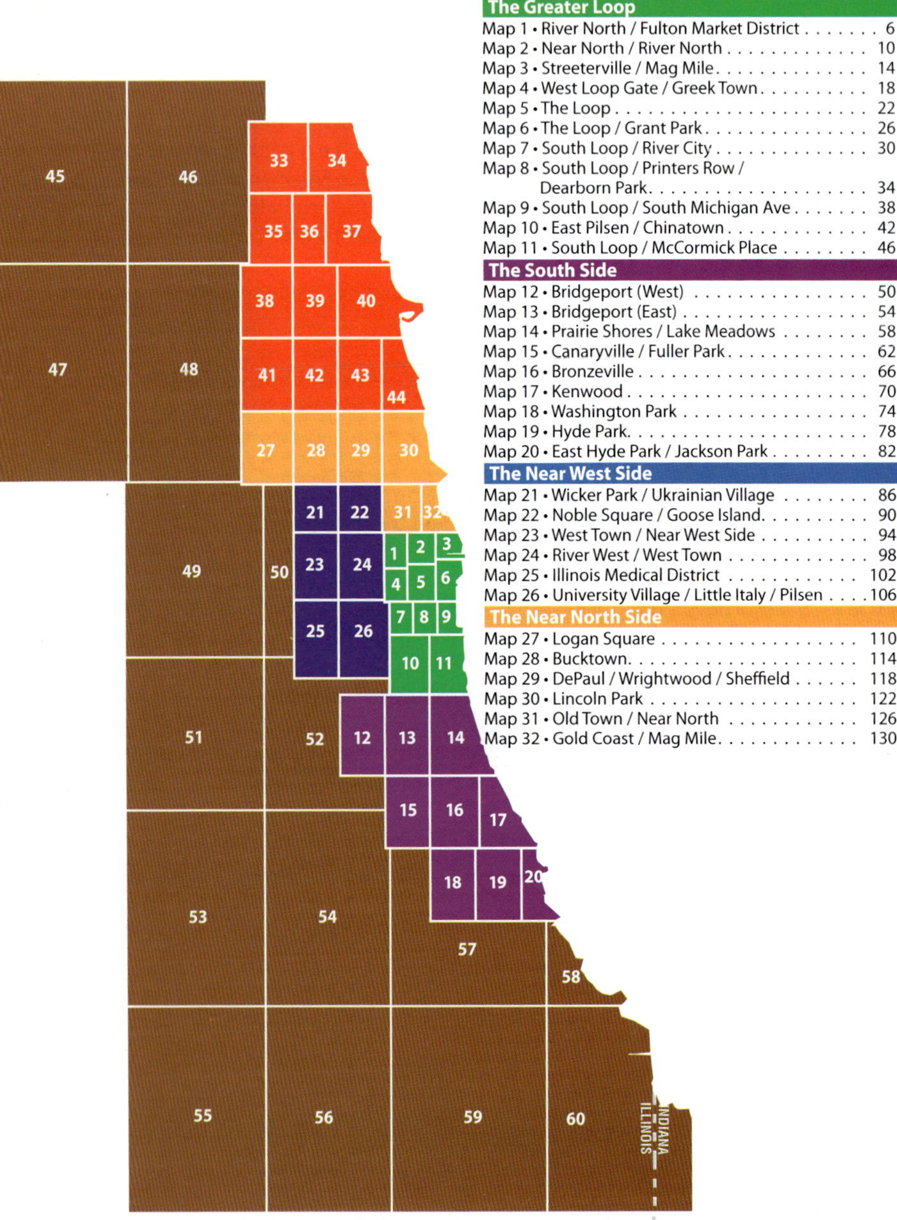

Chicago Neighborhoods

The Greater Loop

The South Side

The Near West Side

The Near North Side

The North Side

Greater Chicago

Parks & Places

Colleges & Universities

Sports

Transit

General Information

Arts & Entertainment

Map 1 • River North / Fulton Market District

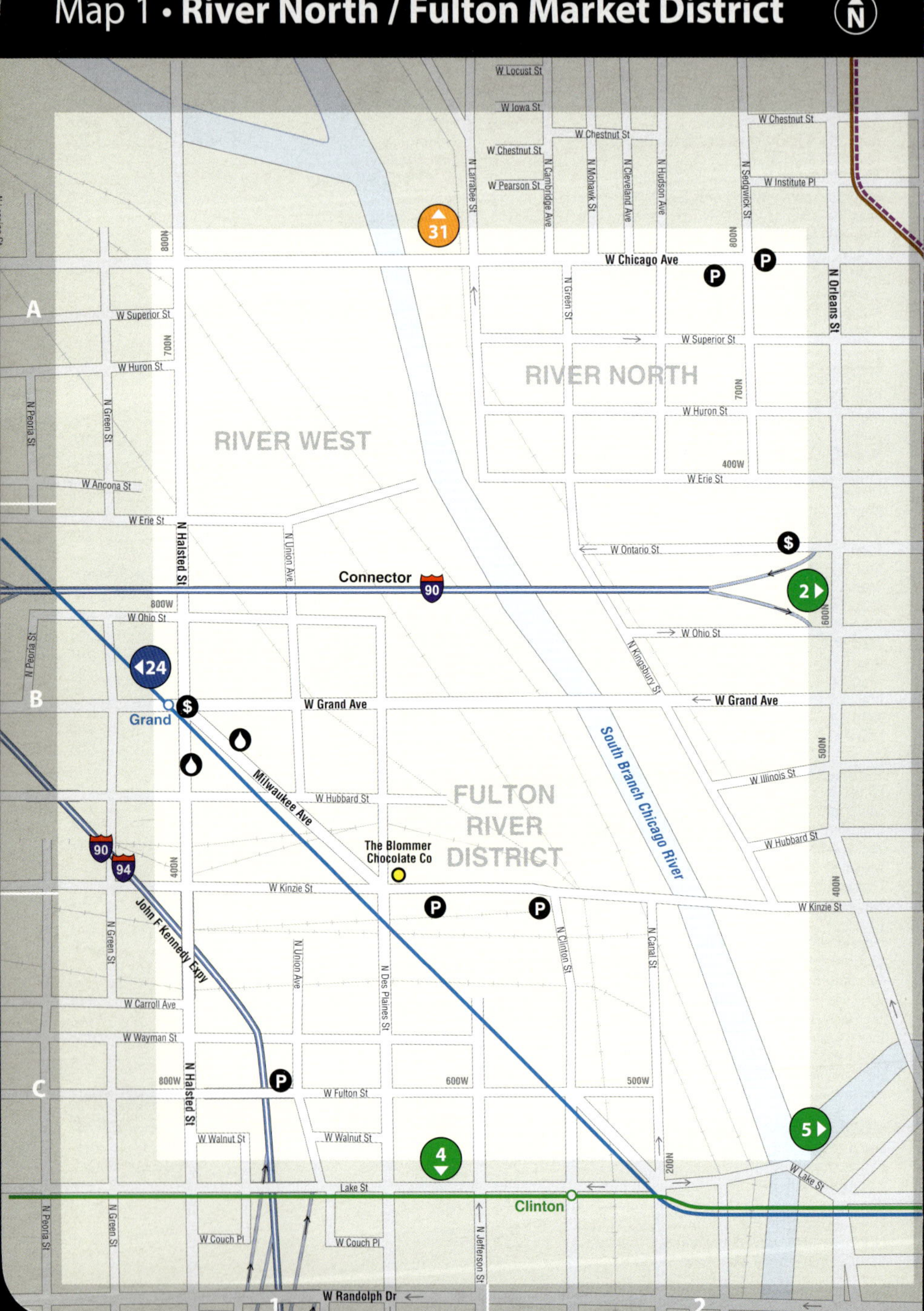

Essentials

Crisscrossed by rail tracks, I-90/94, and the Chicago River, this area is transitioning from industrial to residential as the loft conversion craze in River North, Greek Town, and West Loop Gate expands. The Blommer Chocolate Company pumps sweet, chocolate-coated air into the streets all day. Diabetics, beware.

Banks

- **New Century** • 363 W Ontario St
- **Washington Mutual** • 501 N Milwaukee Ave

Car Washes

- **River West Hand Car Wash** • 478 N Milwaukee Ave
- **We Wash III** • 452 N Halsted St

Landmarks

- **The Blommer Chocolate Co** • 600 W Kinzie St

Parking

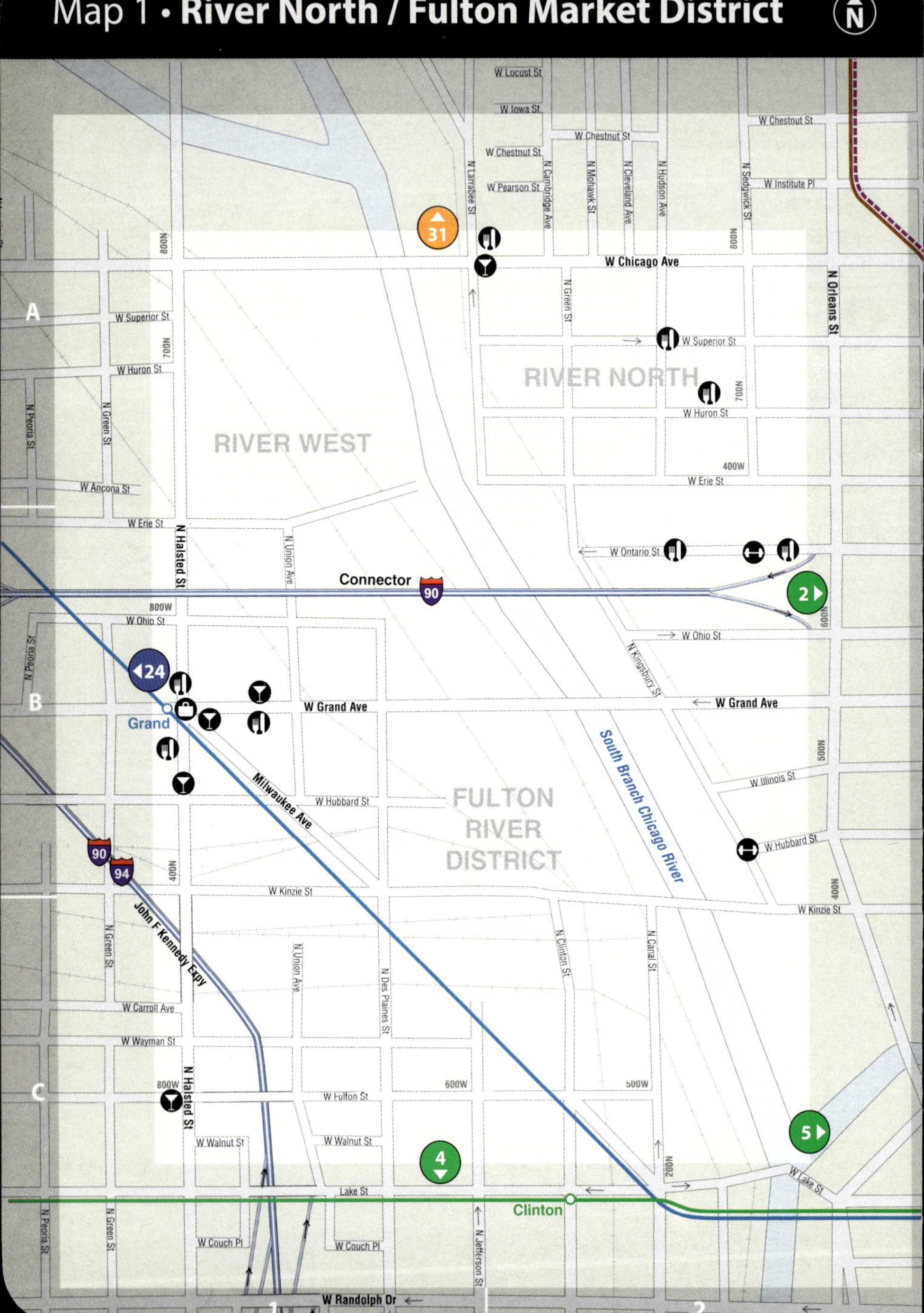
Map 1 • River North / Fulton Market District
N
RIVER NORTH
RIVER WEST
FULTON RIVER DISTRICT
South Branch Chicago River
W Locust St
W Iowa St
W Chestnut St
W Pearson St
W Institute Pl
W Chicago Ave
W Superior St
W Huron St
W Ancona St
W Erie St
W Ontario St
Connector
90
W Ohio St
W Grand Ave
Grand
W Illinois St
W Hubbard St
Milwaukee Ave
W Kinzie St
94
John F Kennedy Expy
W Carroll Ave
W Wayman St
W Fulton St
W Walnut St
Lake St
W Lake St
Clinton
W Couch Pl
W Randolph Dr
N Larrabee St
N Cambridge Ave
N Mohawk St
N Cleveland Ave
N Hudson Ave
N Sedgwick St
N Orleans St
N Green St
N Peoria St
N Halsted St
N Union Ave
N Kingsbury St
N Clinton St
N Canal St
N Des Plaines St
N Jefferson St
800N
700N
600N
500N
400N
200N
800W
600W
500W
400W
31
24
2
4
5
A
B
C
1
2

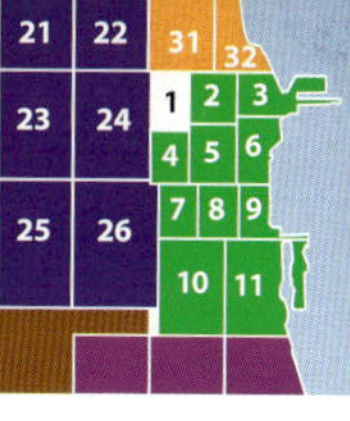

Funky Buddha Lounge and Motel are the bars to scout out Mr. or Ms. Right (or Mr. or Ms. Right NOW). Have beer and burgers with your buddies at Emmit's. French-Japanese fusion restaurant Japonais is one of a handful of trendy concept restaurants pumping new blood into the Chicago restaurant scene.

Gyms

- **East Bank Club** • 500 N Kingsbury St
- **Sharper Fitness** • 401 W Ontario St

Nightlife

- **Emmit's Irish Pub & Eatery** • 495 N Milwaukee Ave
- **Funky Buddha Lounge** • 728 W Grand Ave
- **Motel** • 600 W Chicago Ave
- **Rednofive & Fifth Floor** • 440 N Halsted St
- **Rive Gauche** • 306 N Halsted St

Restaurants

- **Chilpancingo** • 358 W Ontario St
- **Iguana Café** • 517 N Halsted St
- **Japonais** • 600 W Chicago Ave
- **La Scarola** • 721 W Grand Ave
- **Reza's** • 432 W Ontario St
- **Scoozi!** • 410 W Huron St
- **Thyme** • 464 N Halsted St
- **Zealous** • 419 W Superior St

Shopping

- **Doolin's** • 511 N Halsted St

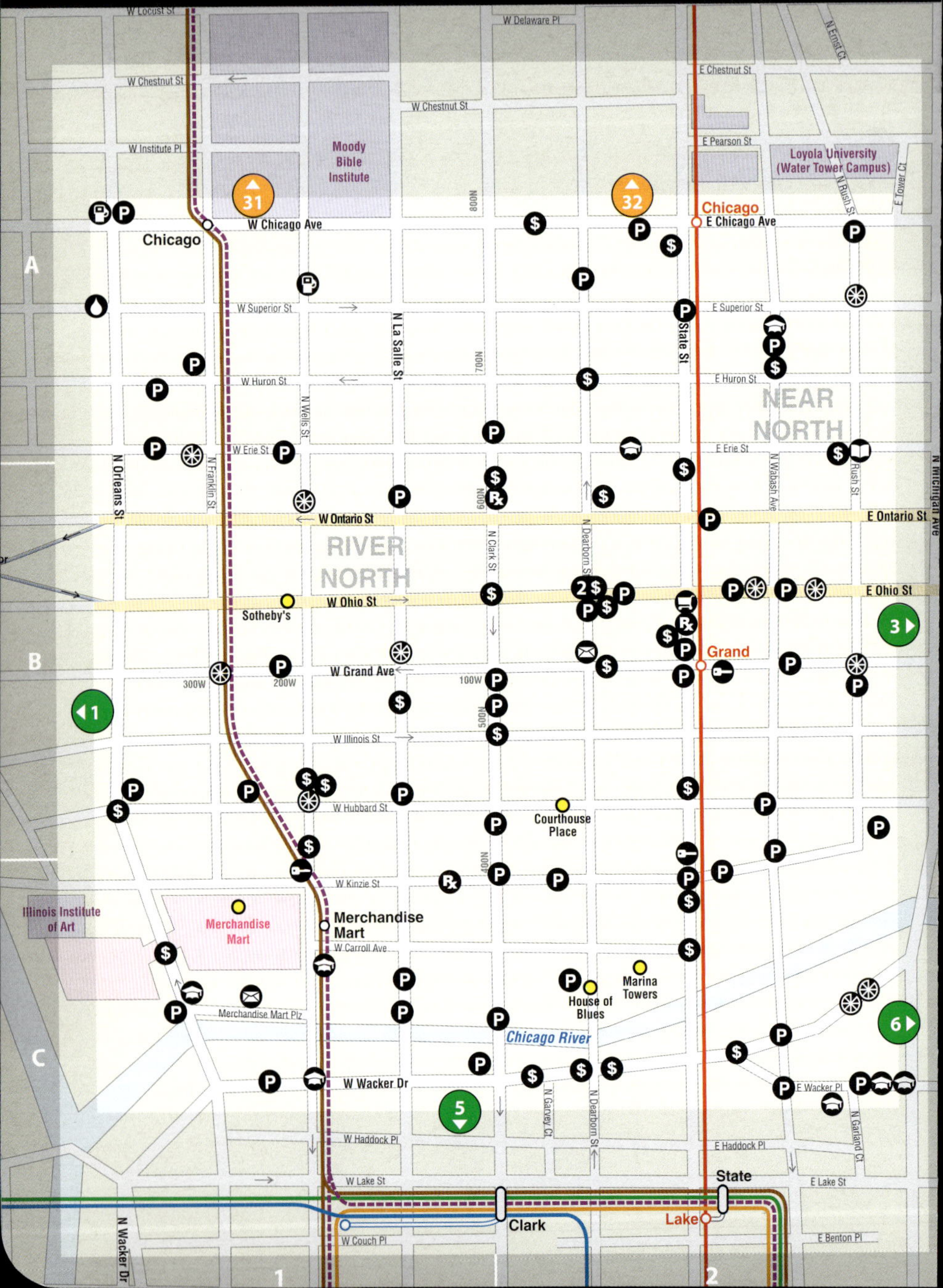

Map 2 • Near North / River North

Essentials

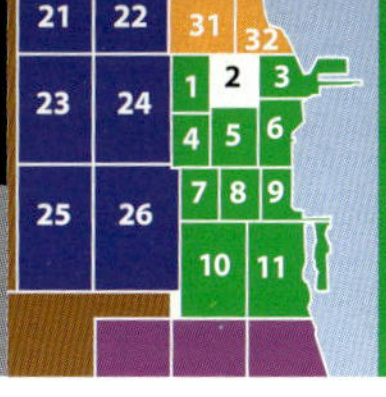

This trendy neighborhood has gone from abandoned warehouse district to artists' haven to tourist mecca. But thankfully, established eateries, comfy bars, independent shopkeepers, and historic architecture hold their ground in making this neighborhood a pulsating place to live. The graceful, old Courthouse Place is where some of Chicago's infamous criminals were tried. Service at the post office on Dearborn Street stinks—go to the UPS Store on Wells Street to get stamps.

Banks

- **Bank of America** • 601 N Dearborn St
- **Bank of America (ATM)** • 444 N Wells St
- **Bank of America (ATM)** • 601 N Dearborn St
- **Bank One** • 340 N State St
- **Bank One** • 35 W Wacker Dr
- **Bank One** • 71 W Chicago Ave
- **Bank One (ATM)** • 101 E Erie St
- **Bank One (ATM)** • 641 N Clark St
- **Charter One** • 33 W Grand Ave
- **Charter One (ATM)** • 35 E Wacker Dr
- **Charter One (ATM)** • 451 N State St
- **Charter One (ATM)** • 645 N State St
- **Citibank** • 600 N Clark St
- **Fifth Third** • 350 Orleans St
- **Fifth Third** • 401 N Wells St
- **Fifth Third** • 431 N Wells St
- **Harris Trust & Savings** • 33 W Ohio St
- **Lakeside** • 55 W Wacker Dr
- **LaSalle** • 515 N La Salle St
- **MB Financial** • 1 E Wacker Dr
- **North** • 501 N Clark St
- **North Community** • 448 N Wells St
- **North Community** • 800 N State St
- **Oak Brook** • 33 W Huron St
- **TCF** • 635 N Dearborn St
- **TCF (ATM)** • 550 N State St
- **Washington Mutual** • 431 N Orleans St
- **Washington Mutual** • 710 N Wabash Ave

Car Rental

- **Enterprise** • 10 E Grand Ave • 312-670-7270
- **Enterprise** • 401 N Wells St • 312-494-3434
- **Hertz** • 401 N State St • 312-372-7600

Car Washes

- **River North Hand Car Wash** • 356 W Superior St

Gas Stations

- **Citgo** • 750 N Wells St
- **Shell** • 350 W Chicago Ave

Landmarks

- **Courthouse Place** • 54 W Hubbard St
- **House of Blues** • 329 N Dearborn St
- **Marina Towers** • 300 N State St
- **Merchandise Mart** • 222 Merchandise Mart Plz
- **Sotheby's** • 215 W Ohio St

Parking

Pharmacies

- **CVS Pharmacy** • 121 W Kinzie St
- **Jewel-Osco** • 550 N State St
- **Walgreens (24 hours)** • 641 N Clark St

Pizza

- **Bacino's** • 75 E Wacker Dr
- **Buca Di Beppo** • 521 N Rush St
- **California Pizza Kitchen** • 52 E Ohio St
- **Gino's East of Chicago** • 633 N Wells St
- **Giordano's** • 730 N Rush St
- **Jay's** • 343 W Erie St
- **Leona's** • 646 N Franklin St
- **Lou Malnati's Pizzeria** • 439 N Wells St
- **Pizzeria Due** • 619 N Wabash Ave
- **Pizzeria Ora** • 545 N La Salle Dr
- **Pizzeria Uno** • 29 E Ohio St
- **Rizzata's Pizzeria** • 300 W Grand Ave
- **Sbarro** • 222 Merchandise Mart Plz

Post Offices

- 222 Merchandise Mart Plz
- 540 N Dearborn St

Schools

- **Adler School of Professional Psychology** • 65 E Wacker Pl
- **Associated Colleges of the Midwest** • 205 W Wacker Dr
- **Chicago School of Professional Psychology** • 325 N Wells St
- **Feltre** • 22 W Erie St
- **Frances Xavier Ward Middle** • 730 N Wabash Ave
- **Illinois Institute of Art** • 350 N Orleans St
- **Institute for Clinical Social Work** • 180 N Michigan Ave

Supermarkets

- **Jewel-Osco** • 550 N State St
- **Whole Foods Market** • 30 W Huron St

Map 2 • Near North / River North

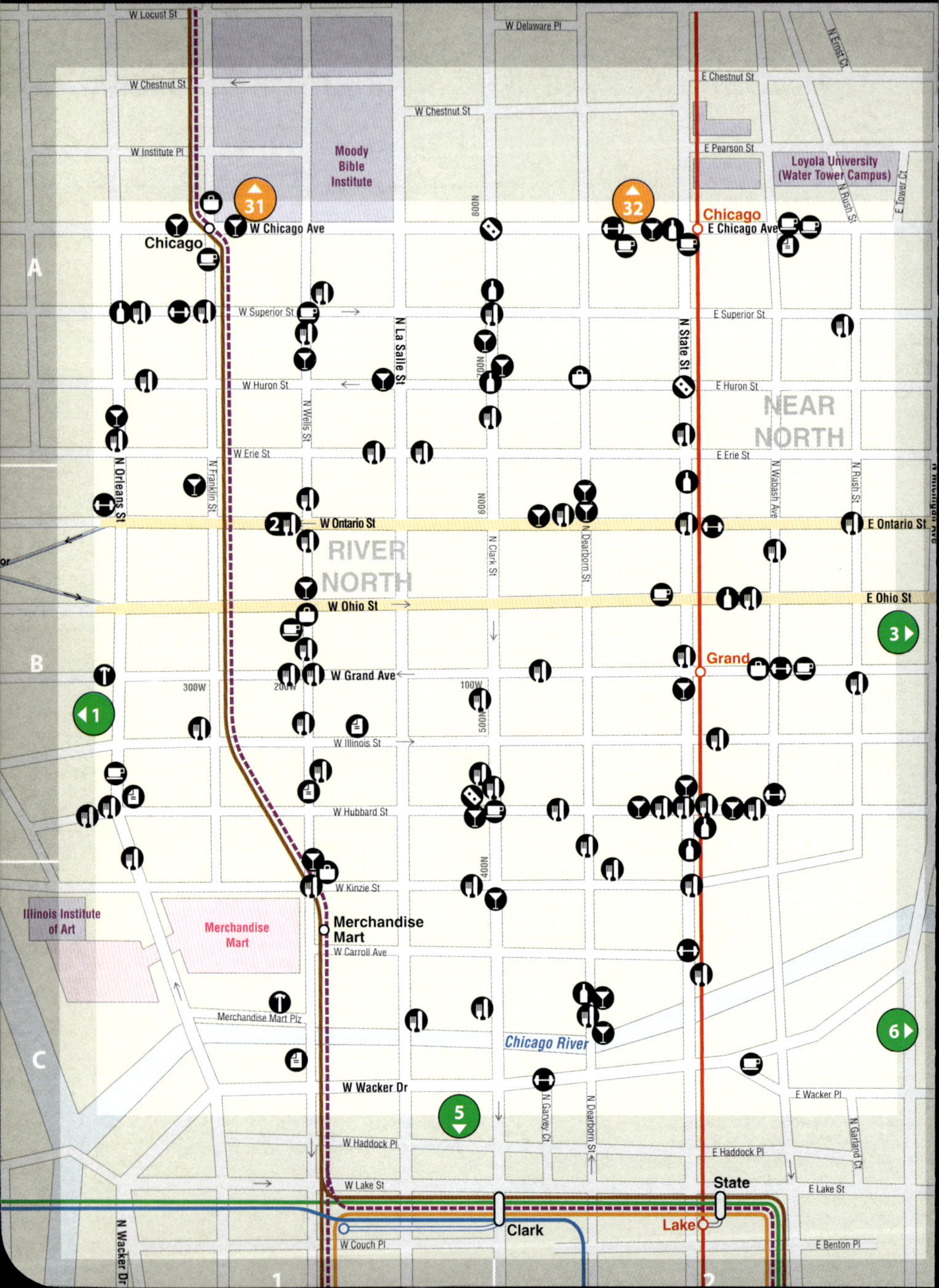

Sundries / Entertainment

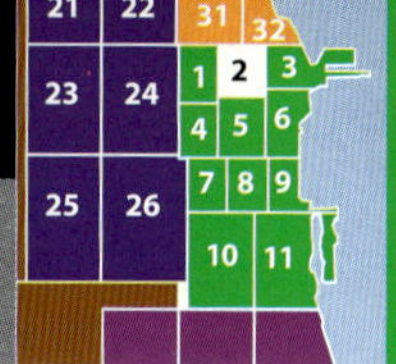

No problem to find places to eat in this 'hood, as long as you have a generous expense account. Narcisse serves up luxury food for luxurious prices. Sugar specializes in sweet things. Those of us on a more limited budget take advantage of the free booze usually available on the Friday night gallery openings. Redhead Piano Bar offers retro swigs to young swingers. Buy the music you heard at the Jazz Record Mart.

Bars

- **Bar Louie** • 226 W Chicago Ave

Coffee

- **Cosi** • 55 E Grand Ave
- **Dunkin' Donuts** • 20 E Chicago Ave
- **Dunkin' Donuts** • 800 N State St
- **Dunkin' Donuts** • Merchandise Mart Plz
- **Ohio House Coffee Shop** • 600 N La Salle Dr
- **Seattle's Best** • 42 E Chicago Ave
- **Starbucks** • 35 E Wacker Dr
- **Starbucks** • 414 N Orleans St
- **Starbucks** • 42 E Chicago Ave
- **Starbucks** • 430 N Clark St
- **Starbucks** • 470 Merchandise Mart Plz
- **Starbucks** • 750 N Franklin St
- **Starbucks (Embassy Suites)** • 600 N State St

Copy Shops

- **Kinko's (24 hours)** • 444 N Wells St
- **Sir Speedy (8 am-5:30)** • 18 W Hubbard St
- **The UPS Store (9 am-6 pm)** • 446 N Wells St
- **The UPS Store (9 am-7 pm)** • 40 E Chicago Ave

Gyms

- **Crunch Fitness** • 350 N State St
- **Crunch Fitness** • 38 E Grand Ave
- **Executive Sports & Fitness Center** • 77 W Wacker Dr
- **Lakeshore Athletic Club** • 441 N Wabash Ave
- **Lawson YMCA** • 30 W Chicago Ave
- **Life Start** • 10 E Ontario St

Hardware Stores

- **Clark & Barlow Hardware** • 353 W Grand Ave
- **Katonah Architectural Hardware** • 222 Merchandise Mart Plz

Liquor Stores

- **Ben'z Liquors** • 15 E Ohio St
- **Bin 36** • 339 N Dearborn St
- **Binny's Beverage Depot** • 213 W Grand Ave
- **Copperfield's** • 70 W Huron St
- **Dalal Food & Liquor** • 414 N State St
- **Galleria Market** • 340 W Superior St
- **Holiday Wines & Spirits** • 6 W Chicago Ave
- **Marina Food & Liquor** • 300 N State St
- **Rossi's Liquors** • 412 N State St
- **Superior Liquor** • 750 N Clark St
- **White Hen Pantry** • 645 N State St

Nightlife

- **Andy's** • 11 E Hubbard St
- **Bin 36** • 339 N Dearborn St
- **Blue Chicago** • 736 N Clark St
- **Blue Frog Bar & Grill** • 676 N La Salle Dr
- **Brehon Pub** • 731 N Wells St
- **Cyrano's Bistrot & Wine Bar** • 546 N Wells St
- **Excalibur** • 632 N Dearborn St
- **Frankie's Blue Room** • 16 W Chicago Ave
- **Gentry** • 440 N State St
- **Green Door Tavern** • 678 N Orleans St
- **House of Blues** • 329 N Dearborn St
- **Howl at the Moon** • 26 W Hubbard St
- **Martini Ranch** • 311 W Chicago Ave
- **Minx** • 111 W Hubbard St
- **Mother Hubbard's** • 5 W Hubbard St
- **Narcisse** • 710 N Clark St
- **Redhead Piano Bar** • 16 W Ontario St
- **Rock Bottom Restaurants & Brewery** • 1 W Grand Ave
- **Spy Bar** • 646 N Franklin St
- **Uncommon Ground Café** • 388 N Clark St
- **Vision** • 640 N Dearborn St

Restaurants

- **1492 Tapas Bar** • 42 E Superior St
- **Allen's New American Café** •' 217 W Huron St
- **Avenues** • 108 E Superior St
- **Ben Pao** • 52 W Illinois St
- **Bijan's Bistro** • 663 N State St
- **Bin 36** • 339 N Dearborn St
- **Bob Chinn's Crab House** • 315 N La Salle Dr
- **Brasserie Jo** • 59 W Hubbard St
- **Brett's Kitchen** • 233 W Superior St
- **Café Iberico** • 739 N La Salle Blvd
- **Carson's Ribs** • 612 N Wells St
- **Cerise** • Le Meridien Hotel, 521 N Rush St
- **Chicago Chop House** • 60 W Ontario St
- **Club Lago** • 331 W Superior St
- **Coco Pazzo** • 300 W Hubbard St
- **Crofton on Wells** • 535 Wells St
- **Cyrano's Bistrot & Wine Bar** • 546 N Wells St
- **Fogo De Chao** • 661 N La Salle St
- **Frontera Grill** • 445 N Clark St
- **Gaylord India** • 678 N Clark St
- **Gene & Georgetti** • 500 N Franklin St
- **Harray Caray's** • 33 W Kinzie St
- **House of Blues** • 329 N Dearborn St
- **Joe's Seafood, Prime Steak & Stone Crab** • 60 E Grand Ave
- **Karyn's Cooked** • 738 N Wells
- **Keefer's** • 20 W Kinzie St
- **Kevin** • 9 W Hubbard St
- **Kinzie Chophouse** • 400 N Wells St
- **Klay Oven** • 414 N Orleans St
- **L8** • 222 W Ontario
- **Lawry's The Prime Rib** • 100 E Ontario St
- **Linos** • 222 W Ontario St
- **Lou Malnati's Pizzeria** • 439 N Wells St
- **Maggiano's Little Italy** • 516 N Clark St
- **Mr Beef** • 666 N Orleans St
- **Nacional 27** • 325 W Huron St
- **Naha** • 500 N Clark St
- **Narcisse** • 710 N Clark St
- **Original Gino's East** • 633 N Wells St
- **Osteria Via Stato** • 620 N State
- **Pizzeria Due** • 619 N Wabash Ave
- **Pizzeria Uno** • 29 E Ohio St
- **Redfish** • 400 N State St
- **Rosebud on Rush** • 720 N Rush St
- **Roy's** • 720 N State St
- **Rumba** • 351 W Hubbard St
- **Ruth's Chris Steak House** • 431 N Dearborn St
- **Shanghai Terrace** • Peninsula Hotel, 108 E Superior St
- **Shaw's Crab House & Blue Crab Lounge** • 21 E Hubbard St
- **Smith & Wollensky** • 318 N State St
- **Sorriso** • 321 N Clark St
- **Star of Siam** • 11 E Illinois St
- **Sugar: A Dessert Bar** • 108 W Kinzie St
- **Sullivan's Steakhouse** • 415 N Dearborn St
- **Sushi Naniwa** • 607 N Wells St
- **Sushisamba Rio** • 504 N Wells St
- **SWK** • 710 N Wells St
- **Thai Star Café** • 660 N State St
- **Tizi Melloul** • 531 N Wells St
- **Topolobampo** • 445 N Clark St
- **Vermillion** • 10 W Hubbard St
- **Vong's Thai Kitchen** • 6 W Hubbard St
- **Weber Grill** • Hilton Garden Inn, 539 N State St
- **Wildfire** • 159 W Erie St

Shopping

- **Jazz Record Mart** • 25 E Illinois St
- **Mary Wolf Gallery** • 705 Dearborn St
- **Mig and Tig Furniture** • 540 N Wells St
- **Montauk** • 401 N Wells
- **Paper Source** • 232 W Chicago Ave

Video Rental

- **Blockbuster Video** • 700 N State St
- **Blockbuster Video** • 806 N Clark St
- **Hubbard's Street Books** • 109 W Hubbard St

Map 3 • Streeterville / Mag Mile

N

E Walton St
N Ernst Ct
N Huguelet Pl
E Delaware Pl
N Dewitt Pl
E Chestnut St
N Mies Van Der Rohe Way
E Pearson St
Lake Michigan
A
Loyola University (Water Tower Campus)
Seneca Park
Lake Shore Park
32
N Rush St
N Tower Ct
800N
E Chicago Ave
GOLD COAST
E Superior St
Northwestern University (Chicago Campus)
N McClurg
N Lake Shore Dr
Lake Shore Dr
Outer Harbor
700N
E Huron St
N Fairbanks Ct
VA Lakeside Med Center
E Erie St
N St Clair St
N Michigan Ave
E Ontario St
Ohio Street Beach
B
2
600N
Navy Pier
PAGE 218
E Ohio St
N Peshtigo Ct
E Grand Ave
Navy Pier
N Seneca St
500N
100E
200E
300E
E Illinois St
Tribune Tower
N Columbus Dr
N Park Dr
N New St
N McClurg Ct
Vyfront Plaza Dr
E Hubbard St
University of Chicago Gleacher Center
STREETERVILLE
E Kinzie St
E North Water St
River Rd
Chicago River
6
C
E Wacker Dr
100E
300E
Du Sable Harbor
N Stetson Ave
N Columbus Dr
N Field Blvd
South Water St
N Garland Ct
N Beaubien Ct
200N
E Lake St
1
2

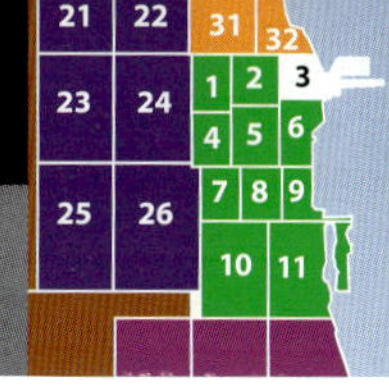

The tiny, densely populated blocks of Streeterville are home to lots of big stores, lots of big restaurants, and lots of big hotels, as well as the maze that is the Northwestern University Medical campus. Hoity-toity residents of the premier high-rises sip their champagne and laugh at the overwhelmed tourists who look like ants so, so far below.

Banks

- **Associated (ATM)** • 401 E Illinois St
- **Banco Popular** • 717 N Michigan Ave
- **Bank of America (ATM)** • 600 N Michigan Ave
- **Bank One** • 605 N Michigan Ave
- **Bank One (ATM)** • 757 N Michigan Ave
- **Charter One (ATM)** • 200 E Ohio St
- **Charter One (ATM)** • 600 N McClurg Ct
- **Citibank** • 539 N Michigan Ave
- **Harris Trust & Savings (ATM)** • 352 E Illinois St
- **Harris Trust & Savings (ATM)** • 455 N Cityfront Plz Dr
- **Metropolitan (ATM)** • 680 N Lake Shore Dr
- **North** • 360 E Ohio St
- **North (ATM)** • 505 N Lake Shore Dr
- **Northern Trust** • 201 E Huron St
- **Northern Trust (ATM)** • 201 E Huron St
- **Northern Trust (ATM)** • 251 E Huron St
- **Northern Trust (ATM)** • 410 N Michigan Ave
- **US** • 400 N Michigan Ave
- **US** • 509 E Illinois St
- **US (ATM)** • 200 E Huron St
- **US (ATM)** • 320 E Superior St
- **US (ATM)** • 357 E Chicago Ave
- **US (ATM)** • 401 E Illinois St
- **US (ATM)** • 710 N Lake Shore Dr

Car Washes

- **River North Experts** • 161 E Chicago Ave

Hospitals

- **Northwestern Memorial** • 251 E Huron St
- **VA Lakeside Medical Center** • 333 E Huron St

Landmarks

- **Navy Pier** • 600 E Grand Ave
- **Tribune Tower** • 435 N Michigan Ave

Parking

Pharmacies

- **Parkway Drugs** • 680 N Lake Shore Dr
- **Walgreens** • 430 N Michigan Ave
- **Walgreens (24 hours)** • 757 N Michigan Ave

Pizza

- **Joey Buona Pizzeria, Grill & Beef Express Café** • 162 E Superior St
- **Sbarro** • 700 N Michigan Ave

Post Offices

- 227 E Ontario St

Schools

- **American College of Surgeons** • 633 N St Clair St
- **Northwestern University** • 211 E Superior St
- **University of Chicago Gleacher Center** • 450 N Cityfront Plaza Dr

Supermarkets

- **Fox & Obel Food Store** • 401 E Illinois St
- **Treasure Island** • 680 N Lake Shore Dr

N
E Walton St
E Delaware Pl
E Chestnut St
E Pearson St
N Ernst Ct
N Huguelet Pl
N Dewitt Pl
N Mies Van Der Rohe Way
Lake Michigan
Loyola University (Water Tower Campus)
Seneca Park
32
Lake Shore Park
N Rush St
E Tower Ct
800N
E Chicago Ave
GOLD COAST
E Superior St
Northwestern University (Chicago Campus)
N McClurg
N Lake Shore Dr
Lake Shore Dr
Outer Harbor
700N
E Huron St
N Fairbanks Ct
VA Lakeside Med Center
E Erie St
N St Clair St
N Michigan Ave
E Ontario St
Ohio Street Beach
2
600N
Navy Pier
PAGE 218
E Ohio St
N Peshtigo Ct
E Grand Ave
N Seneca St
500N
100E
200E
400E
E Illinois St
N Cityfront Plaza Dr
N Columbus Dr
N Park Dr
N New St
N McClurg Ct
E Hubbard St
University of Chicago Gleacher Center
STREETERVILLE
E Kinzie St
E North Water St
River Rd
Chicago River
6
E Wacker Dr
100E
300E
N Stetson Ave
N Columbus Dr
N Field Blvd
Du Sable Harbor
South Water Ct
N Garland Ct
N Beaubien Ct
200N
E Lake St
A
B
C
1
2

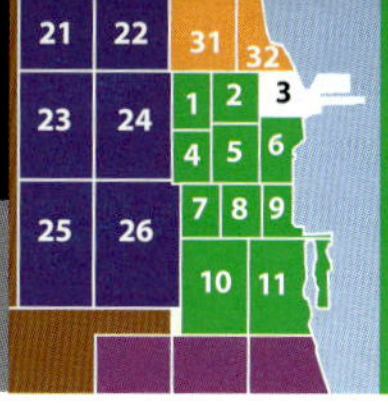

Escape from the shopping bag-toting throngs at comfy Timothy O'Toole's Pub on Fairbank's or go underground on lower Michigan Avenue to Billy Goat Tavern, a Chicago institution. Indian Garden's lunch buffet is an office worker's fave. Bandera brings in the after-work ad execs for roast chicken and also makes great takeout. If you've got bucks to blow and months to wait for a weekend reservation, Tru is for you.

Coffee

- **Dunkin' Donuts** • 200 E Ohio St
- **Dunkin' Donuts** • 401 E Ontario St
- **Starbucks** • 401 E Ontario St
- **Starbucks** • 444 N Michigan Ave
- **Starbucks** • 670 N Michigan Ave
- **Starbucks (Chicago Downtown Courtyard)** • 155 E Ontario St
- **Starbucks (Levy-Navy Pier)** • 600 E Grand Ave
- **Starbucks (Northwestern Memorial Hospital)** • 251 E Huron St
- **Torrefazione Italia** • 680 N Lakeshore Dr
- **Torrefazione Italia** • 700 N Michigan Ave

Copy Shops

- **AlphaGraphics (8 am-6 pm)** • 645 N Michigan Ave
- **Kinko's (7 am-7 pm)** • 540 N Michigan Ave
- **Kwik Kopy (8 am-5:30 pm)** • 500 N Michigan Ave
- **Press Type and Copy (8:30 am-5 pm)** • 541 N Fairbanks Ct
- **The UPS Store (9 am-6:30 pm)** • 207 E Ohio St

Farmer's Markets

- **Museum of Contemporary Art/Streeterville** • E Chicago Ave & Mies Van der Rohe Wy

Gyms

- **Curves** • 200 E Ohio St
- **Holmes Place** • 355 E Grand Ave
- **Lakeshore Athletic Club** • 333 E Ontario St
- **North Pier Athletic Club** • 474 N Lake Shore Dr

Hardware Stores

- **Streeterville Ace Hardware** • 680 N Lake Shore Dr

Liquor Stores

- **Market Place Food** • 393 E Illinois St

Movie Theaters

- **AMC River East** • 322 E Illinois St
- **Loews** • 600 N Michigan Ave
- **Museum of Contemporary Art** • 220 E Chicago Ave
- **Navy Pier IMAX Theatre** • 700 E Grand Ave

Nightlife

- **Billy Goat Tavern** • 430 N Michigan Ave
- **Dick's Last Resort** • 435 E Illinois St
- **O'Neill's Bar & Grill** • 152 E Ontario St
- **Timothy O'Toole's Pub** • 622 N Fairbanks Ct

Pet Shops

- **Streeterville Pet Spa and Boutique** • 401 E Ontario St

Restaurants

- **Bandera** • 535 N Michigan Ave
- **Benihana of Tokyo** • 166 E Superior St
- **Billy Goat Tavern** • 430 N Michigan Ave
- **Bubba Gump Shrimp Co** • Navy Pier, 700 E Grand Ave
- **Cambridge House Grill** • 167 E Ohio St
- **Capital Grille** • 633 N St Clair St
- **Cite** • Lake Point Tower, 70th Fl 505 N Lake Shore Dr
- **Dick's Last Resort** • 435 E Illinois St
- **Eli's the Place for Steaks** • 215 E Chicago Ave
- **Emilio's Tapas Sol y Nieve** • 215 E Ohio St
- **Heaven on Seven** • 600 N Michigan Ave
- **Hot Diggity Dogs** • 251 E Ohio St
- **Indian Garden** • 247 E Ontario St
- **Kamehachi** • 240 E Ontario St
- **Les Nomades** • 222 E Ontario St
- **Nomi** • Park Hyatt Chicago Ave, 800 N Michigan Ave
- **Riva** • Navy Pier 700 E Grand Ave
- **Ron of Japan** • 230 E Ontario St
- **Sayat Nova** • 157 E Ohio St
- **Tru** • 676 N St Clair St
- **Volare** • 201 E Grand Ave
- **Wave** • 644 N Lake Shore Dr

Shopping

- **Apple Store** • 679 N Michigan Ave
- **Chicago Place** • 700 N Michigan Ave
- **Disney Store** • 717 N Michigan Ave
- **Garrett Popcorn Shop** • 670 N Michigan Ave
- **Neiman-Marcus** • 737 N Michigan Ave
- **Niketown** • 669 N Michigan Ave
- **Tiffany & Co** • 730 N Michigan Ave
- **Virgin Megastore** • 540 N Michigan Ave

Video Rental

- **Chicago Video** • 230 E Ohio St
- **Hollywood Video** • 680 N Lake Shore Dr

Map 4 • West Loop Gate / Greek Town

WEST LOOP GATE
GREEK TOWN

W Carroll Ave
W Wayman St
W Fulton St
W Walnut St
W Lake St
W Couch Pl
W Randolph St
W Court Pl
W Washington St
W Warren Ave
W Madison St
W Tilden St
W Arcade Pl
W Monroe St
W Marble Pl
W Adams St
W Quincy St
W Jackson Blvd
W Gladys Ave
W Van Buren St
W Tilden St
W Harrison St

N Peoria St
N Green St
N Halsted St
N Union Ave
N Des Plaines St
N Jefferson St
N Clinton St
N Canal St
N West Water St
N Riverside Plz
N Wacker Drive
S Peoria St
S Green St
S Halsted Ave
S Des Plaines St
S Jefferson St
S Clinton St
S Canal St
S Riverside Plz
S Wacker Drive

Kennedy Expwy
Eisenhower Expy
Chicago River

Clinton
UIC-Halsted
Clinton

Metra Union Pacific
Ogilvie Transportation Center
Union Station
Metra Milwaukee District, North Central Service
Metra Burlington Northern Santa Fe, Heritage Corridor, SouthWest Service
Dugan's Drinking Emporium
Zorba's House Restaurant
University of Illinois at Chicago
Greyhound Bus Terminal

PAGE 280
PAGE 280
PAGE 240

200N
100N
100S
200S
300S
400S
600S
800W
600W
500W
300W

90
94
290

1
5
7
24
26

A
B
C
1
2

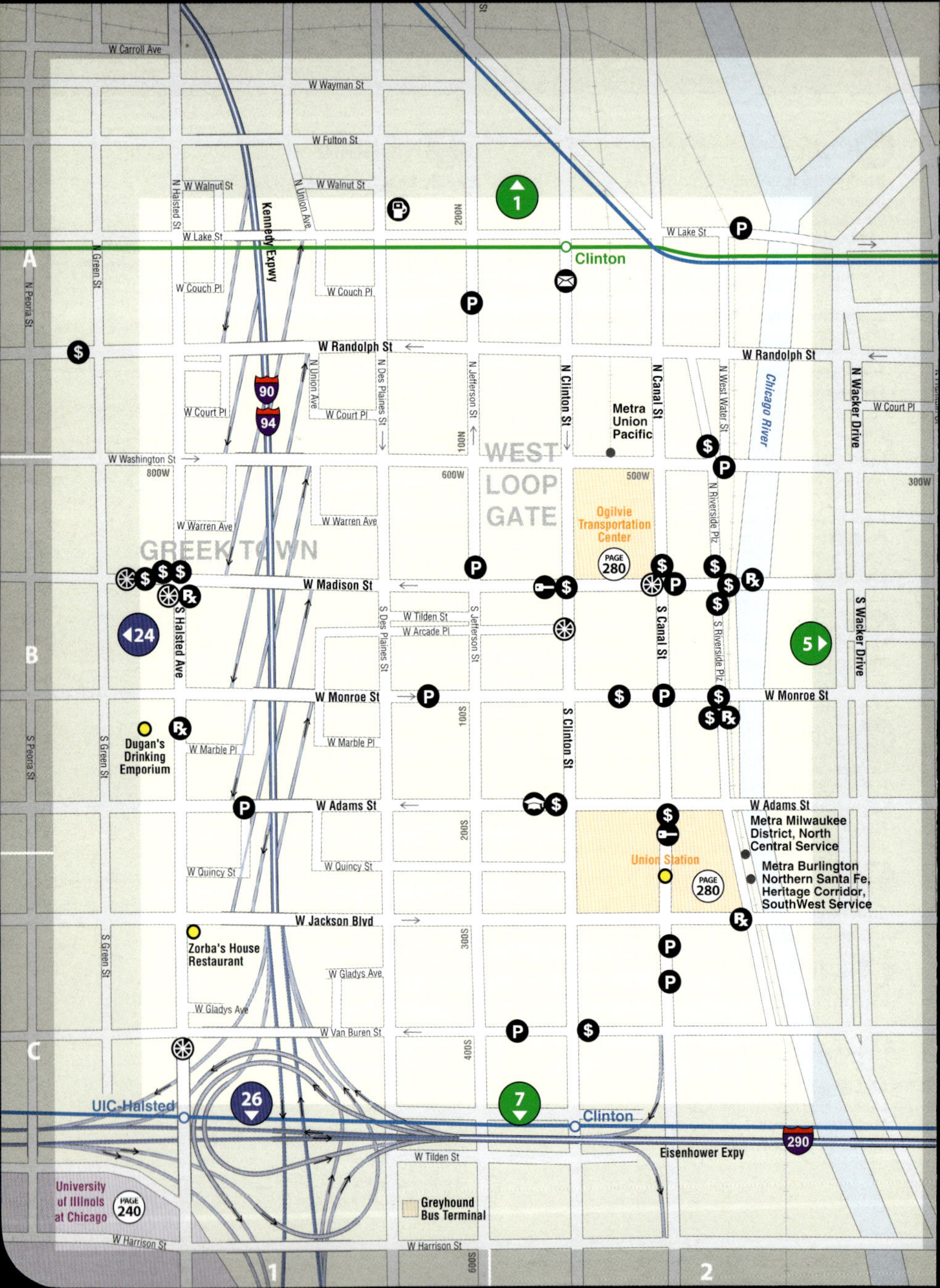

Trains, buses, and gyros define this former warehouse district, which now contains loft residences and office spaces. The gateway for suburbanites into the city, West Loop is the address for the Richard B. Ogilvie Transportation Center (just call it Northwestern Train Station, please), grand Union Station, where Amtrak is based, and the downtown Greyhound Bus Terminal. Just north of Ogilvie, "Metramarket," under construction at this writing, promises the city's hungry residents a Disneyland of fast food and fine dining, along with a French-style market.

Banks

- **American Chartered** • 932 W Randolph St
- **Bank of America** • 2 N Riverside Pl
- **Bank of America (ATM)** • 2 N Riverside Plz
- **Bank of America (ATM)** • 225 S Canal St
- **Bank One** • 1 N Halsted St
- **Bank One** • 300 S Riverside Plz
- **Bank One (ATM)** • 100 N Riverside Plz
- **Bank One (ATM)** • 525 W Monroe St
- **Bank One (ATM)** • 565 W Adams St
- **Citibank** • 500 W Madison St
- **Citibank** • 500 W Monroe St
- **Corus** • 10 S Riverside Plz
- **Harris Trust & Savings (ATM)** • 555 W Madison St
- **LaSalle (ATM)** • 130 S Canal St
- **LaSalle (ATM)** • 550 W Van Buren St
- **MB Financial** • 801 W Madison St
- **MB Financial (ATM)** • 809 W Madison St
- **TCF** • 120 S Riverside Plz
- **TCF (ATM)** • 400 W Madison St
- **US (ATM)** • 11 N Canal St

Car Rental

- **Enterprise** • 555 W Madison St • 312-906-8300
- **Hertz** • 210 S Canal St • 312-928-0538

Gas Stations

- **Fulton & Des Plaines** • 225 N Des Plaines St

Landmarks

- **Dugan's Drinking Emporium** • 128 S Halsted St
- **Union Station** • 200 S Canal St
- **Zorba's House Restaurant** • 301 S Halsted St

Parking

Pharmacies

- **CVS Pharmacy** • 130 S Canal St
- **Dominick's** • 1 N Halsted St
- **Dominick's (Skybridge Building)** • 1 N Halsted St
- **Osco Drug** • 400 W Madison St
- **Walgreens** • 300 S Riverside Plz
- **Walgreens (24 hours)** • 111 S Halsted St

Pizza

- **Bacino's** • 118 S Clinton St
- **Dominick's Finer Foods** • 1 N Halsted St
- **Giordano's** • 815 W Van Buren St
- **Leona's** • 848 W Madison St
- **Sbarro** • 500 W Madison St

Post Offices

- 168 N Clinton St

Schools

- **Chicago-Kent College of Law** • 565 W Adams St

Map 4 • West Loop Gate / Greek Town

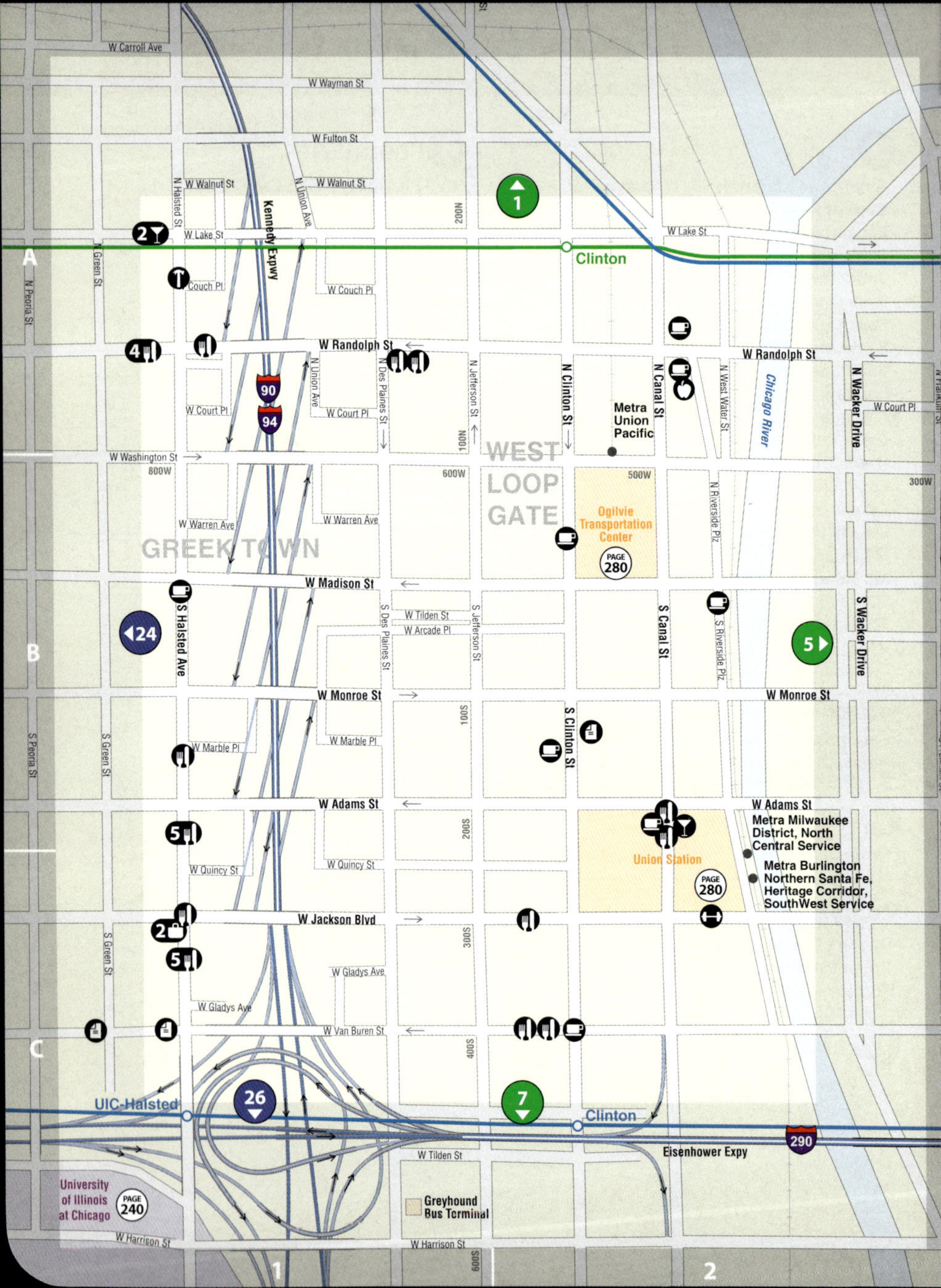

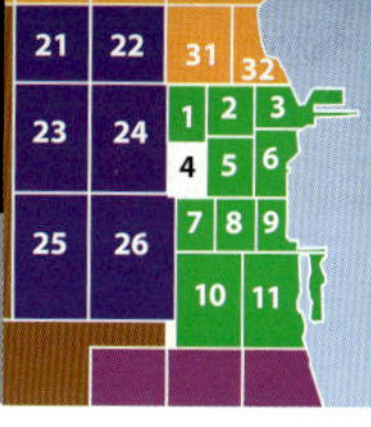

"Opaa!" rings through the streets, especially on summer evenings, when many of the fine Greek restaurants offer patio or rooftop dining. They do grilled octopus right at stylish Costa's, while Greek Islands is a sure-fire hit for birthday parties and other rowdy large-group outings. Seedy Zorba's offers flaming cheese 24 hours a day. Athenian Candle Company is not to be missed—where else can you purchase "Law be Gone" room spray, a 12-foot-tall gilded candle suitable for an Orthodox mass, a smiling Buddha statue, and a female icon allegedly dipped in dove's blood?

Coffee

- **Dunkin' Donuts** • 2 N Riverside Plz
- **Dunkin' Donuts** • 500 W Madison St
- **Krispy Kreme Doughnuts** • 225 S Canal St
- **Starbucks** • 10 S Riverside Plz
- **Starbucks** • 139 S Clinton St
- **Starbucks** • 40 N Clinton St
- **Starbucks** • 400 W Madison St
- **Starbucks** • 550 W Van Buren St
- **Starbucks (Dominick's)** • 1 N Halsted St

Copy Shops

- **Comet Press (9 am-6 pm)** • 812 W Van Buren St
- **Kinko's (24 hours)** • 127 S Clinton St
- **Kinko's (7 am-10 pm)** • 843 W Van Buren St

Farmer's Markets

- **Riverside Plaza** • 2 N Riverside Plz

Gyms

- **Union Station Multiplex** • 444 W Jackson Blvd

Hardware Stores

- **Chicago Wholesale Hardware** • 171 N Halsted St

Nightlife

- **Reserve** • 858 W Lake St
- **Reunion** • 811 W Lake St
- **Snuggery Saloon & Dining Room** • Union Station, Canal & Adams

Restaurants

- **Artopolis Bakery & Café** • 306 S Halsted St
- **Athena** • 212 S Halsted St
- **Avec** • 615 W Randolph St
- **Azure** • 832 W Randolph St
- **Blackbird** • 619 W Randolph St
- **Bluepoint Oyster Bar** • 741 W Randolph St
- **Byzantium** • 232 S Halsted St
- **Costa's** • 340 S Halsted St
- **Gold Coast Dogs** • Union Station, 225 S Canal St
- **Greek Islands** • 200 S Halsted St
- **J&C Inn** • 558 W Van Buren St
- **Lou Mitchell's** • 565 W Jackson Blvd
- **Nine** • 440 W Randolph St
- **Nine Muses** • 315 S Halsted St
- **Parthenon** • 314 S Halsted St
- **Pegasus Restaurant and Taverna** • 130 S Halsted St
- **Red Light** • 820 W Randolph St
- **Robinson's No 1 Ribs** • 225 S Canal St
- **Rodity's** • 222 S Halsted St
- **Santorini** • 800 W Adams St
- **Starfish** • 804 W Randolph St
- **Sushi Wabi** • 842 W Randolph St

Shopping

- **Athenian Candle Co** • 300 S Halsted St
- **Greek Town Music** • 330 S Halsted St

Map 5 • The Loop

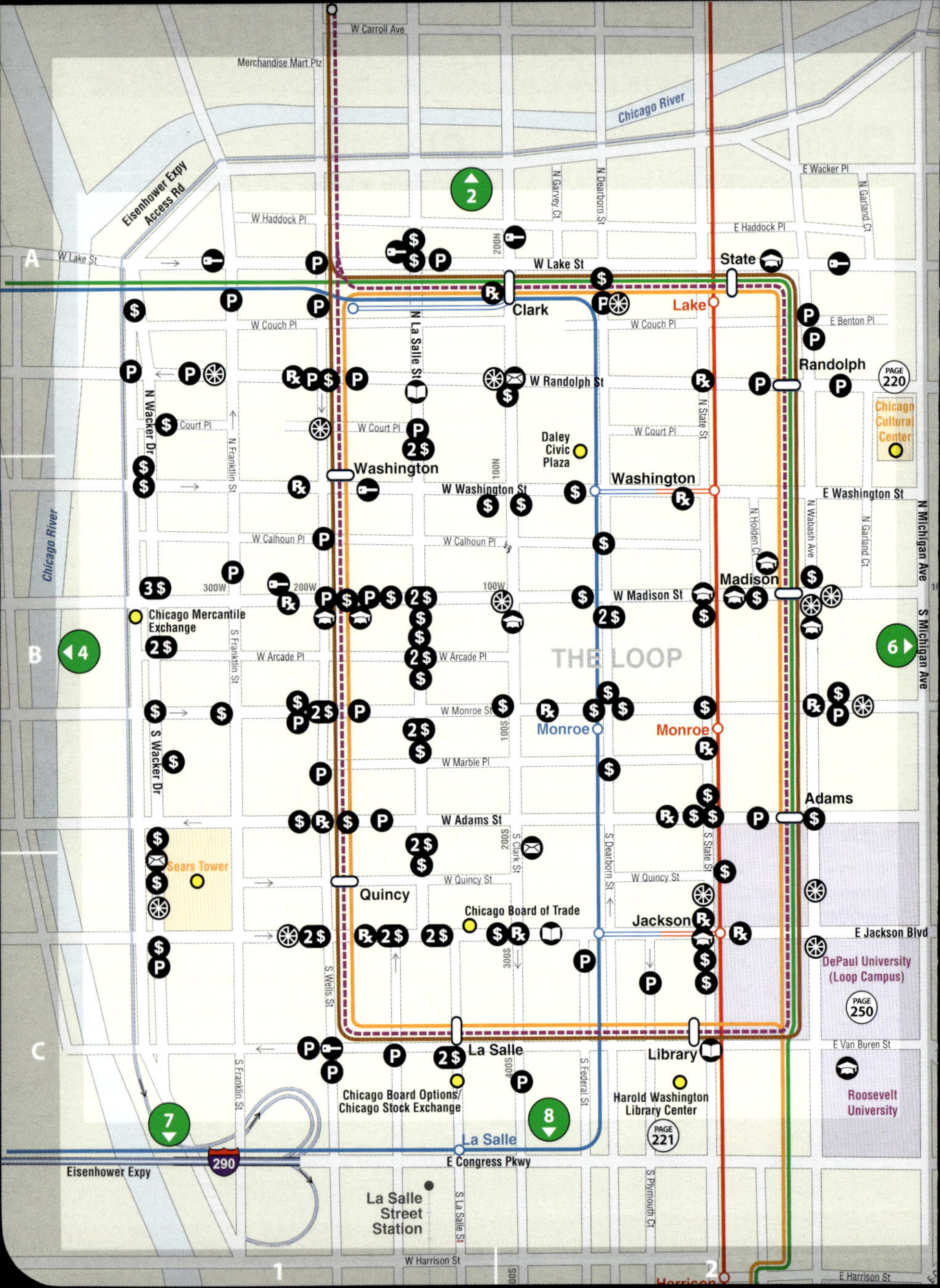

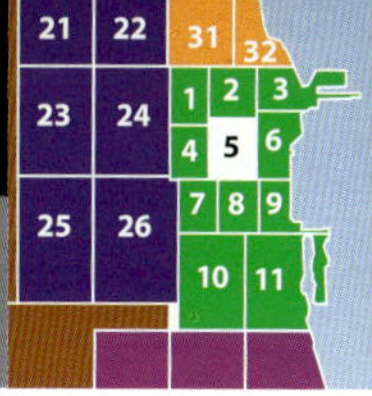

It all starts here, where money changes hands at the CBOT, CBOE, CSE, and CME. The Loop, named after the El tracks lassoing Chicago's heart, is the bustling business and financial district. With all the banks, an ATM is much easier to find than a metered parking space, although pricey parking garages abound. The intersection of State and Madison Streets is the point from which Chicago's simple and efficient street number grid system starts making navigation pretty easy.

Banks

- **Amalgamated Bank of Chicago** • 1 W Monroe St
- **Associated** • 200 N La Salle St
- **Banco Popular** • 415 N La Salle St
- **Bank of America** • 205 W Monroe St
- **Bank of America** • 231 S La Salle St
- **Bank of America** • 33 N Dearborn St
- **Bank of America (ATM)** • 110 N Wacker Dr
- **Bank of America (ATM)** • 205 W Monroe St
- **Bank of America (ATM)** • 231 S La Salle St
- **Bank of America (ATM)** • 233 S Wacker Dr
- **Bank of America (ATM)** • 29 S La Salle St
- **Bank of America (ATM)** • 33 N Dearborn St
- **Bank of Montreal-Harris Bank** • 115 S La Salle St
- **Bank One** • 120 S La Salle St
- **Bank One** • 30 S Wacker Dr
- **Bank One (ATM)** • 140 S Dearborn St
- **Bank One (ATM)** • 16 W Adams St
- **Bank One (ATM)** • 200 W Adams St
- **Bank One (ATM)** • 201 W Madison St
- **Bank One (ATM)** • 30 S Dearborn St
- **Bank One (ATM)** • 55 W Monroe St
- **Bank One (ATM)** • 60 E Monroe St
- **Charter One** • 150 S Wacker Dr
- **Charter One** • 2 S State St
- **Charter One** • 400 S La Salle St
- **Charter One (ATM)** • 200 N Dearborn St
- **Citibank** • 11 S La Salle St
- **Citibank** • 222 W Adams St
- **Citibank** • 69 W Washington St
- **Cole Taylor** • 111 W Washington St
- **Fifth Third** • 1 N Wacker Dr
- **Fifth Third** • 101 N Wacker Dr
- **Fifth Third** • 175 W Jackson Blvd
- **Fifth Third** • 233 S Wacker Dr
- **First American** • 33 W Monroe St
- **First American** • 50 E Adams St
- **First** • 161 N Clark St
- **First** • 20 N Wacker Dr
- **Harris Trust & Savings** • 111 W Monroe St
- **Harris Trust & Savings** • 141 W Jackson Blvd
- **Harris Trust & Savings** • 99 W Washington St
- **Harris Trust & Savings (ATM)** • 311 W Monroe St
- **Lakeside** • 141 W Jackson Blvd
- **LaSalle** • 100 S Wacker Dr
- **LaSalle** • 120 N La Salle St
- **LaSalle** • 135 S La Salle St
- **LaSalle** • 191 N Wacker Dr
- **LaSalle** • 201 S State St
- **LaSalle** • 203 N La Salle St
- **LaSalle** • 77 S Dearborn St
- **LaSalle (ATM)** • 175 W Jackson Blvd
- **LaSalle (ATM)** • 226 W Jackson Blvd
- **MB Financial** • 1 S Wacker Dr
- **MB Financial** • 2 S La Salle St
- **MB Financial (ATM)** • 223 W Jackson Blvd
- **Northern Trust** • 50 S La Salle St
- **Northern Trust (ATM)** • 10 S La Salle St
- **Northern Trust (ATM)** • 181 W Madison St
- **Northern Trust (ATM)** • 50 S La Salle St
- **Shore** • 333 S State St
- **TCF** • 29 E Madison St
- **TCF (ATM)** • Osco, 111 W Jackson Blvd
- **TCF Bank (ATM)** • Osco, 137 S State St
- **US Bank** • 209 S La Salle St
- **US Bank (ATM)** • 333 S Wabash Ave
- **Washington Mutual** • 120 N La Salle St
- **Washington Mutual** • 200 W Randolph St
- **Washington Mutual** • 230 W Monroe St
- **Washington Mutual** • 247 S State St
- **Washington Mutual** • 311 S Wacker Dr
- **Washington Mutual** • 41 N Wabash Ave
- **Washington Mutual** • 70 W Madison St

Car Rental

- **Avis** • 214 N Clark St • 312-782-6825
- **Budget** • 65 E Lake St • 312-960-3100
- **Enterprise** • 201 W Madison St • 312-553-5230
- **Enterprise** • 303 W Lake St • 312-332-7783
- **Enterprise** • 425 S Wells St • 312-939-6001
- **Hertz** • 181 W Washington Blvd • 312-726-1476
- **National/Alamo** • 203 N La Salle St • 312-236-2581

Landmarks

- **Chicago Board of Trade** • 141 W Jackson Blvd
- **Chicago Board Options Exchange** • 400 S La Salle St
- **Chicago Cultural Center** • 78 E Washington St
- **Chicago Mercantile Exchange** • 20 S Wacker Dr
- **Chicago Stock Exchange** • 440 S La Salle St
- **Daley Civic Plaza** • 50 W Washington St
- **Harold Washington Library Center** • 400 S State St
- **Sears Tower** • 233 S Wacker Dr

Libraries

- **Harold Washington Public Library (Chicago Public Library Central Branch)** • 400 S State St
- **US Library** • 77 W Jackson Blvd

Parking

Pharmacies

- **CVS Pharmacy** • 105 S Wabash Ave
- **CVS Pharmacy** • 175 W Jackson Blvd
- **CVS Pharmacy** • 208 W Washington Blvd
- **Osco Drug** • 111 W Jackson Blvd
- **Osco Drug** • 137 S State St
- **Walgreens** • 15 W Washington St
- **Walgreens** • 151 N State St
- **Walgreens** • 16 W Adams St
- **Walgreens** • 191 N Clark St
- **Walgreens** • 200 W Adams St
- **Walgreens** • 201 W Madison St
- **Walgreens** • 240 W Randolph St
- **Walgreens** • 300 S State St
- **Walgreens** • 79 W Monroe St

Pizza

- **Bacci Pizzeria** • 120 N Wells St
- **Exchequer Pub** • 226 S Wabash Ave
- **Giordano's** • 223 W Jackson Blvd
- **Giordano's** • 236 S Wabash Ave
- **Giordano's** • 310 W Randolph St
- **Italian Village** • 71 W Monroe St
- **Mama Falco's** • 5 N Wells St
- **Pizano's Pizza & Pasta** • 61 E Madison St
- **Sbarro** • 100 W Randolph St
- **Sbarro** • 105 W Madison St
- **Sbarro** • 195 N Dearborn St
- **Sbarro** • 233 S Wacker Dr
- **Sbarro** • 333 S State St

Post Offices

- 100 W Randolph St
- 211 S Clark St
- 233 S Wacker Dr

Schools

- **Argosy University** • 20 S Clark St
- **Career Colleges of Chicago** • 11 E Adams St
- **DePaul University** • 1 E Jackson Blvd
- **Harrington College of Design** • 200 W Madison St
- **Harold Washington College** • 30 E Lake St
- **International Academy of Design and Technology** • 1 N State St
- **John Marshall Law School** • 315 S Plymouth Ct
- **Keller Graduate School of Management** • 225 W Washington St
- **MacCormac College** • 29 E Madison St
- **Robert Morris College** • 401 S State St
- **School of the Art Institute** • 37 S Wabash Ave

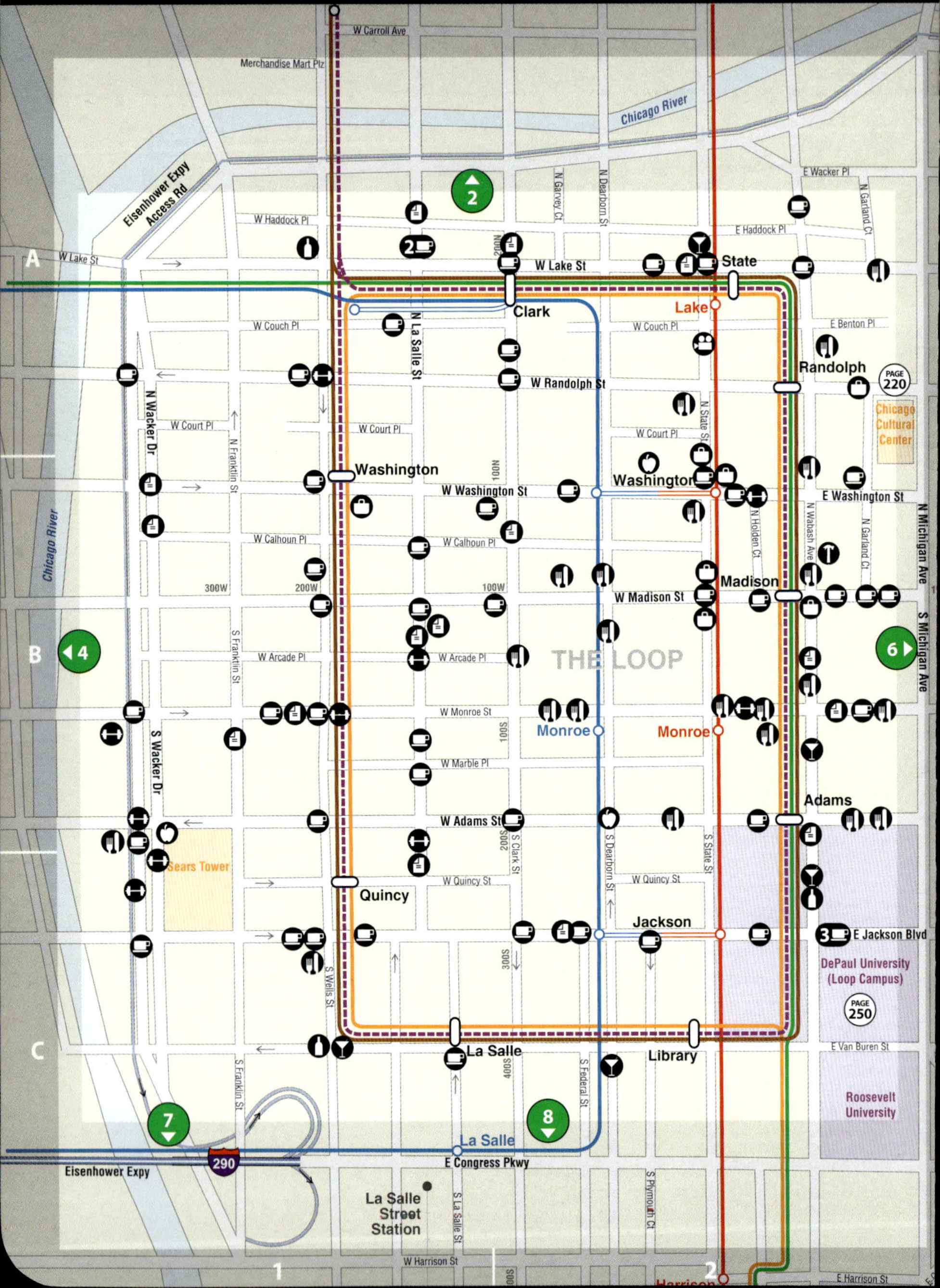

N
W Carroll Ave
Merchandise Mart Plz
Chicago River
Eisenhower Expy Access Rd
E Wacker Pl
W Haddock Pl
E Haddock Pl
N Garvey Ct
N Dearborn St
N Garland Ct
A
W Lake St
W Lake St
State
Lake
Clark
W Couch Pl
W Couch Pl
E Benton Pl
N La Salle St
Randolph
PAGE 220
W Randolph St
Chicago Cultural Center
N Wacker Dr
W Court Pl
N Franklin St
W Court Pl
W Court Pl
N State St
Washington
Washington
W Washington St
E Washington St
100N
Chicago River
W Calhoun Pl
W Calhoun Pl
N Holden Ct
N Wabash Ave
N Garland Ct
N Michigan Ave
300W
200W
100W
Madison
W Madison St
B
4
S Franklin St
W Arcade Pl
W Arcade Pl
THE LOOP
6
S Michigan Ave
W Monroe St
Monroe
Monroe
100S
S Wacker Dr
W Marble Pl
Adams
W Adams St
200S
S Clark St
S Dearborn St
S State St
Sears Tower
W Quincy St
W Quincy St
Quincy
Jackson
3
E Jackson Blvd
300S
S Wells St
DePaul University (Loop Campus)
PAGE 250
La Salle
Library
E Van Buren St
C
400S
S Franklin St
S Federal St
7
8
Roosevelt University
La Salle
290
E Congress Pkwy
Eisenhower Expy
S Plymouth Ct
La Salle Street Station
S La Salle St
W Harrison St
E Harrison St
1
2

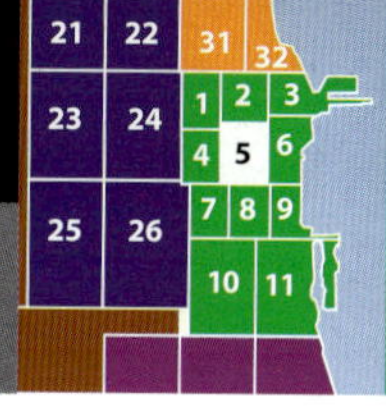

Retail giants Marshall Field's and Carson Pirie Scott anchor State Street. Once a great street that went downhill, it's now making a comeback with new retail blood, renovated hotels, and revitalized theaters. Armies of lawyers and loyal civil servants march among dozens of government buildings located within blocks of each other. Everest is easily the biggest expense report restaurant in the Loop. For decades, spicy Heaven on Seven has drawn Loop workers for Creole home cookin'.

Coffee

- **Caribou Coffee** • 10 S La Salle St
- **Caribou Coffee** • 55 W Monroe St
- **The Coffee Grounds** • 203 N Wabash Ave
- **Cosi** • 203 N La Salle St
- **Cosi** • 230 W Monroe St
- **Cosi** • 230 W Washington St
- **Cosi** • 28 E Jackson Blvd
- **Dunkin' Donuts** • 100 W Randolph St
- **Dunkin' Donuts** • 105 W Madison St
- **Dunkin' Donuts** • 201 N Clark St
- **Dunkin' Donuts** • 201 N State St
- **Dunkin' Donuts** • 201 W Madison St
- **Dunkin' Donuts** • 203 N La Salle St
- **Dunkin' Donuts** • 205 Randolph St
- **Dunkin' Donuts** • 229 W Jackson Blvd
- **Dunkin' Donuts** • 31 E Adams St
- **Dunkin' Donuts** • 39 W Jackson Blvd
- **Dunkin' Donuts** • 6 N Wabash Ave
- **Dunkin' Donuts** • 62 E Jackson Blvd
- **Dunkin' Donuts** • 75 E Washington St
- **Dunkin' Donuts** • 77 W Jackson Blvd
- **Gloria Jean's** • 135 S La Salle St
- **Intelligentsia Coffee & Tea** • 53 W Jackson Blvd
- **Java Java** • 2 N State St
- **Liberty Coffee and Tea** • 401 S La Salle St
- **Millennium Park** • 79 E Madison St
- **Starbucks** • 100 S Wacker Dr
- **Starbucks** • 105 W Adams St
- **Starbucks** • 111 W Washington St
- **Starbucks** • 150 N Wacker Dr
- **Starbucks** • 175 W Jackson Blvd
- **Starbucks** • 180 N La Salle St
- **Starbucks** • 200 W Adams St
- **Starbucks** • 209 W Jackson Blvd
- **Starbucks** • 25 E Washington Blvd
- **Starbucks** • 303 W Madison St
- **Starbucks** • 311 S Wacker Dr
- **Starbucks** • 40 W Lake St
- **Starbucks** • 55 E Jackson Blvd
- **Starbucks** • 66 W Washington St
- **Starbucks** • 68 E Madison St
- **Starbucks** • 70 W Madison St
- **Starbucks (AT&T Building)** • 227 W Monroe St
- **Starbucks (Bank of America Building)** • 231 S La Salle St
- **Starbucks (CT&T Building)** • 161 N Clark St
- **Starbucks (Marshall Fields)** • 111 N State St
- **Starbucks (Sears Tower)** • 233 S Wacker Dr
- **Torrefazione Italia** • 30 N La Salle St

Copy Shops

- **24 Seven Copies (24 hours)** • 222 N La Salle St
- **Acme Copy (8 am-5 pm)** • 218 S Wabash Ave
- **Advance Instant Printing (8:30 am-5 pm)** • 5 S Wabash Ave
- **AlphaGraphics (8 am-6 pm)** • 208 S La Salle St
- **Instant Printing (7 am-5:30)** • 200 S Clark St
- **Kinko's (24 hours)** • 29 S La Salle St
- **Kinko's (6 am-8 pm)** • 55 E Monroe St
- **Kinko's (6 am-8 pm)** • 101 N Wacker Dr
- **Kinko's (6 am-9 pm)** • 227 W Monroe St
- **Kinko's (7 am-11pm)** • 6 W Lake St
- **Kwik Kopy (8 am-5:30 pm)** • 11 S La Salle St
- **The UPS Store (7:30 am-6 pm)** • 27 N Wacker Dr
- **The UPS Store (9 am- 6 pm)** • 122 S Franklin St
- **Viking Printing & Copying (7 am-4 pm)** • 53 W Jackson Blvd

Farmer's Markets

- **Daley Plaza** • W Washington St & S Dearborn St, N of W Washington St
- **Federal Plaza** • Adams St & Dearborn St
- **The Park at Jackson & Wacker** • 311 S Wacker Dr at Sears Tower

Gyms

- **Bally Total Fitness** • 230 W Monroe St
- **Bally Total Fitness** • 25 E Washington St
- **Curves** • 39 S La Salle St
- **Equinox** • 200 W Monroe St
- **Executive Fitness Center** • 17 E Monroe St
- **Metropolitan Fitness Club** • 233 S Wacker Dr
- **Randolph Athletic Club** • 188 W Randolph St
- **River Park Athletic Club** • 200 S Wacker Dr
- **Women's Workout World** • 208 S La Salle St
- **World Gym Fitness Center** • 150 S Wacker Dr

Hardware Stores

- **Ace Hardware** • 26 N Wabash Ave

Liquor Stores

- **Cal's Liquor Store** • 400 S Wells St
- **Lake & Wells Food & Liquor** • 201 W Lake St
- **Wabash Food & Liquor** • 234 S Wabash Ave

Movie Theaters

- **Gene Siskel Film Center** • 164 N State St

Nightlife

- **Cal's** • 400 S Wells St
- **Exchequer Pub** • 226 S Wabash Ave
- **Govnor's Pub** • 207 N State St
- **Manhattans** • 415 S Dearborn St
- **Miller's Pub** • 134 S Wabash Ave

Restaurants

- **Atwood Café** • 1 W Washington St
- **Barro Cantina** • 73 E Lake St
- **Berghoff Restaurant** • 17 W Adams St
- **Billy Goat Tavern** • 330 S Wells St
- **Everest** • 440 S La Salle St
- **French Quarter/Palmer House Hilton** • 17 E Monroe St
- **Gold Coast Dogs** • 159 N Wabash Ave
- **Gold Coast Dogs** • 17 S Wabash Ave
- **Heaven on Seven** • 111 N Wabash Ave
- **Italian Village** • 71 W Monroe St
- **La Cantina Enoteca** • 71 W Monroe St
- **La Rosetta** • 70 W Madison St
- **Miller's Pub** • 134 S Wabash Ave
- **Mrs Levy's Delicatessen** • 233 S Wacker Dr
- **Nick's Fishmarket & Grill** • Bank One Plz, 51 S Clark St
- **Oasis Café** • 21 N Wabash Ave
- **Rhapsody** • Symphony Ctr, 65 E Adams St
- **Russian Tea Time** • 77 E Adams St
- **Trader Vic's** • Palmer House Hilton, 17 E Monroe St
- **Trattoria No 10** • 10 N Dearborn St
- **The Village** • 71 W Monroe St
- **Vivere** • 71 W Monroe St

Shopping

- **American Music World** • 111 N State St
- **Carson Pirie Scott** • 1 S State St
- **Gallery 37 Store** • 66 E Randolph St
- **Jeweler's Mall** • 7 S Wabash Ave
- **Marshall Field's** • 111 N State St
- **Rock Records** • 175 W Washington St
- **Sears** • 2 N State St

Map 6 • The Loop / Grant Park

Essentials

Grant Park is Chicago's front lawn, where grass meets glass. Millennium Park's funky fountain, jellybean and bandstand draw oohs and aahs from tourists and locals alike. Buckingham Fountain is still the number one Chicago photo op.

Banks

- **Associated** • 130 E Randolph St
- **Associated** • 200 E Randolph St
- **Associated** • 225 N Michigan Ave
- **Chicago Community** • 180 N Michigan Ave
- **Citibank** • 100 S Michigan Ave
- **Citibank** • 233 N Michigan Ave
- **MB Financial** • 303 E Wacker Dr
- **Midwest Bank & Trust Company** • 300 S Michigan Ave
- **Midwest Bank & Trust Company (ATM)** • 332 S Michigan Ave
- **North Community** • 180 N Michigan Ave
- **TCF (ATM)** • 150 N Michigan Ave
- **TCF (ATM)** • 224 S Michigan Ave
- **TCF (ATM)** • 500 S Columbus Dr
- **US** • 30 N Michigan Ave
- **US (ATM)** • 111 E Wacker Dr
- **Washington Mutual** • 206 N Michigan Ave

Car Rental

- **Enterprise** • 151 E Wacker Dr • 312-565-6518

Landmarks

- **Art Institute of Chicago** • 111 S Michigan Ave
- **Auditorium Building** • 430 S Michigan Ave
- **Fine Arts Building** • 410 S Michigan Ave
- **Symphony Center** • 22 S Michigan Ave

Parking

Pharmacies

- **CVS Pharmacy** • 205 N Michigan Ave
- **Osco Drug** • 150 N Michigan Ave
- **Walgreens** • 300 N Michigan Ave

Pizza

- **Giordano's** • 135 E Lake St
- **Sbarro** • 233 N Michigan Ave

Post Offices

- 200 E Randolph St

Schools

- **American Academy of Art** • 332 S Michigan Ave
- **National-Louis University** • 122 S Michigan Ave
- **Roosevelt University** • 430 S Michigan Ave

Map 6 • The Loop / Grant Park

Sundries / Entertainment

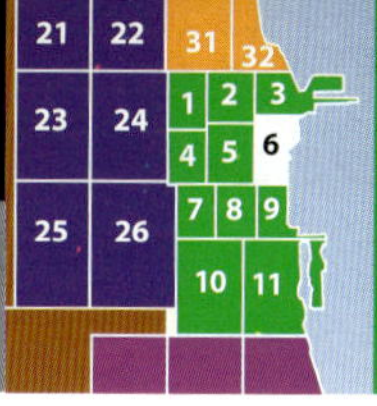

Throngs pack belly-to-belly for the free summer festivals in Grant Park. Take in the finest collection of Impressionist paintings outside of Paris on Tuesdays at the Art Institute, when admission is free. The Bennigan's across the street is the world's busiest—take that as you may. On non-festival days, the park is a lovely place to kill a few hours lounging on the lawn in the shadow of Buckingham Fountain—as long as you can avoid the occasional crazies who also enjoy the park's beautiful expanses.

Coffee

- **Caribou Coffee** • 20 N Michigan Ave
- **Cosi** • 116 S Michigan Ave
- **Cosi** • 233 N Michigan Ave
- **Dunkin' Donuts** • 233 N Michigan Ave
- **Dunkin' Donuts** • 300 E Randolph St
- **Rain Dog Books & Café** • 408 S Michigan Ave
- **Seattle's Best** • 150 N Michigan Ave
- **Starbucks** • 200 N Michigan Ave
- **Starbucks (Chicago Amoco Building)** • 200 E Randolph St
- **Starbucks (Illinois Center)** • 225 N Michigan Ave

Copy Shops

- **AlphaGraphics (8 am-6 pm)** • 180 N Stetson Ave
- **Kinko's (6 am-8 pm)** • 111 E Wacker Dr
- **Sir Speedy (8 am-5:30 pm)** • 180 N Stetson Ave
- **Sir Speedy (8:30 am-5:30 pm)** • 130 E Randolph St

Farmer's Markets

- **Prudential Plaza** • E Lake St & N Beaubien Ct

Gyms

- **Curves** • 180 N Stetson Ave
- **Lakeshore Athletic Club** • 211 N Stetson Ave

Nightlife

- **Alumni Club** • 150 N Michigan Ave
- **Houlihan's** • 111 E Wacker Dr

Restaurants

- **Aria** • 200 N Columbus Dr
- **Art Institute Restaurant on the Park** • 111 S Michigan Ave
- **Artist's Café** • 412 S Michigan Ave
- **Bennigan's** • 150 S Michigan Ave
- **China Grill** • 230 N Michigan
- **Park Grill** • 11 N Michigan Ave
- **Rain Dog Books & Café** • 408 S Michigan Ave

Shopping

- **Art & Artisans** • 108 S Michigan Ave
- **Museum Shop of the Art Institute** • 111 S Michigan Ave
- **Poster Plus** • 200 S Michigan Ave
- **Precious Possessions** • 28 N Michigan Ave
- **Rain Dog Books and Café** • 408 S Michigan Ave
- **The Savvy Traveller** • 310 S Michigan Ave

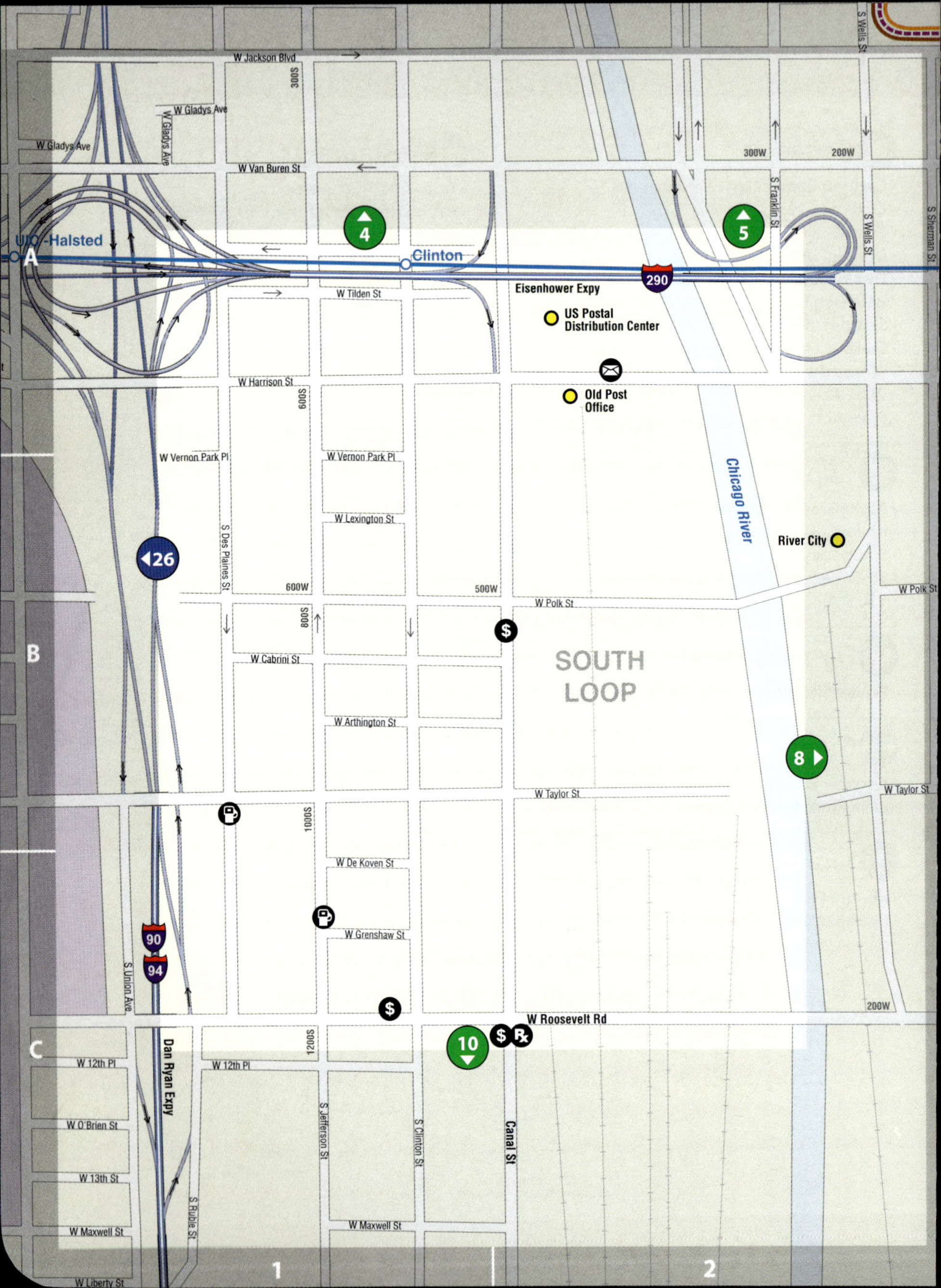

Map 7 • South Loop / River City

W Jackson Blvd
300S
W Gladys Ave
W Gladys Ave
W Gladys Ave
W Van Buren St
300W
200W
S Wells St
S Franklin St
S Sherman St
UIC-Halsted
Clinton
4
5
290
W Tilden St
Eisenhower Expy
US Postal Distribution Center
W Harrison St
600S
Old Post Office
W Vernon Park Pl
W Vernon Park Pl
W Lexington St
Chicago River
River City
26
S Des Plaines St
600W
500W
W Polk St
W Polk St
800S
W Cabrini St
SOUTH LOOP
W Arthington St
8
W Taylor St
W Taylor St
1000S
W De Koven St
W Grenshaw St
90
94
S Union Ave
200W
W Roosevelt Rd
10
1200S
W 12th Pl
W 12th Pl
Dan Ryan Expy
W O'Brien St
S Jefferson St
S Clinton St
Canal St
W 13th St
S Ruble St
W Maxwell St
W Maxwell St
W Liberty St

A
B
C
1
2

Essentials

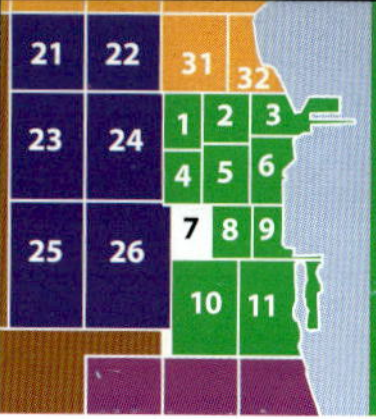

This stretch of South Loop is a tangle of train tracks and expressways, with a dirty river running through it. The old central Post Office could kiss the wrecking ball or go condo. Semis rumble around the giant mail distribution center on Harrison and get lost in the endless knot of the expressway interchange. So your check is on the road, not in the mail.

Banks

- **Bank One (ATM)** • 501 W Roosevelt Rd
- **Northern Trust** • 840 S Canal St
- **South Central** • 525 W Roosevelt Rd

Gas Stations

- **Citgo** • 1004 S Des Plaines St
- **Marathon** • 1121 S Jefferson St

Landmarks

- **Old Post Office** • 404 W Harrison St
- **River City** • 800 S Wells St
- **US Postal Distribution Center** • 433 W Harrison St

Pharmacies

- **Walgreens (24 hours)** • 501 W Roosevelt Rd

Post Offices

- 433 W Harrison St

Map 7 • South Loop / River City

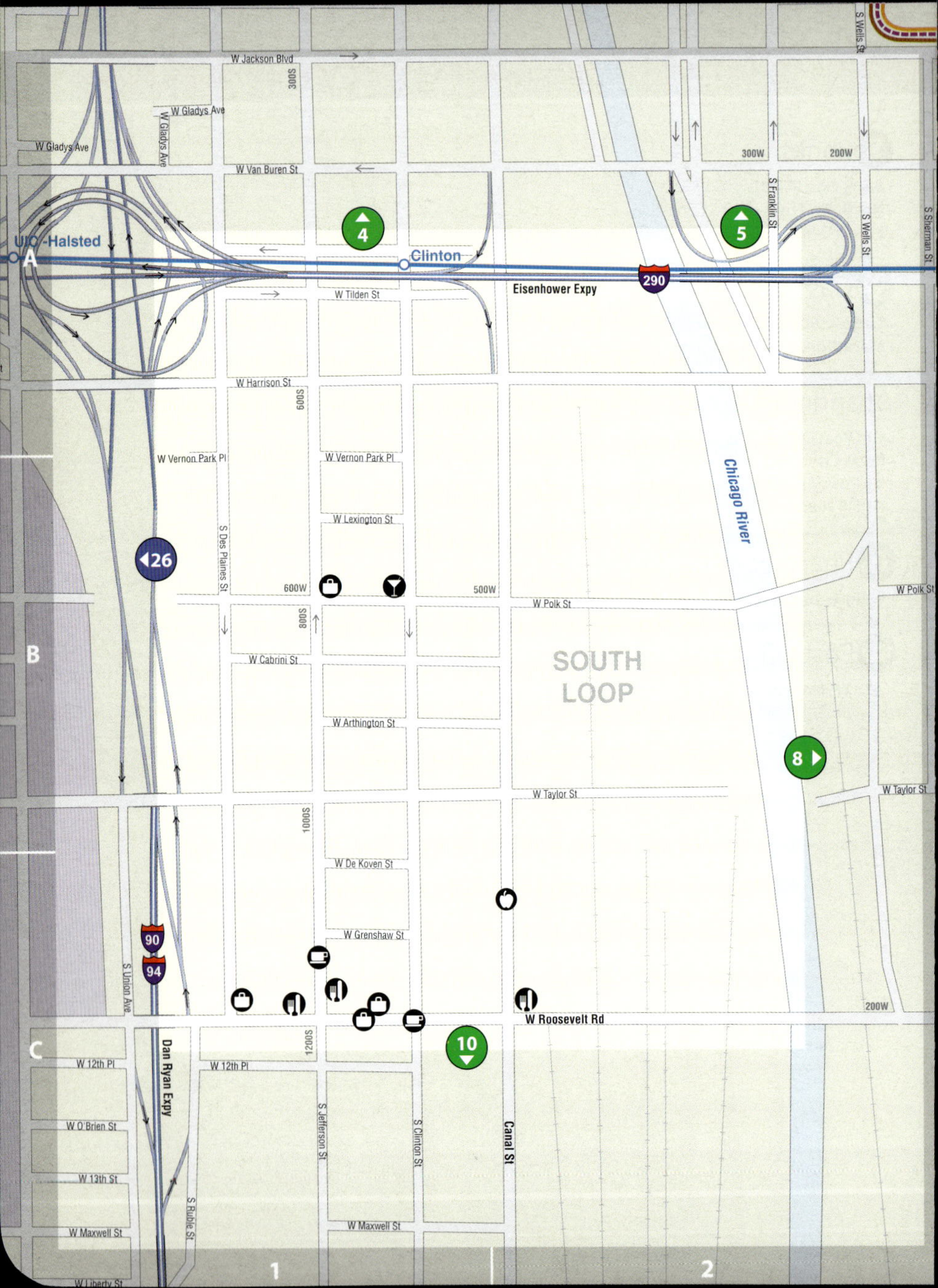

W Jackson Blvd
300S
W Gladys Ave
W Gladys Ave
W Gladys Ave
W Van Buren St
300W
200W
S Franklin St
S Wells St
S Sherman St
UIC-Halsted
A
Clinton
4
5
290
Eisenhower Expy
W Tilden St
W Harrison St
600S
W Vernon Park Pl
W Vernon Park Pl
W Lexington St
Chicago River
S Des Plaines St
26
600W
500W
W Polk St
W Polk St
800S
B
W Cabrini St
SOUTH LOOP
W Arthington St
8
W Taylor St
W Taylor St
1000S
W De Koven St
W Grenshaw St
90
94
S Union Ave
200W
W Roosevelt Rd
C
1200S
10
W 12th Pl
W 12th Pl
Dan Ryan Expy
S Jefferson St
S Clinton St
Canal St
W O'Brien St
W 13th St
S Ruble St
W Maxwell St
W Maxwell St
W Liberty St
1
2

Sundries / Entertainment

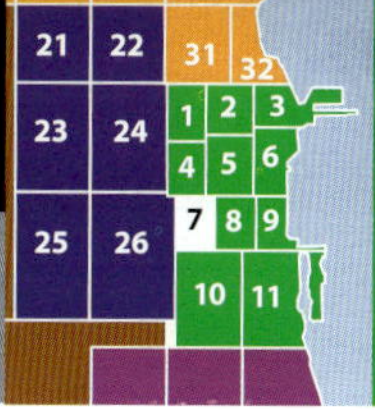

The Maxwell Sunday Market is a shadow of its former self. Sadly, the colorful flea market lost its vibe in the move to Roosevelt Road to make way for UIC's expansion. The Chicago Fire Department Academy on De Koven Street sits on the spot where Mrs. O'Leary's lantern-booting bovine started the Great Chicago Fire of 1871. For kicks, see the fire exhibit and watch the recruits' rappelling exercises.

Coffee

- **Dunkin' Donuts** • 1121 S Jefferson St
- **Dunkin' Donuts** • 500 W Roosevelt Rd

Farmer's Markets

- **Maxwell Sunday Market** • Canal St between Taylor St & Roosevelt Rd

Nightlife

- **Scarlett's Gentleman's** • 750 S Clinton St

Restaurants

- **Bake for Me** • 608 W Roosevelt Rd
- **Manny's Coffee Shop** • 1141 S Jefferson St
- **White Palace Grill** • 1159 S Canal St

Shopping

- **Fishman's Fabrics** • 1101 S Des Plaines St
- **Joseph Adam's Hats** • 544 W Roosevelt Rd
- **Lee's Foreign Car Service** • 727 S Jefferson St
- **Morris & Sons** • 555 W Roosevelt Rd

Map 8 • South Loop / Printers Row / Dearborn Park

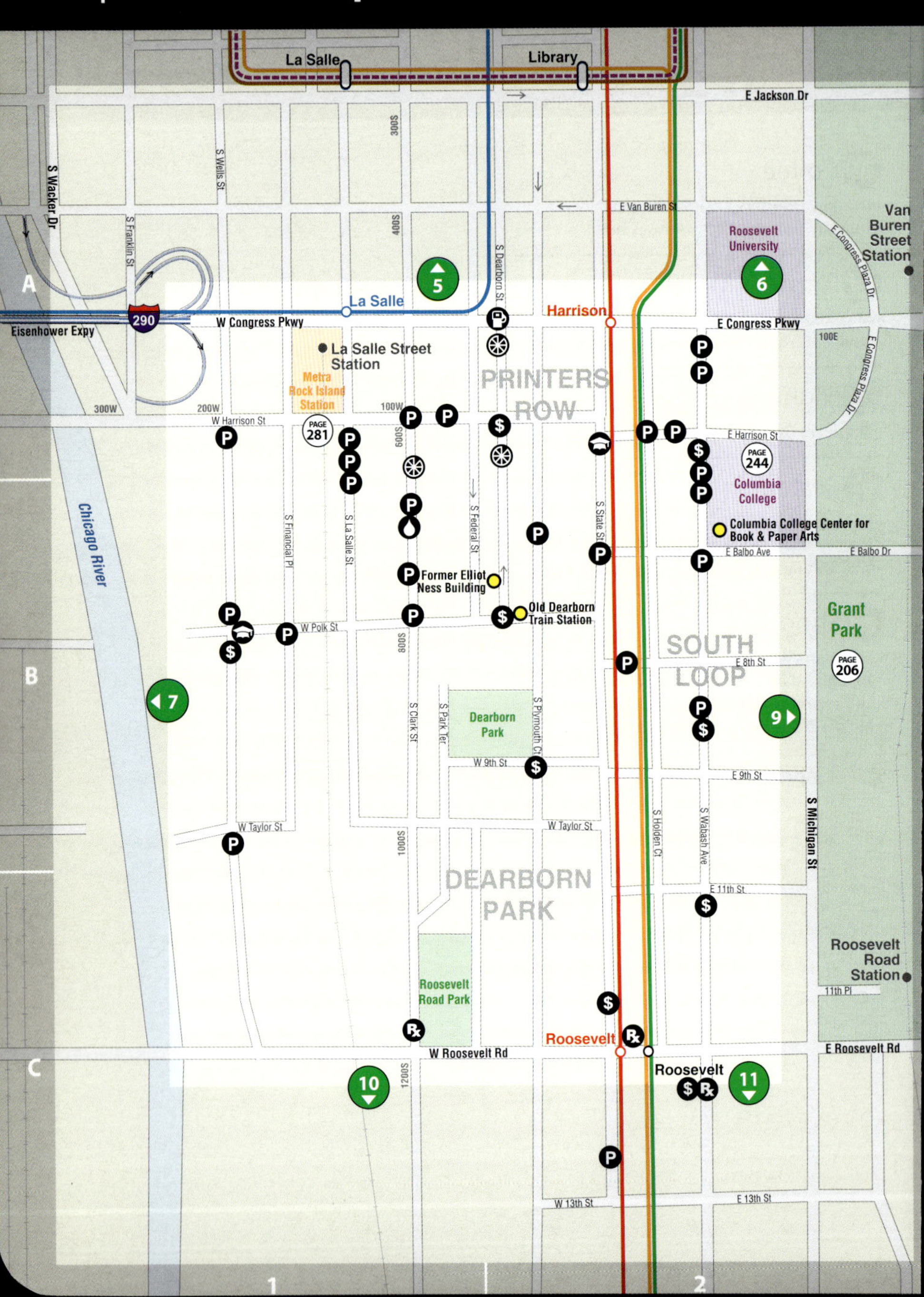

The South Loop is possibly the country's largest urban campus; Columbia, Roosevelt, and DePaul's new massive University Center dorms are all here. Meanwhile, the Mayor's long time dream of moving the sketchy Pacific Garden Mission to a plot of less valuable real estate is finally coming into fruition, clearing the way for a Jones College Prep expansion. A new Target at Clark and Roosevelt seals the deal—so much for the "funky" South Loop.

Banks

- **Bank of America (ATM)** • 1104 S Wabash Ave
- **Bank of America (ATM)** • 623 S Wabash Ave
- **Bank One** • 850 S Wabash Ave
- **Bank One (ATM)** • 800 S Wells St
- **Charter One** • 1143 S State St
- **Charter One (ATM)** • 600 S Dearborn St
- **Charter One (ATM)** • 899 S Plymouth Ct
- **Chicago Community** • 47 W Polk St
- **TCF** • Jewel, 1224 S Wabash Ave

Car Washes

- **Custom Hand Car Wash** • 700 S Clark St

Gas Stations

- **BP** • 50 W Congress Pkwy

Landmarks

- **Columbia College Center for Book & Paper Arts** • 1104 S Wabash Ave, 2nd Fl
- **Former Elliot Ness Building** • 618 S Dearborn St
- **Old Dearborn Train Station** • 47 W Polk St

Parking

Pharmacies

- **Jewel-Osco** • 1224 S Wabash Ave
- **Target** • 1154 S Clark St
- **Walgreens** • 2 E Roosevelt Rd

Pizza

- **Edwardo's Natural Pizza** • 521 S Dearborn St
- **Pat's Pizzeria** • 638 S Clark St
- **Trattoria Caterina** • 616 S Dearborn St

Schools

- **Daystar Education Association** • 800 S Wells St
- **William Jones College Prep** • 606 S State St

La Salle
Library
E Jackson Dr
S Wacker Dr
S Wells St
300S
400S
S Franklin St
E Van Buren St
Roosevelt University
Van Buren Street Station
E Congress Plaza Dr
S Dearborn St
La Salle
Harrison
290
Eisenhower Expy
W Congress Pkwy
E Congress Pkwy
La Salle Street Station
Metra Rock Island Station
PRINTERS ROW
100E
300W
200W
100W
W Harrison St
PAGE 281
600S
E Harrison St
PAGE 244
Columbia College
Chicago River
S Financial Pl
S La Salle St
S Federal St
S State St
E Balbo Ave
E Balbo Dr
Grant Park
W Polk St
800S
SOUTH LOOP
E 8th St
PAGE 206
S Clark St
S Park Ter
Dearborn Park
S Plymouth Ct
W 9th St
E 9th St
W Taylor St
W Taylor St
S Holden Ct
S Wabash Ave
S Michigan St
1000S
DEARBORN PARK
E 11th St
Roosevelt Road Station
11th Pl
Roosevelt Road Park
Roosevelt
W Roosevelt Rd
E Roosevelt Rd
Roosevelt
1200S
W 13th St
E 13th St
A
B
C
1
2
5
6
7
9
10
11

Sundries / Entertainment

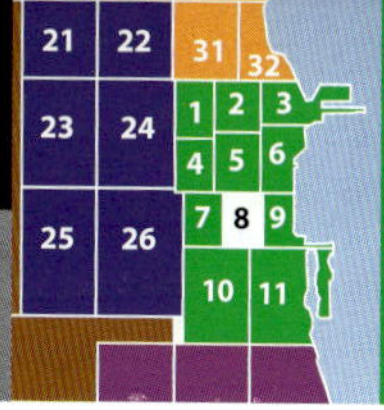

That rumbling you hear is the groundbreaking for another trendy restaurant popping up in one of Chicago's hottest development neighborhoods. Trendy brunchers line up at the South Loop outpost of Lakeview's Orange, while Columbia College students are still throwing back suds at the dumpy Georges, or the South Loop Club. Artier types check out the live world music at Hot House. At this writing, Buddy Guy's Legends is on the verge of moving onto a more stylish space—time will tell how it affects the club's gritty-down home feel.

Coffee

- **Caribou Coffee** • 41 E 8th St
- **Caribou Coffee** • 800 S Wabash Ave
- **Gourmand** • 728 S Dearborn St
- **Starbucks** • 31 E Roosevelt Rd
- **Starbucks** • 555 S Dearborn St
- **Starbucks (Target)** • 1154 S Clark St

Copy Shops

- **Kinko's (7 am-10 pm)** • 700 S Wabash Ave
- **The UPS Store (9 am-6 pm)** • 47 W Polk St

Farmer's Markets

- **Printer's Row** • S Dearborn St & W Polk St

Gyms

- **Bally Total Fitness** • 800 S Wells St
- **Curves** • 47 W Polk St
- **Fitplex** • 1140 S Wabash Ave

Hardware Stores

- **South Loop Ace Hardware** • 725 S State St

Liquor Stores

- **George's Cocktail Lounge** • 646 S Wabash Ave
- **Warehouse Liquors** • 634 S Wabash Ave

Movie Theaters

- **Village Theatres Burnham Plaza** • 826 S Wabash Ave

Nightlife

- **Buddy Guy's Legends** • 754 S Wabash Ave
- **HotHouse** • 31 E Balbo Ave
- **Kasey's Tavern** • 701 S Dearborn St
- **South Loop Club** • 701 S State St
- **Tantrum** • 1023 S State St

Restaurants

- **Blackie's** • 755 S Clark St
- **Hackney's** • 733 S Dearborn St
- **Room 12** • 1152 S Wabash Ave
- **South Loop Club** • 701 S State St
- **SRO** • 610 S Dearborn St
- **Trattoria Caterina** • 616 S Dearborn St

Shopping

- **Kozy's Bike Shop** • 601 S La Salle St
- **Printer's Row Fine and Rare Books** • 715 S Dearborn St
- **Sandmeyer's Book Store** • 714 S Dearborn St

Video Rental

- **Movietime Home Video** • 900 S Wabash Ave

Map 9 • South Loop / South Michigan Ave

East Jackson Dr
Rose Garden
Monroe Street Harbor
E Van Buren St
400S
E Congress Plaza Dr
Roosevelt University
Van Buren Street Station
6
A
E Congress Pkwy
Buckingham Fountain
E Harrison St
Julian and Doris Wineberg Sculpture Garden
600S
Rose Garden
PAGE 206
Grant Park
Columbia College
PAGE 244
Lake Michigan
E Balbo Ave
100E
Chicago Hilton and Towers
S Columbus Dr
S Lake Shore Dr
E 8th St
8
B
Hutchinson Field
S Michigan Ave
E 9th St
E 11th St
S Holden Ct
S Wabash Ave
11th Pl
41
Roosevelt Road Station
Museum Campus
John G Shedd Aquarium
E Roosevelt Rd
Roosevelt
1200S
PAGE 214
C
E Solidarity Dr
E Solidarity Dr
11
Field Museum of Natural History
E 13 St
McFetridge Dr
1
2
E 14th St

Essentials

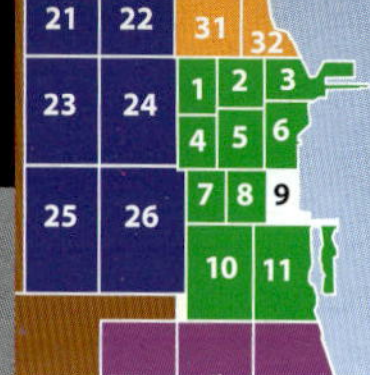

Green could describe this part of the city, from the gardens of Grant Park to the ecologically sensitive Shedd Aquarium on the Museum Campus. Beginning at dusk, Buckingham Fountain's skyrocketing water display, accompanied by lights and music, occurs every hour on the hour for twenty minutes until 11 pm. This routine occurs daily from April to October.

Banks

- **New City** • 900 S Michigan Ave

Landmarks

- **Buckingham Fountain** • Columbus Dr & E Congress Pkwy
- **Chicago Hilton and Towers** • 720 S Michigan Ave
- **Julian and Doris Wineberg Sculpture Garden** • 681 S Michigan Ave
- **Shedd Aquarium** • 1200 S Lake Shore Dr

Libraries

- **Asher Library-Spertus Institute** • 618 S Michigan Ave
- **Library of Columbia College** • 624 S Michigan Ave

Parking

Schools

- **Columbia College** • 600 S Michigan Ave
- **East-West University** • 816 S Michigan Ave
- **Spertus College** • 618 S Michigan Ave

East Jackson Dr
Rose Garden
Monroe Street Harbor
E Van Buren St
400S
E Congress Plaza Dr
Roosevelt University
Van Buren Street Station
6
A
E Congress Pkwy
Buckingham Fountain
E Harrison St
600S
Rose Garden
PAGE 206
Grant Park
Columbia College
PAGE 244
E Balbo Ave
100E
Lake Michigan
S Columbus Dr
S Lake Shore Dr
E 8th St
8
B
Hutchinson Field
S Michigan Ave
E 9th St
E 11th St
S Holden Ct
S Wabash Ave
11th Pl
41
Roosevelt Road Station
Museum Campus
John G Shedd Aquarium
E Roosevelt Rd
Roosevelt
1200S
PAGE 214
C
11
E Solidarity Dr
E Solidarity Dr
Field Museum of Natural History
E 13 St
McFetridge Dr
1
2
E 14th St

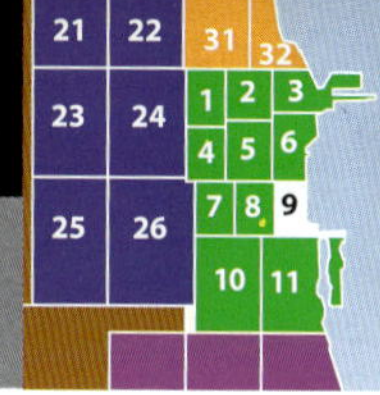

Sundries / Entertainment

The Chicago Hilton and Towers Hotel, at which the cops tossed Tom Hayden through a window during the 1968 Democratic Convention, anchors S Michigan Avenue's gentrification. After a few Killians at Kitty O'Shea's, sneak up to the spectacular 1927 Grand Ballroom for a twirl back in time. A flick at the Fine Arts Theater followed by a honking banana split is a fine way to spend a rainy day.

Nightlife

- **Kitty O'Shea's** • 720 S Michigan Ave
- **Savoy Bar and Grill** • 800 S Michigan Ave

Restaurants

- **Oysy** • 888 S Michigan Ave

Shopping

- **Bariff Shop** • 618 S Michigan Ave

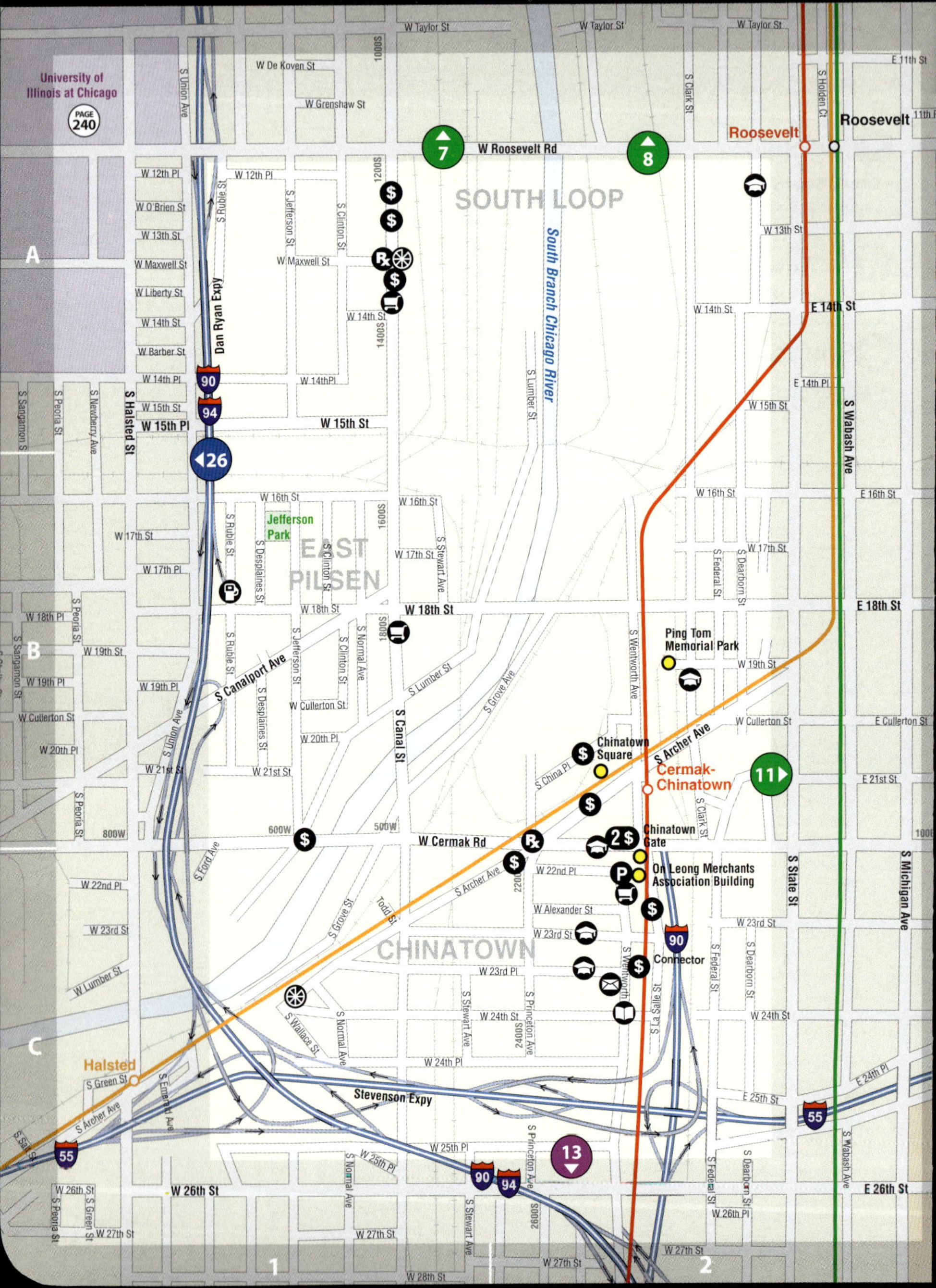

Map 10 • **East Pilsen / Chinatown**

N

University of Illinois at Chicago

PAGE 240

SOUTH LOOP

EAST PILSEN

CHINATOWN

Jefferson Park

Ping Tom Memorial Park

Chinatown Square

Chinatown Gate

On Leong Merchants Association Building

Connector

Roosevelt

Cermak-Chinatown

Halsted

South Branch Chicago River

Dan Ryan Expy

Stevenson Expy

W Roosevelt Rd

W Cermak Rd

W 18th St

W 15th St

W 26th St

S Halsted St

S Canal St

S Canalport Ave

S Archer Ave

S State St

S Michigan Ave

S Wabash Ave

E 14th St

E 18th St

E 26th St

7 8 11 13 26

A B C 1 2

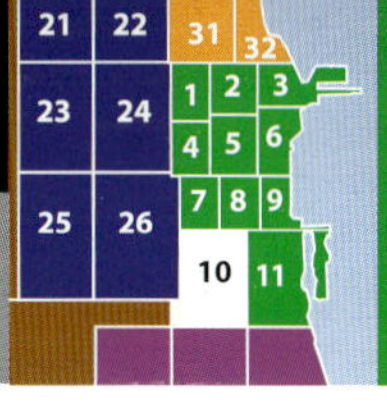

Urban artists still flock to affordable loft spaces in East Pilsen, despite occasional gang uprisings. Development around Chinatown is moving faster than the dim sum carts through the bustling expanse of Three Happiness during its popular Sunday brunch.

Banks

- **American Metro** • 2144 S Archer Ave
- **Bank One** • 1240 S Canal St
- **Bank One** • 1340 S Canal St
- **Charter One** • 2131 S China Pl
- **Charter One** • 2263 S Wentworth Ave
- **Fifth Third** • 600 W Cermak Rd
- **International Bank of Chicago** • 208 W Cermak Rd
- **Lakeside** • 2200 S Archer Ave
- **NAB** • 250 W Cermak Rd
- **New Asia** • 222 W Cermak Rd
- **South Central** • 2335 S Wentworth Ave
- **Washington Mutual** • 1226 S Canal St

Gas Stations

- **Shell** • 1741 S Ruble St

Landmarks

- **Chinatown Gate** • S Wentworth Ave & W Cermak Rd
- **Chinatown Square** • S Archer Ave
- **On Leong Merchants Association Building** • 2216 S Wentworth Ave
- **Ping Tom Memorial Park** • 300 W 19th St

Libraries

- **Chinatown Public Library** • 2353 S Wentworth Ave

Parking

Pharmacies

- **Dominick's** • 1340 S Canal St
- **Walgreens** • 316 W Cermak Rd

Pizza

- **Connie's Pizza** • 2373 S Archer Ave
- **Dominick's Finer Foods** • 1340 S Canal St

Post Offices

- 2345 S Wentworth Ave

Schools

- **John C Haines Elementary** • 247 W 23rd Pl
- **National Teacher's Academy** • 55 W Cermak Rd
- **Perspectives Charter High** • 1930 S Federal St
- **South Loop Elementary** • 1212 S Plymouth Ct
- **St Therese** • 247 W 23rd St

Supermarkets

- **Dominick's** • 1340 S Canal St
- **Richwell Market** • 1835 S Canal St
- **Tai Wah Grocery** • 2226 S Wentworth Ave

Map 10 • East Pilsen / Chinatown

University of Illinois at Chicago
PAGE 240

SOUTH LOOP
EAST PILSEN
CHINATOWN
Jefferson Park
South Branch Chicago River
Roosevelt
Cermak-Chinatown
Halsted

W Taylor St
W De Koven St
W Grenshaw St
W Roosevelt Rd
W 12th Pl
W O'Brien St
W 13th St
W Maxwell St
W Liberty St
W 14th St
W Barber St
W 14th Pl
W 15th St
W 15th Pl
W 16th St
W 17th St
W 17th Pl
W 18th St
W 18th Pl
W 19th St
W 19th Pl
W Cullerton St
W 20th Pl
W 21st St
W Cermak Rd
W 22nd Pl
W Alexander St
W 23rd St
W 23rd Pl
W 24th St
W 24th Pl
W 25th Pl
W 26th St
W 26th Pl
W 27th St
W 28th St
W Lumber St
E 11th St
11th Pl
E 14th St
E 14th Pl
E 16th St
E 18th St
E Cullerton St
E 21st St
E 24th Pl
E 25th St
E 26th St
800W
600W
500W
100E
1000S
1200S
1400S
1600S
1800S
2200S
2400S
2600S

S Union Ave
S Ruble St
S Jefferson St
S Clinton St
S Clark St
S Holden Ct
S Lumber St
S Halsted St
S Sangamon St
S Peoria St
S Newberry Ave
S Desplaines St
S Stewart Ave
S Canal St
S Canalport Ave
S Normal Ave
S Grove Ave
S Wentworth Ave
S Federal St
S Dearborn St
S Wabash Ave
S State St
S Michigan Ave
S Archer Ave
S China Pl
S Ford Ave
S Grove St
Todd St
S Wallace St
S Princeton Ave
S La Salle St
S Green St
S Emerald Ave
S Sally St
Dan Ryan Expy
Stevenson Expy
Connector

90
94
55
7
8
11
13
26
A
B
C
1
2

Sundries / Entertainment

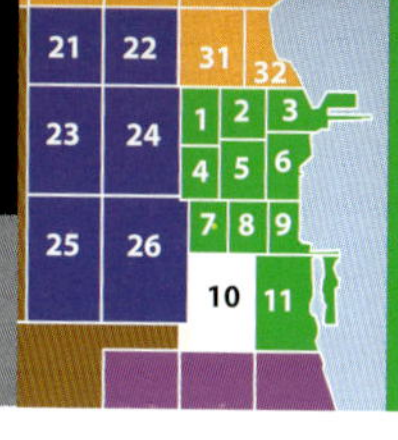

Skip Crate & Barrel and head to Chinatown for great cookware. Browse the shops along Wentworth Avenue for cooking utensils, Chinese furnishings, and imported wares. Woks 'n' Things gets our vote for best cookery. Ten Ren Tea & Ginseng Co. wins for exotic teas and accoutrements. If you haven't done dim sum at the Happy Chef, you should. The Phoenix Café is where the locals go out to eat.

Coffee

- **Starbucks (Dominick's)** • 1340 S Canal St
- **Tasty Place** • 2339 S Wentworth Ave
- **Tea Leaf Café** • 2336 S Wentworth Ave

Copy Shops

- **Kinko's (24 hours)** • 1242 S Canal St

Hardware Stores

- **Turek & Sons** • 1333 S Jefferson St
- **Zweifel True Value Hardware** • 345 W 25th Pl

Restaurants

- **Emperor's Choice** • 2238 S Wentworth Ave
- **Evergreen** • 2411 S Wentworth Ave
- **Happy Chef Dim Sum House** • 2164 S Archer Ave
- **Joy Yee's Noodle Shop** • 2159 Chinatown Sq
- **Lao Sze Chuan Spice City** • 2172 S Archer Ave
- **Penang** • 2201 S Wentworth Ave
- **Phoenix Café** • 2131 S Archer Ave
- **Three Happiness** • 209 W Cermak Rd
- **Won Kow** • 2237 S Wentworth Ave

Shopping

- **Chinatown Bazaar** • 2221 S Wentworth Ave
- **Pacific Imports** • 2200 S Wentworth Ave
- **Sun Sun Tong** • 2260 S Wentworth Ave
- **Ten Ren Tea & Ginseng Co** • 2247 S Wentworth Ave
- **Woks 'n' Things** • 2234 S Wentworth Ave

Video Rental

- **Movie Gallery** • 1258 S Canal St

Map 11 • South Loop / McCormick Place

W Taylor St
E 11th St
S Clark St
S Holden Ct
Roosevelt Road Station
11th Pl
Roosevelt
Roosevelt
E Roosevelt Rd
E Roosevelt Dr
Grant Park
PAGE 206
Lake Michigan
1200S
8
9
P
S Columbus Dr
41
E 13th St
Shedd Aquarium
Field Museum
Museum Campus
A
E Solidarity Dr
Adler Planetarium
PAGE 214
W 14th St
E 14th St
1400S
McFetridge Dr
America's Courtyard
S Wabash Ave
Indiana Ave
Lynne White Dr
E 14th Pl
CENTRAL STATION
Soldier Field
PAGE 264
Burnham Park Yacht Harbor
W 15th St
S Dearborn St
S State St
Northerly Island Park
W 16th St
PRAIRIE DISTRICT
E 16th St
1600S
E Waldron Dr
S Prairie Ave
S Lake Shore Dr
W 17th St
National Vietnam Veterans Art Museum
S Federal St
S Dearborn St
10
E 18th St
Clarke House
S Calumet Ave
E 18th Dr
1800S
18th St Station
Merrill C Meigs Field
S Wentworth Ave
B
W 19th St
Second Presbyterian Church
Hillary Rodham Clinton Women's Park and Gardens of Chicago
S Archer Ave
W Cullerton St
E Cullerton St
The Wheeler Mansion
2000S
Raymond Hilliard Homes
W 21st St
S Clark St
E 21st St
S Calumet Ave
Willie Dixon's Blues Heaven Foundation
100W
100E
200E
300E
S Dr Martin L King Jr Dr
Hyatt Regency McCormick Place
E Cermak Rd
2200S
S Michigan Ave
S Cottage Grove Ave
S Dr Martin L King Jr Dr
23rd St McCormick Place Station
E 23rd Dr
W 23rd St
E 23rd St
400E
Burnham Park
S La Salle St
S Federal St
S Dearborn St
S Calumet Ave
McCormick Place
PAGE 222
Quinn Chapel
The Chicago Daily Defender
W 24th St
E 24th St
2400S
E 24th Pl
C
E 24th Pl
55
Stevenson Expy
W 25th St
E 25th St
S Prairie Ave
S Calumet Ave
S Wabash Ave
S Federal St
S Dearborn St
S Dr Martin L King Jr Dr
S Dr Martin L King Jr Dr
14
E 26th St
W 26th Pl
2600S
Mercy Hospital & Medical Center
E 26th St
E 27th St
27th St Station
W 27th St
S Ellis Ave
Brewery Ave
1
2

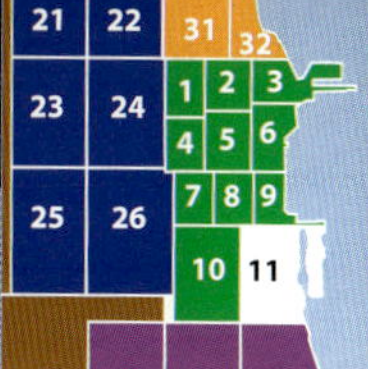

Chicago's economic engine, McCormick Place, helps power the South Loop's steady gentrification. Construction is a way of life here. Now that the new Soldier Field has made its debut, construction is underway for the convention center's new west building, slated for completion in 2008. The Museum Campus is the neighborhoods cultural anchor on the north end, and Burnham Park is its front yard.

Banks

- **Bank One** • 1934 S State St
- **Charter One (ATM)** • 5 E 14th St
- **Fifth Third** • 1300 S Lake Shore Dr
- **Harris Trust & Savings** • 1300 S Wabash Ave
- **Lakeside** • 2141 S Indiana Ave
- **Lakeside (ATM)** • Stevenson Expy & Martin Luther King Dr
- **LaSalle (ATM)** • 450 E 23rd St
- **TCF (ATM)** • 425 E McFetridge Dr
- **Washington Mutual** • 1556 S Michigan Ave

Car Rental

- **Enterprise** • 2460 S Michigan Ave • 312-808-1228
- **Hertz** • 2300 S Dr Martin L King Jr Dr • 312-567-0380

Car Washes

- **State Street Hand Car Wash** • 1701 S State St
- **Strictly By Hand** • 2007 S Wabash Ave

Hospitals

- **Mercy** • 2525 S Michigan Ave

Landmarks

- **America's Courtyard** • South of Adler Planetarium on the lakefront
- **The Chicago Daily Defender** • 2400 S Michigan Ave
- **Clarke House** • 1827 S Indiana Ave
- **Field Museum** • 1400 S Lake Shore Dr
- **Hillary Rodham Clinton Women's Park and Gardens of Chicago** • S Prairie Ave, b/w 18th St & 19th St
- **Hyatt Regency McCormick Place** • 2233 S Dr Martin L King Jr Dr
- **McCormick Place** • 2301 S Lake Shore Dr
- **Merrill C Meigs Field** • Waterfront
- **National Vietnam Veterans Art Museum** • 1801 S Indiana Ave
- **Quinn Chapel, African Methodist Episcopal Church** • 2401 S Wabash Ave
- **Raymond Hilliard Homes** • 2030 S State St
- **Second Presbyterian Church** • 1936 S Michigan Ave
- **Soldier Field** • 425 E McFetridge Dr
- **The Wheeler Mansion** • 2020 S Calumet Ave
- **Willie Dixon's Blues Heaven Foundation** • 2120 S Michigan Ave

Parking

Pharmacies

- **Osco Drug** • 2545 S Dr Martin L King Jr Dr

Pizza

- **Big Daddy's Pizzeria** • 2137 S State St

Police

- **1st District (Central)** • 1718 S State St

Post Offices

- 2035 S State St

Schools

- **Ray Graham Training Center** • 2347 S Wabash Ave

Map 11 • South Loop / McCormick Place

A
B
C
1
2

Lake Michigan
Grant Park
PAGE 206
Roosevelt Road Station
Roosevelt
Roosevelt
8
9
10
14
41
55
E Roosevelt Rd
E Roosevelt Dr
W Taylor St
E 11th St
11th Pl
S Clark St
S Holden Ct
1200S
1400S
1600S
1800S
2000S
2200S
2400S
2600S
E 13th St
S Columbus Dr
Shedd Aquarium
Field Museum
Museum Campus
E Solidarity Dr
PAGE 214
Adler Planetarium
W 14th St
E 14th St
McFetridge Dr
S Wabash Ave
Indiana Ave
CENTRAL STATION
E 14th Pl
W 15th St
S Dearborn St
S State St
Soldier Field
PAGE 264
Burnham Park Yacht Harbor
Lynne White Dr
Northerly Island Park
W 16th St
E 16th St
PRAIRIE DISTRICT
E Waldron Dr
S Wentworth Ave
S Prairie Ave
S Lake Shore Dr
W 17th St
S Federal St
E 18th St
S Calumet Ave
18th St Station
E 18th Dr
Merrill C Meigs Field
W 19th St
S Archer Ave
W Cullerton St
E Cullerton St
W 21st St
S Clark St
E 21st St
100W
100E
200E
300E
400E
E Cermak Rd
S Michigan Ave
S Cottage Grove Ave
S Dr Martin L King Jr Dr
E 23rd Dr
23rd St McCormick Place Station
W 23rd St
E 23rd St
S La Salle St
McCormick Place
PAGE 222
Burnham Park
W 24th St
E 24th St
E 24th Pl
E 24th Pl
Stevenson Expy
W 25th St
E 25th St
E 26th St
W 26th Pl
E 26th St
Mercy Hospital & Medical Center
W 27th St
E 27th St
27th St Station
S Ellis Av
Brewery Av

Theatrical Opera has become a destination restaurant since its opening in 2003, heralding a insurgence of trendy dining options in the 'hood. Old schoolers placate themselves with live jazz at the ramshackle institution, The Velvet Lounge, or tossing back suds at the Wabash Tap. History buffs and culture seekers take day trips to the prestigious addresses of the Prairie Avenue Historic District.

Coffee

- **Dunkin' Donuts** • 1231 S Wabash Ave

Farmer's Markets

- **South Loop Farmers Market** • 18th St & Wabash Ave

Gyms

- **Curves** • 77 E 16th St
- **Phenomenal Fitness** • 1468 S Michigan Ave

Nightlife

- **Chicago Legends** • 2109 S Wabash Ave
- **The Cotton Club** • 1710 S Michigan Ave
- **Velvet Lounge** • 2128 1/2 S Indiana Ave
- **Wabash Tap** • 1233 S Wabash Ave

Restaurants

- **Chef Luciano** • 49 E Cermak Rd
- **Chicago Firehouse Resturant** • 1401 S Michigan Ave
- **Gioco** • 1312 S Wabash Ave
- **NetWorks** • Hyatt Regency McCormick Place, 2231 S Dr Martin L King Jr Dr
- **Opera** • 1301 S Wabash Ave
- **Triad** • 1933 S Indiana Ave

Shopping

- **Blossoms of Hawaii** • 1631 S Michigan Ave
- **Blue Star Auto Stores** • 2001 S State St
- **Cycle Bicycle shop** • 1465 S Michigan Ave
- **Waterware** • 1829 S State St
- **Y'lonn Salon** • 1802 S Wabash Ave

N
Halsted
Ashland
S Archer Ave
W 25th St
W 26th St
W 27th St
W 28th St
W 29th St
W 30th St
W 31st St
W 31st Pl
W 32nd St
W 32nd Pl
W 33rd St
W 33rd Pl
W 34th St
W 34th Pl
W 35th St
W 35th Pl
W 36th St
W 36th Pl
W 37th St
W 37th Pl
W 38th St
W 38th Pl
W Pershing Rd
W Fuller St
S Throop St
S Halsted St
S Ashland Ave
S Racine Ave
S Morgan St
S Sangamon St
S Lituanica Ave
S May St
S Aberdeen St
S Carpenter St
S Justine St
S Laflin Pl
S Jasper Pl
S Loomis Pl
S Iron St
S Paulina St
S Marshfield Ave
S Emerald Ave
S Union Ave
S Green St
S Peoria St
S Senour Ave
S Corbett St
S Mary St
S Stark St
S Hillock Ave
S Eleanor St
S Farrell St
S Bonfield St
S Grove St
S Crowell St
S Short St
S Hanes St
S Lock St
S Grady Ct
S Quinn St
S Hoey St
S Poplar Ave
S Keeley St
S Elias Ct
S Loomis St
S Haynes Ct
S Lyman St
S Bonaparte St
S Arch St
S Lloyd Ave
S Broad St
S Pitney Ct
S Gratten Ave
S Robinson St
S Benson St
Chicago River S Branch
BRIDGEPORT
McGuane Park
Wilson Park
Donovan Park
Monastery of the Holy Cross
Library Fountain
1600W
1200W
800W
2600S
3100S
3500S
3900S
26
13
52
55
A
B
C
1
2

Essentials

Old Style and Chicago fit cheek-to-cheek in Bridgeport. The Irish neighborhood's name is as working class in origin as its closely-knit residents. The neighborhood is home to the final port and bridge on the south branch of the Chicago River, where boats unloaded cargo in the 1800s. Chinatown's and the South Loop's building boom has initiated a Bridgeport Revival. Services have yet to follow the subdivisions.

Banks

- **Bank One** • 3145 S Ashland Ave
- **Chicago Community** • 1110 W 35th St

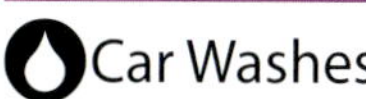

Car Washes

- **Z Best Detailing Center** • 3033 S Archer Ave

Gas Stations

- **Citgo** • 970 W Pershing Rd

Landmarks

- **Library Fountain** • W 34th St & Halsted St
- **Monastery of the Holy Cross** • 3111 S Aberdeen St
- **Wilson Park** • S May St & W 34th Pl

Pharmacies

- **Dominick's** • 3145 S Ashland Ave

Pizza

- **Dominick's** • 3145 S Ashland Ave
- **Lina's Pizza** • 3132 S Morgan St

Schools

- **Charles N Holden Elementary** • 1104 W 31st St
- **Philip D Armour Elementary** • 950 W 33rd Pl
- **St Barbara Elementary** • 2867 S Throop St

Supermarkets

- **Dominick's** • 3145 S Ashland Ave

BRIDGEPORT

Halsted
Ashland
W 25th St
S Archer Ave
S Hillock Ave
S Stark St
S Mary St
S Senour Ave
S Corbett St
S Green St
W 25th St
S Emerald Ave
W 26th St
S Eleanor St
S Farrell St
S Bonfield St
S Grove St
S Crowell St
S Short St
Hanes St
W Fuller St
S Lock St
S Grady Ct
S Throop St
S Quinn St
S Hoey St
S Poplar Ave
S Mary St
S Senour Ave
W 27th St
S Peoria St
W 28th St
W 29th St
S Keeley St
S Farrell St
S Bonfield St
S Elias Ct
S Loomis St
S Haynes Ct
S Lyman St
McGuane Park
S Bonaparte St
S Arch St
S Lloyd Ave
S Gratten Ave
W 30th St
W 31st St
S Archer Ave
S Pitney Ct
S Broad St
W 31st St
S Robinson
W 31st Pl
W 32nd St
S Benson St
W 32nd Pl
W 33rd St
S Throop St
S May St
S Aberdeen St
S Carpenter St
S Lituanica Ave
W 33rd Pl
W 34th St
W 34th Pl
Wilson Park
N Halsted St
S Union Ave
Chicago River S Branch
S Justine St
W 35th St
1600W
1200W
800W
S Iron St
S Morgan St
S Sangamon St
W 35th Pl
W 36th St
W 36th Pl
Donovan Park
W 37th St
W 37th Pl
W 38th St
W 38th Pl
S Paulina St
S Marshfield Ave
S Ashland Ave
S Laflin Pl
S Jasper Pl
S Loomis Pl
S Racine Ave
W Pershing Rd
2600S
3100S
3500S
3900S
26
13
52
55
A
B
C
1
2

Sundries / Entertainment

Hopefully Bridgeport's residential revival will eventually spur business and entertainment in the community. Right now, a big night out is watching a Sox game at a corner tavern or renting a video from Blockbuster.

Gyms

• **Lance's Gym** • 2980 S Archer Ave

Hardware Stores

• **Elston Ace Hardware** • 1514 W 33rd St

Liquor Stores

• **Ashland S** • 3162 S Ashland Ave
• **J & Lee** • 960 W 31st St

Pet Shops

• **Bridgeport Pet Boutique** • 824 W 35th St

Shopping

• **Bridgeport Antiques** • 2963 S Archer Ave

Video Rental

• **Blockbuster Video** • 3145 S Ashland Ave

N
A
B
C
1
2
W 25th St
W 25th Pl
W 26th St
E 26th
W 26th Pl
W 27th St
W 28th St
W 28th Pl
W 29th St
W 29th Pl
W 30th St
W 30th Pl
W 31st St
E 31st St
W 31st Pl
W 32nd St
W 32nd Pl
W 33rd St
W 33rd Pl
W 34th St
W 34th Pl
W 35th St
W 35th Pl
W 36th St
W 37th St
W 37th Pl
W 38th St
W 38th Pl
W De Saible St
W Pershing Rd
W 40th St
E 28th St
E 29th St
E 30th St
E 32nd St
E 34th St
S Halsted St
S Archer Ave
S Green St
S Corbett St
S Senour Ave
S Peoria St
S Poplar Ave
S Lowe Ave
S Normal Ave
S Canal St
S Princeton Ave
S Stewart Ave
S Shields Ave
S Wells St
S Federal St
S Dearborn St
S Wabash Ave
S State St
S La Salle St
S Wentworth Ave
S Emerald Ave
S Union Ave
S Wallace St
S Parnell Ave
S Lituanica Ave
S Sangamon St
Dan Ryan Expy
800W
500W
400W
2600S
3100S
3500S
3900S
BRIDGEPORT
McGuane Park
Williams Park
Armour Square Park
Donovan Park
Stateway Gardens Park
Wentworth Gardens Park
Old Neighborhood Italian American Club
Richard J Daley House
Illinois Institute Of Tech
US Cellular Field
PAGE 248
PAGE 266
35th-Bronzeville-IIT
Sox-35th
55
90
94
10
12
14
15

Bridgeport is home turf to the Daley political dynasty and three other Chicago mayors. This part of Bridgeport is a gritty, and not always hospitable, mix of Irish, Italians, Chinese, and African-Americans. The fancy redesigned IIT campus has drawn new attention to the neighborhood, hopefully for the better.

Banks

- **Bank One** • 757 W 35th St
- **Bank One (ATM)** • 142 W 35th St
- **Bank One (ATM)** • 3241 S Federal St
- **Charter One** • 600 W 37th St
- **Citibank** • 3430 S Halsted St
- **LaSalle (ATM)** • 333 W 35th St
- **South Central** • 3032 S Halsted St
- **TCF (ATM)** • Jewel, 3033 S Halsted
- **TCF (ATM)** • Osco, 741 W 31st St

Car Washes

- **J&J Full Service Car Wash** • 349 W 31st St
- **Looking Good Hand Car Wash** • 3540 S Halsted St

Gas Stations

- **Accutech** • 444 W 26th St
- **BP/Amoco** • 3047 S Halsted St
- **Citgo** • 501 W 31st St
- **Mobil** • 243 W Pershing Rd
- **Shell** • 215 W 31st St

Landmarks

- **McGuane Park** • W 29th St & S Halsted St
- **Old Neighborhood Italian American Club** • 3031 S Shields Ave
- **Richard J Daley House** • 3536 S Lowe Ave

Libraries

- **Daley Public Library** • 3400 S Halsted St

Pharmacies

- **Jewel** • 3033 S Halsted St
- **Osco Drug** • 741 W 31st St
- **Walgreens** • 3000 S Halsted St

Pizza

- **Donnie's Pizza & Café** • 3258 S Wells St
- **Freddie's Pizza & Pasta Parlor** • 701 W 31st St
- **Little Caesar's Pizza** • 3010 S Halsted St
- **Paulie's Pizza & Italian Sandwiches** • 2600 S Wallace St
- **Phil's Pizza** • 3551 S Halsted St
- **Ricobene's Pizzeria** • 252 W 26th St

Police

- **9th District (Deering)** • 3501 S Lowe Ave

Schools

- **Big Picture Company High** • 2710 S Dearborn St
- **Bridgeport Catholic Academy** • 3700 S Lowe Ave
- **Bridgeport Catholic Academy North** • 512 W 28th Pl
- **Crispus Attucks Elementary** • 3813 S Dearborn St
- **George B McClellan Elementary** • 3527 S Wallace St
- **Illinois Institute of Technology** • 3300 S Federal St
- **James Ward Elementary** • 2701 S Shields Ave
- **Mark Sheridan Math & Science Academy** • 533 W 27th St
- **Robert Healy Elementary** • 3010 S Parnell Ave
- **Robert S Abbott Elementary** • 3630 S Wells St
- **Santa Lucia** • 3017 S Wells St
- **St Jerome** • 2805 S Princeton Ave
- **Vandercook College Of Music** • 3140 S Federal St
- **Williams Elementary** • 2710 S Dearborn St
- **Williams Middle** • 2710 S Dearborn St

Supermarkets

- **Chinese Fresh Food Market** • 3001 S Halsted St
- **Jewel** • 3033 S Halsted St

Map 13 • Bridgeport (East)

S Green St
W 25th St
S Archer Ave
S Corbett St
55
S Canal St
S Princeton Ave
W 25th Pl
W 25th Pl
S Lowe Ave
S Normal Ave
90
94
10
S Federal St
S Wabash Ave
E 24th Pl
E 26th
W 26th St
W 26th St
S Peoria St
S Green St
S Senour Ave
W 27th St
2900S
W 27th St
W 26th Pl
W 27th St
W 27th St
W 28th St
S Stewart Ave
S Halsted St
S Dearborn St
A
W 28th Pl
W 28th Pl
E 28th St
Williams Park
800W
500W
400W
W 29th St
E 29th St
W 29th St
W 29th St
S Poplar Ave
McGuane Park
S Shields Ave
S Princeton Ave
S Wells St
S Federal St
W 30th St
W 29th Pl
S Canal St
W 30th St
W 30th St
E 30th St
W 30th Pl
W 31st St
E 31st St
S Green St
3100S
S Federal St
W 31st Pl
W 32nd St
14
E 32nd St
W 32nd St
W 32nd Pl
BRIDGEPORT
Dan Ryan Expy
Illinois Institute Of Tech
W 33rd St
12
B
W 33rd St
E 33rd
S Lituanica Ave
W 33rd Pl
S Emerald Ave
S Union Ave
S Lowe Ave
S Wallace St
S Parnell Ave
S Normal Ave
S Shields Ave
Armour Square Park
S Wentworth Ave
S La Salle St
S Federal St
PAGE 248
S State St
W 34th St
W 34th St
W 34th St
E 34th St
W 34th Pl
800W
35th-Bronzeville-IIT
Illinois Co Of Optom
W 35th St
S Sangamon St
S Lituanica Ave
3500S
Sox-35th
W 35th Pl
US Cellular Field
PAGE 266
S Federal St
E 36t
W 36th St
W 36th St
E 36t
Donovan Park
S Princeton Ave
S Wells St
90
94
W 37th St
W 37th St
W 37th Pl
S Emerald Ave
S Union Ave
S Lowe Ave
S Wallace St
S Parnell Ave
S Normal Ave
W 37th Pl
W 37th Pl
S Shields Ave
W 37th Pl
Stateway Gardens Park
E Carve
E 37th
C
W 38th St
W De Saible St
Wentworth Gardens Park
W 38th St
W 38th St
W 38th St
E 38th St
W 38th St
S Dearborn St
W 38th Pl
W 38th Pl
W 38th Pl
W Pershing Rd
3900S
S Canal St
15
S Princeton Ave
S Wentworth Ave
S La Salle St
S Federal St
E 4
1
2
W 40th Pl
W 40th St

Sundries / Entertainment

Sadly, neighborhood favorite Healthy Foods Lithuanian (and the entire block it sits on) seems to have fallen prey to developer's designs. Meanwhile, Sox fans from the 'hood grab a slice to go from Freddie's and head to Jimbo's after a game at Old Comiskey a.k.a. US Cellular Field. There are some rough patches to this old Chicago neighborhood—outsiders are well advised to stick to well-lit streets after dark.

Coffee

- **Dunkin' Donuts** • 749 W 31st St
- **Nancy's Pantry** • 3500 S Emerald Ave

Gyms

- **Curves** • 3252 S Wallace St

Hardware Stores

- **Joe Harris Paint & Hardware** • 3301 S Wallace St
- **Windy City Hardware** • 3262 S Halsted St

Liquor Stores

- **Bridgeport Liquors** • 3411 S Halsted St
- **Express Food & Liquor** • 3904 S Wentworth Ave

Nightlife

- **Jimbo's Lounge** • 3258 S Princeton Ave
- **Puffer's Bar** • 3356 S Halsted St
- **Schaller's** • 3714 S Halsted St

Restaurants

- **August Moon Restaurant** • 225 W 26th St
- **Franco's Ristorante** • 300 W 31st St
- **Furama** • 2828 S Wentworth Ave
- **Kevin's Hamburger Heaven** • 554 W 39th St
- **Offshore Steak House** • 480 W 26th St
- **Phil's Pizza** • 3551 S Halsted St
- **Ramova Grill** • 3510 S Halsted St
- **Scumaci's Italian Sandwiches** • 220 W 31st St
- **Wing Yip Chop Suey** • 537 W 26th St

Shopping

- **Accutek Printing & Graphics** • 260 W 26th St
- **Ace Bakery** • 3200 S Halsted St
- **Augustine's Spiritual Goods** • 3323 S Halsted St
- **Bridgeport News Travel & Tours** • 3252 S Halsted St
- **Health King Enterprises Chinese Medicinals** • 238 W 31st St
- **Let's Boogie Records & Tapes** • 3321 S Halsted St

Map 14 • Prairie Shores / Lake Meadows

55
W 25th St
E 24th Pl
E 25th St
11
Monument to the Great Northern Migration
E 26th St
PRAIRIE SHORES
Lake Michigan
S Dearborn St
S State St
S Wabash Ave
2600S
S Indiana Ave
S Prairie Ave
S Calumet Ave
E 26th St
E 27th St
27th St
Brewery Ave
S Ellis Ave
Moe Dr
Fort Dearborn Dr
A
E 28th St
S Michigan Ave
SOUTH COMMONS
S Cottage Grove Ave
E 28th St
E 28th Pl
E 29th St
W 29th St
E 29th St
E 29th Pl
S Lake Park Ave
Dunbar Park
S Dr Martin L King Jr Dr
W 30th St
E 30th St
E 30th St
S Vernon Ave
S Ellis Ave
100E
200E
400E
E 31st St
E 31st St
3100S
E 31st Pl
Lake Meadows Park
13
E 32nd St
E 32nd St
S Eberhart Ave
E 32nd St
THE GAP
LAKE MEADOWS
S Rhodes Ave
E 32nd St
S Ellis Ave
E 32nd Pl
B
E 33rd St
E 33rd Blvd
E 33rd St
E 33rd St
S Giles Ave
E 33rd St
E 33rd Pl
Groveland Park
Burnham Park
Illinois Institute Of Tech
E 33rd Pl
41
E Groveland Park
E 34th St
E 34th St
E 34th St
Interesting Benches
S Rhodes Ave
S Lake Shore Dr
E Woodland Park Ave
PAGE 248
Illinois College Of Optometry
Woodland Park
35th-Bronzville-IIT
E 35th St
E 35th St
Douglas Tomb
3500S
S Cottage Grove Ave
E Browning Ave
E 36th St
E 36th St
E 36th St
Chicago Bee Building
E 36th Pl
Ida B Wells/ Barnett Home
E 36th St
E 36th Pl
Ellis Park
Stateway Gardens Park
E 37th St
E Carver Plz
E 37th Pl
E 37th Pl
C
Anderson Park
Madden Park
E 38th St
E 38th St
E 38th St
E 38th St
E 38th Pl
S Langley Ave
S Drexel Blvd
S Vincennes Ave
E Pershing Rd
16
3900S
17
S Lake Park Ave
E Oakwood Blvd
E Oakwood St
1
2

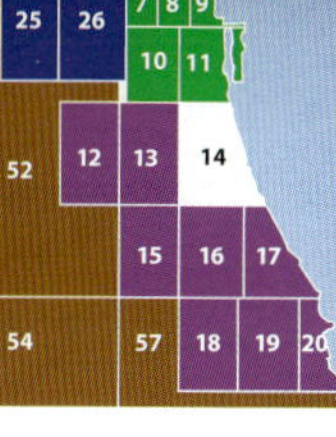

Prairie Shores and Lake Meadows compose a residential high-rise neighborhood along the lakefront. The former Chicago Bee newspaper building, a restored 1929 Art Deco gem, is now the community's public library, housing an impressive African-American history collection. Although undergoing a resurgence, the neighborhood is still quite rough around the western edge on S State Street, where the Robert Taylor Homes, a crime-riddled public housing complex, are located.

Banks

- **Bank One** • 3500 S King Dr
- **Harris Trust & Savings (ATM)** • 3201 S State St
- **Lakeside (ATM)** • 2900 S Ellis Ave
- **Northern Trust (ATM)** • 3851 S Michigan Ave
- **Shore** • 3401 S Dr Martin L King Jr Dr
- **TCF (ATM)** • Jewel, 443 E 34th St
- **Washington Mutual** • 3501 S King Dr

Gas Stations

- **BP** • 343 E 35th St
- **BP/Amoco** • 3101 S Michigan Ave
- **Citgo** • 437 E Pershing Rd

Hospitals

- **Michael Reese** • 2929 S Ellis Ave

Landmarks

- **Chicago Bee Building** • 3647-55 S State
- **Douglas Tomb** • E 35th St & Lake Park
- **Dunbar Park** • S Indiana Ave & E 31st St
- **Ida B Wells / Barnett home** • 3624 S King Dr
- **Interesting Benches** • S Dr Martin L King Jr Dr b/w E 33rd St & E 35th St
- **Monument to the Great Northern Migration** • S Dr Martin L King Jr Dr & E 26th St

Libraries

- **Chicago Bee Public Library** • 3647 S State St
- **King Public Library** • 3436 S Dr Martin L King Jr Dr

Pharmacies

- **Jewel-Osco** • 443 E 34th St
- **Walgreens (24 hours)** • 3405 S Dr Martin L King Jr Dr

Police

- **21st District (Prairie)** • 300 E 29th St

Schools

- **Benjamin W Raymond Elementary** • 3663 S Wabash Ave
- **Chicago Military Academy** • 3519 S Giles Ave
- **Christ the King Lutheran** • 3701 S Lake Park Ave
- **Dawson Technical Institute** • 3901 S State St
- **Doolittle Middle** • 535 E 35th St
- **Doolittle West Primary** • 521 E 35th St
- **Douglas Community Academy** • 3200 S Calumet Ave
- **Drake Elementary** • 2722 S Dr Martin L King Jr Dr
- **Dunbar Vocational Career Academy** • 3000 S Dr Martin L King Jr Dr
- **Illinois College of Optometry** • 3241 S Michigan Ave
- **JJ Pershing School for Humanities** • 3113 S Rhodes Ave
- **McKinley Lakeside High** • 2929 S Wabash Ave
- **Phillips Academy** • 244 E Pershing Rd
- **St James Elementary** • 2920 S Wabash Ave
- **Wells Elementary** • 244 E Pershing Rd
- **William J & Charles H Mayo Elementary** • 249 E 37th St
- **Young Women's Leadership High** • 2641 S Calumet Ave
- **Youth Connection High** • 10 W 35th St

Supermarkets

- **Jewel-Osco** • 443 E 34th St

Map 14 • Prairie Shores / Lake Meadows

Sundries / Entertainment

There are plenty of parks and several architecturally significant sites worth a visit. The Douglas Tomb State Historic Site at E 35th commemorates Illinois Senator Stephen A. Douglas, who faced off against Abe Lincoln in the 1858 debates. Historic Bronzeville starts around Douglas's Tomb. Restored mansions on S 31st Street and further south date from the glitzy 1920s—get a peek inside when the neighborhood sponsors the Bronzeville home tours in late June.

Copy Shops

- **The UPS Store (8 am-7 pm)** • 3437 S Dr Martin L King Jr Dr

Farmer's Markets

- **Bronzeville** • 3000 S Dr Martin L King Jr Dr

Gyms

- **Curves** • 439 E 31 St
- **Wabash YMCA** • 3763 S Wabash Ave

Hardware Stores

- **Meyers Ace Hardware** • 315 E 35th St

Liquor Stores

- **Poorwood Food & Liquors** • 200 E 35th St
- **Rothchild Liquor Marts** • 124 E Pershing Rd

Nightlife

- **Cobblestone's Bar and Grill** • 514 E Pershing Rd
- **Darryl's Den** • 2600 S State St
- **Mr T's Lounge** • 3528 S Indiana Ave

Restaurants

- **Blue Sea Drive Inn** • 427 E Pershing Rd
- **Bronzeville Market & Deli** • 339 E 35th St
- **Chicago Rib House** • 3851 S Michigan Ave
- **Hong Kong Delight** • 327 E 35th St

Shopping

- **Ashley Stewart** • 3455 S Dr Martin L King Jr Dr
- **Avenue** • 3409 S Dr Martin L King Jr Dr

Video Rental

- **Blockbuster Video** • 3349 S Dr Martin L King Jr Dr

N

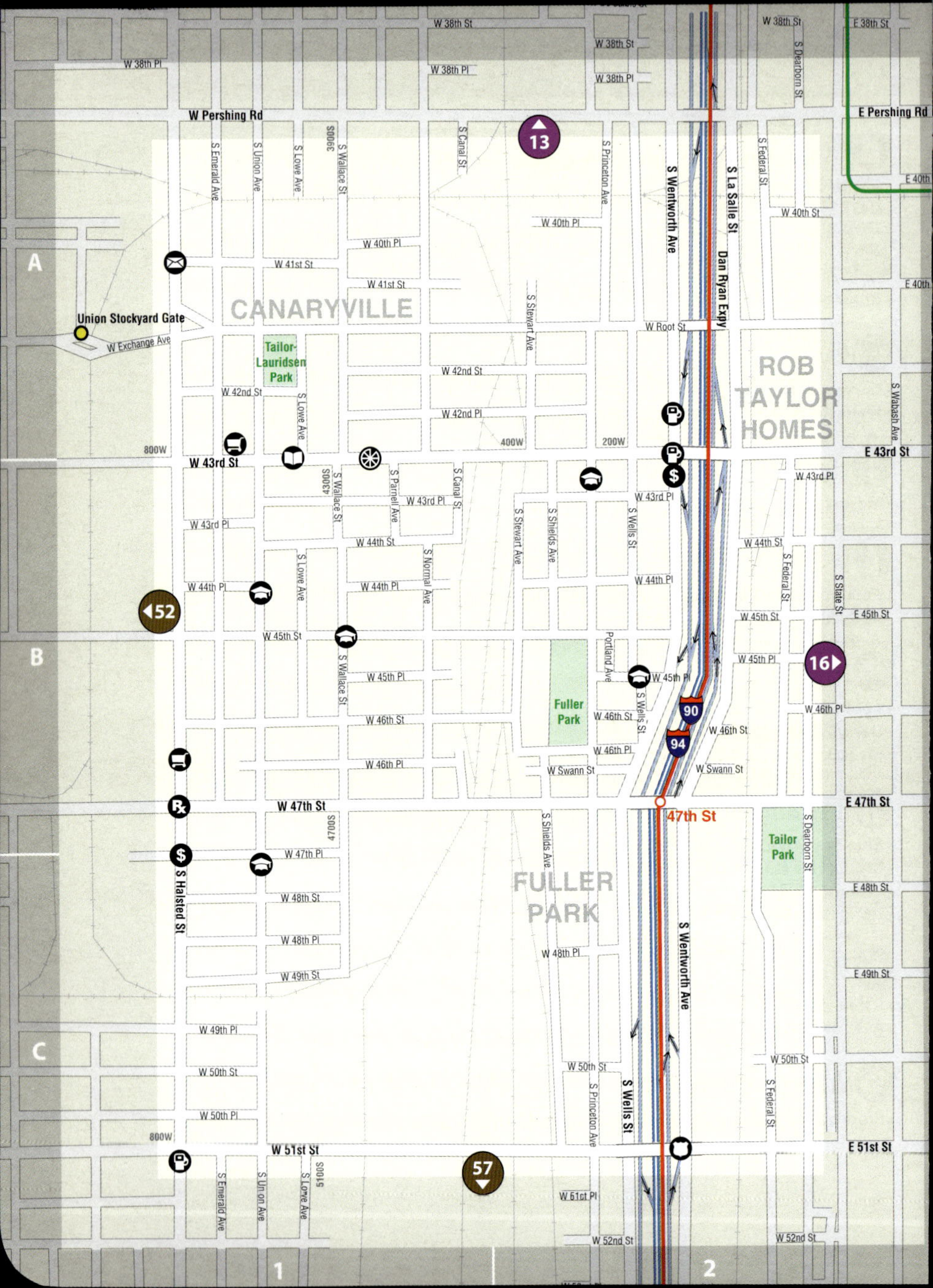

W 38th St
W 38th Pl
W Pershing Rd
E Pershing Rd
13
S Emerald Ave
S Union Ave
S Lowe Ave
S Wallace St
S Canal St
S Princeton Ave
S Wentworth Ave
S La Salle St
S Federal St
S Dearborn St
Dan Ryan Expy
W 40th Pl
W 40th St
E 40th
W 41st St
W 41st Pl
CANARYVILLE
Union Stockyard Gate
W Exchange Ave
Tailor-Lauridsen Park
S Stewart Ave
W Root St
ROB TAYLOR HOMES
W 42nd St
W 42nd Pl
800W
400W
200W
W 43rd St
E 43rd St
W 43rd Pl
S Parnell Ave
S Shields Ave
S Wells St
S Normal Ave
W 44th St
W 44th Pl
S Wabash Ave
S State St
52
W 45th St
E 45th St
W 45th Pl
Portland Ave
Fuller Park
16
W 46th St
W 46th Pl
W Swann St
90
94
W 47th St
E 47th St
47th St
W 47th Pl
S Halsted St
Tailor Park
FULLER PARK
W 48th St
E 48th St
W 48th Pl
W 49th St
E 49th St
W 49th Pl
W 50th St
W 50th Pl
W 51st St
E 51st St
57
W 51st Pl
W 52nd St
A
B
C
1
2

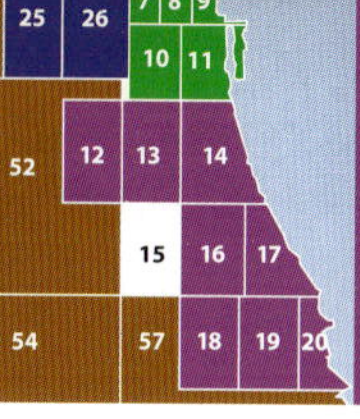

This is a rough neighborhood that you should avoid unless jury duty demands that you travel to the Cook County Criminal Court building on W 51st Street. Public housing projects fraught with gang skirmishes dominate the streets. Here, the Union Stockyards, which earned Chicago's reputation as "hog butcher to the world," once stood. All that's left is the limestone entrance gate to the stockyards. Pass on the sightseeing and keep heading south to upbeat Bronzeville.

Banks

- **Bank One (ATM)** • 4701 S Halsted St
- **TCF (ATM)** • 4300 S Wentworth Ave

Gas Stations

- **Amoco** • 4248 S Wentworth Ave
- **Amoco** • 5101 S Halsted St
- **Citgo** • 4300 S Wentworth Ave

Landmarks

- **Union Stockyard Gate** • Exchange Ave & Peoria St

Libraries

- **Canaryville Public Library** • 642 W 43rd St

Pharmacies

- **Walgreens** • 4700 S Halsted St

Pizza

- **Pizza Nova** • 558 W 43rd St

Police

- **2nd District (Wentworth)** • 5101 S Wentworth Ave

Post Offices

- 4101 S Halsted St

Schools

- **Alexander Graham Elementary** • 4436 S Union Ave
- **Bronzeville Blue Gargoyle High** • 220 W 45th Pl
- **Francis Parkman Elementary** • 245 W 51st St
- **St Gabriel Elementary** • 4500 S Wallace St
- **Thomas A Hendricks Community Academy** • 4316 S Princeton Ave
- **Tilden High** • 4747 S Union Ave

Supermarkets

- **Fairplay Finer Foods** • 4640 S Halsted St
- **Save A Lot** • 710 W 43rd St

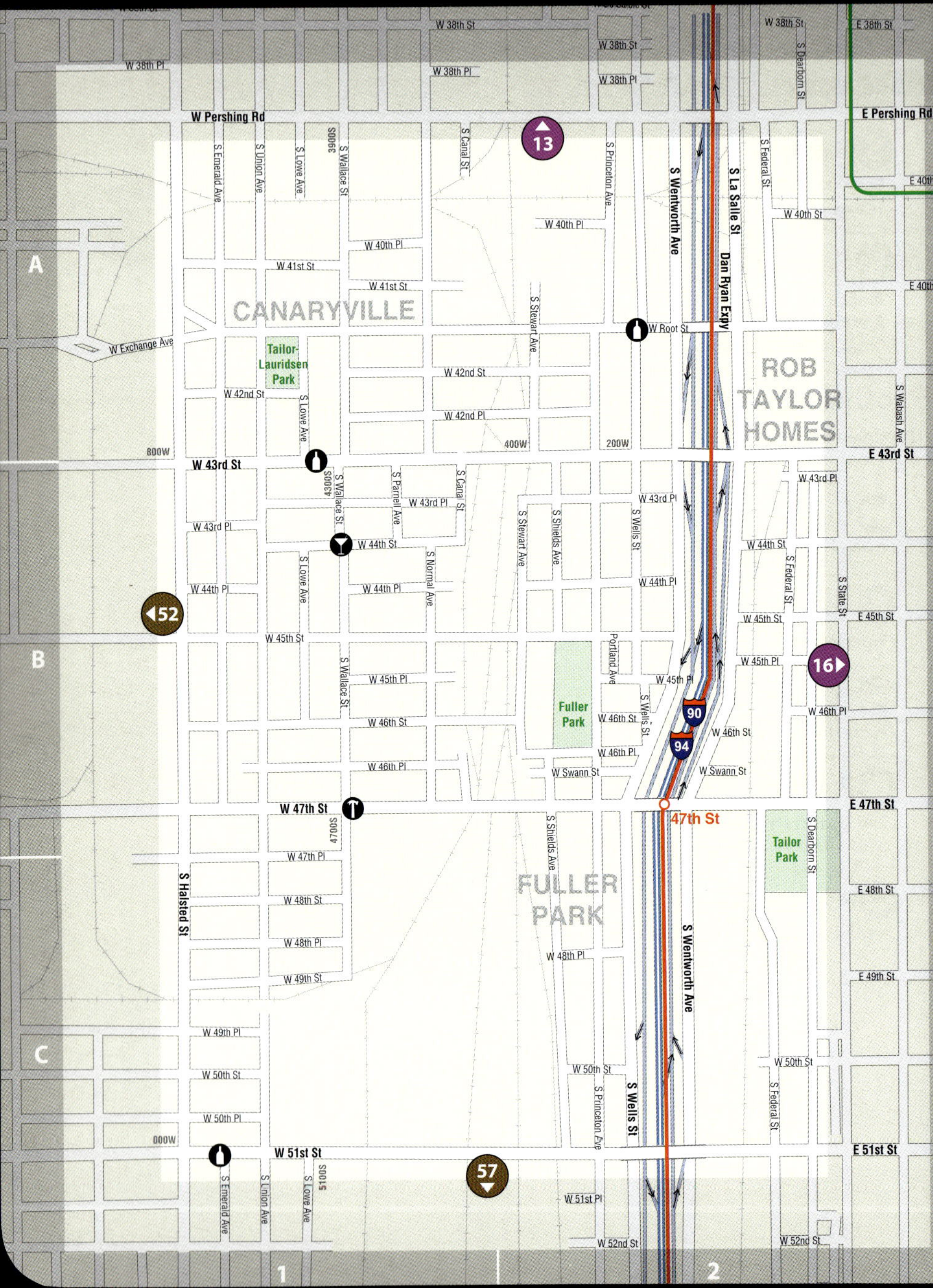

N

CANARYVILLE
FULLER PARK
ROB TAYLOR HOMES
Tailor-Lauridsen Park
Fuller Park
Tailor Park

W Pershing Rd
E Pershing Rd
W 38th St
W 38th Pl
W 40th Pl
W 40th St
W 41st St
W Exchange Ave
W Root St
W 42nd St
W 42nd Pl
W 43rd St
E 43rd St
W 43rd Pl
W 44th St
W 44th Pl
W 45th St
E 45th St
W 45th Pl
W 46th St
W 46th Pl
W Swann St
W 47th St
E 47th St
W 47th Pl
W 48th St
E 48th St
W 48th Pl
W 49th St
E 49th St
W 49th Pl
W 50th St
W 50th Pl
W 51st St
E 51st St
W 51st Pl
W 52nd St

S Halsted St
S Emerald Ave
S Union Ave
S Lowe Ave
S Wallace St
S Parnell Ave
S Normal Ave
S Canal St
S Stewart Ave
S Shields Ave
S Princeton Ave
Portland Ave
S Wells St
S Wentworth Ave
S La Salle St
Dan Ryan Expy
S Federal St
S Dearborn St
S State St
S Wabash Ave

800W
400W
200W
3900S
4300S
4700S
5100S

47th St
90
94

13
16
52
57

A
B
C
1
2

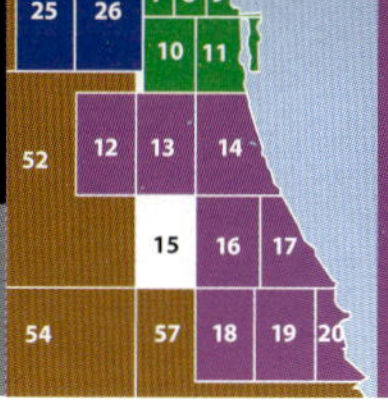

If Chicago ever hosts the Olympics, this will be the perfect neighborhood to host the shooting event.

Hardware Stores

- **Discount Hardware** • 601 W 47th St

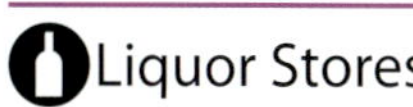

Liquor Stores

- **Bravo Liquors** • 619 W 43rd St
- **Root Inn** • 234 W Root St
- **Shamsan Food & Liquor** • 737 W 51st St

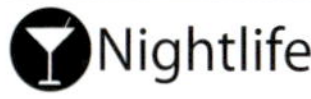

Nightlife

- **Kelley's Tavern** • 4403 S Wallace St

Map 16 • Bronzeville

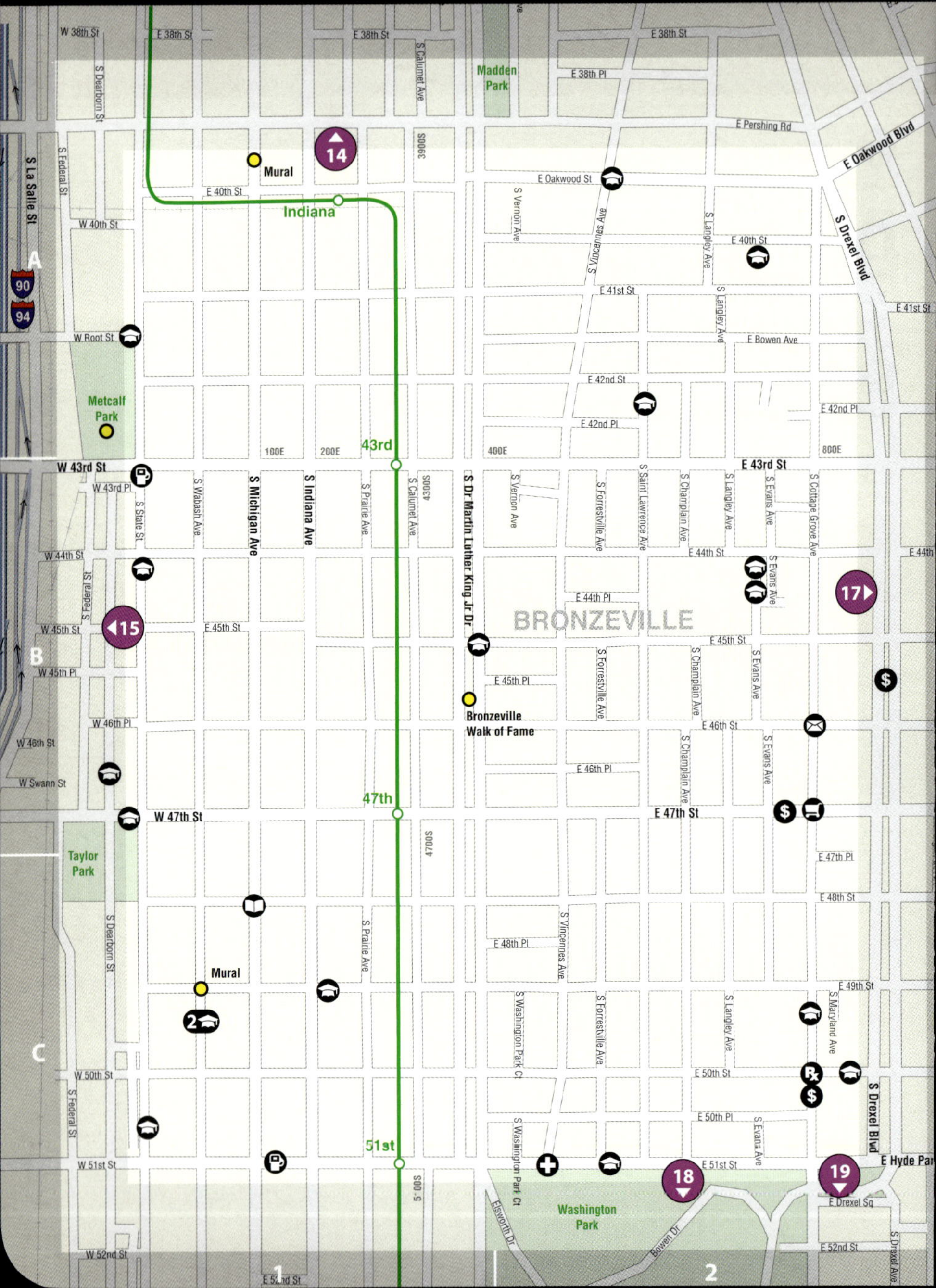

W 38th St
E 38th St
E 38th St
E 38th St
S Dearborn St
S Calumet Ave
Madden Park
E 38th Pl
E Pershing Rd
E Oakwood Blvd
S La Salle St
S Federal St
3900S
14
Mural
E Oakwood St
E 40th St
Indiana
W 40th St
S Vernon Ave
S Vincennes Ave
S Langley Ave
E 40th St
S Drexel Blvd
A
90
94
E 41st St
E 41st St
S Langley Ave
W Root St
E Bowen Ave
Metcalf Park
E 42nd St
E 42nd Pl
E 42nd Pl
100E
200E
43rd
400E
800E
W 43rd St
E 43rd St
W 43rd Pl
S State St
S Wabash Ave
S Michigan Ave
S Indiana Ave
S Prairie Ave
S Calumet Ave
4300S
S Dr Martin Luther King Jr Dr
S Vernon Ave
S Forrestville Ave
S Saint Lawrence Ave
S Champlain Ave
S Langley Ave
S Evans Ave
S Cottage Grove Ave
W 44th St
E 44th St
E 44th
S Evans Ave
S Federal St
E 44th Pl
17
BRONZEVILLE
15
W 45th St
E 45th St
E 45th St
B
W 45th Pl
E 45th Pl
S Forrestville Ave
S Champlain Ave
S Evans Ave
W 46th Pl
Bronzeville Walk of Fame
E 46th St
W 46th St
S Champlain Ave
S Evans Ave
E 46th Pl
W Swann St
47th
W 47th St
E 47th St
4700S
Taylor Park
E 47th Pl
E 48th St
S Dearborn St
S Prairie Ave
S Vincennes Ave
E 48th Pl
Mural
E 49th St
S Washington Park Ct
S Forrestville Ave
S Langley Ave
S Maryland Ave
2
C
W 50th St
E 50th St
S Drexel Blvd
S Federal St
E 50th Pl
S Washington Park Ct
S Evans Ave
51st
W 51st St
E 51st St
E Hyde Par
18
19
S 00S
S Washington Park Ct
Ellsworth Dr
Washington Park
Bowen Dr
E Drexel Sq
W 52nd St
E 52nd St
S Drexel Ave
1
2

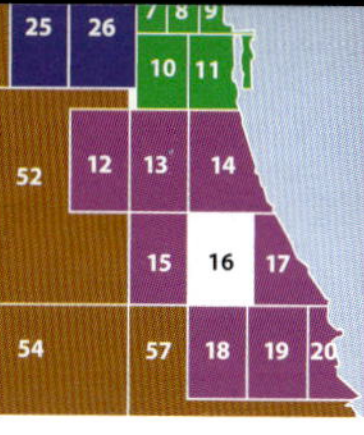

The once-thriving African-American neighborhood of Bronzeville had the vibe of New York's Harlem, and now it's coming back. Bronzeville is experiencing a resurgence, thanks to community efforts to preserve its architecturally significant buildings dating from the 1920s. Neighborhood notables recognized on the Bronzeville Walk of Fame include horn-blower Louis Armstrong, crooner Nat King Cole, astronaut Mae Jemison, choreographer Katherine Dunham (a graduate of the University of Chicago), and architect Walter T. Bailey.

Banks

- **Bank One (ATM)** • 5036 S Cottage Grove Ave
- **Northern Trust (ATM)** • 740 E 47th St
- **Shore** • 4658 S Drexel Blvd

Gas Stations

- **Amoco** • 4300 S State St
- **Citgo** • 123 E 51st St

Hospitals

- **Provident** • 500 E 51st St

Landmarks

- **Bronzeville Walk of Fame** • S Martin Luther King Jr Blvd from 25th St to 47th St
- **Metcalf Park** • 4130-4300 S State St
- **Mural** • 3947 S Michigan Ave
- **Mural** • 49th St & S Wabash Ave

Libraries

- **Hall Public Library** • 4801 S Michigan Ave

Pharmacies

- **Walgreens** • 5036 S Cottage Grove Ave

Post Offices

- 4601 S Cottage Grove Ave

Schools

- **Anthony Overton Elementary** • 221 E 49th St
- **Carter G Woodson North Middle** • 4414 S Evans Ave
- **Carter G Woodson South Elementary** • 4444 S Evans Ave
- **Colman Elementary** • 4655 S Dearborn St
- **Dyett Academy Center** • 555 E 51st St
- **Hales Franciscan High** • 4930 S Cottage Grove Ave
- **Helen J McCorkle Elementary** • 4421 S State St
- **Holy Angel's** • 750 E 40th St
- **Irvin C Mollison Elementary** • 4415 S Dr Martin L King Jr Dr
- **Jean Baptiste Du Sable High** • 4934 S Wabash Ave
- **John Farren Elementary** • 5055 S State St
- **Ludwig Von Beethoven Elementary** • 25 W 47th St
- **Melville W Fuller Elementary** • 4214 S St Lawrence Ave
- **St Elizabeth Elementary** • 4052 S Wabash Ave
- **William Reavis Elementary** • 834 E 50th St
- **Williams Preparatory School of Medicine** • 4934 S Wabash Ave

Supermarkets

- **Save A Lot** • 4701 S Cottage Grove Ave

Map 16 • Bronzeville

W 38th St
E 38th St
E 38th St
E 38th St
S Dearborn St
S Calumet Ave
Madden Park
E 38th Pl
E Pershing Rd
E Oakwood Blvd
3900S
14
S Federal St
S La Salle St
E Oakwood St
E 40th St
Indiana
W 40th St
S Vernon Ave
S Vincennes Ave
S Langley Ave
E 40th St
S Drexel Blvd
A
90
94
E 41st St
S Langley Ave
E 41st St
W Root St
E Bowen Ave
E 42nd St
Metcalf Park
E 42nd Pl
E 42nd Pl
43rd
100E
200E
400E
800E
W 43rd St
E 43rd St
W 43rd Pl
S State St
S Wabash Ave
S Michigan Ave
S Indiana Ave
S Prairie Ave
S Calumet Ave
4300S
S Dr Martin Luther King Jr Dr
S Vernon Ave
S Forrestville Ave
S Saint Lawrence Ave
S Champlain Ave
S Langley Ave
S Evans Ave
S Cottage Grove Ave
W 44th St
E 44th St
E 44th
S Federal St
S Evans Ave
17
E 44th Pl
BRONZEVILLE
W 45th St
15
E 45th St
E 45th St
B
W 45th Pl
S Forrestville Ave
S Champlain Ave
S Evans Ave
E 45th Pl
W 46th Pl
E 46th St
W 46th St
S Champlain Ave
S Evans Ave
E 46th Pl
W Swann St
47th
W 47th St
E 47th St
4700S
Taylor Park
E 47th Pl
E 48th St
S Dearborn St
S Prairie Ave
S Vincennes Ave
E 48th Pl
E 49th St
S Washington Park Ct
S Forrestville Ave
S Langley Ave
S Maryland Ave
C
W 50th St
E 50th St
S Federal St
E 50th Pl
S Evans Ave
S Washington Park Ct
S Drexel Blvd
51st
W 51st St
5100S
E 51st St
18
19
E Hyde Par
E Drexel Sq
Washington Park
Ellsworth Dr
Bowen Dr
E 52nd St
S Drexel Ave
W 52nd St
1
E 52nd St
2

Sundries/ Entertainment

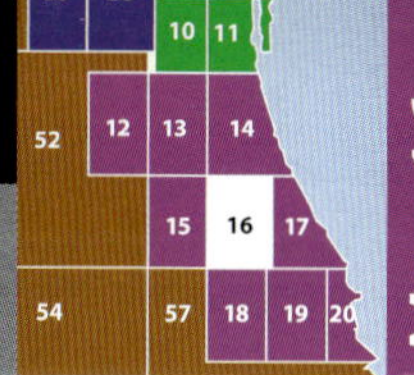

Catch open-mike poetry at the Spoken Word Café. The Negro League Café dishes up nostalgia with its Caribbean-influenced cuisine—the decor commemorates the segregated baseball leagues of the past. Gladys's Luncheonette is a Bronzeville soul legend. Barbara's Soul Food dishes up home-cooked southern cuisine.

Coffee

- **The Negro League Café** • 301 E 43rd St
- **Spoken Word Café** • 4655 S King Dr

Hardware Stores

- **Brooks Hardware** • 103 E 47th St
- **Hyde Park Building Materials** • 4630 S Cottage Grove Ave
- **Tarson Mastercraft Hardware** • 221 E 51st St

Liquor Stores

- **Calumet Food & Liquor** • 315 E 43rd St
- **Pappy's Liquors** • 4700 S Cottage Grove Ave
- **Petra** • 128 E 51st St

Restaurants

- **Barbara's** • 353 E 51st St
- **Gladys' Luncheonette** • 4527 S Indiana Ave
- **Harold's Chicken Shack** • 307 E 51st St
- **Harold's Chicken Shack** • 364 E 47th St

Shopping

- **Afrocentric Bookstore** • 4655 S King Dr
- **Issues Barber & Beauty Salon** • 3958 S Cottage Grove Ave
- **Parker House Sausage Co** • 4601 S State St

Video Rental

- **Blockbuster Video** • 5052 S Cottage Grove Ave

Map 17 • Kenwood

Lake Michigan
OAKLAND
NORTH KENWOOD
KENWOOD
Burnham Park
Kenwood Park
Madison Park
South Kenwood Mansions
Louis Farrakhan Home
47th
41
14
16
19
20
A
B
C
1
2
E Oakwood Blvd
E 38th
3900S
S Drexel Blvd
S Lake Park Ave
S Oakenwald Ave
E 41st St
E 41st Pl
S Ellis Ave
E 42nd St
E 42nd Pl
S Cottage Grove Ave
E 43rd St
4300S
S Berkeley Ave
S Greenwood Ave
E 44th St
E 44th Pl Ext
S University Ave
E 46th St
E 47th St
E 47th Pl
S Ingleside Ave
4700S
S Woodlawn Ave
S Kimbark Ave
S Kenwood Ave
S Dorchester Ave
S Lake Shore Dr
E 48th St
800E
1200E
E 49th St
S Maryland Ave
S East End Ave
S Chicago Beach Dr
E 50th St
E 50th Pl
E Madison Park
E Hyde Park Blvd
E Drexel Sq
5100S
S Drexel Ave
E 52nd St
S Blackstone Ave
S Cornell Ave
S Hyde Park Blvd

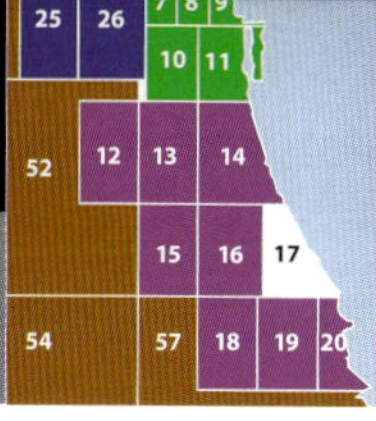

Largely residential, Kenwood is the address for astounding, renovated Victorian mansions. Muhammad Ali once lived in the grand dame at 4944 S Woodlawn Avenue and an 1897 Frank Lloyd Wright house is at 5132 S Woodlawn Avenue The graceful, tree-lined streets of South Kenwood are where the University of Chicago professors live, while students live on campus in neighboring Hyde Park just to the south.

Banks

- **Citibank** • 1320 E 47th St
- **Harris Trust & Savings** • 901 E 47th St

Gas Stations

- **Amoco** • 1158 E 47th St
- **Amoco** • 5048 S Cornell Ave

Landmarks

- **Louis Farrakhan Home** • 4855 S Woodlawn
- **South Kenwood Mansions** • b/w S Dorchester Ave (east), S Ellis Ave (west), E Hyde Park Blvd (south), & E 47th St (north)

Libraries

- **Blackstone Public Library** • 4904 S Lake Park Ave

Pharmacies

- **Walgreens** • 1320 E 47th St

Pizza

- **Domino's** • 1453 E Hyde Park Blvd

Schools

- **Ancona Montessori** • 4770 S Dorchester Ave
- **Ariel Community Academy** • 1119 E 46th St
- **Dr Martin Luther King Jr High** • 4445 S Drexel Blvd
- **Florence B Price Elementary** • 4351 S Drexel Ave
- **Kenwood High** • 5015 S Blackstone Ave
- **Miriam Canter Middle** • 4959 S Blackstone Ave
- **North Kenwood/Oakland Elementary** • 1119 E 46th St
- **North Kenwood/Oakland Middle** • 1014 E 47th St
- **Robinson Elementary** • 4225 S Lake Park Ave
- **Shoesmith Elementary** • 1330 E 50th St

Supermarkets

- **Co-op Market** • 1300 E 47th St
- **Village Foods** • 1521 E Hyde Park Blvd

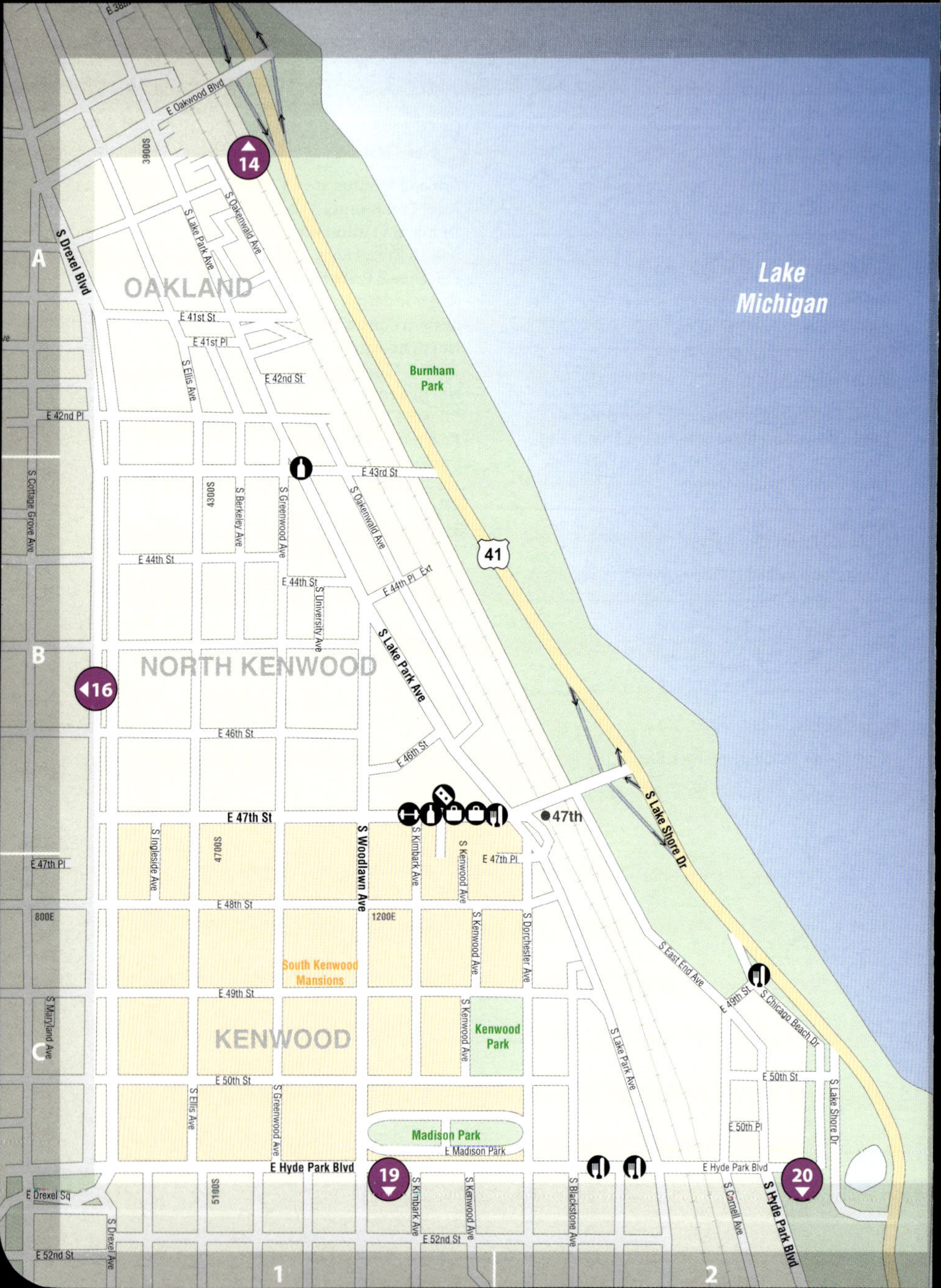

OAKLAND
NORTH KENWOOD
KENWOOD
Lake Michigan
Burnham Park
South Kenwood Mansions
Kenwood Park
Madison Park
47th
41
14
16
19
20
A
B
C
1
2
E Oakwood Blvd
S Drexel Blvd
S Lake Park Ave
S Oakenwald Ave
E 41st St
E 41st Pl
S Ellis Ave
E 42nd St
E 42nd Pl
E 43rd St
S Cottage Grove Ave
S Berkeley Ave
S Greenwood Ave
E 44th St
E 44th Pl Ext
S University Ave
E 46th St
E 47th St
E 47th Pl
S Ingleside Ave
S Woodlawn Ave
S Kimbark Ave
S Kenwood Ave
E 48th St
S Dorchester Ave
E 49th St
S Maryland Ave
S Lake Shore Dr
S East End Ave
S Chicago Beach Dr
E 50th St
E 50th Pl
E Madison Park
E Hyde Park Blvd
E Drexel Sq
S Drexel Ave
E 52nd St
S Blackstone Ave
S Cornell Ave
S Hyde Park Blvd
3900S
4300S
4700S
5100S
800E
1200E

Sundries / Entertainment

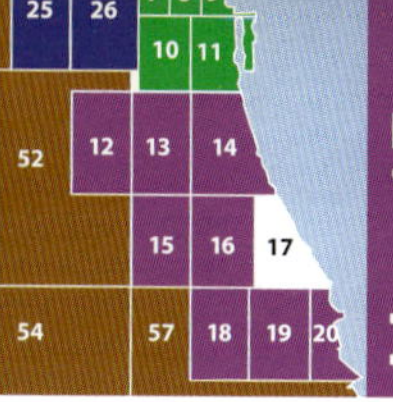

When there are students nearby, count on good, cheap eats. Kenny's on E Hyde Park Boulevard is the go-to place for cheap, finger-lickin'-good ribs. Get your music at Coop's Records and movies at Top Dollar Video and DVD, both on E 47th Street.

Gyms

- **Bally Total Fitness** • 1301 E 47th St

Liquor Stores

- **Co-op Market** • 1300 E 47th St
- **One Stop Food & Liquors** • 4301 S Lake Park Ave

Restaurants

- **Fung's Chop Suey** • 1400 E 47th Dr
- **Kenny's Ribs & Chicken** • 1461 E Hyde Park Blvd
- **Lake Shore Café** • 4900 S Lake Shore Dr
- **The Original Pancake House** • 1517 E Hyde Park Blvd

Shopping

- **Coop's Records** • 1350 E 47th St
- **South Shore Decor** • 1328 E 47th St

Map 18 • Washington Park

N

E 50th St
S Federal St
E 50th Pl
S Evans Ave
51st
W Hyde Park Blvd
16
5100S
S Washington Park Ct
E Hyde Park Blvd
Ellsworth Dr
E Drexel Sq
W 52nd St
Bowen Dr
E 52nd St
S Drexel Ave
E 52nd St
A
E 53rd St
W 53rd St
E 53rd St
S Prairie Ave
S Calumet Ave
E 53rd St
S Maryland Ave
S La Salle St
WASHINGTON PARK
Washington Park
W 54th St
W 54th St
E 54th St
E 54th St
E 54th St
E 54th Pl
W Garfield Blvd
E Garfield Blvd
E Garfield Blvd
E Garfield Blvd
Garfield
S Perry Ave
S Lafayette Ave
5500S
E 55th Pl
Aquatic Center & Refectory
Rainey Dr
E 56th St
E 56th Pl
S Drexel Ave
57
Morgan Dr
Payne Dr
DuSable Museum of African-American History
W 57th St
E 57th St
B
Russell Dr Ramp
19
S Maryland Ave
W 57th Pl
Russell Dr
Lagoon
E 58th St
S Calumet Ave
S Cottage Grove Ave
University of Chicago
PAGE 242
E 59th St
W 59th St
E 59th St
S Lafayette Ave
Midway Plaisance
Best Dr
Best Dr
Best Dr
Former Home of Black Panther Jesse Binga
E 60th St
W 60th St
100E
200E
300E
400E
800E
S Drexel Ave
S La Salle St
S Perry Ave
S Lafayette Ave
S State St
61st St
S Wabash Ave
6100S
S Indiana Ave
S Michigan St
S Prairie Ave
S Dr Martin Luther King Dr
S Vernon Ave
S Eberhart Ave
S Rhodes Ave
S St Lawrence Ave
W 61st St
E 61st Pl
C
E 62nd St
W 62nd St
S Champlain Ave
S Langley Ave
S Evans Ave
East 63rd-Cottage Grove
King Dr
W 63rd St
E 63rd St
57
S Maryland Ave
E 63rd Pl

Designed in 1871 and one of the sites for the 1893 World Columbian Exposition, Washington Park dominates the neighborhood. Lorado Taft's depressing but impressive Fountain of Time stone sculpture portrays how life goes on while the clock tick-tocks. Within the 367-acre park's confines is the oftenoverlooked DuSable Museum of African-American History. The museum's collections preserve and interpret the African-American experience.

Car Washes

- **Adam's Car Wash** • 48 E Garfield Blvd

Gas Stations

- **Marathon** • 48 E Garfield Blvd

Landmarks

- **Aquatic Center & Refectory** • 5531 S Dr Martin L King Jr Dr
- **DuSable Museum of African-American History** • 740 E 56th Pl
- **Former Home of Black Panther Jesse Binga** • 5922 S Dr Martin L King Jr Dr
- **Washington Park** • E 60th St thru E 51st St, from S Cottage Grove Ave to S Dr Martin L King Jr Dr

Libraries

- **Bessie Coleman Public Library** • 731 E 63rd St

Pizza

- **B&B Pizza King** • 4 W Garfield Blvd

Post Offices

- 700 E 61st St

Schools

- **ACE Technical High** • 5410 S State St
- **Austin O Sexton Elementary** • 6020 S Langley Ave
- **Beasley Academic Elementary** • 5255 S State St
- **Betsy Ross Elementary** • 6059 S Wabash Ave
- **Chicago International Elementary - Washington Park Campus** • 6105 S Michigan Ave
- **Edmund Burke Elementary** • 5356 S King Dr
- **John Foster Dulles High** • 6311 S Calumet Ave
- **William W Carter Elementary** • 5740 S Michigan Ave
- **Woodlawn Intergenerational High** • 448 E 61st St

Supermarkets

- **Brothers Food Market** • 723 E 63rd St

N
E 50th St
S Federal St
E 50th Pl
S Evans Ave
51st
W Hyde Park Blvd
E Hyde Park Blvd
S Washington Park Ct
16
5100S
Ellsworth Dr
E Drexel Sq
Bowen Dr
W 52nd St
E 52nd St
S Drexel Ave
E 53rd St
A
W 53rd St
E 53rd St
S Prairie Ave
S Calumet Ave
S Maryland Ave
S La Salle St
WASHINGTON PARK
Washington Park
W 54th St
W 54th St
E 54th St
E 54th St
E 54th Pl
W Garfield Blvd
E Garfield Blvd
E Garfield Blvd
E Garfield Blvd
Garfield
S Perry Ave
S Lafayette Ave
5500S
E 55th Pl
Rainey Dr
E 56th St
E 56th Pl
57
Morgan Dr
Payne Dr
S Drexel Ave
W 57th St
E 57th St
B
W 57th Pl
Russell Dr Ramp
S Maryland Ave
19
Russell Dr
Lagoon
E 58th St
S Calumet Ave
S Cottage Grove Ave
University of Chicago
PAGE 242
W 59th St
E 59th St
E 59th St
S Lafayette Ave
Midway Plaisance
Best Dr
Best Dr
Best Dr
E 60th St
W 60th St
100E
200E
300E
400E
800E
S La Salle St
S Perry Ave
S Lafayette Ave
S State St
S Drexel Ave
E 61st St
S Wabash Ave
S Michigan St
6100S
S Indiana Ave
S Prairie Ave
S Dr Martin Luther King Dr
S Vernon Ave
S Eberhart Ave
S Rhodes Ave
S St Lawrence Ave
W 61st St
E 61st Pl
C
W 62nd St
E 62nd St
S Champlain Ave
S Langley Ave
S Evans Ave
East 63rd-Cottage Gro
King Dr
W 63rd St
E 63rd St
57
S Maryland Ave
E 63rd Pl
1
2

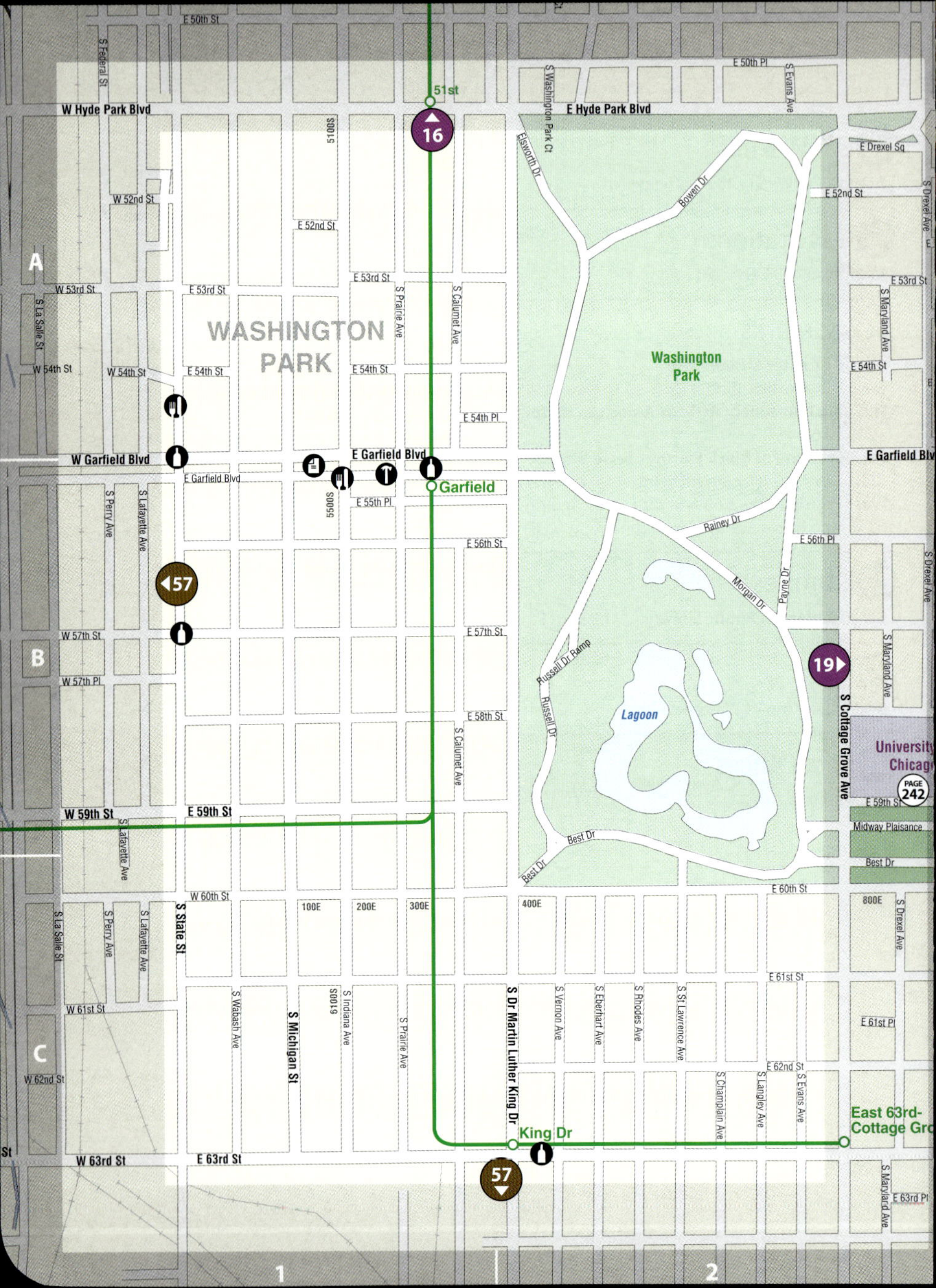

Sundries / Entertainment

Washington Park exudes a relaxed attitude. Lots of great fried chicken joints can be found in this neighborhood, making it perfect for picnics. Look to the park for things to do. Its outdoor swimming pool, playing fields, fishing lagoons, and peaceful nature areas keep residents outdoors and active. The food at Rose's BBQ on S State Street satisfies a hearty appetite.

Copy Shops

- **JJC Creative Services (9 am-5:30 pm)** • 130 E Garfield Blvd

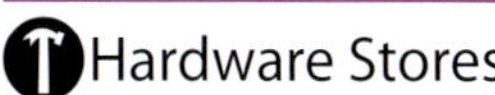

Hardware Stores

- **Boulevard Ace Hardware** • 227 E Garfield Blvd

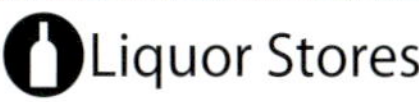

Liquor Stores

- **Garden State Liquors** • 5701 S State St
- **Jordan Food & Liquor** • 315 E Garfield Blvd
- **Midway Food & Liquor** • 5500 S State St
- **Rothschild Liquor Marts** • 425 E 63rd St

Restaurants

- **Ms Lee's Good Food** • 205 E Garfield Blvd
- **Rose's BBQ Chicken** • 5426 S State St

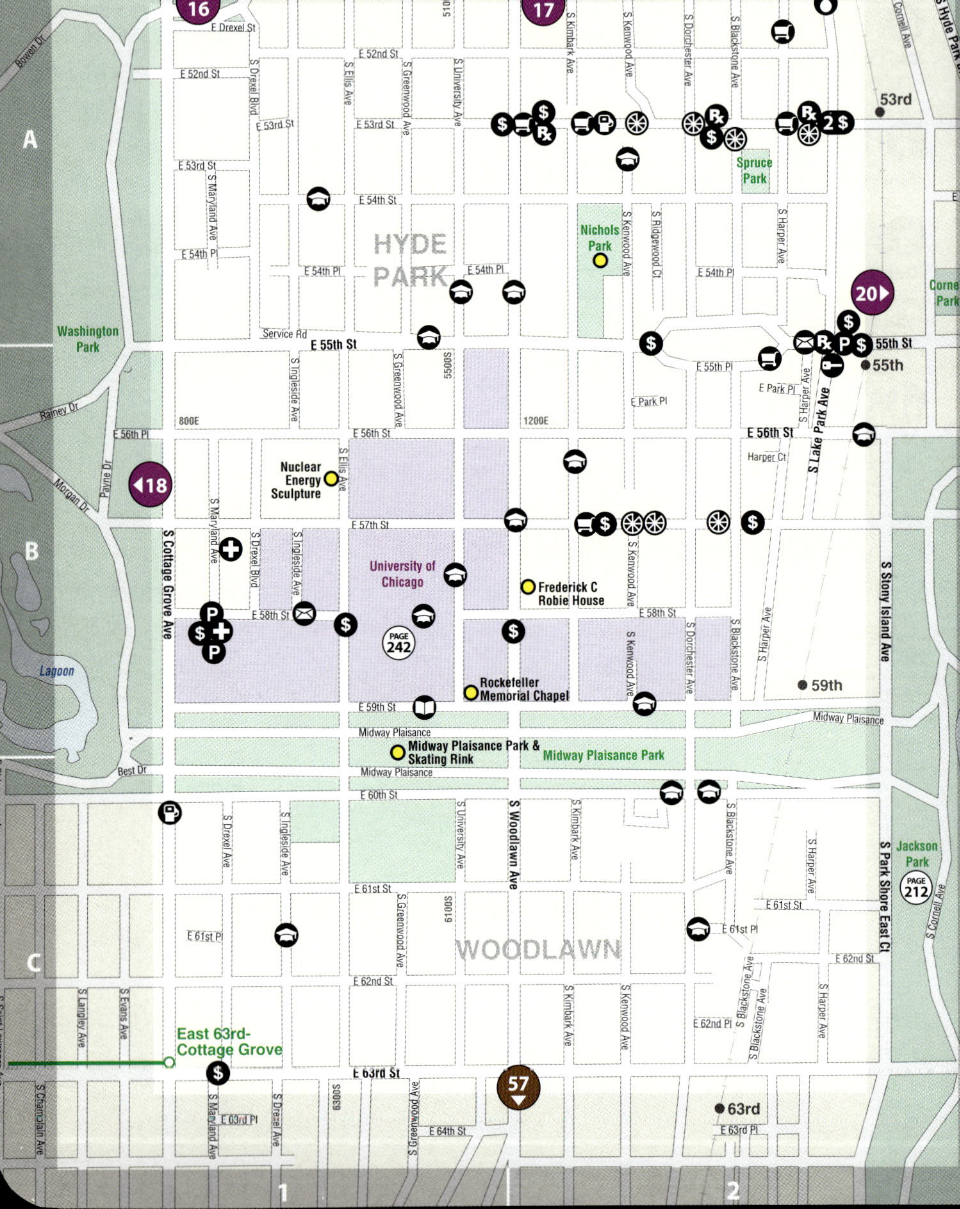

E 50th St
E 50th Pl
S Evans Ave
Madison Park
E Madison Park
E Hyde Park Blvd
S Lake Park Ave
S Cornell Ave
S Hyde Park Blvd
16
17
E Drexel St
Bowen Dr
E 52nd St
S Drexel Blvd
S Ellis Ave
S Greenwood Ave
S University Ave
S Kimbark Ave
S Kenwood Ave
S Dorchester Ave
S Blackstone Ave
53rd
E 53rd St
A
Spruce Park
S Maryland Ave
E 54th St
HYDE PARK
Nichols Park
S Ridgewood Ct
S Harper Ave
E 54th Pl
20
Cornell Park
Washington Park
Service Rd
E 55th St
55th St
55th
E 55th Pl
S Ingleside Ave
E Park Pl
Rainey Dr
800E
1200E
E 56th Pl
E 56th St
Harper Ct
Payne Dr
Morgan Dr
18
Nuclear Energy Sculpture
E 57th St
B
S Cottage Grove Ave
University of Chicago
Frederick C Robie House
S Stony Island Ave
E 58th St
PAGE 242
Lagoon
Rockefeller Memorial Chapel
59th
E 59th St
Midway Plaisance
Midway Plaisance Park & Skating Rink
Midway Plaisance Park
Best Dr
E 60th St
S Woodlawn Ave
Jackson Park
S Park Shore East Ct
PAGE 212
E 61st St
E 61st Pl
WOODLAWN
C
E 62nd St
E 62nd Pl
S Langley Ave
East 63rd-Cottage Grove
S Saint Lawrence Ave
E 63rd St
57
63rd
S Champlain Ave
E 63rd Pl
E 64th St
1
2

Essentials

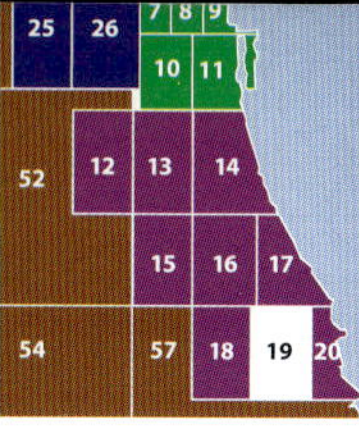

Infused with the ivy-laden University of Chicago, Hyde Park is a great mix of academia and cultural diversity. Though the Rockefeller Memorial Chapel, Oriental Institute and Frank Lloyd Wright-designed Robie House are the architectural gems of the neighborhood, the charm of wild parrot nests dotting the trees of Nichols Park is unmatched. Residents run the gamut of cultures, which brings unique flavor to the tree-lined streets of Hyde Park.

Banks

- **Bank One** • 1204 E 53rd St
- **Bank One (ATM)** • 1554 E 55th St
- **Bank One (ATM)** • 5815 S Maryland Ave
- **Citibank** • 5807 S Woodlawn Ave
- **Citibank** • 5812 S Ellis Ave
- **Cole Taylor** • 824 E 63rd St
- **Hyde Park** • 1311 E 57th St
- **Hyde Park** • 1525 E 53rd St
- **Hyde Park (ATM)** • 1518 E 53rd St
- **Hyde Park (ATM)** • 1526 E 55th St
- **TCF (ATM)** • 1214 E 53rd St
- **TCF (ATM)** • 1455 E 57th St
- **TCF (ATM)** • Osco, 1420 E 53rd St
- **University National** • 1354 E 55th St

Car Washes

- **BP/Amoco** • 5130 S Lake Park Ave

Car Rental

- **Enterprise** • 5508 S Lake Park Ave • 773-288-0500

Gas Stations

- **Amoco** • 6011 S Cottage Grove Ave
- **Mobil** • 1330 E 53rd St

Hospitals

- **University of Chicago** • 5841 S Maryland Ave
- **University of Chicago Children's Hospital** • 5721 S Maryland Ave

Landmarks

- **Frederick C Robie House** • 5757 S Woodlawn Ave
- **Midway Plaisance Park & Skating Rink** • S Ellis Ave & S University Ave, from E 59th to E 60th Sts
- **Nichol's Park** • 1300 E 55th St
- **Nuclear Energy Sculpture** • 5600 Block S Ellis
- **Rockefeller Memorial Chapel** • 5850 S Woodlawn Ave

Libraries

- **University of Chicago Harper Memorial Library** • 1116 E 59th St

Parking

Pharmacies

- **CVS Pharmacy** • 1228 E 53rd St
- **Katsaros Pharmacy** • 1521 E 53rd St
- **Osco Drug** • 1420 E 53rd St
- **Walgreens (24 hours)** • 1554 E 55th St

Pizza

- **Caffe Florian** • 1450 E 57th St
- **Edwardo's Natural Pizza** • 1321 E 57th St
- **Giordano's** • 5309 S Blackstone Ave
- **Medici on 57th** • 1327 E 57th St
- **Pizza Capri** • 1501 E 53rd St
- **Pizza Hut** • 1406 E 53rd St

Post Offices

- 1526 E 55th St
- 956 E 58th St

Schools

- **Andrew Carnegie Elementary** • 1414 E 61st Pl
- **Bret Harte Elementary** • 1556 E 56th St
- **Charles Kozminski Elementary** • 936 E 54th St
- **Chicago Theological Seminary** • 5757 S University Ave
- **John Fiske Elementary** • 6145 S Ingleside Ave
- **Lutheran School of Theology at Chicago** • 1100 E 55th St
- **McCormick Seminary** • 5460 S University Ave
- **Meadville Lombard Theological School** • 5701 S Woodlawn Ave
- **Phillip Murray Language Academy** • 5335 S Kenwood Ave
- **Sonia Sahnkman Orthogenic** • 1365 E 60th St
- **St Thomas the Apostle Elementary** • 5467 S Woodlawn Ave
- **Toyota Technological Institute at Chicago** • 1427 E 60th St
- **University of Chicago** • 5801 S Ellis Ave
- **University of Chicago Laboratory Schools** • 1362 E 59th St
- **William H Ray Elementary** • 5631 S Kimbark Ave

Supermarkets

- **Bonne Sante Health Food** • 1512 E 53rd St
- **Co-op Market** • 1526 E 55th St
- **Co-op Market Express** • 1226 E 53rd St
- **Hyde Park Produce** • 1312 E 53rd St
- **Sunflower Seed Health Food** • 5210-C S Harper Ave
- **University Market** • 1323 E 57th St

Map 19 • Hyde Park

Sundries / Entertainment

While Hyde Park struggles to identify a 'nightlife', the Woodlawn Tap is consistently there for the college crowd and neighborhood regulars alike. Bookstore Row on 57th Street provides a literary surge to the neighborhood. Restaurants range from the delivery-and-counter-seating-only Ribs and Bibs, to the upscale La Petite Folie, and finally to the ever-necessary Noodles, Etc.

Coffee

- **Dunkin' Donuts** • 1411 E 53rd St
- **Einstein Bros Bagels (University of Chicago)** • 1135 E 57th St
- **Starbucks** • 1174 E 55th St
- **Starbucks** • 1508 E 53rd St
- **Third World Café** • 1301 E 53rd St

Copy Shops

- **Copy Works (8:30 am-6 pm)** • 5210 S Harper Ave
- **Kinko's (6 am-12 am)** • 1315 E 57th St
- **The UPS Store (8:30 am-6:30 pm)** • 1507 E 53rd St

Farmer's Markets

- **Hyde Park** • E 52nd Pl & Harper Ave

Gyms

- **Curves** • 1424 E 53rd St
- **Curves** • 1514 E 63rd St

Hardware Stores

- **Elston Ace Hardware** • 5420 S Lake Park Ave

Liquor Stores

- **Binny's Beverage Depot** • 1531 E 53rd St
- **Fair Discount** • 801 E 63rd St
- **Kimbark Liquors & Wine Shop** • 1214 E 53rd St

Movie Theaters

- **University of Chicago Doc Films** • 1212 E 59th St

Nightlife

- **Lucky Strike** • 1055 E 55th St
- **Woodlawn Tap** • 1172 E 55th St

Pet Shops

- **Hyde Park Pet** • 5210 S Harper Ct

Restaurants

- **Bonjour Café Bakery** • 1550 E 55th St
- **C'Est Si Bon** • 5225-F S Harper Ave
- **Calypso Café** • 5211 S Harper Ave
- **Cedars Mediterranean Kitchen** • 1206 E 53rd St
- **Daley's Restaurant** • 809 E 63rd St
- **Dixie Kitchen and Bait Shop** • 5225 S Harper Ave
- **Hyde Park Gyros** • 1368 E 53rd St
- **Kikuya Japanese Restaurant** • 1601 E 55th St
- **La Petite Folie** • 1504 E 55th St
- **Maravilla's Mexican Restaurant** • 5211 S Harper Ave
- **Medici on 57th** • 1327 E 57th St
- **Mellow Yellow** • 1508-10 E 53rd St
- **Nathan's** • 1372 E 53rd St
- **Noodles Etc** • 1333 E 57th St
- **Rajun Cajun** • 1459 E 53rd St
- **Ribs N Bibs** • 5300 S Dorchester Ave
- **Salonica** • 1440 E 57th St
- **Thai 55 Restaurant** • 1607 E 55th St
- **Valois** • 1518 E 53rd St

Shopping

- **57th Street Books** • 1301 E 57th St
- **Akente Express II** • 5210 S Harper Ave
- **The Baby PhD Store** • 5225-I S Harper Ave
- **Border's Books and Music** • 1539 E 53rd St
- **Coconuts** • 1506 E 53rd St
- **Cohn & Stern For Men** • 1500 E 55th St
- **Dr Wax Records and Tapes** • 5225-D S Harper Ave
- **Futons N More** • 1370 E 53rd St
- **House of Africa** • 1352 E 53rd St
- **Hyde Park Records** • 1377 E 53rd St
- **O'Gara and Wilson** • 1448 E 57th St
- **Powell's Bookstore** • 1501 E 57th St
- **Toys Et Cetera** • 5211-A S Harper Ave
- **Wesley's Shoe Corral** • 1506 E 55th St
- **Wheels and Things** • 5210-E S Harper Ave

Video Rental

- **Hollywood Video** • 1530 E 53rd St

Lake Michigan
HYDE PARK
E 50th St
E 50th Pl
E Hyde Park Blvd
S Hyde Park Blvd
S Lake Shore Dr
Model Yacht Basin
17
53rd
E 53rd St
E 54th St
S Cornell Ave
Cornell Park
S Everett Ave
S South Shore Dr
S Shore Dr
Promontory Point Park
E 54th Pl
E 55th St
E 55th Pl
55th
E Park Pl
S Harper Ave
S Lake Park Ave
E 56th St
Harper Ct
S Stony Island Ave
E 57th St
E Museum Dr
E 57th Dr
Columbia Dr
57th Street Beach
Hyde Park Hospital
Museum of Science and Industry
E Columbia Dr Cutoff
S Dorchester Ave
S Blackstone Ave
E 58th St
19
University of Chicago
PAGE 242
59th
E 59th St
Midway Plaisance
Plaisance Park
41
Jackson Park Beach
Wooded Island
West Lagoon
East Lagoon
Osaka Garden
E 61st St
E 61st Pl
S Park Shore East Ct
E 62nd Pl
PAGE 212
Jackson Park
E 63rd St
58
E Hayes Dr
Coast Gd Dr Cut Off
63rd
E 63rd Pl
South Lagoon
Yacht Harbor
A
B
C
1
2

This is a great neighborhood in which to relax. Recently, the Chicago Park District dumped money into upgrading the neighborhood's lakefront. The 57th Street and 63rd Street beaches are less crowded than those on the North Side. The Museum of Science and Industry deserves multiple visits, but beware, brain freeze sets in fast from all the information the institute presents. Osaka Garden on Wooded Island and Promontory Point Park are prime places to chill out.

Landmarks

- **Osaka Garden/Wooded Island** • just south of the Museum of Science and Industry, b/w the West and East Lagoons
- **Promontory Point Park** • 5491 S Shore Dr

Pizza

- **Cholie's Pizza** • 1601 E 53rd St

Schools

- **Akiba-Schechter Jewish Day School** • 5235 S Cornell Ave
- **Catholic Theological Union** • 5420 S Cornell Ave
- **Hyde Park Academy** • 6220 S Stony Island Ave

Map 20 • East Hyde Park / Jackson Park

Sundries / Entertainment

Home to previous Chicago Mayor Harold Washington, this neighborhood relies on parks and the lakefront to set the mood. Hunt through Jackson Park to discover remnants of the 1893 World's Fair. Keep on moving with Art's Cycle on E 55th St and go nation-hopping with the restaurant selection on the same block.

Copy Shops

- **Post Link** • 1634 E 53rd St

Gyms

- **Southside YMCA** • 6330 S Stony Island Ave

Movie Theaters

- **Omnimax Theatre** • Museum of Science & Industry, E 57th St & Lake Shore Dr

Nightlife

- **Bar Louie** • 5500 S South Shore Dr
- **The Cove** • 1750 E 55th St

Restaurants

- **Café Corea** • 1603 E 55th St
- **Marina Café** • 6401 S Coast Guard Dr
- **Morry's Deli** • 5500 S Cornell Ave
- **Nile Restaurant** • 1611 E 55th St
- **Orly's Café** • 1660 E 55th St
- **Piccolo Mondo** • 1642 E 56th St
- **Siam Thai Cuisine** • 1639 E 55th St
- **Snail's Thai Cuisine** • 1649 E 55th St

Shopping

- **Art's Cycle Sales & Service** • 1636 E 55th St

Video Rental

- **Blockbuster Video** • 1644 E 53rd St

Map 21 • Wicker Park / Ukranian Village

N

Western
Ehler Park
W Homer St
W Cortland St
Clybourn
W Moffat St
N Wilmot Ave
N Winnebago Ave
W Moffat St
W Churchill St
Churchill Park
W Bloomingdale Ave
W Willow St
Churchill
W Saint Paul Ave
W Saint Paul Ave
Dan Ryan Expy
90
94
W Wabansia Ave
W Wabansia Ave
W Wabansia Ave
N Milwaukee Ave
W Caton St
W Concord Pl
W Concord Pl
N Oakley Ave
N Bell Ave
N Leavitt St
N Honore St
N Wood St
N Hermitage Ave
N Paulina St
N Marshfield Ave
A
28
Damen
Coyote Building
Crumbling Bucktown
Flat Iron Building
W North Ave
1600W
N Maplewood Ave
N Campbell Ave
N Artesian Ave
W Pierce Ave
W Pierce Ave
N Elk Grove Ave
W Le Moyne St
W Le Moyne St
W Le Moyne St
W Le Moyne St
N Rockwell St
W Julian St
N Bosworth Ave
N Greenview Ave
N Honore St
Wicker Park
WICKER PARK
N Wicker Park Ave
W Beach Ave
W Schiller St
N Dean St
W Blackhawk St
W Hirsch St
N Western Ave
N Claremont Ave
N Oakley Ave
N Bell Ave
N Leavitt St
W Evergreen Ave
N Wicker Park Ave
W Evergreen Ave
W Ellen St
N Bauwans St
W Potomac Ave
W Potomac Ave
N Marion Ct
N Honore St
W Potomac Ave
N Hermitage Ave
N Moorman St
W Crystal St
W Crystal St
N Paulina St
N Mautene Ct
Clemente Park
Division
N Milwaukee Ave
B
W Division St
2400W
2000W
Division Street Russian Bath
22
50
W Haddon Ave
W Haddon Ave
W Haddon Ave
W Haddon Ave
Holy Trinity Orthodox Cathedral and Rectory
W Thomas St
N Hoyne Ave
N Damen Ave
N Winchester Ave
N Wolcott Ave
N Honore St
N Wood St
N Hermitage Ave
N Marshfield Ave
N Ashland Ave
W Thomas St
UKRAINIAN VILLAGE
W Cortez St
W Cortez St
W Cortez St
W Augusta Blvd
EAST UKRAINIAN VILLAGE
2 $
W Walton St
W Walton St
W Walton St
N Greenview Ave
W Iowa St
N Oakley Blvd
W Pearson St
W Pearson St
W Rice St
W Rice St
W Fry St
N Greenview Ave
800N
23
W Chicago Ave
C
W Lee Pl
N Armour St
W Superior St
Superior Park
W Superior St
W Huron St
W Erie St
600N
W Ontario St
W Ohio St
W Race Ave
W Race Ave
N Artesian Ave
N Hartland Ct
N Hermitage Ave
N Paulina St
N Marshfield Ave
1
2

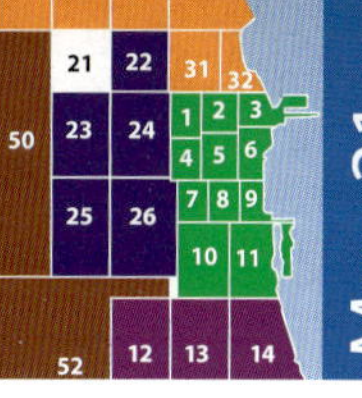

While yuppies rehab Victorians and developers strike for gold, the young arty community that paved the way is finding it harder and harder to stomach rising rents in this former ethnic enclave. Proximity to downtown and the expressway, as well as many cool boutiques, coffeeshops, and bakeries, still makes this a desirable place to live, even though weekend parking and traffic rival those of Lincoln Park.

Banks

- **Bank One** • 1849 W North Ave
- **Bank One** • 1959 W Division St
- **MB Financial** • 936 N Western Ave
- **Midwest Bank & Trust Company** • 1601 Milwaukee Ave
- **North Community** • 1555 N Damen Ave
- **North Community** • 2000 W Division St
- **TCF** • Jewel, 1341 N Paulina St
- **Washington Mutual** • 1811 W North Ave

Car Washes

- **Elite Car Wash** • 823 N Western Ave

Gas Stations

- **Citgo** • 1720 W North Ave
- **Citgo** • 823 N Western Ave
- **Clark Oil** • 1949 W Augusta Blvd
- **Shell** • 1600 N Western Ave
- **Shell** • 1950 W Division St

Hospitals

- **St Elizabeth's** • 1431 N Claremont Ave
- **St Mary of Nazareth** • 2233 W Division St

Landmarks

- **Coyote Building** • 1600 N Milwaukee Ave
- **Crumbling Bucktown** • 1579 N Milwaukee Ave
- **Division Street Russian Bath** • 1916 W Division St
- **Flat Iron Building** • 1579 N Milwaukee Ave
- **Holy Trinity Orthodox Cathedral and Rectory** • 1121 N Leavitt St
- **Wicker Park** • Pierce St & Hoyne St

Pharmacies

- **Jewel-Osco** • 1341 N Paulina St
- **Osco Drug** • 2418 W Division St
- **Walgreens** • 1372 N Milwaukee Ave
- **Walgreens** • 2440 W North Ave

Pizza

- **Leona's** • 1936 W Augusta Blvd
- **Piece** • 1927 W North Ave
- **Pizza Hut** • 1601 N Western Ave
- **Pizza Metro** • 1707 W Division St

Police

- **13th District (Wood)** • 937 N Wood St

Schools

- **A N Pritzker Elementary** • 2009 W Schiller St
- **Albert R Sabin** • 2216 W Hirsch St
- **Association House High** • 2150 W North Ave
- **Christopher Columbus Elementary** • 1003 N Leavitt St
- **De Diego Elementary** • 1313 N Claremont Ave
- **Hans Christian Andersen Elementary** • 1148 N Honore St
- **Josephinum High** • 1501 N Oakley Blvd
- **Roberto Clemente Community High** • 1147 N Western Ave
- **St Helen Elementary** • 2135 W Augusta Blvd
- **St Nicholas** • 2238 W Rice St

Supermarkets

- **Jewel-Osco** • 1341 N Paulina St

N
Western
Damen
Division
Clybourn
Ehler Park
Churchill Park
Wicker Park
Clemente Park
Superior Park
WICKER PARK
UKRAINIAN VILLAGE
EAST UKRAINIAN VILLAGE
W Homer St
W Cortland St
W Moffat St
W Churchill St
W Willow St
W Saint Paul Ave
W Bloomingdale Ave
W Wabansia Ave
W Caton St
W Concord Pl
N Milwaukee Ave
W North Ave
W Pierce Ave
W Le Moyne St
W Julian St
W Beach Ave
W Blackhawk St
W Schiller St
W Hirsch St
W Evergreen Ave
W Ellen St
W Potomac Ave
W Crystal St
W Division St
W Haddon Ave
W Thomas St
W Cortez St
W Augusta Blvd
W Walton St
W Iowa St
W Pearson St
W Fry St
W Rice St
W Chicago Ave
W Lee Pl
W Superior St
W Huron St
W Erie St
W Ontario St
W Ohio St
W Race Ave
N Winnebago Ave
N Wilmot Ave
N Western Ave
N Oakley Ave
N Oakley Blvd
N Bell Ave
N Leavitt St
N Claremont Ave
N Maplewood Ave
N Campbell Ave
N Artesian Ave
N Rockwell St
N Damen Ave
N Hoyne Ave
N Winchester Ave
N Wolcott Ave
N Honore St
N Wood St
N Hermitage Ave
N Paulina St
N Marshfield Ave
N Ashland Ave
N Elk Grove Ave
N Wicker Park Ave
N Dean St
N Bauwans St
N Moorman St
N Mautene Ct
N Marion Ct
N Bosworth Ave
N Greenview Ave
N Armour St
N Harland Ct
Dan Ryan Expy
90
94
2400W
2000W
1600W
1600N
800N
600N
28
22
50
23
A
B
C
1
2

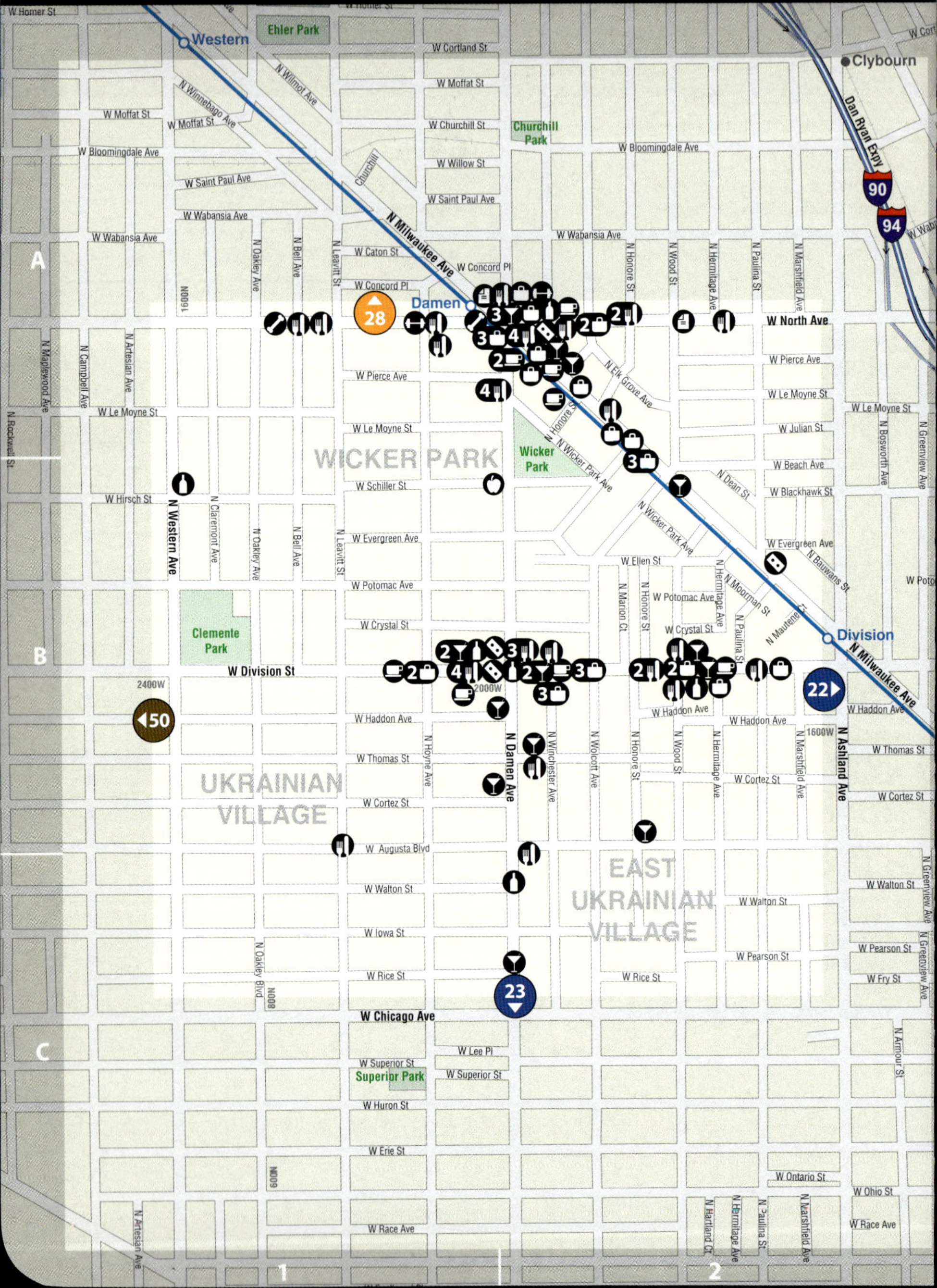

Sundries / Entertainment

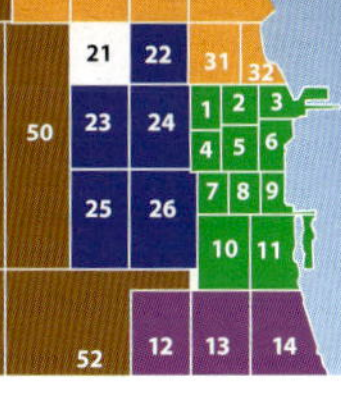

Heads turn when you walk in at the see-and-be-seen Earwax Café. Leo's Lunchroom offers hearty, tasty lunch options, and more adventurous dinners. Spring is widely considered to be one of the city's finest dining destinations. Indie bands and avante garde jazz wail through the night from the peculiar-smelling Empty Bottle. Brainy hipsters haunt the aisles at Quimby's and Myopic Books.

Coffee

- **Alliance Bakery** • 1736 W Division St
- **Caffe Gelto** • 2034 W Division St
- **Filter** • 1585 N Milwaukee Ave
- **Half & Half** • 1560 N Damen Ave
- **Jinx** • 1928 W Division St
- **Letizia's Natural Bakery** • 2144 W Division St
- **Starbucks** • 1588 N Milwaukee Ave
- **Starbucks** • 1701 N Division St
- **Sweet Thang** • 1921 W North Ave

Copy Shops

- **Copymax (9 am-7 pm)** • 1573 N Milwaukee Ave
- **Kinko's (24 hours)** • 1800 W North Ave

Farmer's Markets

- **Wicker Park/Bucktown** • W Schiller St & N Damen Ave

Gyms

- **Bucktown Fitness Club** • 2100 W North Ave
- **Cheetah Gym** • 1934 W North Ave
- **Curves** • 2010 W Pierce Ave

Liquor Stores

- **Carlos Food & Liquor** • 1401 N Western Ave
- **D+D Liquor** • 2018 W Division St
- **Ola's Liquor** • 947 N Damen Ave
- **Sahar Food & Liquor** • 1761 W Division St
- **Taste Wine & Cheese** • 1922 W North Ave
- **Wicker Park Liquor** • 2006 W Division St

Nightlife

- **Bar Thirteen** • 1944 W Division St
- **Borderline** • 1954 W North Ave
- **Club Foot** • 1824 W Augusta Blvd
- **D'Vine** • 1950 W North Ave
- **Davenport's** • 1383 N Milwaukee Ave
- **Double Door** • 1572 N Milwaukee Ave
- **Empty Bottle** • 1035 N Western Ave
- **Estelle's Café & Lounge** • 2013 W North Ave
- **Gold Star Bar** • 1755 W Division St
- **Iggy's** • 1840 W North Ave
- **Inn Joy** • 2051 W Division St
- **Inner Town Pub** • 1935 W Thomas St
- **Lava Lounge** • 859 N Damen Ave
- **The Note** • 1565 N Milwaukee Ave
- **Phyllis' Musical Inn** • 1800 W Division St
- **Pontiac Café** • 1531 N Damen Ave
- **Rainbo Club** • 1150 N Damen Ave
- **Rodan** • 1530 N Milwaukee Ave
- **Small Bar** • 2049 W Division St
- **Subterranean Cabaret & Lounge** • 2011 W North Ave
- **Ten56** • 1056 N Damen Ave
- **Vintage Wine Bar** • 1942 W Division St

Pet Shops

- **For Dog's Sake** • 2257 W North Ave
- **Wicker Pet** • 2029 W North Ave

Restaurants

- **Adobo Grill** • 2005 W Division St
- **Blue Line Club Car** • 1548 N Damen Ave
- **Bluefin** • 1952 W North Ave
- **Bob San** • 1805 W Division St
- **The Bongo Room** • 1470 N Milwaukee Ave
- **Cleo's** • 1935 W Chicago Ave
- **Cold Comfort Café & Deli** • 2211 W North Ave
- **D'Vine Restaurant & Wine Bar** • 1950 W North Ave
- **Earwax** • 1561 N Milwaukee Ave
- **Feast** • 1616 N Damen Ave
- **Green Ginger** • 2050 W Division St
- **Half & Half** • 1560 N Damen Ave
- **Iggy's** • 1840 W North Ave
- **Las Palmas** • 1835 W North Ave
- **Leo's Lunchroom** • 1809 W Division St
- **Leona's** • 1936 W Augusta Blvd
- **Lulu's Hot Dogs** • 1000 S Leavitt St
- **Mas** • 1670 W Division St
- **Milk & Honey** • 1920 W Division St
- **Mirai Sushi** • 2020 W Division St
- **MOD** • 1520 N Damen Ave
- **Moonshine** • 1824 W Division St
- **Pacific Café** • 1619 N Damen Ave
- **Parlor** • 1745 W North Ave
- **Picante** • 2016 W Division St
- **Piece** • 1927 W North Ave
- **Settimana Café** • 2056 W Division St
- **Sigara Hookah Café & Lounge** • 2013 W Division St
- **Smoke Daddy** • 1804 W Division St
- **Souk** • 1552 N Milwaukee Ave
- **Spring** • 2039 W North Ave
- **Sultan's Market** • 2057 W North Ave
- **Thai Lagoon** • 2223 W North Ave
- **Thai Village** • 2053 W Division St
- **Tre Via** • 1575 N Milwaukee Ave

Shopping

- **American Apparel** • 1563 N Milwaukee Ave
- **Asian Essence** • 2121 W Division St
- **Asrai Garden** • 1935 W North Ave
- **Casa de Soul** • 1919 W Division St
- **Cattails** • 1935 W Division St
- **City Soles/Niche** • 2001 W North Ave
- **DeciBel Audio** • 1407 N Milwaukee Ave
- **House of Monsters** • 1579 N Milwaukee Ave, Gallery 218
- **Lille** • 1923 W North Ave
- **Modern Times** • 1538 N Milwaukee Ave
- **Myopic Bookstore** • 1564 N Milwaukee Ave
- **Nina** • 1655 W Division St
- **Noir** • 1726 W Division St
- **Noir-Men** • 1740 W Division St
- **Orange Skin** • 1429 N Milwaukee Ave
- **Paper Doll** • 1747 W Division St
- **Penelope's** • 1913 W Division St
- **Porte Rouge** • 1911 W Division St
- **Quimby's Bookstore** • 1854 W North Ave
- **Ragstock** • 1433 N Milwaukee Ave
- **Reckless Records** • 1532 N Milwaukee Ave
- **The Silver Room** • 1410 N Milwaukee Ave
- **Stinkerbelle** • 1951 W Division St
- **Symmetry** • 1925 W Division St
- **Una Mae's Freak Boutique** • 1422 N Milwaukee Ave
- **Untitled** • 1941 W North Ave
- **Wag Artworks** • 2121 W Division St

Video Rental

- **Blockbuster Video** • 1303 N Milwaukee Ave
- **Earwax** • 1561 N Milwaukee Ave
- **Mass Video** • 2014 W Division St
- **North Coast Video** • 2014-16 W Division St

Map 22 • Noble Square / Goose Island

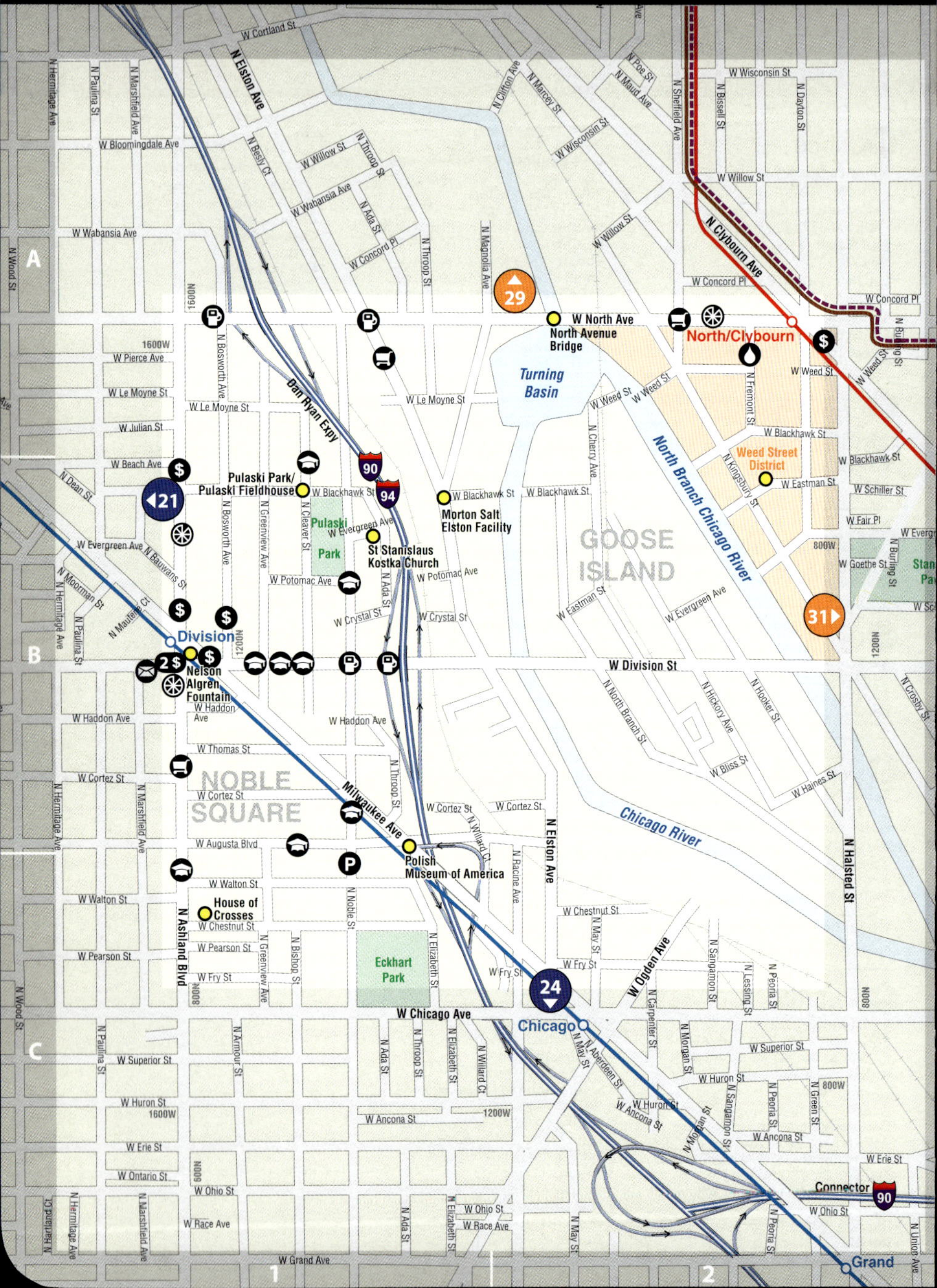
N
A
B
C
1
2
29
31
21
24
90
94
W Cortland St
N Elston Ave
N Hermitage Ave
N Paulina St
N Marshfield Ave
W Bloomingdale Ave
N Besly Ct
W Willow St
N Throop St
W Wabansia Ave
N Ada St
W Concord Pl
N Throop St
N Magnolia Ave
N Clifton Ave
N Marcey St
W Wisconsin St
N Poe St
N Maud Ave
N Sheffield Ave
N Bissell St
N Dayton St
W Wisconsin St
W Willow St
N Clybourn Ave
W Concord Pl
W Wabansia Ave
N Wood St
1600W
W North Ave
North Avenue Bridge
North/Clybourn
W Pierce Ave
W Le Moyne St
W Julian St
W Beach Ave
N Bosworth Ave
Dan Ryan Expy
W Le Moyne St
Turning Basin
W Weed St
N Cherry Ave
North Branch Chicago River
N Fremont St
W Blackhawk St
Weed Street District
N Kingsbury St
W Eastman St
W Schiller St
W Fair Pl
W Evergreen Ave
N Burling St
W Goethe St
800W
N Dean St
Pulaski Park/ Pulaski Fieldhouse
W Blackhawk St
Morton Salt Elston Facility
N Greenview Ave
N Cleaver St
Pulaski Park
W Evergreen Ave
St Stanislaus Kostka Church
GOOSE ISLAND
W Evergreen Ave
N Bauwans St
N Moorman St
N Mautene Ct
W Potomac Ave
W Crystal St
W Eastman St
Division
1200N
Nelson Algren Fountain
W Division St
N North Branch St
N Hickory Ave
N Hooker St
N Crosby St
W Haddon Ave
W Thomas St
W Cortez St
NOBLE SQUARE
Milwaukee Ave
W Bliss St
W Haines St
Chicago River
N Willard Ct
N Racine Ave
N Elston Ave
N Halsted St
W Augusta Blvd
Polish Museum of America
W Walton St
House of Crosses
W Chestnut St
N Ashland Blvd
W Pearson St
N Bishop St
N Noble St
Eckhart Park
N Elizabeth St
W Fry St
N May St
W Ogden Ave
N Carpenter St
N Sangamon St
N Lessing St
N Peoria St
800N
W Chicago Ave
Chicago
N Armour St
W Superior St
N Morgan St
N Aberdeen St
W Huron St
W Ancona St
N Green St
W Erie St
W Ontario St
600N
W Ohio St
W Race Ave
1200W
Connector
N Hartland Ct
N Union Ave
W Grand Ave
Grand

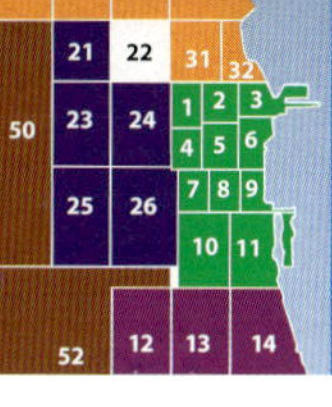

Gritty industry, healthy retail, and alternative culture swirl together throughout this spicy neighborhood, which thrives on artistic ingenuity and Latin spirit. On Saturdays, it seems like the whole city drives here to fill up and go to Home Depot. Traffic on North Avenue Bridge is wretched. This area is a clubber's haven, while jazz fans bee-bop at Joe's on Weed Street, and yuppies cruise each other at Slow Down, Life's Too Short. El Barco Mariscos offers fresh Latin seafood.

Banks

- **Bank of America (ATM)** • 1590 N Clybourn Ave
- **Bank One** • 1230 N Milwaukee Ave
- **Fifth Third** • 1209 N Milwaukee Ave
- **Fifth Third** • 1220 N Bosworth Ave
- **Harris Trust & Savings** • 1242 N Ashland Blvd
- **MB Financial** • 1200 N Ashland Ave
- **New Century** • 1414 N Ashland Ave

Car Washes

- **Turtle Wax Car Wash** • 1550 N Fremont St

Gas Stations

- **Amoco** • 1600 N Elston Ave
- **BP** • 1334 W Division St
- **Gas Depot** • 1551 W North Ave
- **Shell** • 1400 W Division St

Landmarks

- **House of Crosses** • 1544 W Chestnut St
- **Morton Salt Elston Facility** • Elston Ave & Blackhawk St
- **Nelson Algren Fountain** • Division St & Ashland Blvd
- **North Avenue Bridge** • W North Ave
- **Polish Museum of America** • 984 N Milwaukee Ave
- **Pulaski Park/Pulaski Fieldhouse** • Blackhawk St & Cleaver St
- **St Stanislaus Kostka Church** • 1351 W Evergreen Ave
- **Weed Street District** • b/w Chicago River & Halsted St

Parking

Pizza

- **California Pizza Kitchen** • 939 W North Ave
- **Little Caesar's Pizza (Kmart)** • 1360 N Ashland Ave
- **Pizza Hut** • 1601 W Division St

Post Offices

- 1635 W Division St

Schools

- **College of Office Technology** • 1520 W Division St
- **Elizabeth Peabody Elementary** • 1444 W Augusta Blvd
- **Holy Trinity High** • 1443 W Division St
- **Montessori School-Near North** • 1434 W Division St
- **Noble Street High** • 1010 N Nobel St
- **Rudy Lozano Elementary** • 1424 N Cleaver St
- **St Stanislaus Kosta Elementary** • 1255 N Noble St
- **William H Wells High** • 936 N Ashland Ave

Supermarkets

- **Guanajuato Grocery** • 1051 N Ashland Ave
- **Stanley's Fresh Fruit & Vegetables** • 1558 N Elston Ave
- **Whole Foods Market** • 1000 W North Ave

Map 22 • Noble Square / Goose Island

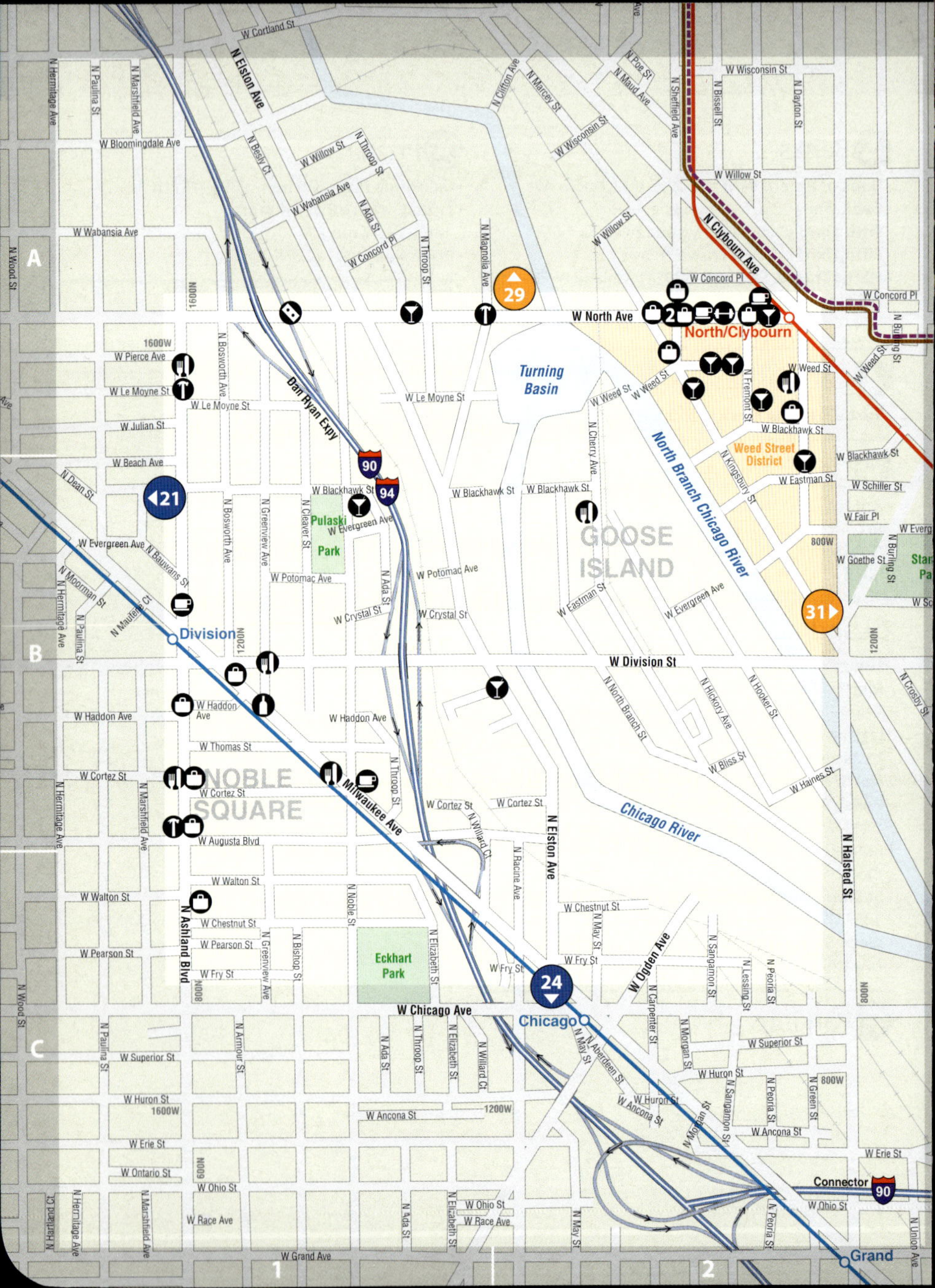
N
W Cortland St
N Elston Ave
N Hermitage Ave
N Paulina St
N Marshfield Ave
W Bloomingdale Ave
N Besly Ct
W Willow St
N Throop St
W Wabansia Ave
N Ada St
W Concord Pl
N Magnolia Ave
N Clifton Ave
N Marcey St
W Wisconsin St
N Poe St
N Maud Ave
N Sheffield Ave
W Wisconsin St
N Bissell St
N Dayton St
W Willow St
N Clybourn Ave
W Concord Pl
W Wabansia Ave
N Wood St
A
1600N
29
W North Ave
North/Clybourn
1600W
W Pierce Ave
N Bosworth Ave
W Le Moyne St
W Le Moyne St
W Le Moyne St
Turning Basin
W Weed St
W Weed St
W Weed St
N Fremont St
N Cherry Ave
W Julian St
Dan Ryan Expy
W Beach Ave
90
94
N Dean St
W Blackhawk St
W Blackhawk St
W Blackhawk St
W Blackhawk St
W Blackhawk St
Weed Street District
N Kingsbury St
North Branch Chicago River
W Eastman St
W Schiller St
W Fair Pl
21
N Bosworth Ave
N Greenview Ave
N Cleaver St
Pulaski Park
W Evergreen Ave
W Evergreen Ave
GOOSE ISLAND
800W
W Goethe St
N Burling St
W Potomac Ave
W Potomac Ave
N Ada St
W Eastman St
W Evergreen Ave
N Bauwans St
N Moorman St
N Hermitage Ave
N Paulina St
N Mautene Ct
W Crystal St
W Crystal St
31
Division
1200N
B
W Division St
W Haddon Ave
W Haddon Ave
W Haddon Ave
N North Branch St
N Hickory Ave
N Hooker St
N Crosby St
W Thomas St
W Bliss St
W Haines St
W Cortez St
NOBLE SQUARE
W Cortez St
N Hermitage Ave
N Marshfield Ave
Milwaukee Ave
N Throop St
W Cortez St
W Cortez St
N Willard Ct
Chicago River
W Augusta Blvd
N Elston Ave
N Racine Ave
N Halsted St
W Walton St
W Walton St
N Noble St
W Chestnut St
W Chestnut St
N Ashland Blvd
W Pearson St
W Pearson St
N Greenview Ave
N Bishop St
Eckhart Park
N Elizabeth St
N May St
W Fry St
W Fry St
W Fry St
W Ogden Ave
N Sangamon St
N Lessing St
N Peoria St
24
800N
W Chicago Ave
Chicago
N Paulina St
W Superior St
N Armour St
N Ada St
N Throop St
N Elizabeth St
N Willard Ct
N May St
N Aberdeen St
N Carpenter St
N Morgan St
W Superior St
C
N Wood St
W Huron St
1600W
W Huron St
W Huron St
N Sangamon St
N Peoria St
N Green St
800W
W Ancona St
1200W
W Ancona St
N Morgan St
W Ancona St
W Erie St
W Erie St
W Ontario St
600N
W Ohio St
Connector
90
N Hartland Ct
N Hermitage Ave
N Marshfield Ave
W Race Ave
N Ada St
N Elizabeth St
W Ohio St
W Race Ave
N May St
N Peoria St
W Ohio St
N Union Ave
W Grand Ave
Grand
1
2

Sundries / Entertainment

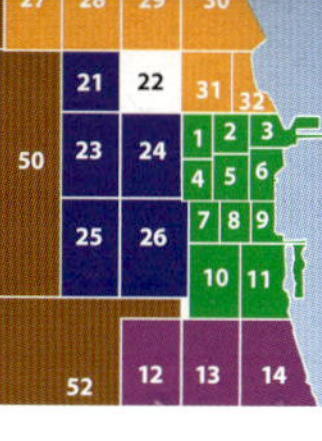

United Center draws the faithful to Bulls and Blackhawks games. Hip Ukrainian Village seeps down into West Town's north end, making this area a mix of young professionals, working-class folk, and students from nearby University of Illinois at Chicago. Along Grand and Western are the city's best hand car washes and detailing outfits.

Coffee

- **Coffee on Milwaukee** • 1046 N Milwaukee Ave
- **Dunkin' Donuts** • 1244 N Ashland Ave
- **Peet's Coffee and Tea** • 1000 W North Ave
- **Starbucks** • 1001E W North Ave

Gyms

- **Crunch Fitness** • 939 W North Ave

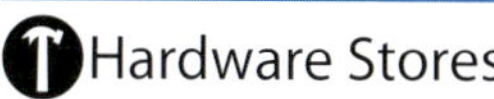

Hardware Stores

- **Ace Hardware** • 1013 N Ashland Ave
- **Home Depot** • 1232 W North Ave
- **Paragon Hardware & Mill Supply** • 1512 N Ashland Ave

Liquor Stores

- **Crater Food & Liquor** • 1144 N Milwaukee Ave

Nightlife

- **Biology Bar** • 1520 N Fremont St
- **Crobar** • 1543 N Kingsbury St
- **Exit** • 1315 W North Ave
- **Four** • 1551 W Division St
- **Hot Shots** • 1440 N Dayton St
- **Joe's** • 940 W Weed St
- **Slow Down, Life's Too Short** • 1177 N Elston Ave
- **Zentra** • 923 W Weed St

Restaurants

- **Corosh** • 1072 N Milwaukee Ave
- **El Barco Mariscos Seafood** • 1035 N Ashland Blvd
- **Hilary's Urban Eatery** • 1500 W Division St
- **Luc Thang** • 1524 N Ashland Blvd
- **NYC Bagel** • 1001 W North Ave
- **Sangria Restaurant and Tapas Bar** • 901 W Weed St

Shopping

- **Best Buy** • 1000 W North Ave
- **Cost Plus World Market** • 1623 N Sheffield Ave
- **Dusty Groove Records** • 1120 N Ashland Ave
- **Expo Design Center** • 1500 N Dayton St
- **Irv's Luggage Warehouse** • 820 W North Ave
- **Nocturnal Dominion** • 913 N Ashland Ave
- **Old Navy** • 1569 N Kingsbury
- **Olga's Flower Shop** • 1041 N Ashland Ave
- **Restoration Hardware** • 938 W North Ave
- **Right-On Futon** • 1184 N Milwaukee Ave
- **Transitions Bookplace** • 1000 W North Ave
- **Wax Addict Records** • 1014 N Ashland Ave

Video Rental

- **Blockbuster Video** • 1500 W North Ave

Map 23 • West Town / Near West Side

Essentials

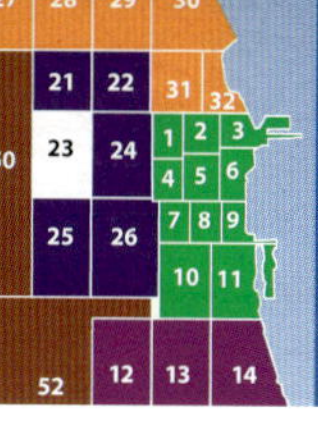

The warehouse commercial district around Damen Avenue and Kinzie Street is a burgeoning shopping district. If you're in the market for gargoyles or vintage marble fireplace mantles, go to Salvage One on Hubbard. For Cuban cigars, head to Donofrio's on Chicago. Ethnic eateries reflect the area's mish-mash of influences. Tiny, tasty, artsy Munch serves solid breakfasts.

Banks

- **Bank One (ATM)** • 1700 W Van Buren St
- **Citibank** • 2005 W Chicago Ave
- **Fifth Third** • 1901 W Madison St
- **LaSalle (ATM)** • 1900 W Van Buren St
- **MB Financial** • 820 N Western Ave
- **MidAmerica** • 2154 W Madison St
- **Self Reliance Ukrainian Credit Union** • 2332 W Chicago Ave
- **TCF (ATM)** • Osco, 2427 W Chicago Ave

Car Washes

- **Boss Hand Car Wash** • 25 S Western Ave
- **Quiroga's Detail & Hand Car** • 2036 W Grand Ave

Gas Stations

- **Marathon** • 101 N Western Ave
- **Shell** • 45 N Western Ave

Landmarks

- **First Baptist Congregational Church** • 1613 W Washington Blvd
- **Metropolitan Missionary Baptist Church** • 2151 W Washington Blvd
- **Ukrainian Cultural Center** • 2247 W Chicago Ave
- **Ukrainian National Museum** • 721 N Oakley Blvd
- **United Center** • 1901 W Madison St

Libraries

- **Mabel Manning Public Library** • 6 S Hoyne Ave
- **Malcolm X College Library** • 1900 W Van Buren St
- **Midwest Public Library** • 2335 W Chicago Ave

Pharmacies

- **Osco Drug** • 2427 W Chicago Ave
- **Walgreens** • 2340 W Madison St

Pizza

- **Angie's Restaurant** • 1715 W Chicago Ave
- **Bacci Pizzeria** • 2356 W Chicago Ave
- **Bella's Pizza & Restaurant** • 1952 W Chicago Ave
- **Naty's Pizza 2** • 1757 W Chicago Ave

Post Offices

- 116 S Western Ave

Schools

- **Best Practice High** • 2040 W Adams St
- **Crane Achievement Academy** • 2245 W Jackson Blvd
- **Dett R Nathaniel Elementary** • 2306 W Maypole Ave
- **Ellen Mitchell Elementary** • 2233 W Ohio St
- **Foundations Elementary** • 2040 W Adams St
- **Healy High** • 100 N Western Ave
- **Henry Suder Elementary** • 2022 W Washington Blvd
- **Irene C Hernandez Achievement Center** • 2245 W Jackson Blvd
- **Malcolm X College** • 1900 W Van Buren St
- **Mancel Talcott Elementary** • 1840 W Ohio St
- **Nia Middle** • 2040 W Adams St
- **St Malachy Elementary** • 2252 W Washington Blvd
- **Ulysses S Grant Community Academy** • 145 S Campbell Ave
- **Victor Herbert Elementary** • 2131 W Monroe St
- **West Town High** • 2021 W Fulton St
- **William H Brown Elementary** • 54 N Hermitage Ave
- **Wilma Rudolph Learning Center** • 110 N Paulina St

Supermarkets

- **Edmar Foods** • 2019 W Chicago Ave
- **Ukrainian Village Grocery** • 2204 W Chicago Ave

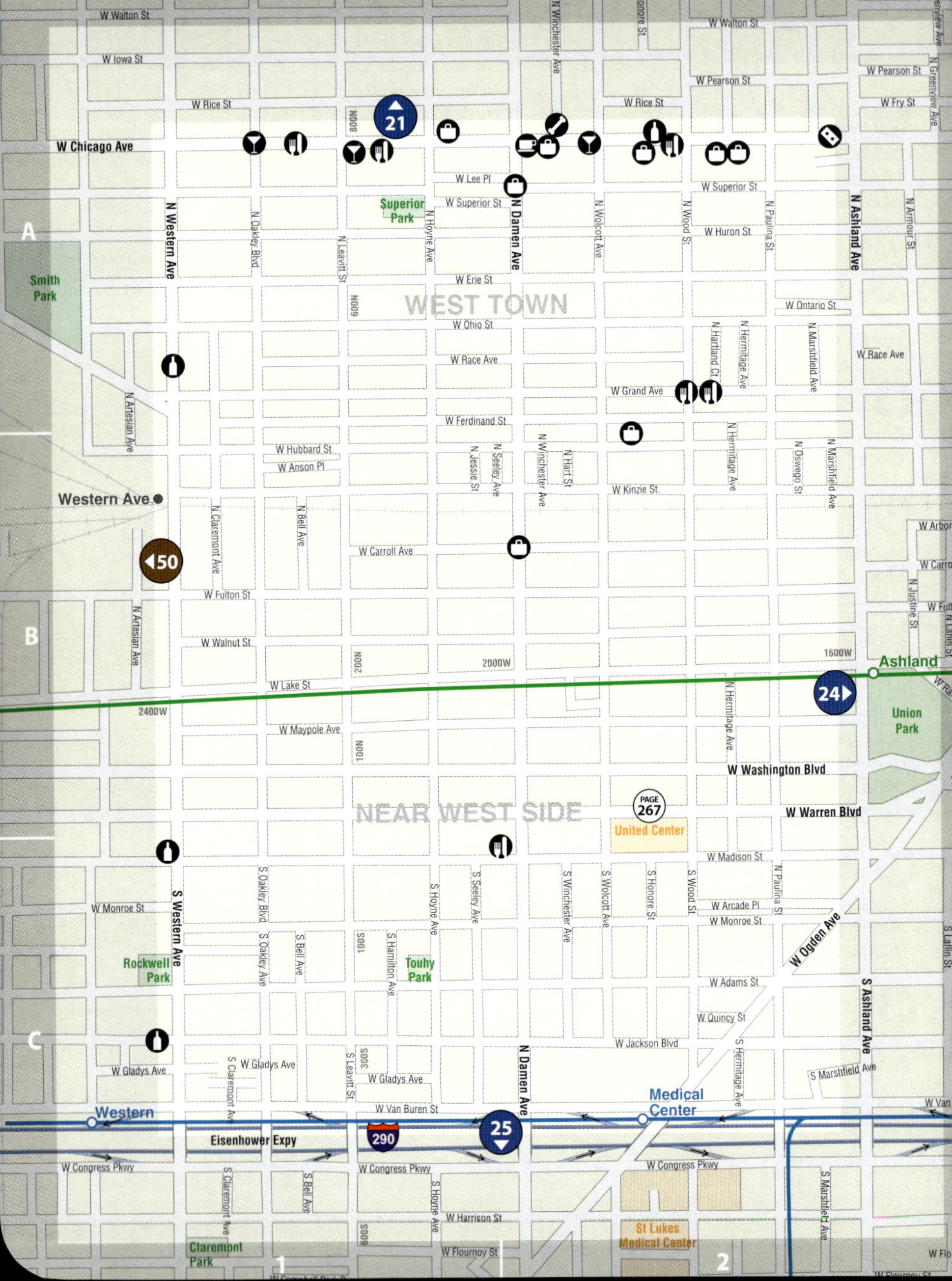
N
W Walton St
W Iowa St
W Rice St
W Chicago Ave
W Pearson St
W Fry St
W Lee Pl
W Superior St
W Huron St
Superior Park
Smith Park
N Western Ave
N Oakley Blvd
N Leavitt St
N Hoyne Ave
N Damen Ave
N Wolcott Ave
N Wood St
N Paulina St
N Ashland Ave
N Armour St
N Winchester Ave
N Honore St
N Greenview Ave
W Erie St
WEST TOWN
W Ontario St
W Ohio St
W Race Ave
W Grand Ave
W Ferdinand St
W Hubbard St
W Anson Pl
W Kinzie St
N Hartland Ct
N Hermitage Ave
N Marshfield Ave
N Oswego St
N Artesian Ave
N Jessie St
N Seeley Ave
N Hart St
Western Ave
N Claremont Ave
N Bell Ave
W Carroll Ave
W Arbor
W Carroll
W Fulton St
W Walnut St
N Justine St
N Laflin St
W Lake St
2400W
2000W
1600W
Ashland
Union Park
W Maypole Ave
W Washington Blvd
W Warren Blvd
NEAR WEST SIDE
PAGE 267
United Center
W Madison St
W Arcade Pl
W Monroe St
W Adams St
W Quincy St
W Jackson Blvd
W Ogden Ave
S Western Ave
S Oakley Blvd
S Bell Ave
S Hamilton Ave
S Hoyne Ave
S Seeley Ave
S Winchester Ave
S Wolcott Ave
S Honore St
S Wood St
N Paulina St
S Laflin St
S Ashland Ave
Rockwell Park
Touhy Park
W Gladys Ave
S Claremont Ave
S Leavitt St
S Hermitage Ave
S Marshfield Ave
W Van Buren St
Western
Medical Center
Eisenhower Expy
290
W Congress Pkwy
W Harrison St
W Flournoy St
St Lukes Medical Center
Claremont Park
800N
600N
200N
100N
100S
300S
600S
21
24
25
50
A
B
C
1
2

Sundries / Entertainment

This neighborhood was once the heart of the city's produce and meat markets, and a few food supplier warehouses still exist, mixing in with loft conversions. Randolph Street is Chicago's hottest restaurant row and a growing gallery district. The high priestess of talk, Oprah Winfrey, reigns over West Town from her broadcasting palace, Harpo Studios on Washington. D'Amato's Bakery supplies eateries all over the city with its crusty loaves.

Coffee

- **Atomix** • 1957 W Chicago Ave

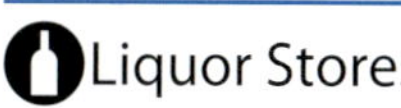

Liquor Stores

- **Campbell Food & Liquor** • 2459 W Madison St
- **DiCarlo's Armanetti Liquors** • 515 N Western Ave
- **J&L** • 1801 W Chicago Ave
- **S&F** • 2458 W Jackson Blvd

Nightlife

- **Darkroom** • 2210 W Chicago Ave
- **Sak's Ukrainian Village Restaurant** • 2301 W Chicago Ave
- **Tuman's** • 2159 W Chicago Ave

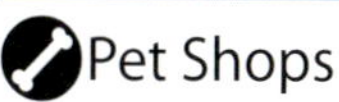

Pet Shops

- **Liz's Bird Shop** • 1931 W Chicago Ave

Restaurants

- **A Tavola** • 2148 W Chicago Ave
- **China Dragon Restaurant** • 2008 W Madison St
- **Il Jack's Italian Restaurant** • 1758 W Grand Ave
- **Munch** • 1800 W Grand Ave
- **Old Lviv** • 2228 W Chicago Ave
- **Tecalitlan Restaurant** • 1814 W Chicago Ave

Shopping

- **Alcala's** • 1733 W Chicago Ave
- **Decoro Studio** • 2000 W Carroll St
- **Donofrio's Double Corona Cigars** • 2058 W Chicago Ave
- **H&R Sports** • 1741 W Chicago Ave
- **Rotofugi** • 1953 W Chicago Ave
- **Salvage One Architectural Artifacts** • 1840 W Hubbard St
- **Sprout Home** • 745 N Damen Ave
- **Tomato Tattoo** • 1855 W Chicago Ave

Video Rental

- **Fredie's Video** • 1618 W Chicago Ave

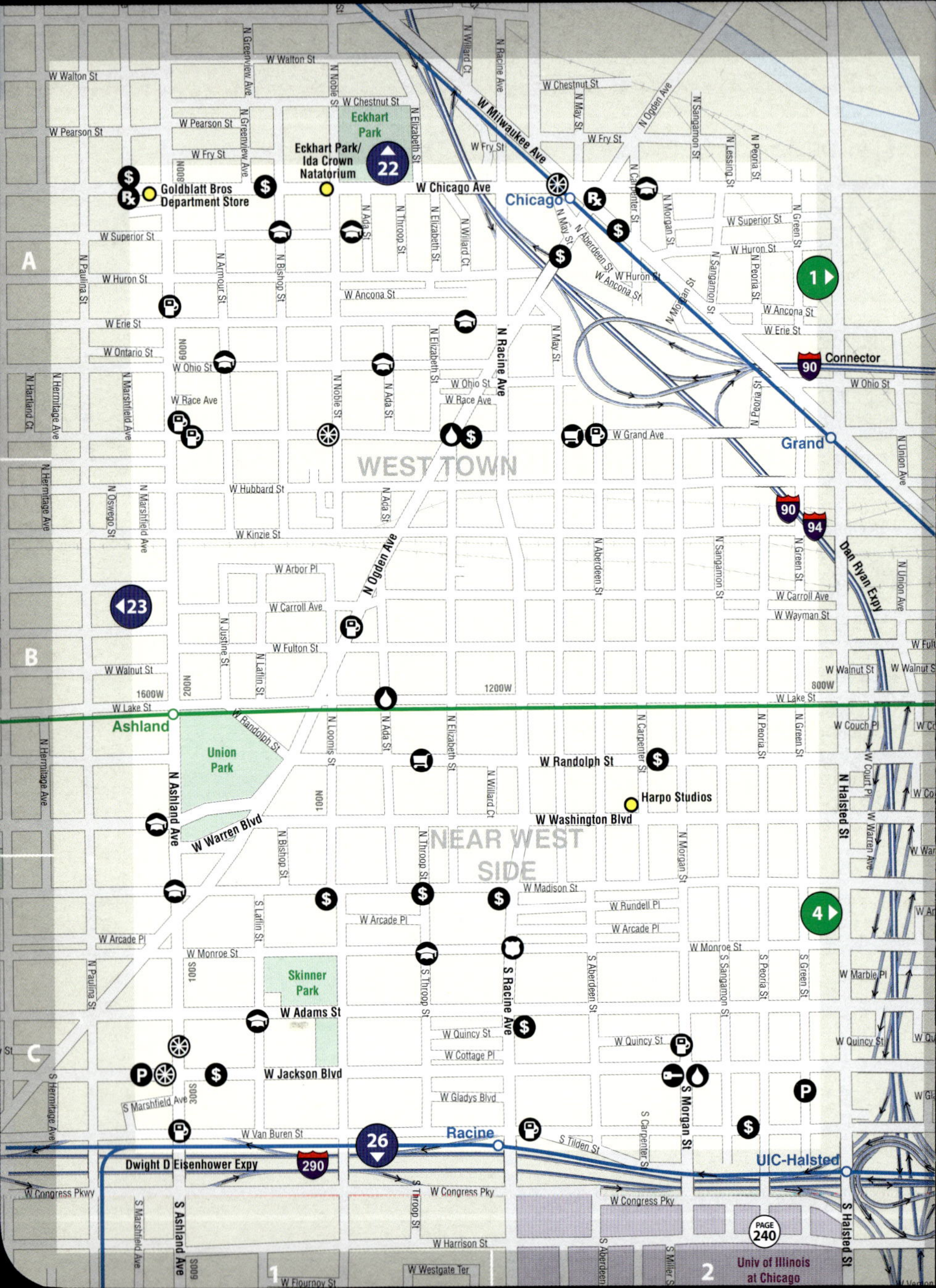
N
A
B
C
1
2
W Walton St
W Pearson St
W Fry St
W Chestnut St
N Greenview Ave
N Noble St
Eckhart Park
Eckhart Park/
Ida Crown
Natatorium
22
N Elizabeth St
N Willard Ct
N Racine Ave
W Milwaukee Ave
N May St
N Ogden Ave
N Sangamon St
N Lessing St
N Peoria St
Goldblatt Bros
Department Store
W Chicago Ave
Chicago
N Carpenter St
N Morgan St
W Superior St
N Green St
W Huron St
N Paulina St
N Armour St
N Bishop St
N Ada St
N Throop St
N Aberdeen St
W Ancona St
1
W Erie St
W Ontario St
W Ohio St
W Race Ave
N Hermitage Ave
N Harland Ct
N Marshfield Ave
Connector
90
N Peoria St
Grand
W Grand Ave
WEST TOWN
N Union Ave
W Hubbard St
N Oswego St
W Kinzie St
90
94
Dan Ryan Expy
W Arbor Pl
W Carroll Ave
W Wayman St
23
N Justine St
N Laflin St
W Fulton St
W Walnut St
1600W
1200W
800W
W Lake St
Ashland
Union
Park
W Randolph St
N Loomis St
W Couch Pl
W Court Pl
N Halsted St
N Ashland Ave
1000N
Harpo Studios
W Washington Blvd
W Warren Blvd
W Warren Ave
NEAR WEST
SIDE
W Madison St
W Rundell Pl
W Arcade Pl
4
W Monroe St
S Laflin St
Skinner
Park
S Throop St
S Racine Ave
S Aberdeen St
S Sangamon St
S Peoria St
S Green St
W Marble Pl
W Adams St
W Quincy St
W Cottage Pl
W Jackson Blvd
S Hermitage Ave
S Marshfield Ave
W Gladys Blvd
S Morgan St
S Carpenter St
W Van Buren St
26
Racine
S Tilden St
UIC-Halsted
Dwight D Eisenhower Expy
290
W Congress Pkwy
W Congress Pky
S Marshfield Ave
S Ashland Ave
S Throop St
S Aberdeen St
S Miller St
PAGE
240
Univ of Illinois
at Chicago
S Halsted St
W Harrison St
W Westgate Ter
W Flournoy St

Essentials

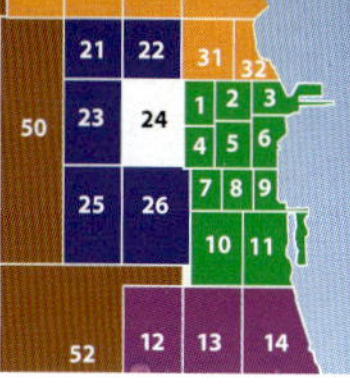

West Town has some great dining. We recommend breakfast at Wishbone, seafood at Crab Street Saloon and Marché for theatrical French. Matchbox is as trendy as Jack's Tap is basic. Construction booms on plenty of corners, but services have been slow to follow. Residents badly need a Dominick's.

Banks

- **American Chartered (ATM)** • 1032 W Randolph St
- **Banco Popular** • 1445 W Chicago Ave
- **Broadway** • 900 W Van Buren St
- **Charter One (ATM)** • 200 S Racine Ave
- **Charter One (ATM)** • 833 W Van Buren St
- **First Eagle National** • 1201 W Madison St
- **MB Financial** • 1420 W Madison St
- **MB Financial (ATM)** • 843 W Randolph St
- **MB Financial (ATM)** • 9 S Green St
- **North Community** • 1244 W Grand Ave
- **TCF (ATM)** • 1645 W Jackson Blvd
- **TCF (ATM)** • Osco, 771 N Ogden Ave
- **US** • 745 N Milwaukee Ave
- **Washington Mutual** • 1301 W Madison St
- **Washington Mutual** • 1656 W Chicago Ave

Car Rental

- **Enterprise** • 318 S Morgan St • 312-432-9780

Car Washes

- **A&A Automobile Service** • 1352 W Lake St
- **Bert's Car Wash** • 1231 W Grand Ave
- **Shell** • 1001 W Jackson Blvd

Gas Stations

- **BP** • 1600 W Van Buren St
- **Citgo** • 1535 W Grand Ave
- **Marathon** • 1100 W Grand Ave
- **Marathon** • 335 N Ogden Ave
- **Marathon** • 649 N Ashland Ave
- **Shell** • 1001 W Jackson Blvd
- **Shell** • 1160 W Van Buren St
- **Shell** • 505 N Ashland Ave

Landmarks

- **Eckhart Park/Ida Crown Natatorium** • Noble St & Chicago Ave
- **Goldblatt Bros Department Store** • 1613-35 W Chicago Ave
- **Harpo Studios** • 1058 W Washington Blvd

Parking

Pharmacies

- **Osco Drug** • 771 N Ogden Ave
- **Walgreens** • 1650 W Chicago Ave

Pizza

- **Moretti's** • 1645 W Jackson Blvd
- **Penny's Pizza** • 234 S Ashland Ave
- **Pie-Eyed Pizza** • 1111 W Chicago Ave
- **Salerno's Restaurant** • 1201 W Grand Ave

Police

- **12th District (Monroe)** • 100 S Racine Ave

Schools

- **Chicago Academy for the Arts** • 1010 W Chicago Ave
- **James Otis Elementary** • 525 N Armour St
- **Jesse Spaulding** • 1628 W Washington Blvd
- **Mark Skinner Classical** • 111 S Throop St
- **Midwest Apostolic Bible College** • 14 S Ashland Ave
- **Milburn High** • 1448 W Superior St
- **Near North Special Ed Center** • 739 N Ada St
- **Philo Carpenter Elementary** • 1250 W Erie St
- **Santa Maria Addolorata** • 1337 W Ohio St
- **Whitney Young High** • 211 S Laflin St

Supermarkets

- **Bari Foods** • 1120 W Grand Ave
- **Cyd & D'Pano** • 1325 W Randolph St

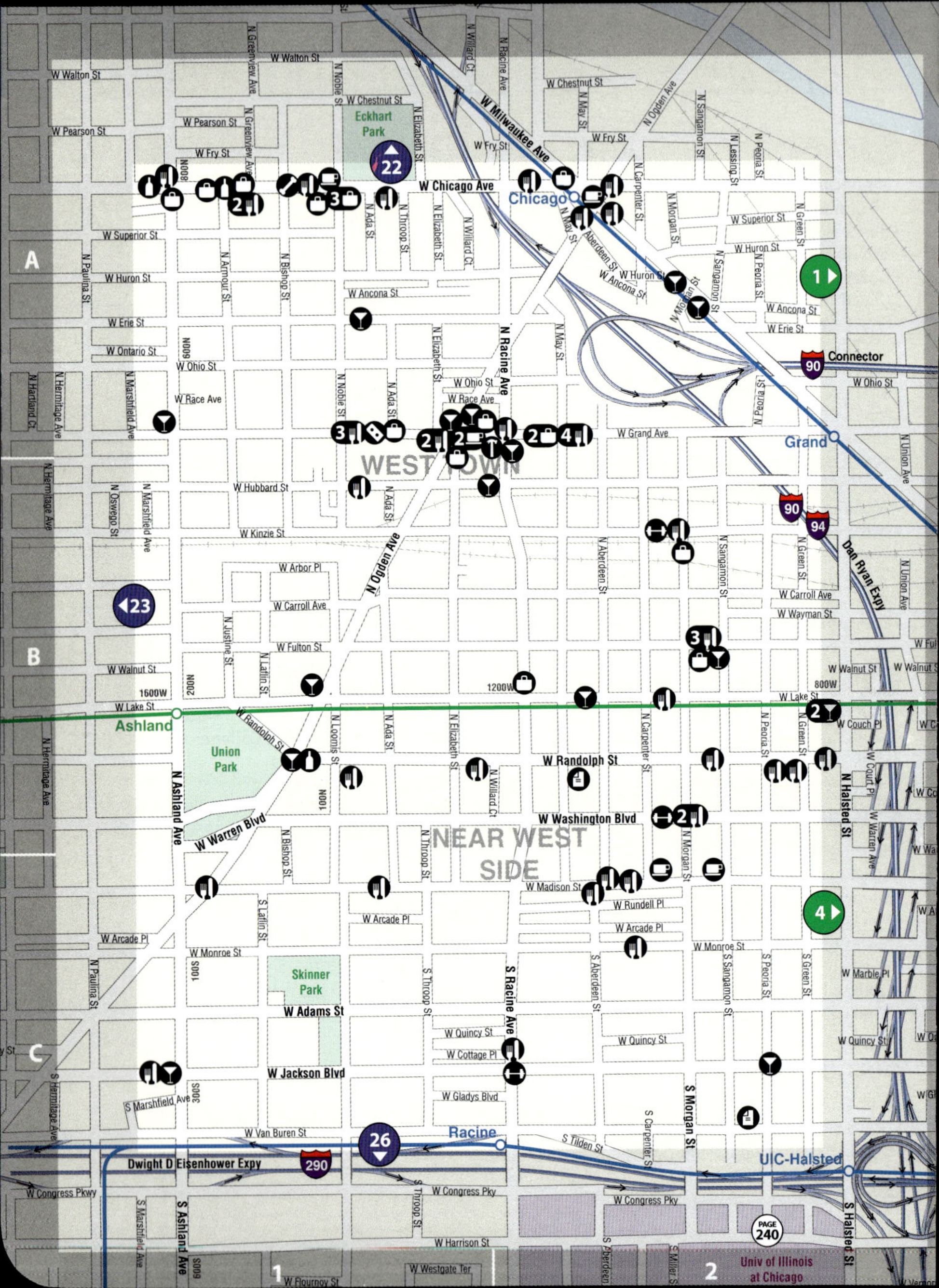

N

WEST TOWN

NEAR WEST SIDE

Eckhart Park

Union Park

Skinner Park

Chicago

Grand

Ashland

Racine

UIC-Halsted

Univ of Illinois at Chicago

W Chicago Ave

W Grand Ave

W Randolph St

W Washington Blvd

W Madison St

W Adams St

W Jackson Blvd

W Van Buren St

Dwight D Eisenhower Expy

Dan Ryan Expy

W Milwaukee Ave

N Ogden Ave

N Racine Ave

S Racine Ave

N Ashland Ave

S Ashland Ave

N Halsted St

S Halsted St

S Morgan St

Connector

22

23

26

1

4

PAGE 240

Sundries / Entertainment

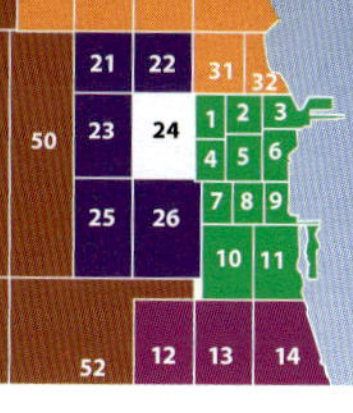

It seems like River West is getting a new eatery every other week. Gentrification is well underway, but a few authentic spots remain. While popular options like Twisted Spoke continue to attract regulars with beer and burgers, young urban couples flock to trendies like Green Zebra and The Tasting Room. A good food market is still nowhere to be found, but the area just got its first Starbucks. For an immeasurably more pleasant experience, go to Sip Coffee House.

Coffee

- **Bialy's Café** • 1425 W Chicago Ave
- **Bon Appetit Café & Coffeehouse** • 817 N Milwaukee Ave
- **Sip Coffee House** • 1223 W Grand Ave
- **Starbucks** • 1001A W Madison St
- **Starbucks** • 520 N Ogden Ave
- **West Gate Coffeehouse** • 924 W Madison St

Copy Shops

- **AlphaGraphics (8 am-6 pm)** • 1017 W Washington Blvd
- **The UPS Store (9 am-6:30 pm)** • 910 W Van Buren St

Gyms

- **Naturally Fit** • 310 S Racine Ave
- **West Loop Gym** • 1024 W Kinzie St

Hardware Stores

- **Imperial Hardware** • 1208 W Grand Ave

Liquor Stores

- **Loop Tavern** • 1610 W Chicago Ave
- **Rothchild Liquor Marts** • 1532 W Chicago Ave
- **Tasting Room** • 1415 W Randolph St

Nightlife

- **Babalu** • 1645 W Jackson Blvd
- **Betty's Blue Star Lounge** • 1600 W Grand Ave
- **Café Fresco** • 1202 W Grand Ave
- **Chromium** • 817 W Lake St
- **Dante's** • 1200 W Hubbard St
- **Estate** • 1111 W Lake St
- **Fulton Lounge** • 955 W Fulton Market
- **Guess Bar** • 820 W Lake St
- **J Patricks** • 1367 W Erie St
- **Jack's Tap** • 901 W Jackson Blvd
- **Matchbox** • 679 N Milwaukee Ave
- **Sonotheque** • 1444 W Chicago Ave
- **Tasting Room** • 1415 W Randolph St
- **Transit** • 1431 W Lake St
- **Twisted Spoke** • 501 N Ogden Ave

Pet Shops

- **VCA - Lake Shore Animal Hospital** • 960 W Chicago Ave

Restaurants

- **160 Blue** • 160 N Loomis St
- **Amelia's Mexican Grille** • 1235 W Grand Ave
- **Amore Ristorante** • 1330 W Madison St
- **Aroma** • 941 W Randolph St
- **Bella Notte** • 1374 W Grand Ave
- **Billy Goat Tavern** • 1535 W Madison St
- **Blyss** • 1061 W Madison St
- **Breakfast Club** • 1381 W Hubbard St
- **Buongiorno Café** • 1123 W Grand Ave
- **Burger Baron** • 1381 W Grand Ave
- **Cannella's on Grand** • 1132 W Grand Ave
- **Carmichaels Chicago Steakhouse** • 1052 W Monroe St
- **D'Agostino's Pizzeria** • 752 N Ogden Ave
- **D'Amotos Italian Bakery** • 1124 W Grand Ave
- **De Cero** • 814 W Randolph St
- **Dragonfly Mandarin Restaurants** • 832 W Randolph St
- **Flo** • 1434 W Chicago Ave
- **Follia** • 953 W Fulton St
- **Green Zebra** • 1460 W Chicago Ave
- **Hacienda Tecalitlan** • 820 N Ashland Blvd
- **Ina's** • 1235 W Randolph St
- **Jerry's Sandwiches** • 1045 W Madison St
- **La Borsa** • 375 N Morgan St
- **La Sardine** • 111 N Carpenter St
- **Le Peep Grill** • 1000 W Washington Blvd
- **Marche** • 833 W Randolph St
- **Misto** • 1118 W Grand Ave
- **Moretti's** • 1645 W Jackson Blvd
- **Moto** • 945 W Fulton Market
- **Oggi Trattoria Café** • 1378 W Grand Ave
- **Rushmore** • 1023 W Lake St
- **Salerno's Pizza and Pasta** • 1201 W Grand Ave
- **Silver Palm** • 768 N Milwaukee Ave
- **Sushi X** • 1136 W Chicago Ave
- **Twisted Spoke** • 501 N Ogden Ave
- **Union Park** • 228 S Racine Ave
- **Vinnie's Sandwich Shop** • 1204 W Grand Ave
- **Vivo** • 838 W Randolph St
- **West Town Tavern** • 1329 W Chicago Ave
- **Windy City Café** • 1062 W Chicago Ave
- **Wishbone** • 1001 W Washington Blvd

Shopping

- **3 Design Three** • 1431 W Chicago Ave
- **Aesthetic Eye** • 1520 W Chicago Ave
- **Casati** • 949 W Fulton Market
- **Design Inc** • 1359 W Grand Ave
- **Douglas Dawson Gallery** • 400 N Morgan St
- **Jan's Antiques** • 225 N Racine Ave
- **PakMail** • 1461 W Chicago Ave
- **Pet Care Plus** • 1212 W Grand Ave
- **The Realm** • 1430 W Chicago Ave
- **Roots** • 1140 W Grand Ave
- **RR#1 Chicago Apothecary** • 814 N Ashland Blvd
- **Snap** • 470 N Ogden Ave
- **Spiced** • 1162 W Grand Ave
- **Upgrade Cycle Works** • 1130 W Chicago Ave
- **X/S Salon** • 1433a W Chicago Ave
- **Xyloform** • 1423 W Chicago Ave

Video Rental

- **Grand Slam Video** • 1369 W Grand Ave

Map 25 • Illinois Medical District

Western
Medical Center
23
290
Eisenhower Expy
W Van Buren St
W Gladys Ave
W Congress Pkwy
W Harrison St
W Flournoy St
W Campbell Park Dr
W Lexington St
W Polk St
W Arthington St
W Taylor St
W Fillmore St
W Grenshaw St
W Roosevelt Rd
W Washburne Ave
W 13th St
W Hastings St
W 14th St
W 14th Pl
W 15th St
W 15th Pl
W 16th St
W 17th St
W 18th St
W 18th Pl
W 19th St
W Cullerton St
W 21st St
W 21st Pl
W Cermak Rd
W 22nd Pl
S Campbell Ave
S Western Ave
S Claremont Ave
S Oakley Ave
S Oakley Blvd
S Bell Ave
S Leavitt St
S Hoyne Ave
S Seeley Ave
S Hamilton Ave
Almond St
S Ogden Ave W
S Bowler St
W Bowler St
W Boone St
S Damen Ave
S Honore St
S Winchester Ave
S Wolcott Ave
S Wood St
S Hermitage Ave
S Paulina St
S Marshfield Ave
Garibaldi Pl
S Laflin St
S Ashland Ave
S Blue Island Ave
Claremont Park
VA Medical Center
St Lukes Medical Center
University of Illinois Hospital
ILLINOIS MEDICAL DISTRICT
Harrison Park
HEART OF CHICAGO
Polk
18th
Western Ave
Western
Hoyne
2400W
2000W
1600W
600S
1200S
1600S
2200S
26
50
52
A
B
C
1
2

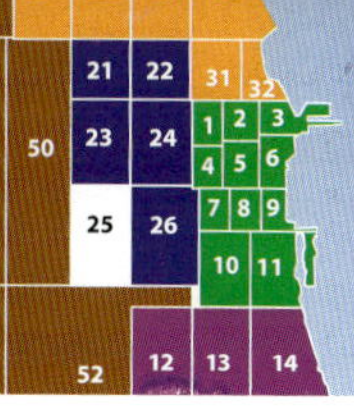

Health is at the heart of this neighborhood. Several hospitals and UIC's medical school are centered here, including publicly funded Cook County Hospital built in 1913. Doc-shock TV show ER was inspired by Cook's hectic emergency room treatment of some of Chicago's gang crime victims. If you get shot, this is where you want to go.

Banks

- **Bank One** • 2000 W Cermak Rd
- **Bank One (ATM)** • 600 S Paulina St
- **LaSalle (ATM)** • 1701 W Taylor St
- **LaSalle (ATM)** • 1717 W Polk St
- **LaSalle (ATM)** • 818 S Wolcott Ave
- **Metropolitan** • 2201 W Cermak Rd
- **Metropolitan** • 2235 W Cermak Rd

Car Washes

- **G Express Hand Car Wash** • 2323 W 18th St
- **Shell** • 2401 W Roosevelt Rd

Gas Stations

- **Citgo** • 2107 S Western Ave
- **Clark Oil** • 1721 S Paulina St
- **Mobil** • 2401 W Ogden Ave
- **Shell** • 2401 W Roosevelt Rd

Hospitals

- **John H Stroger** • 1901 W Harrison
- **Rush-Presbyterian St Luke's** • 1725 W Harrison St
- **St Anthony's** • 2875 W 19th St
- **University of Illinois at Chicago** • 1740 W Taylor St
- **VA Medical Center** • 820 S Damen Ave

Parking

Pharmacies

- **Walgreens (24 hours)** • 1931 W Cermak Rd

Pizza

- **Bacci Pizzeria** • 2248 W Taylor St
- **Damenzo's Pizza** • 2324 W Taylor St
- **Pisa Pizza** • 2050 W Cermak Rd
- **Pizza Hut** • 2337 W Cermak Rd
- **Pizza Nova** • 1842 W 18th St

Schools

- **Chicago Hope Academy** • 2189 W Bowler St
- **Children of Peace Elementary** • 1900 W Taylor St
- **Children of Peace St Callistus** • 2187 W Bowler St
- **Josiah L Pickard Elementary** • 2301 W 21st Pl
- **Nancy Jefferson** • 1100 S Hamilton Ave
- **Octavio Paz Middle** • 2401 W Congress Pkwy
- **Orozco Elementary** • 1940 W 18th St
- **Rush University** • 600 S Paulina St
- **St Ann Grade School** • 2211 W 18th Pl
- **University of Illinois College of Medicine** • 1853 W Polk St
- **Washington Irving Elementary** • 749 S Oakley Blvd
- **William E Gladstone Elementary** • 1231 S Damen Ave

Supermarkets

- **Aldi** • 1739 W Cermak Rd
- **Fairplay Finer Foods** • 2200 S Western Ave

Map 25 • Illinois Medical District

W Gladys Ave
S Claremont Ave
S Leavitt St
W Gladys Ave
S Seeley Ave
S Hermitage Ave
S Marshfield Ave
Western
Medical Center
23
W Van Buren St
290
Eisenhower Expy
W Congress Pkwy
S Honore St
St Lukes Medical Center
S Campbell Ave
S Claremont Ave
S Oakley Ave
S Bell Ave
S Hoyne Ave
W Harrison St
W Harrison St
S Marshfield Ave
Claremont Park
600S
S Wolcott Ave
S Winchester Ave
W Flournoy St
W Flournoy St
W Campbell Park Dr
W Flournoy St
A
W Lexington St
S Western Ave
W Lexington St
S Bowler St
W Lexington
Polk
W Polk St
W Bowler St
S Ogden Ave W
W Polk St
S Claremont Ave
S Oakley Blvd
S Bell Ave
W Boone St
S Damen Ave
University of Illinois Hospital
S Hermitage Ave
S Paulina St
S Marshfield Ave
S Laflin St
W Arthington St
VA Medical Center
Garibaldi Pl
W Taylor St
W Taylor St
W Fillmore St
Almond St
S Seeley Ave
W Fillmore St
W Fillmore St
S Wood St
W Grenshaw St
W Grenshaw St
S Hoyne Ave
S Hoyne Ave
S Hamilton Ave
W Roosevelt Rd
2400W
2000W
1200S
ILLINOIS MEDICAL DISTRICT
1600W
S Laflin St
W Washburne Ave
S Oakley Ave
W Washburne Ave
W 13th St
S Claremont Ave
S Heath Ave
S Bell Ave
S Leavitt St
W Hastings St
W Hastings St
S Laflin St
B
26
W 14th St
W 14th St
W 14th St
S Wolcott Ave
50
W 14th Pl
W 15th St
S Ashland Ave
W 15th Pl
S Laflin St
W 16th St
W 16th St
1600S
W 17th St
S Hoyne Ave
Western Ave
S Hamilton Ave
S Leavitt St
18th
W 18th St
S Marshfield Ave
W 18th Pl
S Western Ave
S Oakley Ave
Harrison Park
W 18th Pl
S Damen Ave
C
W 19th St
HEART OF CHICAGO
W Cullerton St
W Cullerton St
Western
Hoyne
W 21st St
W 21st St
S Leavitt St
S Hoyne Ave
S Wolcott Ave
S Wood St
S Paulina St
S Laflin St
W 21st Pl
W 21st Pl
S Blue Island Ave
W Cermak Rd
52
S Bell Ave
2200S
W 22nd Pl
W 22nd Pl
1
2

Sundries/ Entertainment

It's a Blockbuster night.

Coffee

- **Dunkin' Donuts** • 1710 W 18th St
- **Dunkin' Donuts** • 1713 W Polk St
- **Dunkin' Donuts** • 2356 W Cermak Rd
- **Dunkin' Donuts** • 2401 W Ogden Ave

Gyms

- **Curves** • 600 S Western Ave

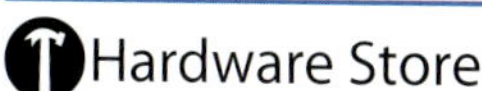

Hardware Stores

- **Mitchell Hardware & Paints** • 2141 W Cermak Rd

Liquor Stores

- **Helen's Grocery & Liquors** • 2300 W 21st St

Nightlife

- **White Horse Lounge** • 2059 W 19th St

Restaurants

- **Carnitas Uruapan Restaurant** • 1725 W 18th St
- **El Charco Verde** • 2253 W Taylor St
- **TJ's Family Restaurant** • 1928 W Cermak Rd

Video Rental

- **Blockbuster Video** • 2425 W Cermak Rd
- **Pedraza Video** • 1758 W 19th St

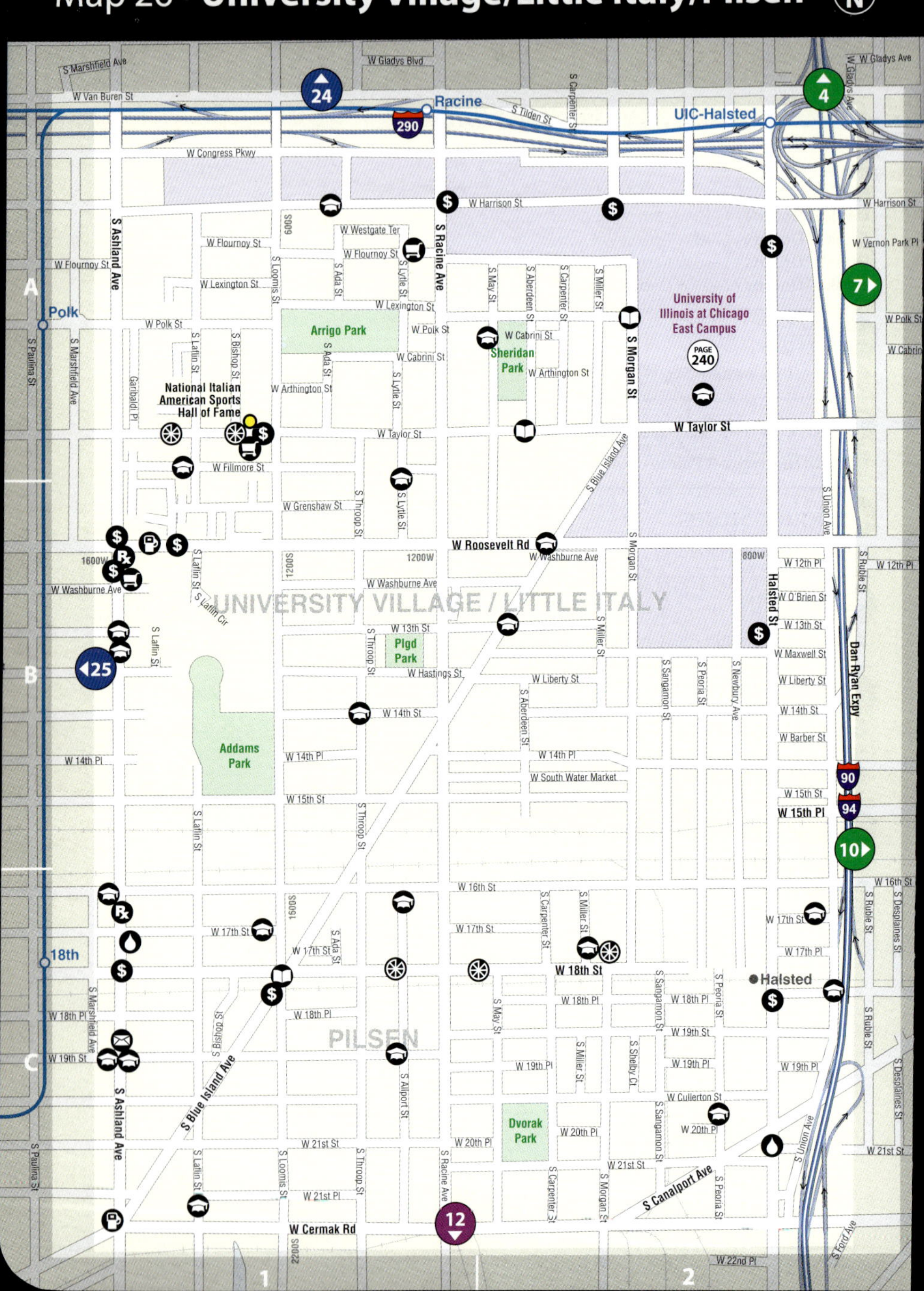

N
Racine
UIC-Halsted
Polk
18th
Halsted
24
4
7
25
10
12
290
90
94
University of Illinois at Chicago East Campus
PAGE 240
National Italian American Sports Hall of Fame
Arrigo Park
Sheridan Park
Plgd Park
Addams Park
Dvorak Park
UNIVERSITY VILLAGE / LITTLE ITALY
PILSEN
W Van Buren St
W Congress Pkwy
W Harrison St
W Roosevelt Rd
W Taylor St
W 18th St
W Cermak Rd
S Ashland Ave
S Racine Ave
S Morgan St
Halsted St
S Blue Island Ave
S Canalport Ave
Dan Ryan Expy
W 15th Pl
1600W
1200W
800W
A
B
C
1
2

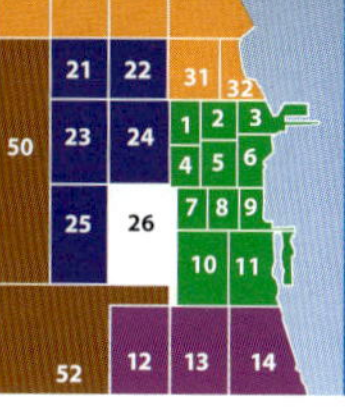

University of Illinois at Chicago is consuming blocks like the Great Chicago Fire of 1871, which started nearby. The campus expansion stretches south of Roosevelt Road. What's left of Little Italy from the last UIC expansion centers around Taylor Street, where Tuscan and Sicilian are spoken. Any pizza parlor is a good pick, but Pompeii's pies rule. The vibrant Latino Pilsen neighborhood starts here and spreads south.

Banks

- **Charter One (ATM)** • 1524 W Taylor St
- **Chicago Community** • 1800 S Halsted St
- **LaSalle** • 1212 S Ashland Ave
- **LaSalle (ATM)** • 1200 W Harrison St
- **LaSalle (ATM)** • 601 S Morgan St
- **LaSalle (ATM)** • 750 S Halsted St
- **MB Financial** • 1618 W 18th St
- **MidAmerica** • 1314 S Halsted St
- **Midwest Bank & Trust Company (ATM)** • 1810 South Blue Island Ave
- **TCF** • Jewel, 1220 S Ashland Ave
- **Washington Federal** • 1410 W Taylor St

Car Washes

- **Pilsen Car Wash** • 2042 S Halsted St
- **Speed Hand Car Wash** • 1700 S Ashland Ave

Gas Stations

- **BP** • 1602 W Cermak Rd
- **Marathon** • 1549 W Roosevelt Rd

Landmarks

- **National Italian American Sports Hall of Fame** • 1431 W Taylor St

Libraries

- **Lozano Public Library** • 1805 S Loomis St
- **Roosevelt Public Library** • 1101 W Taylor St
- **University of Illinois at Chicago Library** • 801 S Morgan St

Pharmacies

- **Jewel-Osco** • 1220 S Ashland Ave
- **Osco Drug** • 1713 S Ashland Ave

Pizza

- **Benny's Pizza II** • 1244 W 18th St
- **Caire's Pizza** • 1166 W 18th St
- **Leona's Pizzeria** • 1419 W Taylor St
- **Pizza Tango** • 1013 W 18th St
- **Pompeii Bakery** • 1531 W Taylor St

Post Offices

- 1859 S Ashland Ave

Schools

- **Andrew Jackson Language Academy** • 1340 W Harrison St
- **Benito Juarez High** • 2150 S Laflin St
- **City as Classroom High** • 1814 S Union Ave
- **Galileo Scholastic Academy** • 820 S Carpenter St
- **John A Walsh Elementary** • 2031 S Peoria St
- **John M Smyth Elementary** • 1059 W 13th St
- **Joseph Jungman Elementary** • 1746 S Miller St
- **Joseph Medill Elementary** • 1301 W 14th St
- **Manuel Perez Elementary** • 1241 W 19th St
- **Montefiore High** • 1310 S Ashland Ave
- **Moses Montefiore Middle** • 1310 S Ashland Ave
- **Peter Cooper Dual Language Academy** • 1624 W 19th St
- **Pilsen Academy** • 1420 W 17th St
- **Simpson Academy for Young Women** • 1321 S Paulina St
- **St Ignatius College Prep** • 1076 W Roosevelt Rd
- **St Pius V Elementary** • 1919 S Ashland Ave
- **St Procopius** • 1625 S Allport St
- **Thomas Jefferson Elementary** • 1522 W Fillmore St
- **University of Illinois at Chicago East Campus** • 840 S Wood St

Supermarkets

- **Conte Di Savoia** • 1438 W Taylor St
- **Jewel** • 1240 W Harrison St
- **Jewel-Osco** • 1220 S Ashland Ave

UNIVERSITY VILLAGE / LITTLE ITALY

PILSEN

University of Illinois at Chicago East Campus

PAGE 240

Arrigo Park

Sheridan Park

Plgd Park

Addams Park

Dvorak Park

Racine

UIC-Halsted

Polk

18th

Halsted

W Van Buren St
W Congress Pkwy
W Harrison St
W Flournoy St
W Lexington St
W Polk St
W Cabrini St
W Arthington St
W Taylor St
W Fillmore St
W Grenshaw St
W Roosevelt Rd
W Washburne Ave
W 13th St
W Hastings St
W Liberty St
W 14th St
W 14th Pl
W South Water Market
W 15th St
W 15th Pl
W 16th St
W 17th St
W 17th Pl
W 18th St
W 18th Pl
W 19th St
W 19th Pl
W Cullerton St
W 20th Pl
W 21st St
W 21st Pl
W Cermak Rd
W 22nd Pl
W 12th Pl
W O'Brien St
W Maxwell St
W Barber St
W Gladys Blvd
W Gladys Ave
W Vernon Park Pl
W Westgate Ter
S Ashland Ave
S Racine Ave
S Morgan St
S Halsted St
S Blue Island Ave
S Canalport Ave
Dan Ryan Expy
S Paulina St
S Marshfield Ave
S Laflin St
S Loomis St
S Throop St
S Lytle St
S Ada St
S Bishop St
S May St
S Aberdeen St
S Carpenter St
S Miller St
S Sangamon St
S Peoria St
S Newbury Ave
S Union Ave
S Ruble St
S Desplaines St
S Allport St
S Shelby Ct
S Tilden St
S Ford Ave
Garibaldi Pl
S Laflin Cir

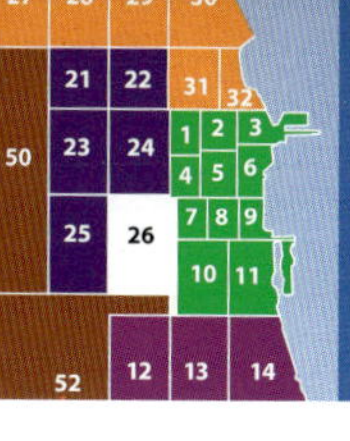

Try Taylor Street for authentic Italian. Sports fans chow down here before games at the United Center. Just like mama, Gennaro's dishes up generous portions. Where's the beef? At Al's. Buy Scafuri Bakery's cannoli by the dozen. The murals in Pilsen, especially at the 18th Street El station, are outstanding. Come here for authentic Mexican tacos as restaurants and bodegas line the streets.

Coffee

- **Café Jumping Bean** • 1439 W 18th St
- **Café Mestizo** • 2123 S Ashland Ave
- **Caribou Coffee** • 1328 S Halsted St
- **Caribou Coffee** • 811 W Maxwell St
- **Jamoch's Caffe** • 1066 W Taylor St
- **Kristoffer's Café & Bakery** • 1733 S Halsted St
- **Mi Cafetal** • 1519 W 18th St
- **Starbucks** • 1430 W Taylor St

Copy Shops

- **Postnet (9 am-7 pm)** • 1258 S Halsted St

Gyms

- **Curves** • 960-62 W 18th St
- **Duncan YMCA** • 1001 W Roosevelt Rd
- **Group Fitness** • 750 S Halsted St
- **Pilsen YMCA** • 1608 W 21st Pl
- **Temoc's Gym Fitness Center** • 2118 S Halsted St

Hardware Stores

- **Ace Hardware** • 1514 S Ashland Ave
- **Alvarez Hardware** • 1323 W 18th St
- **Chiarugi Hardware** • 1449 W Taylor St
- **La Brocha Gorda** • 974 W 18th St
- **Seigle's Lumber (lumber only)** • 977 W Cermak Rd
- **Torres Hardware** • 1836 S Ashland Ave

Liquor Stores

- **Amador Liquors** • 1167 W 18th St
- **Conte Di Savoia** • 1438 W Taylor St
- **F&R Liquor** • 2129 S Halsted St
- **Guadalajara Food & Liquors** • 1527 W 18th St
- **Three Sons Food & Liquor** • 1311 W Taylor St

Nightlife

- **Bar Louie** • 1321 W Taylor St
- **Bevi Amo Wine Bar** • 1358 W Taylor St
- **Hawkeye's Bar & Grill** • 1458 W Taylor St
- **The Illinois Bar & Grill** • 1421 W Taylor St
- **Skylark** • 2149 S Halsted St

Restaurants

- **Al's Number 1 Italian Beef** • 1079 W Taylor St
- **Café Viaggio** • 1435 W Taylor St
- **Caffe La Scala** • 626 S Racine Ave
- **Carm's Beef and Snack Shop** • 1057 W Polk St
- **Chez Joel** • 1119 W Taylor St
- **Couscous** • 1445 W Taylor St
- **De Pasada** • 1519 W Taylor St
- **Francesca's** • 1400 W Taylor St
- **Gennaro's** • 1352 W Taylor St
- **Golden Thai** • 1509 W Taylor St
- **La Vita** • 1359 W Taylor St
- **Little China** • 1520 W Taylor St
- **May Street Café** • 1136 W Cermak
- **New Rosebud Café** • 1500 W Taylor St
- **Nuevo Leon** • 1515 W 18th St
- **Playa Azul** • 1514 W 18th St
- **Siam Pot** • 1509 Taylor St
- **Sweet Maple Café** • 1339 W Taylor St
- **Taj Mahal** • 1512 W Taylor St
- **Taylor Street Taco Grill** • 1412 W Taylor St
- **Tuscany** • 1014 W Taylor St

Shopping

- **Scafuri Bakery** • 1337 W Taylor St

Video Rental

- **Manny's Video** • 1546 W 21st St

Map 27 • Logan Square

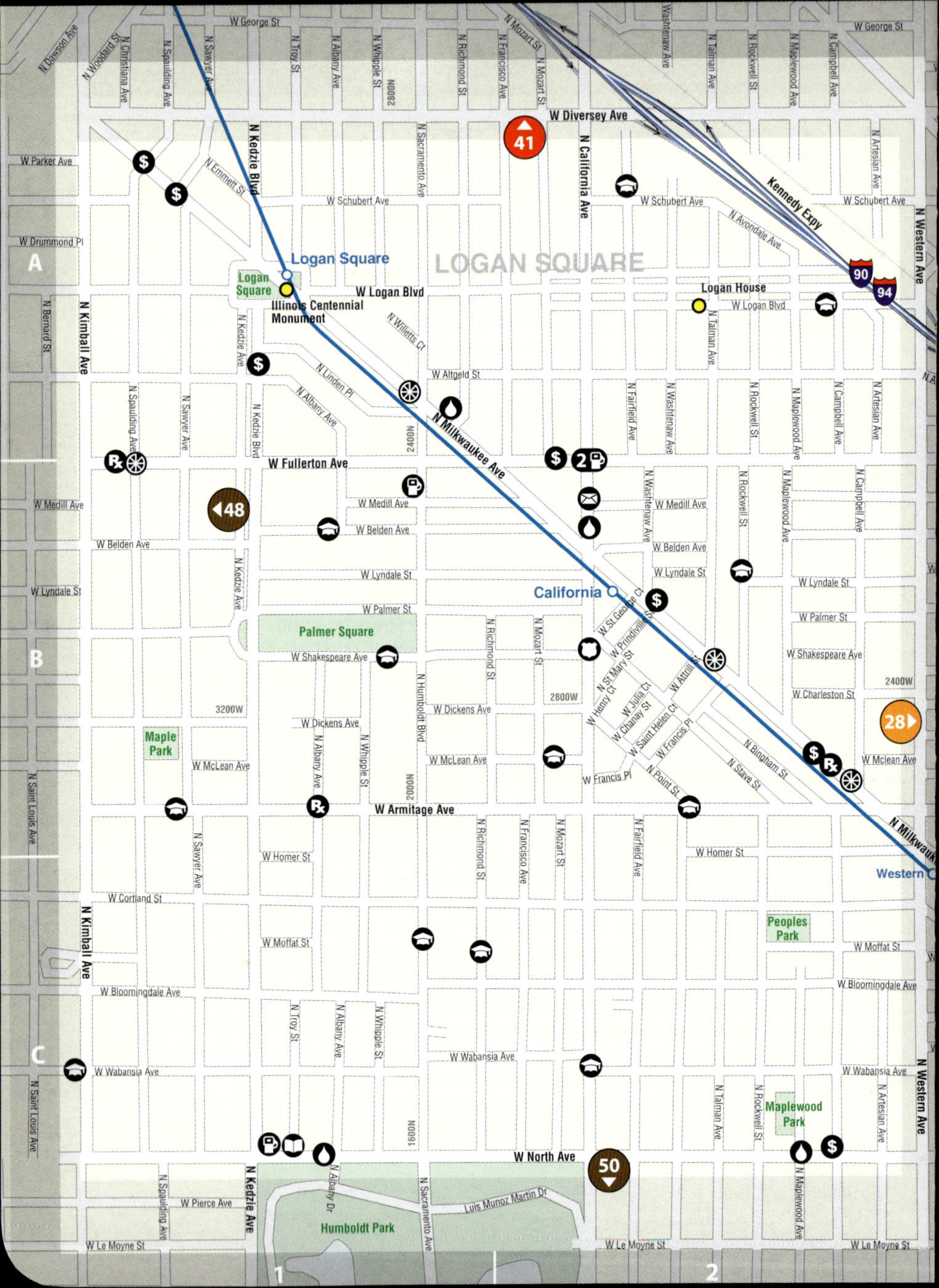

LOGAN SQUARE

Logan Square
California
Western

Logan Square
Illinois Centennial Monument
Logan House
Palmer Square
Maple Park
Peoples Park
Maplewood Park
Humboldt Park

Kennedy Expy
90
94

W George St
W Diversey Ave
W Parker Ave
W Schubert Ave
W Drummond Pl
W Logan Blvd
W Altgeld St
W Fullerton Ave
W Medill Ave
W Belden Ave
W Lyndale St
W Palmer St
W Shakespeare Ave
W Charleston St
W Dickens Ave
W McLean Ave
W Mclean Ave
W Francis Pl
W Armitage Ave
W Homer St
W Cortland St
W Moffat St
W Bloomingdale Ave
W Wabansia Ave
W North Ave
W Pierce Ave
W Le Moyne St
Luis Munoz Martin Dr

N Dawson Ave
N Woodard St
N Christiana Ave
N Spaulding Ave
N Sawyer Ave
N Troy St
N Albany Ave
N Whipple St
N Richmond St
N Francisco Ave
N Mozart St
N Washtenaw Ave
N Talman Ave
N Rockwell St
N Maplewood Ave
N Campbell Ave
N Artesian Ave
N Western Ave
N Kedzie Blvd
N Kedzie Ave
N Emmett St
N Sacramento Ave
N California Ave
N Avondale Ave
N Kimball Ave
N Bernard St
N Saint Louis Ave
N Willetts Ct
N Linden Pl
N Albany Ave
N Milwaukee Ave
N Fairfield Ave
N Humboldt Blvd
W St George Ct
W Prindiville St
W St Mary St
N St Henry Ct
W Julia Ct
W Chanay St
W Saint Helen Ct
W Francis Pl
W Attrill St
N Point St
N Bingham St
N Stave St
N Albany Dr

2800W
2400W
2000N
1600N
3200W
2800W
2400W
2000N
1600N

41
48
28
50
2

A
B
C
1
2

Essentials

It's come to pass that this former rough and ready 'hood is now drawing renovators in droves as rents start to inch their way upwards. No surprise with the stately graystones lining tree-lined boulevards, as well as access to both the expressway and public transportation. The only wonder is that it took this long.

Banks

- **Banco Popular** • 2525 N Kedzie Blvd
- **Bank One** • 2235 N Milwaukee Ave
- **Charter One** • 2500 W North Ave
- **Citibank** • 2707 N Milwaukee Ave
- **Northern Trust** • 2814 W Fullerton Ave
- **TCF (ATM)** • Osco, 2053 N Milwaukee Ave
- **Washington Mutual** • 2741 N Milwaukee Ave

Car Washes

- **California Car Wash** • 2340 N California Ave
- **Dreamwash** • 2524 W North Ave
- **Logan Square Car Wash** • 2436 N Milwaukee Ave
- **Puerto Rico Car Wash** • 3110 W North Ave

Gas Stations

- **Amoco** • 2800 W Fullerton Ave
- **Citgo** • 2338 N Sacramento Ave
- **Citgo** • 3142 W North Ave
- **Shell** • 2801 W Fullerton Ave

Landmarks

- **Illinois Centennial Monument** • 3100 W Logan Blvd
- **Logan House** • 2656 W Logan Blvd

Libraries

- **Humboldt Park Public Library** • 1605 N Troy St

Pharmacies

- **Osco Drug** • 2053 N Milwaukee Ave
- **Walgreens** • 3110 W Armitage Ave
- **Walgreens** • 3320 W Fullerton Ave

Pizza

- **Big Tony's Pizza** • 3276 W Fullerton Ave
- **Congress Pizzeria** • 2033 N Milwaukee Ave
- **Father & Son Pizza** • 2475 N Milwaukee Ave
- **Lucky Vito's Pizzeria** • 2171 N Milwaukee Ave

Police

- **14th District (Shakespeare)** • 2150 N California Ave

Post Offices

- 2339 N California Ave

Schools

- **Bernhard Moos Elementary** • 1711 N California Ave
- **Charles R Darwin Elementary** • 3116 W Belden Ave
- **Harriet Beecher Stowe Elementary** • 3444 W Wabansia Ave
- **Humboldt Community Christian** • 1847 N Humboldt Blvd
- **J W Von Goethe Elementary** • 2236 N Rockwell St
- **Lorenz Brentano Math & Science Academy** • 2723 N Fairfield Ave
- **Richard Yates Elementary** • 1839 N Richmond St
- **Salem Christian** • 2845 W McLean Ave
- **Salomon P Chase Elementary** • 2021 N Point St
- **St Augustine College West** • 3255 W Armitage Ave
- **St John Berchman's** • 2511 W Logan Blvd
- **St Sylvester's** • 3027 W Palmer Blvd

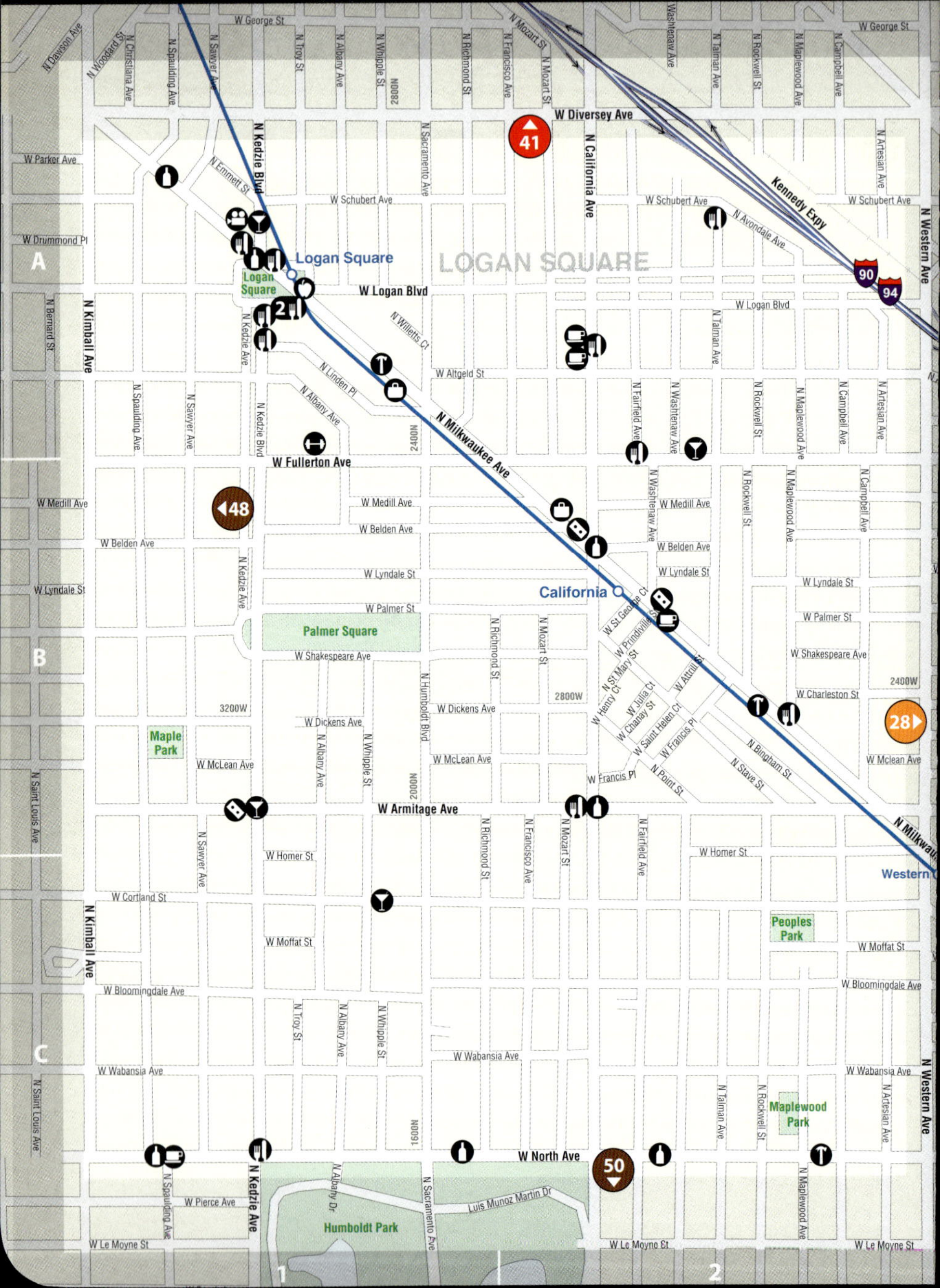

Map 27 • Logan Square

LOGAN SQUARE

W George St, W Diversey Ave, W Parker Ave, W Schubert Ave, W Drummond Pl, W Logan Blvd, W Altgeld St, W Fullerton Ave, W Medill Ave, W Belden Ave, W Lyndale St, W Palmer St, W Shakespeare Ave, W Charleston St, W Dickens Ave, W McLean Ave, W Francis Pl, W Armitage Ave, W Homer St, W Cortland St, W Moffat St, W Bloomingdale Ave, W Wabansia Ave, W North Ave, W Pierce Ave, W Le Moyne St

N Kedzie Blvd, N Kedzie Ave, N Kimball Ave, N Spaulding Ave, N Sawyer Ave, N Troy St, N Albany Ave, N Whipple St, N Sacramento Ave, N Richmond St, N Francisco Ave, N Mozart St, N California Ave, N Washtenaw Ave, N Talman Ave, N Rockwell St, N Maplewood Ave, N Campbell Ave, N Artesian Ave, N Western Ave, N Fairfield Ave, N Humboldt Blvd, N Milwaukee Ave, N Avondale Ave, Kennedy Expy

Logan Square, California, Western

Logan Square, Palmer Square, Maple Park, Peoples Park, Maplewood Park, Humboldt Park

41, 48, 28, 50, 90, 94

A, B, C, 1, 2

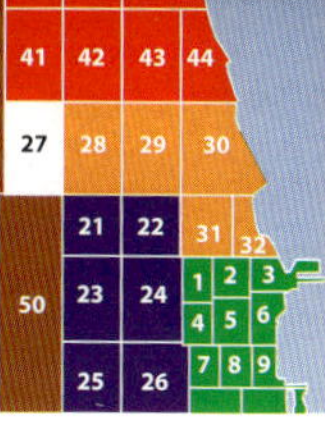

The Fireside Bowl, perpetually threatening to close, is Chicago's all-age punk-rock haven—it's been a while, I think, since anyone's actually gone there to knock down pins. The Winds is the place to go for an after-work drink. Lula Café has gone from neighborhood treasure to funky destination dining. The Congress Theater draws eclectic shows, from national touring acts to drag kings.

Coffee

- **Dunkin' Donuts** • 2247 N Milwaukee Ave
- **Dunkin' Donuts** • 3309 W North Ave
- **No Friction Café** • 2502 N California Ave
- **Starbucks** • 2543 N California Ave

Farmer's Markets

- **Logan Square** • W Logan Blvd & N Kedzie Blvd, Southeast Corner

Gyms

- **Curves** • 3143 W Fullerton Ave

Hardware Stores

- **Gillman's Hardware** • 2118 N Milwaukee Ave
- **Monroy's Hardware Store** • 2511 W North Ave
- **Tony's Tools** • 2500 N Milwaukee Ave

Liquor Stores

- **D&D Liquors** • 2958 W North Ave
- **Foremost Liquor Store** • 2300 N Milwaukee Ave
- **Foremost Liquor Store** • 3301 W North Ave
- **International Liquor Store** • 2001 N California Ave
- **Logan Liquors** • 2639 N Kedzie Ave
- **Red Star Liquors** • 2715 N Milwaukee Ave
- **Yafai Liquors** • 2700 W North Ave

Movie Theaters

- **Logan Theater** • 2646 N Milwaukee Ave

Nightlife

- **3030** • 3030 W Cortland St
- **Fireside Bowl** • 2648 W Fullerton Ave
- **Streetside Café** • 3201 W Armitage Ave
- **The Winds Café** • 2657 N Kedzie Blvd

Restaurants

- **Abril Mexican Restaurant** • 2607 N Milwaukee Ave
- **Buona Terra Ristorante** • 2535 N California Ave
- **Café Bolero** • 2252 N Western Ave
- **Choi's Chinese Restaurant** • 2638 N Milwaukee Ave
- **Dunlay's on the Square** • 3137 W Logan Blvd
- **El Cid** • 2116 N Milwaukee Ave
- **El Nandu** • 2731 N Fullerton Ave
- **Hot Spot** • 2824 W Armitage Ave
- **Johnny's Grill** • 2545 N Kedzie Blvd
- **Lula Café** • 2537 N Kedzie Blvd
- **Mama Kitty's** • 1616 N Kedzie Ave

Shopping

- **MegaMall** • 2502 N Milwaukee Ave
- **Threads, Etc** • 2327 N Milwaukee Ave

Video Rental

- **Blockbuster Video** • 2251 N Milwaukee Ave
- **Hi-Fi Video** • 3129 W Armitage Ave
- **Morelia Video** • 2381 N Milwaukee Ave

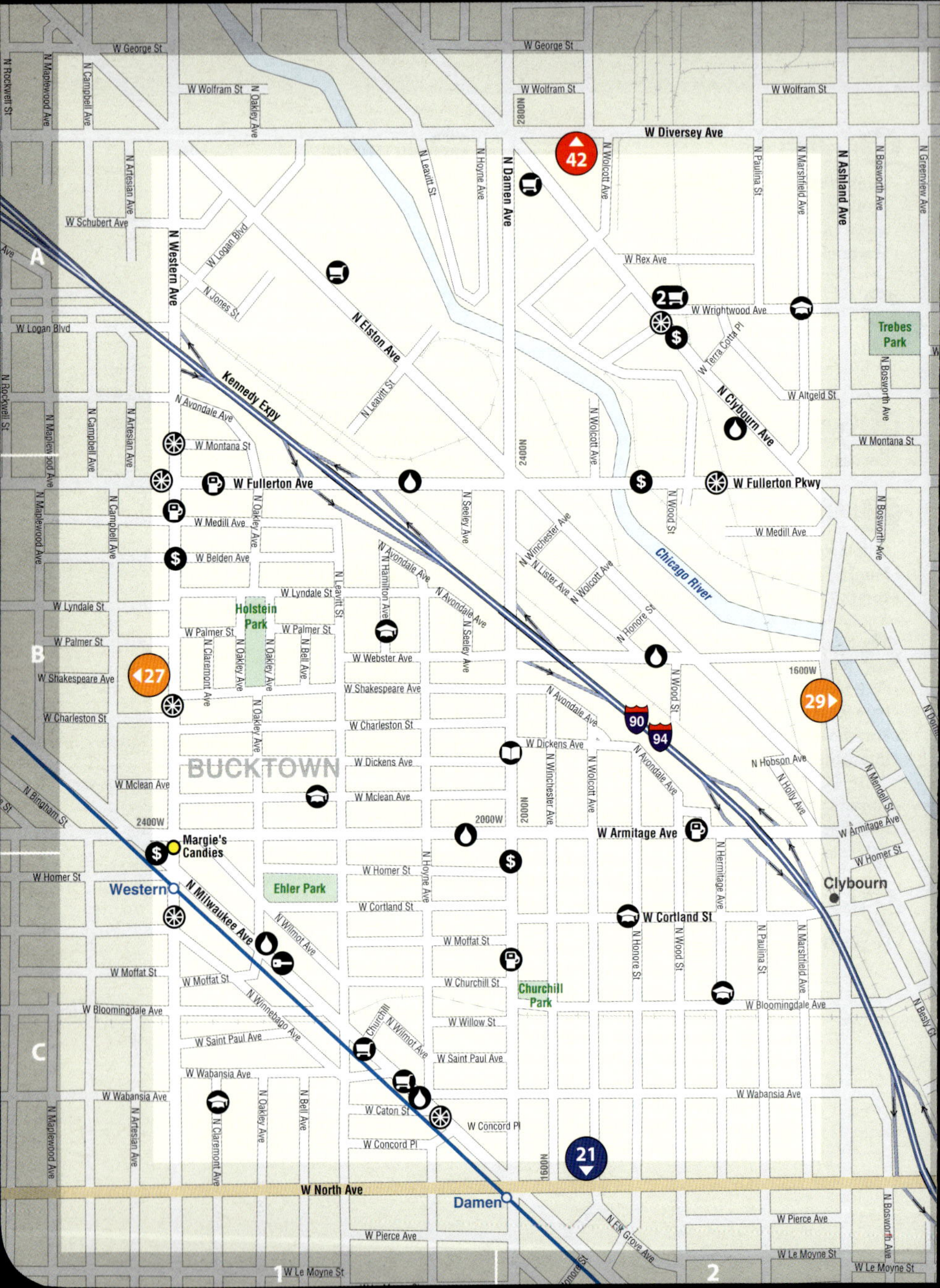

Map 28 • Bucktown

W George St
W Wolfram St
W Diversey Ave
W Schubert Ave
W Logan Blvd
W Rex Ave
W Wrightwood Ave
W Terra Cotta Pl
W Altgeld St
W Montana St
W Fullerton Ave
W Fullerton Pkwy
W Medill Ave
W Belden Ave
W Lyndale St
W Palmer St
W Webster Ave
W Shakespeare Ave
W Charleston St
W Dickens Ave
W Mclean Ave
W Armitage Ave
W Homer St
W Cortland St
W Moffat St
W Churchill St
W Bloomingdale Ave
W Willow St
W Saint Paul Ave
W Wabansia Ave
W Caton St
W Concord Pl
W North Ave
W Pierce Ave
W Le Moyne St
N Rockwell St
N Maplewood Ave
N Campbell Ave
N Artesian Ave
N Western Ave
N Oakley Ave
N Claremont Ave
N Bell Ave
N Leavitt St
N Hamilton Ave
N Hoyne Ave
N Seeley Ave
N Damen Ave
N Winchester Ave
N Lister Ave
N Wolcott Ave
N Honore St
N Wood St
N Hermitage Ave
N Paulina St
N Marshfield Ave
N Ashland Ave
N Bosworth Ave
N Greenview Ave
N Logan Blvd
N Jones St
N Elston Ave
N Avondale Ave
N Clybourn Ave
N Hobson Ave
N Holly Ave
N Mendell St
N Milwaukee Ave
N Wilmot Ave
N Winnebago Ave
N Bingham St
N Elk Grove Ave
Kennedy Expy
Chicago River
Holstein Park
Ehler Park
Churchill Park
Trebes Park
BUCKTOWN
Margie's Candies
Western
Damen
Clybourn
2800N
2400N
2000N
1600N
2400W
2000W
1600W
90
94
42
27
29
21
A
B
C
1
2

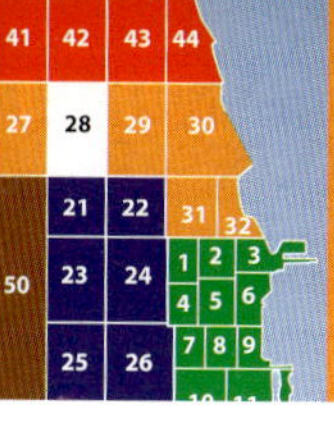

As Bucktown's once-thriving art scene fades further into oblivion, real estate becomes out of reach for all but the young executives who are attracted to the area's upscale boutiques, restaurants, and arty-urban reputation.

Banks

- **Bank One** • 1757 W Fullerton Ave
- **Charter One** • 2550 N Clybourn Ave
- **Citibank** • 1737 W Fullerton Ave
- **Citibank** • 1951 N Western Ave
- **Cole Taylor** • 1965 N Milwaukee Ave
- **MidAmerica** • 1830 W Fullerton Ave
- **MidAmerica** • 1955 N Damen Ave
- **MidAmerica** • 2300 N Western Ave
- **Northern Trust (ATM)** • 2346 N Western Ave
- **TCF** • 2627 Elston Ave
- **Washington Mutual** • 2790 N Clybourn Ave

Car Washes

- **Bucktown Hand Car Wash** • 2036 W Armitage Ave
- **Clybourn Express & Car Wash** • 2452 N Clybourn Ave
- **Express Car Wash** • 2111 W Fullerton Ave
- **Fast Eddie's Hand Car Wash** • 1828 W Webster Ave
- **Prestige Hand Wash** • 1843 N Milwaukee Ave
- **Wash Express** • 1657 N Milwaukee Ave

Car Rental

- **Enterprise** • 1842 N Milwaukee Ave • 773-862-4700

Gas Stations

- **Amoco** • 1768 W Armitage Ave
- **Amoco** • 2357 W Fullerton Ave
- **Citgo** • 1768 W Armitage Ave
- **Citgo** • 2501 N Western Ave
- **Marathon** • 2346 N Western Ave
- **Mobil** • 1750 N Western Ave

Landmarks

- **Margie's Candies** • 1960 N Western Ave

Libraries

- **Damen Avenue Library** • 2056 N Damen Ave

Pharmacies

- **Dominick's** • 2550 N Clybourn Ave

Pizza

- **Barcello's Pizzeria** • 1647 N Milwaukee Ave
- **Chuck E Cheese's** • 1730 W Fullerton Ave
- **Dominick's Finer Foods** • 2550 N Clybourn Ave
- **John's Restaurant & Lounge** • 2104 N Western Ave
- **Li'l Guys/My Pie** • 2010 N Damen Ave
- **Plazzio's Pizza** • 1901 N Western Ave
- **Sonny's Pizza** • 2431 N Western Ave

Schools

- **Antonia Pantoja High** • 2435 N Western Ave
- **Casimir Pulaski Fine Arts Academy** • 2230 W McLean Ave
- **Chicago International Elementary - Bucktown Campus** • 2235 N Hamilton Ave
- **Frederick Funston Elementary** • 2010 W Armitage Ave
- **St Mary of the Angels** • 1810 N Hermitage Ave
- **Thomas Drummond Elementary** • 1845 W Cortland St
- **William H Prescott Elementary** • 1632 W Wrightwood Ave

Supermarkets

- **Aldi** • 1767 N Milwaukee Ave
- **Aldi** • 2600 N Clybourn Ave
- **Always Open** • 1704 N Milwaukee Ave
- **Costco** • 2746 N Clybourn Ave
- **Cub Foods** • 2627 N Elston Ave
- **Dominick's** • 2550 N Clybourn Ave

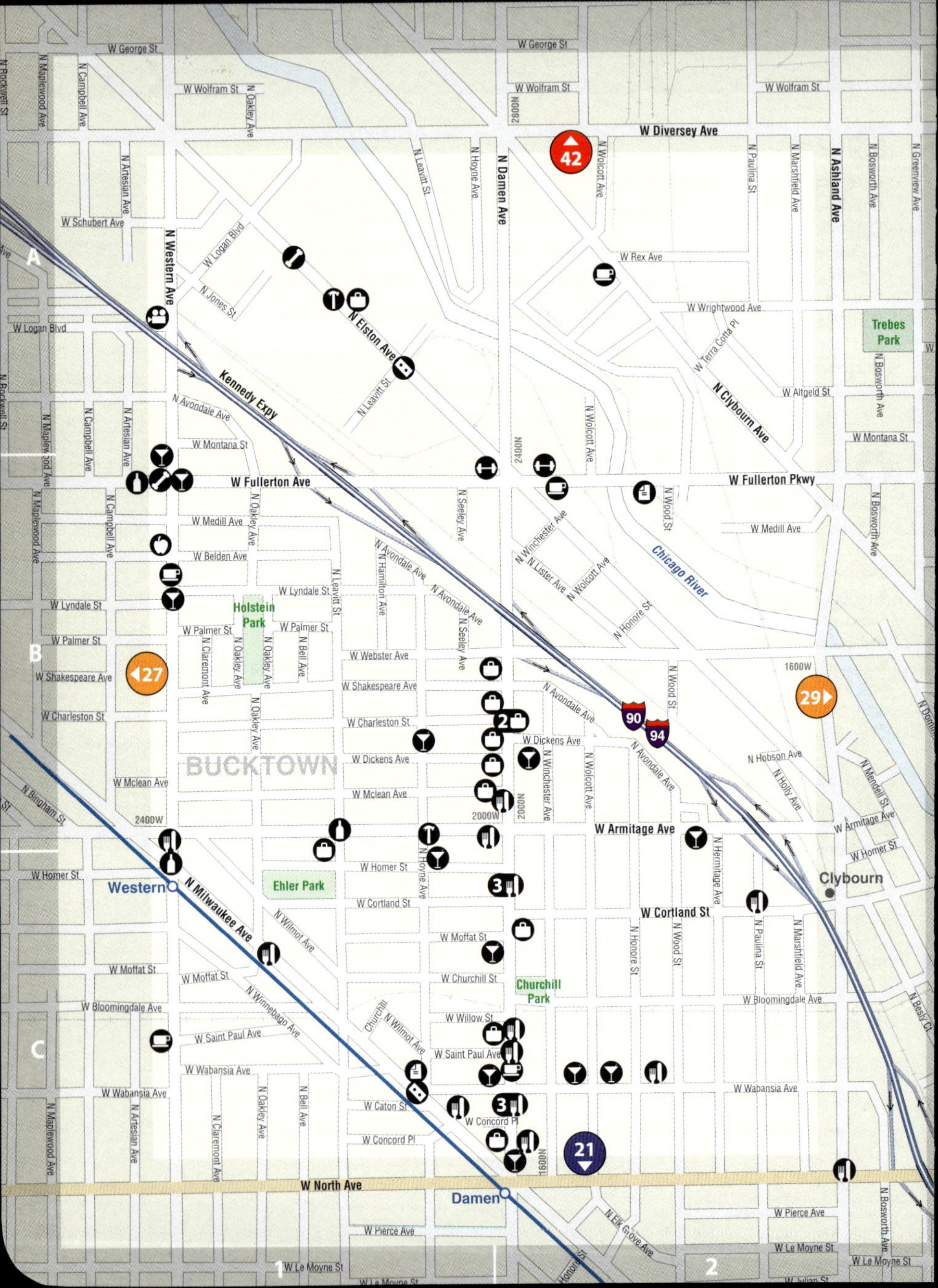

W George St
W Wolfram St
W Diversey Ave
W Schubert Ave
W Logan Blvd
N Jones St
N Elston Ave
N Leavitt St
W Rex Ave
W Wrightwood Ave
W Terra Cotta Pl
W Altgeld St
N Clybourn Ave
Trebes Park
Kennedy Expy
N Avondale Ave
W Montana St
W Fullerton Ave
W Fullerton Pkwy
W Medill Ave
W Belden Ave
W Lyndale St
W Palmer St
Holstein Park
W Shakespeare Ave
W Webster Ave
W Charleston St
W Dickens Ave
BUCKTOWN
W Mclean Ave
W Armitage Ave
W Homer St
W Cortland St
W Moffat St
W Churchill St
Churchill Park
Ehler Park
W Willow St
W Bloomingdale Ave
W Saint Paul Ave
W Wabansia Ave
W Caton St
W Concord Pl
W North Ave
W Pierce Ave
W Le Moyne St
W Julian St
N Milwaukee Ave
N Wilmot Ave
N Winnebago Ave
N Elk Grove Ave
Chicago River
N Western Ave
N Rockwell St
N Maplewood Ave
N Campbell Ave
N Artesian Ave
N Oakley Ave
N Claremont Ave
N Bell Ave
N Hamilton Ave
N Seeley Ave
N Hoyne Ave
N Damen Ave
N Winchester Ave
N Lister Ave
N Wolcott Ave
N Honore St
N Wood St
N Hermitage Ave
N Paulina St
N Marshfield Ave
N Ashland Ave
N Bosworth Ave
N Greenview Ave
N Hobson Ave
N Holly Ave
N Mendell St
N Besly Ct
N Dominick St
N Bingham St
2800N
2400N
2000N
1600N
2400W
2000W
1600W
Western
Damen
Clybourn
42
27
29
21
90
94
A
B
C
1
2

Sundries / Entertainment

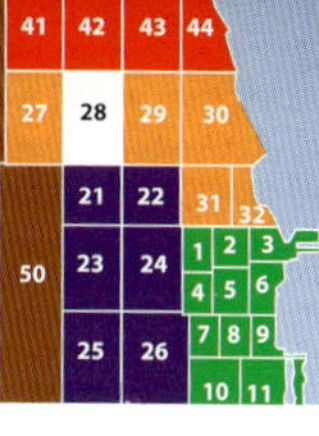

Café Matou is a hidden gem on Milwaukee Avenue. Punters still crowd the Northside Café, especially popular in the summer for its patios and fruity drink concoctions. Of all the upscale neighborhood taverns populating the streets, perhaps Lemmings has the most indicative name.

Coffee

- **Art Gallery Kafe** • 1907 N Milwaukee Ave
- **Caffe De Luca** • 1721 N Damen Ave
- **Dunkin' Donuts** • 1746 N Western Ave
- **Dunkin' Donuts** • 1909 N Western Ave
- **Dunkin' Donuts** • 1927 W Fullerton Ave
- **Red Hen Bread** • 1623 N Milwaukee Ave
- **Starbucks (Dominick's)** • 2550 N Clybourn Ave
- **Starbucks (Target)** • 2656 N Elston Ave

Copy Shops

- **Copy Max (7 am-9 pm)** • 1829 W Fullerton Ave
- **The UPS Store (8:30 am-8 pm)** • 1658 Milwaukee Ave

Farmer's Markets

- **Bucktown** • W Belden Ave & N Western Ave

Gyms

- **Children's Fitness Center** • 1880 W Fullerton Ave

Hardware Stores

- **Home Depot** • 2570 N Elston Ave

Liquor Stores

- **Bon Song Liquors** • 2000 N Leavitt St
- **Bucktown Food & Liquor** • 2422 W Fullerton Ave
- **Danny's Buy Low** • 2222 N Western Ave
- **MW Food & Liquor** • 1950 N Milwaukee Ave

Movie Theaters

- **AMC** • 2600 N Western Ave

Nightlife

- **Artful Dodger Pub** • 1734 W Wabansia Ave
- **Bar Louie** • 1704 N Damen Ave
- **Cans** • 1640 N Damen Ave
- **Charleston Tavern** • 2076 N Hoyne Ave
- **Danny's** • 1951 W Dickens Ave
- **Danny's** • 2222 N Western Ave
- **Gallery Cabaret** • 2020 N Oakley Ave
- **Lemmings** • 1850 N Damen Ave
- **The Liar's Club** • 1665 W Fullerton Ave
- **Lincoln Tavern** • 1858 W Wabansia Ave
- **The Map Room** • 1949 N Hoyne Ave
- **Marie's Rip Tide Lounge** • 1745 W Armitage Ave
- **The Mutiny** • 2428 N Western Ave
- **Northside Café** • 1635 N Damen Ave
- **Quenchers Saloon** • 2401 N Western Ave

Pet Shops

- **Petsmart** • 2665 N Elston Ave

Restaurants

- **Café De Luca** • 1721 N Damen Ave
- **Café Laguardia** • 2111 W Armitage Ave
- **Café Matou** • 1846 N Milwaukee Ave
- **Club Lucky** • 1824 W Wabansia Ave
- **Darwin's** • 1935 N Damen Ave
- **Hollywood Grill** • 1601 W North Ave
- **Hot Chocolate** • 1747 N Damen
- **Jane's** • 1655 W Cortland St
- **Le Bouchon** • 1958 N Damen Ave
- **Margie's Candies** • 1960 N Western Ave
- **Meritage** • 2118 N Damen Ave
- **My Pie Pizza** • 2010 N Damen Ave
- **Northside Bar & Grill** • 1635 N Damen Ave
- **Rinconcito Sudamericano** • 1954 W Armitage Ave
- **Roong Thai Restaurant** • 1633 N Milwaukee Ave
- **Scylla** • 1952 N Damen
- **Silver Cloud Club & Grill** • 1700 N Damen Ave
- **Think** • 2235 N Western
- **Toast** • 2046 N Damen Ave

Shopping

- **Bleeker Street Antiques** • 1946 N Leavitt St
- **G Boutique** • 2131 N Damen Ave
- **Goddess and the Grocer** • 1646 N Damen
- **Jean Alan** • 2134 N Damen Ave
- **Jolie Joli** • 1623 N Damen Ave
- **Mark Shale Outlet** • 2593 N Elston Ave
- **Pagoda Red** • 1714 N Damen Ave
- **Pavilion Antiques** • 2055 N Damen Ave
- **Red Balloon Company** • 2060 N Damen Ave
- **T-Shirt Deli** • 1739 N Damen Ave
- **Viva La Femme** • 2115 N Damen Ave
- **Yardifacts** • 1864 N Damen Ave

Video Rental

- **Blockbuster Video** • 1704 N Milwaukee Ave

Map 29 • DePaul / Wrightwood / Sheffield

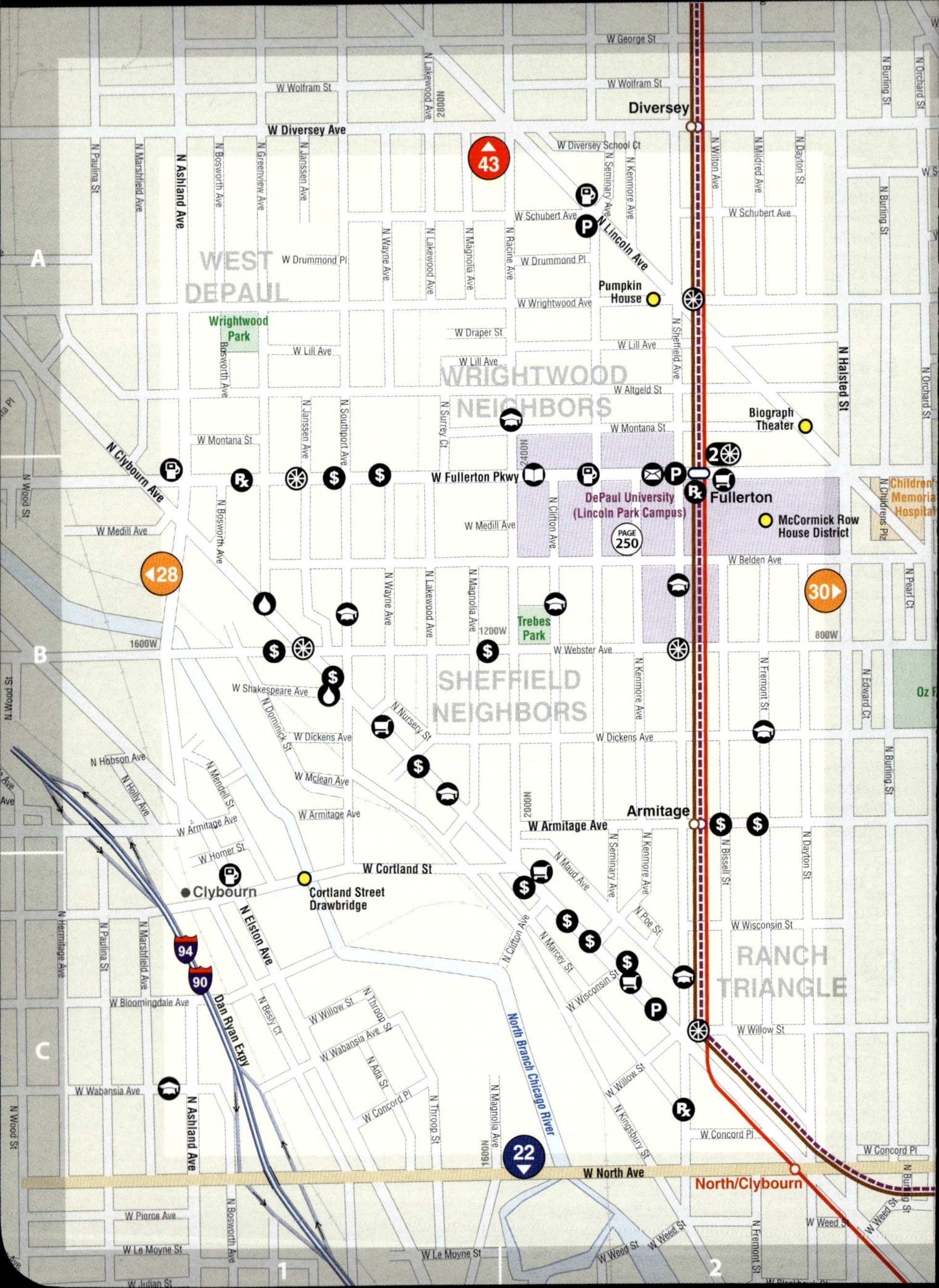

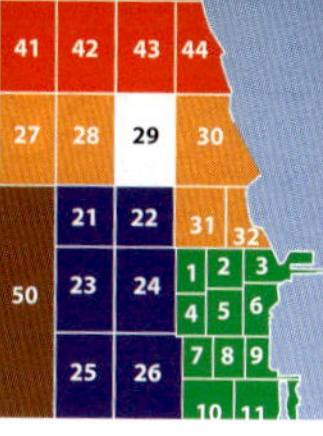

Abodes on the quiet, shady streets around DePaul University and west of the El tracks command big mortgages and high rents. Always super-size when ordering Stefani's pizza, because you'll want some for breakfast. The Clybourn Corrider's heavy traffic can be infuriating and narrow side streets crowded with parked cars and SUVs don't offer much relief. Around the area's eastern half, it's wiser to take the El and hoof it.

Banks

- **Associated (ATM)** • 1224 W Webster Ave
- **Bank of America (ATM)** • 1471 W Webster Ave
- **Bank of America (ATM)** • 1845 N Clybourn Ave
- **Bank One** • 2170 N Clybourn Ave
- **Bank One** • 935 W Armitage Ave
- **Charter One (ATM)** • 1349 W Fullerton Ave
- **Charter One (ATM)** • 2710 N Lincoln Ave
- **Fifth Third** • 900 W Armitage Ave
- **TCF** • Osco, 1400 W Fullerton Ave
- **US** • 1953 N Clybourn Ave
- **Washington Mutual** • 2053 N Clybourne Ave
- **Washington Mutual** • 2662 N Lincoln Ave

Car Washes

- **We'll Clean** • 2261 N Clybourn Ave
- **White Glove Car Wash** • 1415 W Shakespeare Ave

Gas Stations

- **BP** • 1607 W Fullerton Ave
- **Mobil** • 1106 W Fullerton Ave
- **Mobil** • 1901 N Elston Ave
- **Mobil** • 2670 N Lincoln Ave

Landmarks

- **Biograph Theater** • 2433 N Lincoln Ave
- **Courtland Street Drawbridge** • 1440 W Cortland St
- **McCormick Row House District** • W Chalmers Pl, W Belden Ave, & W Fullerton Pkwy
- **Pumpkin House** • 1052 W Wrightwood Ave

Libraries

- **Lincoln Park Public Library** • 1150 W Fullerton Ave

Parking

Pharmacies

- **CVS Pharmacy (24 hours)** • 1714 N Sheffield Ave
- **Dominick's** • 959 W Fullerton Ave
- **Walgreens (24 hours)** • 1520 W Fullerton Ave

Pizza

- **Amato's Pizza** • 953 W Willow St
- **Dominick's Finer Foods** • 959 W Fullerton Ave
- **Lou Malnati's Pizzeria** • 958 W Wrightwood Ave
- **Pequod's Pizzeria** • 2207 N Clybourn Ave
- **Stefani's** • 1418 W Fullerton Ave
- **Tomato Head Pizza Kitchen** • 1001 W Webster Ave
- **Via-Carducci's Italian Eatery** • 1419 W Fullerton Ave

Post Offices

- 2405 N Sheffield Ave

Schools

- **Anixter** • 2032 N Clybourn Ave
- **Arts of Living** • 1855 N Sheffield Ave
- **DePaul University (Lincoln Park Campus)** • 2250 N Sheffield Ave
- **Frederic Chopin Elementary** • 2450 W Racine Ave
- **Jonathan Burr Elementary** • 1621 W Wabansia Ave
- **Oscar F Mayer Elementary** • 2250 N Clifton Ave
- **St James Lutheran** • 2101 N Fremont St
- **St Josephat** • 2245 N Southport Ave

Supermarkets

- **Dominick's** • 959 W Fullerton Ave
- **Save A Lot** • 1953 N Clybourn Ave
- **Trader Joe's** • 1840 N Clybourn Ave
- **Treasure Island** • 2121 N Clybourn Ave

N

A
B
C
1
2

WEST DEPAUL
WRIGHTWOOD NEIGHBORS
SHEFFIELD NEIGHBORS
RANCH TRIANGLE

Wrightwood Park
Trebes Park
DePaul University (Lincoln Park Campus)
Children's Memorial Hospital
Oz Park

Diversey
Fullerton
Armitage
Clybourn
North/Clybourn

43
28
30
22
PAGE 250

W George St
W Wolfram St
W Diversey Ave
W Diversey School Ct
W Schubert Ave
W Drummond Pl
W Wrightwood Ave
W Draper St
W Lill Ave
W Altgeld St
W Montana St
W Fullerton Pkwy
W Medill Ave
W Belden Ave
W Webster Ave
W Shakespeare Ave
W Dickens Ave
N Hobson Ave
W Mclean Ave
W Armitage Ave
W Homer St
W Cortland St
W Wisconsin St
W Bloomingdale Ave
W Willow St
W Wabansia Ave
W Concord Pl
W North Ave
W Pierce Ave
W Le Moyne St
W Weed St
W Wood St

N Paulina St
N Marshfield Ave
N Ashland Ave
N Bosworth Ave
N Greenview Ave
N Janssen Ave
N Lakewood Ave
N Wayne Ave
N Magnolia Ave
N Racine Ave
N Seminary Ave
N Kenmore Ave
N Lincoln Ave
N Sheffield Ave
N Wilton Ave
N Mildred Ave
N Dayton St
N Burling St
N Orchard St
N Halsted St
N Clybourn Ave
N Southport Ave
N Surrey Ct
N Clifton Ave
N Childrens Plz
N Pearl Ct
N Fremont St
N Edward Ct
N Wood St
N Dominick St
N Nursery St
N Mendell St
N Holly Ave
N Maud Ave
N Bissell St
N Poe St
N Elston Ave
N Hermitage Ave
N Marcey St
N Besly Ct
N Throop St
N Ada St
N Kingsbury St
N Burling Plz

2800N
2400N
2000N
1600N
1600W
1200W
800W

94
90
Dan Ryan Expy
North Branch Chicago River

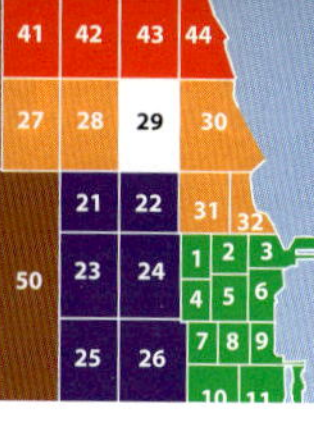

An afternoon is well spent swigging suds at one of the neighborhood's local taverns. Wrightwood Tap and Kincade's are our favorites. If you haven't had the fish 'n' chips at the Red Lion, you should—it's across from the Biograph Theater on Lincoln where notorious bank robber John Dillinger was gunned down by G-men. Be wary if your date wears red. Wine Discount Center on Elston is the ultimate bottle shop for wine enthusiasts.

Coffee

- **Bean Café (DePaul University)** • 2235 N Sheffield Ave
- **Einstein Bros Bagels** • 2212 N Clybourn Ave
- **Savor the Flavor** • 2545 N Sheffield Ave
- **Starbucks** • 1001 W Armitage Ave
- **Starbucks** • 1157 W Wrightwood Ave
- **Starbucks** • 2200 N Clybourn Ave
- **Starbucks** • 2454 N Ashland Ave
- **Starbucks** • 2475 N Lincoln Ave
- **Starbucks (Dominick's)** • 959 W Fullerton Ave

Copy Shops

- **Kinko's (24 hours)** • 2300 N Clybourn Ave
- **Sir Speedy (8 am-6 pm)** • 1711 N Clybourn Ave
- **The UPS Store (8:30 am-7 pm)** • 1341 W Fullerton Ave
- **The UPS Store (8:30 am-7 pm)** • 858 W Armitage Ave

Gyms

- **Bally Total Fitness** • 1455 W Webster Ave
- **Crunch Fitness** • 2727 N Lincoln Ave
- **Curves** • 1156 W Armitage Ave
- **Lakeshore Athletic Club** • 1320 W Fullerton Ave
- **Webster Fitness Club** • 957 W Webster Ave

Hardware Stores

- **Armitage Hardware & Building Supply** • 925 W Armitage Ave
- **Hollywood Industrial Supply** • 1524 W Fullerton Ave

Liquor Stores

- **J&R Liquor & Foods** • 2401 N Ashland Ave
- **Kegs to Go** • 2581 N Lincoln Ave
- **Sam's Wine and Liquor Warehouse** • 1720 N Marcey St
- **Wine Discount Center** • 1826 N Elston Ave

Movie Theaters

- **Facets Multimedia Theatre** • 1517 W Fullerton Ave
- **Loews** • 1471 W Webster Ave

Nightlife

- **Big House** • 2354 N Clybourn Ave
- **Charlie's Ale House** • 1224 W Webster Ave
- **Delilah's** • 2771 N Lincoln Ave
- **Gin Mill** • 2462 N Lincoln Ave
- **Green Dolphin Street** • 2200 N Ashland Ave
- **Hideout** • 1354 W Wabansia Ave
- **Hog Head McDunna's** • 1505 W Fullerton Ave
- **Irish Eyes** • 2519 N Lincoln Ave
- **Jack Sullivan's** • 2142 N Clybourn Ave
- **Kincade's** • 950 W Armitage Ave
- **Local Option** • 1102 W Webster Ave
- **Nic and Dino's Tripoli Tavern** • 1147 W Armitage Ave
- **The (Prop) House** • 1675 N Elston Ave
- **Red Lion Pub** • 2446 N Lincoln Ave
- **Webster Wine Bar** • 1480 Webster Ave
- **Wrightwood Tap** • 1059 W Wrightwood Ave
- **Zella** • 1983 N Clybourn Ave

Pet Shops

- **Barker & Meowsky** • 1003 W Armitage Ave
- **Galloping Gourmutts** • 2736 N Lincoln Ave
- **Petco** • 2000 N Clybourn Ave

Restaurants

- **Buffalo Wild Wings** • 2464 N Lincoln Ave
- **Charlie's Ale House** • 1224 W Webster Ave
- **Clarke's Pancake House & Restaurant** • 2441 N Lincoln Ave
- **Demon Dogs** • 944 W Fullerton Ave
- **Good Island Brewing Company** • 1800 N Clybourn Ave
- **Green Dolphin Street** • 2200 N Ashland Ave
- **John's Place** • 1200 W Webster Ave
- **Lindo Mexico** • 2642 N Lincoln Ave
- **Red Lion Pub** • 2446 N Lincoln Ave
- **Sai Café** • 2010 N Sheffield
- **Salt & Pepper Diner** • 2575 N Lincoln Ave
- **Shine & Morida** • 901 W Armitage Ave
- **Taco & Burrito House** • 1548 W Fullerton Ave
- **Tsuki** • 1441 W Fullerton Ave
- **Twisted Lizard** • 1964 N Sheffield Ave

Shopping

- **Active Endeavors** • 853 W Armitage Ave
- **Isabella Fine Lingerie** • 1127 W Webster Ave
- **Jayson Home & Garden** • 1885 N Clybourn Ave
- **Sam's Wine and Liquor Warehouse** • 1720 N Marcey St
- **SOULPassion** • 1745 N Clybourn Ave
- **Tabula Tua** • 1015 W Armitage Ave
- **Uncle Dan's** • 2440 N Lincoln Ave
- **Vosges Haut Chocolat** • 951 W Armitage Ave
- **Wine Discount Center** • 1826 1/2 N Elston Ave

Video Rental

- **Blockbuster Video** • 2037 N Clybourn Ave
- **Blockbuster Video** • 2400 N Sheffield Ave
- **Facets Multimedia** • 1517 W Fullerton Ave
- **Hollywood Video** • 1940 N Elston Ave

W Surf St
N Pine Grove Ave
N Commonwealth Ave
W Surf St
N Cambridge Ave
N Pine Grove Ave
N Sheridan Rd
N Burling St
N Orchard St
2800N
W Diversey Ave
W Diversey Dr
W Diversey Ave
44
N Mildred Ave
N Dayton St
W Schubert Ave
W Drummond Pl
N Lehmann Ct
N Hampden Ct
W Wrightwood Ave
W Schubert Ave
W Drummond Pl
Dewes Mansion
A
PARK WEST
W Wrightwood Ave
W Deming Pl
North Pond
N Cannon Dr
Lake Michigan
W Deming Pl
W Saint James Pl
W Roslyn Pl
N Burling St
N Orchard St
N Geneva Ter
W Arlington Pl
Theurer-Wrigley House
N Lakeview Ave
W Arlington Pl
Peggy Notebaert Nature Museum
2400N
N Cambridge Ave
W Fullerton Pkwy
W Fullerton Pky
Lincoln Park Boat Club
De Paul University (Lincoln Park Campus)
N Halsted St
Children's Memorial Hospital
W Kemper Pl
W Kemper Ave
N Commonwealth Ave
N Lincoln Park West
N Stockton Dr
Lincoln Park Conservatory
N Cannon Dr
PAGE 250
Kauffman Store and Flats
W Belden Ave
N Meyer Ave
29
N Pearl Ct
W Grant Pl
800W
400W
Lincoln Park
PAGE 210
B
N Edward Ct
W Webster Ave
N Dayton St
Oz Park
N Lincoln Ave
N Hudson Ave
Lake Shore Dr
W Dickens Ave
N Ridge Dr
N Fremont St
N Burling St
N Howe St
2000N
LINCOLN PARK
N Orleans St
Lincoln Park Cultural Center
Lincoln Park Zoo
W Armitage Ave
N Clark St
N Mohawk St
N Cleveland Ave
N Hudson Ave
W Ridge Dr
South Pond
N Ridge Dr
W Wisconsin St
Bauler Park
N Sedgwick St
N Orleans St
N Lincoln Park West
41
Old Town Triangle Historic District
Stockton Dr
W Menomonee St
N Crilly Ct
N Wells St
Lincoln Park
C
W Willow St
W Willow St
N Hudson Ave
N Fern Ct
N Orleans St
W Willow St
W Saint Paul Ave
N Vine St
N Larrabee St
W Eugenie St
N North Park Ave
N Crilly Ct
N Saint Michaels Ct
N Meyer Ct
W Concord Pl
W Concord Ln
31
32
W Concord Pl
1600N
W North Ave
North/Clybourn
W Lutz Pl
Sedgwick
W Weed St
W Weed St
N Burling St
N Frontier Ave
N Orleans St
N Wieland St
N La Salle St
W Germania Pl
N Dearborn Pkwy
N State St
N Astor St
N Fremont
W Blackhawk St
1
W Burton Pl
W Burton Pl
2
E Burton Pl

Essentials

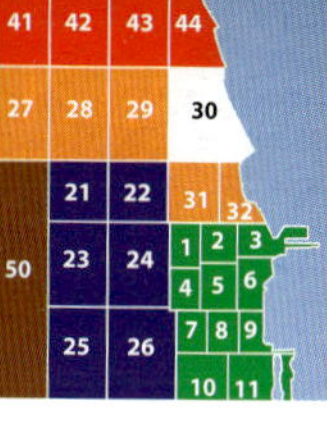

Lincoln Park is either heaven or hell, depending on your tolerance for yuppies, the fratboy mentalities of local students, and horrendous traffic congestion. On the upside, it IS awfully pretty and residents don't lack for upscale shopping and dinner options.

Banks

- **Bank of America** • 2401 N Clark St
- **Bank One** • 1700 N Wells St
- **Bank One** • 2501 N Clark St
- **Bank One** • 2603 N Halsted St
- **Bridgeview** • 1970 N Halsted St
- **Charter One** • 1640 N Wells St
- **Charter One (ATM)** • 2757 N Pine Grove Ave
- **Citibank** • 2001 N Halsted St
- **Citibank** • 2400 N Lincoln Ave
- **Citibank** • 2555 N Clark St
- **Citibank** • 2635 N Clark St
- **Corus** • 2401 N Halsted St
- **First American** • 356 W Armitage Ave
- **MidAmerica** • 2021 N Clark St
- **North Community** • 2000 N Halsted St
- **North Community** • 2201 N Halsted St
- **North Community** • 2335 N Clark St
- **North Community** • 2500 N Clark St
- **TCF (ATM)** • 1730 N Clark St
- **TCF (ATM)** • Osco, 2414 Lincoln Ave
- **Washington Mutual** • 2744 N Clark St

Gas Stations

- **BP** • 1647 N La Salle Dr
- **Shell** • 2600 N Halsted St

Hospitals

- **Children's Memorial** • 707 W Fullerton Ave
- **Lincoln Park** • 550 W Webster Ave

Landmarks

- **Dewes Mansion** • 503 N Wrightwood Ave
- **Kauffman Store and Flats** • 2312 N Lincoln Ave
- **Lincoln Park Boat Club** • N Cannon Dr & W Fullerton Pkwy
- **Lincoln Park Conservatory** • 2391 N Stockton Dr
- **Lincoln Park Cultural Center** • 2045 N Lincoln Park W
- **Lincoln Park Zoo** • N Cannon Dr, south of W Fullerton Pkwy
- **Peggy Notebaert Nature Museum** • 2430 N Cannon Dr
- **Theurer-Wrigley House** • 2466 N Lakeview Ave

Parking

Pharmacies

- **CVS Pharmacy** • 401 W Armitage Ave
- **Osco Drug** • 2414 N Lincoln Ave
- **Parkway Drugs** • 2346 N Clark St
- **Walgreens** • 2317 N Clark St

Pizza

- **Bacino's** • 2204 N Lincoln Ave
- **Bricks** • 1909 N Lincoln Ave
- **Café Luigi** • 2548 N Clark St
- **Chicago Red Eyes Hot Off the Grill** • 350 W Armitage Ave
- **Chicago's Pizza & Oven Grinder Co** • 2121 N Clark St
- **Domino's** • 2231 N Lincoln Ave
- **Edwardo's Natural Pizza** • 2622 N Halsted St
- **Gioio's Beef Stand Pizzeria** • 2572 N Clark St
- **Lincoln Park Pizza** • 2245 N Lincoln Ave
- **My Pie Pizzeria** • 2417 N Clark St
- **O' Fame** • 750 W Webster Ave
- **Pizza Capri** • 1733 N Halsted St
- **Ranalli's** • 1925 N Lincoln Ave

Post Offices

- 2643 N Clark St

Schools

- **Abraham Lincoln Elementary** • 615 W Kemper Pl
- **Francis W Parker High** • 330 W Webster Ave
- **La Salle Language Academy** • 1734 N Orleans St
- **Lincoln Park High** • 2001 N Orchard St
- **Louisa May Alcott Elementary** • 2625 N Orchard St
- **St Clement** • 2524 N Orchard St
- **Walter L Newberry Math & Science Academy** • 700 W Willow St

Supermarkets

- **Big Apple Finer Foods** • 2345 N Clark St
- **Lincoln Park Market** • 2500 N Clark St
- **Treasure Island** • 1639 N Wells St

Map 30 • Lincoln Park

N

W Surf St
W Diversey Ave
W Diversey Dr
W Schubert Ave
W Drummond Pl
W Wrightwood Ave
W Deming Pl
W Saint James Pl
W Roslyn Pl
W Arlington Pl
W Fullerton Pkwy
W Fullerton Pky
W Kemper Pl
W Kemper Ave
W Belden Ave
W Grant Pl
W Webster Ave
W Dickens Ave
W Armitage Ave
W Wisconsin St
W Menomonee St
W Willow St
W Saint Paul Ave
W Eugenie St
W Concord Pl
W Concord Ln
W North Ave
W Lutz Pl
W Weed St
W Blackhawk St
W Germania Pl
W Burton Pl
E Burton Pl
N Burling St
N Orchard St
N Cambridge Ave
N Pine Grove Ave
N Sheridan Rd
N Commonwealth Ave
N Mildred Ave
N Dayton St
N Hampden Ct
N Lehmann Ct
N Geneva Ter
N Lakeview Ave
N Cannon Dr
N Stockton Dr
N Lincoln Park West
N Meyer Ave
N Halsted St
N Pearl Ct
N Edward Ct
N Hudson Ave
N Lincoln Ave
N Fremont St
N Howe St
N Orleans St
N Clark St
N Ridge Dr
N Mohawk St
N Cleveland Ave
N Sedgwick St
N Crilly Ct
N Wells St
N Vine St
N Larrabee St
N Meyer Ct
N Saint Michaels Ct
N Fern Ct
N North Park Ave
N Frontier Ave
N Wieland St
N La Salle St
N Dearborn Pkwy
N State St
N Astor St
N Weed St
Lake Shore Dr
Stockton Dr
2800N
2400N
2000N
1600N
800W
400W
PARK WEST
LINCOLN PARK
De Paul University (Lincoln Park Campus)
Children's Memorial Hospital
North Pond
South Pond
Oz Park
Bauler Park
Old Town Triangle Historic District
Lincoln Park
Lake Michigan
North/Clybourn
Sedgwick
41
A
B
C
1
2

44
PAGE 250
29
PAGE 210
31
32

Sundries / Entertainment

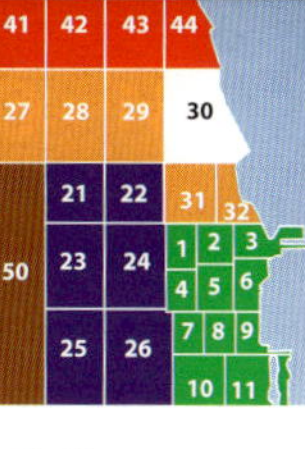

Lincoln Park provides great outdoor entertainment in this high-rent district. Lincoln Park Zoo is the nation's oldest free zoo. Recent habitat improvements make visits a little less gloomy. Neo plays retro grooves for black-clad clubbers stranded in the Eighties. Late-night punters sop it up with a side of abuse offered by the rude, raucous servers at the infamous Wiener's Circle. Those wanting to drop a mortgage payment on Chicago's most celebrated restaurant make reservations for Charlie Trotter's several months in advance.

Coffee

- **Box Car Café** • 723 W Wrightwood Ave
- **Caribou Coffee** • 2453 N Clark St
- **Einstein Bros Bagels** • 2530 N Clark St
- **Monterotondo** • 612 W Wrightwood Ave
- **Savories** • 1651 N Wells St
- **Screenz Digital Universe** • 2717 N Clark St
- **Siena Coffee** • 2308 N Clark St
- **Starbucks** • 2063 N Clark St
- **Starbucks** • 2200 N Halsted St
- **Starbucks** • 2275 N Lincoln Ave
- **Starbucks** • 2525 1/2 N Clark St
- **Starbucks** • 2529 N Clark St

Copy Shops

- **The UPS Store (8 am-7 pm)** • 2506 N Clark St
- **The UPS Store (9 am-6 pm)** • 2038 N Clark St

Farmer's Markets

- **Chicago's Green City Market** • 1750 N Clark St
- **Lincoln Park** • W Armitage Ave & N Orchard St
- **Lincoln Park Zoo** • 2001 N Stockton Dr

Gyms

- **Equinox** • 1750 N Clark St
- **Lincoln Park Fitness Center** • 444 W Fullerton Pkwy

Hardware Stores

- **Home Depot** • 2665 N Halsted St
- **Wahler Brothers True Value** • 2551 N Halsted St

Liquor Stores

- **Chalet Wine & Cheese Shop** • 2000 N Clark St
- **Country Fresh Finer Foods** • 2583 N Clark St
- **Dynamic Liquors** • 2132 N Halsted St
- **Field House** • 2455 N Clark St
- **Miska's Liquor** • 2353 N Clark St
- **Old Town Sundries Liquors** • 1820 N Clark St

Movie Theaters

- **Three Penny Cinema** • 2424 N Lincoln Ave

Nightlife

- **B.L.U.E.S.** • 2519 N Halsted St
- **Bacchus** • 2242 N Lincoln Ave
- **Bar Louie** • 1800 N Lincoln Ave
- **Blu** • 2247 N Lincoln Ave
- **Corner Pocket** • 2610 N Halsted St
- **Gamekeepers** • 345 W Armitage Ave
- **Glascott's** • 2158 N Halsted St
- **GoodBar** • 2512 N Halsted St
- **Griffin's Public House** • 2710 N Halsted St
- **Hidden Shamrock** • 2723 N Halsted St
- **Katacomb** • 1909 N Lincoln Ave
- **Kingston Mines** • 2548 N Halsted St
- **Lion Head Pub & The Apartment** • 2251 N Lincoln Ave
- **Neo** • 2350 N Clark St
- **Park West** • 322 W Armitage Ave
- **Sauce** • 1750 N Clark St
- **Second City** • 1616 N Wells St
- **Tequila Roadhouse** • 1653 N Wells St
- **Wise Fools Pub** • 2270 N Lincoln Ave

Restaurants

- **Aladdin Café** • 2269 N Lincoln Ave
- **Ambria** • 2300 N Lincoln Park W
- **Asiana** • 2546 N Clark St
- **Athenian Room** • 807 W Webster Ave
- **Boka** • 1729 N Halsted St
- **Café Ba-Ba-Reeba!** • 2024 N Halsted St
- **Café Bernard** • 2100 N Halsted St
- **Charlie Trotter's** • 816 W Armitage Ave
- **Dunlay's** • 2600 N Clark St
- **Emilio's Tapas** • 444 Fullerton Pkwy
- **Fattoush** • 2652 N Halsted St
- **Frances' Deli** • 2552 N Clark St
- **Geja's Café** • 340 W Armitage Ave
- **Itto Sushi** • 2616 N Halsted St
- **Karyn's** • 1901 N Halsted Ave
- **King Crab** • 1816 N Halsted St
- **Mon Ami Gabi** • 2300 N Lincoln Park W
- **My Pie Pizza** • 2417 N Clark St
- **Nookies** • 1746 N Wells St
- **Nookies, Too** • 2114 N Halsted St
- **North Pond** • 2610 N Cannon Dr
- **O' Fame** • 750 W Webster Ave
- **Original Pancake House** • 2020 N Lincoln Park W
- **PS Bangkok** • 2521 N Halsted St
- **Piattini** • 934 W Webster Ave
- **Ranalli's** • 1925 N Lincoln Ave
- **Ranalli's** • 2301 N Clark St
- **RJ Grunt's** • 2056 N Lincoln Park W
- **Robinson's No 1 Ribs** • 655 W Armitage Ave
- **Salvatore's Ristorante** • 525 W Arlington Pl
- **Sushi O Sushi** • 346 W Armitage Ave
- **Taco Burrito Palace #2** • 2441 N Halsted St
- **Tilli's** • 1952 N Halsted St
- **Twin Anchors** • 1655 N Sedgwick St
- **Via Emilia Ristorante** • 2119 N Clark St
- **Vinci** • 1732 N Halsted St
- **Wiener's Circle** • 2622 N Clark St

Shopping

- **Art & Science** • 1971 N Halsted St
- **Cynthia Rowley** • 808 W Armitage Ave
- **Ethan Allen** • 1700 N Halsted St
- **Gallery 1756** • 1756 N Sedgwick St
- **GNC** • 2740 N Clark St
- **Lori's Designer Shoes** • 824 W Armitage Ave
- **Sally Beauty Supply** • 2727 N Clark St
- **Triangle Gallery of Old Town** • 1763 N North Park Ave

Video Rental

- **Blockbuster Video** • 2200 N Clark St
- **Blockbuster Video** • 2577 N Clark St
- **Odd Obsession Movies** • 1659 N Halsted St
- **Tokyo Video of Chicago (Japanese)** • 2755 N Pine Grove Ave

N

Lincoln Park
PAGE 210
South Pond
OLD TOWN
CABRINI GREEN
NEAR NORTH
Stanton Schiller Park
Seward Park
Washington Square Park
Moody Bible Institute
Loyola Univ (Water Tower Ca
Chicago River
North/ Clybourn
Sedgwick
Chicago
Grand
Clar Divi
Connector
90
1
2
22
30
32
A
B
C
800W
200W
100W
1600N
1200N
800N

W Wisconsin St
W Menomonee St
W Willow St
W Saint Paul Ave
W Eugenie St
W Concord Pl
W Concord Ln
W North Ave
W Lutz Pl
W Germania Pl
W Weed St
W Blackhawk St
W Burton Pl
W Eastman St
W Schiller St
W Fair Pl
W Evergreen Ave
W Goethe St
W Sullivan St
W Scott St
W Division St
W Elm St
W Hill St
W Maple St
W Wendell St
W Hobbie St
W Oak St
W Walton St
W Delaware Pl
W Locust St
W Iowa St
W Chestnut St
W Pearson St
W Institute Pl
W Chicago Ave
W Superior St
W Huron St
W Ancona St
W Erie St
W Ontario St
W Ohio St
W Grand Ave
W Illinois St
W Bliss St
W Haines St
W Ogden Ave
E North Av
E Scot
E Su
E Ch

N Bissell St
N Dayton St
N Halsted St
N Burling St
N Vine St
N Mohawk St
N Cleveland Ave
N Hudson Ave
N Sedgwick St
N Orleans St
N Lincoln Park W
N Crilly Ct
N Fern Ct
N Meyer Ct
N Saint Michaels Ct
N Kingsbury St
N Fremont St
N Frontier Ave
N Ogden Ave
N Clybourn Ave
N Schick Pl
N North Park Ave
N Wieland St
N Sandburg Ter
N La Salle St
N Clark St
N Sutton Pl
N Dearborn Pkwy
N State Pkwy
N State St
N Astor St
N Orchard St
N Howe St
N Crosby St
N Larrabee St
N Cambridge Ave
N Felton Ct
N Franklin St
N Wells St
N Rush St
N Dearborn St
N Hooker St
N Hickory Ave
N North Branch St
N Sangamon St
N Lessing St
N Peoria St
N Carpenter St
N Morgan St
N Green St
N Union Ave
N Desplaines St
Stockton Dr

Essentials

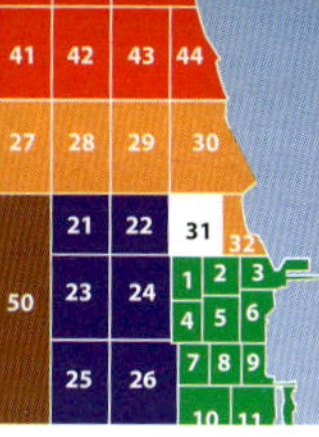

Close to all the action on Mag Mile and the lakefront, this area is packed with people, history, and significant architecture. Old Town Triangle District is on the National Registry of Historic Places. The neighborhood's sophisticated, artsy flair is showcased during the annual Old Town Art Fair (June). The well-heeled live along State Street near the park in exquisite single-family homes.

Banks

- **Bank of America** • 1590 N Clybourn Ave
- **Bank of America (ATM)** • 1608 N Wells St
- **Bank One** • 424 W Division St
- **Bank One (ATM)** • 1601 N Wells St
- **Fifth Third** • 837 W North Ave
- **LaSalle** • 1565 N Clybourn Ave
- **North Community** • 1561 N Wells St
- **Washington Mutual** • 1565 N La Salle Blvd
- **Washington Mutual** • 609 W North Ave

Car Rental

- **Enterprise** • 523 W North Ave • 312-482-8322

Car Washes

- **Gold Coast Car Wash** • 875 N Orleans St
- **We'll Clean** • 1520 N Halsted St

Gas Stations

- **Amoco** • 1560 N Halsted St
- **Mobil** • 1234 N Halsted Ave

Libraries

- **Near North Public Library** • 310 W Division St

Parking

Pharmacies

- **Dominick's** • 424 W Division St
- **Walgreens (24 hours)** • 1601 N Wells St

Pizza

- **Casa Del Pacci** • 349 W Oak St
- **Dominick's Finer Foods** • 424 W Division St
- **Domino's** • 143 W Division St
- **Father & Son Restaurant** • 645 W North Ave

Police

- **18th District (Near North)** • 1160 N Larrabee St

Schools

- **Catherine Cook Elementary** • 226 W Schiller St
- **Edward Jenner Academy of the Arts** • 1119 N Cleveland Ave
- **Franklin Fine Arts Center** • 225 W Evergreen Ave
- **Friedrick Von Schiller Middle** • 640 W Scott St
- **George Manierre Elementary** • 1420 N Hudson Ave
- **Immaculate Conception** • 1431 N North Park Ave
- **Moody Bible Institute** • 820 N La Salle Blvd
- **Richard E Byrd Elementary** • 363 W Hill St
- **Ruben Salazar Bilingual Education Center** • 160 W Wendell St
- **Sojourner Truth Elementary** • 1443 N Ogden Ave
- **Walter Payton Preparatory** • 1034 N Wells St

Supermarkets

- **Dominick's** • 424 W Division St

Map 31 • Old Town / Near North

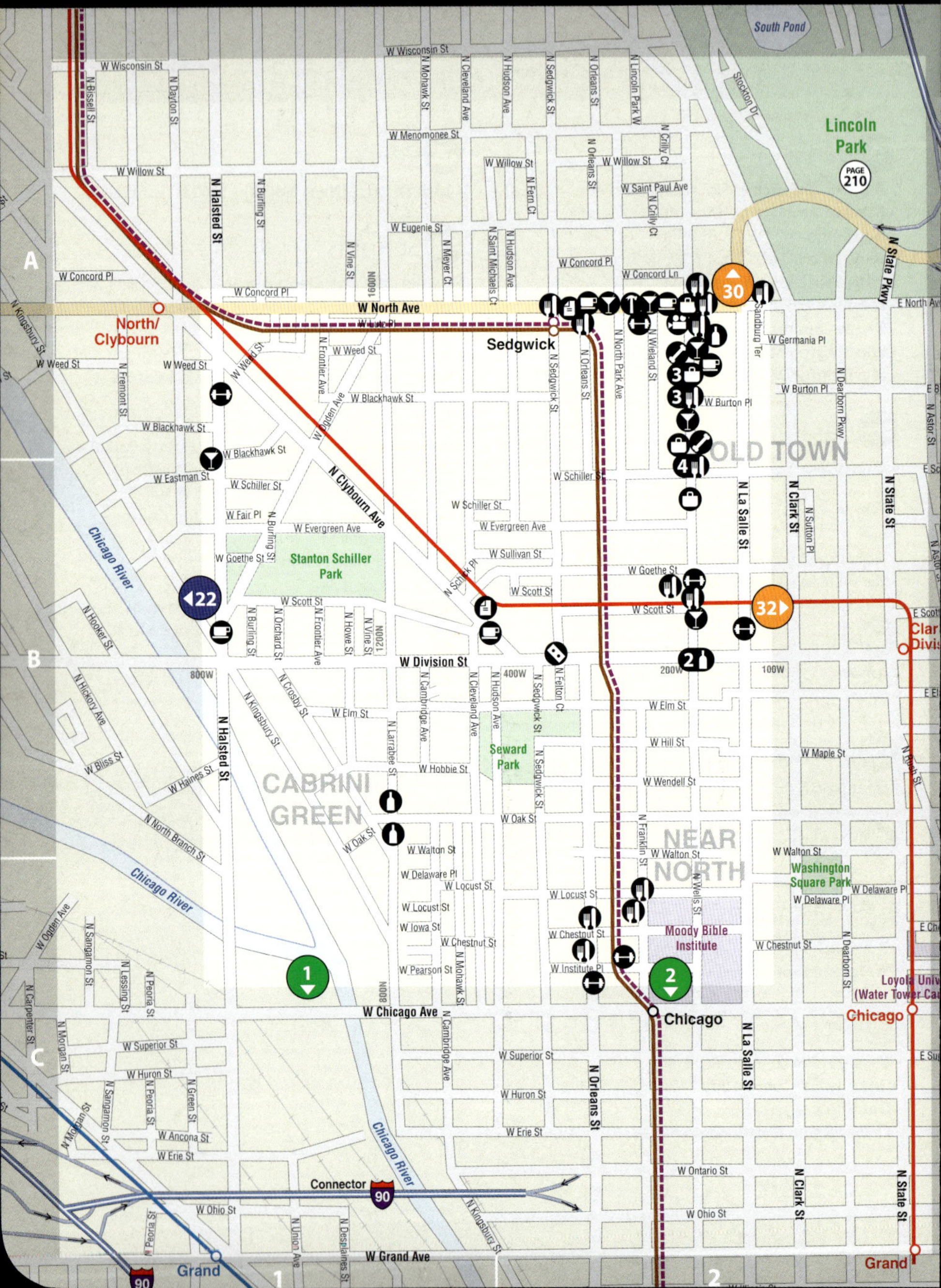

South Pond
Lincoln Park
PAGE 210
OLD TOWN
NEAR NORTH
CABRINI GREEN
Stanton Schiller Park
Seward Park
Washington Square Park
Moody Bible Institute
Loyola Univ (Water Tower Ca
Chicago River
North/ Clybourn
Sedgwick
Chicago
Chicago
Grand
Grand
Clar Divis
Connector
90
90
30
32
22
1
2
A
B
C
1
2
W Wisconsin St
W Menomonee St
W Willow St
W Saint Paul Ave
W Eugenie St
W Concord Pl
W Concord Ln
W North Ave
E North Av
W Weed St
W Blackhawk St
W Eastman St
W Schiller St
W Fair Pl
W Evergreen Ave
W Goethe St
W Sullivan St
W Scott St
E Scott
W Germania Pl
W Burton Pl
W Division St
W Elm St
W Hill St
W Maple St
W Wendell St
W Hobbie St
W Oak St
W Walton St
W Delaware Pl
W Locust St
W Iowa St
W Chestnut St
W Pearson St
W Institute Pl
W Chicago Ave
W Superior St
W Huron St
W Erie St
W Ontario St
W Ohio St
W Ancona St
W Grand Ave
W Bliss St
W Haines St
N Bissell St
N Dayton St
N Halsted St
N Burling St
N Vine St
N Meyer Ct
N Mohawk St
N Cleveland Ave
N Hudson Ave
N Sedgwick St
N Orleans St
N Lincoln Park W
N Crilly Ct
N Fern Ct
N Saint Michaels Ct
N Wieland St
N North Park Ave
N Sandburg Ter
N Dearborn Pkwy
N Astor St
N State Pkwy
Stockton Dr
N Kingsbury St
N Fremont St
N Frontier Ave
N Ogden Ave
N Clybourn Ave
N Schick Pl
N Orchard St
N Howe St
N La Salle St
N Clark St
N Sutton Pl
N State St
N Hooker St
N Hickory Ave
N Crosby St
N Larrabee St
N Cambridge Ave
N Felton Ct
N Franklin St
N Wells St
N Rush St
N Dearborn St
N North Branch St
N Sangamon St
N Lessing St
N Peoria St
N Carpenter St
N Morgan St
N Green St
N Union Ave
N Desplaines St
800W
400W
200W
100W
1600N
1200N
800N

Sundries / Entertainment

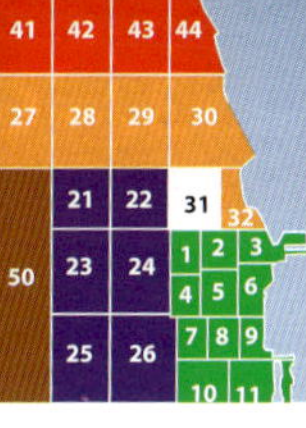

You could be laughing with a rising star at Second City, Chicago's famed improv club, where John Belushi, Bill Murray, Gilda Radner, Rick Moranis, and Mike Myers got their starts. When in town, Minnie Driver and Gary Sinise browse for books at Barbara's. Topo Gigio's grilled calamari is never rubbery, and for sushi as fresh as fish can be out of water, go to Kamehachi.

Coffee

- **Dunkin' Donuts** • 1234 N Halsted St
- **Dunkin' Donuts** • 333 W North Ave
- **Einstein Bros Bagels** • 1549 N Wells St
- **Starbucks** • 1229 N Clybourn Ave
- **Starbucks** • 210 W North Ave

Copy Shops

- **The UPS Store (8 am-7 pm)** • 333 W North Ave
- **The UPS Store (8:30 am-7 pm)** • 1235 N Clybourn Ave

Gyms

- **Crunch Fitness** • 820 N Orleans St
- **Curves** • 314 W Institute Pl
- **Fitplex** • 1235 N La Salle Dr
- **New City YMCA** • 1515 N Halsted St
- **A Women's Gym** • 1248 N Wells St
- **XSport Fitness** • 230 W North Ave

Hardware Stores

- **Tipre Hardware** • 229 W North Ave

Liquor Stores

- **Galleria Liquor** • 1559 N Wells St
- **Green Oak Food & Liquor** • 956 N Larrabee St
- **House of Glunz** • 1206 N Wells St
- **Old Town Liquors** • 1200 N Wells St
- **Ollie's Food** • 1012 N Larrabee St

Movie Theaters

- **Lowes Piper Alley Theater** • 1608 N Wells St

Nightlife

- **Burton Place** • 1447 N Wells St
- **Dragon Room** • 809 W Evergreen Ave
- **North Park Tap** • 313 W North Ave
- **Old Town Ale House** • 219 W North Ave
- **Spoon** • 1240 N Wells St
- **Weeds** • 1555 N Dayton St
- **Zanies Comedy Club** • 1548 N Wells St

Pet Shops

- **Collar & Leash** • 1435 N Wells St
- **Old Town Aquarium** • 1538 N Wells St

Restaurants

- **Bistrot Margot** • 1437 N Wells St
- **Chic Café** • 361 W Chestnut St
- **Cucina Bella Osteria & Wine Bar** • 1612 N Sedgwick St
- **Fireplace Inn** • 1448 N Wells St
- **Flat Top Grill** • 319 W North Ave
- **Fresh Choice** • 1534 N Wells St
- **Kamehachi** • 1400 N Wells St
- **Kiki's Bistro** • 900 N Franklin St
- **Las Pinatas** • 1552 N Wells St
- **Mitchell's** • 101 W North Ave
- **MK** • 868 N Franklin St
- **O'Brien's** • 1528 N Wells St
- **Old Jerusalem** • 1411 N Wells St
- **Pluton** • 873 N Orleans St
- **Salpicon** • 1252 N Wells St
- **Topo Gigio Ristorante** • 1516 N Wells St

Shopping

- **Crate & Barrel Outlet Store** • 1864 N Clybourn Ave
- **Etre** • 1361 N Wells St
- **Fleet Feet Sports** • 210 W North Ave
- **Fudge Pot** • 1532 N Wells St
- **Jumbalia** • 1427 N Wells St
- **Old Town Gardens** • 1555 N Wells St
- **The Spice House** • 1512 N Wells St
- **Village Cycle** • 1337 N Wells St

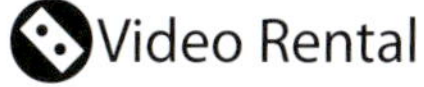

Video Rental

- **Blockbuster Video** • 400 W Division St

Map 32 • Gold Coast / Mag Mile

Lincoln Park
PAGE 210
Lake Michigan
GOLD COAST
Sedgwick
Clark/Division
Chicago
Grand
Water Tower and Park
Dr Scholl College of Podiatry
Moody Bible Institute
Loyola University (Water Tower Campus)
Seneca Park
Lake Shore Park
Milton Lee Olive Park
30
31
2
3
41
A
B
C
1
2

N Sedgwick St
N Orleans St
N Lincoln Park W
W Menomonee St
W Willow St
N Cleveland Ave
W Saint Paul Ave
W Eugenie St
N Cleveland Ave
N Wells St
W Concord Pl
W Concord Ln
1600N
Stockton Dr
W North Blvd
W Germania Pl
N Sandburg Ter
N Dearborn Pkwy
N State St
N Lake Shore Dr
N Orleans St
N North Park Ave
N Wieland St
W Burton Pl
E Burton Pl
N Astor St
N La Salle St
W Schiller St
E Schiller St
N Ritchie Ct
E Banks St
N Sutton Pl
W Evergreen Ave
N Astor St
N Stone St
W Goethe St
W Scott St
E Scott St
N Felton Ct
1200N
E Division St
E Elm St
W Elm St
E Cedar St
W Hill St
W Maple St
E Bellevue Pl
W Wendell St
N Lake Shore Dr
W Oak St
200W
100W
100E
W Walton St
E Walton St
W Delaware Pl
N Ernst Ct
N Huguelet Pl
N Dewitt Pl
W Locust St
W Delaware Pl
W Chestnut St
E Chestnut St
N Mies Van Der Rohe Way
W Institute Pl
800N
E Pearson St
N Tower Ct
W Chicago Ave
E Chicago Ave
W Superior St
E Superior St
N La Salle St
N Dearborn St
N Fairbanks Ct
W Huron St
E Huron St
N Orleans St
N Franklin St
N Wabash Ave
N Rush St
N Michigan Ave
N Mcclurg Ct
W Erie St
E Erie St
N Lake Shore Dr
W Ontario St
E Ontario St
600N
N Clark St
N State St
N Saint Clair St
W Ohio St
E Ohio St
N Mies Van Der Rohe Way
E Grand Ave
N Peshtigo Ct
W Illinois St
E Illinois St

Money, money, money equals location, location, location. The butter-yellow stone Water Tower, which survived the Great Chicago Fire of 1871, anchors the city's most expensive and exclusive place to live and play. You'll drop about $400 bucks for a bed at The Ritz, Park Hyatt, Peninsula, or Four Seasons. A high school education at the private, pricey Latin School of Chicago could buy a fleet of Mercedes.

Banks

- **Bank of America (ATM)** • 1167 N State St
- **Bank of America (ATM)** • 1201 N Dearborn St
- **Bank of America (ATM)** • 58 E Oak St
- **Bank One** • 1122 N Clark St
- **Bank One** • 875 N Michigan Ave
- **Bank One (ATM)** • 1200 N Clark St
- **Bank One (ATM)** • 1200 N Dearborn St
- **Charter One** • 1201 N Clark St
- **Citibank** • 68 E Oak St
- **Cosmopolitan Bank and Trust** • 801 N Clark St
- **Delaware Place** • 190 E Delaware Pl
- **Harris Trust & Savings** • 1000 N Lakeshore Dr
- **Harris Trust & Savings (ATM)** • 25 W Pearson St
- **LaSalle** • 940 N Michigan Ave
- **LaSalle (ATM)** • 1201 N State St
- **North Community** • 2 W Elm St
- **North Federal Savings** • 100 W North Ave
- **Northern Trust** • 120 E Oak St
- **Northern Trust (ATM)** • 120 E Oak St
- **Oak** • 1000 N Rush St
- **TCF** • Jewel, 1210 N Clark St
- **TCF (ATM)** • 1165 N Clark St
- **TCF (ATM)** • 1400 N Lakeshore Dr
- **TCF (ATM)** • 1525 N Clark St
- **Washington Mutual** • 1200 N State Pkwy

Car Rental

- **Enterprise** • 850 N State St • 312-951-6262
- **Hertz** • 1025 N Clark St • 312-951-2930

Gas Stations

- **Shell** • 130 W North Ave

Landmarks

- **Water Tower Place and Park** • 845 N Michigan Ave

Libraries

- **Newberry Library** • 60 W Walton St

Parking

Pharmacies

- **CVS Pharmacy (24 hours)** • 1201 N State Pkwy
- **Jewel** • 1210 N Clark St
- **Osco Drug** • 1165 N Clark St
- **Walgreens (24 hours)** • 1200 N Dearborn St

Pizza

- **California Pizza Kitchen** • 835 N Michigan Ave
- **Chi-Town Pizza** • 11 E Division St
- **Edwardo's Natural Pizza** • 1212 N Dearborn St
- **Gino's Pizzeria** • 930 N Rush St
- **Pizano's Pizza & Pasta** • 864 N State St

Schools

- **Archbishop Quigley Prep Seminary** • 103 E Chestnut St
- **Dr Scholl College of Podiatry** • 1001 N Dearborn St
- **Latin School of Chicago** • 59 W North Blvd
- **Loyola University (Downtown Campus)** • 820 N Michigan Ave
- **William B Ogden Elementary** • 24 W Walton St

Supermarkets

- **Jewel-Osco** • 1210 N Clark St
- **Potash Brothers** • 875 N State St
- **Treasure Island** • 75 W Elm St

Lincoln Park
PAGE 210
Lake Michigan
GOLD COAST
Sedgwick
Clark/Division
Chicago
Grand
Dr Scholl College of Podiatry
Moody Bible Institute
Loyola University (Water Tower Campus)
Seneca Park
Lake Shore Park
Milton Lee Olive Park
W North Blvd
N Lake Shore Dr
N State St
N La Salle St
N Clark St
N Michigan Ave
E Division St
W Chicago Ave
E Chicago Ave
W Ontario St
E Ontario St
W Ohio St
E Ohio St
N Orleans St
30
31
41
2
3

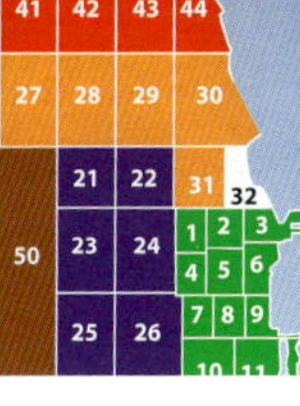

Shopping, shopping, shopping. Oak Street is Chicago's answer to Rodeo Drive—high-priced designer duds for the status-conscious. Bars surrounding the Rush and Division intersections draw tourists and frat boys with wet t-shirt contests and upside down margaritas. Le Passage is a one-stop dinner and nightclub destination for the thin and wan set.

Coffee

- **Coffee Expressions** • 100 W Oak St
- **Dunkin' Donuts** • 101 W Division St
- **Dunkin' Donuts** • 130 W North Ave
- **Einstein Bros Bagels** • 44 E Walton St
- **Starbucks** • 111 E Chestnut St
- **Starbucks** • 1538 N Clark St
- **Starbucks** • 39 W Division St
- **Starbucks** • 828 N State St
- **Starbucks** • 932 N Rush St
- **Wolf & Kettle** • 101 E Pearson St

Copy Shops

- **Kinko's (6 am-12 am)** • 1201 N Dearborn St
- **The UPS Store (8 am-7 pm)** • 47 W Division St

Farmer's Markets

- **Near North** • 15 W Division St

Gyms

- **Equinox** • 900 N Michigan Ave
- **Gold Coast Multiplex** • 1030 N Clark St

Hardware Stores

- **Gordon's Ace Hardware** • 24 W Maple St
- **Potash Bros Ace Hardware** • 110 W Germania Pl

Liquor Stores

- **Chalet Wine & Cheese Shop** • 40 E Delaware Pl
- **Potash Brothers Supermart** • 1525 N Clark St

Movie Theaters

- **Lowes Esquire** • 58 E Oak St
- **Village Theater** • 1548 N Clark St

Nightlife

- **Backroom** • 1007 N Rush St
- **Bar Chicago** • 9 W Division St
- **Butch McGuire's** • 20 W Division St
- **Cru Wine Bar** • 888 N Wabash Ave
- **Dublin's** • 1050 N State St
- **The Hunt Club** • 1100 N State St
- **Jilly's Retro Club** • 1007 N Rush St
- **Le Passage** • 937 N Rush St
- **Leg Room** • 7 W Division St
- **Mothers** • 26 W Division St
- **She-nanigans** • 16 W Division St
- **Signature Lounge** • 875 N Michigan Ave
- **Underground Wonder Bar** • 10 E Walton St
- **The Whisky** • 1015 N Rush St
- **Zebra Lounge** • 1220 N State St

Pet Shops

- **Paws-a-Tively** • 109 W North Ave

Restaurants

- **Ashkenaz** • 12 E Cedar St
- **Bistro 110** • 110 E Pearson St
- **Bistrot Zinc** • 1131 N State St
- **Café des Architectes** • 20 E Chestnut St
- **Café Spiaggia** • 980 N Michigan Ave
- **Cape Cod Room** • 140 E Walton St
- **Cheesecake Factory** • 875 N Michigan Ave
- **Cru Wine Bar & Café** • 888 N Wabash Ave
- **Dave & Buster's** • 1030 N Clark St
- **Foodlife** • 835 N Michigan Ave
- **Gibson's Steakhouse** • 1028 N Rush St
- **Hugo's Frog Bar** • 1024 N Rush St
- **Johnny Rockets** • 901 N Rush St
- **Le Colonial** • 937 N Rush St
- **McCormick & Schmick's** • 41 E Chestnut St
- **Mike Ditka's** • 100 E Chestnut St
- **Morton's of Chicago** • 1050 N State St
- **Original Pancake House** • 22 E Bellevue Pl
- **Pane Caldo** • 72 E Walton St
- **Pump Room** • Omni Ambassador East Hotel, 1301 N State Pkwy
- **Ra Sushi** • 1139 N State St
- **Ritz-Carlton Dining Room** • Ritz Carlton Hotel, 160 E Pearson St
- **Signature Room at the 95th** • 875 N Michigan Ave
- **Spiaggia** • 980 N Michigan Ave
- **Tavern on Rush** • 1031 N Rush St
- **Tempo** • 6 E Chestnut St
- **Tsunami** • 1160 N Dearborn St
- **Whiskey Bar and Grill** • 1015 N Rush St

Shopping

- **Anthropologie** • 1120 N State St
- **Barney's New York** • 25 E Oak St
- **BCBG** • 55 E Oak St
- **Bloomingdale's** • 900 N Michigan Ave
- **Bravco Beauty Center** • 43 E Oak St
- **Chanel at the Drake Hotel** • 935 N Michigan Ave
- **Elements** • 102 E Oak St
- **Europa Books** • 832 N State St
- **Fitigues Surplus** • 939 N Rush St
- **Frette** • 41 E Oak St
- **G'bani** • 949 N State St
- **Gucci** • 900 N Michigan Ave
- **H&M** • 840 N Michigan Ave
- **Hermes** • 110 E Oak St
- **Lord & Taylor** • 835 N Michigan Ave
- **MAC** • 40 E Oak St
- **Nicole Miller** • 63 E Oak St
- **Paul Stuart X/S** • 875 N Michigan Ave
- **Portico** • 48 E Walton St
- **Prada** • 30 E Oak St
- **Pratesi** • 67 E Oak St
- **Tod's** • 121 E Oak St
- **Ultimate Bride** • 106 E Oak St
- **Ultimo** • 114 E Oak St
- **Urban Outfitters** • 935 N Rush St
- **Water Tower** • 845 N Michigan Ave

Video Rental

- **Blockbuster Video** • 1201 N Clark St
- **Video Shmideo** • 907 N State St

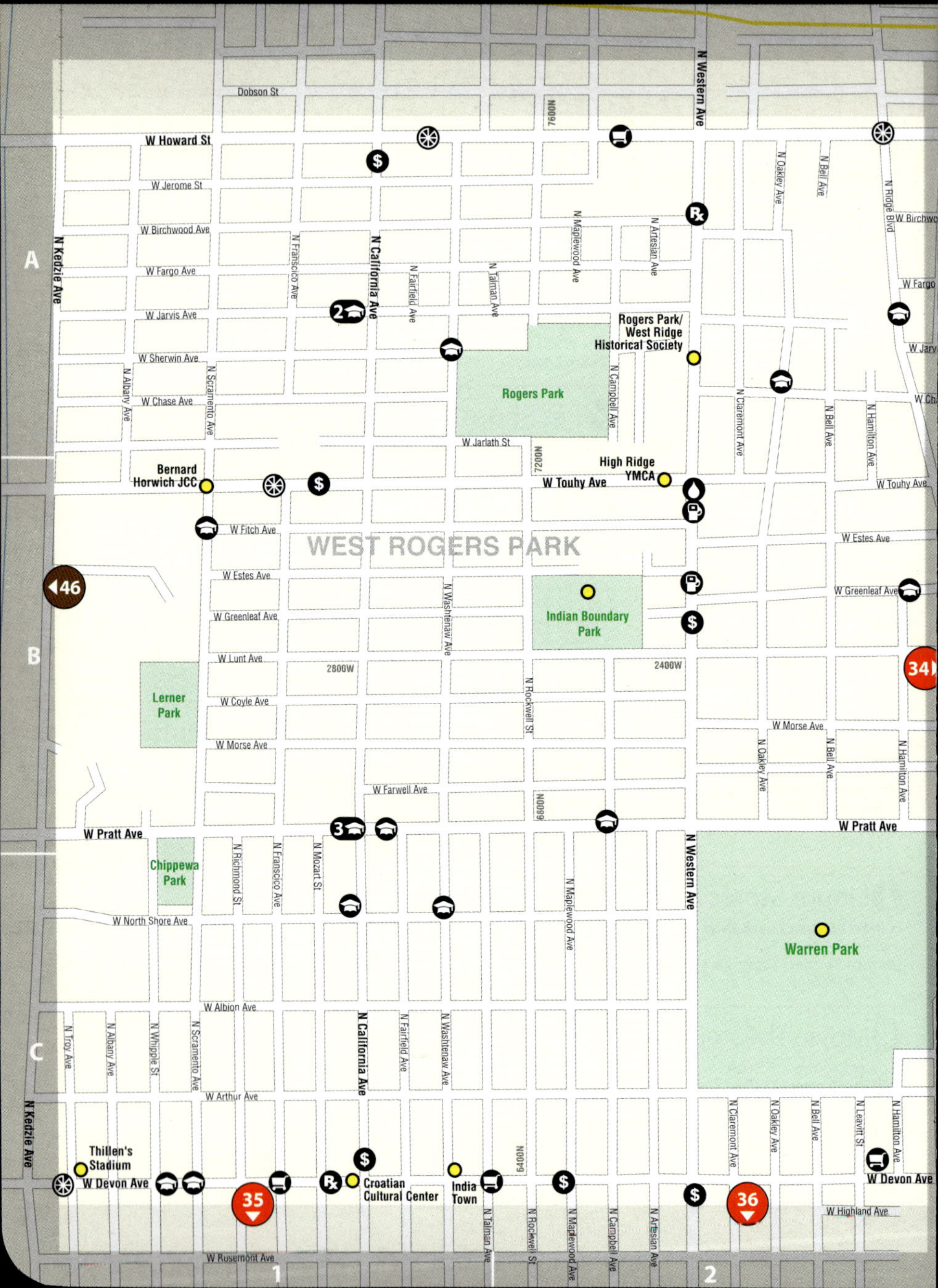

Map 33 • West Rogers Park

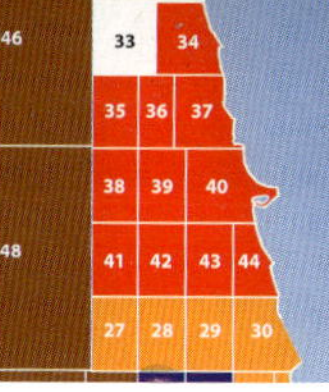

Turbans, tandoori chicken, fedoras, kosher pizza, saris, live chickens, and chop suey. Devon Avenue is a chaotic global marketplace where shopkeepers know how to make a buck in any language. Devon is a parking lot on weekends. Walking is the only way to negotiate this tempting and tasty international stretch. Side streets off Pratt and Touhy look like Skokie with modest single-family homes on compact lots lining the surprisingly bucolic streets.

Banks

- **Bank One** • 7015 N Western Ave
- **Citibank** • 2801 W Devon Ave
- **Devon** • 6445 N Western Ave
- **First Commercial** • 2201 W Howard St
- **Greater Chicago** • 7555 N California Ave
- **LaSalle** • 2545 W Devon Ave
- **LaSalle** • 2855 W Touhy Ave

Car Washes

- **Fast Carwash** • 7130 N Western Ave

Gas Stations

- **Clark Oil** • 7050 N Western Ave
- **Marathon** • 7130 N Western Ave

Landmarks

- **Bernard Horwich JCC** • 3003 W Touhy Ave
- **Croatian Cultural Center** • 2845 W Devon Ave
- **High Ridge YMCA** • 2430 W Touhy Ave
- **India Town** • W Devon Ave, near N Washtenaw Ave
- **Indian Boundary Park** • 2500 W Lunt Ave
- **Rogers Park/West Ridge Historical Society** • 7344 N Western Ave
- **Thillen's Stadium** • Devon Ave & Kedzie Ave
- **Warren Park** • 6601 N Western Ave

Libraries

- **Northtown Public Library** • 6435 N California Ave

Pharmacies

- **Osco Drug** • 2825 W Devon Ave
- **Walgreens** • 7510 N Western Ave

Pizza

- **Domino's** • 3144 W Devon Ave
- **Eastern Style Pizza** • 2911 W Touhy Ave
- **Gulliver's Pizzeria & Restaurant** • 2727 W Howard St
- **Pizza Hut** • 957 Howard St

Schools

- **ATT Ptach Special Education Program** • 2828 W Pratt Blvd
- **Bethesda Lutheran Elementary** • 6803 N Campbell Ave
- **Brisk Academy - Yeshivas Brisk** • 3000 W Devon Ave
- **Cheder Lubavitch Hebrew Boy's School** • 2809 W Jarvis Ave
- **Cheder Lubavitch Hebrew Girls' School** • 2809 W Jarvis Ave
- **Consolidated Hebrew High** • 2828 W Pratt Blvd
- **Daniel Boone Elementary** • 6710 N Washtenaw Ave
- **Decatur Classical** • 7030 N Sacramento Ave
- **George Armstrong Elementary** • 2110 W Greenleaf Ave
- **Hanna Sacks Girls' High** • 3021 W Devon Ave
- **Hebrew Academy of Chicago** • 2800 W North Shore Ave
- **Ida Crown Jewish Academy** • 2828 W Pratt Blvd
- **Rogers Elementary** • 7345 N Washtenaw Ave
- **St Margaret Mary Elementary** • 7318 N Oakley Ave
- **St Scholastica High** • 7416 N Ridge Blvd

Supermarkets

- **Jewel** • 2485 W Howard St
- **New York Kosher** • 2900 W Devon Ave
- **North Water Market** • 2626 W Devon Ave
- **Save A Lot** • 2151 W Devon Ave

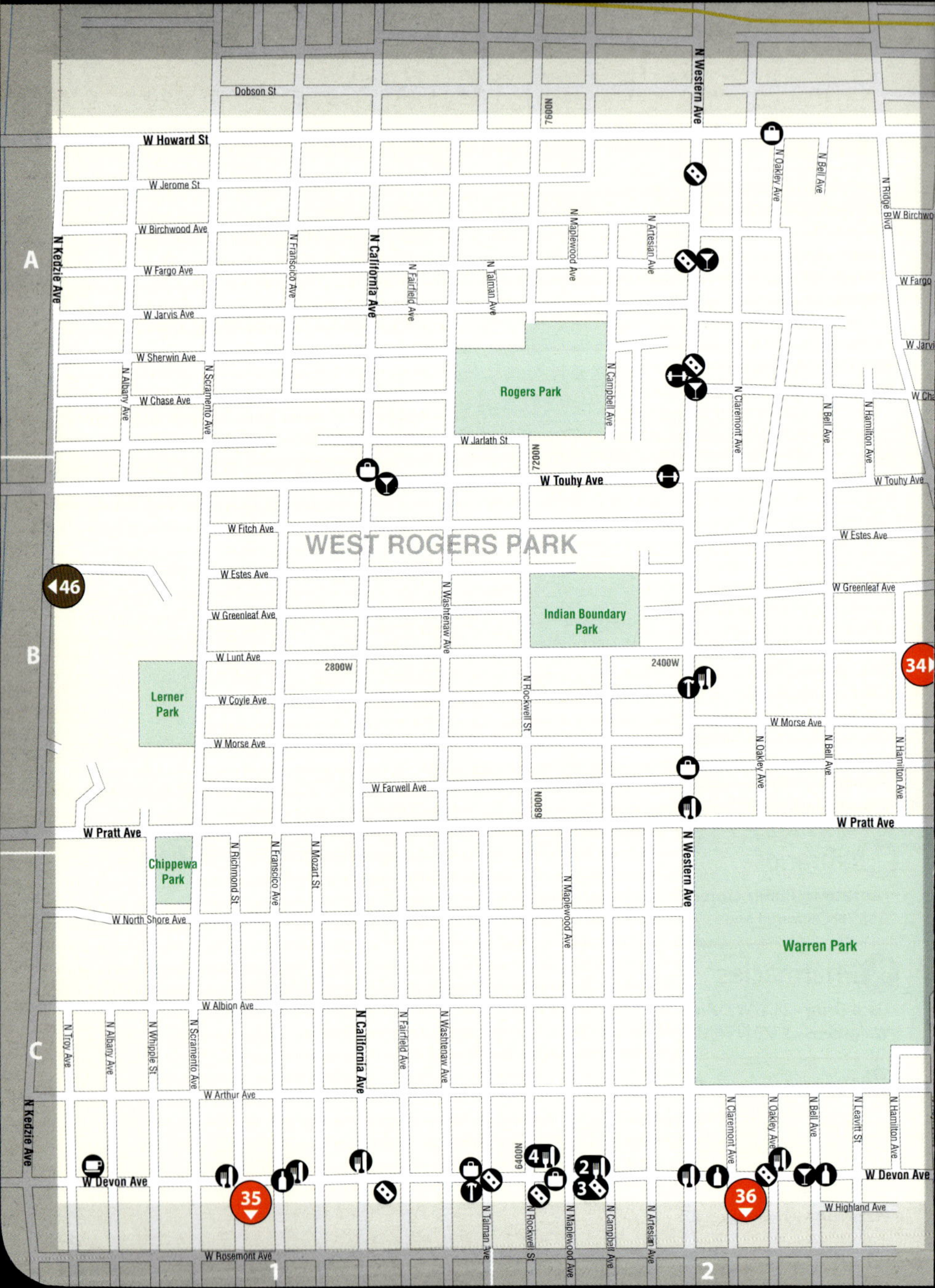

N
Dobson St
W Howard St
W Jerome St
W Birchwood Ave
W Fargo Ave
W Jarvis Ave
W Sherwin Ave
W Chase Ave
N Kedzie Ave
N Albany Ave
N Sacramento Ave
N Francisco Ave
N California Ave
N Fairfield Ave
N Talman Ave
N Maplewood Ave
N Artesian Ave
N Western Ave
N Oakley Ave
N Bell Ave
N Ridge Blvd
W Birchwo
W Fargo
W Jarvi
W Cha
7600N
Rogers Park
N Campbell Ave
N Claremont Ave
N Bell Ave
N Hamilton Ave
W Jarlath St
7200N
W Touhy Ave
W Touhy Ave
W Fitch Ave
WEST ROGERS PARK
W Estes Ave
W Estes Ave
46
W Greenleaf Ave
W Greenleaf Ave
N Washtenaw Ave
Indian Boundary Park
W Lunt Ave
2800W
2400W
34
Lerner Park
W Coyle Ave
N Rockwell St
W Morse Ave
W Morse Ave
N Oakley Ave
N Bell Ave
N Hamilton Ave
W Farwell Ave
6800N
W Pratt Ave
W Pratt Ave
Chippewa Park
N Richmond St
N Francisco Ave
N Mozart St
N Western Ave
N Maplewood Ave
W North Shore Ave
Warren Park
W Albion Ave
N Troy Ave
N Albany Ave
N Whipple St
N Sacramento Ave
N California Ave
N Fairfield Ave
N Washtenaw Ave
W Arthur Ave
N Claremont Ave
N Oakley Ave
N Bell Ave
N Leavitt St
N Hamilton Ave
N Kedzie Ave
6400N
4
2
3
W Devon Ave
W Devon Ave
35
36
W Highland Ave
N Talman Ave
N Rockwell St
N Maplewood Ave
N Campbell Ave
N Artesian Ave
W Rosemont Ave
A
B
C
1
2

Sundries / Entertainment

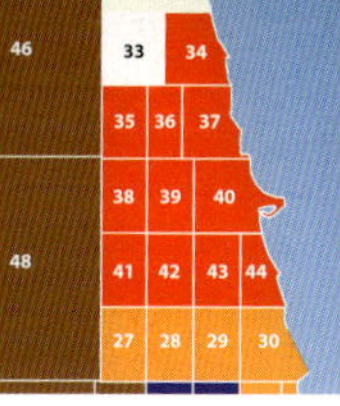

Just stand on a street corner and watch the world walk by. If you're feeling active, we recommend the batting cages at Indian Boundary Park. Warren Park's sledding hill makes for a great dog run. The fabrics at Taj Sari Palace on Devon are frameable art. See what's playing in India's theaters at Bombay Video. Inexpensive kebabs and tandoori are the fare of this 'hood.

Coffee

- **Dunkin' Donuts** • 3132 W Devon Ave

Gyms

- **Curves** • 7300 N Western Ave
- **High Ridge YMCA** • 2424 W Touhy Ave

Hardware Stores

- **Basco Plumbing & True Value** • 2650 W Devon Ave
- **Coast To Coast Store** • 6942 N Western Ave

Liquor Stores

- **Adelphi Liquors** • 2351 W Devon Ave
- **Beatrice Liquor** • 2901 W Devon Ave
- **M&Y Liquor & Grocery Store** • 2252 W Devon Ave

Nightlife

- **Cary's Lounge** • 2251 W Devon Ave
- **Mark II Chicago** • 7436 N Western Ave
- **McKellin's** • 2800 W Touhy Ave
- **Mullen's Sports Bar and Grill** • 7301 N Western Ave

Restaurants

- **Arya Bhavan** • 2508 W Devon Ave
- **Café Montenegro** • 6954 N Western Ave
- **Delhi Darbar Kabab House** • 6403 N California Ave
- **Desi Island** • 2401 W Devon Ave
- **Fluky's** • 6821 N Western Ave
- **Ghandi India Restaurant** • 2601 W Devon Ave
- **Good Morgan Kosher Fish Market** • 2948 W Devon Ave
- **Hashalom** • 2905 W Devon Ave
- **Hema's Kitchen** • 6406 N Oakley
- **Mysore Woodland's** • 2548 W Devon Ave
- **Tiffin** • 2536 W Devon Ave
- **Udupi Palace** • 2543 W Devon Ave
- **Viceroy of India** • 2520 W Devon Ave

Shopping

- **Cheesecakes by JR** • 2841 W Howard St
- **Chicago Harley Davidson** • 6868 N Western Ave
- **Dilshad** • 2645 W Devon Ave
- **Office Mart** • 2801 W Touhy Ave
- **Taj Sari Palace** • 2553 W Devon Ave

Video Rental

- **Atlantic Video Rentals (Indian)** • 2541 W Devon Ave
- **Blockbuster Video** • 7300 N Western Ave
- **Blockbuster Video** • 7574 N Western Ave
- **Bombay Video (Indian)** • 2634 W Devon Ave
- **Elita Video (Russian)** • 2753 W Devon Ave
- **New Devon Video** • 2304 W Devon Ave
- **New Jhankar Video (Indian)** • 2521 W Devon Ave
- **Super Star Video (Indian)** • 2538 W Devon Ave
- **Video Vision** • 2524 W Devon Ave
- **Western Video** • 7439 N Western Ave

Map 34 • East Rogers Park

Essentials

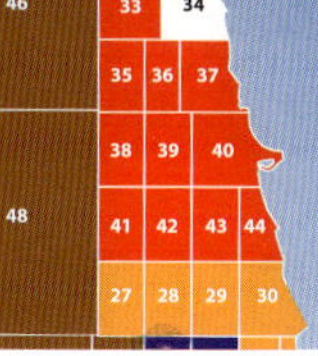

Students, seniors, liberals, and everyday urbanites mix in East Rogers Park. Loyola University anchors the southeast corner of the neighborhood. Renovated three-flats flank the tree-lined streets west of campus. A wall of ugly high-rises line the lake. Sheridan Road traffic heading into suburban Evanston is hellish during rush hours and on weekends.

Banks

- **Bank One** • 1763 W Howard St
- **Bank One** • 6623 N Damen Ave
- **Charter One (ATM)** • 6801 N Sheridan Rd
- **First Commercial** • 6930 N Clark St
- **First Commercial** • 6945 N Clark St
- **Harris Trust & Savings** • 6538 N Sheridan Rd
- **Harris Trust & Savings (ATM)** • Loyola University, 6633 N Winthrop Ave
- **LaSalle** • 7516 N Clark St
- **MB Financial** • 6443 N Sheridan Rd
- **Washington Mutual** • 1425 W Morse Ave

Car Washes

- **Roger's Park Hand Car Wash** • 6828 N Clark St

Gas Stations

- **BP** • 1841 W Devon Ave
- **Citgo** • 1500 W Devon Ave
- **Citgo** • 7138 N Sheridan Rd
- **Marathon** • 7550 N Sheridan Rd
- **Mobil** • 7201 N Clark St
- **Shell** • 6346 N Clark St
- **Shell** • 6401 N Ridge Blvd

Landmarks

- **Angel Guardian Croatian Catholic Church** • 6346 N Ridge Ave
- **Robert A Black Golf Course** • 2045 W Pratt Blvd

Libraries

- **Rogers Park Public Library** • 6907 N Clark St

Pizza

- **Carmen's of Loyola Pizzeria** • 6568 N Sheridan Rd
- **Giordano's** • 6836 N Sheridan Rd
- **Hamilton's Pizza & Pub** • 6341 N Broadway St
- **Leona's** • 6935 N Sheridan Rd
- **Riccardo's Pizza** • 6349 N Clark St
- **Vince's Pizzeria** • 1527 W Devon Ave

Police

- **24th District (Rogers Park)** • 6464 N Clark St

Post Offices

- 1723 W Devon Ave
- 7056 N Clark St
- 7617 N Paulina St

Schools

- **Chicago Math & Science Academy** • 1709 W Lunt Ave
- **Chicago Waldorf** • 1300 W Loyola Ave
- **Eugene Field Elementary** • 7019 N Ashland Blvd
- **Jordan Elementary** • 7414 N Wolcott Ave
- **Joyce Kilmer Elementary** • 6700 N Greenview Ave
- **Loyola University of Chicago** • 6525 N Sheridan Rd
- **New Field Primary** • 1707 W Morse Ave
- **North Shore Elementary** • 1217 W Chase Ave
- **Pactt Learning Center** • 7101 N Greenview Ave
- **Roger C Sullivan High** • 6631 N Bosworth Ave

Supermarkets

- **Dominick's** • 1763 W Howard St (in mall near Howard Red Line Stop)
- **Dominick's** • 6623 N Damen Ave
- **New Leaf Natural Grocery** • 1261 W Loyola Ave
- **Rogers Park Fruit Market** • 7401 N Clark St

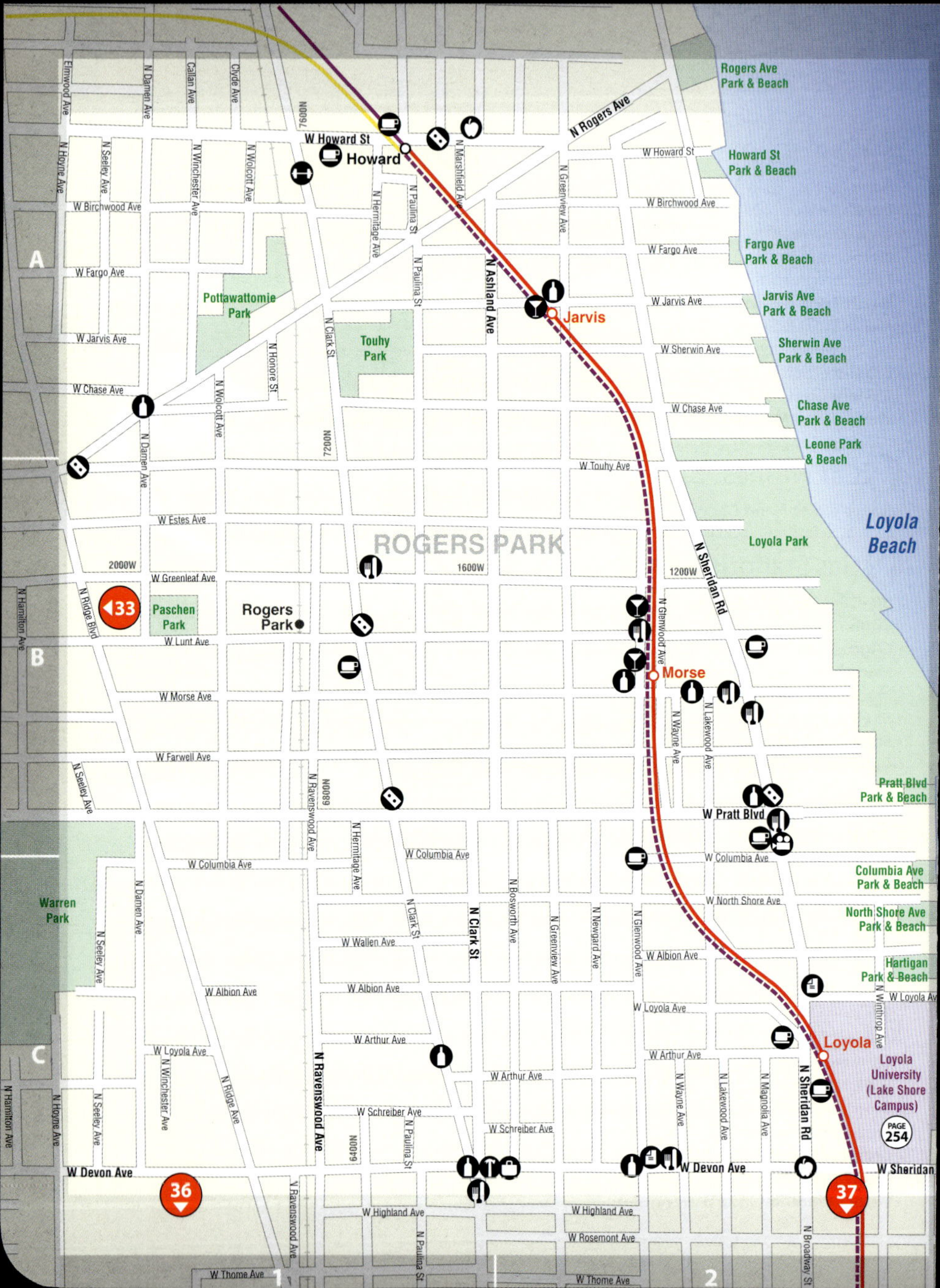

Rogers Ave Park & Beach
Howard St Park & Beach
Fargo Ave Park & Beach
Jarvis Ave Park & Beach
Sherwin Ave Park & Beach
Chase Ave Park & Beach
Leone Park & Beach
Loyola Beach
Loyola Park
Pratt Blvd Park & Beach
Columbia Ave Park & Beach
North Shore Ave Park & Beach
Hartigan Park & Beach
Loyola University (Lake Shore Campus)
PAGE 254
Howard
Jarvis
Morse
Loyola
ROGERS PARK
Rogers Park
Pottawattomie Park
Touhy Park
Paschen Park
Warren Park
W Howard St
N Rogers Ave
W Birchwood Ave
W Fargo Ave
W Jarvis Ave
W Sherwin Ave
W Chase Ave
W Touhy Ave
W Estes Ave
W Greenleaf Ave
W Lunt Ave
W Morse Ave
W Farwell Ave
W Pratt Blvd
W Columbia Ave
W North Shore Ave
W Wallen Ave
W Albion Ave
W Loyola Ave
W Arthur Ave
W Schreiber Ave
W Devon Ave
W Sheridan
W Highland Ave
W Rosemont Ave
W Thorne Ave
Elmwood Ave
N Damen Ave
Callan Ave
Clyde Ave
N Hoyne Ave
N Seeley Ave
N Winchester Ave
N Wolcott Ave
N Hermitage Ave
N Paulina St
N Marshfield Ave
N Ashland Ave
N Greenview Ave
N Honore St
N Clark St
N Ridge Blvd
N Hamilton Ave
N Ravenswood Ave
N Bosworth Ave
N Newgard Ave
N Glenwood Ave
N Wayne Ave
N Lakewood Ave
N Magnolia Ave
N Sheridan Rd
N Winthrop Ave
N Broadway St
2000W
1600W
1200W
7600N
7200N
6800N
6400N
A
B
C
1
2
33
36
37

Sundries / Entertainment

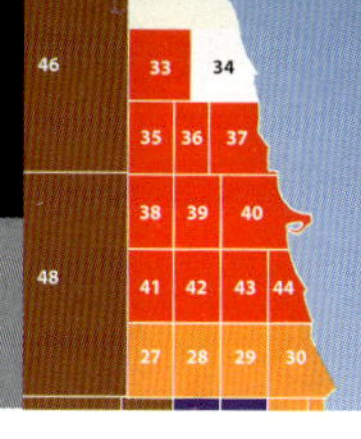

Locals adore the Korean couple who run Hahn liquors. Loyola students chill in the many crunchy neighborhood coffeehouses, and speaking of crunchy, the Heartland Café, serving up organic grub and live folk music, is the favored spot for the tie-dye set. Gay neighborhood bar Charmers dates back to 1929—its Art Nouveau décor is wonderfully intact.

Coffee

- **Dunkin' Donuts** • 1200 W Loyola Ave
- **Dunkin' Donuts** • 1763 W Howard St
- **Dunkin' Donuts** • 6970 N Clark St
- **Ennui** • 6981 N Sheridan Rd
- **Kaffeccino** • 6441 N Sheridan Rd
- **Starbuck's** • 6738 N Sheridan Rd
- **Starbucks (Dominick's)** • 1763 W Howard St

Copy Shops

- **Asos Copies & More (9 am-7 pm)** • 6604 N Sheridan Rd
- **The UPS Store (9 am-7 pm)** • 1400 W Devon Ave

Farmer's Markets

- **Loyola/Rogers Park** • W Devon Ave & N Broadway Ave
- **Rogers Park** • W Howard St & N Marshfield Ave

Gyms

- **Bally Total Fitness** • 7529 N Clark St

Hardware Stores

- **Clark-Devon Hardware** • 6401 N Clark St

Liquor Stores

- **Dino's Liquors** • 6400 N Clark St
- **Hahn Liquors** • 1410 W Devon Ave
- **Isam's Food & Liquor** • 6816 N Sheridan Rd
- **Jarvis Liquors** • 1508 W Jarvis Ave
- **Lian's Liquor & Grocery** • 6507 N Clark St
- **Morse Liquors** • 1400 W Morse Ave
- **Soo Liquors** • 1420 W Morse Ave
- **Summit Grocery** • 7300 N Rogers Ave

Movie Theaters

- **Village North Theaters** • 6746 N Sheridan Rd

Nightlife

- **Charmers** • 1502 W Jarvis Ave
- **Heartland Café** • 7000 N Glenwood Ave
- **No Exit** • 6970 N Glenwood Ave

Restaurants

- **Deluxe Diner** • 6349 N Clark St
- **El Famous Burrito** • 7047 N Clark St
- **Ennui Café** • 6981 N Sheridan Rd
- **Heartland Café** • 7000 N Glenwood Ave
- **Morseland** • 1218 W Morse Ave
- **Panini Panini** • 6764 N Sheridan Rd
- **Speakeasy Supperclub** • 1401 W Devon Ave

Shopping

- **Mar-Jen Discount Furniture** • 1536 W Devon Ave

Video Rental

- **Blockbuster Video** • 7007 N Clark St
- **Hollywood Video** • 1751 W Howard St
- **Pratt Video** • 6810 N Sheridan Rd
- **Syed Video** • 6808 N Clark St

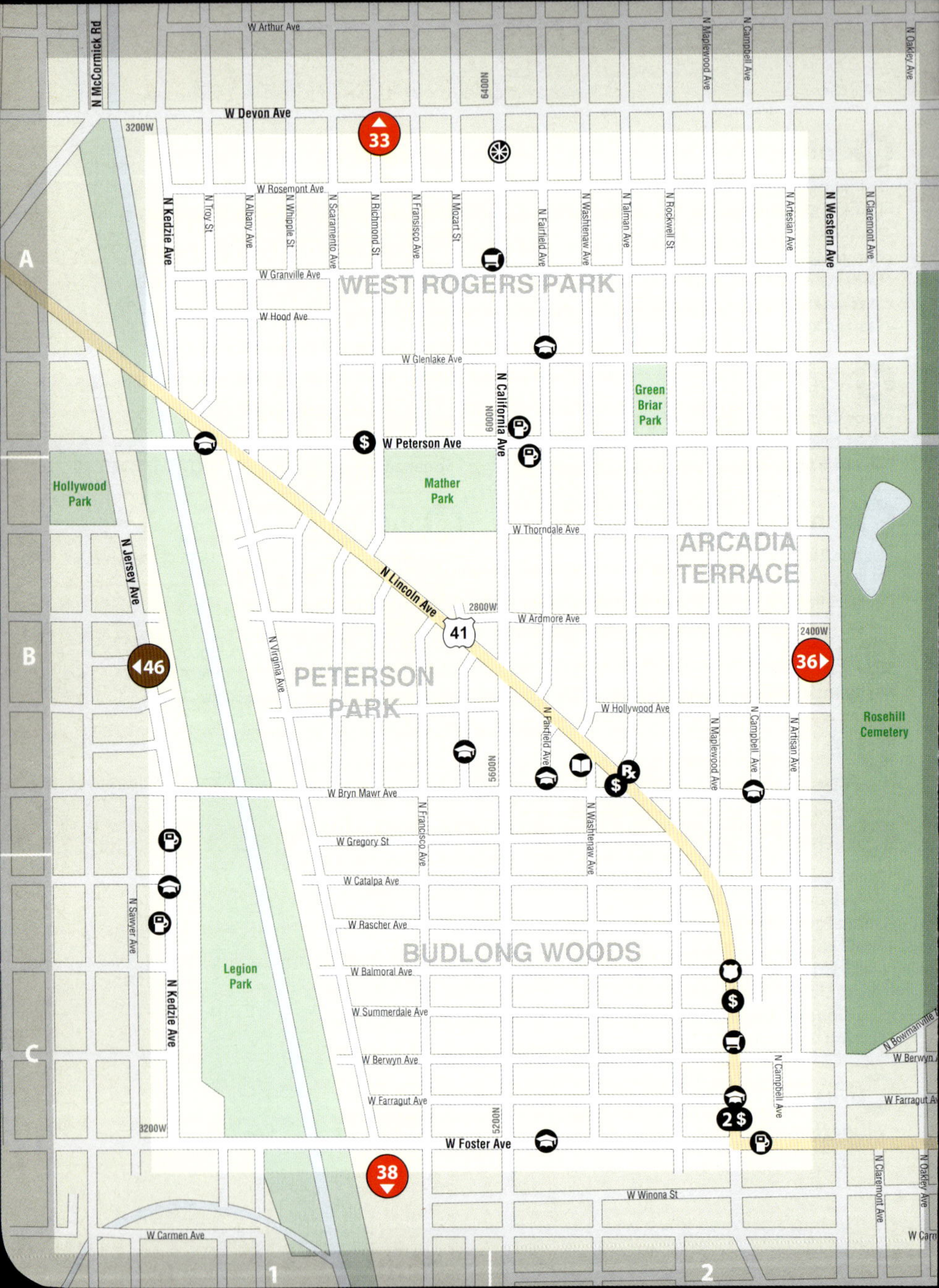

N

W Arthur Ave
N McCormick Rd
6400N
N Maplewood Ave
N Campbell Ave
N Oakley Ave
W Devon Ave
3200W
33
W Rosemont Ave
N Kedzie Ave
N Troy St
N Albany Ave
N Whipple St
N Sacramento Ave
N Richmond St
N Fransisco Ave
N Mozart St
N Fairfield Ave
N Washtenaw Ave
N Talman Ave
N Rockwell St
N Artesian Ave
N Western Ave
N Claremont Ave
A
W Granville Ave
WEST ROGERS PARK
W Hood Ave
W Glenlake Ave
N California Ave
6000N
Green Briar Park
W Peterson Ave
Hollywood Park
Mather Park
W Thorndale Ave
ARCADIA TERRACE
N Jersey Ave
N Lincoln Ave
2800W
41
W Ardmore Ave
2400W
B
46
36
N Virginia Ave
PETERSON PARK
W Hollywood Ave
N Fairfield Ave
N Maplewood Ave
N Campbell Ave
N Artisan Ave
Rosehill Cemetery
5600N
W Bryn Mawr Ave
N Francisco Ave
N Washtenaw Ave
W Gregory St
W Catalpa Ave
N Sawyer Ave
W Rascher Ave
BUDLONG WOODS
Legion Park
W Balmoral Ave
N Kedzie Ave
W Summerdale Ave
C
W Berwyn Ave
N Bowmanville
W Berwyn
N Campbell Ave
W Farragut Ave
W Farragut
3200W
5200N
2
W Foster Ave
38
N Claremont Ave
N Oakley Ave
W Winona St
W Carmen Ave
W Carm

1
2

Near, Middle, and Far East meet in Arcadia Terrace and Peterson Park.

Banks

- **Bank One** • 5224 N Lincoln Ave
- **Bank One (ATM)** • 5627 N Lincoln Ave
- **Charter One (ATM)** • 5233 N Lincoln Ave
- **First Commercial** • 2935 W Peterson Ave
- **Washington Mutual** • 5341 N Lincoln Ave

Gas Stations

- **BP** • 2751 W Peterson Ave
- **Citgo** • 2464 W Foster Ave
- **Citgo** • 5447 N Kedzie Ave
- **Citgo** • 5547 N Kedzie Ave
- **Mobil** • 2758 W Peterson Ave

Libraries

- **Budlong Woods Public Library** • 5630 N Lincoln Ave

Pharmacies

- **Walgreens** • 5627 N Lincoln Ave

Pizza

- **Tel Aviv Kosher Pizza** • 6349 N California Ave

Police

- **20th District (Foster)** • 5400 N Lincoln Ave

Schools

- **Budlong Elementary** • 2701 W Foster Ave
- **DeWitt Clinton Elementary** • 6110 N Fairfield Ave
- **Joan Dachs Bais Yaakov Elementary** • 3200 W Peterson Ave
- **Lyman A Budlong Elementary** • 2701 W Foster Ave
- **Minnie Mars Jamieson Elementary** • 5650 N Mozart St
- **NAES College** • 2838 W Paterson Ave
- **Northside College Preparatory** • 5501 N Kedzie Ave
- **St Hilary Elementary** • 5614 N Fairfield Ave
- **St Philip Lutheran** • 2500 W Bryn Mawr Ave
- **Telshe Yeshiva Chicago** • 3535 W Foster Ave

Supermarkets

- **Aldi** • 6220 N California Ave
- **Dominick's** • 5233 N Lincoln Ave

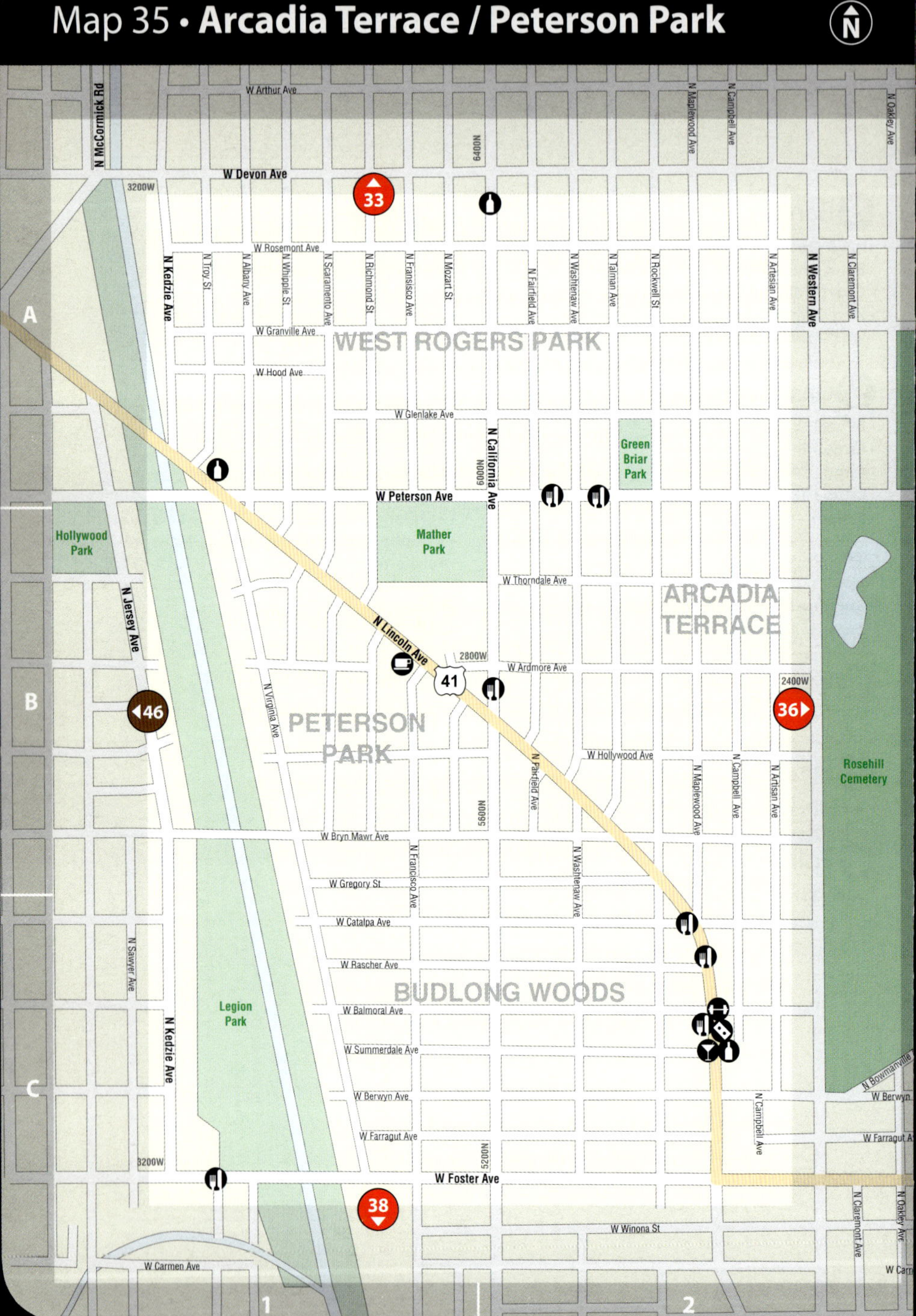
N
W Arthur Ave
N McCormick Rd
6400N
N Maplewood Ave
N Campbell Ave
N Oakley Ave
W Devon Ave
3200W
33
W Rosemont Ave
N Kedzie Ave
N Troy St
N Albany Ave
N Whipple St
N Sacramento Ave
N Richmond St
N Fransisco Ave
N Mozart St
N Fairfield Ave
N Washtenaw Ave
N Talman Ave
N Rockwell St
N Artesian Ave
N Western Ave
N Claremont Ave
A
W Granville Ave
WEST ROGERS PARK
W Hood Ave
W Glenlake Ave
N California Ave
Green Briar Park
6000N
W Peterson Ave
Hollywood Park
Mather Park
W Thorndale Ave
ARCADIA TERRACE
N Jersey Ave
N Lincoln Ave
2800W
W Ardmore Ave
41
2400W
B
46
36
N Virginia Ave
PETERSON PARK
W Hollywood Ave
N Fairfield Ave
N Maplewood Ave
N Campbell Ave
N Artisan Ave
Rosehill Cemetery
5600N
W Bryn Mawr Ave
W Gregory St
N Francisco Ave
N Washtenaw Ave
W Catalpa Ave
W Rascher Ave
N Sawyer Ave
BUDLONG WOODS
W Balmoral Ave
Legion Park
N Kedzie Ave
W Summerdale Ave
C
N Bowmanville
W Berwyn Ave
W Berwyn
N Campbell Ave
W Farragut Ave
W Farragut A
3200W
5200N
W Foster Ave
38
N Claremont Ave
N Oakley Ave
W Winona St
W Carmen Ave
W Carm
1
2

Those in the market for wheels cruise Western Avenue's car dealerships. Fondue Stube is an unsung gem—gooey pots of melted cheese and chocolate for a fraction of the price of Lincoln Park's Gejas.

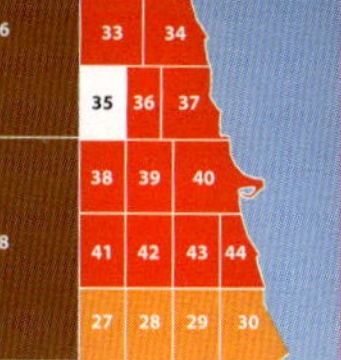

Coffee

- **Internet Café Chicago** • 5809 N Lincoln Ave

Gyms

- **Curves** • 5360 N Lincoln Ave

Liquor Stores

- **Buy Low Liquors** • 6015 N Lincoln Ave
- **Eden Liquor Store & Foods** • 5359 N Lincoln Ave
- **K&B Food & Liquor** • 6343 N California Ave

Nightlife

- **Hidden Cove** • 5338 N Lincoln Ave

Restaurants

- **Aztecas Mexican Taqueria** • 5421 N Lincoln Ave
- **Charcoal Delights** • 3139 W Foster Ave
- **Fondue Stube** • 2717 W Peterson Ave
- **Garden Buffet** • 5347 N Lincoln Ave
- **Katsu** • 2651 W Peterson Ave
- **Pueblito Viejo** • 5429 N Lincoln Ave
- **Woo Chon** • 5744 N California Ave

Video Rental

- **New York Video** • 5340 N Lincoln Ave

Map 36 • Bryn Mawr
N
W Arthur Ave
W Loyola Ave
N Clark St
N Winchester Ave
N Ridge Ave
W Arthur Ave
W Schreiber Ave
N Paulina St
W Schreiber
N Rockwell St
N Maplewood Ave
N Campbell Ave
N Oakley Ave
N Bell Ave
N Leavitt St
N Hamilton Ave
N Hoyne Ave
N Seeley Ave
6400N
W Devon Ave
33
34
W Highland Ave
W Rosemont Ave
WEST
ROGERS
PARK
W Thorne Ave
Emerson
Park
W Thome Ave
W Highland
N Paulina St
W Thorne
A
N Western Ave
N Ashland Ave
W Granville Ave
N Artesian Ave
N Claremont Ave
N Hamilton Ave
N Seeley Ave
N Damen Ave
W Hood Ave
N Winchester Ave
N Wolcott Ave
N Ravenswood Ave
N Hermitage Ave
W Glenlake Ave
W Glenlake Ave
Green
Briar
Park
W Norwood St
6000N
2400W
2000W
14
W Peterson Ave
W Peterson
Ridge Ave
35
N Ravenswood Ave
N Hermitage Ave
N Paulina St
W Thorndale Ave
W Thorndale Ave
37
W Ardmore Ave
B
W Ardmore Ave
N Clark St
W Rosehill Dr
1600W
Rosehill
Cemetery
W Edgewater Ave
5600N
W Hollywood Ave
W Hollywood Ave
W Olive Ave
W Bryn Mawr Ave
W Bryn Mawr Ave
N Paulina St
W Gregory St
Lincoln Ave
N Damen Ave
W Catalpa Ave
N Campbell Ave
W Rascher Ave
W Rascher Ave
N Bowmanville Ave
N Hoyne Ave
BOWMANVILLE
W Balmoral Ave
N Winchester Ave
N Wolcott Ave
N Ravenswood Ave
N Ravenswood Ave
C
W Summerdale Ave
W Summerdale Ave
N Bell Ave
N Oakley Ave
W Berwyn Ave
W Berwyn Ave
W Farragut Ave
W Farragut Ave
N Honore St
5200N
41
W Foster Ave
39
2400W
1600W
N Ashland Ave
W Winona St
W Winona St
W Winona St
N Claremont Ave
N Western Ave
1
W Carmen Ave
Winnemac
Park
2
W Carmen Ave

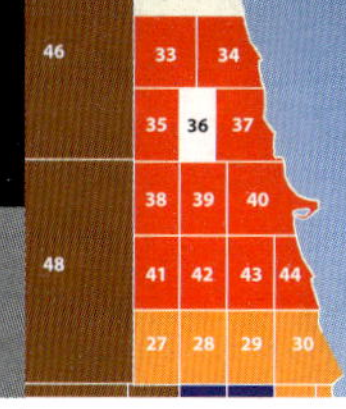

Bryn Mawr is residential—living and dead. Rosehill Cemetery takes up much of the neighborhood's real estate. The magnificent mausoleum houses mail-order magnates Montgomery Ward and Richard Warren Sears. Bryn Mawr has affordable homes, turn-of-the-century apartment buildings, and a burgeoning art scene.

Banks

- **Bank One** • 6210 N Western Ave
- **Charter One (ATM)** • 6128 N Ravenswood Ave
- **North Community** • 5241 N Western Ave

Car Washes

- **Norwood 2 Hand Carwash** • 5462 N Damen Ave

Car Rental

- **Enterprise** • 5844 N Western Ave • 773-989-3390
- **Hertz** • 5543 N Western Ave • 773-506-2125

Gas Stations

- **Citgo** • 1840 W Peterson Ave
- **Citgo** • 5300 N Western Ave
- **Shell** • 5201 N Western Ave
- **Shell** • 6000 N Western Ave

Landmarks

- **Rosehill Cemetery and Mausoleum** • 5800 N Ravenswood Ave

Pharmacies

- **Walgreens** • 6236 N Western Ave

Pizza

- **Fireside Restaurant & Lounge** • 5739 N Ravenswood Ave

Schools

- **Eliza Chappell Elementary** • 2135 W Foster Ave
- **Stone Scholastic Academy** • 6239 N Leavitt St

N
WEST ROGERS PARK
Emerson Park
Green Briar Park
Rosehill Cemetery
BOWMANVILLE
Winnemac Park
W Devon Ave
W Peterson Ave
W Foster Ave
N Western Ave
N Ravenswood Ave
N Ashland Ave
N Clark St
N Ridge Ave
Ridge Ave
Lincoln Ave
N Bowmanville Ave
W Loyola Ave
W Arthur Ave
W Schreiber Ave
W Highland Ave
W Rosemont Ave
W Thome Ave
W Granville Ave
W Hood Ave
W Norwood St
W Glenlake Ave
W Thorndale Ave
W Ardmore Ave
W Rosehill Dr
W Edgewater Ave
W Hollywood Ave
W Olive Ave
W Bryn Mawr Ave
W Gregory St
W Catalpa Ave
W Rascher Ave
W Balmoral Ave
W Summerdale Ave
W Berwyn Ave
W Farragut Ave
W Winona St
W Carmen Ave
N Rockwell St
N Maplewood Ave
N Campbell Ave
N Oakley Ave
N Bell Ave
N Leavitt St
N Hamilton Ave
N Hoyne Ave
N Seeley Ave
N Winchester Ave
N Paulina St
N Artesian Ave
N Claremont Ave
N Damen Ave
N Wolcott Ave
N Hermitage Ave
N Honore St
6400N
6000N
5600N
5200N
2400W
2000W
1600W
14
41
33
34
35
37
39
A
B
C
1
2

Sundries / Entertainment

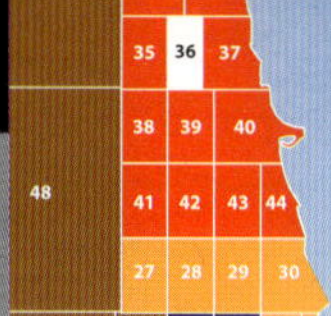

Bryn Mawr residents say that Rosehill Cemetery's mausoleum is haunted. Stop by local taverns where ghost stories might come up in everyday chatter. San Soo Gap San is popular for accesible Korean fare. The Fireside serves up Cajun-inspired comfort food and features a four-season patio.

Coffee

- **Dunkin' Donuts** • 1954 W Peterson Ave
- **Dunkin' Donuts** • 6254 N Western Ave

Liquor Stores

- **A&B Grocery & Liquors** • 6320 N Western Ave
- **Aces & Eights** • 5306 N Damen Ave
- **Diala Grocery & Liquor** • 1935 W Foster Ave
- **Foster Food & Liquor** • 1900 W Foster Ave
- **L&M Food & Liquor** • 1968 W Peterson Ave
- **Leadway Liquors** • 5233 N Damen Ave

Nightlife

- **Claddagh Ring** • 2306 W Foster Ave
- **Leadway Bar & Café** • 5233 N Damen Ave

Restaurants

- **El Tipico** • 1836 W Foster Ave
- **Fireside Restaurant & Lounge** • 5739 N Ravenswood Ave
- **Max's Italian Beef** • 5754 N Western Ave
- **San Soo Gap San Korean Restaurant and Sushi House** • 5247 N Western Ave

Map 37 • Edgewater / Andersonville

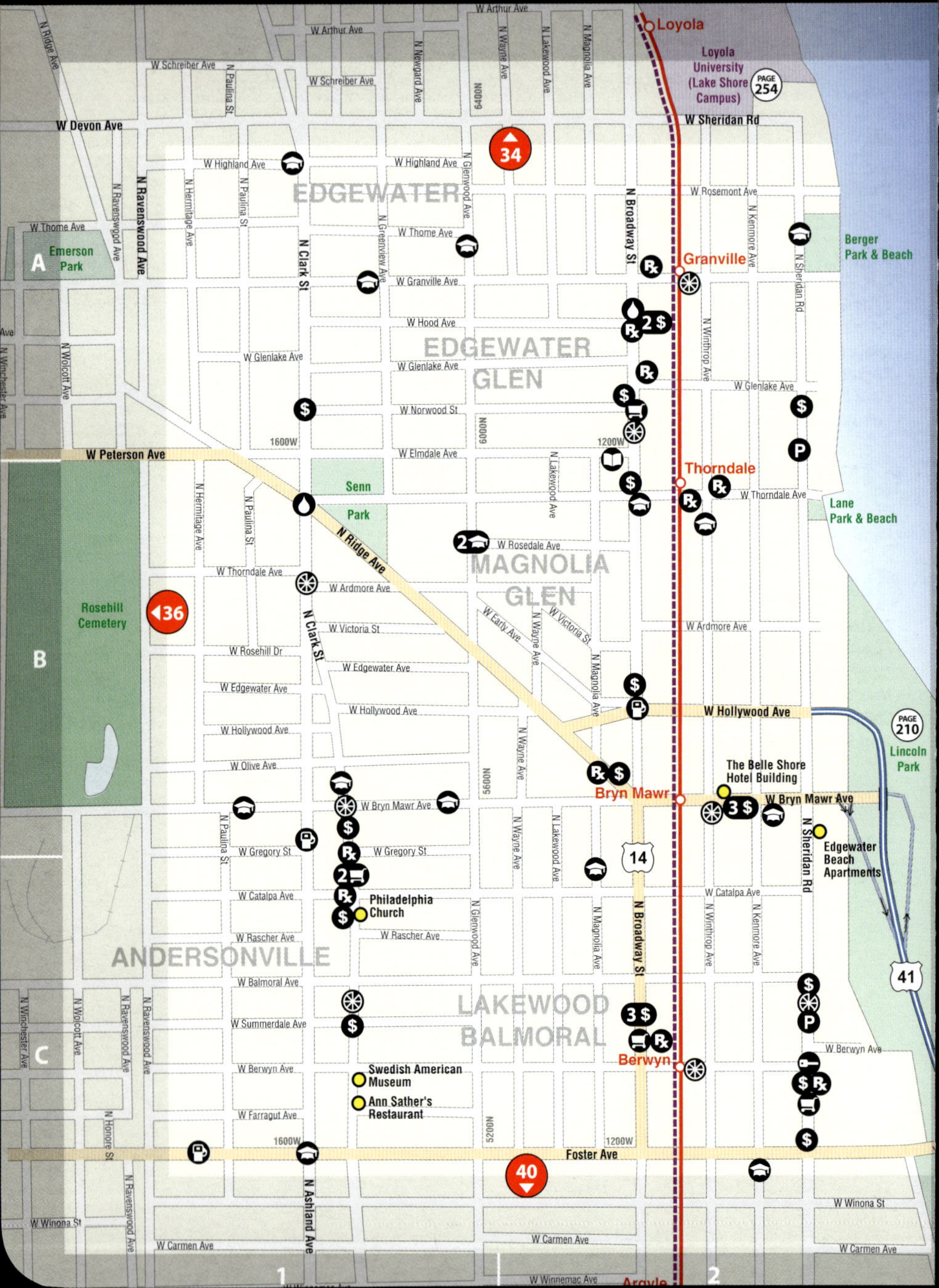

N
Loyola
Loyola University (Lake Shore Campus)
PAGE 254
W Arthur Ave
W Schreiber Ave
W Devon Ave
W Sheridan Rd
34
W Highland Ave
EDGEWATER
W Rosemont Ave
W Thome Ave
Emerson Park
A
Berger Park & Beach
Granville
W Granville Ave
W Hood Ave
EDGEWATER GLEN
W Glenlake Ave
W Norwood St
1600W
1200W
W Peterson Ave
W Elmdale Ave
Thorndale
Senn Park
N Ridge Ave
W Thorndale Ave
Lane Park & Beach
W Rosedale Ave
MAGNOLIA GLEN
W Ardmore Ave
Rosehill Cemetery
36
B
W Victoria St
W Early Ave
W Rosehill Dr
W Edgewater Ave
W Hollywood Ave
PAGE 210
Lincoln Park
W Olive Ave
The Belle Shore Hotel Building
Bryn Mawr
W Bryn Mawr Ave
Edgewater Beach Apartments
W Gregory St
14
W Catalpa Ave
Philadelphia Church
W Rascher Ave
ANDERSONVILLE
W Balmoral Ave
41
LAKEWOOD BALMORAL
W Summerdale Ave
C
Berwyn
W Berwyn Ave
Swedish American Museum
Ann Sather's Restaurant
W Farragut Ave
1600W
1200W
5200N
Foster Ave
40
W Winona St
W Carmen Ave
W Winnemac Ave
Argyle
N Ridge Ave
N Paulina St
N Newgard Ave
N Wayne Ave
N Lakewood Ave
N Magnolia Ave
N Ravenswood Ave
N Hermitage Ave
N Clark St
N Greenview Ave
N Glenwood Ave
N Broadway St
N Kenmore Ave
N Sheridan Rd
N Winthrop Ave
N Wolcott Ave
N Winchester Ave
N Honore St
N Ashland Ave
6400N
6000N
5600N
1
2

Essentials

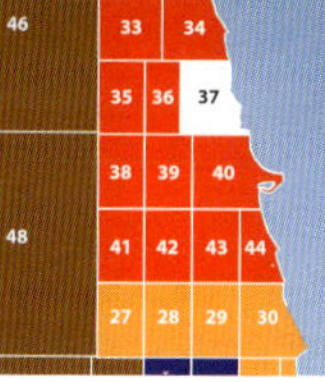

A range of housing types and small businesses (neighborhood groups start grumbling whenever the chains come knocking), along with cultural diversity, make Andersonville and Edgewater bastions for so-called "lakefront liberals." Besides beautiful residential areas and stroll-friendly commercial districts, Edgewater boasts the city's gay beach at Hollywood and the lakefront, not to mention the "lesbian Jewel."

$ Banks

- **Bank One** • 1055 W Bryn Mawr Ave
- **Bank One** • 6009 N Broadway St
- **Bank One (ATM)** • 1036 W Bryn Mawr Ave
- **Bank One (ATM)** • 5625 N Ridge Ave
- **Bank One (ATM)** • 6125 N Broadway St
- **Bridgeview** • 1058 W Bryn Mawr Ave
- **Bridgeview** • 5345 N Sheridan Rd
- **Bridgeview** • 6041 N Clark St
- **Broadway** • 5960 N Broadway St
- **Charter One (ATM)** • 5235 N Sheridan Rd
- **Charter One (ATM)** • 5457 N Clark St
- **First Commercial** • 6033 N Sheridan Rd
- **Harris Trust & Savings (ATM)** • 6125 N Broadway St
- **Metropolitan (ATM)** • 5342 N Broadway St
- **North Community** • 5342 N Broadway St
- **TCF** • 5343 N Broadway St
- **US** • 5340 N Clark St
- **Washington Mutual** • 5200 N Sheridan Rd
- **Washington Mutual** • 5531 N Clark St
- **Washington Mutual** • 5725 N Broadway St

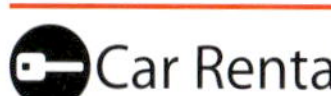

Car Rental

- **Enterprise** • 5313 N Sheridan Rd • 773-271-4500

Car Washes

- **Snappy Hand Car Wash** • 5961 N Ridge Ave
- **Superior Hand Car Wash** • 6147 N Broadway St

Gas Stations

- **Marathon** • 5550 N Ashland Ave
- **Ravenswood Clark Oil** • 1745 W Foster Ave
- **Shell** • 5701 N Broadway St

Landmarks

- **Ann Sather's Restaurant** • 5207 N Clark St
- **The Belle Shore Hotel Building** • 1062 W Bryn Mawr Ave
- **Edgewater Beach Apartments** • 5555 N Sheridan Rd
- **Philadelphia Church** • 5437 N Clark St
- **Swedish American Museum** • 5211 N Clark St

Libraries

- **Edgewater Public Library** • 1210 W Elmdale Ave

Parking

Pharmacies

- **Dominick's** • 5235 N Sheridan Rd
- **Gordono Pharmacy** • 5501 N Clark St
- **Granville Medical Pharmacy** • 6212 N Broadway St
- **Jewel-Osco** • 5345 N Broadway St
- **Jewel-Osco** • 5516 N Clark St
- **Osco Drug** • 6150 N Broadway St
- **Thorndale Pharmacy** • 1104 W Thorndale Ave
- **Walgreens** • 5625 N Ridge Ave
- **Walgreens** • 6125 N Broadway St

Pizza

- **Calo Pizzeria Restaurant** • 5343 N Clark St
- **Dominick's Finer Foods** • 6009 N Broadway St
- **Domino's** • 5912 N Clark St
- **Franko's Pizza Express** • 1109 W Bryn Mawr Ave
- **Gino's North Pizzeria** • 1111 W Granville Ave
- **Pizzeria Aroma** • 1125 W Berwyn Ave
- **Primo Pizza** • 5600 N Clark St
- **Tedino's** • 5335 N Sheridan Rd

Schools

- **Helen C Peirce School of International Studies** • 1423 W Bryn Mawr Ave
- **Jose J Marti Elementary** • 5126 N Kenmore Ave
- **Lake Shore** • 5611 N Clark St
- **Northside Catholic Academy** • 5525 N Magnolia Ave
- **Northside Catholic Academy (St Gertrude Campus)** • 6214 N Glenwood Ave
- **Rogers Park Montessori (Bryn Mawr)** • 1020 W Bryn Mawr Ave
- **Rogers Park Montessori (Thorndale)** • 1244 W Thorndale Ave
- **Sacred Heart** • 6250 N Sheridan Rd
- **Senn High** • 5900 N Glenwood Ave
- **St Gregory High** • 1677 W Bryn Mawr Ave
- **Stephen K Hayt Elementary** • 1518 W Granville Ave
- **Swift Elementary** • 5900 N Winthrop Ave
- **Trumbull Elementary** • 5200 N Ashland Ave
- **William E Rodriguez Academic Preparatory** • 5900 N Glenwood Ave

Supermarkets

- **DelRay Farms** • 5205 N Broadway St
- **Dominick's** • 5235 N Sheridan Rd
- **Dominick's** • 6009 N Broadway St
- **Edgewater Produce** • 5515 N Clark St
- **Jewel-Osco** • 5345 N Broadway St
- **Jewel-Osco** • 5516 N Clark St

N

W Arthur Ave
Loyola
Loyola University (Lake Shore Campus)
PAGE 254
W Schreiber Ave
W Sheridan Rd
W Devon Ave
34
W Highland Ave
EDGEWATER
W Rosemont Ave
W Thome Ave
Emerson Park
Granville
Berger Park & Beach
W Granville Ave
W Hood Ave
W Glenlake Ave
EDGEWATER GLEN
W Norwood St
W Elmdale Ave
W Peterson Ave
Senn Park
Thorndale
W Thorndale Ave
Lane Park & Beach
N Ridge Ave
W Rosedale Ave
MAGNOLIA GLEN
W Ardmore Ave
Rosehill Cemetery
36
W Victoria St
W Rosehill Dr
W Early Ave
W Edgewater Ave
W Hollywood Ave
PAGE 210
Lincoln Park
W Olive Ave
Bryn Mawr
W Bryn Mawr Ave
14
W Gregory St
W Catalpa Ave
W Rascher Ave
ANDERSONVILLE
W Balmoral Ave
41
W Summerdale Ave
LAKEWOOD BALMORAL
Berwyn
W Berwyn Ave
W Farragut Ave
Foster Ave
40
W Winona St
W Carmen Ave
W Winnemac Ave
Argyle
N Clark St
N Broadway St
N Sheridan Rd
N Ashland Ave
N Ravenswood Ave
N Paulina St
N Hermitage Ave
N Wolcott Ave
N Winchester Ave
N Glenwood Ave
N Greenview Ave
N Wayne Ave
N Lakewood Ave
N Magnolia Ave
N Kenmore Ave
N Winthrop Ave
N Newgard Ave
N Honore St
N Ridge Ave
1600W
1200W
6400N
6000N
5600N
5200N
A
B
C
1
2

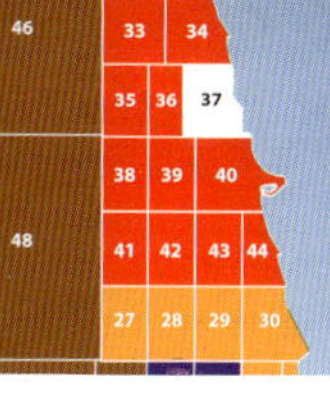

While there's Boystown with its pride pylons, boys bars and flamboyant parades, Andersonville is the center of gay and lesbian residential life in Chicago. The liberal community around Clark and Foster has great depth. Pick up a read at Women & Children First bookstore and devour it at global Kopi Cafe. The area offers many great brunch options, from M.Henry, to Angels to Svea, making it perhaps one of the most pleasant of all neighborhoods, anywhere, ever, to stroll about on the weekends.

Coffee

- **Café Boost** • 5400 N Clark St
- **Coffee Chicago** • 5256 N Broadway St
- **Dunkin' Donuts** • 1127 W Bryn Mawr Ave
- **Dunkin' Donuts** • 6250 N Clark St
- **Dunkin' Donuts** • 6332 N Broadway St
- **Einstein Bros Bagels** • 5318 N Clark St
- **Kopi, A Traveler's Café** • 5317 N Clark St
- **Metropolis Coffee Co** • 1039 W Granville Ave
- **Pause** • 1107 W Berwyn Ave
- **The Peacock Café** • 5440 N Sheridan Rd
- **Starbucks** • 1070 W Bryn Mawr Ave
- **Starbucks** • 5300 N Clark St
- **Starbucks (Dominick's)** • 6009 N Broadway St
- **Viva Java** • 1147 W Granville Ave

Copy Shops

- **The UPS Store (8 am-7 pm)** • 1055 W Bryn Mawr Ave
- **The UPS Store (9 am-7 pm)** • 5315 N Clark St

Farmer's Markets

- **Edgewater** • N Broadway St & W Thorndale Ave

Gyms

- **Cheetah Gym** • 5248 N Clark St
- **Cheetah Gym** • 5838 N Broadway St
- **Curves** • 5339 N Sheridan Rd
- **Curves** • 6118 N Broadway St

Hardware Stores

- **Cas Hardware Store** • 5305 N Clark St
- **Clarendon Electric & Hardware** • 6050 N Broadway St
- **Dadop Hardware** • 5943 N Broadway St
- **Marx Ace Hardware** • 5830 N Clark St

Liquor Stores

- **Buy Low Liquors** • 5201 N Clark St
- **Castle Wines & Spirits** • 1128 W Thorndale Ave
- **Granville Liquors** • 1100 W Granville Ave
- **In Fine Spirits** • 5418 N Clark St
- **M&D Food Liquors** •5652 N Clark St
- **Sovereign Liquors** • 6202 N Broadway St
- **Sun Liquors** • 1101 W Granville Ave

Movie Theaters

- **Chicago Filmmakers** • 5243 N Clark St

Nightlife

- **Atmosphere** • 5355 N Clark St
- **Charlie's Ale House** • 5308 N Clark St
- **Edgewater Lounge** • 5600 N Ashland Ave
- **Farraguts Tavern** • 5240 N Clark St
- **George's Cocktail Lounge** • 646 S Wabash Ave
- **Granville Anvil** • 1137 Granville Ave
- **Joie de Vine** • 1744 W Balmoral Ave
- **Madrigals** • 5316 N Clark St
- **Moody's Pub** • 5910 N Broadway St
- **Ollie's** • 1064 W Berwyn Ave
- **Simon's** • 5210 N Clark St
- **StarGaze** • 5419 N Clark St

Pet Shops

- **The Dog Scene** • 5637 N Ashland Ave
- **Park View Pet Shop** • 5358 N Broadway St
- **Ruff N'Stuff Dog Obedience** • 5430 N Clark St

Restaurants

- **Andie's** • 5253 N Clark St
- **Ann Sather** • 5207 N Clark St
- **Carson's Ribs** • 5970 N Ridge Ave
- **Corner Grille** • 5200 N Clark St
- **Francesca's Bryn Mawr** • 1039 W Bryn Mawr Ave
- **Indie Café** • 5951 N Broadway St
- **Jin Ju** • 5203 N Clark St
- **La Fonda Latino** • 5350 N Broadway St
- **La Tache** • 1475 W Balmoral Ave
- **M Henry** • 5707 N Clark St
- **Moody's Pub** • 5910 N Broadway St
- **Pasteur** • 5525 N Broadway St
- **Pauline's** • 1754 W Balmoral Ave
- **Reza's** • 5255 N Clark St
- **South** • 5900 N Broadway St
- **Sushi Luxe** • 5204 N Clark St
- **Svea** • 5236 N Clark St
- **Swedish Bakery** • 5348 N Clark St
- **Tanoshii** • 5547 N Clark St
- **Taste of Lebanon** • 1509 W Foster Ave
- **Tomboy** • 5402 N Clark St
- **Urban Epicure** • 1512 W Berwyn Ave

Shopping

- **Alamo Shoes** • 5321 N Clark St
- **Atelier Asia** • 1477 W Balmoral Ave
- **Bon Bon** • 5410 N Clark St
- **Brown Elephant** • 5228 N Clark St
- **Cassona** • 5241 N Clark St
- **Early to Bed** • 5232 N Sheridan Rd
- **Elda de la Rosa** • 5407 N Clark St
- **Erickson Jewelers** • 5304 N Clark St
- **Gethsemane Garden Center** • 5739 N Clark St
- **Johnny Sprocket's** • 1052 W Bryn Mawr
- **Paper Trail** • 5309 N Clark St
- **Presence** • 5216 N Clark St
- **Scout** • 5221 N Clark St
- **Surrender** • 5225 N Clark St
- **Toys & Treasures** • 5311 N Clark St
- **White Attic** • 5408 N Clark St
- **Women & Children First** • 5233 N Clark St

Video Rental

- **BJ Video** • 5552 N Broadway St
- **Blockbuster Video** • 5300 N Broadway St
- **Diamond Grocery & Video (Indian)** • 6322 N Broadway St
- **Hollywood Video** • 6201 N Clark St
- **Lion Video** • 5218 N Sheridan Rd
- **National Video** • 1108 W Granville Ave
- **Select Video** • 5358 N Clark St
- **Specialty Video** • 5307 N Clark St
- **Video Town** • 1127 W Thorndale Ave

Map 38 • Ravenswood / Albany Park

RAVENSWOOD
LINCOLN SQUARE
ALBANY PARK
HORNER PARK

River Park
Ronan Park
Gross Park
Jacob Park
Horner Park
California Park

Albany Park Community Center
Fish Furniture Co Building
Willis Building
North Branch Pumping Station
Ronan Park Walking Trail
Ravenswood Manor Park
Paradise

Kimball
Kedzie
Francisco
Rockwell
Western

W Foster Ave
W Winona St
W Carmen Ave
W Winnemac Ave
W Argyle St
W Ainslie St
W Gunnison St
W Lawrence Ave
W Giddings St
W Leland Ave
W Eastwood Ave
W Wilson Ave
W Windsor Ave
W Sunnyside Ave
W Agatite Ave
W Montrose Ave
W Pensacola Ave
W Cullom Ave
W Hutchinson St
W Berteau Ave
W Warner Ave
W Belle Plaine Ave
W Cuyler Ave
W Irving Park Rd
W Dakin St
W Byron St

N St Louis Ave
N Bernard Ave
N Kimball Ave
N Christiana Ave
N Spaulding Ave
N Sawyer Ave
North Park College
N Kedzie Ave
N Troy St
N Albany Ave
N Whipple St
N Sacramento Ave
N Richmond St
N Francisco Ave
N Mozart St
N Manor Ave
N California Ave
N Virginia Ave
N Fairfield Ave
N Washtenaw Ave
N Talman Ave
N Rockwell St
N Maplewood Ave
N Campbell Ave
N Artesian Ave
N Western Ave
N Lincoln Ave

5200N
4800N
4400N
4000N
3200W
2800W
2400W

35
48
39
41

A
B
C
1
2

Essentials

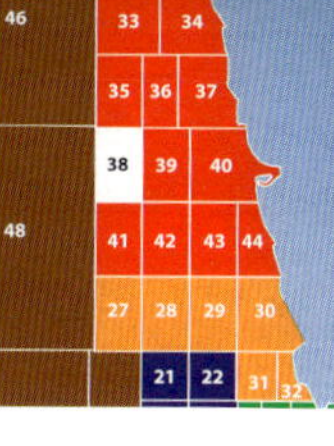

Within the Ravenswood neighborhood is The Manor, a small area of about a quarter of a mile that packs a lot of power and wealth. Generations of Chicago's elite live in this haven next to the river, where owls nest in trees and boat owners have private docks. Further west, Albany Park is one of the hottest spots for new condo conversions in the city. Urban pioneers enjoy lots of space, and a plethora of excellent ethnic shops and restaurants.

Banks

- **Albany** • 3400 W Lawrence Ave
- **Bank One** • 2959 W Irving Park Rd
- **Bank One** • 4801 N Lincoln Ave
- **Bank One** • 4843 N Kedzie Ave
- **Charter One** • 2752 W Montrose Ave
- **Charter One (ATM)** • 5050 N Lincoln Ave
- **TCF (ATM)** • Osco, 5158 N Lincoln Ave

Car Washes

- **Minute Man Car Wash** • 3218 W Irving Park Rd
- **Ruby Hand Carwash** • 4334 N California Ave

Gas Stations

- **BP** • 3201 W Montrose Ave
- **Citgo** • 2800 W Lawrence Ave
- **Citgo** • 2816 W Irving Park Rd
- **Shell** • 5155 N Kimball Ave

Hospitals

- **Swedish Covenant** • 5145 N California Ave

Landmarks

- **Albany Park Community Center** • 3401 W Ainslie St
- **Fish Furniture Co Building** • 3322 W Lawrence Ave
- **North Branch Pumping Station** • Lawrence Ave & the Chicago River
- **Paradise** • 2916 W Montrose Ave
- **Ravenswood Manor Park** • 4626 N Manor Ave
- **River Park** • 5100 N Francisco Ave
- **Ronan Park Walking Trail** • 3000 W Argyle St
- **Willis Building** • 3221 W Lawrence Ave

Libraries

- **Albany Park Public Library** • 5150 N Kimball Ave

Pharmacies

- **Osco Drug** • 5158 N Lincoln Ave
- **Walgreens** • 3153 W Irving Park Rd
- **Walgreens** • 4343 N Kedzie Ave
- **Walgreens** • 4801 N Lincoln Ave

Pizza

- **Angelo's Pizza & Restaurant** • 3026 W Montrose Ave
- **Boomer's** • 5035 N Lincoln Ave
- **Bravo International Pizzaria** • 3256 W Lawrence Ave
- **Golden Crust Pizzeria** • 4620 N Kedzie Ave
- **La Roma Pizzeria** • 3213 W Irving Park Rd
- **Little Caesars Pizza** • 2501 W Lawrence Ave
- **Noli's Pizza** • 4839 N Kedzie Ave
- **Papa Giorgio's** • 2604 W Lawrence Ave

Post Offices

- 2522 W Lawrence Ave

Schools

- **Albany Park Multicultural Academy** • 5039 N Kimball Ave
- **Lawrence Hall Youth Services** • 4833 N Francisco Ave
- **Newton Bateman Elementary** • 4220 N Richmond St
- **North Park University** • 3225 W Foster Ave
- **North River Elementary** • 4416 N Troy St
- **Thomas J Waters Fine Arts Elementary** • 4540 N Campbell Ave
- **Transfiguration** • 5044 N Rockwell St
- **Von Steuben Metropolitan Science Center** • 5039 N Kimball Ave
- **Waters Fine Arts Academy** • 4540 N Campbell Ave
- **William G Hibbard Elementary** • 3244 W Ainslie St

Supermarkets

- **Al-Khayyam Bakery and Market** • 4738 N Kedzie Ave
- **Aldi** • 2431 W Montrose Ave
- **Andy's Fruit Ranch** • 4733 N Kedzie Ave
- **Cermak Produce** • 4234 N Kimball Ave
- **Clark Market** • 4853 N Kedzie Ave
- **Harvestime Foods** • 2632 W Lawrence Ave
- **Holy Land Grocery** • 4806 N Kedzie Ave
- **Peter Grocery** • 4947 N Kedzie Ave
- **Sahar Meat Market** • Albany Plaza Mall, 4829 N Kedzie Ave

35
39
41
48

A
B
C
1
2

RAVENSWOOD
LINCOLN SQUARE
HORNER PARK
ALBANY PARK

River Park
Ronan Park
Gross Park
Jacob Park
Horner Park
California Park

Kimball
Kedzie
Francisco
Rockwell
Western

W Foster Ave
W Winona St
W Carmen Ave
W Winnemac Ave
W Argyle St
W Ainslie St
W Gunnison St
W Lawrence Ave
W Giddings St
W Leland Ave
W Eastwood Ave
W Wilson Ave
W Windsor Ave
W Sunnyside Ave
W Agatite Ave
W Montrose Ave
W Pensacola Ave
W Cullom Ave
W Hutchinson St
W Berteau Ave
W Warner Ave
W Belle Plaine Ave
W Cuyler Ave
W Irving Park Rd
W Dakin St
W Byron St

N St Louis Ave
N Bernard Ave
N Kimball Ave
N Christiana Ave
N Spaulding Ave
N Sawyer Ave
N Kedzie Ave
N Troy St
N Albany Ave
N Whipple St
N Sacramento Ave
N Richmond St
N Francisco Ave
N Mozart St
N California Ave
N Fairfield Ave
N Virginia Ave
N Manor Ave
N Washtenaw Ave
N Talman Ave
N Rockwell St
N Maplewood Ave
N Campbell Ave
N Artesian Ave
N Western Ave
N Lincoln Ave
North Park College

5200N
4800N
4400N
4000N
3200W
2800W
2400W

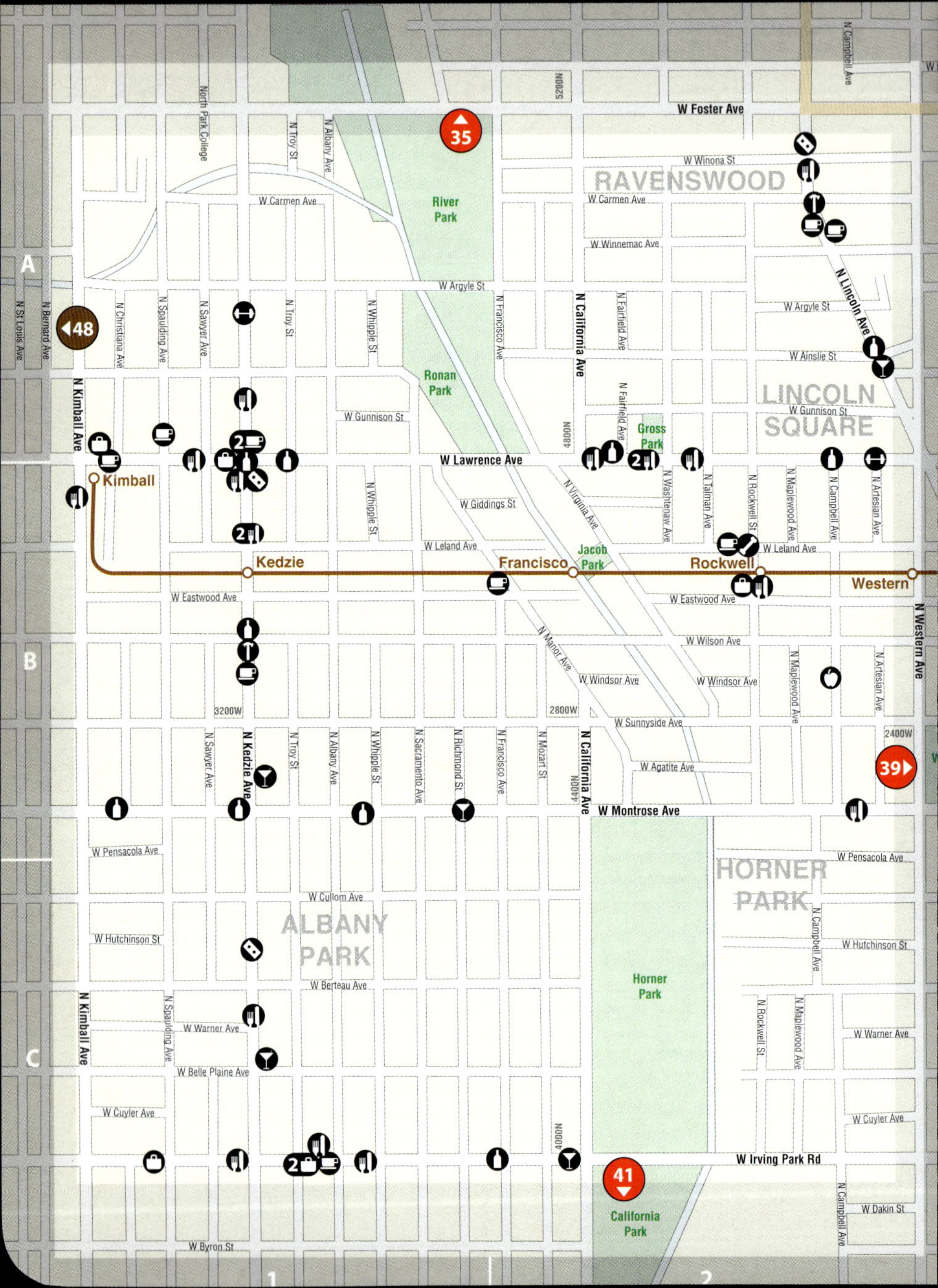

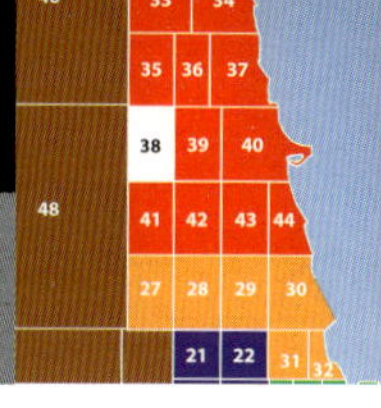

Noon O'Kebab is perhaps the most highly regarded of the many kebab emporiums of Albany Park. Meanwhile, the neighborhood is still looking for a friendly local watering hole. In the meantime, residents can head south to Brisku's Bistro for cevapas and brew, or west to Lincoln Square Lanes, where they can toss back a few between frames.

Coffee

- **Beans & Bagels** • 2601 W Leland Ave
- **Café Origin** • 5062 N Lincoln Ave
- **Coffee Liberte** • 4807 N Spaulding Ave
- **Donut Doctor** • 3342 W Lawrence Ave
- **Dunkin' Donuts** • 3101 W Irving Park Rd
- **Dunkin' Donuts** • 4811 N Kedzie Ave
- **Jaafer Sweets** • Albany Plz Mall, 4825 N Kedzie Ave
- **Merle's Coffee House** • 4642 N Francisco Ave
- **Royal Coffee** • 5074 N Lincoln Ave
- **Starbucks** • 4558 N Kedzie Ave

Farmer's Markets

- **Chicago World Market** • 4540 N Campbell Ave

Gyms

- **Curves** • 4953 N Kedzie Ave
- **Women's Workout World** • 2540 W Lawrence Ave

Hardware Stores

- **Jay's Hardware** • 4608 N Kedzie Ave
- **Singer's True Value Hardware** • 5075 N Lincoln Ave

Liquor Stores

- **Buy Low Liquor Store** • 3360 W Montrose Ave
- **Cardinal Wine & Spirits** • 4905 N Lincoln Ave
- **Food & Liquors Express** • 2752 W Lawrence Ave
- **Foremost Liquor Store** • 4616 N Kedzie Ave
- **J&A Liquors** • 3213 W Lawrence Ave
- **Jerusalem Liquors** • 3133 W Lawrence Ave
- **Peacock Liquors** • 3056 W Montrose Ave
- **Prestige Liquors** • 3210 W Montrose Ave
- **Quick Stop** • 2901 W Irving Park Rd

Nightlife

- **Brisku's Bistro** • 4100 N Kedzie Ave
- **Candlestick Maker** • 4432 N Kedzie Ave
- **Lincoln Square Lanes** • 4874 N Lincoln Ave
- **Montrose Saloon** • 2933 W Montrose Ave
- **Peek Inn** • 2825 W Irving Park Rd

Pet Shops

- **Ruff Haus Pets** • 4652 N Rockwell St

Restaurants

- **Arun's** • 4156 N Kedzie Ave
- **Cousin's Turkish Restaurants** • 3038 W Irving Park Rd
- **Dharma Garden Thai Restaurants** • 3111 W Irving Park Rd
- **Great Sea Chinese Restaurants** • 3254 W Lawrence Ave
- **Han Bat** • 2723 W Lawrence Ave
- **Huddle House** • 4748 N Kimball Ave
- **Jimmy's Fast Food** • 4810 N Drake Ave
- **Kang Nam** • 4849 N Kedzie Ave
- **Korean Restaurants** • 2659 W Lawrence Ave
- **Lutz Continental Café** • 2458 W Montrose Ave
- **Manzo's Ristorante** • 3210 W Irving Park Rd
- **Noon O Kabab** • 4661 N Kedzie Ave
- **Penguin** • 2723 W Lawrence Ave
- **Rockwell's Neighborhood Grill** • 4632 N Rockwell St
- **Santa Rita Taqueria** • 2752 W Lawrence Ave
- **Shelly's Freez** • 5119 N Lincoln Ave
- **Thai Little Home Café** • 4747 N Kedzie Ave

Shopping

- **Lincoln Antique Mall** • 3115 W Irving Park Rd
- **The Music Store** • 3121 W Irving Park Rd
- **Odin Tatu** • 3313 W Irving Park Rd
- **Rave Sports** • 3346 W Lawrence Ave
- **Sassy Boutique** • 3210 W Lawrence Ave
- **Scents & Sensibility** • 4654 N Rockwell St

Video Rental

- **AV Video Center** • 5153 N Lincoln Ave
- **Hollywood Video** • 4246 N Kedzie Ave
- **V&K Video** • 4750 N Kedzie Ave

W Berwyn Ave
N Campbell Ave
N Oakley Ave
W Farragut Ave
N Hoyne Ave
5200N
N Ravenswood Ave
N Honore St
W Farragut Ave
W Farragut
Foster Ave
41
36
37
W Winona St
Winnemac Park
W Winona St
N Claremont Ave
W Carmen Ave
N Winchester Ave
N Wolcott Ave
N Ravenswood Ave
W Carmen Ave
W Winnemac Ave
W Winnemac Ave
A
W Argyle St
W Argyle St
N Jannsen Ave
N Claremont Ave
N Bell Ave
N Hamilton Ave
N Hoyne Ave
N Seeley Ave
W Ainslie St
W Ainslie St
W Ainslie St
LINCOLN SQUARE
RAVENSWOOD
N Clark St
W Gunnison St
N Lincoln Ave
4800N
W Lawrence Ave
Ravenswood
N Rockwell St
N Maplewood Ave
N Campbell Ave
N Artesian Ave
N Hamilton Ave
N Seeley Ave
N Winchester Ave
N Ashland Ave
W Giddings St
W Leland Ave
W Leland Ave
Western
Damen
N Ravenswood Ave
N Ravenswood Ave
N Hermitage Ave
N Greenview Ave
W Eastwood Ave
W Eastwood Ave
W Wilson Ave
W Wilson Ave
B
Old Town School of Folk Music
W Windsor Ave
N Claremont Ave
N Damen Ave
38
40
W Sunnyside Ave
N Maplewood Ave
N Artesian Ave
Welles Park
W Agatite Ave
4400N
N Paulina St
N Greenview Ave
Montrose
Montrose Ave
2400W
N Western Ave
N Campbell Ave
N Claremont Ave
N Oakley Ave
N Bell Ave
N Leavitt St
N Hoyne Ave
2000W
N Wolcott Ave
1600W
W Pensacola Ave
W Pensacola Ave
W Pensac
W Cullom Ave
W Cullom Ave
W Hutchinson St
W Hutchinson St
W Hutchinson St
N Honore St
W Hutchi
W Berteau Ave
NORTH CENTER
W Berteau Ave
N Rockwell St
N Campbell Ave
N Claremont Ave
N Wolcott Ave
N Ravenswood Ave
W Warner Ave
W Warner Ave
W Warne
C
N Maplewood Ave
W Belle Plaine Ave
W Cuyler Ave
W Cuyler Ave
W Cuyler Ave
W Cuyle
St Benedict's Church
4000N
Irving Park
W Irving Park Rd
N Bell Ave
N Hamilton Ave
42
N Seeley Ave
W Larchmont Ave
Revere Park
W Dakin St
N Lincoln Ave
W Byron St
1
2

Essentials

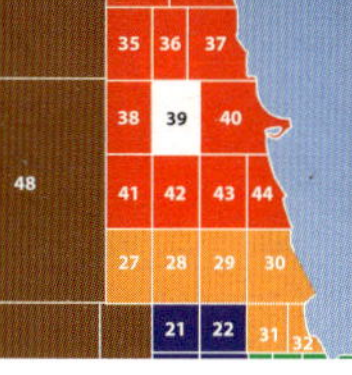

Germans, Eastern Europeans, and Latinos share these increasingly pricey neighborhoods. The heart of ethnically diverse Ravenswood is Lincoln Square, the locus of German life in Chicago. The closest you'll get to Munich for Octoberfest without boarding a plane is here. The blocks around St Benedict's Church have spawned a growing, family-friendly neighborhood that goes by "St Ben's".

Banks

- **Albany** • 4400 N Western Ave
- **Bank One** • 1825 W Lawrence Ave
- **Bank One** • 4711 N Lincoln Ave
- **Bank One (ATM)** • 2301 W Irving Park Rd
- **Bridgeview** • 4553 N Lincoln Ave
- **Charter One** • 4037 N Lincoln Ave
- **Charter One (ATM)** • 2323 W Lawrence Ave
- **Community Bank of Ravenswood** • 2300 W Lawrence Ave
- **Corus** • 3959 N Lincoln Ave
- **Corus** • 4800 N Western Ave
- **Great Bank of Lincoln Square** • 4725 N Western Ave
- **Lincoln Park Savings** • 1946 W Irving Park Rd
- **Lincoln Park Savings** • 2139 W Irving Park Rd
- **TCF** • Jewel, 4250 N Lincoln Ave
- **TCF** • Osco, 4051 N Lincoln Ave
- **Washington Mutual** • 4000 N Lincoln Ave
- **Washington Mutual** • 4605 N Lincoln Ave

Gas Stations

- **Mobil** • 4000 N Western Ave
- **Mobil** • 4638 N Damen Ave
- **Phil & Son's Gas For Less** • 4201 N Lincoln Ave
- **Shell** • 4346 N Western Ave

Hospitals

- **Methodist Hospital of Chicago** • 5025 N Paulina St

Landmarks

- **Old Town School of Folk Music** • 4544 N Lincoln Ave
- **St Benedict's Church** • 2215 W Irving Park Rd

Libraries

- **Sullzer Public Library** • 4455 N Lincoln Ave

Pharmacies

- **Jewel** • 4250 N Lincoln Ave
- **Osco Drug** • 4051 N Lincoln Ave
- **Walgreens** • 2301 W Irving Park Rd

Pizza

- **Chicago's Pizza** • 1919 W Montrose Ave
- **Pizza DOC** • 2251 W Lawrence Ave
- **Pizza Hut** • 2309 W Lawrence Ave
- **Stefano's** • 2124 W Lawrence Ave

Post Offices

- 2011 W Montrose Ave

Schools

- **American English Academy** • 4627 N Winchester Ave
- **Infinity Chicago North Elementary** • 1713 W Cullom Ave
- **James B McPherson Elementary** • 4728 N Wolcott Ave
- **Jane Addams High** • 1800 W Cuyler Ave
- **John C Coonley Elementary** • 4046 N Leavitt St
- **Mary E Courtenay Language Arts Center** • 1726 W Berteau Ave
- **North Park Elementary** • 2017 W Montrose Ave
- **Pilgrim Lutheran** • 4300 N Winchester Ave
- **Queen of Angels** • 4520 N Western Ave
- **Ravenswood Baptist Christian** • 4437 N Seeley Ave
- **Ravenswood Elementary** • 4332 N Paulina St
- **Roald Amundsen High** • 5110 N Damen Ave
- **St Matthias** • 4910 N Claremont Ave

Supermarkets

- **Deal$** • 4738 N Western Ave
- **Jewel** • 4250 N Lincoln Ave

N
Foster Ave
41
W Berwyn Ave
W Farragut Ave
W Winona St
W Carmen Ave
W Winnemac Ave
W Argyle St
W Ainslie St
W Gunnison St
W Lawrence Ave
W Giddings St
W Leland Ave
W Eastwood Ave
W Wilson Ave
W Windsor Ave
W Sunnyside Ave
W Agatite Ave
Montrose Ave
W Pensacola Ave
W Cullom Ave
W Hutchinson St
W Berteau Ave
W Warner Ave
W Belle Plaine Ave
W Cuyler Ave
W Irving Park Rd
W Dakin St
W Larchmont Ave
W Byron St
N Lincoln Ave
N Campbell Ave
N Oakley Ave
N Hoyne Ave
N Claremont Ave
N Bell Ave
N Hamilton Ave
N Seeley Ave
N Winchester Ave
N Wolcott Ave
N Ravenswood Ave
N Honore St
N Rockwell St
N Maplewood Ave
N Artesian Ave
N Western Ave
N Leavitt St
N Damen Ave
N Hermitage Ave
N Paulina St
N Ashland Ave
N Greenview Ave
N Clark St
5200N
4800N
4400N
4000N
2400W
2000W
1600W
Winnemac Park
Welles Park
Revere Park
LINCOLN SQUARE
RAVENSWOOD
NORTH CENTER
Ravenswood
Western
Damen
Montrose
Irving Park
36
37
38
40
42
A
B
C
1
2

Sundries / Entertainment

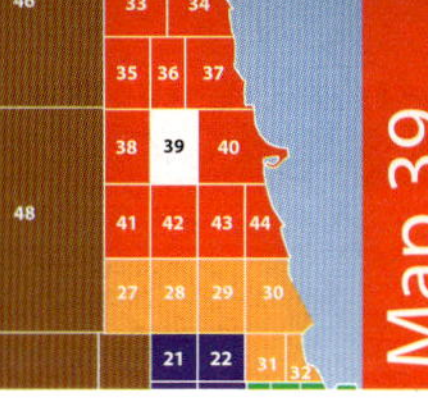

Lincoln Avenue is exploding with new dining options. The organic bistro fare at Bistro Campagne packs in locals every night of the week, while Andalucia offers inexpensive, authentic tapas. The Old Town School of Folk Music is a destination spot for cultural world music and folk concerts. Afterwards, toss back a stein at the Chicago Brauhaus.

Coffee

- **Beans & Bagels** • 1812 W Montrose Ave
- **Big E's Coffee Lounge** • 5131 N Damen Ave
- **Bourbon** • 4768 N Lincoln Ave
- **Café Marrakech Expresso** • 4747 N Damen Ave
- **Dunkin' Donuts** • 1743 W Lawrence Ave
- **Dunkin' Donuts** • 4010 N Western Ave
- **Katerina's** • 1920 W Irving Park Rd
- **Perfect Cup** • 4700 N Damen Ave
- **Red Eye Café** • 4164 N Lincoln Ave
- **Starbucks** • 1900 W Montrose Ave
- **Starbucks** • 4015 N Lincoln Ave
- **Starbucks** • 4553 N Lincoln Ave

Copy Shops

- **AlphaGraphics (8 am-6 pm)** • 1611 W Irving Park Rd
- **The UPS Store (8 am-7 pm)** • 4064 N Lincoln Ave

Farmer's Markets

- **Lincoln Square** • W Leland Ave & N Lincoln Ave
- **North Center** • W Belle Plaine Ave & N Damen Ave

Gyms

- **Curves** • 4351 N Lincoln Ave

Hardware Stores

- **Lincoln Square Ace Hardware** • 4250 N Lincoln Ave

Liquor Stores

- **Best Buy Food & Liquor** • 1832 W Montrose Ave
- **Bozic's Imports & Wholesale** • 4725 N Western Ave
- **Bright** • 1628 W Lawrence Ave
- **Cotler's Liquors** • 4959 N Damen Ave
- **Fine Wine Brokers** • 4621 N Lincoln Ave
- **Fox Liquors** • 4707 N Damen Ave
- **George's Liquors** • 1964 W Lawrence Ave
- **Houston Liquor & Foods** • 1829 W Irving Park Rd
- **Leland Inn** • 4662 N Western Ave

Movie Theaters

- **Davis Cinema** • 4614 N Lincoln Ave

Nightlife

- **Chicago Brauhaus** • 4732 N Lincoln Ave
- **Daily Bar & Grill** • 4560 N Lincoln Ave
- **The Long Room** • 1612 W Irving Park Rd
- **Lyon's Den** • 1934 W Irving Park Rd
- **Resi's Bierstube** • 2034 W Irving Park Rd

Pet Shops

- **Barking Lot** • 2442 W Irving Park Rd
- **Vahle's Bird & Pet Shop** • 4710 N Damen Ave

Restaurants

- **Andalucia** • 1820 W Montrose Ave
- **Bistro Campagne** • 4518 N Lincoln Ave
- **Café 28** • 1800 W Irving Park Rd
- **Café Selmarie** • 4729 N Lincoln Ave
- **Chicago Brauhaus** • 4732 N Lincoln Ave
- **Daily Bar & Grill** • 4560 N Lincoln Ave
- **Garcia's** • 4749 N Western Ave
- **Glunz Bavarian Haus** • 4128 N Lincoln Ave
- **Jury's Food & Drink** • 4337 N Lincoln Ave
- **La Boca della Verita** • 4618 N Lincoln Ave
- **O'Donovan's** • 2100 W Irving Park Rd
- **Opart Thai House** • 4658 N Western Ave
- **Pizza DOC** • 2251 W Lawrence Ave
- **Roong Petch** • 1828 W Montrose Ave
- **She She** • 4539 N Lincoln Ave
- **Smokin' Woody's** • 4160 N Lincoln Ave
- **Tank Sushi** • 4515 N Lincoln Ave
- **Thai Oscar** • 4638 N Western Ave
- **Toucan** • 4603 N Lincoln Ave
- **Tournesol** • 4343 N Lincoln Ave

Shopping

- **Architectural Artifacts** • 4325 N Ravenswood Ave
- **The Book Cellar** • 4736-37 N Lincoln Ave
- **The Cheese Stands Alone** • 4547 N Western Ave
- **The Chopping Block** • 4747 N Lincoln Ave
- **Delicatessen Meyer** • 4750 N Lincoln Ave
- **Different Strummer** • 4544 N Lincoln Ave
- **East Meets West** • 2118 W Lawrence Ave
- **European Import Center** • 4752 N Lincoln Ave
- **Gallimaufry Gallery** • 4712 N Lincoln Ave
- **Glass Art & Decorative Studio** • 4507 N Lincoln Ave
- **Griffins & Gargoyles Antiques** • 2140 W Lawrence Ave
- **Laurie's Planet of Sound** • 4639 N Lincoln Ave
- **Martin's Big & Tall Store for Men** • 4745 N Lincoln Ave
- **Merz Apothecary** • 4716 N Lincoln Ave
- **Nbahri Rhythms** • 4726 N Lincoln Ave
- **Play It Again Sports** • 2102 W Irving Park Rd
- **Quake Collectables** • 4628 N Lincoln Ave
- **Timeless Toys** • 4749 N Lincoln Ave

Video Rental

- **Blockbuster Video** • 1958 W Irving Park Rd
- **Blockbuster Video** • 2301 W Lawrence Ave
- **Darkstar Video** • 4353 N Lincoln Ave
- **Decade DVD** • 4612 N Lincoln Ave
- **Tom's Video** • 1830 W Wilson Ave

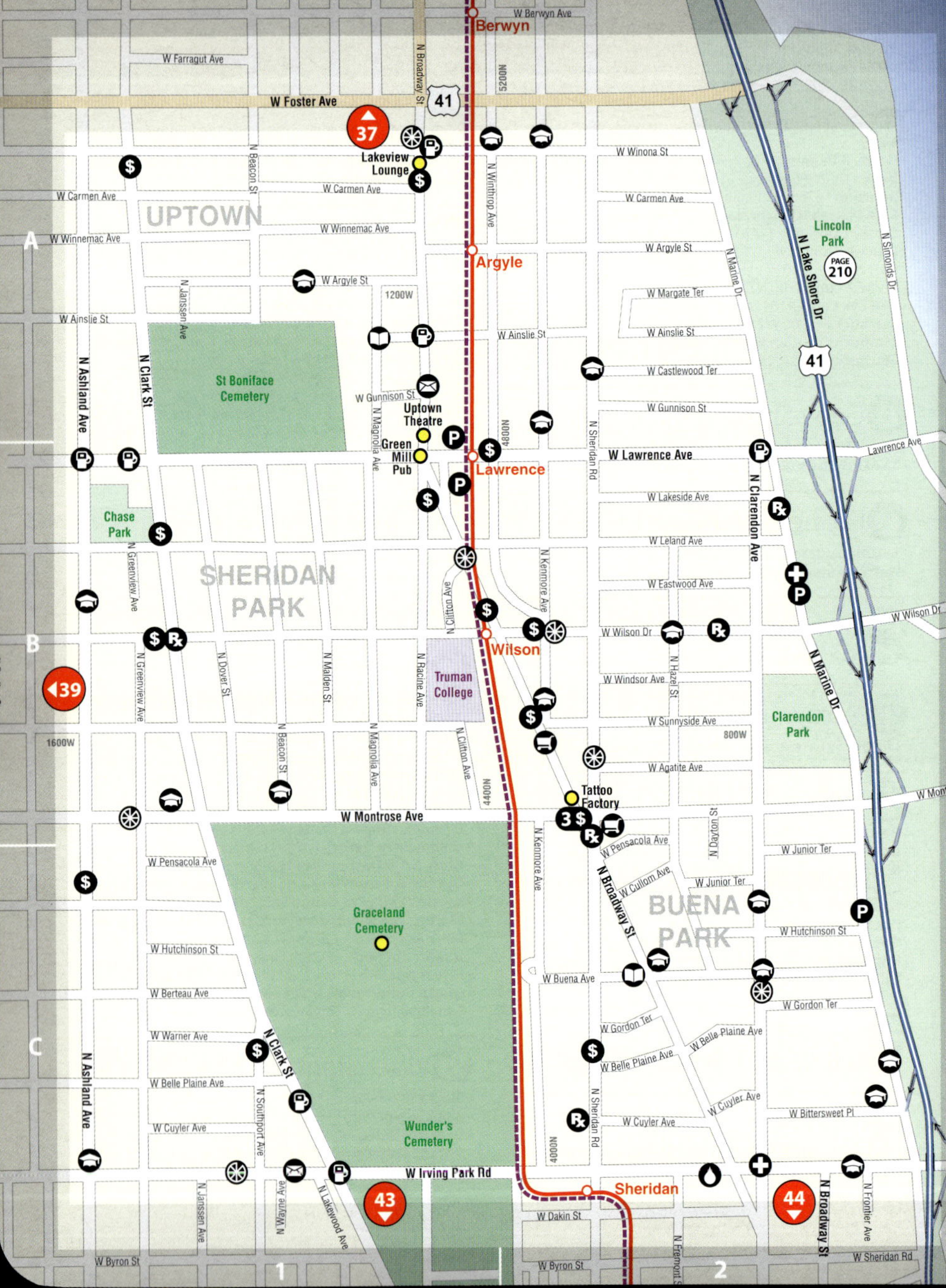
Berwyn
W Berwyn Ave
W Farragut Ave
N Broadway St
5200N
W Foster Ave
41
37
Lakeview Lounge
N Beacon St
W Carmen Ave
W Winona St
N Winthrop Ave
W Carmen Ave
UPTOWN
W Winnemac Ave
A
W Winnemac Ave
Argyle
W Argyle St
W Argyle St
N Marine Dr
N Lake Shore Dr
Lincoln Park
PAGE 210
N Simonds Dr
1200W
W Margate Ter
N Janssen Ave
W Ainslie St
W Ainslie St
W Ainslie St
41
N Ashland Ave
N Clark St
St Boniface Cemetery
W Castlewood Ter
W Gunnison St
Uptown Theatre
W Gunnison St
N Magnolia Ave
4800N
N Sheridan Rd
Green Mill Pub
Lawrence
W Lawrence Ave
Lawrence Ave
W Lakeside Ave
N Clarendon Ave
Chase Park
W Leland Ave
N Greenview Ave
SHERIDAN PARK
N Clifton Ave
N Kenmore Ave
W Eastwood Ave
W Wilson Dr
W Wilson Dr
B
Wilson
N Greenview Ave
N Dover St
N Malden St
N Racine Ave
Truman College
W Windsor Ave
N Hazel St
N Marine Dr
39
W Sunnyside Ave
800W
Clarendon Park
1600W
N Beacon St
N Magnolia Ave
N Clifton Ave
4400N
W Agatite Ave
Tattoo Factory
W Montrose Ave
W Mont
N Kenmore Ave
N Dayton St
W Pensacola Ave
W Pensacola Ave
W Junior Ter
W Cullom Ave
W Junior Ter
N Broadway St
BUENA PARK
Graceland Cemetery
W Hutchinson St
W Hutchinson St
W Berteau Ave
W Buena Ave
W Gordon Ter
W Gordon Ter
W Warner Ave
C
N Clark St
W Belle Plaine Ave
W Belle Plaine Ave
N Ashland Ave
W Belle Plaine Ave
N Southport Ave
N Sheridan Rd
W Cuyler Ave
W Cuyler Ave
W Bittersweet Pl
W Cuyler Ave
Wunder's Cemetery
4000N
W Irving Park Rd
Sheridan
N Janssen Ave
N Wayne Ave
N Lakewood Ave
43
44
N Broadway St
N Frontier Ave
W Dakin St
N Fremont St
W Byron St
W Byron St
W Sheridan Rd
1
2

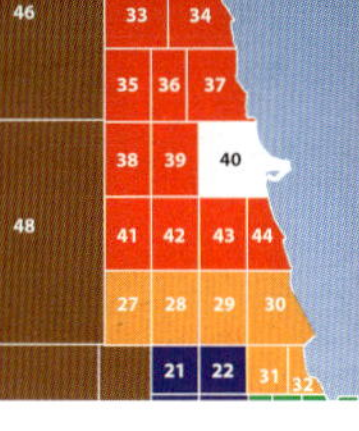

Politically, Uptown is divided between development-minded pro-gentrification guppies and grassroots, anti-gentrification hippies. Time will tell which group will prevail (though we have a guess...). Meanwhile, SOFO (the area defined by Argyle, Foster, Broadway, and Ashland) is where the gay and lesbian vibe of Andersonville bleeds southward towards somewhat more accessible rents and condo prices.

Banks

- **American Metro** • 4878 N Broadway St
- **Bank One** • 1101 W Lawrence Ave
- **Bank One** • 3956 N Sheridan Rd
- **Bank One** • 5134 N Clark St
- **Bank One (ATM)** • 1500 W Wilson Ave
- **Bridgeview** • 4753 N Broadway St
- **Bridgeview** • 5117 N Clark St
- **Charter One (ATM)** • 4116 N Clark St
- **Harris Trust & Savings** • 4531 N Broadway St
- **International Bank Of Chicago** • 5069 N Broadway St
- **Marquette** • 4322 Ashland Ave
- **North Community** • 4701 N Clark St
- **TCF** • 1050 W Wilson Ave
- **TCF** • 4355 N Sheridan Rd
- **TCF (ATM)** • 4106 N Sheridan Rd
- **Washington Mutual** • 4356 N Broadway St

Car Washes

- **Motor City Lube and Spa Detail** • 939 W Irving Park Rd

Gas Stations

- **Amoco** • 755 W Lawrence Ave
- **Citgo** • 1530 W Lawrence Ave
- **Citgo** • 4000 N Clark St
- **Gas City** • 4070 N Clark St
- **Marathon** • 5156 N Broadway St
- **Shell** • 4800 N Ashland Ave
- **Uptown Service Station** • 4900 N Broadway St

Hospitals

- **Louis A Weiss Memorial** • 4646 N Marine Dr
- **Thorek** • 850 W Irving Park Rd

Landmarks

- **Graceland Cemetery** • 4001 N Clark St
- **Green Mill Pub** • 4802 N Broadway St
- **Lakeview Lounge** • 5110 N Broadway St
- **Tattoo Factory** • 4408 N Broadway St
- **Uptown Theatre** • 4707 N Broadway St

Libraries

- **Bezazian Public Library** • 1226 W Ainslie St
- **Uptown Public Library** • 929 W Buena Ave

Parking

Pharmacies

- **Jewel-Osco** • 4355 N Sheridan Rd
- **Osco Drug** • 845 W Wilson Ave
- **Walgreens** • 1500 W Wilson Ave
- **Walgreens** • 4025 N Sheridan Rd
- **Walgreens** • 4646 N Marine Dr

Pizza

- **Bo Jono's Pizzeria** • 4185 N Clarendon Ave
- **Domino's** • 1415 W Irving Park Rd
- **Gigio's Pizzeria** • 4643 N Broadway St
- **Laurie's Pizzeria & Liquors** • 5153 N Broadway St
- **Pizza Factory** • 4443 N Sheridan Rd
- **Ranalli's Up North** • 1522 W Montrose Ave
- **Uptown Pizza** • 1031 W Wilson Ave

Post Offices

- 1343 W Irving Park Rd
- 4850 N Broadway St

Schools

- **Day School** • 800 W Buena Ave
- **Joan F Arai Middle** • 900 W Wilson Ave
- **John T McCutcheon Elementary** • 4865 N Sheridan Rd
- **Joseph Brennemann Elementary** • 4251 N Clarendon Ave
- **Lakeview High** • 4015 N Ashland Ave
- **Lycee Francais de Chicago** • 613 W Bittersweet Pl
- **Our Lady of Lourdes** • 4641 N Ashland Ave
- **Passages Elementary** • 1447 W Montrose Ave
- **Prologue High** • 640 W Irving Park Rd
- **St Augustine College** • 1333 W Argyle St
- **St Mary of the Lake Elementary** • 1026 W Buena Ave
- **St Thomas of Canterbury** • 4827 N Kenmore Ave
- **A Step Ahead Learning Center** • 4208 N Broadway St
- **Stewart Elementary** • 4525 N Kenmore Ave
- **Stockton Elementary** • 4420 N Beacon St
- **Truman College** • 1145 W Wilson Ave
- **Walt Disney Elementary** • 4140 N Marine Dr
- **William C Goudy Elementary** • 5120 N Winthrop Ave

Supermarkets

- **Aldi** • 4450 N Broadway St
- **Jewel-Osco** • 4355 N Sheridan Rd

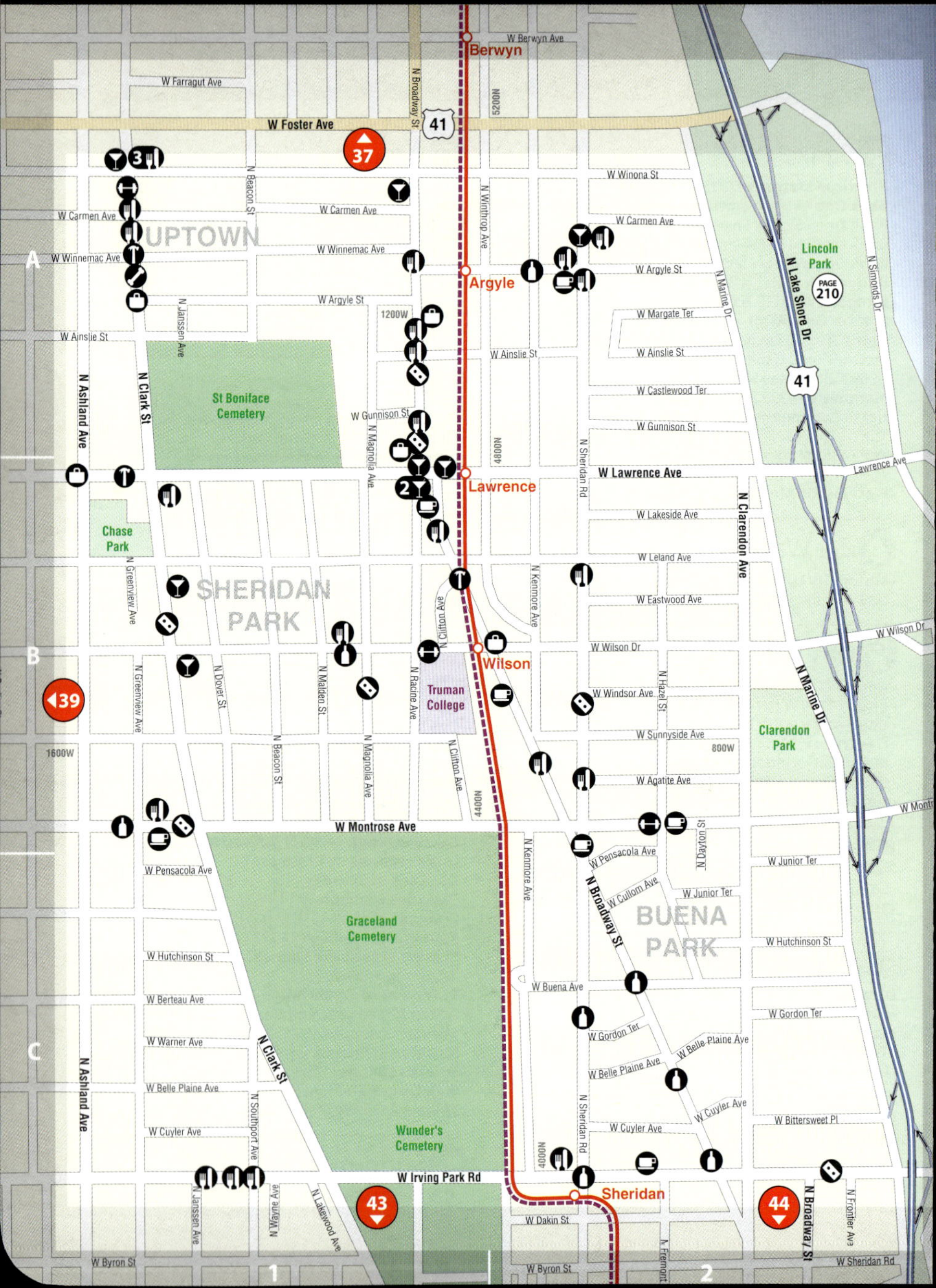

N

Berwyn
Argyle
Lawrence
Wilson
Sheridan

UPTOWN
SHERIDAN PARK
BUENA PARK

St Boniface Cemetery
Chase Park
Truman College
Graceland Cemetery
Wunder's Cemetery
Lincoln Park
Clarendon Park

W Berwyn Ave
W Farragut Ave
W Foster Ave
W Winona St
W Carmen Ave
W Winnemac Ave
W Argyle St
W Margate Ter
W Ainslie St
W Castlewood Ter
W Gunnison St
W Lawrence Ave
Lawrence Ave
W Lakeside Ave
W Leland Ave
W Eastwood Ave
W Wilson Dr
W Wilson Dr
W Windsor Ave
W Sunnyside Ave
W Agatite Ave
W Montrose Ave
W Montr
W Pensacola Ave
W Cullom Ave
W Junior Ter
W Hutchinson St
W Berteau Ave
W Buena Ave
W Gordon Ter
W Warner Ave
W Belle Plaine Ave
W Cuyler Ave
W Bittersweet Pl
W Irving Park Rd
W Dakin St
W Byron St
W Sheridan Rd

N Broadway St
N Winthrop Ave
N Beacon St
N Janssen Ave
N Ashland Ave
N Clark St
N Magnolia Ave
N Greenview Ave
N Dover St
N Malden St
N Racine Ave
N Clifton Ave
N Kenmore Ave
N Sheridan Rd
N Hazel St
N Dayton St
N Clarendon Ave
N Marine Dr
N Lake Shore Dr
N Simonds Dr
N Southport Ave
N Wayne Ave
N Lakewood Ave
N Fremont
N Frontier Ave

5200N
4800N
4400N
4000N
1200W
1600W
800W

41

37
39
43
44
PAGE 210

A
B
C
1
2

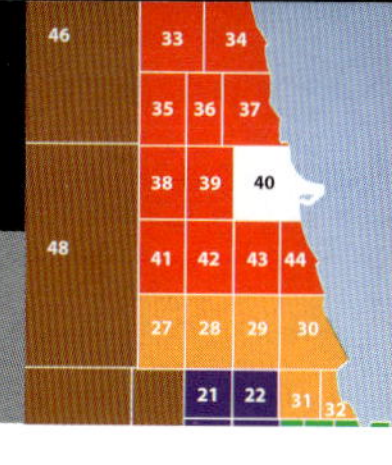

The nightlife of SOFO (South of Foster) is hopping. Standbys such as the Green Mill (famed for gangland connections and the Sunday night poetry slam) and Big Chicks (a favored gay neighborhood bar with superb art collection) have long drawn folks to uptown. Now diners flock to Tweet, Hama Matsu, and Hopleaf (which also serves up an impressive selection of Belgian beer). Hey—be careful walking around drunk and/or alone at night. Parts of this 'hood are still rather sketchy.

Coffee

- **Corona's Coffee Shop** • 909 W Irving Park Rd
- **Dunkin' Donuts** • 1441 W Montrose Ave
- **Dunkin' Donuts** • 4547 N Broadway St
- **New Chinatown Bakery & Coffee Shop** • 1019 W Argyle St
- **Starbucks** • 4355 N Sheridan Rd
- **Starbucks** • 4753 N Broadway St
- **Urban Tea Lounge** • 838 W Montrose Ave

Gyms

- **Curves** • 1144 W Wilson Ave
- **Know No Limits** • 5121 N Clark St
- **World Gym Fitness Center** • 909 W Montrose Ave

Hardware Stores

- **Andersonville Hardware** • 5036 N Clark St
- **Crafty Beaver Home Center** • 1522 W Lawrence Ave
- **Uptown Ace Hardware** • 4654 N Broadway St

Liquor Stores

- **GNS Food & Liquor** • 4092 N Broadway St
- **Laurie's Pizzeria & Liquors** • 5153 N Broadway St
- **Manhattan Liquors** • 4200 N Broadway St
- **Rayan's Discount Liquors** • 1532 W Montrose Ave
- **Sheridan Park Food & Liquor** • 1255 W Wilson Ave
- **Sheridan-Irving Liquor** • 3944 N Sheridan Rd
- **Thomas Food & Liquor** • 4141 N Sheridan Rd
- **Wine Store** • 1040 W Argyle St

Nightlife

- **Big Chicks** • 5024 N Sheridan Rd
- **Carol's Pub** • 4659 N Clark St
- **Crew Bar & Grill** • 4804 N Broadway St
- **Green Mill Pub** • 4802 N Broadway St
- **Hopleaf** • 5148 N Clark St
- **Joy-Blue** • 3998 N Southport Ave
- **Lakeview Lounge** • 5110 N Broadway St
- **Riveria** • 4746 N Racine Ave
- **T's** • 5025 N Clark St
- **The Uptown Lounge** • 1136 W Lawrence Ave

Pet Shops

- **Chicago Aquarium** • 5028 N Clark St

Restaurants

- **Andie's** • 1467 W Montrose Ave
- **Atlantique** • 5101 N Clark St
- **Bale French Bakery** • 5018 N Broadway St
- **Deleece** • 4004 N Southport Ave
- **Don Quijote** • 4761 N Clark St
- **Frankie J's, An American Theatre and Grill** • 4437 N Broadway St
- **Furama** • 4936 N Broadway St
- **Golden House Restaurant** • 4744 N Broadway St
- **Hama Matsu** • 5143 N Clark
- **Holiday Club** • 4000 N Sheridan Rd
- **Jim's Grill** • 1429 W Irving Pk
- **La Donna** • 5146 N Clark St
- **Magnolia Café** • 1224 W Wilson Ave
- **Pho Xe Tang** • 1007 W Argyle
- **Riques** • 5004 N Sheridan Rd
- **Siam Noodle & Rice** • 4654 N Sheridan Rd
- **Silver Seafood** • 4829 N Broadway St
- **Smoke Country House** • 1465 W Irving Park Rd
- **Thai Pastry and Restaurants** • 4925 N Broadway St
- **Tokyo Marina** • 5058 N Clark St
- **Tweet** • 5020 N Sheridan Rd

Shopping

- **Arcadia Knitting** • 1613 W Lawrence Ave
- **Eagle Leathers** • 5005 N Clark St
- **Shake Rattle and Read Book Box** • 4812 N Broadway St
- **Tai Nam Market Center** • 4925 N Broadway St
- **Wilson Broadway Mall** • 1114 W Wilson Ave

Video Rental

- **Albert Video** • 1435 W Montrose Ave
- **Blockbuster Video** • 4620 N Clark St
- **Hollywood Video** • 4883 N Broadway St
- **Line Video** • 4554 N Magnolia Ave
- **Nationwide Video** • 736 W Irving Park Rd
- **Suan Thu (Vietnamese)** • 4820 N Broadway St
- **United Video** • 4519 N Sheridan Rd
- **Vietnam Video (Vietnamese/Chinese)** • 4820 N Broadway St

N

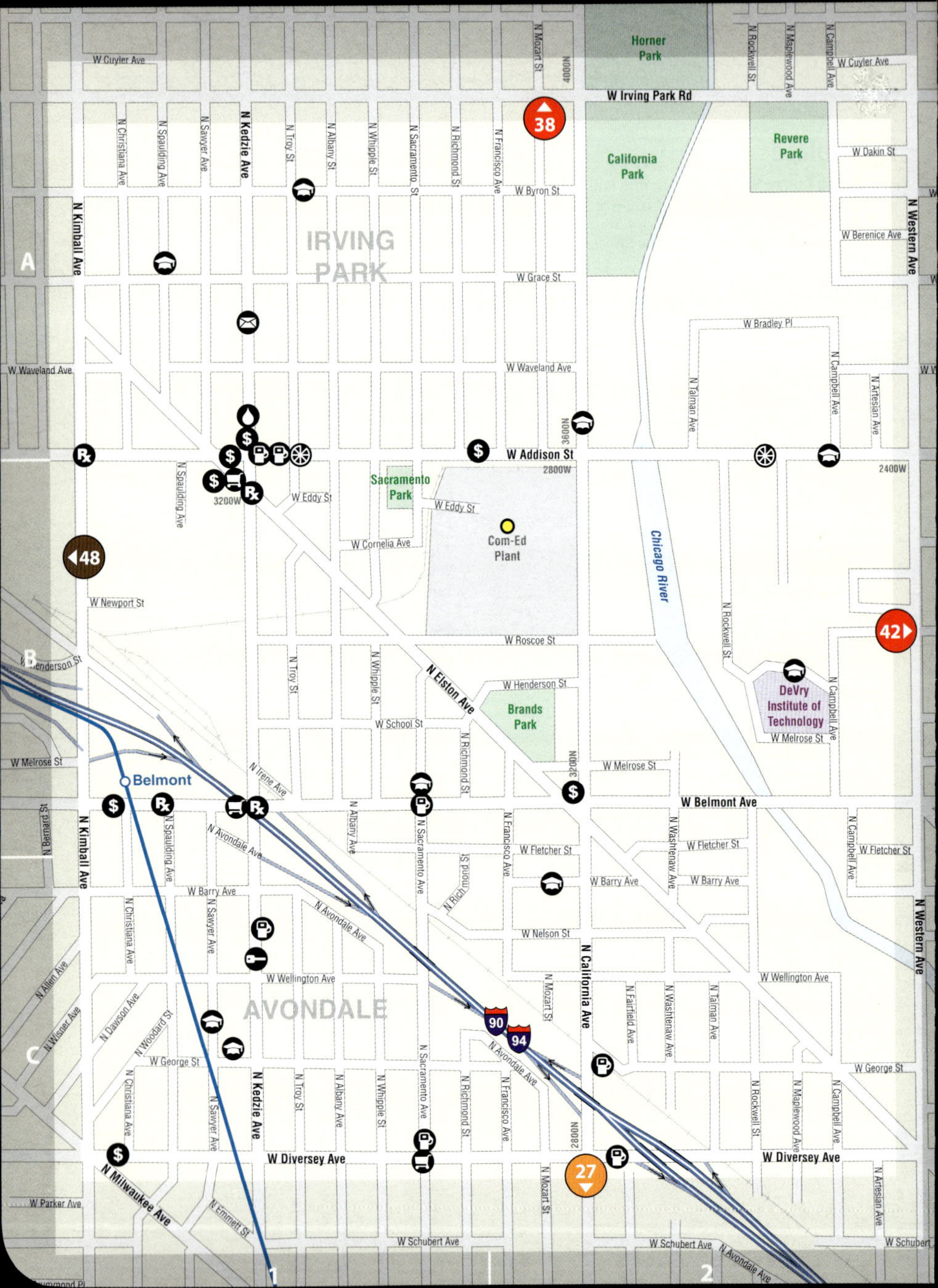

IRVING PARK
AVONDALE
Horner Park
California Park
Revere Park
Sacramento Park
Brands Park
Com-Ed Plant
DeVry Institute of Technology
Chicago River
Belmont
W Irving Park Rd
W Addison St
W Belmont Ave
W Diversey Ave
N Elston Ave
N Milwaukee Ave
N Kedzie Ave
N California Ave
N Western Ave
N Kimball Ave
W Cuyler Ave
W Byron St
W Grace St
W Waveland Ave
W Eddy St
W Cornelia Ave
W Newport St
W Roscoe St
W Henderson St
W School St
W Melrose St
W Fletcher St
W Barry Ave
W Nelson St
W Wellington Ave
W George St
W Parker Ave
W Schubert Ave
W Dakin St
W Berenice Ave
W Bradley Pl
N Avondale Ave
N Irene Ave
38
42
48
27
90
94
4000N
3600N
3200N
2800N
3200W
2800W
2400W
A
B
C
1
2

If hipster sightings are any indication, blue-collar Avondale is positioning itself as the new frontier of north-side gentrification. Roscoe Villagers and Logan Square residents branch ever outward, searching for affordable housing and elusive street parking. Old Irving streets are lined with stately historic homes and fast food joints.

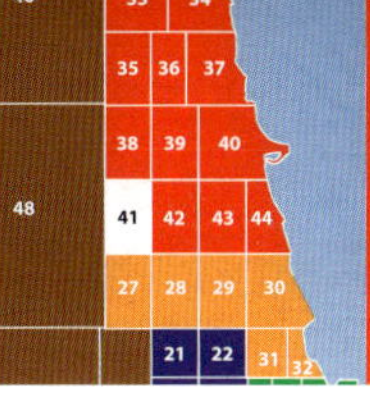

Banks

- **Bank One** • 3227 W Addison St
- **Harris Trust & Savings** • 2927 W Addison St
- **LaSalle** • 3350 W Diversey Ave
- **North Community** • 2758 W Belmont Ave
- **TCF** • Jewel, 3570 N Elston Ave
- **US** • 3611 N Kedzie Ave
- **Washington Mutual** • 3339 W Belmont Ave

Car Washes

- **123 Hand Car Wash** • 3635 N Kedzie Ave

Car Rental

- **Enterprise** • 3029 N Kedzie Ave • 773-478-3310

Gas Stations

- **Citgo** • 2920 N California Ave
- **Citgo** • 3001 W Belmont Ave
- **James Standard Service** • 3201 W Addison St
- **Marathon** • 3057 N Kedzie Ave
- **Martin** • 2811 N Sacramento Ave
- **Mobil** • 2801 W Diversey Ave
- **Shell** • 3159 W Addison St

Landmarks

- **Com-Ed Plant** • N California Ave & W Roscoe St

Pharmacies

- **CVS Pharmacy (24 hours)** • 3411 W Addison St
- **Dominick's** • 3300 W Belmont Ave
- **Jewel-Osco** • 3572 N Elston Ave
- **Walgreens** • 3302 W Belmont Ave

Pizza

- **Little Caesar's Pizza** • 3135 W Addison St
- **Pipo's Pizza** • 2550 W Addison St

Post Offices

- 3750 N Kedzie Ave

Schools

- **Albert G Lane Tech** • 2501 W Addison St
- **Avondale Elementary** • 2945 N Sawyer Ave
- **Carl Von Linne Elementary** • 3221 N Sacramento Ave
- **DeVry Institute of Technology** • 3300 N Campbell Ave
- **Gordon Technical High** • 3633 N California Ave
- **Grover Cleveland Elementary** • 3121 W Byron St
- **Immaculate Heart of Mary** • 3820 N Spaulding Ave
- **Logandale Middle** • 3212 W George St
- **Resurrection Catholic Academy** • 2845 W Barry Ave

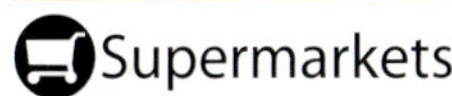

Supermarkets

- **Dominick's** • 3300 W Belmont Ave
- **Jewel Osco** • 3570 N Elston Ave
- **Naseen Food Market** • 3001 W Diversey Ave

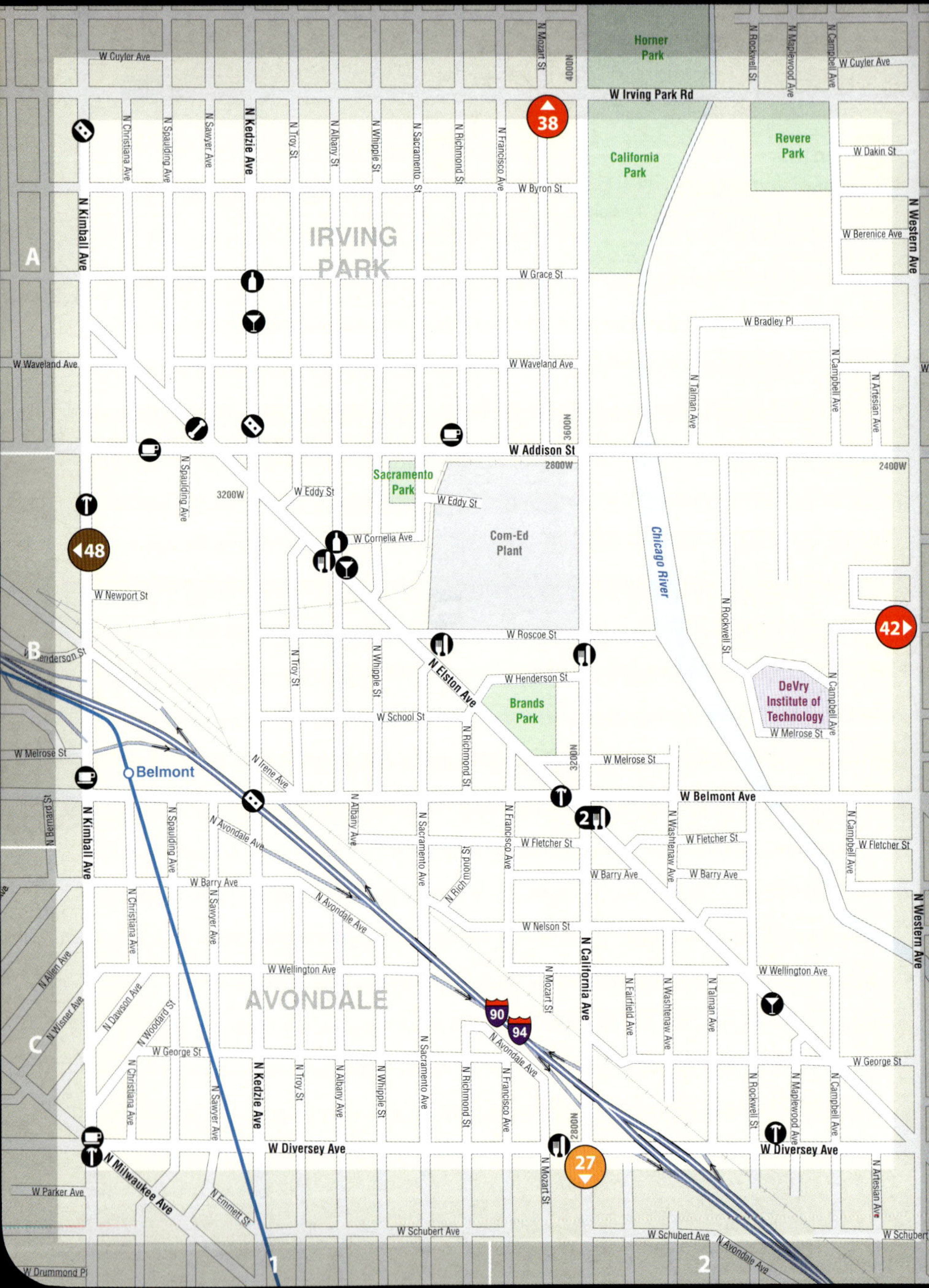

Map 41 • Avondale / Old Irving

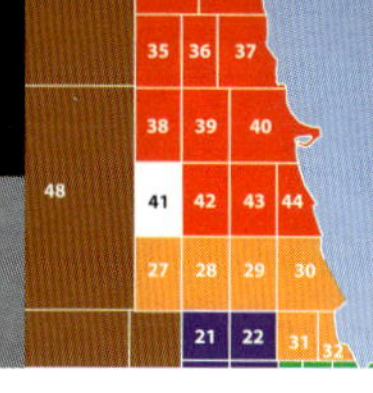

The Polish and Puerto Rican communities comingle in the local taverns dotting every corner. Younger crowds catch live Celtic music at Chief O'Neills or sip cosmos and bob their heads to techno music at N. Taqueria Trespazada has some of the best greasy Mexican take-out in town, or you can sit down and sip a margarita at homey La Finca.

Coffee

- **Dunkin' Donuts** • 3214 N Kimball Ave
- **Dunkin' Donuts** • 3310 W Addison St
- **Dunkin' Donuts** • 3427 W Diversey Ave
- **Starbucks (Target)** • 2939 W Addison St

Hardware Stores

- **Cobey True Value Hardware** • 3429 W Diversey Ave
- **Elston Ace Hardware** • 2825 W Belmont Ave
- **Home Depot** • 3500 N Kimball Ave
- **Kabbe True Value Hardware** • 2550 W Diversey Ave

Liquor Stores

- **Discount Store** • 3457 N Albany Ave
- **JJ Peppers** • 3201 W Diversey Ave

Nightlife

- **Chief O'Neill's** • 3471 N Elston Ave
- **Christina's Place** • 3759 N Kedzie Ave
- **N** • 2977 N Elston Ave

Pet Shops

- **Pet Supplies Plus** • 3640 N Elston Ave

Restaurants

- **Chief O'Neill's** • 3471 N Elston Ave
- **Clara's** • 3159 N California Ave
- **Hot Doug's** • 3324 N California Ave
- **IHOP** • 2818 W Diversey Ave
- **La Finca** • 3361 N Elston Ave
- **Taqueria Trespazada** • 3144 N California Ave

Video Rental

- **Blockbuster Video** • 3233 W Addison St
- **Blockbuster Video** • 3326 W Belmont Ave
- **Blockbuster Video** • 3951 N Kimball Ave

A
B
C
1
2
NORTH CENTER
ROSCOE VILLAGE
LAKEVIEW
Revere Park
DeVry Institute of Technology
Gross Park
Hamlin Park
Chicago River
Irving Park
Addison
Paulina
39
41
43
28
W Belle Plaine Ave
W Cuyler Ave
W Irving Park Rd
W Larchmont Ave
W Dakin St
W Byron St
W Berenice Ave
W Grace St
W Bradley Pl
W Waveland Ave
W Patterson Ave
W Addison St
W Eddy St
W Cornelia Ave
W Newport Ave
W Roscoe St
W Henderson St
W School St
W Melrose St
W Belmont Ave
W Fletcher St
W Barry Ave
W Nelson St
W Wellington Ave
W Oakdale Ave
W George St
W Wolfram St
W Diversey Ave
W Schubert Ave
N Logan Blvd
N Clybourn Ave
N Lincoln Ave
N Maplewood Ave
N Campbell Ave
N Western Ave
N Artesian Ave
N Claremont Ave
N Oakley Ave
N Bell Ave
N Rockwell St
N Leavitt St
N Hamilton Ave
N Hoyne Ave
N Seeley Ave
N Damen Ave
N Wolcott Ave
N Ravenswood Ave
N Hermitage Ave
N Paulina St
N Marshfield Ave
N Ashland Ave
N Bosworth Ave
N Greenview Ave
N Honore St
4000N
3600N
3200N
2800N
2400W
2000W
1600W

Essentials

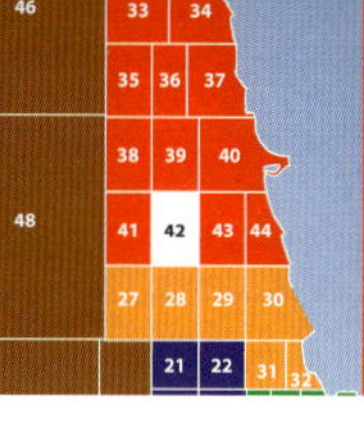

The busy intersection of Western and Belmont was the grounds for Riverview Park, once the world's largest amusement park. Now it's a playground filled with funky bars, clubs, and trendy restaurants. Within this recently gentrified area is small but popular Roscoe Village.

Banks

- **Bank of America (ATM)** • 3435 N Western Ave
- **Bank One** • 3531 N Western Ave
- **Bank One** • 3868 N Lincoln Ave
- **Bank One (ATM)** • 1649 W Belmont Ave
- **Charter One (ATM)** • 3350 N Western Ave
- **Harris Trust & Savings (ATM)** • 3354 N Damen Ave
- **Lincoln Park Savings** • 3234 N Damen Ave
- **North Community** • 2800 N Western Ave
- **North Community** • 3401 N Western Ave
- **TCF** • Jewel, 3400 N Western Ave
- **Washington Mutual** • 3348 N Western Ave

Car Washes

- **Ultra Sonic Car Wash** • 3650 N Western Ave

Car Rental

- **Enterprise** • 3844 N Western Ave • 773-539-5900
- **Priceless** • 3535 N Lincoln Ave • 773-836-8888

Gas Stations

- **BP/Amoco** • 3955 N Western Ave
- **Citgo** • 2401 W Diversey Ave
- **Gas for Less** • 2801 N Damen Ave
- **Marathon** • 3145 N Western Ave

Libraries

- **Lincoln-Belmont Public Library** • 1659 W Melrose St

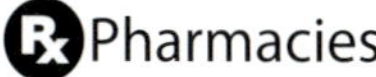

Pharmacies

- **CVS Pharmacy (24 hours)** • 2815 N Western Ave
- **CVS Pharmacy (24 hours)** • 3944 N Western Ave
- **Dominick's** • 3350 N Western Ave
- **Jewel-Osco** • 3400 N Western Ave
- **Walgreens** • 1649 W Belmont Ave
- **Walgreens** • 3358 N Western Ave

Pizza

- **Dominick's Finer Foods** • 3350 N Western Ave
- **Pete's Pizza** • 3737 N Western Ave
- **Robey Pizza** • 1954 W Roscoe St

Police

- **19th District (Belmont)** • 2452 W Belmont Ave

Schools

- **Alex Bell Elementary** • 3730 N Oakley Ave
- **Alexander Hamilton Elementary** • 1650 W Cornelia Ave
- **Friedrich L Jahn Elementary** • 3149 N Wolcott Ave
- **George Schneider Elementary** • 2957 N Hoyne Ave
- **John L Audubon Elementary** • 3500 N Hoyne Ave
- **St Andrew Elementary** • 1710 W Addison St
- **St Benedict High** • 3900 N Leavitt St
- **St Benedict Middle** • 3920 N Leavitt St

Supermarkets

- **Dominick's** • 3350 N Western Ave
- **Jewel-Osco** • 3400 N Western Ave
- **Paulina Meat Market** • 3501 N Lincoln Ave
- **Trader Joe's** • 3745 N Lincoln Ave

NORTH CENTER
ROSCOE VILLAGE
LAKEVIEW
Revere Park
DeVry Institute of Technology
Gross Park
Hamlin Park
Chicago River
Irving Park
Addison
Paulina
39
41
43
28
W Irving Park Rd
W Addison St
W Belmont Ave
W Diversey Ave
N Western Ave
N Damen Ave
N Ashland Ave
N Lincoln Ave
N Clybourn Ave
W Belle Plaine Ave
W Cuyler Ave
W Dakin St
W Larchmont Ave
W Byron St
W Berenice Ave
W Grace St
W Bradley Pl
W Waveland Ave
W Patterson Ave
W Eddy St
W Cornelia Ave
W Newport Ave
W Roscoe St
W Henderson St
W School St
W Melrose St
W Fletcher St
W Barry Ave
W Nelson St
W Wellington Ave
W Oakdale Ave
W George St
W Wolfram St
W Schubert Ave
N Logan Blvd
N Maplewood Ave
N Campbell Ave
N Rockwell St
N Artesian Ave
N Claremont Ave
N Oakley Ave
N Bell Ave
N Leavitt St
N Hamilton Ave
N Hoyne Ave
N Seeley Ave
N Wolcott Ave
N Ravenswood Ave
N Hermitage Ave
N Paulina St
N Marshfield Ave
N Bosworth Ave
N Greenview Ave
N Honore St
4000N
3600N
3200N
2800N
2400W
2000W
1600W
A
B
C
1
2

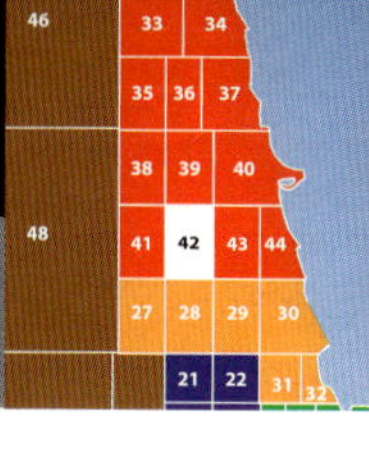

Restaurant Row is Roscoe Avenue between Damen and Western. While there are lots of new eateries to choose from, we still like The Village Tap. Pull up a bar stool for good grease and cold beer and jaw a while. Belmont Avenue between Ashland and Western is lined with antique shops.

Coffee

- **Dinkel's Bakery** • 3329 N Lincoln Ave
- **Dunkin' Donuts** • 1755 W Addison St
- **Dunkin' Donuts** • 3535 N Western Ave
- **Mojoe's Café Lounge** • 2256 W Roscoe St
- **Starbucks** • 1700 W Diversey Pkwy
- **Starbucks** • 2023 W Roscoe St
- **Starbucks** • 2159 W Belmont Ave
- **Starbucks** • 3350 N Lincoln Ave
- **Starbucks** • 3356 N Lincoln Ave
- **Starbucks (Albertsons)** • 3400 N Western Ave
- **Su Van's Café and Bake Shop** • 3351 Lincoln Ave
- **Thai Linda Café** • 2022 W Roscoe St

Copy Shops

- **Kinko's (6 am-10 pm)** • 3435 N Western Ave

Farmer's Markets

- **Roscoe Village** • W Belmont Ave & N Wolcott Ave

Gyms

- **Curves** • 2037 W Roscoe St
- **Lakeview YMCA** • 3333 N Marshfield Ave

Hardware Stores

- **Staubers Ace Hardware** • 3911 N Lincoln Ave

Liquor Stores

- **Armanetti Wine Shop** • 3530 N Lincoln Ave
- **Damen Food & Liquor** • 1956 W School St
- **Grace & Leavitt Liquors** • 2157 W Grace St
- **Miller's Tap & Liquor Store** • 2204 W Roscoe St
- **Miska's Liquor** • 2156 W Belmont Ave
- **Pelly's Liquors** • 3444 N Lincoln Ave
- **R&S Liquor** • 2425 W Diversey Ave
- **West Lakeview Liquors** • 2156 W Addison St

Nightlife

- **Art of Sports** • 2444 W Diversey Ave
- **Beat Kitchen** • 2100 W Belmont Ave
- **Black Rock** • 3614 N Damen Ave
- **Cabo Grill** • 3407 N Paulina
- **Cody's Public House** • 1658 W Barry Ave
- **Four Moon Tavern** • 1847 W Roscoe St
- **Four Treys** • 3333 N Damen Ave
- **G&L Fire Escape** • 2157 W Grace St
- **Hungry Brain** • 2319 W Belmont Ave
- **Martyrs'** • 3855 N Lincoln Ave
- **Mulligan's Public House** • 2000 W Roscoe St
- **Riverview Tavern & Restaurant** • 1958 W Roscoe St
- **Seanchai** • 2345 W Belmont Ave
- **Tiny Lounge** • 1814 W Addison St
- **The Village Tap** • 2055 W Roscoe St
- **Xippo** • 3759 N Damen Ave

Restaurants

- **Brett's Café Americain** • 2011 W Roscoe St
- **Costello Sandwich & Sides** • 2015 W Roscoe St
- **El Tinajon** • 2054 W Roscoe St
- **Four Moon Tavern** • 1847 W Roscoe St
- **Kaze Sushi** • 2032 W Roscoe
- **Kitsch'n on Roscoe** • 2005 W Roscoe St
- **La Mora** • 2132 W Roscoe St
- **Lee's Chop Suey** • 2415 W Diversey Ave
- **Piazza Bella Trattoria** • 2116 W Roscoe St
- **Riverview Tavern & Grill** • 1958 W Roscoe St
- **Thai Linda Café** • 2022 W Roscoe St
- **Victory's Banner** • 2100 W Roscoe St
- **The Village Tap** • 2055 W Roscoe St
- **Wishbone** • 3300 N Lincoln Ave

Shopping

- **Antique Resources** • 1741 W Belmont Ave
- **Father Time Antiques** • 2108 W Belmont Ave
- **Glam to Go** • 2002 W Roscoe St
- **Good Old Days Antiques** • 2138 W Belmont Ave
- **Lynn's Hallmark** • 3353 N Lincoln Ave
- **My Closet** • 3350 N Paulina St
- **Sam & Willy's** • 3405 N Paulina St

Video Rental

- **Blockbuster Video** • 1645 W School St
- **Blockbuster Video** • 3322 N Western Ave
- **Hard Boiled Records and Video** • 2010 W Roscoe St

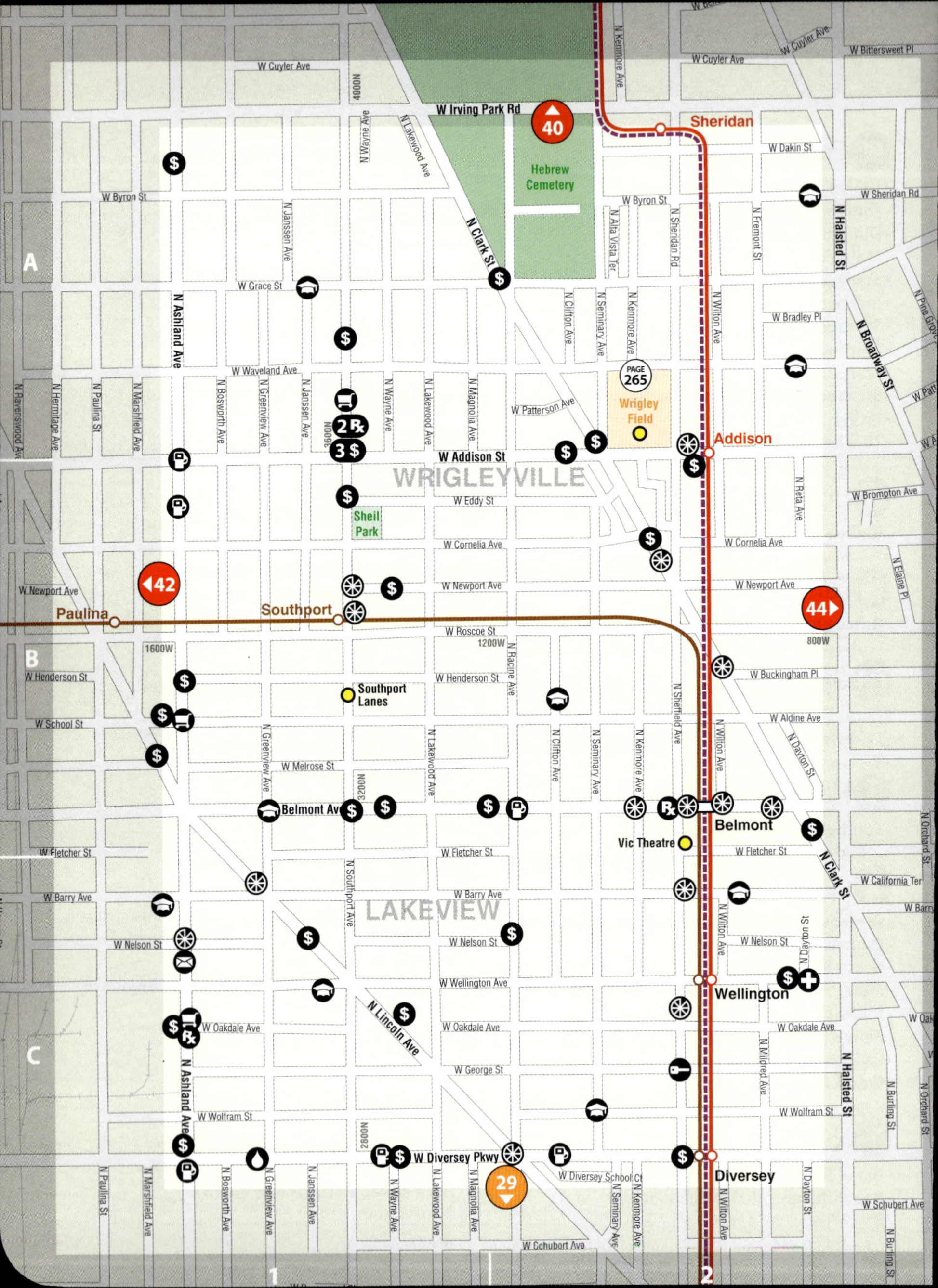

N

WRIGLEYVILLE
LAKEVIEW

Hebrew Cemetery
Wrigley Field
PAGE 265
Sheil Park
Southport Lanes
Vic Theatre

Sheridan
Addison
Belmont
Wellington
Diversey
Paulina
Southport

40
42
44
29

A
B
C
1
2

W Irving Park Rd
W Cuyler Ave
W Bittersweet Pl
W Dakin St
W Sheridan Rd
W Byron St
W Grace St
W Bradley Pl
W Waveland Ave
W Patterson Ave
W Addison St
W Eddy St
W Brompton Ave
W Cornelia Ave
W Newport Ave
W Roscoe St
W Henderson St
W Buckingham Pl
W School St
W Aldine Ave
W Melrose St
Belmont Ave
W Fletcher St
W Barry Ave
W California Ter
W Nelson St
W Wellington Ave
W Oakdale Ave
W George St
W Wolfram St
W Diversey Pkwy
W Diversey School Ct
W Schubert Ave

N Clark St
N Lakewood Ave
N Wayne Ave
N Janssen Ave
N Kenmore Ave
N Alta Vista Ter
N Sheridan Rd
N Fremont St
N Halsted St
N Broadway St
N Pine Grove
N Clifton Ave
N Seminary Ave
N Wilton Ave
N Ashland Ave
N Ravenswood Ave
N Hermitage Ave
N Paulina St
N Marshfield Ave
N Bosworth Ave
N Greenview Ave
N Magnolia Ave
N Racine Ave
N Sheffield Ave
N Reta Ave
N Elaine Pl
N Dayton St
N Southport Ave
N Lincoln Ave
N Mildred Ave
N Orchard St
N Burling St

4000N
3900N
3200N
2800N
1600W
1200W
800W

Essentials

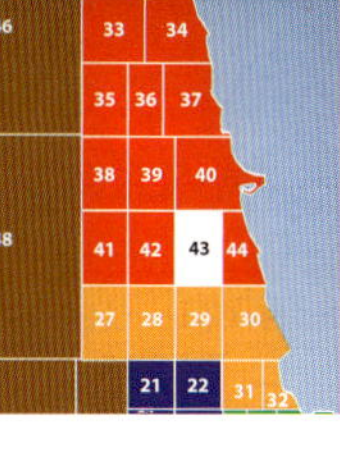

Pleasant, pretty streets belie atrocious traffic and parking, as well as the constant summertime disturbance of drunken Cubs fans roaming the streets and urinating in alleys and doorways. On the plus side, residents don't have to travel far for anything—tons of good restaurants, a variety of nightlife, the lakefront, and loads of services from groceries to video rentals cram into this youthful 'hood.

Banks

- **Bank One** • 1240 W Belmont Ave
- **Bank One** • 2968 N Lincoln Ave
- **Bank One** • 3335 N Ashland Ave
- **Bank One** • 3730 N Southport Ave
- **Bank One (ATM)** • 940 W Addison St
- **Charter One** • 3066 N Lincoln Ave
- **Charter One** • 3948 N Ashland Ave
- **Charter One (ATM)** • 958 W Diversey Pkwy
- **Citibank** • 3620 N Clark St
- **Corus** • 3179 N Clark St
- **Corus** • 3604 N Southport Ave
- **First American** • 1345 W Diversey Pkwy
- **Lakeside** • 2800 N Ashland Ave
- **LaSalle** • 3201 N Ashland Ave
- **LaSalle** • 3301 N Ashland Ave
- **North Community** • 1401 W Belmont Ave
- **Northern Trust (ATM)** • 836 W Wellington Ave
- **TCF** • Jewel, 2940 N Ashland Ave
- **TCF** • Jewel, 3630 N Southport Ave
- **TCF (ATM)** • 1344 W Newport Ave
- **TCF (ATM)** • 1362 W Belmont Ave
- **TCF (ATM)** • 3056 N Racine Ave
- **TCF (ATM)** • 3800 N Clark St
- **TCF (ATM)** • Osco, 3637 N Southport Ave
- **TCF (ATM)** • Taco Bell, 1111 W Addison St
- **Washington Mutual** • 3252 N Lincoln Ave
- **Washington Mutual** • 3500 N Clark St
- **Washington Mutual** • 3556 N Southport Ave

Car Rental

- **Enterprise** • 2900 N Sheffield Ave • 773-880-5001

Car Washes

- **We'll Clean** • 1515 W Diversey Pkwy

Gas Stations

- **Amoco** • 1200 W Belmont Ave
- **BP** • 1355 W Diversey Pkwy
- **Citgo** • 3600 N Ashland Ave
- **Shell** • 1160 W Diversey Pkwy
- **Shell** • 2801 N Ashland Ave
- **Shell** • 3552 N Ashland Ave

Hospitals

- **Advocate Illinois Masonic Medical Center** • 836 W Wellington Ave

Landmarks

- **Southport Lanes** • 3325 N Southport Ave
- **Vic Theatre** • 3145 N Sheffield Ave
- **Wrigley Field** • 1060 W Addison St

Pharmacies

- **Jewel** • 3630 N Southport Ave
- **Jewel-Osco** • 2940 N Ashland Ave
- **Osco Drug** • 3637 N Southport Ave
- **Walgreens** • 1001 W Belmont Ave

Pizza

- **Art of Pizza** • 3033 N Ashland Ave
- **Bacci Pizzeria** • 950 W Addison St
- **Chicago's Pizza & Pasta** • 3114 N Lincoln Ave
- **Gino's East of Chicago** • 2801 N Lincoln Ave
- **Giordano's** • 1040 W Belmont Ave
- **Homemade Pizza Co** • 3430 N Southport Ave
- **Leona's** • 3215 N Sheffield Ave
- **Pat's Pizzeria** • 3114 N Sheffield Ave
- **Philly's Best** • 907 W Belmont Ave
- **Pizano's Pizza & Pasta** • 3466 N Clark St
- **Pizza Capri** • 962 W Belmont Ave
- **Pompeii Bakery** • 2955 N Sheffield Ave
- **Red Tomato** • 3417 N Southport Ave

Post Offices

- 3024 N Ashland Ave

Schools

- **Augustus H Burley Elementary** • 1630 W Barry Ave
- **Hawthorne Scholastic Academy** • 3319 N Clifton Ave
- **Horace Greeley Elementary** • 832 W Sheridan Rd
- **Inter-American Elementary** • 919 W Barry Ave
- **James G Blaine Elementary** • 1420 W Grace St
- **John V LeMoyne Elementary** • 851 W Waveland Ave
- **Louis J Agassiz Elementary** • 2851 N Seminary Ave
- **St Alphonsus Academy** • 1439 W Wellington Ave
- **St Luke Academy** • 1500 W Belmont Ave

Supermarkets

- **Jewel** • 3630 N Southport Ave
- **Jewel-Osco** • 2940 N Ashland Ave
- **Whole Foods Market** • 3300 N Ashland Ave

N
WRIGLEYVILLE
LAKEVIEW
Hebrew Cemetery
Wrigley Field
PAGE 265
Sheil Park
Sheridan
Addison
Belmont
Wellington
Diversey
Paulina
Southport
40
42
44
29
A
B
C
1
2
W Cuyler Ave
W Irving Park Rd
W Byron St
W Grace St
W Waveland Ave
W Addison St
W Eddy St
W Cornelia Ave
W Newport Ave
W Roscoe St
W Henderson St
W School St
W Melrose St
W Belmont Ave
W Fletcher St
W Barry Ave
W Nelson St
W Wellington Ave
W Oakdale Ave
W George St
W Wolfram St
W Diversey Pkwy
W Diversey School Ct
W Schubert Ave
W Patterson Ave
W Dakin St
W Sheridan Rd
W Bittersweet Pl
W Bradley Pl
W Brompton Ave
W Buckingham Pl
W Aldine Ave
W California Ter
N Ashland Ave
N Clark St
N Lincoln Ave
N Halsted St
N Broadway St
N Sheffield Ave
N Sheridan Rd
N Wilton Ave
N Kenmore Ave
N Seminary Ave
N Clifton Ave
N Racine Ave
N Magnolia Ave
N Lakewood Ave
N Wayne Ave
N Janssen Ave
N Greenview Ave
N Bosworth Ave
N Marshfield Ave
N Paulina St
N Hermitage Ave
N Ravenswood Ave
N Southport Ave
N Alta Vista Ter
N Fremont St
N Reta Ave
N Elaine Pl
N Dayton St
N Mildred Ave
N Burling St
N Orchard St
4000N
3600N
3200N
2800N
1600W
1200W
800W

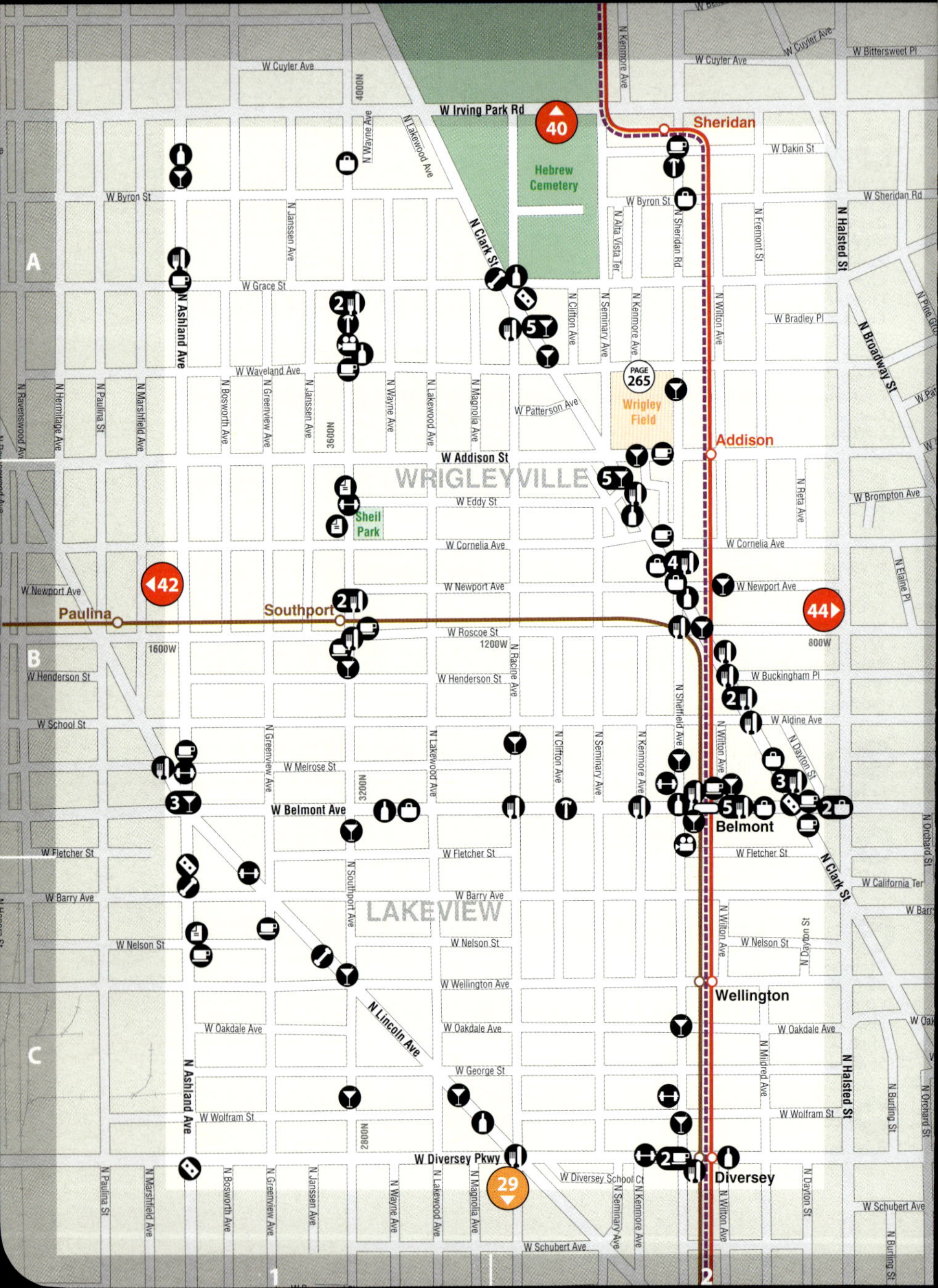

Sundries / Entertainment

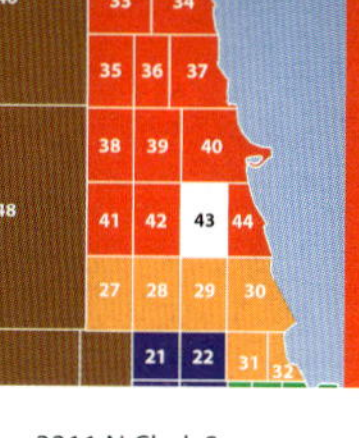

Live music venue Metro has been rocking the area for 25 + years. The beautiful Music Box Theatre is the place to go for art house films—especially on weekends when they feature a live organist (their occasional sing-a-longs to musicals are also big hits). Spice lovers (and silverware haters) know to gnaw at Mama Desta's Red Sea Ethiopian restaurant. Touristy spots near the ballpark all cater to Cubs fans—caveat emptor. Further south at Clark and Belmont is the Punkin' Donuts—prime hang-out area for the city's pierced and pouty youth.

Coffee

- **Café Avanti** • 3706 N Southport Ave
- **Caribou Coffee** • 3240 N Ashland Ave
- **Dunkin' Donuts** • 3000 N Ashland Ave
- **Dunkin' Donuts** • 3200 N Clark St
- **Einstein Bros Bagels** • 3420 N Southport Ave
- **Einstein Bros Bagels** • 3455 N Clark St
- **Einstein Bros Bagels** • 949 W Diversey Pkwy
- **Emerald City Coffee** • 3928 N Sheridan Rd
- **Mellow Grounds Coffee Lounge** • 3807 N Ashland Ave
- **My Place for Tea** • 901 W Belmont Ave
- **Starbucks** • 1000 W Diversey Ave
- **Starbucks** • 1023 W Addison St
- **Starbucks** • 3045 N Greenview Ave
- **Starbucks** • 3184 N Clark St
- **Starbucks** • 3359 N Southport Ave

Copy Shops

- **Kinko's (24 hours)** • 3524 N Southport Ave
- **Mail Boxes Etc (9 am-7 pm)** • 3105 N Ashland Ave
- **The UPS Store (9 am-7 pm)** • 3540 N Southport Ave

Gyms

- **Chicago Fitness Center** • 3131 N Lincoln Ave
- **Curves** • 2825 N Sheffield Ave
- **Curves** • 3556 N Southport Ave
- **Lincoln Park Athletic Club** • 1019 W Diversey Pkwy
- **Number One Gym** • 3232 N Sheffield Ave
- **XSport Fitness** • 3240 N Ashland Ave

Hardware Stores

- **Ace Hardware** • 3921 N Sheridan Rd
- **Alhambra** • 3737 N Southport Ave
- **Tenenbaum Hardware & Paint** • 1138 W Belmont Ave

Liquor Stores

- **1000 Liquors** • 1000 W Belmont Ave
- **Bel-Port Food & Liquor** • 1362 W Belmont Ave
- **East Lake View Food & Liquor** • 3814 N Clark St
- **Foremost Liquor Store** • 3014 N Ashland Ave
- **Gilday Liquors** • 946 W Diversey Pkwy
- **Gold Crown Liquors Store** • 3425 N Clark St
- **Kent Certified Wine Cellar** • 2858 N Lincoln Ave
- **Que Syrah Fine Wines** • 3726 N Southport Ave
- **Wrigleyville Food & Liquor** • 3515 N Clark St

Movie Theaters

- **Music Box Theatre** • 3733 N Southport Ave
- **Vic Theatre Brew & View** • 3145 N Sheffield Ave

Nightlife

- **Berlin** • 954 W Belmont Ave
- **Bottom Lounge** • 3206 N Wilton St
- **Bungalow Bar and Lounge** • 1622 W Belmont Ave
- **Cherry Red** • 2833 N Sheffield Ave
- **Cubby Bear** • 1059 W Addison St
- **Elbo Room** • 2871 N Lincoln Ave
- **Fizz Bar and Grill** • 3220 N Lincoln Ave
- **Fly Me to the Moon** • 3400 N Clark St
- **Ginger Man Tavern** • 3740 N Clark St
- **Goose Island Brewery** • 3535 N Clark St
- **Gunther Murphy's** • 1638 W Belmont Ave
- **Guthrie's Tavern** • 1300 W Addison St
- **Higgin's Tavern** • 3259 N Racine Ave
- **Improv Olympic** • 3541 N Clark St
- **Jack's Bar & Grill** • 2856 N Southport Ave
- **John Barleycorn** • 3524 N Clark St
- **Justin's** • 3358 N Southport Ave
- **Lincoln Tap Room** • 3010 N Lincoln Ave
- **Metro** • 3730 N Clark St
- **Murphy's Bleachers** • 3655 N Sheffield Ave
- **Pops for Champagne** • 2934 N Sheffield Ave
- **Raw Bar** • 3720 N Clark St
- **Schuba's** • 3159 N Southport Ave
- **Sheffield's** • 3258 N Sheffield Ave
- **Slugger's** • 3540 N Clark St
- **Smart Bar** • 3730 N Clark St
- **Ten Cat Tavern** • 3931 N Ashland Ave
- **Trace** • 3714 N Clark St
- **Underground Lounge** • 952 W Newport Ave
- **Wild Hare** • 3530 N Clark St
- **Y*k-zies-Clark** • 3710 N Clark St

Pet Shops

- **4 Legs** • 3809 N Clark St
- **Aquatic World (fish only)** • 3039 N Lincoln Ave
- **Petco** • 3112 N Ashland Ave

Restaurants

- **Ann Sather** • 929 W Belmont Ave
- **Blue Bayou** • 3734 N Southport Ave
- **Bolat** • 3346 N Clark St
- **Clarke's Diner** • 930 W Belmont Ave
- **Coobah** • 3423 N Southport Ave
- **Cy's Crab House** • 3819 N Ashland Ave
- **Duck Walk** • 919 W Belmont Ave
- **Heaven on Seven** • 3478 N Clark St
- **Mama Desta's Red Sea** • 3216 N Clark St
- **Matsu Yama** • 1059 W Belmont Ave
- **Matsuya** • 3469 N Clark St
- **Menagerie** • 1232 W Belmont Ave
- **Mia Francesca** • 3311 N Clark St
- **Moti Mahal** • 1031-35 W Belmont Ave
- **Orange** • 3231 N Clark St
- **Original Gino's East** • 2801 N Lincoln Ave
- **Outpost** • 3438 N Clark St
- **Penny's Noodle Shop** • 3400 N Sheffield Ave
- **Penny's Noodle Shop** • 950 W Diversey Ave
- **Pepper Lounge** • 3441 N Sheffield Ave
- **Platiyo** • 3313 N Clark St
- **PS Bangkok** • 3345 N Clark St
- **Rise** • 3401 N Southport Ave
- **Salt & Pepper Diner** • 3537 N Clark St
- **Shiroi Hana** • 3242 N Clark St
- **Socca** • 3301 N Clark St
- **Standard India** • 917 W Belmont Ave
- **Strega Nona** • 3747 N Southport Ave
- **Tango Sur** • 3763 N Southport Ave
- **Tombo Kitchen** • 3244 N Lincoln Ave
- **Wrigleyville Dog** • 3737 N Clark St

Shopping

- **Alley** • 3228 N Clark St
- **Bookworks** • 3444 N Clark St
- **Hollywood Mirror** • 812 W Belmont
- **Midwest Pro Stereo** • 1613 W Belmont Ave
- **Namascar** • 3946 N Southport Ave
- **Ragstock** • Belmont Ave & Dayton St, 2nd Fl
- **Strange Cargo** • 3448 N Clark St
- **Uncle Fun** • 1338 W Belmont Ave

Video Rental

- **Blockbuster Video** • 2803 N Ashland Ave
- **Blockbuster Video** • 3753 N Clark St
- **Hollywood Video** • 3128 N Ashland Ave
- **Nationwide Video** • 843 1/2 W Belmont Ave

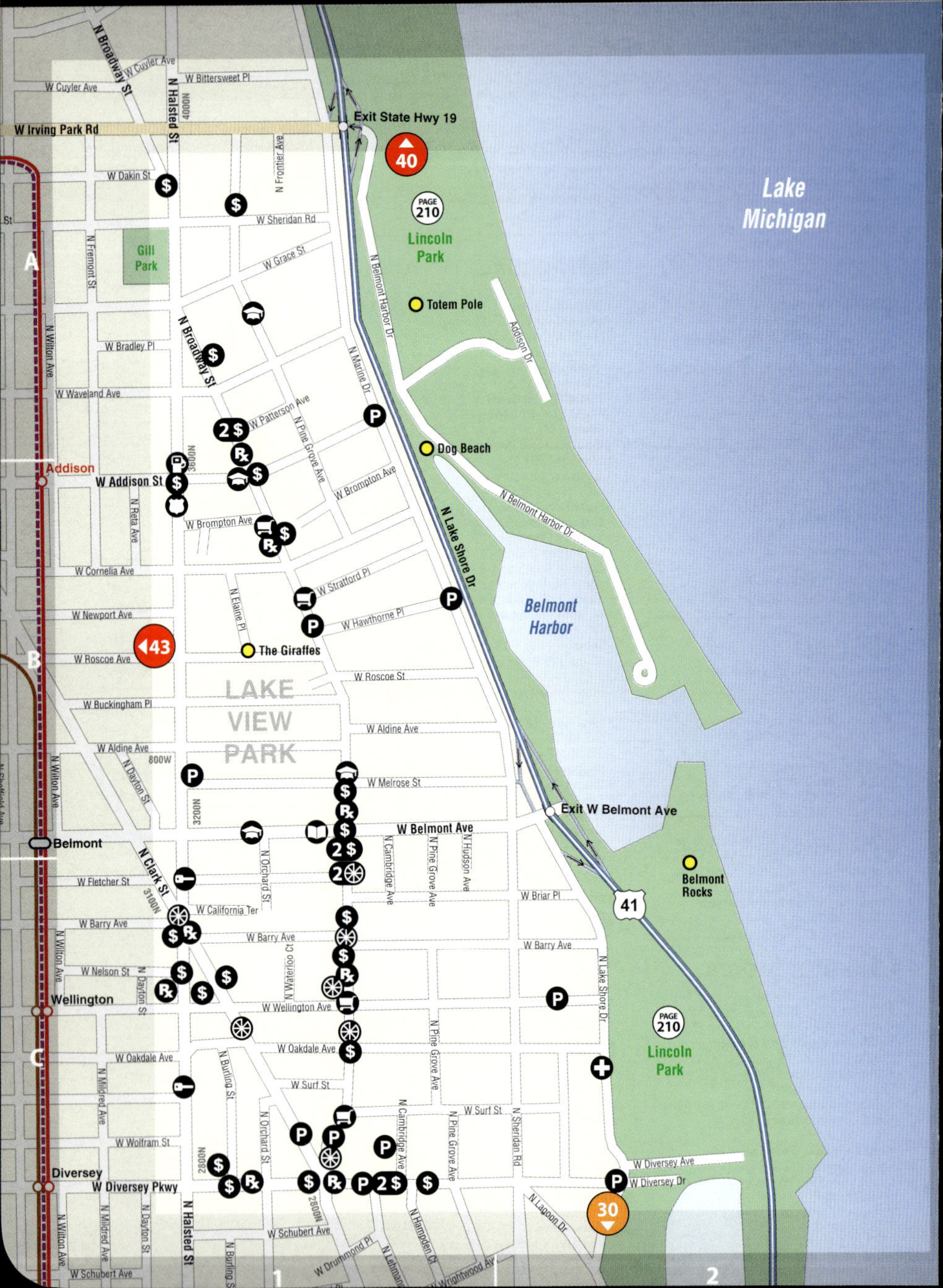
N
Lake Michigan
Lincoln Park
PAGE 210
40
Exit State Hwy 19
Totem Pole
Dog Beach
Belmont Harbor
Belmont Rocks
41
Exit W Belmont Ave
Gill Park
The Giraffes
LAKE VIEW PARK
43
30
Addison
Belmont
Wellington
Diversey
A
B
C
1
2
W Cuyler Ave
W Bittersweet Pl
W Irving Park Rd
W Dakin St
W Sheridan Rd
W Grace St
W Bradley Pl
W Waveland Ave
W Patterson Ave
W Addison St
W Brompton Ave
W Cornelia Ave
W Stratford Pl
W Hawthorne Pl
W Newport Ave
W Roscoe Ave
W Roscoe St
W Buckingham Pl
W Aldine Ave
W Melrose St
W Belmont Ave
W Fletcher St
W California Ter
W Barry Ave
W Briar Pl
W Nelson St
W Wellington Ave
W Oakdale Ave
W Surf St
W Wolfram St
W Diversey Pkwy
W Diversey Ave
W Diversey Dr
W Schubert Ave
W Drummond Pl
W Wrightwood Ave
N Broadway St
N Halsted St
N Frontier Ave
N Fremont St
N Wilton Ave
N Belmont Harbor Dr
Addison Dr
N Marine Dr
N Pine Grove Ave
N Lake Shore Dr
N Reta Ave
N Elaine Pl
N Dayton St
N Clark St
N Orchard St
N Cambridge Ave
N Hudson Ave
N Waterloo Ct
N Burling St
N Mildred Ave
N Sheridan Rd
N Lagoon Dr
N Hampden Ct
N Lehmann Ct
4000N
3600N
3200N
3100N
2800N
800W

Essentials

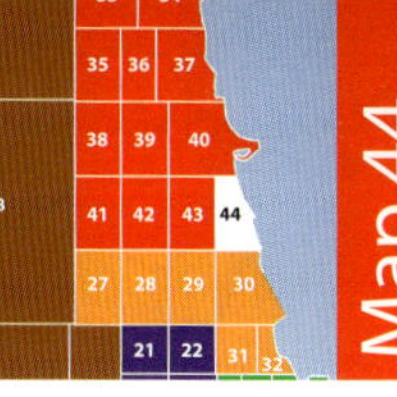

Known equally as New Town, East Lakeview, and Boys Town (due to its highly visible gay community), East Lakeview is home to the city's annual gay pride parade (which attracts hundreds of thousands of participants and spectators every year), as well as the equally flamboyant Halsted Street Market Days. South of Belmont, things tone down a bit, as brownstones and greystone condos are occupied by young married couples. Active nightlife and residential zoning make parking in East Lakeview some of the worst in the city.

Banks

- **Bank One** • 3032 N Clark St
- **Bank One** • 3714 N Broadway St
- **Bank One (ATM)** • 3046 N Halsted St
- **Bank One (ATM)** • 3107 N Broadway St
- **Bank One (ATM)** • 3201 N Broadway St
- **Bank One (ATM)** • 3646 N Broadway St
- **Central Savings** • 2800 N Broadway St
- **Charter One** • 664 W Diversey Pkwy
- **Charter One (ATM)** • 3601 N Broadway St
- **Charter One (ATM)** • 3930 N Pine Grove Ave
- **Harris Trust & Savings** • 3601 N Halsted St
- **Harris Trust & Savings** • 558 W Diversey Pkwy
- **LaSalle** • 3051 N Clark St
- **LaSalle** • 538 W Diversey Pkwy
- **MidAmerica** • 3020 N Broadway St
- **NAB** • 2949 N Broadway St
- **North Community** • 3180 N Broadway St
- **North Community** • 3639 N Broadway St
- **North Community** • 742 W Diversey Pkwy
- **North Community** • 742 W Diversey Pkwy
- **TCF** • Jewel, 3531 N Broadway St
- **TCF (ATM)** • 3158 N Broadway St
- **TCF (ATM)** • 3241 N Broadway St
- **TCF (ATM)** • 3932 N Broadway St
- **TCF (ATM)** • Osco, 3101 N Clark St

Car Rental

- **Budget** • 2901 N Halsted St • 773-528-1770
- **Hertz** • 3151 N Halsted St • 773-832-1912

Gas Stations

- **Shell** • 801 W Addison St

Hospitals

- **St Joseph's** • 2900 N Lake Shore Dr

Landmarks

- **Belmont Rocks** • W Briar Pl at the lake
- **Dog Beach** • Northern tip of Belmont Harbor
- **The Giraffes** • N Elaine Pl & W Roscoe Ave
- **Totem Pole** • N Waveland Ave & N Belmont Harbor Dr

Libraries

- **John Merlo Public Library** • 644 W Belmont Ave

Parking

Pharmacies

- **CVS Pharmacy** • 3033 N Broadway St
- **Jewel-Osco** • 3531 N Broadway St
- **Osco Drug** • 3101 N Clark St
- **Walgreens** • 2801 N Broadway St
- **Walgreens** • 3646 N Broadway St
- **Walgreens** • 740 W Diversey Pkwy
- **Walgreens (24 Hours)** • 3046 N Halsted St
- **Walgreens (24 hours)** • 3201 N Broadway St

Pizza

- **Buca Di Beppo** • 2941 N Clark St
- **Dominick's Finer Foods** • 3012 N Broadway St
- **Domino's** • 3103 N Clark St
- **Mac's Pizza** • 3152 N Broadway St
- **Mac's Pizza** • 606 W Briar Pl
- **Nancy's Pizza** • 2930 N Broadway St
- **Pizza Hut** • 3034 N Broadway St
- **Renaldi's Pizza Pub** • 2827 N Broadway St

Police

- **23rd District (Town Hall)** • 3600 N Halsted St

Schools

- **Bernard Zell Ansche Emet Day School** • 3760 N Pine Grove Ave
- **Lake View Academy** • 716 W Addison St
- **Mt Carmel Academy** • 720 W Belmont Ave
- **Nettelhorst Elementary** • 3252 N Broadway St

Supermarkets

- **Dominick's** • 3012 N Broadway St
- **Jewel-Osco** • 3531 N Broadway St
- **Treasure Island** • 3460 N Broadway St

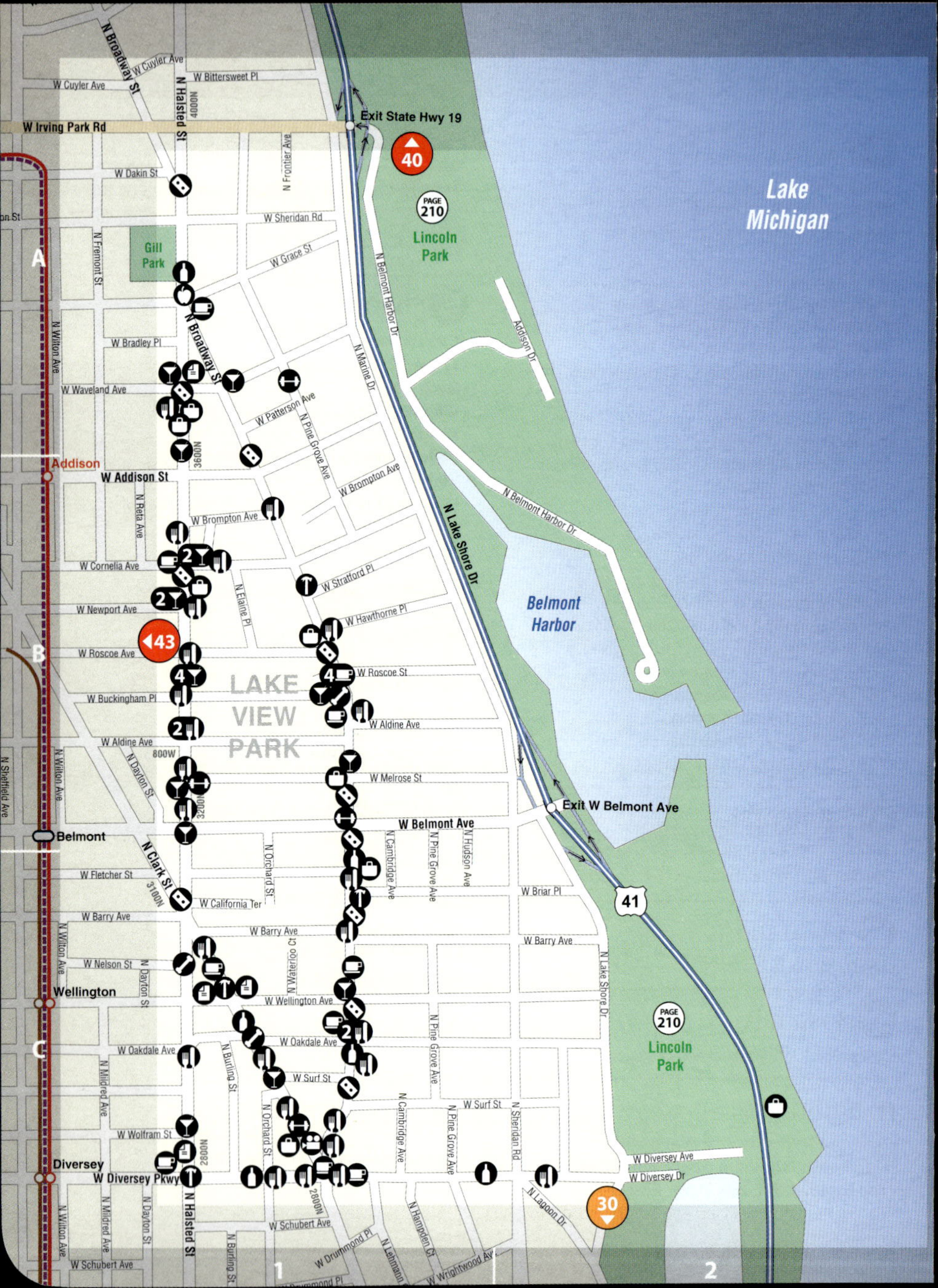
N
Lake Michigan
Lincoln Park
Belmont Harbor
LAKE VIEW PARK
Gill Park
Exit State Hwy 19
Exit W Belmont Ave
40
43
30
41
PAGE 210
A
B
C
1
2
Addison
Belmont
Wellington
Diversey
W Irving Park Rd
W Cuyler Ave
W Bittersweet Pl
N Broadway St
N Halsted St
4000N
W Dakin St
W Sheridan Rd
W Grace St
N Frontier Ave
N Fremont St
W Bradley Pl
W Waveland Ave
W Patterson Ave
N Pine Grove Ave
N Marine Dr
N Belmont Harbor Dr
Addison Dr
3600N
W Addison St
N Reta Ave
W Brompton Ave
W Cornelia Ave
W Newport Ave
N Elaine Pl
W Stratford Pl
W Hawthorne Pl
N Lake Shore Dr
W Roscoe Ave
W Roscoe St
W Buckingham Pl
W Aldine Ave
800W
N Dayton St
N Wilton Ave
N Sheffield Ave
W Melrose St
3200N
W Belmont Ave
N Cambridge Ave
N Hudson Ave
N Orchard St
N Clark St
3100N
W Fletcher St
W California Ter
W Barry Ave
W Briar Pl
W Nelson St
N Waterloo Ct
W Wellington Ave
W Oakdale Ave
N Burling St
N Mildred Ave
W Surf St
N Sheridan Rd
W Wolfram St
2800N
W Diversey Pkwy
W Diversey Ave
W Diversey Dr
N Lagoon Dr
W Schubert Ave
W Drummond Pl
N Hampden Ct
N Lehmann
W Wrightwood Ave

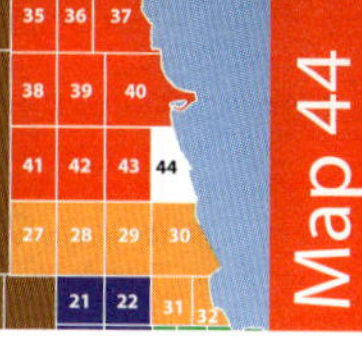

Heaps of good casual restaurants, a thriving bar scene (gay clubs mostly north of Belmont, Irish Pubs, south), and a first-rate cinema make East Lakeview a destination spot for nightlife. La Creperie is tiny and charming and frequently has live French music. Roscoe's and Sidetracks are two cavernous gay bars that really pack 'em in. Las Mananitas serves lethal margaritas on an outdoor patio great for people watching. Clark Street Dog is there to help you sop it up if you've had one too many. If you come to East Lakeview, do yourself a huge favor and cab it—taxis are abundant in these parts, and it's a cinch to hail one at any hour.

Coffee

- **Borders Books & Music** • 2817 N Clark St
- **Caribou Coffee** • 3025 N Clark St
- **Caribou Coffee** • 3300 N Broadway St
- **Caribou Coffee** • 3500 N Halsted St
- **Coffee & Tea Exchange** • 3311 N Broadway St
- **Dunkin' Donuts** • 801 W Diversey Pkwy
- **Einstein Bros Bagels** • 3330 N Broadway St
- **Intelligentsia Coffee Roasters** • 3123 N Broadway St
- **Starbucks** • 3358 N Broadway St
- **Starbucks** • 3845 N Broadway St
- **Starbucks** • 617 W Diversey Pkwy

Copy Shops

- **Kinko's (24 hours)** • 3001 N Clark St
- **Sir Speedy (8 am-5:30 pm)** • 2818 N Halsted St
- **The UPS Store (8 am-7 pm)** • 3023 N Clark St
- **The UPS Store (8 am-7 pm)** • 3712 N Broadway St

Farmer's Markets

- **North Halsted Chicago Farmers Market** • N Halsted St north of W Bradley Pl

Gyms

- **Bally Total Fitness** • 2828 N Clark St
- **Chicago Sweat Shop** • 3215 N Broadway St
- **East Lakeview Multiplex** • 3657 N Pine Grove
- **Halsted Street Multiplex** • 3228 N Halsted St

Hardware Stores

- **Clark Street Ace Hardware** • 3011 N Clark St
- **Edwards True Value Hardware** • 2804 N Halsted St
- **Lehman's True Value Hardware** • 3473 N Broadway St
- **Midtown True Value Hardware** • 3130 N Broadway St

Liquor Stores

- **Binny's Beverage Depot** • 3000 N Clark St
- **Broadway Food & Liquor** • 3158 N Broadway St
- **Eastgate Wine & Spirits** • 446 W Diversey Pkwy
- **Gold Medal Liquors** • 3823 N Broadway St
- **Paradise Liquors** • 2934 N Broadway St
- **Sysha Food and Liquor** • 702 W Diversey Pkwy

Movie Theaters

- **Landmark Century Centre Cinema** • 2828 N Clark St

Nightlife

- **Charlie's Chicago** • 3726 N Broadway St
- **Circuit** • 3641 N Halsted St
- **The Closet** • 3325 N Broadway St
- **Cocktail** • 3359 N Halsted St
- **Crush** • 2843 N Halsted St
- **Duke of Perth** • 2913 N Clark St
- **Gentry on Halsted** • 3320 N Halsted St
- **Hydrate** • 3458 N Halsted St
- **Kit Kat Lounge** • 3700 N Halsted St
- **Little Jim's** • 3501 N Halsted St
- **Monsignor Murphy's** • 3019 N Broadway St
- **Roscoe's** • 3354 N Halsted St
- **Sidetrack** • 3349 N Halsted St
- **Spin** • 800 W Belmont Ave
- **Town Hall Pub** • 3340 N Halsted St

Pet Shops

- **Paradise Pet Salon** • 3920 N Broadway St
- **Petco** • 3046 N Halsted St
- **Scrub Your Pup** • 2935 N Clark St

Restaurants

- **Aladdin's Eatery** • 614 W Diversey Pkwy
- **Angelina Ristorante** • 3561 N Broadway St
- **Ann Sather** • 3411 N Broadway St
- **Arco de Cuchilleros** • 3445 N Halsted St
- **The Bagel** • 3107 N Broadway St
- **Café Bordeaux and Crepes** • 2932 N Broadway St
- **Chicago Diner** • 3411 N Halsted St
- **Clark Street Dog** • 3040 N Clark St
- **Cornelia's Restaurant** • 750 W Cornelia Ave
- **Cousin's** • 2833 N Broadway St
- **Duke of Perth** • 2913 N Clark St
- **Erwin, An American Café & Bar** • 2925 N Halsted St
- **Firefly** • 3335 N Halsted St
- **Half Shell** • 676 W Diversey Pkwy
- **Jack's on Halsted** • 3201 N Halsted St
- **Kit Kit Lounge & Supper Club** • 3700 N Halsted St
- **Koryo** • 2936 N Broadway St
- **La Creperie** • 2845 N Clark St
- **Las Mananitas** • 3523 N Halsted St
- **Mark's Chop Suey** • 3343 N Halsted St
- **Mars** • 3124 N Broadway St
- **Melrose** • 3233 N Broadway St
- **Monsoon** • 2813 N Broadway St
- **Nancy's Original Stuffed Pizza** • 2930 N Broadway St
- **Nookie's Tree** • 3334 N Halsted St
- **Sinbad's** • 921 W Belmont Ave
- **X/O** • 3441 N Halsted St
- **Yoshi's Café** • 3257 N Halsted St

Shopping

- **The Brown Elephant Resale** • 3651 N Halsted St
- **Century Mall** • 2828 N Clark St
- **Equinox** • 3401 N Broadway St
- **GayMart** • 3457 N Halsted St
- **The Pleasure Chest** • 3155 N Broadway St
- **Unabridged Bookstore** • 3251 N Broadway St

Video Rental

- **Blockbuster Video** • 3120 N Clark St
- **Broadway Video** • 3916 N Broadway St
- **Golden Video** • 3619 N Broadway St
- **Hollywood Video** • 2868 N Broadway St
- **Mr Video** • 3356 N Broadway St
- **Nationwide Video** • 2827 N Broadway St
- **Nationwide Video** • 3936 N Clarendon Ave
- **RJ's Video** • 3452 N Halsted St
- **Specialty Video** • 3221 N Broadway St
- **West Coast Video** • 3114 N Broadway St
- **Windy City Video** • 3701 N Halsted St

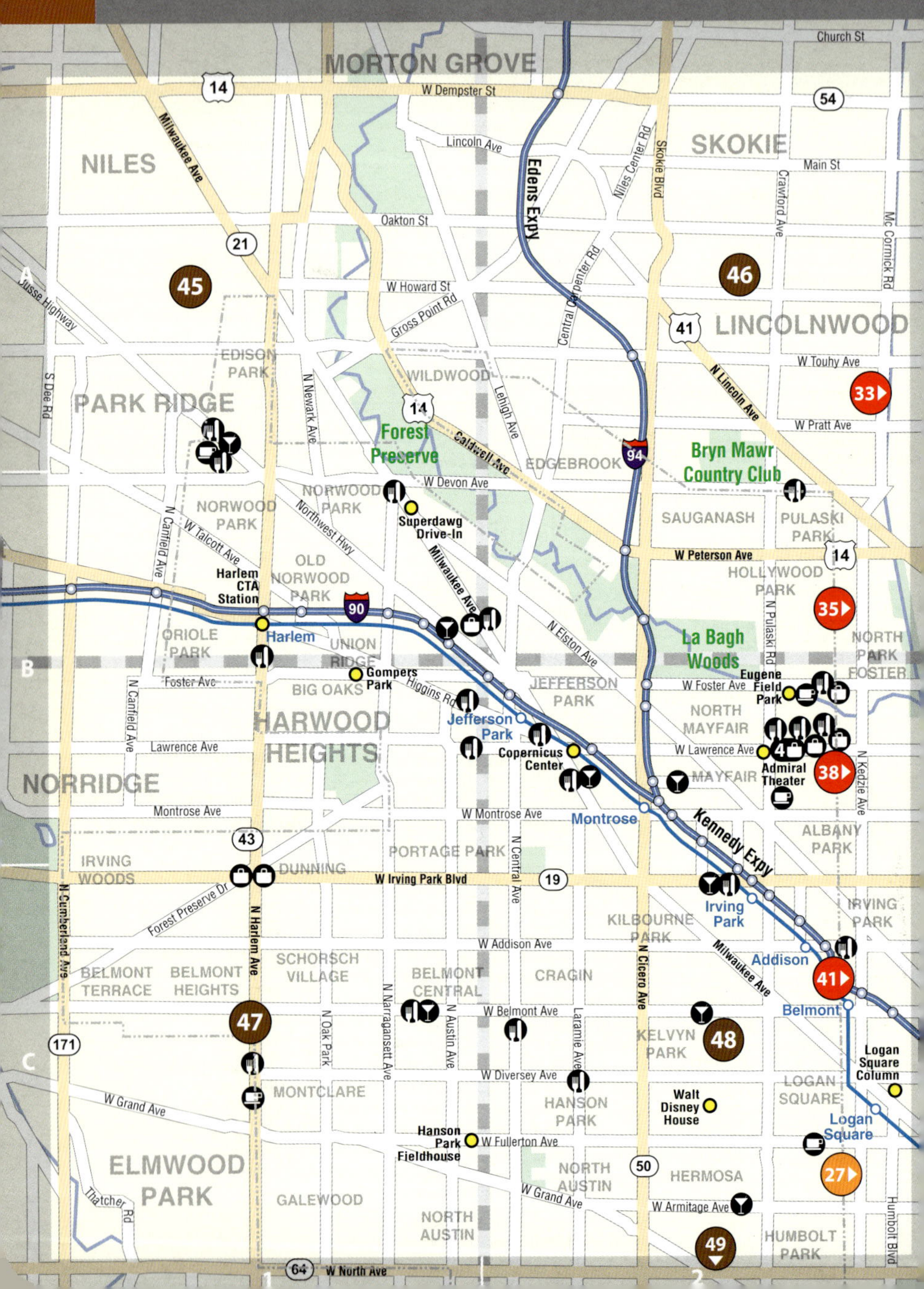

MORTON GROVE
W Dempster St
NILES
SKOKIE
Church St
Main St
Lincoln Ave
Milwaukee Ave
Edens Expy
Niles Center Rd
Skokie Blvd
Crawford Ave
Mc Cormick Rd
Oakton St
W Howard St
Gross Point Rd
Central Carpenter Rd
LINCOLNWOOD
W Touhy Ave
N Lincoln Ave
W Pratt Ave
Tousse Highway
S Dee Rd
EDISON PARK
PARK RIDGE
WILDWOOD
N Newark Ave
Lehigh Ave
Forest Preserve
Caldwell Ave
EDGEBROOK
Bryn Mawr Country Club
W Devon Ave
NORWOOD PARK
Northwest Hwy
Superdawg Drive-In
SAUGANASH
PULASKI PARK
N Canfield Ave
W Talcott Ave
OLD NORWOOD PARK
W Peterson Ave
HOLLYWOOD PARK
Harlem CTA Station
Harlem
UNION RIDGE
N Elston Ave
La Bagh Woods
N Pulaski Rd
NORTH PARK
FOSTER
ORIOLE PARK
Gompers Park
BIG OAKS
Higgins Rd
JEFFERSON PARK
W Foster Ave
Eugene Field Park
Foster Ave
NORTH MAYFAIR
HARWOOD HEIGHTS
Jefferson Park
Copernicus Center
W Lawrence Ave
Admiral Theater
Lawrence Ave
MAYFAIR
N Kedzie Ave
NORRIDGE
Montrose Ave
W Montrose Ave
Montrose
Kennedy Expy
ALBANY PARK
IRVING WOODS
DUNNING
PORTAGE PARK
N Central Ave
W Irving Park Blvd
Forest Preserve Dr
N Cumberland Ave
N Harlem Ave
KILBOURNE PARK
Irving Park
IRVING PARK
W Addison Ave
Milwaukee Ave
Addison
BELMONT TERRACE
BELMONT HEIGHTS
SCHORSCH VILLAGE
BELMONT CENTRAL
CRAGIN
N Cicero Ave
Belmont
W Belmont Ave
N Narragansett Ave
N Oak Park
N Austin Ave
Laramie Ave
KELVYN PARK
Logan Square Column
W Diversey Ave
MONTCLARE
W Grand Ave
HANSON PARK
Walt Disney House
LOGAN SQUARE
Logan Square
Hanson Park Fieldhouse
W Fullerton Ave
ELMWOOD PARK
NORTH AUSTIN
HERMOSA
W Grand Ave
Thatcher Rd
GALEWOOD
W Armitage Ave
NORTH AUSTIN
HUMBOLT PARK
Humbolt Blvd
W North Ave
14
54
21
41
14
94
14
90
43
19
171
50
64
45
46
33
35
38
4
41
47
48
27
49
A
B
C
1
2

Essentials

If there's one thing you can count on in Northwest Chicago, it's that you can count on just about everything. Compared to other sections of the city, the Northwest is a bastion of stability. Most of the people and businesses have been around forever, and even typically transitory ethnic enclaves are fairly entrenched. This includes a crazy quilt of Eastern European, Middle Eastern, Korean, and Italian quarters, blocks, and streets. Northwest Chicago is blessed with an abundance of small parks and field houses, as well as a large hunk of forest preserve, giving much of the area a bucolic, suburban feel.

Landmarks

- **Admiral Theater** • 3940 W Lawrence Ave
- **Copernicus Center** • 5216 W Lawrence Ave
- **Eugene Field Park** • 5100 N Ridgeway Ave
- **Gompers Park** • 4222 W Foster Ave
- **Hanson Park Fieldhouse** • 5501 W Fullerton Ave
- **Harlem CTA Station** • N Harlem Ave & Kennedy Expy
- **Logan Square Column** • 3100 W Logan Blvd
- **Superdawg Drive-In** • 6363 N Milwaukee Ave
- **Walt Disney House** • 2156 N Tripp Ave

Sundries / Entertainment

Northwest Chicago wears its blue-collar ethnic proclivities on its sleeve. Local shops and restaurants don't go out of their way to attract clientele outside of their own, and signs, menus, and even the staff at the area's abundant Korean and Eastern European businesses make little effort to communicate in English. (The same can be said for the clientele at many of the area's numerous ostensibly English-speaking corner taverns.) Adventuresome diners rise to the challenge—some of the city's best unsung gems are to be found here, including Hungarian Paprikash, Thai vegan spot Amitabul, and the Swedish Tre Kronor. Toss back authentic pints at the 5th Province Pub. Located in the Irish-American Heritage Center, it's only open on Friday and Saturday nights. Rosa's Lounge is a venerable, beloved Chicago jazz and blues venue.

Nightlife

- **5th Province Pub** • Irish-American Heritage Center, 4626 N Knox Ave
- **Abbey Pub** • 3420 W Grace St
- **Emerald Isle** • 6686 N Northwest Hwy
- **Fischman Liquors** • 4780 N Milwaukee Ave
- **Hollywood Lounge** • 3301 W Bryn Mawr Ave
- **Little Rascals** • 4356 W Belmont Ave
- **New Polonia Club** • 6103 W Belmont Ave
- **Old Irving Park Sports Bar & Grill** • 4217 W Irving Park Blvd
- **Rosa's Lounge** • 3420 W Armitage Ave
- **Vaughan's Pub** • 5485 N Northwest Hwy

Coffee

- **Café Italia** • 2625 N Harlem Ave
- **Edison Perk** • 6701 N Olmstead Ave
- **Hotti Biscotti** • 3545 W Fullerton Ave
- **Nefertiti Café** • 3737 W Lawrence Ave
- **Schlegl's Bakery & Café** • 3334 W Foster Ave

Restaurants

- **Amitabul** • 6207 N Milwaukee Ave
- **Basta Pasta** • 6733 N Olmstead Ave
- **Blue Angel** • 5310 N Milwaukee Ave
- **Don Juan** • 6730 N Northwest Hwy
- **Gale Street Inn** • 4914 N Milwaukee Ave
- **Grota Smorgasborg** • 3112 N Central Ave
- **Halina's Polish Delights** • 5914 W Lawrence Ave
- **Hiromi's** • 3609 W Lawrence Ave
- **Mario's Café** • 5241 N Harlem Ave
- **Mayan Sol** • 3830 W Lawrence Ave
- **Mirabell Restaurant** • 3454 W Addison Ave
- **Montasero's Ristorante** • 3935 W Devon Ave
- **Noodles** • 5956 W Higgins Rd
- **Paprikash** • 5210 W Diversey Ave
- **Red Apple** • 3121 N Milwaukee Ave
- **Ristorante Agostino** • 2817 N Harlem Ave
- **Sabatino's** • 4441 W Irving Park Blvd
- **Seo Hae** • 3534 W Lawrence Ave
- **Taqueria La Oaxaquena** • 6113 W Diversey
- **Teresa II Polish & Lounge** • 4751 N Milwaukee Ave
- **Trattoria Pasta D'Arte** • 6311 N Milwaukee Ave
- **Tre Kronor** • 3258 W Foster Ave

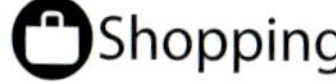

Shopping

- **Albany Office Supply** • 3419 W Lawrence Ave
- **American Science & Surplus** • 5316 N Milwaukee Ave
- **Chicago Produce** • 3500 W Lawrence Ave
- **El Mundo Del Dulce** • 4806 N Drake Ave
- **Harlem Irving Plaza** • N Harlem Ave & W Irving Park Blvd
- **NY Shoes Imports** • 3546 W Lawrence Ave
- **Perfumes 'R' Us** • 3608 W Lawrence Ave
- **Rolling Stone Records** • 7300 W Irving Park Rd
- **Srpska Tradicija** • 3615 W Lawrence Ave
- **Sweden Shop** • 3304 W Foster Ave

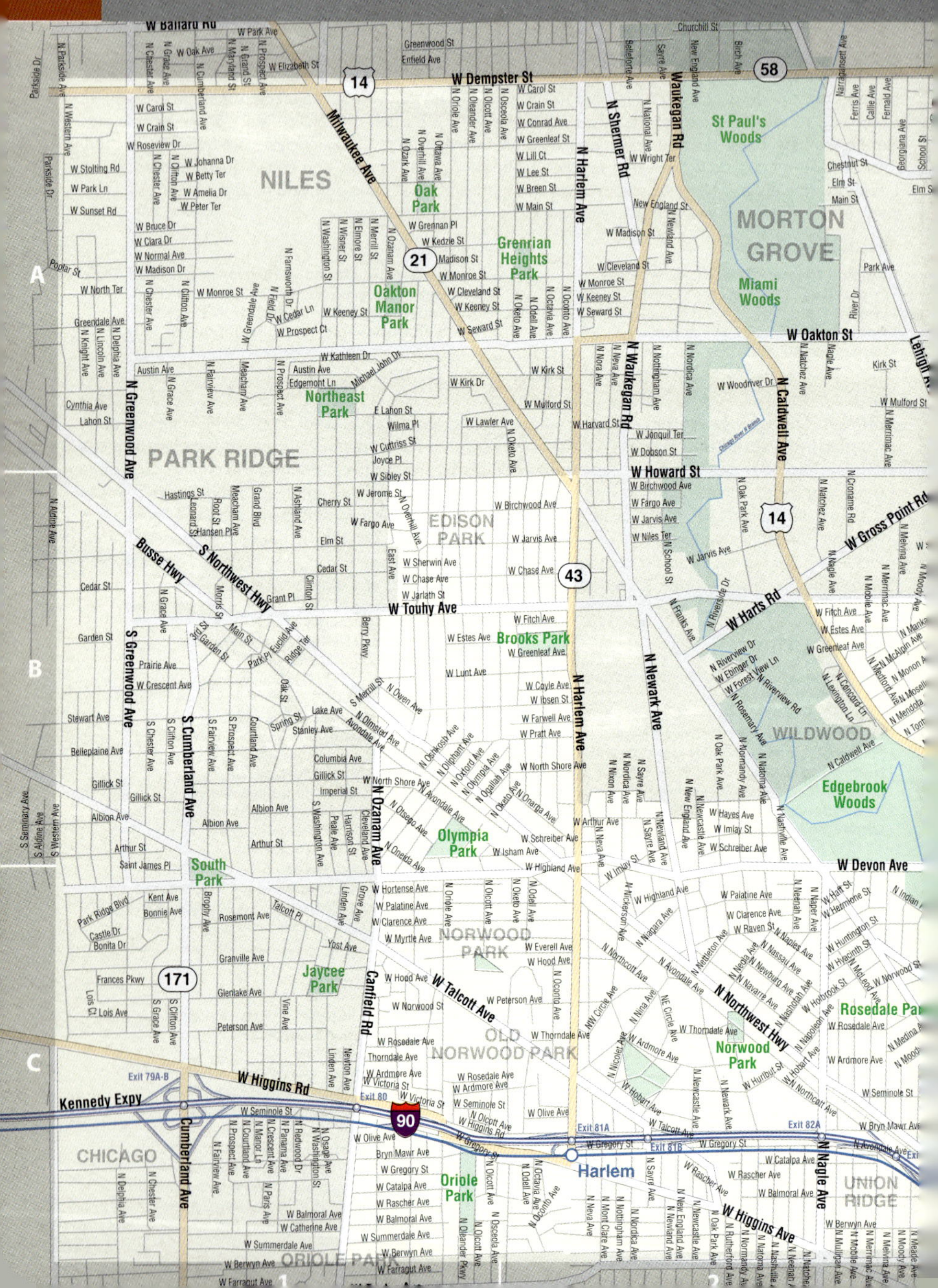
NILES
PARK RIDGE
MORTON GROVE
EDISON PARK
WILDWOOD
NORWOOD PARK
OLD NORWOOD PARK
CHICAGO
UNION RIDGE
Harlem
St Paul's Woods
Miami Woods
Oak Park
Grennan Heights Park
Oakton Manor Park
Northeast Park
Brooks Park
Olympia Park
South Park
Jaycee Park
Oriole Park
Norwood Park
Edgebrook Woods
Rosedale Park
W Dempster St
W Oakton St
W Howard St
W Touhy Ave
W Devon Ave
W Higgins Rd
W Higgins Ave
Kennedy Expy
Milwaukee Ave
N Harlem Ave
N Waukegan Rd
N Caldwell Ave
N Greenwood Ave
S Greenwood Ave
S Cumberland Ave
Cumberland Ave
N Ozanam Ave
Canfield Rd
N Newark Ave
N Nagle Ave
S Northwest Hwy
N Northwest Hwy
Busse Hwy
W Talcott Ave
W Harts Rd
W Gross Point Rd
N Sherman Rd
14
21
43
58
90
171
Exit 79A-B
Exit 80
Exit 81A
Exit 81B
Exit 82A
A
B
C
1
2

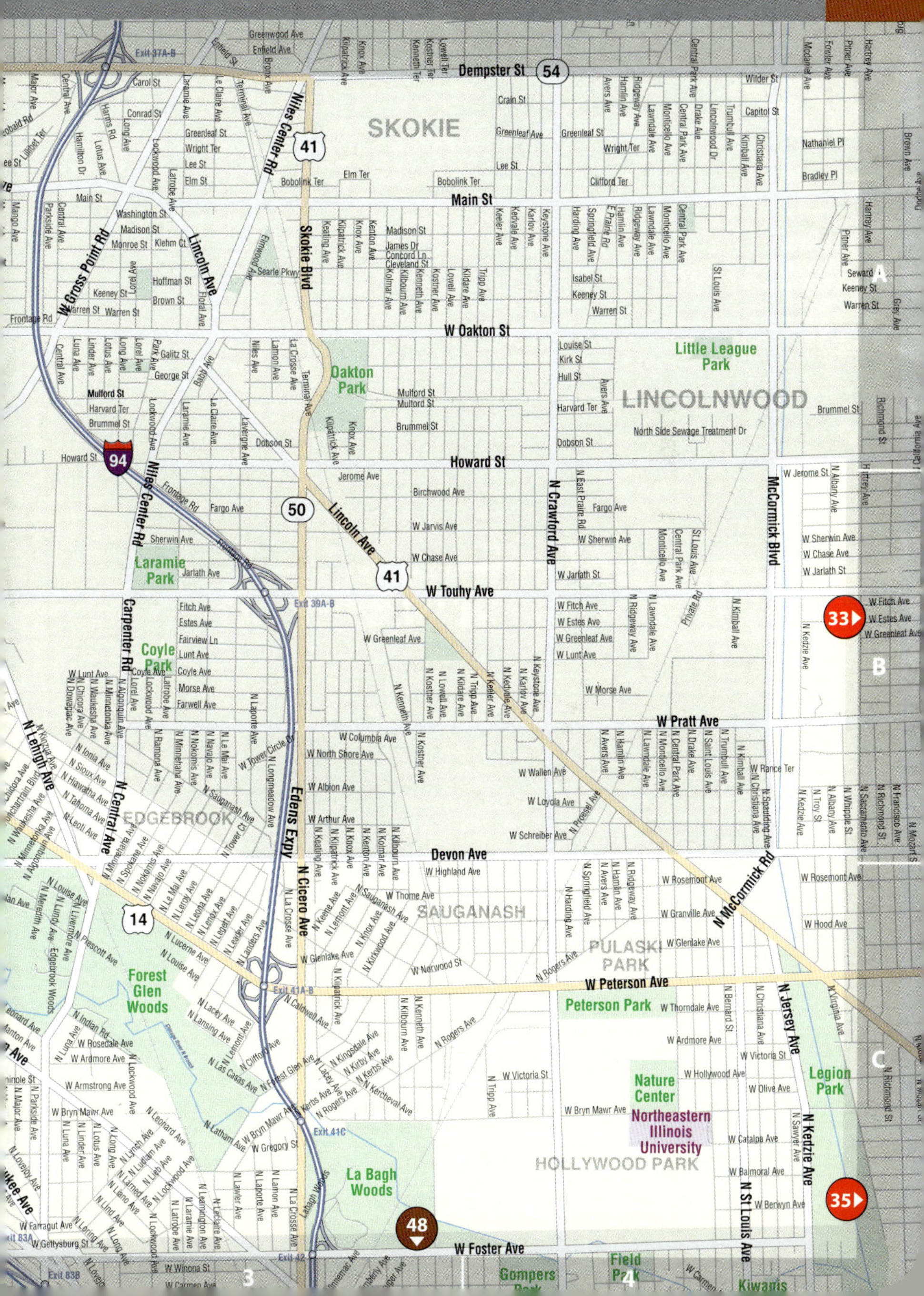
SKOKIE
LINCOLNWOOD
EDGEBROOK
SAUGANASH
PULASKI PARK
HOLLYWOOD PARK
Dempster St
Main St
W Oakton St
Howard St
W Touhy Ave
W Pratt Ave
Devon Ave
W Peterson Ave
W Foster Ave
Skokie Blvd
Niles Center Rd
Lincoln Ave
W Gross Point Rd
N Crawford Ave
McCormick Blvd
N McCormick Rd
Edens Expy
N Cicero Ave
N Central Ave
N Lehigh Ave
Carpenter Rd
N Jersey Ave
N Kedzie Ave
N St Louis Ave
Oakton Park
Little League Park
Laramie Park
Coyle Park
Forest Glen Woods
Peterson Park
Nature Center
Northeastern Illinois University
Legion Park
La Bagh Woods
Gompers Park
Field Park
Kiwanis
North Side Sewage Treatment Dr
Exit 37A-B
Exit 39A-B
Exit 41A-B
Exit 41C
Exit 42
Exit 83A
Exit 83B
54
41
94
50
14
33
35
48
A
B
C
3
4

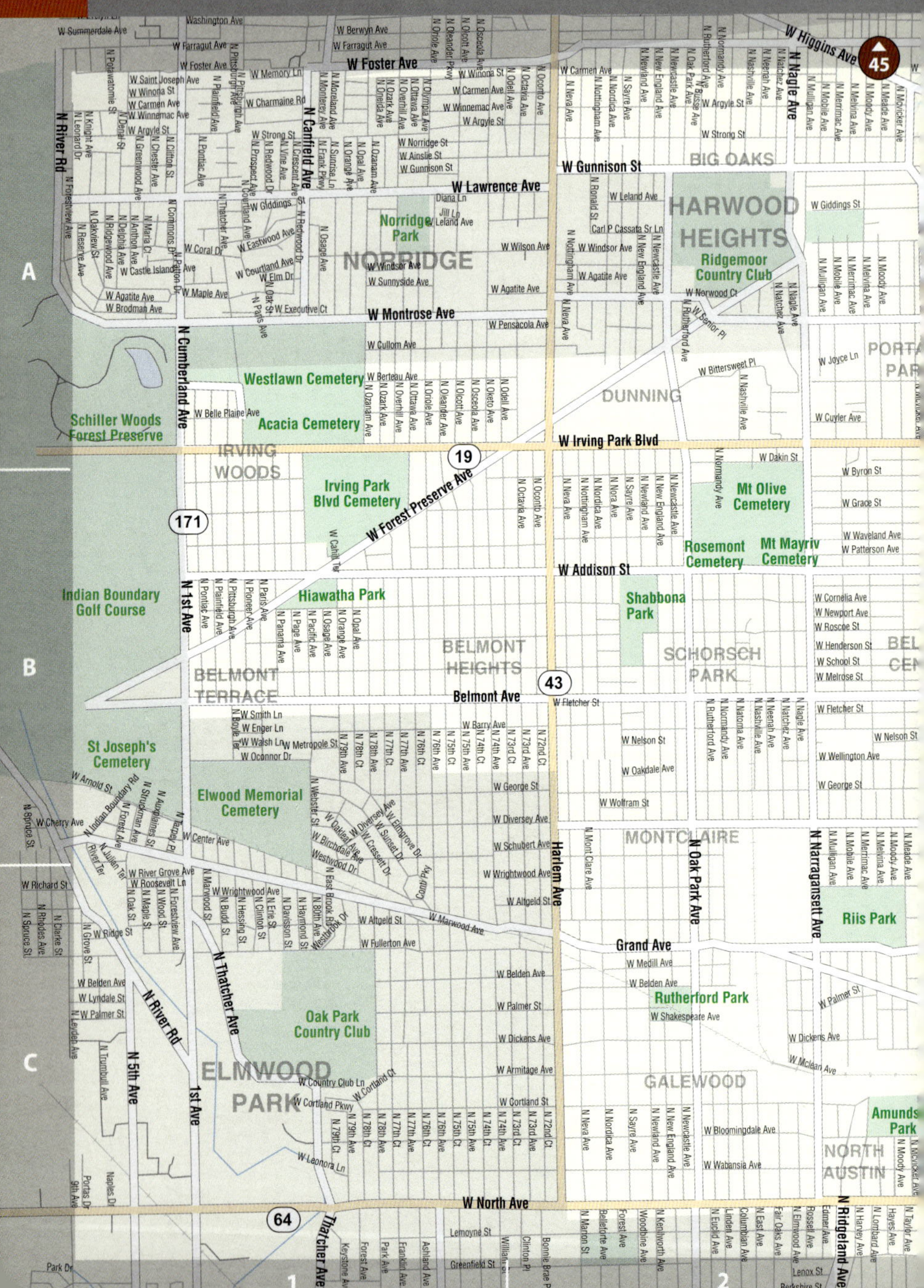
45
W Higgins Ave
W Foster Ave
W Lawrence Ave
W Gunnison St
W Montrose Ave
W Irving Park Blvd
W Addison St
Belmont Ave
Grand Ave
W North Ave
W Forest Preserve Ave
N River Rd
N Cumberland Ave
N Canfield Ave
N 1st Ave
Harlem Ave
N Oak Park Ave
N Narragansett Ave
N Nagle Ave
N Thatcher Ave
N 5th Ave
1st Ave
Thatcher Ave
N Ridgeland Ave
19
43
64
171
NORRIDGE
Norridge Park
BIG OAKS
HARWOOD HEIGHTS
Ridgemoor Country Club
DUNNING
PORTAGE PARK
Westlawn Cemetery
Acacia Cemetery
Schiller Woods Forest Preserve
IRVING WOODS
Irving Park Blvd Cemetery
Mt Olive Cemetery
Rosemont Cemetery
Mt Mayriv Cemetery
Indian Boundary Golf Course
Hiawatha Park
Shabbona Park
BELMONT HEIGHTS
BELMONT TERRACE
SCHORSCH PARK
St Joseph's Cemetery
Elwood Memorial Cemetery
MONTCLAIRE
Riis Park
Rutherford Park
Oak Park Country Club
ELMWOOD PARK
GALEWOOD
Amundsen Park
NORTH AUSTIN
A
B
C
1
2

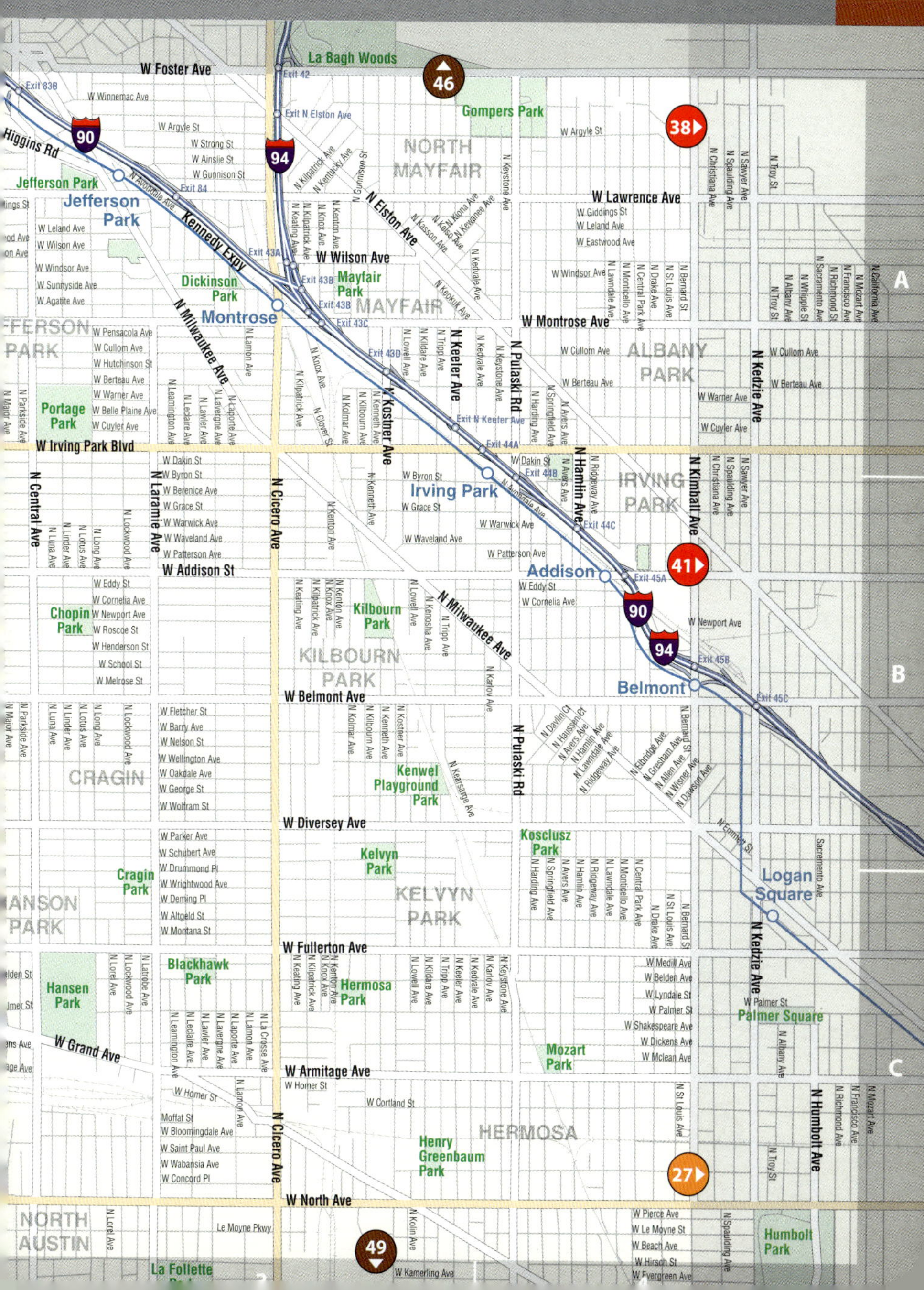

La Bagh Woods
46
Gompers Park
38
NORTH MAYFAIR
Jefferson Park
Jefferson Park
Dickinson Park
Montrose
Mayfair Park
MAYFAIR
ALBANY PARK
Portage Park
Irving Park
IRVING PARK
Addison
41
Belmont
Chopin Park
Kilbourn Park
KILBOURN PARK
CRAGIN
Kenwel Playground Park
Kosciusz Park
Logan Square
Cragin Park
Kelvyn Park
KELVYN PARK
Blackhawk Park
Hansen Park
Hermosa Park
Palmer Square
Mozart Park
HERMOSA
Henry Greenbaum Park
27
NORTH AUSTIN
49
Humbolt Park
La Follette
W Foster Ave
W Lawrence Ave
W Wilson Ave
W Montrose Ave
W Irving Park Blvd
W Addison St
W Belmont Ave
W Diversey Ave
W Fullerton Ave
W Armitage Ave
W North Ave
Kennedy Expy
N Milwaukee Ave
N Elston Ave
N Cicero Ave
N Pulaski Rd
N Kostner Ave
N Keeler Ave
N Kimball Ave
N Kedzie Ave
N Hamlin Ave
N Laramie Ave
N Central Ave
N Humbolt Ave
W Grand Ave
Higgins Rd
A
B
C

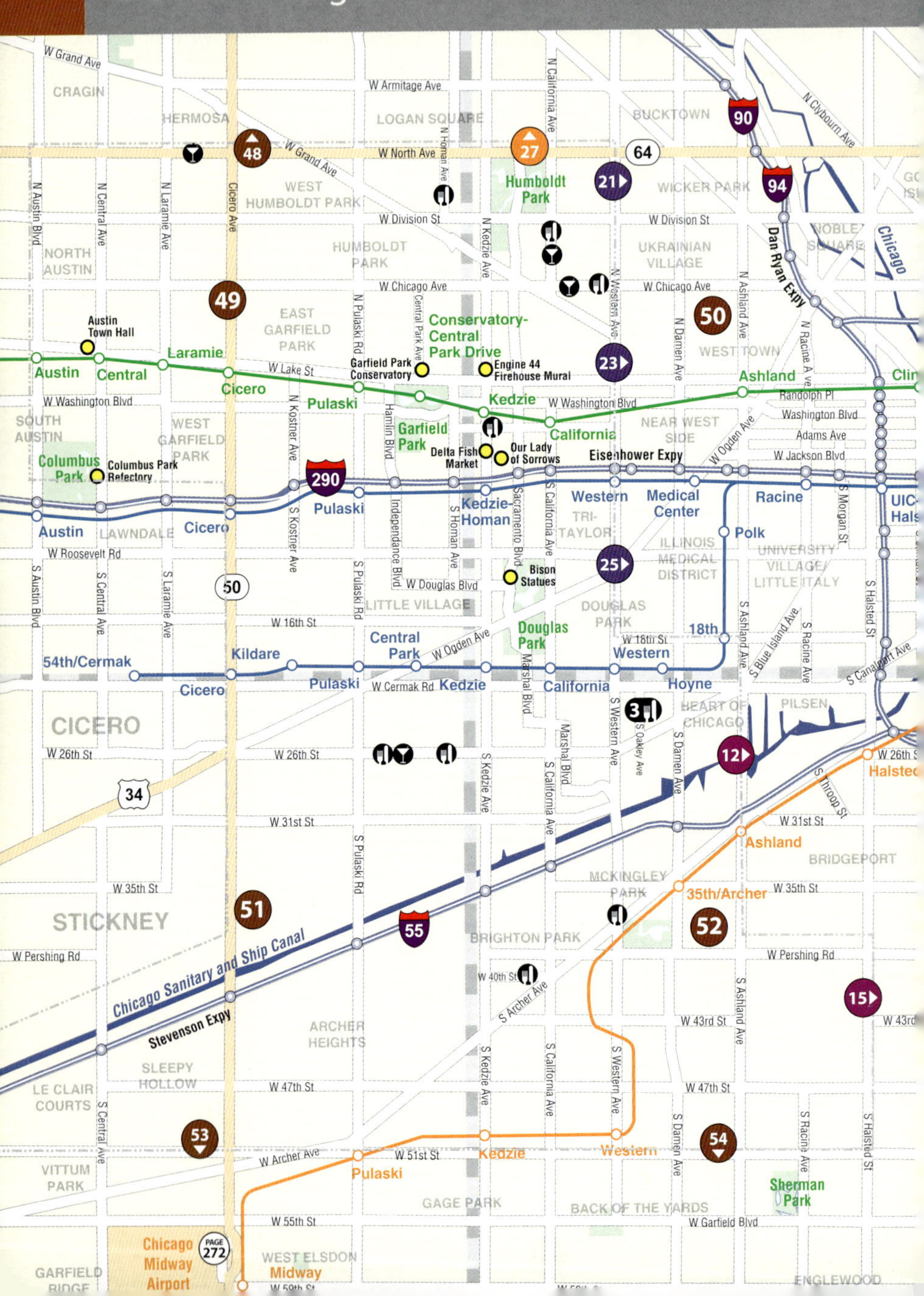

CRAGIN
HERMOSA
LOGAN SQUARE
BUCKTOWN
WEST HUMBOLDT PARK
Humboldt Park
WICKER PARK
HUMBOLDT PARK
UKRAINIAN VILLAGE
NOBLE SQUARE
NORTH AUSTIN
EAST GARFIELD PARK
WEST TOWN
Austin Town Hall
Conservatory-Central Park Drive
Garfield Park Conservatory
Engine 44 Firehouse Mural
SOUTH AUSTIN
WEST GARFIELD PARK
Garfield Park
NEAR WEST SIDE
Delta Fish Market
Our Lady of Sorrows
Eisenhower Expy
Columbus Park
Columbus Park Refectory
LAWNDALE
TRI-TAYLOR
Medical Center
ILLINOIS MEDICAL DISTRICT
UNIVERSITY VILLAGE/ LITTLE ITALY
Bison Statues
LITTLE VILLAGE
DOUGLAS PARK
Douglas Park
CICERO
HEART OF CHICAGO
PILSEN
BRIDGEPORT
MCKINLEY PARK
STICKNEY
BRIGHTON PARK
Chicago Sanitary and Ship Canal
Stevenson Expy
ARCHER HEIGHTS
SLEEPY HOLLOW
LE CLAIR COURTS
VITTUM PARK
GAGE PARK
BACK OF THE YARDS
Sherman Park
Chicago Midway Airport
PAGE 272
WEST ELSDON
Midway
GARFIELD RIDGE
ENGLEWOOD
Austin
Central
Laramie
Cicero
Pulaski
Kedzie
California
Ashland
Racine
Polk
18th
Western
Hoyne
Kildare
54th/Cermak
Central Park
Kedzie-Homan
Ashland
35th/Archer
Halsted
Kedzie
W Grand Ave
W Armitage Ave
W North Ave
W Division St
W Chicago Ave
W Lake St
W Washington Blvd
Randolph Pl
Washington Blvd
Adams Ave
W Jackson Blvd
W Roosevelt Rd
W Douglas Blvd
W 16th St
W 18th St
W Ogden Ave
W Cermak Rd
W 26th St
W 31st St
W 35th St
W Pershing Rd
W 40th St
S Archer Ave
W 43rd St
W 47th St
W Archer Ave
W 51st St
W 55th St
W Garfield Blvd
N Austin Blvd
N Central Ave
N Laramie Ave
Cicero Ave
N Pulaski Rd
N Kostner Ave
Central Park Ave
Hamlin Blvd
N Homan Ave
N Kedzie Ave
N California Ave
N Western Ave
N Damen Ave
N Ashland Ave
N Racine Ave
N Clybourn Ave
Dan Ryan Expy
S Austin Blvd
S Central Ave
S Laramie Ave
S Kostner Ave
S Pulaski Rd
Independence Blvd
S Homan Ave
Sacramento Blvd
S California Ave
Marshal Blvd
S Western Ave
S Oakley Ave
S Damen Ave
S Ashland Ave
S Blue Island Ave
S Racine Ave
S Morgan St
S Halsted St
S Canalport Ave
S Throop St
S Kedzie Ave
48
27
64
90
94
21
49
50
23
290
25
12
3
34
51
55
52
15
53
54

Essentials

Some of Chicago's roughest areas are encompassed by this territory, specifically from Douglas Park to Austin. Come for the parks—over 300 acres worth, with lakes, beaches, even a waterfall—but park nearby and skedaddle before dark. Heart of Chicago houses a proud Italian immigrant community, mixing peacefully with West Pilsen's Latin vibe. The Chicago Sanitary and Ship Canal boasts a couple of Chicago's oldest draw bridges, long out of commission.

Landmarks

- **Austin Town Hall** • 5610 W Lake St
- **Bison Statues at Humboldt Park** • 1400 N Sacramento Ave
- **Columbus Park Refectory** • 500 S Central Ave
- **Delta Fish Market** • 228 S Kedzie Ave
- **Engine 44 Firehouse Mural** • 412 N Kedzie Ave
- **Garfield Park Conservatory** • 300 N Central Park Ave
- **Our Lady of Sorrows** • 3121 W Jackson

Sundries / Entertainment

There's no absence of take-out rib joints, chop suey, or taquerias on the west side. Finding a place where you can actually sit down to enjoy a meal presents more of a challenge. For those so inclined, Edna's serves up some of the city's best soul food—save room for dessert. Puerto Rican stews are the specialty at cafeteria-style La Palma. The 2400 block of South Oakley rivals Taylor Street for authentic Italian feasts. Hipsters nostalgic for their grandparents' era hang out at the retro-styled California Clipper.

Nightlife

- **The 5105 Club** • 5105 W North Ave
- **Black Beetle** • 2532 W Chicago Ave
- **California Clipper** • 1002 N California Ave
- **La Justicia** • 3901 W 26th St

Restaurants

- **Bacchanalia Ristorante** • 2413 S Oakley Ave
- **Bruna's** • 2424 S Oakley Ave
- **Edna's Restaurant** • 3175 W Madison St
- **Falco's Pizza** • 2806 W 40th St
- **Flying Saucer** • 1123 N California Ave
- **Ignotz** • 2421 S Oakley Ave
- **La Palma** • 1340 N Homan Ave
- **Lalo's** • 3515 W 26th St
- **Lindy's and Gertie's** • 3685 S Archer Ave
- **Taquerias Atotonilco** • 3916 W 26th St
- **Tommy's Rock-n-Roll Café** • 2500 W Chicago

OAK PARK
WEST HUMBOLDT PARK
HUMBOLDT PARK
NORTH AUSTIN
EAST GARFIELD PARK
SOUTH AUSTIN
WEST GARFIELD PARK
CICERO
LITTLE VILLAGE
W North Ave
Division St
Chicago Ave
W Lake St
W Washington Blvd
Roosevelt Rd
W 16th St
Cermak Rd
Tri-State Tollway
N Ridgeland Ave
N Central Ave
N Laramie Ave
N Austin Blvd
S Laramie Ave
S Cicero Ave
S Kostner Ave
S Pulaski Rd
S Hamlin Blvd
S Independence Blvd
S Homan Blvd
S Central Ave
S Austin Blvd
S Ridgeland Ave
Oak Park
Austin
Austin Town Hall Park
Central
Levin Park
Laramie
Cicero
Pulaski
Conservatory Central Park
La Follette Park
Augusta Park
Garfield Park
Moore Playground Park
Clark Playground Park
Columbus Park
North Warren Park
Warren Park
Parkholm Park
Franklin Park
54th/Cermak
Kildare
Central Park
64
48
50
290
51
PAGE 234
PAGE 216
A
B
C

Damen
BUCKTOWN
W North Ave
64
94
21
22
WICKER PARK
Division
W Division St
E Division St
NOBLE SQUARE
UKRAINIAN VILLAGE
Eckhan Park
Dan Ryan Expy
Chicago
W Chicago Ave
24
Smithfield Park
Grand Ave
23
Grand
WEST TOWN
90
Chicago River
Ashland
California
W Lake St
Lake St
Union Park
Randolph St
W Washington Blvd
W Warren Blvd
NEAR WEST SIDE
Washington St
Madison St
Monroe St
Adams St
Adams Blvd
Medical Center
Jackson Blvd
Racine
UIC Halsted
Western
Eisenhower Expy
290
Altgeld Park
Campbell Park
Polk
W Harrison St
TRI-TAYLOR
W Roosevelt Rd
UNIVERSITY VILLAGE/ LITTLE ITALY
25
26
Addams Park
ILLINOIS MEDICAL DISTRICT
W 15th Pl
W 18th St
18th
Harrison Park
52
27
California
Western
Hoyne
W Cermak Rd
Canalport Ave
S Blue Island Ave
A
B
C

49
54th/Cermak
Cicero
Kildare
Pulaski
Central Par
W Cermak Rd
50
W Ogden Ave
W 26th St
34
S Austin Blvd
S Laramie Ave
W 35th St
S Central Ave
Cicero Ave
CICERO
Piotrowski Park
S Pulaski Rd
W 31st St
Hawthorne Race Course
W Pershing Rd
Chicago Sanitary and Ship Canal
55
STICKNEY
ARCHER HEIGHTS
LeClaire Courts
SLEEPY HOLLOW
LE CLAIR COURTS
W 47th St
Archer Park
Vittum Park
53
Pulaski
Archer Ave
VITTUM PARK
Strohacker Park
W 55th St
Chicago Midway Airport
PAGE 272
WEST ELSDON
Pasteur Park
Midway
Airport Dr
A
B
C
1
2

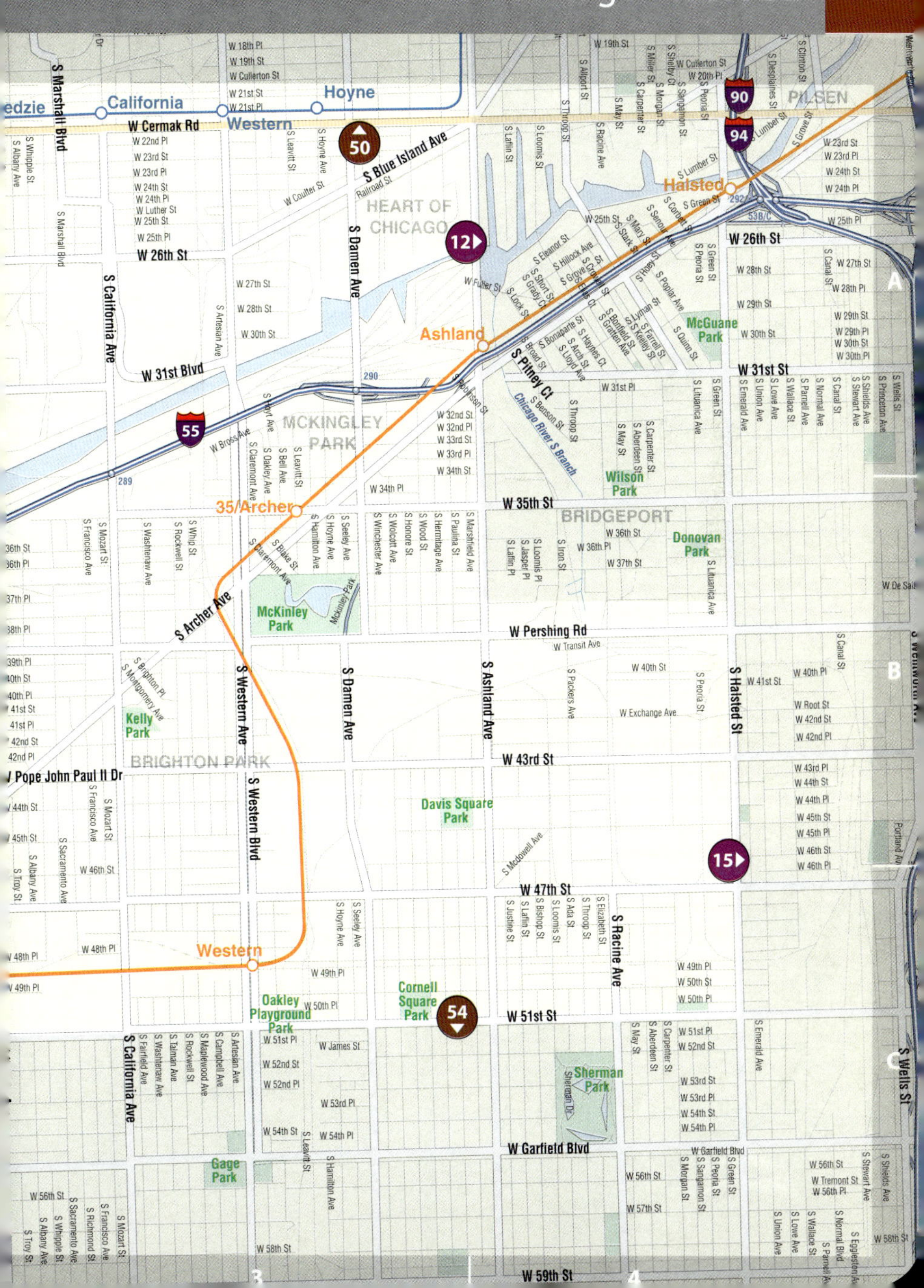

California
Western
Hoyne
W Cermak Rd
50
S Blue Island Ave
HEART OF CHICAGO
12
PILSEN
90
94
Halsted
W 26th St
W 31st Blvd
Ashland
McGuane Park
W 31st St
55
MCKINGLEY PARK
35/Archer
W 35th St
BRIDGEPORT
Donovan Park
Wilson Park
S Pitney Ct
Chicago River S Branch
McKinley Park
S Archer Ave
W Pershing Rd
S Western Ave
S Damen Ave
S Ashland Ave
S Halsted St
Kelly Park
BRIGHTON PARK
W 43rd St
W Pope John Paul II Dr
S Western Blvd
Davis Square Park
15
W 47th St
S Racine Ave
Western
Oakley Playground Park
Cornell Square Park
54
W 51st St
S California Ave
S California Ave
S Marshall Blvd
Sherman Park
W Garfield Blvd
Gage Park
S Wells St
W 59th St
A
B
C
3
4

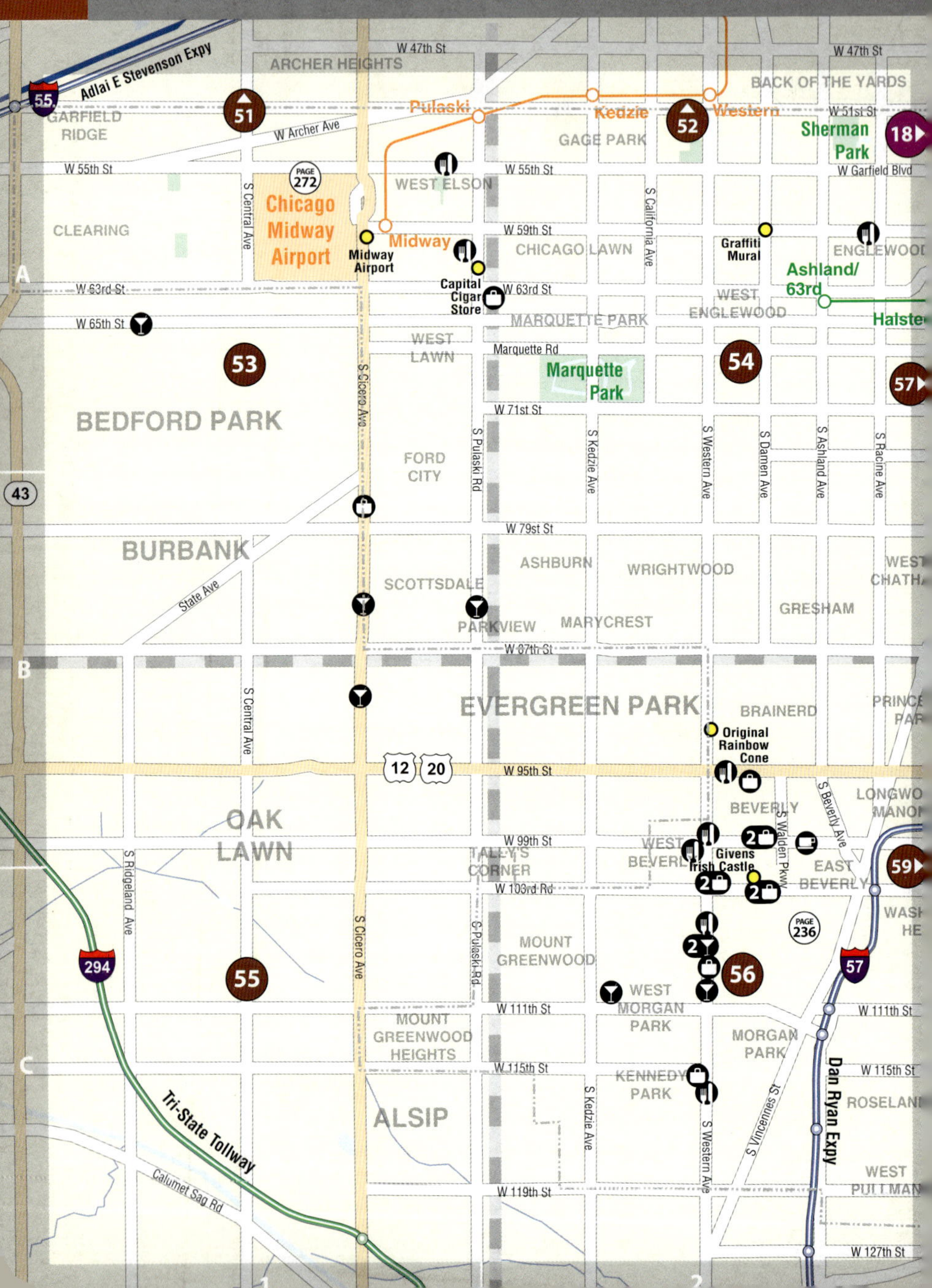

Adlai E Stevenson Expy
55
W 47th St
ARCHER HEIGHTS
BACK OF THE YARDS
W 51st St
51
Pulaski
Kedzie
52
Western
Sherman Park
18
GARFIELD RIDGE
W Archer Ave
GAGE PARK
W 55th St
PAGE 272
W Garfield Blvd
Chicago Midway Airport
WEST ELSON
S Central Ave
S California Ave
CLEARING
Midway Airport
Midway
W 59th St
CHICAGO LAWN
Graffiti Mural
ENGLEWOOD
Capital Cigar Store
Ashland/ 63rd
W 63rd St
WEST ENGLEWOOD
W 65th St
MARQUETTE PARK
Halsted
WEST LAWN
Marquette Rd
53
54
Marquette Park
57
BEDFORD PARK
W 71st St
S Cicero Ave
S Pulaski Rd
S Kedzie Ave
S Western Ave
S Damen Ave
S Ashland Ave
S Racine Ave
FORD CITY
43
W 79st St
BURBANK
ASHBURN
WRIGHTWOOD
WEST CHATHAM
SCOTTSDALE
State Ave
GRESHAM
PARKVIEW
MARYCREST
W 87th St
EVERGREEN PARK
BRAINERD
PRINCE PARK
Original Rainbow Cone
12
20
W 95th St
S Beverly Ave
LONGWOOD MANOR
BEVERLY
OAK LAWN
W 99th St
S Walden Pkwy
WEST BEVERLY
TALLY'S CORNER
Givens Irish Castle
EAST BEVERLY
59
W 103rd Rd
S Ridgeland Ave
PAGE 236
WASHINGTON HEIGHTS
MOUNT GREENWOOD
294
56
57
55
WEST MORGAN PARK
W 111th St
MOUNT GREENWOOD HEIGHTS
MORGAN PARK
W 115th St
KENNEDY PARK
ALSIP
S Vincennes St
Dan Ryan Expy
ROSELAND
Tri-State Tollway
Calumet Sag Rd
WEST PULLMAN
W 119th St
W 127th St
A
B
C
1
2

Essentials

Perhaps the most racially and ethnically diverse area in all of Chicagoland, the Southwest side, home to Midway Airport and the infamous Southside Irish Parade, is a cultural stew where shared blue-collar values override perceived differences. This is true in the rougher areas, such as Englewood and Gresham, as well as in the more prosperous (and historically significant) Beverly and Morgan Park 'hoods. Marquette Park is a popular hangout, as much for local gangs as for golfers and fishermen. The area surrounding it has a strong Arab-American vibe. This is the place to go on the Southwest side for falafel and shawerma.

Landmarks

- **Capital Cigar Store** • 6258 S Pulaski Rd
- **Givens Irish Castle** • 10244 S Longwood Dr
- **Graffiti Mural** • W 59th St & S Damen Ave
- **Midway Airport** • 5700 S Cicero Ave
- **Original Rainbow Cone** • 9233 S Western Ave

Sundries/Entertainment

Irish pubs lining the Western Avenue Irish Parade route are too numerous to list. Meanwhile, Inn Exile is the Southwest side's gay video bar. Diners on the Southwest Side usually take it to go. Shoppers converge on the Ford City Shopping Center, where the cinema features 16 screens, while juvenile comedians gear up with fake vomit and whoopee cushions at Izzy Rizzy's House of Tricks.

Nightlife

- **Cork & Kerry** • 10614 S Western Ave
- **Dubliner** • 10910 S Western Ave
- **Groucho's** • 8355 S Pulaski Rd
- **Inn Exile** • 5758 W 65th St
- **Jeremy Lanigan's Irish Pub** • 3119 W 111th St
- **Keegan's Pub** • 10618 S Western Ave
- **Murphy's Law** • 9247 S Cicero Ave, Oak Lawn
- **TC's Pub** • 9700 S Cicero Ave, Oak Lawn

Restaurants

- **Franconello's Italian Restaurant** • 10222 S Western Ave
- **Hoe China Tea** • 4020 W 55th St
- **Janson's Drive-In / Snyder's Red Hots** • 9900 S Western Ave
- **Leon's Bar-B-Que** • 1206 W 59th St
- **Lume's** • 11601 S Western Ave
- **Tatra Inn** • 6040 S Pulaski Rd
- **Top Notch Beefburger** • 2116 W 95th St

Coffee

- **Café Luna** • 1742 W 99th St

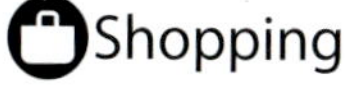

Shopping

- **African American Images Bookstore** • 1909 W 95th St
- **Bev Art Brewer and Winemaker Supply** • 10033 S Western Ave
- **Beverly Records** • 11612 S Western Ave
- **Calabria Imports** • 1905 W 103rd St
- **Ford City Center** • 7601 S Cicero Ave
- **Grich Antiques** • 10857 S Western Ave
- **Izzy Rizzy's House of Tricks** • 6356 S Pulaski Rd
- **Ms Priss** • 9915 S Walden Pkwy
- **Optimo Hat** • 10215 S Western Ave
- **Reading on Walden** • 9913 S Walden Pkwy
- **World Folk Music** • 1808 W 103rd St

Adlai E Stevenson Expy
55
W 51st St
W 47th St
S Central Ave
Vittum Park
Archer Park
ARCHER HEIGHTS
Pulaski
W Archer Ave
W 55th St
GARFIELD RIDGE
Park Number 468
WEST ELSON
Pasteur Park
Wentworth Kinzie Park
Minuteman Park
Chicago Midway Airport
Airport Dr
Midway
W 59th St
S Harlem Ave
Valley Forge Park
Nathan Hale Park
W 63rd St
WEST LAWN
Lawler Park
West Lawn Park
S Cicero Ave
BEDFORD PARK
S Pulaski Rd
Rainey Hancock Park
79th St
SCOTTSDALE
BURBANK
Scottsdale Park
Durkin Center Park
W 87th St
Harlem Ave
43
50
51
55
PAGE 272
A
B
C
1
2

W 47th St
Kedzie
Western
BACK OF THE YARDS
Cornell Square Park
W 51st St
GAGE PARK
Sherman Park
S Halsted St
W 55th St
Gage Park
W Garfield Blvd
S Kedzie Ave
S California Ave
S Western Ave
S Damen Ave
S Ashland Ave
S Racine Ave
Hermitage Park
W 59th St
CHICAGO LAWN
Lindblum Park
ENGLEWOOD
S Union Ave
S Halsted Pkwy
Ashland/63rd
W 63rd St
Halsted
WEST ENGLEWOOD
Oakley Playlot
Odgen Park
Montgomery Park
W Marquette Rd
Marquette Park
No 44 Playlot
W 71st St
Hamilton Park
Murray Playground Park
W 74th St
S Eggleston Ave
W 79th St
ASHBURN
WRIGHTWOOD
Dawes Park
MARYCREST
GRESHAM
WEST CHATHAM
W 83rd St
Ashburn Park
O' Hallaren Park
Foster Park
Dan Ryan Woods
S Vincennes Ave
Evergreen Cemetery
52
15
18
57
56

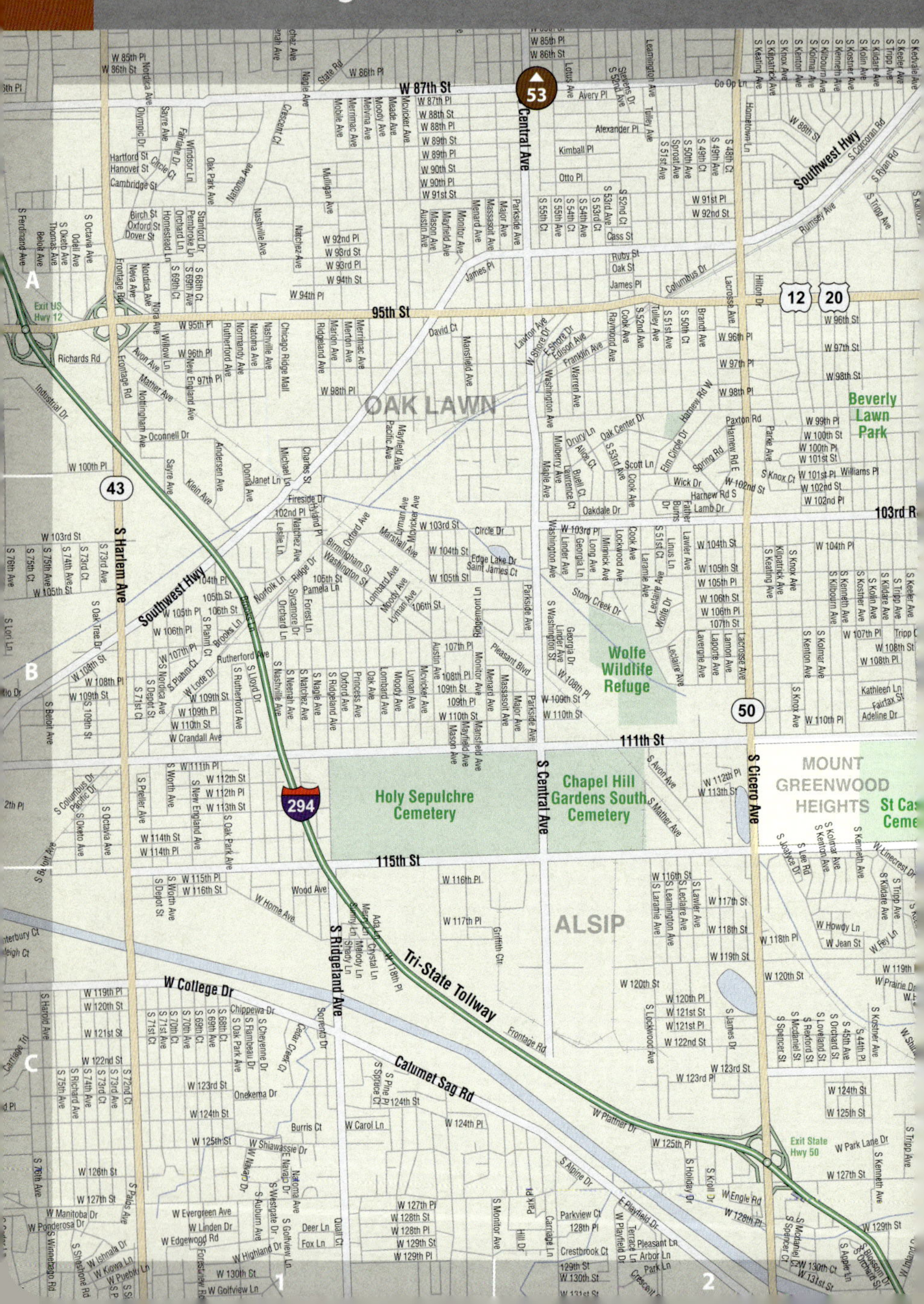
W 87th St
53
Central Ave
Southwest Hwy
95th St
12
20
Exit US Hwy 12
OAK LAWN
Beverly Lawn Park
43
S Harlem Ave
W 100th Pl
103rd Rd
Oakdale Dr
W 103rd St
Wolfe Wildlife Refuge
50
111th St
MOUNT GREENWOOD HEIGHTS
294
Holy Sepulchre Cemetery
Chapel Hill Gardens South Cemetery
S Central Ave
S Cicero Ave
115th St
ALSIP
S Ridgeland Ave
Tri-State Tollway
W College Dr
Calumet Sag Rd
Exit State Hwy 50
Richards Rd
Industrial Dr
Columbus Dr
Rumsey Ave
James Pl
Stony Creek Dr
Pleasant Blvd
W Home Ave
Wood Ave
W Platner Dr
S Alpine Dr
W 127th St
W 129th Pl
W 130th St
A
B
C
1
2

EVERGREEN PARK
BEVERLY
BRAINERD
PRINCETON PARK
WEST BEVERLY
EAST BEVERLY
LONGWOOD MANOR
MORGAN PARK
MOUNT GREENWOOD
WEST MORGAN PARK
KENNEDY PARK
ROSELAND
PULLMAN
Dan Ryan Park
Longwood Park
Ridge Park
Oakdale Park
Euclid Park
Fernwood Park
Crescent Park
Kennedy Park
Ade Park
Cooper Park
Morgan Field
White Park
Memorial Park
Central Park
W 87th St
W 95th St
W 103rd St
W 111th St
W 115th St
W 119th St
123rd St
W 127th St
Burr Oak Ave
W Vermont Ave
Western Ave
S Vincennes Ave
S Beverly Ave
S Halsted St
Halsted St
Dan Ryan Expy
S Ashland Ave
S Kedzie Ave
S Vincennes Rd
Exit 357
Exit W 103Rd St
Exit 355
Exit W 112th Pl
Exit 354
Exit 353
12
20
57
54
59
PAGE 236
A
B
C
3
4

Greater Chicago • South

Essentials

The far Southside still lives in the shadows of the abandoned steel mills that built this area. With them went the regional economy. What remaining scraps that were left are now being tugged at by the pull of legalized casinos a few miles down the road in Indiana. Meanwhile, south central Chicago, from Chatham southward, comprises the comfortable middle-class area dubbed the black bungalow belt. Here, strong community ties defy the Southside's rough-and-tumble reputation. Further afield, the white ethnic enclave of Hegewisch lives in a world of its own, fenced in by forest preserves and industrial wasteland.

Landmarks

- **Chicago Skyway** • 8801 S Anthony St
- **New Regal Theatre** • 1645 E 79th St
- **Oak Woods Cemetery** • 1035 E 67th St
- **Pullman Clock Tower** • E 111th St & S Cottage Grove Ave
- **South Shore Cultural Center** • 7059 South Shore Dr

Sundries / Entertainment

Many of the Southside's more upscale lounges are restricted to those 25 and over. The Jeffrey Pub is a long-standing gay dance club. Lee's Unleaded is a classy place to catch live blues, while jazz legend Von Freeman jams every Tuesday night at the New Apartment Lounge. Most of the city's barbeque shacks serve their take-out through bulletproof glass. For excellent, authentic soul food, go no further than Army & Lou's on E 75th Street. Vegetarians flock down the street to the always-bustling Soul Vegetarian East.

Nightlife

- **Jeffrey Pub** • 7041 S Jeffery Blvd
- **Lee's Unleaded Blues** • 7401 S Jeffrey Blvd
- **New Apartment Lounge** • 504 E 75th St
- **Pullman's Pub** • 611 E 113th St
- **Reds** • 6926 S Stony Island Ave

Restaurants

- **Army & Lou's** • 422 E 75th St
- **Atomic Sub** • 6353 S Cottage Grove Ave
- **Captain Hard Times** • 436 E 79th St
- **Chatham Pancake House** • 700 E 87th St
- **Dat's Donuts** • 8251 S Cottage Grove Ave
- **Helen's Restaurant** • 1732 E 79th St
- **Leon's Bar-B-Que** • 8249 S Cottage Grove Ave
- **Phil's Kastle** • 9232 S Commercial Ave
- **Soul Queen** • 9031 S Stony Island Ave
- **Soul Vegetarian East** • 205 E 75th St
- **Tropic Island Jerk Chicken** • 1922 E 79th St

Shopping

- **Underground Afrocentric Bookstore** • 1727 E 87th St

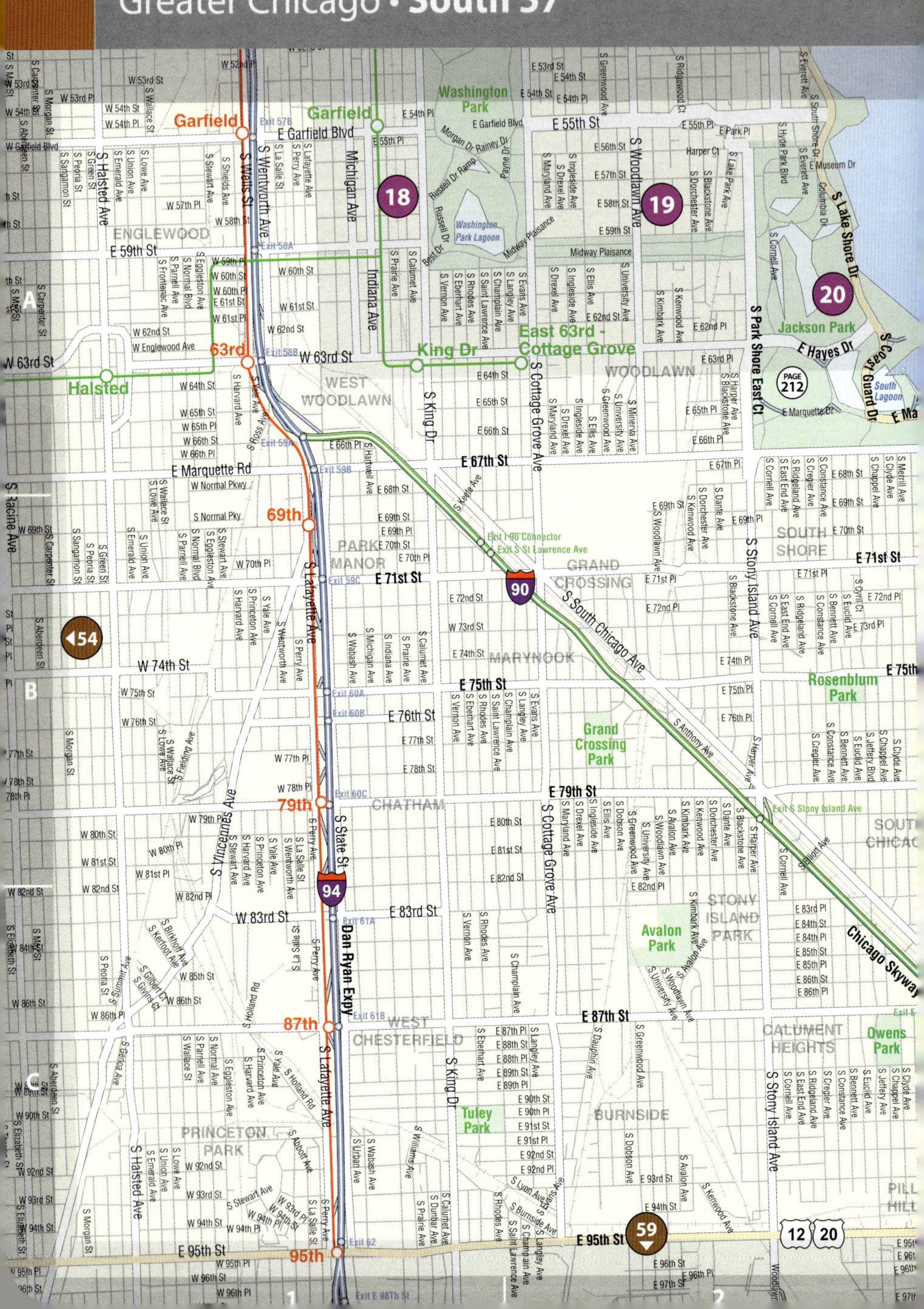
Garfield
Garfield
Washington Park
Washington Park Lagoon
Midway Plaisance
18
19
20
Jackson Park
South Lagoon
PAGE 212
ENGLEWOOD
WEST WOODLAWN
WOODLAWN
63rd
Halsted
King Dr
East 63rd - Cottage Grove
E Hayes Dr
S Coast Guard Dr
S Lake Shore Dr
S Park Shore East Ct
E Marquette Dr
E Marquette Rd
69th
PARK MANOR
GRAND CROSSING
SOUTH SHORE
E 71st St
90
S South Chicago Ave
MARYNOOK
54
W 74th St
E 75th St
Rosenblum Park
Grand Crossing Park
E 79th St
79th
CHATHAM
SOUTH CHICAGO
94
S State St
Dan Ryan Expy
W 83rd St
E 83rd St
STONY ISLAND PARK
Avalon Park
Chicago Skyway
87th
E 87th St
WEST CHESTERFIELD
CALUMENT HEIGHTS
Owens Park
Tuley Park
BURNSIDE
PRINCETON PARK
S Stony Island Ave
S Halsted Ave
S Lafayette Ave
S Cottage Grove Ave
S Woodlawn Ave
S Wentworth Ave
S Wells St
Michigan Ave
Indiana Ave
S King Dr
S Racine Ave
S Vincennes Ave
W 95th St
E 95th St
95th
59
12
20
A
B
C
1
2

Lake Michigan

A

B

C

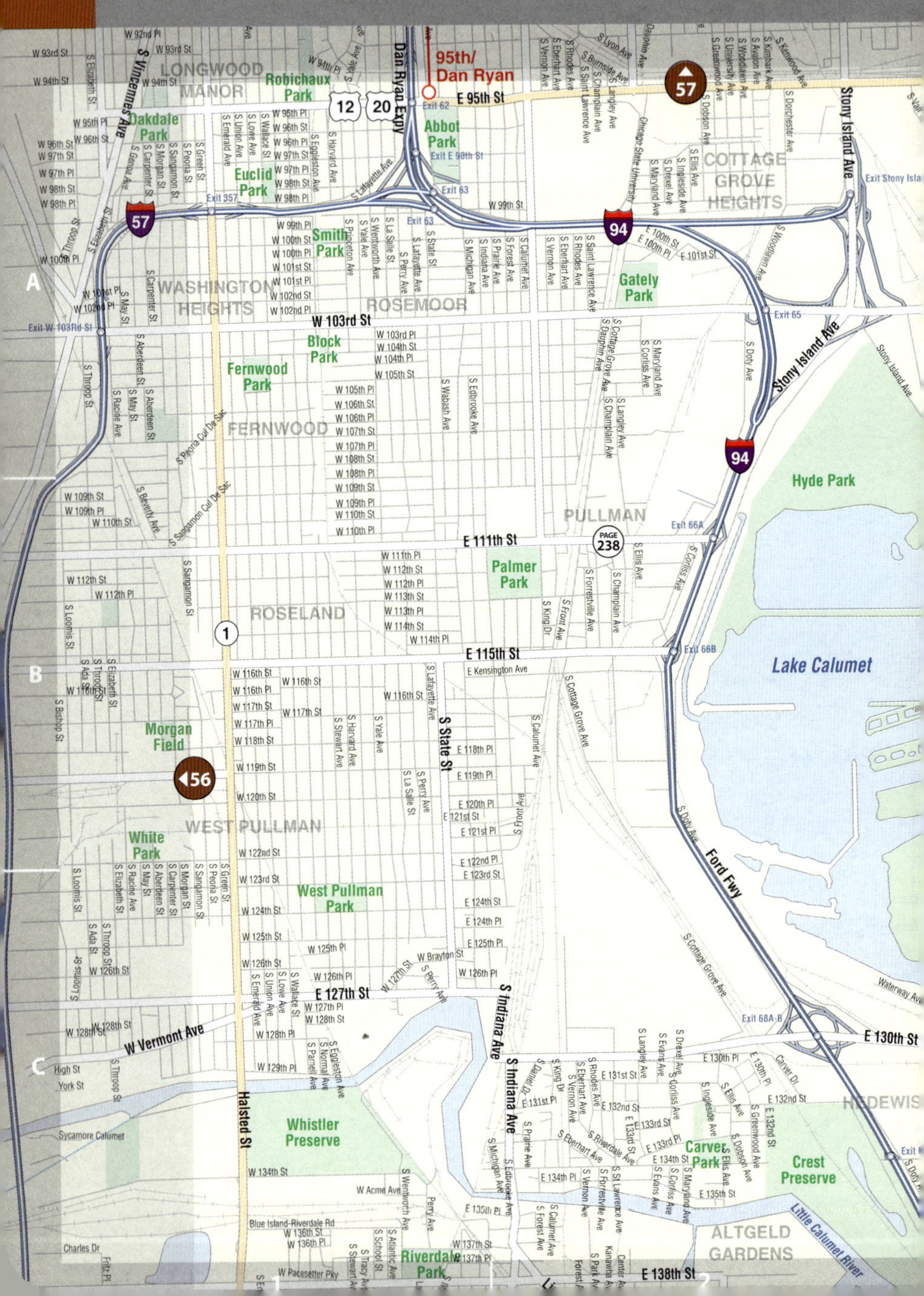
95th/
Dan Ryan
Dan Ryan Expy
E 95th St
Exit 62
Exit E 98th St
Exit 63
Exit 357
Exit W 103Rd St
Exit 65
Exit 66A
Exit 66B
Exit 68A-B
Exit Stony Island
LONGWOOD
MANOR
Robichaux
Park
Oakdale
Park
Abbot
Park
Euclid
Park
COTTAGE
GROVE
HEIGHTS
Smith
Park
WASHINGTON
HEIGHTS
ROSEMOOR
Gately
Park
W 103rd St
Block
Park
Fernwood
Park
FERNWOOD
Stony Island Ave
Hyde Park
PULLMAN
E 111th St
PAGE
238
Palmer
Park
ROSELAND
E 115th St
E Kensington Ave
Lake Calumet
Morgan
Field
56
57
WEST PULLMAN
White
Park
West Pullman
Park
S State St
Ford Fwy
E 127th St
W Vermont Ave
S Indiana Ave
E 130th St
Halsted St
Whistler
Preserve
Carver
Park
Crest
Preserve
HEGEWISCH
ALTGELD
GARDENS
Little Calumet River
Riverdale
Park
E 138th St
W 134th St
W Acme Ave
Blue Island-Riverdale Rd
W Pacesetter Pky
Charles Dr
Sycamore Calumet
High St
York St
Waterway Av
E 130th Pl
E 132nd St
E 134th St
E 135th St
A
B
C
1
2

Lake Michigan
Calumet Park
Veterans Memorial Park
Trumbull Park
Wolfe Plg Park
Rowen Park
Eggers Woods
Wolf Lake Park
Wolf Lake
Forsyth Park
Menn Park
Burnham Woods
Pulaski Park
JEFFERY MANOR
SOUTH DEERING
HEGEWISCH
Calumet River
Chicago Skyway
S Indianapolis Ave
Calumet Ave
E 95th St
E 100th St
E 103rd St
E 106th St
E 130th St
S Colfax Ave
S Torrence Ave
S Avenue O
S Ewing Ave
S Avenue L
S Brainard Ave
S Saginaw Ave
INDIANA
ILLINOIS
58
12
20
41
90
912
A
B
C
3
4

Randolph
E Randolph St
Chicago Cultural Center
PAGE 220
Randolph Street Station
Washington
E Washington St
Millennium Park Music Pavilion
Daley Bicentennial Plaza
Madison
E Madison St
Millennium Park
PAGE 208
MAP 6
Monroe
E Monroe St
E Monroe Dr
Adams
E Adams St
Art Institute of Chicago
PAGE 334
Butler Field
Petrillo Music Shell
Monroe St Harbor
Jackson
E Jackson Blvd
E Jackson Dr
Rose Garden
E Van Buren St
Van Buren Street Station
W Congress Pkwy
E Congress Dr
Buckingham Fountain
Lake Michigan
Harrison
E Harrison St
Spirit of Music Garden
41
E Balbo Ave
E Balbo Dr
Grant Park
E 8th St
Hutchinson Field
E 9th St
S Michigan Ave
Columbus Dr
S Lake Shore Dr
MAP 9
E 11th St
Roosevelt Road Station
Roosevelt/ Wabash
W Roosevelt Rd
E Roosevelt Rd
Field Plaza Dr
John G Shedd Aquarium
Field Museum of Natural History
Adler Planetarium
E 13th St
Wm McFetridge Dr
Burnham Park
Museum Campus
PAGE 214
Soldier Field
PAGE 264
MAP 11
Burnham Harbor
E 14th St
S State St
S Wabash Ave
S Indiana Ave
E Waldron Dr
Field Blvd
Harbor Dr

Overview

Called Chicago's "front lawn," Grant Park stretches along the lakeshore from Randolph Street south to Roosevelt Road and west to Michigan Avenue where grass meets glass. While the city's massive summer festivals turn the park into Chicago's dirty doormat, Grant Park is usually a quiet place with open space to relax, play, and panhandle.

The park's history can be traced back to 1835, when concerned citizens lobbied to prevent development along their pristine waterfront. The State of Illinois ruled to preserve the land as "public ground forever to remain vacant of buildings." Architect and city planner Daniel Burnham laid the groundwork for the park and made plans to erect museums and civic buildings along the waterfront. Chicagoans can thank homeboy and mail-order king Aaron Montgomery Ward for pressuring the State of Illinois in 1911 to preserve the land as an undeveloped open space.

Nature

Grant Park's lawns, gardens, lakefront, and bench-lined paths attract a mixed crowd of lunching office workers, runners, bikers, readers, and thinkers (some disguised as snoozing homeless folks). South and north of Buckingham Fountain are the formal Spirit of Music Garden and Rose Garden, respectively. Near Daley Bicentennial Plaza is the riotously colorful Wildflower Garden, recalling Illinois' prairie past. There are also 18 sculptures strewn with abandon throughout the park.

Sports

On the park's north side is Daley Bicentennial Plaza (337 E Randolph St, 312-742-7648) equipped with a fitness center, skating rink, and 12 outdoor tennis courts. The courts are open year-round from 7 am to 10 pm on weekdays and from 9 am to 5 pm on weekends. Court time costs $7 per hour (and there's a two-hour limit). We recommend making reservations (312-742-7650). The skating rink is open daily from November to March for ice-skating ($4-$5 skate rental available), and open for free in-line skating on off-ice months. On the south end of the park, baseball diamonds and tennis courts are available on a first-come basis (unless they are reserved for league play).

Buckingham Fountain

Buckingham Fountain is Grant Park's spouting centerpiece at the intersection of Congress Parkway and Columbus Drive. Designed by Edward Bennett, the fountain has been showering onlookers with wind-blown spray since 1927, and is notable for its role in the opening sequence of the sitcom *Married with Children*. Today, the water flows April through October from 10 am to 11 pm daily. For 20 minutes each hour, the center basin jettisons water 150 feet into the air. The skyrocketing water display is accompanied by lights and music during evening hours. Food concessions and restrooms can be found nearby.

Festivals & Events

Chicagoans used to gather at the Petrillo Music Shell for free Grant Park Orchestra and Chorus concerts during the summer. Now they go to the Millennium Park Music Pavilion, located between Michigan and Columbus Avenues. Concerts take place June through August (312-742-4763; www.grantparkmusicfestival.com). You can't always pass up a free headliner concert at Grant Park's monstrous Summer Festivals. Avoid the gut-to-gut, al fresco feeding frenzy at the ten-day Taste of Chicago by going, if you must, on a weekday. For a complete event schedule, contact the Mayor's Office of Special Events at 312-744-3370, or check out their website at www.cityofchicago.org/specialevents.

How to Get There

By Car: Exits off Lake Shore Drive west to Grant Park are Randolph Street, Monroe Drive, Jackson Drive, Balbo Drive, and Roosevelt Road. Also, enter the park from Michigan Avenue heading east on the same streets. The underground East Monroe Garage is off Monroe Drive. Columbus Drive runs through Grant Park's center and has metered parking.

By Train: From the Richard B. Ogilvie Transportation Center, travel east to Michigan Avenue and Grant Park on CTA buses 14, 56, and 20 ($1.75 one-way). From Union Station, board CTA buses 60, 157, 123, and 151.

Metra trains coming from the south stop at the Roosevelt Road station on the south end of Grant Park before terminating at the underground Randolph Street station below Millennium Park.

By L: Get off at any L stop in the Loop between Randolph Street and Van Buren Street ($1.75 one-way). Walk two blocks east to Grant Park.

By Bus: CTA buses 151, 145, 146, 147, 3, and 10 (weekends only) stop along Michigan Avenue in front of Grant Park ($1.75 one-way).

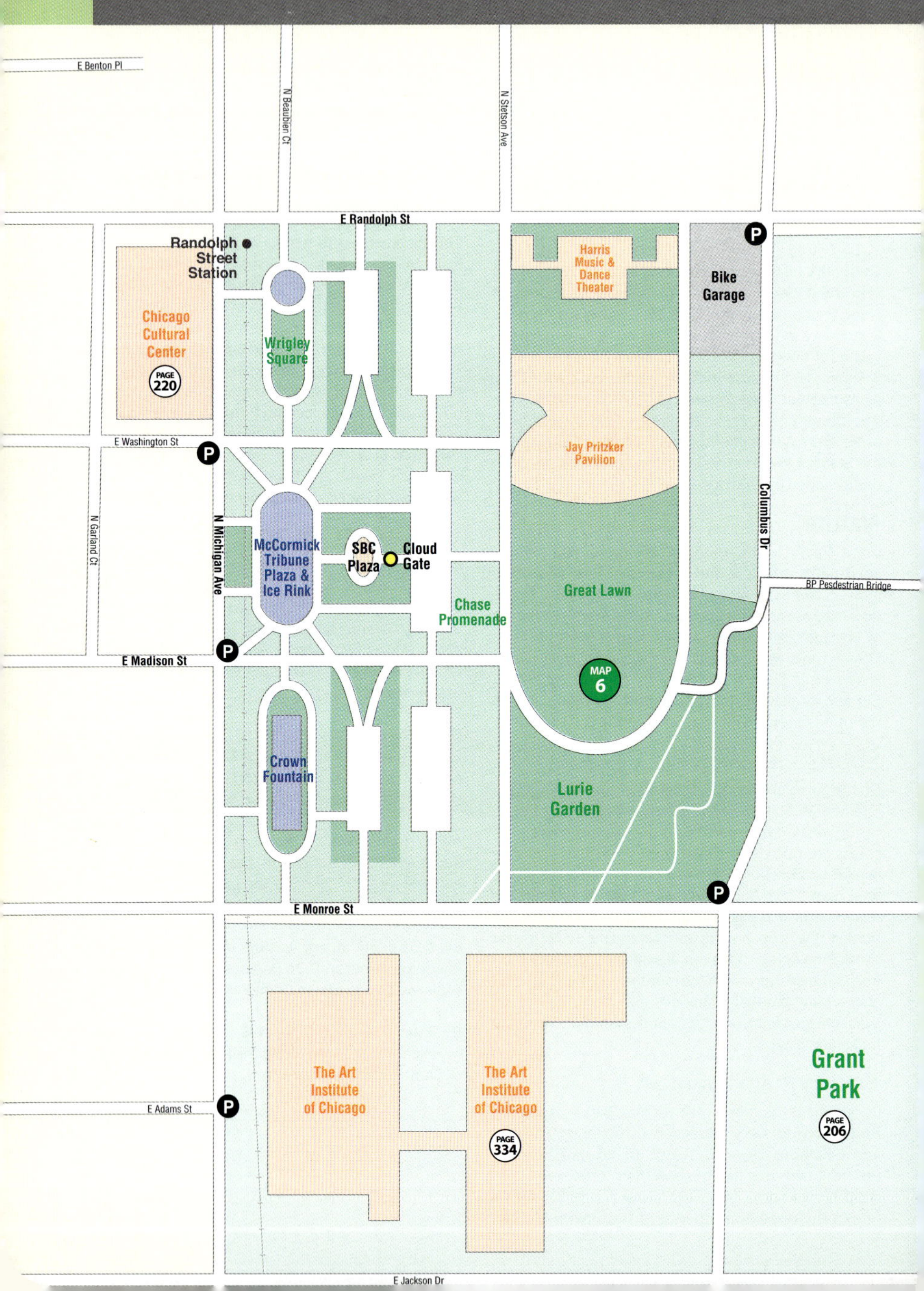
E Benton Pl
N Beaubien Ct
N Stetson Ave
E Randolph St
Randolph Street Station
Chicago Cultural Center
PAGE 220
Wrigley Square
Harris Music & Dance Theater
Bike Garage
E Washington St
Jay Pritzker Pavilion
Columbus Dr
N Garland Ct
N Michigan Ave
McCormick Tribune Plaza & Ice Rink
SBC Plaza
Cloud Gate
Chase Promenade
Great Lawn
BP Pesdestrian Bridge
E Madison St
MAP 6
Crown Fountain
Lurie Garden
E Monroe St
The Art Institute of Chicago
The Art Institute of Chicago
PAGE 334
Grant Park
PAGE 206
E Adams St
E Jackson Dr

Overview

Four years behind schedule and hundreds of millions of dollars over budget, Millennium Park has *finally* launched itself as the cultural epicenter Daley Da Mare promised us it would be, even if it did take myriad stop-gap funding measures to eternally endow us with the SBC Plaza, McCormick Tribune Plaza & Ice Rink, and the Chase Promenade. While gaped-mouth denizens ooh and aah, even nay-sayers will have to admit that, with all said and done, it's really pretty swell. Now we're just waiting for the Art Institute expansion, scheduled for tape-cutting in 2007, to complete the vision and finally send the construction crews home.

Jay Pritzker Pavilion

The cornerstone of Millennium Park, it seems as though the whole park may have been conceived to give the Gehry architectural masterpiece an appropriate setting. Spectacularly innovative, the pavilion's façade features immense stainless steel ribbons unfurling 40 feet into the sky. The pavilion's stage area is as big as Orchestra Hall across the street, and can accommodate a 120-person orchestra and a 150-person choir. Seating for the free concert events includes a 4,000-seat terrace and an additional 95,000-square-foot lawn area that can accommodate 7,000 picnickers. A one-of-a-kind integrated sound system offers outdoor acoustics to rival Ravinia. Meanwhile, the now obsolete Petrillo Bandshell sulks from across the way in Butler Field.

Harris Music & Dance Theater

Several dance and theatrical troupes share the 1,500-seat underground space behind Gehry's behemoth bandshell, including Hubbard Street Dance, the Chicago Children's Choir, and the Jazz Institute of Chicago. Two underground parking garages flank the theater.

Tickets and schedule available at www.madtchi.com.

Nature & Sculpture

The park has several different defined green spaces, including Wrigley Square, with its neoclassical peristyle (a great place to eat a sandwich on a nice day); the Chase Promenade, gearing up to house art fairs and ethnic festivals; and SBC Plaza, between the skating rink and promenade, home to Anish Kapoor's 100-ton stainless steel jelly-bean sculpture entitled *Cloud Gate*. Flanking the skating rink to the south is the modernist Crown Fountain. The Lurie Garden, a ridiculously conceptual assemblage of seasonal foliage, offers a beautiful public gathering space, as well as more contemplative environments. A pedestrian bridge, also designed by Gehry, connects the park with Daley Bicentennial Plaza, across Columbus Drive.

Sports

The 15,910-square-foot McCormick Tribune ice skating rink opens annually in November. Admission is free and skates are available for rental. The park also houses a state-of-the-art bicycle garage. The heated space provides parking for 300 bikes, showers, a repair facility, and a café.

Dining

The 300-seat Park Grill, overlooking the skating rink, offers burgers, steaks, and salads year round. In the summer, carry-away grub is available from a variety of kiosks throughout the park.

How to Get There

No matter your mode of travel, approach the area around Millennium Park with patience and allow extra time. For train, L, and bus transportation recommendations, see NFT's Grant Park or Art Institute sections. Metra's Randolph Street train station, servicing only south-bound trains, is located under Millennium Park.

If you choose to drive, underground parking is available. Access the Grant Park North Garage from Michigan Avenue. Enter Millennium Park Garage from the lower levels of Randolph Street and mid-level of Columbus Drive.

Overview

The largest of Chicago's 552 parks, Lincoln Park stretches 1,208 acres along the lakefront from the breeder cruising scene at the North Avenue Beach to the gay cruising scene at Hollywood Beach. The park boasts one of the world's longest bike trails, but thanks to an ever-increasing abundance of stroller-pushers, leashless dogs, and headphone-wearing rollerbladers, the path proves treacherous for cyclists and pedestrians alike. Nonetheless, sporty types and summertime cruisers still find satisfaction indoors and out at Lincoln Park. Public buildings, including animal houses at the Lincoln Park Zoo, Café Brauer, Peggy Notebaert Nature Museum, and vintage beach bath houses, make the park as architecturally attractive as it is naturally beautiful.

Nature

Much of southern Lincoln Park is open green space popular for football, soccer, dog play, and barbeques. Paths shaded by mature trees lead to stoic statues. Until the 1860s, Lincoln Park was nothing more than a municipal cemetery filled with the shallow graves of cholera and small pox victims. Although the city attempted to relocate all the bodies in the cemetery-to-park conversion of 1869, digging doggies may unearth more than picnickers' chicken bones.

In spring, bird watchers flock to Lincoln Park's ponds and nature trails. Addison Bird Sanctuary Viewing Platform north of Belmont Harbor overlooks five fenced-in acres of wetlands and woods. Birding programs around North Pond are run by the Lincoln Park Conservancy and the Chicago Ornithological Society (773-883-7275; Chicago, IL 60614, www.friendslp.org). Free guided walks are held on Wednesdays, starting at 7 am. Bring binoculars and plenty of coffee. The Fort Dearborn Chapter of the Illinois Audubon Society hosts free park and zoo bird walks (847-675-3622). Migratory birds gather around the revamped 1889 lily pond at Fullerton Parkway and North Cannon Drive.

Sports

Baseball diamonds on the park's south end are bordered by La Salle Drive and Lake Shore Drive, next to the newly renovated field house and NorthStar Eatery. Upgrades planned for the area include a running track, soccer field, and basketball and volleyball courts. Bicyclists and runners race along Lincoln Park Lagoon to the footbridge over Lake Shore Drive to North Avenue Beach, Chicago's volleyball mecca. To reserve courts and rent equipment, go to the south end of the landmark, boat-shaped bath house (312-742-3224). Just north of the bath house is a seasonal rollerblade rink and fitness club. North of Montrose Harbor on lakefront North Wilson Drive is a new, free skateboard park.

The nine-hole Sydney R. Marovitz Public Golf Course (3600 Recreation Dr, 312-742-7930) hosts hackers year-round. Snail-slow play allows plenty of time to enjoy skyline views from this lakefront cow pasture, which is always crowded. Greens fees are $19 weekdays, $22 on weekends, and you can rent clubs for $10. Reserve tee times by calling 312-245-0909, or show up at sunrise. The starter sits in the northeast corner of the clock tower field house.

Recreational Drive, north of Belmont Harbor, is the site of 20 first-come-first-served tennis courts, located beside baseball diamonds (which are dominated by lesbian softball leagues in the summer), playing fields, and a playground. There are four clay courts (the last ones left in Chicago!) next to the new Diversey Miniature Golf Course. The clay courts are open 7 am-8 pm and cost $16 per hour (the 7 am-9 am early bird special costs $24) ; tennis shoes are required. For reservations and further information, call 312-742-7821. Also nearby is the Diversey Golf Range (141 W Diversey Ave, 312-742-7929), open year-round (100 balls for $11, 50 balls for $7.50). The free courts at Montrose are preferred by budget-conscious folks in the know.

Members of the Lincoln Park Boat Club row in Lincoln Park Lagoon. Rowing classes for the public are offered May through September (773-549-2628; www.lpbc.net).

Whimsical, swan-shaped paddleboats at South Pond next to Café Brauer are as boring to paddle as you'd guess. Located at 2021 N Stockton Drive, this restored Prairie School national landmark houses seasonal restaurants and an upstairs ballroom, and is a popular venue for weddings and other private functions. Fishermen frequent South Pond and the lagoon. Belmont, Montrose, and Diversey Harbors also allow shore fishing.

Lincoln Park Zoo

Address: *220 N Cannon Dr*
Chicago, IL 60614
Phone: *312-742-2000*
Website: *www.lpzoo.com*
Hours: *Daily, 9 am-6 pm; animal buildings, 10 am-5 pm*
Admission: *FREE*

Established in 1868, Lincoln Park Zoo is the country's oldest free zoo. National TV shows *Zoo Parade* and Ray Rayner's show *Ark in the Park* were filmed here. The monkeys are livin' large in Lincoln Park: the cushy Regenstein Center for African Apes, which opened in 2004, cost $26 million to build and covers 29,000 square feet of living space. (Don't worry, it's supported by corporate sponsorships and private funds, not your tax dollars.) Flanking the zoo's northwest side is the free Lincoln Park Conservatory, which is a fantastic source of oxygen renewal recommended for hangover sufferers.

Peggy Notebaert Nature Museum

Address: *2430 N Cannon Dr*
Chicago, IL 60614
Phone: *773-755-5100*
Website: *www.naturemuseum.org*
Hours: *Mon-Fri 9 am-4:30 pm; Sat-Sun 10 am-5 pm*
Admission: *$7 adults, $6 Chicago residents, $5 seniors & students,$4 children under 12, Thursdays free*

The Peggy Notebaert Nature Museum succeeds in making Illinois' level landscape interesting. The contemporary version of the 1857 Chicago Academy of Sciences, this hands-on museum depicts the close connection between urban and natural environments, and represents global environmental issues through a local lens. A flowing water lab and flitting butterfly haven invite return visits. A must-see for anyone with a passion for taxidermy and/or *Silence of the Lambs*.

Chicago Historical Society

Address: *Clark St & North Ave*
Chicago, IL 60614
Phone: *312-642-4600*
Website: *www.chicagohistory.org*
Hours: *Mon-Sat 9:30 am-4:30 pm; Sun, 12 pm-5 pm*
Admission: *$5 adults,$3 seniors & students, $1 children ages 6-12, Mondays free*

The Chicago Historical Society holds over 20 million primary documents relating to the history of the Chicago area. Exhibits about the city's pioneer roots, architecture, music, fashion, neighborhoods, windy politics, and oral histories breathe life into an otherwise dry history. Locals can access the excellent free research center (open Tuesday through Saturday) for genealogical information and housing history. Big Shoulders Café (312-587-7766) is an affordable, light lunch spot nearby.

Performances

Lincoln Park Cultural Center (2045 N Lincoln Park W, 312-742-7726) stages plays, theater workshops, and family-friendly performances year-round. Theater on the Lake (Fullerton Ave & Lake Shore Dr, 312-742-7529) performs nine weeks of alternative drama in summer. The newly renovated theater now hosts events throughout the calendar year, thanks to much-needed climate control improvements. Lincoln Park Zoo hosts outdoor summer concerts as well. Call the events hotline at 312-742-2283.

How to Get There

By Car: Lake Shore Drive exits to Lincoln Park are Bryn Mawr Avenue, Foster Avenue, Lawrence Avenue, Wilson Drive, Montrose Drive, Irving Park Parkway, Belmont Avenue, Fullerton Avenue, and North Avenue.

Free parking lots are at Recreational Drive near Belmont Harbor and Simonds Drive near Montrose Harbor. Paid lots are at North Avenue Beach, Chicago Historical Society, Lincoln Park Zoo, and Grant Hospital Garage. Stockton Drive and Cannon Drive have free street parking. A metered lot is on Diversey Parkway, next to the golf range.

By Bus: CTA buses 151, 156, 77, 146, and 147 travel through Lincoln Park ($1.75 one-way). For schedules and fares, contact the RTA Information Center (312-836-7000; www.rtachicago.com).

By L: Get off the Red Line at any stop between Fullerton and Bryn Mawr Avenues ($1.75 one-way), then head one mile east.

E 55th St
55th St
S Harper Ave
S Lake Park Ave
S Cornell Ave
S Hyde Park Blvd
S South Shore Dr
57th St Beach
E 56th St
E 57th St
S Everett Ave
E Museum Dr
E 57th St
Museum of Science and Industry
Doctors Hospital of Hyde Park
Columbia Dr
Science Dr
Columbia Basin
50th Street Harbor
Lake Michigan
59th St
Perennial Garden
Columbia Dr
E 59th St
Midway Plaisance
Midway Plaisance Park
Osaka Garden
41
E 60th St
S Stony Island Ave
S Lake Shore Dr
S Harper Ave
West Lagoon
Wooded Island (Paul H Douglas Nature Sanctuary)
East Lagoon
Jackson Park Beach
E 61st St
MAP 20
E 62nd St
Tennis Courts
Hayes Dr
Jackson Park
Outdoor Basketball/ Tennis Courts
E 63rd St
Hayes Dr
Coast Guard Station
Jackson Park Field House
Hayes Dr
Coast Gd Dr Cut Off
E 64th St
S Cornell Ave
Jackson Park Golf Course
S Richards Dr
South Lagoon
S Coast Guard Dr
S Promontory Dr
La Rabida Childrens Hospital & Research Center
Yacht Harbor
E 65th St
E 65th Pl
E Marquette Dr
E Marquette Dr
E 66th St
67th St Beach
MAP 58
E 66th Pl
Basketball Courts
MAP 57
E 67th St
E 67th St
E 67th Pl
S Cornell Ave
East End Ave
Ridgeland Ave
S Cregier Ave
Constance Ave
Bennett Ave
Euclid Ave
Jeffery Ave
Chappel Ave
Clyde Ave
S Merrill Ave
S Paxton Ave
Crandon Ave
S Oglesby Ave

Overview

Historic Jackson Park, which borders Lake Michigan, Hyde Park, and Woodlawn, was, for a long time, an unused tract of fallow land. The 500-acre parcel was eventually transformed into a real city park in the 1870s, thanks to Frederick Law Olmsted of Central Park fame. The Midway Plaisance connects Jackson Park to its sister park, Washington Park. Jackson Park experienced its 15 minutes of worldwide fame in 1893, when the park played host to the World's Fair Columbian Exposition. Today, the Museum of Science and Industry and La Rabida Children's Hospital and Research Center occupy two of the former fair structures.

Until recently, Jackson Park had gone to seed. But thanks to Mayor Daley's green thumb, the government has been pumping money into park-rehabilitation projects, and Jackson Park is reaping the benefits. Major improvements to the area's lakefront, bike path, athletic centers, and beaches have Jackson Park shimmering again.

Museum of Science and Industry

Address: *57th St & Lake Shore Dr*
Chicago, IL 60637
Phone: *773-684-1414*
Website: *www.msichicago.org*
Hours: *Mon-Sat 9:30 am-4 pm; Sun 11 am-4 pm*
Admission: *$9 adults, ($8 for Chicagoans); $5 children ages 3-11, ($4.25 Chicagoans); $7.50 seniors, ($6.75 for Chicagoans)*

The 1893 World's Fair Arts Palace is now home to the Museum of Science and Industry. The mammoth 350,000 square-foot palace is one of the largest science museums in the world. Generations of Chicagoans and visitors have been wowed by hatching baby chicks, U-505 (the only World War II German submarine captured), and the Walk-Through Heart. The model railroad, another favorite exhibit, has been expanded to the now 3,500-square-foot *Great Train Journey*, which depicts the route from Chicago to Seattle. Other popular attractions include the fast food toy exhibit, the coal mine, and the Fairy Castle.

Nature

Two lagoons surround Wooded Island, aka Paul H. Douglas Nature Sanctuary. Osaka Garden, a serene Japanese garden with an authentic tea house and entrance gate, sits at the island's northern tip. The ceremonial garden, like the golden Statue of the Republic on Hayes Avenue, recalls the park's 1893 Exposition origins. The Chicago Audubon Society (773-539-6793; www.chicagoaudubon.org) conducts bird walks in the park. These sites and the Perennial Garden at 59th Street and Cornell Drive are also butterfly havens.

Sports

Back in the very beginning of the 20th century, the Jackson Park Golf Course was the only public course in the Midwest. Today, the historic 18-hole course is certified by the Audubon Cooperative Sanctuary and has beautiful wilderness habitats. (Or are those scruffy fairways?) Greens fees cost $22 during the week and $25 on weekends (all rates are discounted for residents). A driving range is adjacent to the course (312-245-0909).

In the past six years, the city has spent over $10 million to improve fitness facilities in its parks, and the Jackson Park field house was the happy recipient of a much-needed facelift. The swanky new weight room and gymnasium are open to adults weekdays from 9:30 am to 2 pm and from 6 pm to 9 pm, and weekends from 9:30 am to 4:30 pm. The facilities are open to teens from 2 pm to 6 pm. Adult membership passes cost $50 for ten weeks, and teens work out for free. From Hayes Drive north along Cornell Avenue are outdoor tennis courts, baseball diamonds, and a running track. Tennis courts are on the west side of Lakeshore Drive at 63rd Street. Jackson Park's beaches are at 57th Street and 63rd Street (water playground, too). Inner and Outer Harbors allow shore fishing (6401 S Stony Island Ave, 773-256-0903).

Neighboring Parks

North of Jackson Park at 55th Street and Lake Shore Drive is Promontory Point, a scenic lakeside picnic spot. Harold Washington Park, 51st Street and Lake Shore Drive, has a model yacht basin and eight tennis courts on 53rd Street.

To the west, 460-acre Washington Park (5531 S Martin Luther King Dr, 773-256-1248) has an outdoor swimming pool, playing fields, and nature areas. It's also worth stopping by to see Lorado Taft's 1922 Fountain of Time sculpture and the DuSable Museum of African-American History (740 E 56th Pl, 773-947-0600; www.dusablemuseum.org).

At 71st Street and South Shore Drive are South Shore Beach, a harbor, bird sanctuary, and South Shore Cultural Center (7059 South Shore Dr, 773-256-0149). South Shore Golf Course is a nine-hole public course. Greens fees cost $13.60 weekdays and $15 on weekends (312-245-0909).

How to Get There

By Car: From the Loop, drive south on Lake Shore Drive, exit west on 57th Street. From the south, take I-94 W. Exit on Stony Island Avenue heading north to 57th Drive. The museum's parking garage entrance is on 57th Drive. The Music Court lot is behind the museum. A free parking lot is on Hayes Drive.

By Bus: From the Loop, CTA buses 6 and 10 (weekends and daily in summer) stop by the museum.

By L (the quickest way to get to Jackson Park): Take the Green Line to the Garfield Boulevard (55th Street) stop ($1.75 one-way); transfer to the eastbound 55 bus.

By Train: Sporadic service. From the Loop's Randolph Street and Van Buren Street stations, take Metra Electric service ($2.05 one-way). Trains stop at the 55th, 56th, and 57th Street Station platform (may be under construction). Walk two blocks east. From the Richard B. Ogilvie Transportation Center, walk two blocks south to Union Station on Canal Street and catch CTA bus 1.

Grant Park
PAGE 206
41
Water Taxi Dock
Ped Underpass
E Roosevelt Rd
Main Entrance
Shedd Aquarium
Handicap Entrance
Group Entrance
North Main Entrance
Free Trolley Stop
S Columbus Dr
Handicap Entrance
The Field Museum
South Main Entrance
Solidarity Dr
Solidarity Dr
Free Trolley Stop
North Entrance
Adler Planetarium
Free Trolley Stop
Planetarium Lot
Group & Handicap Entrance
Free Trolley Stop
McFetridge Dr
North Garage
Lynne White Dr
12th St Beach
Museum Campus Dr
Burnham Harbor
Soldier Field
PAGE 264
Northerly Island Park
Merrill C Meigs Field
Waldron Dr
S Prairie Ave
MAP 11
S Lake Shore Dr
Waldron Garage
Burnham Park
18th St Station
S Calumet Ave
Main Museum Visitor Entrance
E 18th St
South Lot
E Cullerton St
E 21st St
S Calumet Ave
Lake Michigan
200E
300E
E Cermak Rd
S Dr Martin L King Jr Dr
S Dr Martin L King Jr Dr
S Cottage Grove Ave
McCormick Place
23rd St McCormick Place Station
E 23rd Dr
E 23rd St
400E
S Calumet Ave
Burnham Park
McCormick Place
PAGE 222
S Prairie Ave
E 24th St
E 24th Pl
E 24th Pl
Stevenson Expy
55

Overview

The Museum Campus is the ultimate destination for educational field trips. South of Grant Park at the intersection of Roosevelt Road and Lake Shore Drive, Museum Campus' 57 acres of uninterrupted lakefront parkland connect three world-renowned Chicago institutions: The Field Museum, Shedd Aquarium, and the Adler Planetarium & Astronomy Museum. You've got Mayor Daley to thank for all of this beautiful space; it was the bossman himself who championed the rerouting of Lake Shore Drive to create the Museum Campus, which opened in 1998.

The Field Museum

Address: *1400 S Lake Shore Dr*
Chicago, IL 60605
Phone: *312-922-9410*
Website: *www.fieldmuseum.org*
Hours: *Open everyday 9 am-5 pm, except Christmas,*
Admission: *$19 adults, $14 students & seniors, discount for Chicagoans*

The massive, classical Greek architectural-style museum constructed in 1921 houses over 20 million artifacts. From dinosaurs, diamonds, and earthworms to man-eating lions, totem poles, and mummies, there is just too much to savor in a single visit. Some temporary exhibits and the Underground Adventure cost an additional $7 on top of admission fees. Free museum tours are held weekdays at 11 am and 2 pm.

John G. Shedd Aquarium

Address: *1200 S Lake Shore Dr*
Chicago, IL 60605
Phone: *312-939-2438*
Website: *www.shedd.org*
Hours: *Memorial Day-Labor Day: Daily, 9 am-6 pm (open 'til 10 pm on Thurs)*
Labor Day-Memorial Day: Mon-Fri: 9 am-5 pm; Sat-Sun: 9 am-6 pm. Closed Christmas
Admission: *$23 adults ($17 Chicagoans), $16 seniors over 65 and children under 11 ($12 Chicagoans)*

In Spring 2003, the John G. Shedd Aquarium unveiled an extremely cool underwater exhibit, *Philippine Island*, a coral reef shark habitat. Visitors walk through 385,000 gallons of water where sharks cruise. The ten-room, $45-million addition showcases Indo-Pacific animals, corals, and tropical fish. Opened in 1929, the Beaux Arts architectural-style aquarium's six wings radiate from a giant, circular coral reef tank.

Burnham Park

Burnham Park, the site of the 1933 Century of Progress exhibition, encompasses McCormick Place, Burnham Harbor, the former Merrill C. Meigs Airport (closed by political coup by Mayor Daley in 2003), and Soldier Field. A free skateboard park is located at Lake Shore Drive and 31st Street. The 12th Street Beach is on Northerly Island. Other beaches are at 31st Street and 49th Street. Outdoor basketball courts are east of Lake Shore Drive around 35th Street and 47th Street. Along Solidarity Drive and Burnham Harbor shore, fishing is welcome. The wilderness Nature Area at 47th Street attracts butterflies and birds.

Adler Planetarium

Address: *1300 S Lake Shore Dr*
Chicago, IL 60605
Phone: *312-922-7827*
Website: *www.adlerplanetarium.org*
Hours: *9:30 am-4:30 pm daily; First Friday of every month: 9:30 am-10 pm; Closed Thanksgiving and Christmas.*
Admission: *$13 for adults ($11 Chicagoans), $11 kids ages 4-17 ($10 Chicagoans), $12 seniors over 65 ($10 Chicagoans)*

The Adler Planetarium & Astronomy Museum has interactive exhibits explaining space phenomena and intergalactic events. The museum's 2,000 historic astronomical and navigational instruments form the western hemisphere's largest collection. Chicago skyline views from planetarium grounds are out of this world.

How to Get There

By Car: From the Loop, take Columbus Drive south; turn east on McFetridge Drive. From the south, take Lake Shore Drive to McFetridge Drive. Area parking lots are near Soldier Field, Field Museum, Adler Planetarium, and McCormick Place. All parking on Museum Campus costs $12 per day. Metered parking is available on Solidarity Drive.

By Bus: CTA buses 2, 6, 10, 12, 14, 127, 130, and 146 serve the area ($1.75 one-way). For schedules and fares, contact the RTA Information Center at 312-913-3110; www.rtachicago.com.

By L: Ride the Orange, Red, or Green Lines to the Roosevelt Road stop ($1.75). Walk east through the pedestrian underpass at Roosevelt Road.

By Train: From Richard B. Ogilvie Transportation Center, travel east on CTA bus 20 to State Street; transfer to the 146 ($1.80 one-way). From Union Station take CTA bus 1, 151, or 126; transfer at State Street to the 146 or 10. From La Salle Street station, take the 146 ($1.75 one-way). South Shore and Metra trains stop at the Roosevelt Road station.

By Trolley: Free trolleys travel to the Museum Campus from public transportation stations and some parking lots during the warmer months. See www.cityofchicago.org/transportation, or call 1-877-CHICAGO for more details.

On Foot: Walk south through Grant Park past bobbing boats and the gushing Buckingham Fountain to the Museum Campus.

Water Taxis: Seasonally, water taxis operate between Navy Pier and the Museum Campus (312-222-9328; www.shorelinesightseeing.com).

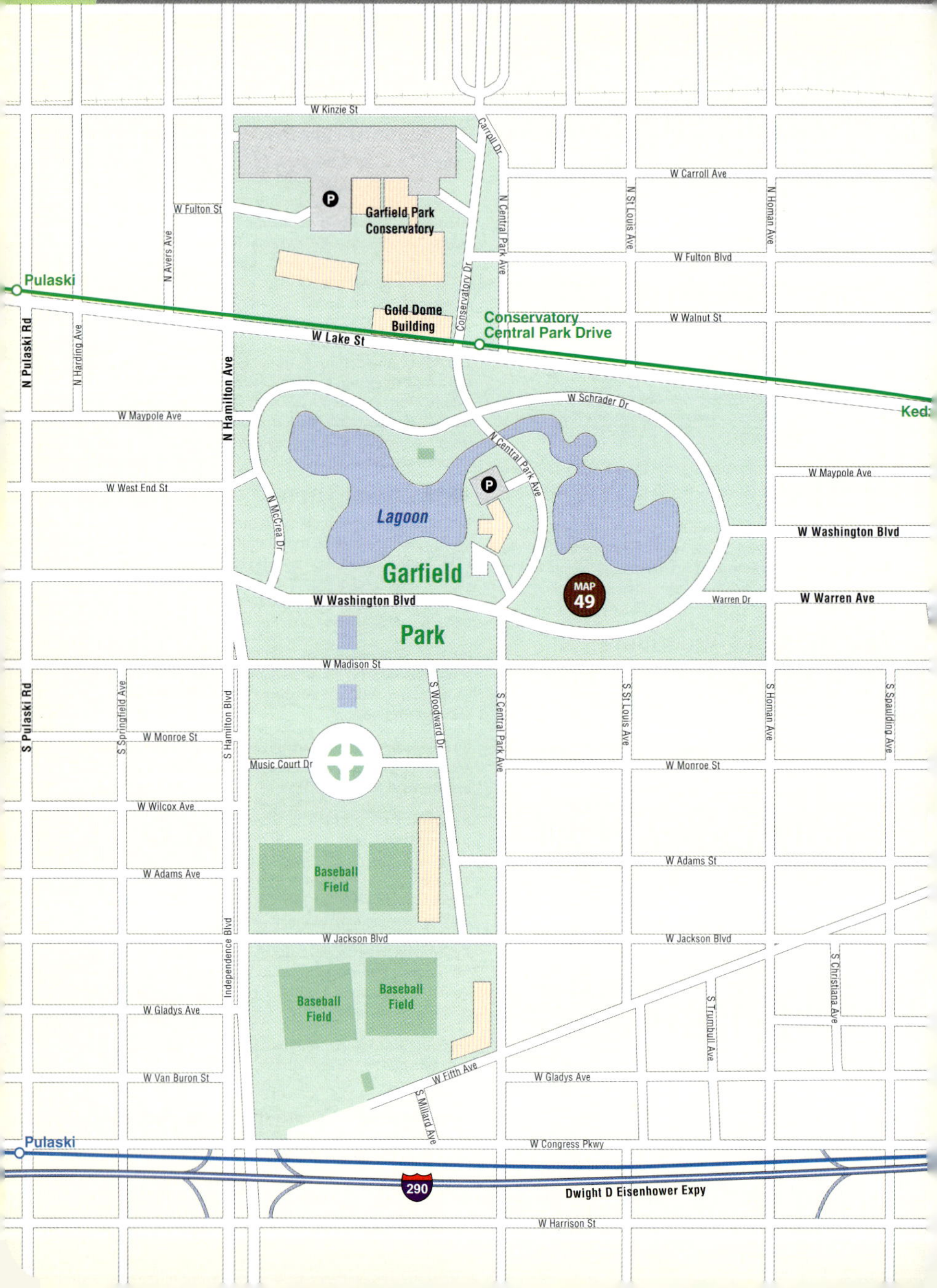

W Kinzie St
Carroll Dr
Garfield Park Conservatory
W Fulton St
N Avers Ave
W Carroll Ave
N Central Park Ave
N St Louis Ave
N Homan Ave
W Fulton Blvd
Conservatory Dr
Pulaski
Gold Dome Building
Conservatory Central Park Drive
W Walnut St
W Lake St
N Pulaski Rd
N Harding Ave
N Hamilton Ave
W Schrader Dr
Ked
W Maypole Ave
N Central Park Ave
W Maypole Ave
W West End St
N McCrea Dr
Lagoon
W Washington Blvd
Garfield
MAP 49
W Washington Blvd
Warren Dr
W Warren Ave
Park
W Madison St
S Pulaski Rd
S Springfield Ave
S Hamilton Blvd
S Woodward Dr
S Central Park Ave
S St Louis Ave
S Homan Ave
S Spaulding Ave
W Monroe St
Music Court Dr
W Monroe St
W Wilcox Ave
Baseball Field
W Adams Ave
W Adams St
W Jackson Blvd
W Jackson Blvd
Independence Blvd
Baseball Field
Baseball Field
S Trumbull Ave
S Christiana Ave
W Gladys Ave
W Fifth Ave
W Van Buron St
W Gladys Ave
S Millard Ave
Pulaski
W Congress Pkwy
290
Dwight D Eisenhower Expy
W Harrison St

Overview

Until recently, the slowly gentrifying (read: sketchy) West Side was the home of the city's best kept secret garden—Garfield Park Conservatory. But the secret has been unveiled since the Chicago Park District invested over $12 million to restore this national landmark. The 185-acre park boasts fishing lagoons, a swimming pool, an ice rink, baseball diamonds, and basketball and tennis courts. Garfield Park's landmark Gold Dome Building houses a fitness center, a basketball court, and the Peace Museum.

Garfield Park and its sister parks—Humboldt Park (1400 N Sacramento Ave, 312-742-7549) and Douglas Park (1401 S Sacramento Ave, 312-747-7670)—constitute a grand system of sprawling green spaces linked by broad boulevards designed in 1869 by William Le Baron Jenney (better known as the "father of the skyscraper.") However, Jenney's plan didn't bear fruit until almost 40 years later (after the uprooting of corrupt park officials), when Danish immigrant and former park laborer Jens Jensen became chief landscape architect. In 1908, Jensen completed the parks and consolidated their three small conservatories under the 1.8-acre Garfield Park Conservatory's curvaceous glass dome, designed to resemble a "great Midwestern haystack."

Garfield Park Conservatory

Address: *300 N Central Park Ave*
Chicago, IL 60624
Phone: *773-638-5100*
Website: *www.garfield-conservatory.org*
Hours: *9 am-5 pm daily; Thurs: 9 am-8 pm*
Admission: *FREE*

One of the nation's largest conservatories, Garfield Park has six thematic plant houses with 1,000 species and more than 10,000 individual plants from around the world. *Plants Alive!*, a 5,000-square-foot children's garden, has touchable plants, a soil pool for digging, a Jurassic Park-sized bumble bee, and a two-story, twisting flower stem that doubles as a slide. School groups often book the garden for field trips, so call first to determine public access hours. Annual Conservatory events include the Spring Flower Show, Azalea/Camellia Show, Chocolate Festival, Summer Tropical Show, Chrysanthemum (Chicago's city flower) Show, and Holiday Garden Show. A snack-café cart operates weekends. You can also score great deals on produce at the farmer's market.

The Peace Museum

Address: *100 N Central Park Ave*
Chicago, IL 60624
Phone: *773-638-6450*
Website: *www.peacemuseum.org*
Hours: *Thurs, Fri, Sat: 11 am-4 pm; Sun: 1 pm-4 pm*
Admission: *$5*

Located on the top floor of the landmark Garfield Park Gold Dome Building is the Peace Museum. The tiny museum's collection of 10,000 artworks, photographs, and artifacts promoting non-violence are displayed through rotating, thematic exhibits. Special exhibits include a John Lennon guitar, an original U2 song sheet, and moving drawings by Nagasaki and Hiroshima survivors. Call for information on current and traveling exhibits.

Fishing

Garfield Park's two lagoons at Washington Boulevard and Central Park Avenue and those at Douglas and Humboldt Parks are favorite West Side fishing holes. Seasonally, they are stocked with bluegill, crappie, channel catfish, and largemouth bass, along with an occasional unfortunate gang member. Review your health insurance plan before eating what you hook. Kids can take free fishing classes at the park lagoons during the summer through the Chicago Park District (312-747-6067). Groups of ten kids or more fish every day of the week at a new location. You'll have to call in advance, as groups are organized by appointment only. The program runs June 20-August 12, Mon-Fri, between 10 am and 4 pm.

Nature

The Chicago Park District leads free nature walks and has created marked trails with information plaques at the city's bigger parks, Garfield and Humboldt Parks included. Seasonally, visitors can view as many as 100 species of colorful butterflies at the formal gardens of Garfield Park, Humboldt Park, and Douglas Park. The parks' lagoons are officially designated Chicago "birding parks," so take binoculars. Picnics for 50 people or more and tent set-up require party-throwers to obtain permits issued by the Chicago Park District.

How to Get There

By Car: Garfield Park is ten minutes from the Loop. Take I-290 W; exit on Independence Boulevard and drive north. Turn east on Washington Boulevard to Central Park Avenue. Go north on Central Park Avenue two blocks past the Golden Dome field house and Lake Street to the Conservatory. A free parking lot is on the building's south side, just after Lake Street. Street parking is available on Central Park Avenue, Madison Street, and Washington Boulevard.

By L: From the Loop, take the Green Line west ($1.75 one-way) to the new Conservatory-Central Park Drive stop, a renovated Victorian train station at Lake Street and Central Park Avenue.

By Bus: From the Loop, board CTA 20 Madison Street bus westbound ($1.75 one-way). Get off at Madison Street and Central Park Avenue. Walk four blocks north to the Conservatory.

Additional Information

Chicago Park District, 312-742-7529;
www.chicagoparkdistrict.com
Nature Chicago Program - City of Chicago and Department of the Environment, 312-744-7606;
www.cityofchicago.org
Chicago Ornithological Society, 312-409-9678;
www.chicagobirder.org

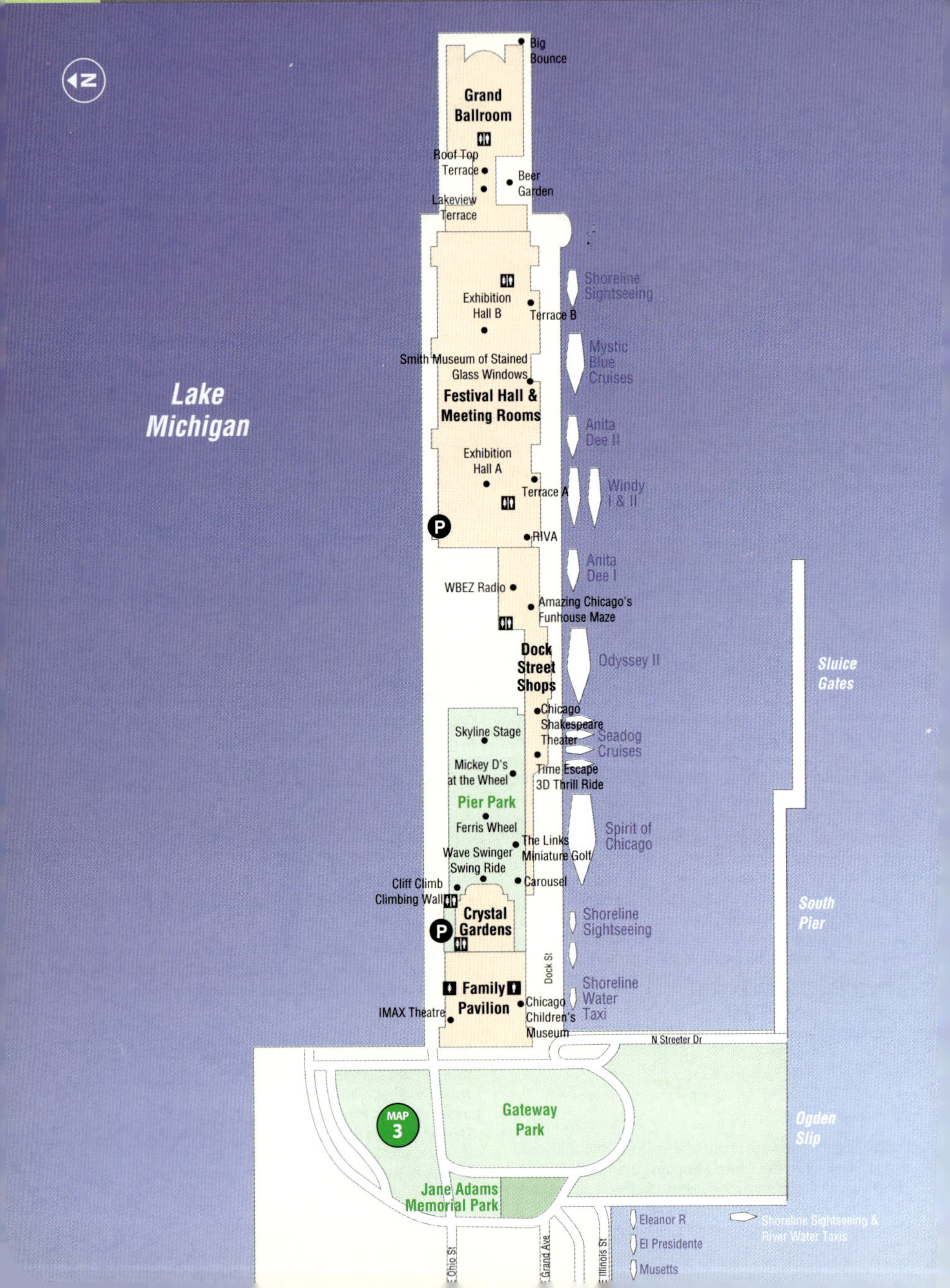

Parks & Places • Navy Pier

Big Bounce

Grand Ballroom

Roof Top Terrace

Beer Garden

Lakeview Terrace

Shoreline Sightseeing

Exhibition Hall B

Terrace B

Smith Museum of Stained Glass Windows

Mystic Blue Cruises

Lake Michigan

Festival Hall & Meeting Rooms

Anita Dee II

Exhibition Hall A

Terrace A

Windy I & II

P

RIVA

Anita Dee I

WBEZ Radio

Amazing Chicago's Funhouse Maze

Dock Street Shops

Odyssey II

Sluice Gates

Chicago Shakespeare Theater

Seadog Cruises

Skyline Stage

Mickey D's at the Wheel

Time Escape 3D Thrill Ride

Pier Park

Ferris Wheel

Spirit of Chicago

The Links Miniature Golf

Wave Swinger Swing Ride

Carousel

Cliff Climb Climbing Wall

South Pier

Crystal Gardens

P

Shoreline Sightseeing

Dock St

Family Pavilion

Shoreline Water Taxi

IMAX Theatre

Chicago Children's Museum

N Streeter Dr

MAP 3

Gateway Park

Ogden Slip

Jane Adams Memorial Park

Eleanor R

Shoreline Sightseeing & River Water Taxis

El Presidente

Musetts

Ohio St

Grand Ave

Illinois St

General Information

NFT Map:	3
Address:	600 E Grand Ave Chicago, IL 60611
Phone:	312-595-7437
Website:	www.navypier.com
Pier Hours:	Opens 10 am daily. Closing times of restaurants, shops, and attractions vary by season, holiday, and public exhibitions/events.
Skyline Stage:	1,500-seat, outdoor performance pavilion in Pier Park; performances are May through September, 312-595-5005
IMAX Theatre:	312-595-5629
Free Fireworks Displays:	Memorial Day to Labor Day nights, Wednesdays (9:30 pm) & Saturdays (10:15 pm)
WBEZ Radio:	National Public Radio's local station, 312-948-4600; www.wbez.org.
Exhibit Space:	Festival Hall, Lakeview Terrace, Ballroom Lobby, Grand Ballroom; 36 meeting rooms

Overview

A playground for the uninspired tourist, Navy Pier (a.k.a. the mall on the lake) is often avoided by real Chicagoans, who scoff at its self-consciously inoffensive blandness. Save for an occasional Skyline Stage concert or high-end nosh at RIVA, a trek to the pier is best reserved for those times when you have Grandma and a bevy of nieces and nephews in tow.

Built in 1916 as a municipal wharf, the pier has also done time as a) the University of Illinois at Chicago's campus, b) a hospital, c) a military training facility, d) a concert venue, and e) a white elephant. In 1989, the Metropolitan Pier and Exposition Authority invested $150 million to transform the crumbling pier into a peninsular entertainment-exhibition complex that attracts 8 million uninspired people a year. In addition to convention space, Navy Pier has two museums, the Shakespeare Theater, the Crystal Gardens, outdoor concert pavilion, vintage grand ballroom, 15-story Ferris wheel, IMAX Theatre, and, just for the hell of it, a radio station.

Chicago Shakespeare Theater

The professional Chicago Shakespeare Theater has a 510-seat, courtyard-style theater and a 185-seat studio theater that are Chicago's sole venues dedicated to performing wordsmith Willy's works. In addition to the season's plays, the theater produces Shakespeare "shorts" for younger patrons. A bookstore and teacher resource center are also on-site (312-595-5600; www.chicagoshakes.com).

Chicago Children's Museum

The Chicago Children's Museum features daily activities, a creative crafts studio, and 15 interactive exhibits ranging from dinosaur digs and waterworks to a toddler tree house, safety town, and construction zone. The museum is open Monday through Saturday 10 am to 8 pm, and Sunday until 7 pm. Admission is $7 for adults and children; free Thursdays 5 pm to 8 pm (312-527-1000; www.chichildrensmuseum.org).

Smith Museum of Stained Glass Windows

This is the first stained-glass-only museum in the country. The 150 windows installed in the lower level of Festival Hall are mainly from Chicago-area buildings and the city's renowned stained glass studios. Windows representing over a century of artistic styles include works by Louis Comfort Tiffany, Frank Lloyd Wright, Louis Sullivan, and John LaFarge. The free museum is open during Pier hours (312-595-5024).

Getting There

By Car: From the north, exit Lake Shore Drive at Grand Avenue; proceed east. From the southeast, exit Lake Shore Drive at Illinois Street; go east. Three garages are on the Pier's north side, and plenty of parking lots are just west of Lake Shore Drive in Streeterville (Map 3).

By Bus: CTA buses 29, 56, 65, 66, 120, 121, and 124 serve Navy Pier.

By L: Take the Green or Red Line to Grand Avenue ($1.75 one-way). Board eastbound CTA Bus 29 (additional 25¢) or take the free trolley.

By Train: From Richard B. Ogilvie Transportation Center, take CTA buses 56 or 124. From Union Station, board bus 121.

By Trolley: Free, daily trolleys that typically run every 20 minutes travel between Navy Pier and State Street along Grand Avenue and Illinois Street. Pick-up points are indicated by "Navy Pier Trolley Stop" signs along the route. Go to: www.tylin.com/chicago/tma

By Boat: Seasonal water shuttles (one-way $12 adults, $6 kids) travel between Navy Pier and the Museum Campus and along the Chicago River to the Sears Tower (312-222-9328; www.shorelinesightseeing.com).

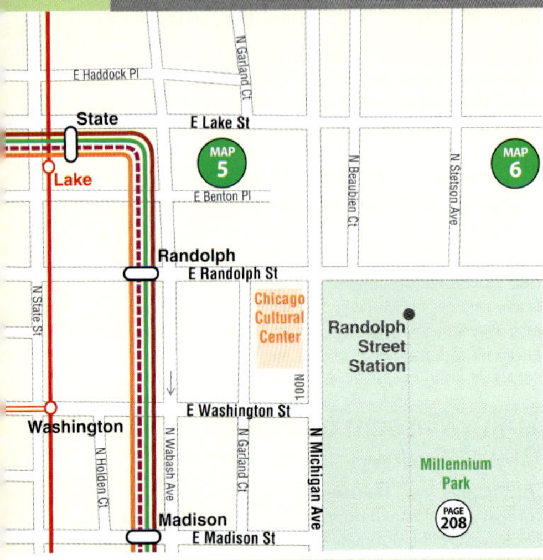

General Information

NFT Maps: 5, 6
Address: 78 E Washington St
Chicago, IL 60602
Phone: 312-744-6630
Website: www.cityofchicago.org/culturalcenter/
Hours: Mon-Thurs 10 am -7 pm; Fri 10 am-6 pm; Sat 10 am-5 pm; Sun 11 am-5 pm; closed on holidays

Overview

The Chicago Cultural Center is the Loop's public arts center. Free—that's right, we said FREE—concerts, theatrical performances, films, lectures, and exhibits are offered daily. Admission to the Cultural Center and its art galleries are all free, too. Call 312-346-3278 for weekly event updates.

The building itself, constructed in 1897, is a neoclassical landmark featuring intricate glass and marble mosaics on its walls and grand stairways. Once the city's central public library, the Cultural Center boasts the world's largest Tiffany dome in Preston Bradley Hall and the Renaissance-style Grand Army of the Republic Exhibition Hall. Free (there's that lovely word again) 45-minute architectural tours are held on Wednesdays, Fridays, and Saturdays at 1:15 pm. If you're interested in a guided group tour highlighting the building's history, call 312-744-8032 for more information.

Performances

The Cultural Center's free "LunchBreak" series provides downtown working stiffs with a welcome midday respite. The jazz concerts are held at 12:15 pm in the Randolph Café every Tuesday and Friday, while the classical concerts and opera are performed Mondays at 12:15 pm in Preston Bradley Hall. Call 312-744-6630 for information on frequently scheduled special programs.

Off-Loop theater productions appear regularly in the Center's Studio Theater, including the seasonal ShawChicago series featuring plays by Bernard Shaw on Saturdays, Sundays, and Mondays. Performances are free but reservations are required (312-409-5605; www.shawchicago.org).

Art Galleries

A permanent exhibit in the Landmark Gallery, *Chicago Landmarks Before the Lens* is a stunning black-and-white photographic survey of Chicago architecture. Five additional galleries regularly rotate exhibits, showcasing work in many media by renowned and local artists. Tours of current exhibits are Thursdays at 12:15 pm.

How to Get There

By Car: Travel down Michigan Avenue to Randolph Street. From Lake Shore Drive, exit at Randolph Street. For parking garages in the area, see Map 6.

By Train: From the Richard B. Ogilvie Transportation Center, travel east to Michigan Avenue on CTA buses 157, 20, 56, and 127. From Union Station, take CTA buses 60, 157, and 151. From the Randolph Street station below Millennium Park, walk west across Michigan Avenue. For schedules and fares, contact the RTA Information Center (312-836-7000; www.rtachicago.com).

By L: Take the Green Line to the Randolph stop. Walk east one block.

By Bus: CTA buses 151, 145, 147, and 3 stop on Michigan Avenue in front of the Cultural Center.

General Information

NFT Map: 5
Address: 400 S State St
Chicago, IL 60605
Phone: 312-747-4999
Website: www.chipublib.org

Overview

Harold Washington Library Center is the world's largest public library. Named after Chicago's first African-American mayor, the 756,640-square-foot architectural monstrosity has over 70 miles of shelves storing more than 9 million books, microforms, serials, and government documents. Over 50 works of notable sculpture, painting, and mosaic adorn the free library visited by over 6,000 patrons daily.

The library's collections are located on floors three through eight. Roam the outer walls for a windowed alcove in which to read, write, or snooze in blissful quiet. The Winter Garden on the ninth floor is a welcome escape from bad weather, while Secondhand Prose, a used bookstore on the first floor, is perfect for those of us who don't want the hassle of pesky late fees. Frequent free public programs are held in the lower level's 385-seat auditorium, video theater, exhibit hall, and meeting rooms. Call 312-747-4649 for information on scheduled events.

Library hours are Monday through Thursday 9 am to 7 pm, Friday and Saturday 9 am to 5 pm, and Sunday 1 pm to 5 pm. Free library tours can be arranged for groups by calling 312-747-4136.

Research Services

To check the availability or location of an item, call Catalog Information at 312-747-4340, or search the library's Online Catalog on www.chipublib.org. Their Email Reference Service responds to information requests within two days. For faster answers to common research questions, check out the website's handy Virtual Library Service under Selected Internet Resources, then click on "Reference Shelf."

Computer Services

The library's 96 computers with Internet access and 37 more with word processing, desktop publishing, graphic presentation, and spreadsheet applications are located on the third floor in the Computer Commons. Computer use is free and available on a first-come-first-served basis. You can reserve computers for up to one hour per day based on walk-in availability. Limited time slots are also available via phone reservation at 312-747-4540. For downloads, bring your own formatted disk or purchase one at the library for $2. Free laser printing is also provided. Operating hours are Monday through Thursday 9 am-7 pm, Friday and Saturday 9 am-5 pm, and Sunday 1 pm-5 pm.

Thomas Hughes Children's Library

The 18,000-square-foot Thomas Hughes Children's Library on the second floor serves children through age 14. In addition to more than 120,000 books representing 40 foreign languages, there is a reference collection on children's literature for adults. Twenty free computers, twelve with Internet connections, are also available. Children's programs are hosted weekly (312-747-4200).

Special Collections

The library's Special Collections & Preservation Division's highlights include: Harold Washington Collection, Civil War & American History Research Collection, Chicago Authors & Publishing Collection, Chicago Blues Archives, Chicago Theater Collection, World's Columbian Exposition Collection, and Neighborhood History Research Collection. The collections' reading room is closed Thursday, Friday, and Sunday.

How to Get There

By Car: The library is at the intersection of State Street and Congress Parkway in South Loop. Take I-290 E into the Loop. See Map 5 for area parking garages.

By L: The Brown Line, Purple Line, and Orange Line stop at the Library Station. Exit the Red Line and O'Hare Airport Blue Line at Van Buren Station; walk one block south. Change from the Harlem/Lake Street Green Line to the northbound Orange Line at Roosevelt Road station; get off at Library Station.

By Bus: CTA buses that stop on State Street in front of the library are the 2, 6, 29, 36, 62, 151, 145, 146, and 147.

N
Michigan Ave
Indiana Ave
Prairie Ave
MAP 11
21st St
Calumet St
Mines Dr
Moe Dr
Soldier Field Parking Lot
P
North Building
Level 4
Meeting Rooms (N426-N427)
Level 3
Exhibition Halls
Level 2
Meeting Rooms (N226-N231)
Level 1
Exhibition Halls
Meeting Rooms (N126-N140)
Lakeside Technology
Conference Center
E Cermak Rd (E 22nd St)
Lake Shore Dr
41
Burnham Park
Lakeside Center (East Building)
Level 4
Meeting Rooms (E450-E451)
Level 3
Exhibition Halls
Meeting Rooms (E350-E354)
Arie Crown Balcony
Level 2
Exhibition Hall E
Meeting Rooms (E250-E272)
Arie Crown Theater
Level 1
Offices
Parking Lot A
Hyatt Parking Garage
Hyatt Hotel
Martin Luther King Dr
McCormick Square
Gate 22
North Building
Taxi Pick Up/Drop Off
Gate 4
South Building
Taxi Pick Up/Drop Off
South Building
Level 5
Meeting Rooms (S501-S505)
Level 4
Vista Room (S406)
Meeting Rooms (S401-S405)
Level 3
Exhibition Halls
Grand Concourse
Level 2.5
Food Court/Restaurant
Shops & Services
Metra Trains
Level 1
Grand Ballroom (S100)
Meeting Rooms (S101-S106)
McCormick Place West Expansion Area
E 24th St
E 24th Pl
Gate 30
Lakeside
Taxi Pick Up/Drop Off
Underground Parking Lot C
Fort Dearborn Dr
55
E 25th St
Mercy Hospital
Mines Dr
Mc 8th Dr
Moe Dr
Parking Lot B
Burnham Park
Lake Michiga

General Information

NFT Map:	11
Mailing Address:	2301 S Lake Shore Dr Chicago, IL 60616
Phone:	312-791-7000
Website:	www.mccormickplace.com
South Building:	Exhibit Hall A; charter bus stop
North Building:	Exhibit Halls B and C; Metra train station
Lakeside Center:	Exhibit Halls D and E; 4,249-seat Arie Crown Theater (Level 2); underground parking garage

Overview

When it comes to the convention business, size matters. With 2.2 million square feet of exhibit space spread among three buildings, McCormick Place is the largest convention center in the country. The center sees more than three million visitors a year attending its trade shows and public exhibitions in the South Building, North Building, and Lakeside Center (East Building). The city's colossal cash cow is about to get even bigger with the addition of a new $850 million West Building. Slated for completion in 2008, the expansion will add 470,000 square feet of exhibit space and 250,000 square feet of meeting rooms to the already gargantuan center.

McCormick Place's growth continues to bolster the rapid gentrification of South Loop and with each expansion, the complex's overall aesthetic appeal steadily improves. But despite major renovations, Chicagoans still refer to the complex as "the mistake on the lake," and Mayor Daley called the black boxy behemoth the "Berlin Wall" that separates Chicagoans from their beloved lakefront.

Finding Your Way Around

Getting to McCormick Place is the easy part. Then you have to navigate the inside. The main entrance is off Martin Luther King Drive, next to the Hyatt Hotel. Here's how to crack the code names for meeting rooms and exhibit halls:

All meeting room locations start with E (Lakeside Center/East Building), N (North Building), or S (South Building). The first numeral represents the floor level, and the last two digits specify which room. Room numbers are never duplicated among the complex's three buildings.

Exhibit halls are named by consecutive letters starting with the South Building where Hall A (Level 3) is located. North Building houses Halls B (Level 3) and C (Level 1). Exhibit Halls D (Level 3) and E (Level 2) are in Lakeside Center.

Restaurants & Services

Connie's Pizza and McDonald's Express are in the North Building (Level 2). The Plate Room Food Court is in the Grand Concourse (Level 2.5 and 3), where Starbucks, shops, a shoe shine, and massage services are also located. (Aren't convention centers just *great?*) Business centers and ATMs are in the Grand Concourse (Level 2.5), North Building (Level 2), and Lakeside Center (Level 2). If you're totally lost, there are Visitor Information Centers in all three buildings.

How to Get There

By Car: From the Loop, take Lake Shore Drive south; from the southeast, travel north on Lake Shore Drive. Signage to McCormick Place on Lake Shore Drive is frequent and clear. Parking garages are in Lakeside Center and the Hyatt. Lots are at 31st Street and Lake Shore Drive and at Martin Luther King Drive across from the South Building. Additional lots are north of McCormick Place at Burnham Harbor and Soldier Field.

By Bus: From the Loop, CTA buses 3 and 4 stop in front of the South Building. From Richard B. Ogilvie Transportation Center, take buses 124, 125, or 157 to Michigan Avenue; transfer to a southbound 3 or 4 ($1.75 with transfer one-way). From Union Station, board eastbound bus 1 to Michigan Avenue; transfer to a southbound 3 or 4.

During major shows, countless charter buses circle downtown hotels, transporting conventioneers to McCormick Place for free. With the new express busway, charter buses travel from Randolph Street to the South Building in less than ten minutes. For schedules, check with the hotels and at McCormick Place information desks.

By Train: A Metra train ride from the Loop's Randolph Street and Van Buren Street stations to the McCormick Place Station takes nine minutes ($1.85 one-way). Escalators to the train platform are on the west side of the Grand Concourse (Level 2.5).

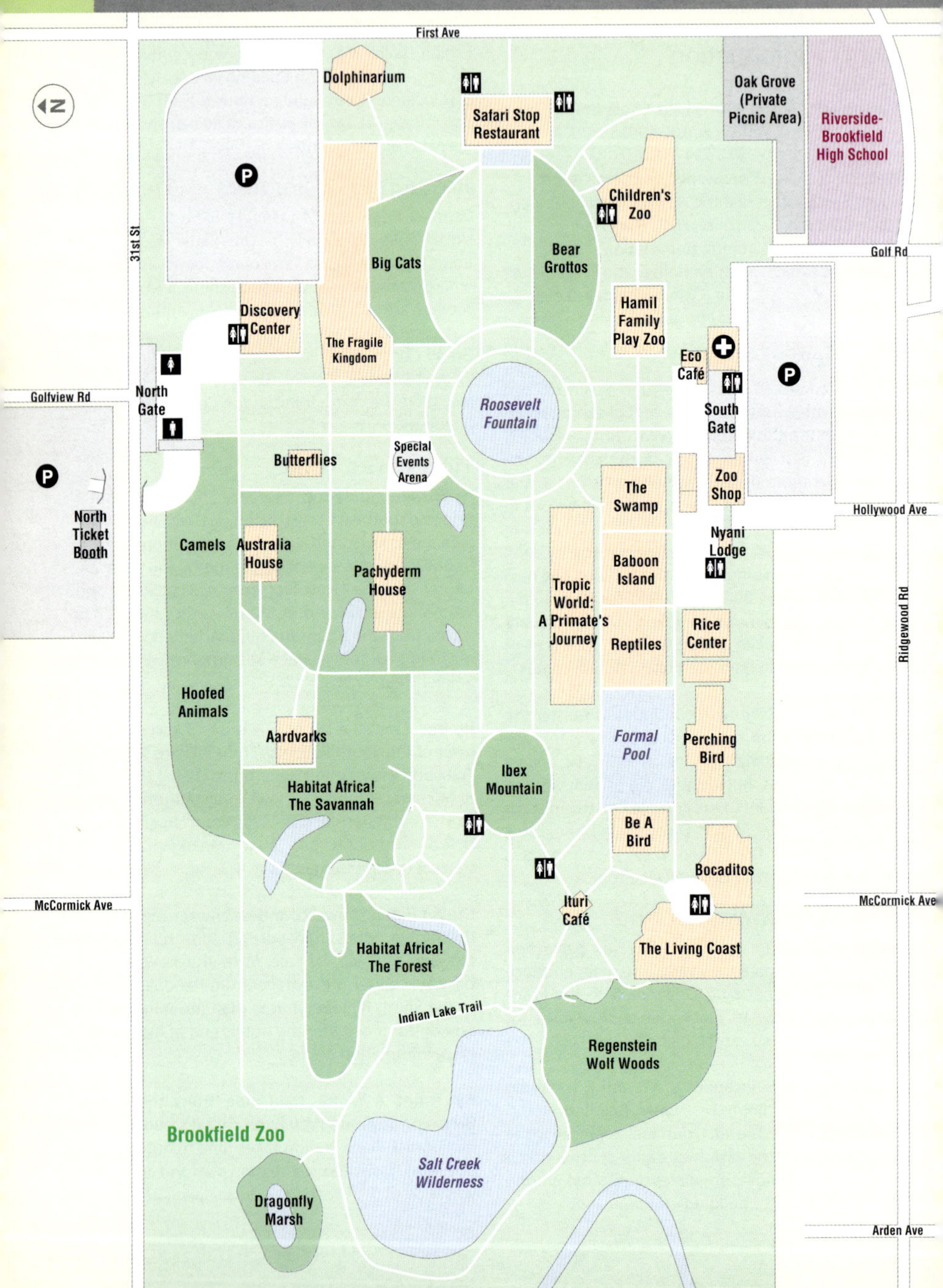
First Ave
Dolphinarium
Safari Stop Restaurant
Oak Grove (Private Picnic Area)
Riverside-Brookfield High School
Children's Zoo
Bear Grottos
Big Cats
31st St
Golf Rd
Discovery Center
The Fragile Kingdom
Hamil Family Play Zoo
Eco Café
North Gate
Golfview Rd
Roosevelt Fountain
South Gate
Butterflies
Special Events Arena
Zoo Shop
Hollywood Ave
North Ticket Booth
Camels
Australia House
Pachyderm House
The Swamp
Baboon Island
Nyani Lodge
Tropic World: A Primate's Journey
Reptiles
Rice Center
Ridgewood Rd
Hoofed Animals
Aardvarks
Formal Pool
Perching Bird
Ibex Mountain
Habitat Africa! The Savannah
Be A Bird
Bocaditos
McCormick Ave
Ituri Café
The Living Coast
Habitat Africa! The Forest
Indian Lake Trail
Regenstein Wolf Woods
Brookfield Zoo
Salt Creek Wilderness
Dragonfly Marsh
Arden Ave

General Information

Address:	31st St & First Ave Brookfield, IL 60513
Phone:	708-485-0236
Website:	www.brookfieldzoo.org
Hours:	Open daily from 10 am-5 pm, and until 7:30 on Sundays from Labor Day to Memorial Day
Admission:	$8 adults, $4 children 3-11 & seniors, free children 2 and under

Overview

While Lincoln Park Zoo is the city's free zoo, Brookfield Zoo offers a far more comprehensive wild animal experience, with a strong emphasis on conservation education. 216 acres of creepy critters make for a memorable day trip. We'll skip the analogy with the Joliet Riverboat Casino.

Hamill Family Play Zoo

This interactive play area is part of a program to create a huge new wing of the zoo dedicated solely to kids. Great—just what a zoo needs: more kids. Children get to interact in a variety of ways, including donning costumes to play "zoo keeper" or "ring-tailed lemur," creating and frolicking in their own simulated habitats, planting seeds in the greenhouse, or spotting creepy insects in the outdoor bug path. Think a grownup would look silly dressed like a lemur? We want to play!

Regenstein Wolf Woods

Opened in 2004, the zoo's new wolf exhibit allows visitors to follow the progress of a small pack of endangered male wolves as they do the wolfy things wolves do. One-way glass allows spectators to get up close and personal with the wolves without freaking them out.

Other Exhibits

Of course the zoo is full of exhibits, some more fascinating than others. Among them are the seasonal butterfly exhibit and the dragonfly march. Here are some other worthwhile sights:

- **Habitat Africa**: This is broken up into two sections: The Rainforest, with its zebras and African millipedes (heebie-jeebies), and The Savannah, with our favorite, the giraffes.
- **Dolphinarium**: Dolphin shows are scheduled at regular intervals two or three times a day (sometimes more during peak seasons and on weekends).
- **Tropic World**: Visit Kamba, the baby gorilla born in front of a captivated, slightly disgusted crowd of zoo visitors last fall. Mother Koola now knows how Marie Antoinette felt when she shared the delivery of her offspring with the French peasantry.

Eating at the Zoo

- **La Gran Cocina**: At the South American Marketplace. Walk-up stir-fry, chicken, pizza, and fruit.
- **Eco Café**: Near the Hamill Family Play Zoo. Brookfield Zoo teamed up with Whole Foods to create the Eco Café offering yogurt, organic chips, and other healthy snacks. The green theme goes far beyond the menu, too. Much of the café's structure and function are of the tree-hugging sort.
- **Bocaditos**: Table service dining on the second floor of the South American Marketplace. Peruvian fare with a "familiar" twist (read: blanded down for white-bread palates).
- **Ituri Café**: Near the Habitat Africa playground. Walk-up food vendor with picnic tables.

How to Get There

By Car: From the Eisenhower or Stevens Expressway, exit at 1st Avenue. From there, signs will direct you the short distance to the zoo. Lot parking is $8.

By Train: From downtown Chicago, take the Burlington Northern line to Zoo Stop/Hollywood Station.

By Bus: Pace buses 304 and 331 stop right at the zoo's gates.

Stone Gate Dr
Ravinia Festival
Green Bay Rd
Cherokee R
Marion Rd
Melvin Dr
Marquette Rd
Hastings Ave
Turnbull Woods Ct
Turnbull Woods Ct
Lake Cook Rd
Main Entrance
Botanic Garden Center
Chicago Botanic Garden
Woods & Nature Trail
Fruit & Vegetable Garden
Bulb Garden
Gateway Visitor Center
Aquatic Garden
Native Plant Garden
Landscape Gardens
Heritage Garden
Rose Garden
Education Center
Dwarf Conifer
Japanese Garden
Circle Garden
English Walled Garden
English Oak Meadow
Spider Land
The Greenhouses
Waterfall Garden
Japanese Garden
Enabling Garden
Lakeside Gardens
Japanese Garden
Skokie River
41
Sensory Garden
Water Gardens
Edens Expy Spur
Edens Expy
Evening Island
94
Skokie Blvd
Sun Evaluation Garden
Glencoe Golf Club
Henrici Dr
Prairie
Children's Garden
Shade Evaluation
33
34

General Information

Address: 1000 Lake Cook Rd, Glencoe, IL 60022
Phone: 847-835-5440
Website: www.chicagobotanic.org
Hours: Open 364 days, 8 am to sunset; closed December 25
Admission: Free

Overview

Spanning 385 acres, the serene and lovely Chicago Botanic Garden has been the backdrop for many a chi-chi wedding since they opened the gates in 1972.

Nature

Twenty-three gardens and two prairie habitats make up the Botanic Garden. Among them are a specialized Japanese garden, a rose garden, a bulb garden, a greenhouse full of tropical vegetation, and several beds solely dedicated to indigenous plants and flowers.

Where to Eat

• **Garden Café:** Serves breakfast and café fare—salads, sandwiches, beer and wine. Open November to March: 8 am-4 pm; April to October: 8 am-5 pm weekdays, 8 am-5:30 pm weekends, and open to 7 pm on Carillion Concert Mondays.

• **Rose Terrace Café:** Ice cream and sandwiches. Open late May or early June to late September, 11:30 am-2:30 pm.

• **Garden Grill:** Grill being the operative word, serves burgers, dogs, and the like. Open April to October 31 for lunch Friday to Sunday 11:30 am-2:30 pm, weather permitting. Open for dinner from late May to late September, 5:30 pm-8 pm, featuring a barbeque buffet and beer garden.

Note: picnicking allowed in designated areas only.

How to Get to There

By Car: Take I-90/94 W (The Kennedy) to the I-94 (The Edens), and US 41. Exit on Lake Cook Road, then go a half-mile east to the garden.

By Train: Take the Union Pacific North Line to Central (in Evanston) and catch the Pace bus 213 to Lake Cook and Nyoda, or take the same Metra train to Highland Park, and catch the Pace 473 to Lake Cook and Skokie. Easy Pace connections are also available from the Metra Glencoe stop.

By Bicycle: The Chicago Bikeway System winds through the forest preserves all the way up to the garden. Join it near the Billy Caldwell Golf Club at 6200 N Caldwell. A bicycle map is available on the Botanic Garden website.

Where to Stay

You can make an excursion of your visit to Ravinia and/or the Botanic Garden by booking a room at:

Renaissance Chicago North Shore (933 Skokie Blvd, Northbrook, 847-498-6500); **Residence Inn Chicago** (530 Lake Cook Rd, Deerfield, 847-940-4644); **Hyatt Deerfield** (1750 Lake Cook Rd, 800-233-1234); **Highland Park Courtyard** (1505 Lake Cook Rd, 847-831-3338).

Ravinia Festival

Address: 200 Ravinia Park Rd, Highland Park, IL 60035
Phone: 847-266-5100
Website: www.ravinia.org
Hours: June through mid-September, gates open at 5 pm

Overview

Not to be outdone, the adjoining Ravinia Festival, the nation's oldest outdoor concert venue, has been hosting classical music concerts since 1904. The summer home of the CSO, Ravinia eventually added pop and jazz to their bill, including such notables as Janis Joplin, Aretha Franklin (a Ravinia regular), k.d. lang, Tony Bennet, and other top names from opera and world music.

The Pavilion—Those who are serious about the music experience pay a premium for one of the 3,200 seats in this covered, open-air pavilion, affording them a view of the stage and better acoustics.

The Lawn—Although you can't see the stage, great outdoor acoustics bring the concert to you on the lawn, where blanket rights come cheap—typically $5-$10 a pop.

The Martin Theatre—The only remaining building original to the Festival, the 1904 Martin Theatre now hosts "Martinis at the Martin," a cabaret series celebrating the Great American Songbook.

Eating at Ravinia

Ravinia is well known for lawn picnickers who compete to outdo each other with elaborate spreads, including roll-up tables, table linens, candelabras, champagne, and caviar. For those less ambitious, Ravinia offers take-out sandwiches and picnic fare at The Gatehouse, burgers and dogs at Le Café, ice cream and other sweet treats at Carousel Market, or you can make reservations to eat in at their fine-dining restaurant, Mirabelle. Wine, beer, and soft drinks are also available at concession stands throughout the park.

How to Get There

By Car: The I-94 and I-294 have marked exits for Ravinia. Skip traffic back-ups on Lake Cook Road by exiting at Deerfield, Central, or Clavey Roads, and following directions to Park and Ride lots, which offer free parking and shuttle buses to Ravinia. The West Lot, Ravinia's closest parking spot, costs $7-$10 for parking and fills up early for the most popular concerts.

By Train: During festival season, the Union Pacific North Line offers the "Ravinia Special." For $5 round-trip, the train departs Madison and Canal at 5:50 pm, with stops at Clybourn, Ravenswood, Rogers Park, and Evanston, arriving at the Ravinia gates at 6:30 pm, and departing for the city 15 minutes after the concert's end.

Six Flags
Great America
W Big Hollow Rd
W Belvidere Rd
W Belvidere Rd
W Peterson Rd
Skokie Hwy
W Half Day Rd
W Half Day Rd
N Rand Rd
W Lake Cook Rd
E Dundee Rd
Elmhurst Rd
Northwest Hwy
Palatine Rd
Willow Rd
Edens Expy
Rand Rd
Golf Rd
Algonquin Rd
Higgins Rd
Elmhurst Rd
Elgin Ohare Expy
N York Rd
Kennedy Expy
Edens Expy
8
8
21
94
137
45
60
176
21
60
60
22
8
53
45
68
53
294
58
290
8
18

General Information

Address: 542 N Rte 21
Gurnee, IL 60031
Phone: 847-249-4363
Website: www.sixflags.com/parks/greatamerica
Hours: Open May to October. Hours are generally 10 am-10 pm, but vary by season. See website for specific hours and dates.
Entry: $44.99 adults, $29.99 children & seniors

Overview

Long lines, crappy food, hokey entertainment...if that isn't the stuff dreams are made of, then baby, we don't know what is.

Tickets

Reduced rates are available for advanced purchase through the website, and via promotions throughout the season—look for discounted deals at Dominick's, as well as on specially marked Coke cans. For die-hard thrill seekers, season passes offer the best deal at $89.99 per person, with special rates for families of four or more.

For the Kiddies

Camp Cartoon Network and Looney Tunes National Park offer easy-going rides and games for tykes 54 inches and under, while Bugs, Yosemite Sam, and the rest amble around for photo ops. The double-decker classic kiddie ride Columbia Carousel, located just past the park's main entrance, may be too tame for young 'uns hopped up on funnel cake and Tweety-pops.

Thrill Rides

Every few years, Six Flags tries to outdo itself with a new, even more death-defying and harrowing ride. Most recently, this magnificent feat was accomplished with the opening of the Superman-Ultimate Flight ride. Passengers soar through the air head-first as though they were flying, nearly brushing the ground below them on the giant loop-de-loop. Other thrills include the Raging Bull "hyper-twister," where you drop at incredible degrees and speeds into subterranean depths. Batman The Ride allows your feet to dangle free, while riders remain standing during the Iron Wolf. We had serious misgivings about the decision to ride the Déjà Vu as we sat suspended, face-down, 120-something feet above the ground, secured only by a shoulder harness before dropping down at a 90 degree angle. (We survived unscathed.) Meanwhile, the classic wooden American Eagle coaster offers vintage, but no-less-worrisome, rickety thrills.

Hurricane Harbor Water Park

Opened in 2005, Great America's adjoining Hurricane Harbor water park introduced attractions such as "Skull Island," which press materials dub the thrill-evoking "world's largest interactive water play structure." How's that for screaming "fun?" The park also features a 1,000+ gallon water drop that dumps itself upon unsuspecting visitors every ten minutes. Leave the Prada at home.

Fright Fest

Avoid the heat and long lines of the summer season and creep into the park during the month of October (mostly on weekends) among the Halloween-themed décor and scary music playing over the P.A. Areas are marked according to levels of scariness, so those with young children or weak hearts can plan accordingly. In the spookiest parts of the park, actors in ghoulish costumes sneak around startling visitors (hope we didn't ruin the surprise). There are also two haunted houses that charge separate admission fees.

Also in the 'hood

Gurnee Mills Outlet Mall

Address: 6170 W Grand Ave, Gurnee, IL 60031
Phone: 847-263-7500
Hours: Open Mon-Sat 10 am-9 pm, Sun 10 am-7 pm

Gurnee Mills is a theme park for the avid shopper. Included among the usual chain grub and garb are outlet stores for fashion and housewares such as Abercrombie & Fitch, Athlete's Foot, Banana Republic, Levi's, Saks Fifth Avenue, and more. We'll refrain from saying that going to an outlet mall makes you even more of a jackass than going to a regular mall.

Make a Night of It

Where to stay in Gurnee:

- **Baymont Inn & Suites**, 5688 N Ridge Rd, 847-662-7600
- **Country Inn & Suites**, 5420 Grand Ave, 847-625-9700
- **Fairfield Inn**, 6090 Gurnee Mills Cir East, 847-855-8868
- **Grand Hotel & Suites**, 5520 Grand Ave, 847-249-7777
- **Hampton Inn**, 5550 Grand Ave, 847-662-1100

How to Get There

By Car: Take I-94 or I-294 west, exit at Grand Avenue. Be aware that traffic is very congested in July and August! Arrive extra early or extra late to beat the crowds.

By Train & Bus: Take the Metra Union Pacific North Line to Waukegan, where you can catch the Pace bus 565 to Great America. Note: Public transportation to Great America from the Ogilvie Transportation Center and Madison and Canal takes just over two hours each way.

White Harbour
Lake Michigan
Linden
Central
Noyes
Foster
Davis
Dempster
Main
South Blvd
Howard
Northwestern University
PAGE 252
Block Museum
Evanston Hospital
Ryan Field
Peter N Jans Community Golf Course
Chandler Park
Leahy Park
Kendall College
Noyes Cultural Arts Center
Ingraham Park
Civic Center
Gross Point Lighthouse Park
Long Field
Lovelace Park
Mitchell Indian Museum
Bent Park
Dwight Perkins Wood Forest Preserve
Eggleston Park
Ladd Arboretum and Ecology Center
Twiggs Park
McCormick Park
North Shore Channel
ETHS Park
Evanston Township High School
Evanston Public Library
Home of Francis E Willard
Homestead Hotel
Centennial Park
Dawes Park
Evanston Historical Society (Dawes House)
Harbert Park
Robert Crown Park
Burnham Shore Park
Clark Square
South Beach Park
Calvary Cemetery
Robert E James Park
Elks Memorial Park
Isabella St
Central St
Emerson St
Church St
Dempster St
Main St
Oakton St
Howard St
South Blvd
Green Bay Rd
Elgin Rd
McCormick Blvd
Sheridan Rd
Chicago Ave
Ridge Ave
Dodge Ave
Lake Shore Blvd
N Rogers Ave
46

Overview

Although the suburb is a short 13 miles from Chicago's bustling Loop, Evanston seems a world away. Spacious Victorian and Prairie Style homes with mini-vans and Mercedes parked on tree-lined streets overlook Lake Michigan and surround the quaint college town's downtown.

Once home to Potawatami Indians, Evanston was actually founded after the establishment of the town's most well-known landmark, Northwestern University. Plans for the school began in 1851, and after the university opened for business four years later, its founder John Evans (along with a bunch of other Methodist dudes) proposed the establishment of the city, and so the town was named Evanston in 1857. Today, residents are as devoted to cultural and intellectual pursuits as the morally minded patriarchs were to enforcing prohibition. The sophisticated, racially diverse suburb of over 74,000 packs a lot of business and entertainment into its 8.5 square miles. Superb museums, many national historic landmarks, parks, artistic events, eclectic shops, and theaters make up for the poor sports performances by Northwestern University's Wildcats in recent Big Ten football and basketball seasons.

Culture

Evanston has several museums and some interesting festivals that warrant investigation. Besides Northwestern's Block Museum of Art, the impressive Mitchell Museum of the American Indian showcases life of the Midwest's Native Americans (2600 Central Park Ave, 847-475-1030). The 1865 home of Frances E. Willard, founder of the Women's Christian Temperance Union and women's suffrage leader, is located at 1730 Chicago Avenue (847-328-7500). Tours of the historic home are offered on the afternoons of every first and third Sunday of each month. Admission costs $5 for adults and $3 for children 12 and under.

Festivals & Events

- **May**: Evanston goes Baroque during Bach Week, 847-236-0452, www.bachweek.org.
- **June:** Fountain Square Arts Festival, 847-328-1500, and free Starlight Concerts hosted in many of the city's 80 parks through August, 847-448-8058
- **July**: Ethnic Arts Festival, 847-448-8058
- **September**: Town architectural walking tour, 312-922-3432, www.architecture.org.
- **December**: First Night, a city-wide arts celebration, rings in the New Year, 866-475-6483, www.firstnighte vanston.org;

Nature

Evanston is blessed with six public beaches open June 10th through Labor Day. For hours, fees, and boating information, contact the City of Evanston's Recreation Division (847-866-2910; www.cityofevanston.org). The town's most popular parks encircle its beaches: Grosse Point Lighthouse Park, Centennial Park, Burnham Shores Park, Dawes Park, and South Boulevard Beach Park. All are connected by a bike path and fitness trail. On clear days, Chicago's skyline is visible from Northwestern's campus. West of downtown, McCormick, Twiggs, and Herbert Parks flank the North Shore Channel. Bicycle trails thread along the shore from Green Bay Road south to Main Street. North of Green Bay Road is Peter N Jans Community Golf Course, a short 18-hole, par 60 public links at 1031 Central Street (847-475-9173) and the Ladd Memorial Arboretum and Ecology Center, located at 2024 McCormick Boulevard (847-864-5181).

How to Get There

By Car: Lake Shore Drive to Sheridan Road is the most direct and scenic route from Chicago to Evanston. Drive north on LSD, which ends at Hollywood; then drive west to Sheridan and continue north. Near downtown, Sheridan becomes Burnham Place briefly, then Forest Avenue. Go north on Forest, which turns into Sheridan again by lakefront Centennial Park.

By Train: Metra's Union Pacific North Line departing from the Richard B. Ogilvie Transportation Center in West Loop stops at the downtown Davis Street CTA Center station, 25 minutes from the Loop ($2.90 one-way). This station is the town transportation hub, where Metra and L trains and buses interconnect. For all Metra, L, and CTA bus schedules, call 312-836-7000; www.rtachicago.com.

By L: The CTA Purple Line Express L train travels direct to and from the Loop during rush hours ($1.75 one-way). Other hours, ride the Howard-Dan Ryan Red Line to Howard Street, transfer (additional 25¢) to Purple Line.

By Bus: From Chicago's Howard Street Station, CTA and Pace Suburban buses service Evanston ($1.50 rush hours one-way; other, $1.25).

Additional Information

Evanston Convention & Visitors' Bureau,
847-328-1500;
Chicago's North Shore Convention & Visitors Bureau
847-763-0011; www.visitchicagonorthshore.com
Evanston Public Library, 1703 Orrington Ave, 847-866-0300; www.epl.org

Rosalie St
Chandler Park
Leahy Park
North Shore Channel
McCormick Park
Milburn St
Long Field
Lincoln St
Kendall College
Colfax St
Bryant Ave
Noyes Ct
Grant St
Dartmouth Pl
Noyes St
Noyes
Wesley Ave
Leonard Pl
Maple Ave
Northwestern University
PAGE 252
Ingraham Park
Ridge Ave
Gaffield Pl
Philbrick Park
Haven Pl
Garrett Pl
Simpson St
Green Bay Rd
Firemen's Park
Hamlin St
Library Pl
Leon Pl
Pratt Ct
Foster
Foster St
Garnett Pl
Sherman Ave
Orrington Ave
Sheridan Rd
Block Museum
Emerson St
University Pl
University Pl
Elgin Rd
Railroad Ave
Lyons St
Clark St
Lake Michigan
Benson Ave
Orrington Ave
Chicago Ave
Clark St
Church St
Home of Francis E Willard
Hinman Ave
Centennial Park
Davis
Evanston Public Library
Church St
Judson Ave
Davis St
Davis
Alexander Park
Homestead Hotel
Grove St
Davis St
Forest Pl
Wesley Ave
Ashbury Ave
Ridge Ave
Oak Ave
Maple Ave
Grove St
Raymond Park
Dawes Park
Lake St
Elmwood Ave
Evanston Historical Society (Dawes House)
Greenwood St
Forest Ave
Dempster
Dempster St
Burnharm Pl

Where to Drink

- **Tommy Nevin's Pub**, 1450 Sherman Ave, 847-869-0450. Bar food, live music, drink specials.
- **Keg of Evanston**, 810 Grove St, 847-869-9987. DJ on the weekends. Dollar drafts on Wednesdays!
- **1800 Club**, 1800 Sherman Ave, 847-733-7900. Always busy, thanks to cheap drinks and trivia night.
- **Prairie Moon**, 1502 Sherman Ave, 847-864-8328. Weekly drink specials.

Where to Eat

- **Trio**, 1625 Hinman Ave, in the Homestead Hotel, 847-733-8746. French. Deep-pocketed regulars gush about the daring food combinations. A favorite for foodies. Open Wed-Sun.
- **Blind Faith Café**, 525 Dempster St, 847-328-6875. Vegetarian. Healthy, fiber-filled fare for the Birkenstock set. Food so earthy, you'll need to floss dirt from your teeth.
- **Va Pensiero**, 1566 Oak Ave, in the Margarita Inn, 847-475-7779. Italian. Classy, romantic supper club offering over 250 Italian wines. A "pop the question" kind of place.
- **Pete Miller's Original Steakhouse**, 1557 Sherman Ave, 847-328-0399. American. Beef bubbas stake out this joint as one of Chicago's best for red meat served in a cozy dining room; fist-thick burgers slung in live jazz lounge.
- **Tapas Barcelona**, 1615 W Chicago Ave, 847-866-9900. Spanish. Lick your fingers with friends over tasty tapas and sangria.
- **Las Palmas**, 817 University Pl, 847-328-2555. High-priced margaritas; fresh Mexican fare.
- **Unicorn Café,** 1723 Sherman Ave, 847-332-2312. Quaint and reasonably priced.
- **Clarke's**, 720 Clark St, 847-864-1610. Inexpensive sandwiches and omelettes.
- **Trattoria Demi**, 1571 Sherman Ave, 847-332-2330. Good Italian food in a cozy setting.
- **Hecky's Barbeque**, 1902 Green Bay Rd, 847-492-1182. It's the sauce that's the boss.
- **Joy Yee Noodles**, 521 Davis St, 847-733-1900. Pricey, trendy "bubble tea" specialists.
- **Olive Mountain**, 610 Davis St, 847-475-0380. Middle Eastern specialties.
- **Lulu's Dim Sum and Then Sum**, 804 Davis St, 847-869-4343. Best Pad Thai in Evanston. Huge portions, reasonably priced.
- **Café Mozart**, 600 Davis St, 847-492-8056. Wireless Internet, leopard couch, snarky staff.
- **Kafein Café**, 1621 Chicago Ave, 847-491-1621. Open 'til 2 am on weeknights and 3 am on weekends, perfect for those late-night cram sessions.
- **Mt Everest**, 630 Church St, 847-491-1069. Nepalese and Indian food with lunch buffet.
- **Noodles & Company**, 930 Church St, 847-733-1200. Thai noodles, pasta, even mac and cheese!

Where to Shop

- **Asinamali Women's Boutique**, 1722 Sherman Ave, 847-866-6219. Great clothes in a reasonable price range.
- **William's Shoes**, 710 Church St, 847-328-0527. Great boot and sneaker selection.
- **Campus Gear**, 1717 Sherman Ave, 847-869-7033. Cheaper than the campus bookstore for Northwestern apparel. If that's your thing.
- **Art & Science Hair Salon**, 811 Church St, 847-864-4247. Beakers bring you back to science class. Student discounts available.

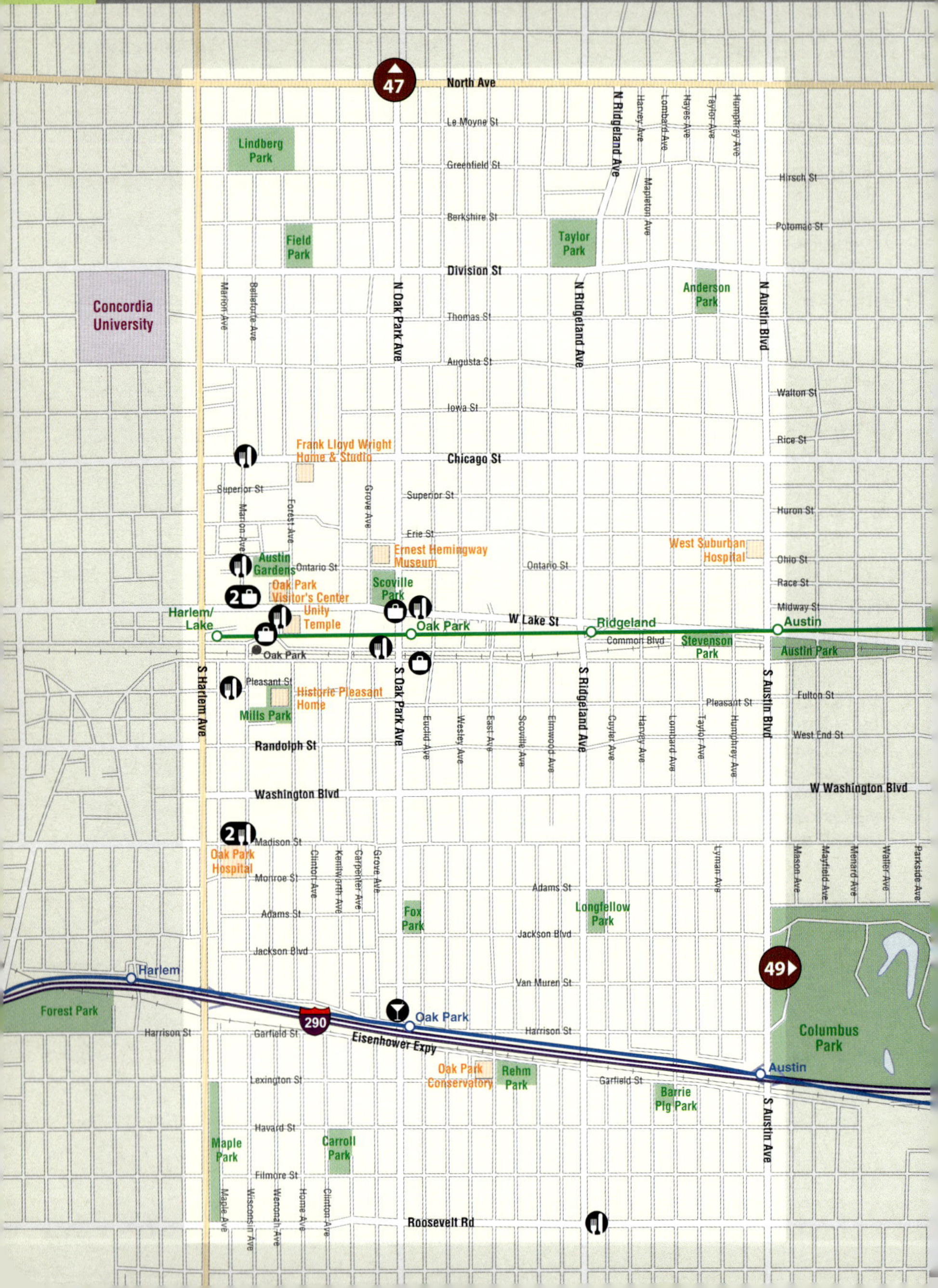

47
North Ave
Le Moyne St
Greenfield St
Berkshire St
Division St
Thomas St
Augusta St
Iowa St
Chicago St
Superior St
Erie St
Ontario St
W Lake St
Common Blvd
Pleasant St
Randolph St
Washington Blvd
W Washington Blvd
Madison St
Monroe St
Adams St
Jackson Blvd
Van Buren St
Harrison St
Garfield St
Lexington St
Harvard St
Filmore St
Roosevelt Rd
Hirsch St
Potomac St
Walton St
Rice St
Huron St
Ohio St
Race St
Midway St
Fulton St
West End St
N Ridgeland Ave
Harvey Ave
Lombard Ave
Hayes Ave
Taylor Ave
Humphrey Ave
Mapleton Ave
N Oak Park Ave
N Austin Blvd
Marion Ave
Belleforte Ave
Forest Ave
Grove Ave
S Harlem Ave
S Oak Park Ave
S Ridgeland Ave
S Austin Blvd
Euclid Ave
Wesley Ave
East Ave
Scoville Ave
Elmwood Ave
Cuyler Ave
Clinton Ave
Kenilworth Ave
Carpenter Ave
Lyman Ave
Mason Ave
Mayfield Ave
Menard Ave
Walter Ave
Parkside Ave
Maple Ave
Wisconsin Ave
Wenonah Ave
Home Ave
S Austin Ave
Lindberg Park
Field Park
Taylor Park
Anderson Park
Concordia University
Frank Lloyd Wright Home & Studio
Ernest Hemingway Museum
West Suburban Hospital
Austin Gardens
Oak Park Visitor's Center
Scoville Park
Unity Temple
Harlem/ Lake
Oak Park
Ridgeland
Austin
Stevenson Park
Austin Park
Historic Pleasant Home
Mills Park
2
Oak Park Hospital
Fox Park
Longfellow Park
Columbus Park
49
Harlem
Forest Park
290
Eisenhower Expy
Oak Park Conservatory
Rehm Park
Barrie Pig Park
Maple Park
Carroll Park

General Information

Oak Park Visitors Bureau: 708-524-7800; www.visitoakpark.com
Oak Park Tourist: www.oprf.com

Overview

You can thank Oak Park for McDonald's, *Tarzan*, *A Moveable Feast*, and Prairie style architecture. Their creators called the charming suburb their home: Ray Kroc, Edgar Rice Burroughs, Ernest Hemingway, and Frank Lloyd Wright, respectively.

Best known for its architectural gems and strong public schools, Oak Park is a happy hunting ground for homebuyers seeking an upscale, integrated suburb 10 miles from the Loop. Less impressed than most with his picture-perfect hometown of 52,500, Hemingway described Oak Park as "a village of wide lawns and narrow minds."

Village trustees must still be smarting from Hemingway's crack, because they publicize an official policy on maintaining diversity. The "diversity statement" sounds like some sort of disclaimer or zealot's vision for heaven on Earth: "Ours is a community that encourages contributions of all citizens regardless of race, gender, ethnicity, sexual orientation, disability, religion . . ."

Architecture

Oak Park harbors the nation's largest concentration of Frank Lloyd Wright buildings, 25 in the village and another six in neighboring River Forest. The village's must-see sites are located in a compact area bordered by Division Street, Lake Street, Forest Avenue, and Ridgeland Avenue. Designs by Wright, William Drummond, George W. Maher, John Van Bergen, and E.E. Roberts are represented throughout.

You can ground yourself in Prairie style architectural principles at the brilliant Frank Lloyd Wright Home and Studio. Maintained by the Frank Lloyd Wright Preservation Trust, guided tours of the designer's personal space are offered daily at 11:20 am, 1:20 pm, and 3:20 pm (951 Chicago Ave, 708-848-1976; www.wrightplus.org). Only 15 people are allowed per tour and tickets can be purchased on the foundation's website or on-site (early arrival recommended) at a cost of $9 for adults, $7 for students and seniors. Worthwhile walking tours of the surrounding streets are also offered for an additional $9, though a combined $16 ticket ($12 for students and seniors) covers both the home-studio site and walking tour at a discount.

Completed in 1908, Unity Temple (875 Lake St, 708-383-8873; www.unitytemple-utrf.org) was Wright's first commissioned public building, and is now open daily for self-directed tours and on weekends for guided tours ($6 for adults, $4 for students and seniors). Designed by George W. Maher, Historic Pleasant Home (217 S Home Ave, 708-383-2654; www.pleasanthome.org) aptly illustrates the architectural evolution from Victorian design to early Prairie style with tours held Thursday through Sunday at 12:30 pm, 1:30 pm, and 2:30 pm ($5, Fridays free).

The Oak Park Visitors Center offers maps and a PDA walking tour of the Ridgeland Historic District highlighting 15 of the area's Victorian "Painted Ladies" ($9 for adults, $6 for students and seniors) 10 am-3:30 pm daily. Call 708-524-7800, or visit www.visitoakpark.com for more information.

Culture & Events

Once a year in May, the public gets to snoop inside Wright-designed private residences during the popular Wright Plus Housewalk ($85). His home-studio and Robie House in Hyde Park (shuttle provided) are also included in the tour (708-848-9518; www.wrightplus.org).

Get your fill of he-man author Hemingway at the Ernest Hemingway Museum (200 N Oak Park Ave, 708-848-2222; www.hemingway.org), open Sunday through Friday 1 pm-5 pm, and Saturday 10 am-5 pm ($7 adults, $5.50 students and seniors). His birthplace, also included with the price of admission, is located just up the street at 339 N Oak Park Avenue.

Summer evenings, catch Shakespeare's works performed outdoors in Austin Gardens by the Oak Park Festival Theatre company (708-524-2050; www.oakparkfestival.com). The lush Oak Park Conservatory, originally built in 1929 to provide a place for all of the exotic plants Oak Park residents collected on their travels abroad, is located at 615 Garfield Street (708-386-4700; suggested $1 donation) and definitely worth a visit.

Where to Drink

- **Avenue Ale House**, 825 S Oak Park Ave, 708-848-2801. Really great place to grab a beer (or frozen margarita or sangria) and watch a game. Tasty grub. Great patio.

Where to Eat

- **Café Le Coq**, 734 Lake St, 708-848-2233. French Bistro wows Oak Park foodies.
- **Cucina Paradiso**, 814 North Blvd, 708-848-3434. Italian. Fork-twirling Oak Parkers patronize this friendly pasta place.
- **Khyber Pass**, 1031 Lake St, 708-445-9032. Indian. Taxi drivers and curry-loving locals fill up on lunch and dinner buffets.
- **Mama Thai**, 1112 W Madison St, 708-386-0100. Inexpensive, charming, and delicious. Plus, they deliver!
- **Marion Street Grill**, 189 N Marion St, 708-383-1551. Inviting, upscale restaurant featuring fresh seafood, steaks, and chops. Impressive wine list.
- **New Rebozo**, 1116 Madison St, 708-445-0370. Best Mexican in town with specials that deviate from your average fare.
- **Petersen Ice Cream**, 1100 Chicago Ave, 708-386-6131. American. Comfort food and silky ice cream make this diner a popular destination.
- **Pete's Red Hots,** 6346 W Roosevelt Rd, 708-383-6122. Fast food at its finest. Best fries ever.
- **Philander's Oak Park in the Carleton Hotel**, 1120 Pleasant St, 708-848-4250. Seafood. Marine cuisine served in handsome atmosphere; nightly, fishtail to live jazz.

Where to Shop

- **Alphabet Soup**, 1107 W Lake St, 708-848-0300. A treasure trove of eclectic gifts, jewelry, and home accessories.
- **Antiques, Etc,** 125 N Marion St, 708-386-9194. 30+ dealers in one spot. Beautiful furniture, art, jewelry, rugs, and more.
- **Magic Tree Bookstore**, 141 N Oak Park Ave, 708-848-0770. Children's bookstore that has music, puzzles, and gifts.
- **Pumpkin Moon**, 1028 North Blvd, 708-524-8144. The place for nostalgic collectables. Includes toys, T-shirts, and candy. Super fun.
- **Val's Halla Records**, 723 1/2 South Blvd, 708-524-1004. New and used CDs tapes and LPs, bought and sold by a rather knowledgeable staff. Don't miss the Elvis shrine.

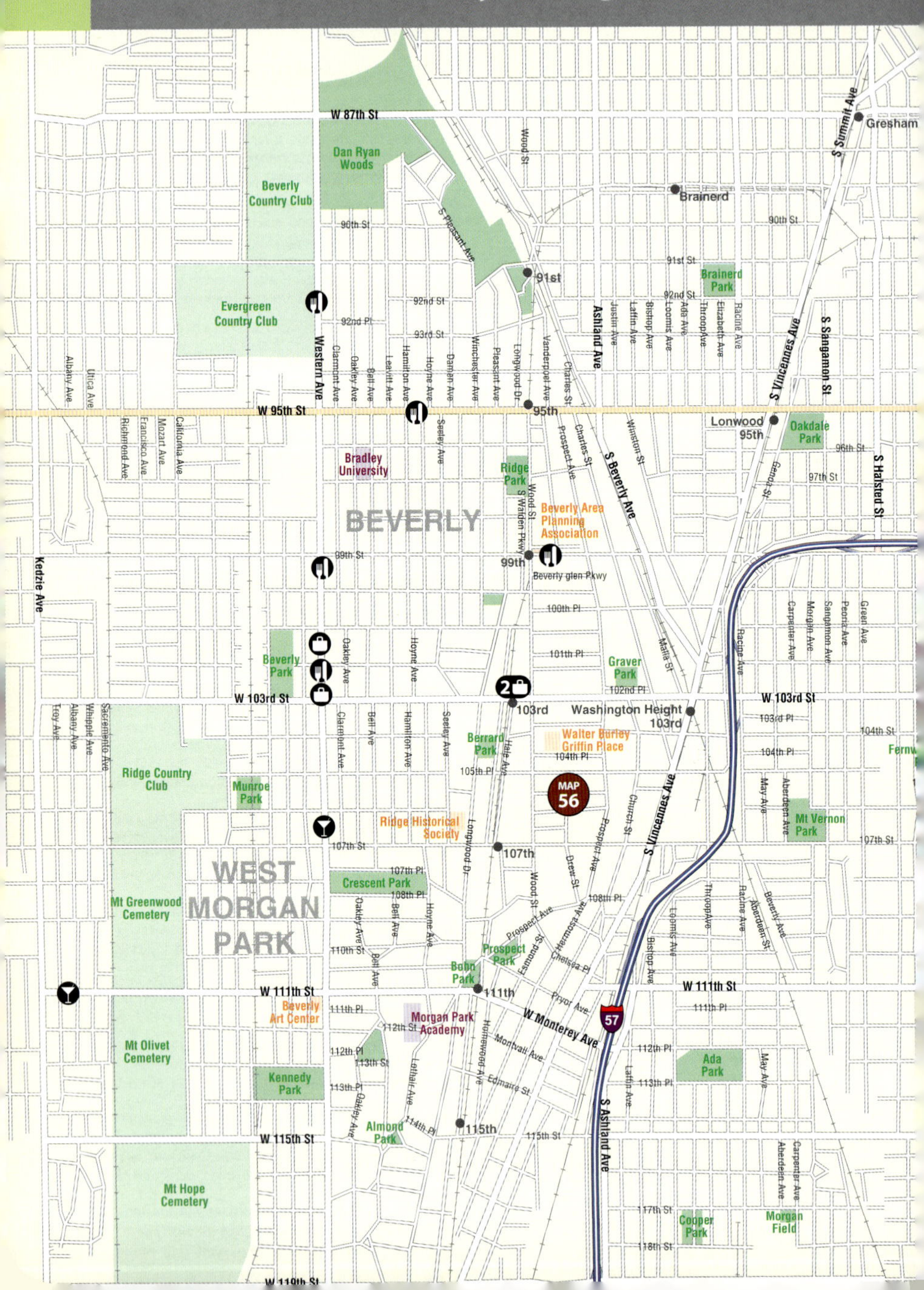
W 87th St
Dan Ryan Woods
Beverly Country Club
Evergreen Country Club
Gresham
Brainerd
91st
Brainerd Park
W 95th St
95th
Lonwood 95th
Oakdale Park
Bradley University
Ridge Park
BEVERLY
Beverly Area Planning Association
99th
Graver Park
Beverly Park
W 103rd St
103rd
Washington Height 103rd
Walter Burley Griffin Place
Berrard Park
Ridge Country Club
Munroe Park
MAP 56
Ridge Historical Society
107th
Mt Vernon Park
Crescent Park
WEST MORGAN PARK
Mt Greenwood Cemetery
Prospect Park
Bohn Park
W 111th St
111th
Beverly Art Center
Morgan Park Academy
W Monterey Ave
Mt Olivet Cemetery
Kennedy Park
Ada Park
Almond Park
115th
W 115th St
Mt Hope Cemetery
Cooper Park
Morgan Field
W 119th St
Western Ave
Kedzie Ave
Ashland Ave
S Ashland Ave
S Beverly Ave
S Vincennes Ave
S Halsted St
S Sangamon St
S Summit Ave
Longwood Dr
Wood St
57

Overview

Beverly Hills, best known simply as Beverly, is the stronghold of Chicago's heralded "South Side Irish" community. An authentic medieval castle, baronial mansions, rolling hills, and plenty of pubs compose Chicago's Emerald Isle of 39,000 residents.

Once populated by Illinois and Potawatomi Indian tribes, Beverly is now home to clans of Irish-American families who moved here after the Great Chicago Fire. Famous residents include: Andrew Greeley, Brian Piccolo, George Wendt, the Schwinn Bicycle family, and decades of loyal Chicago civil servants.

Proud and protective of their turf, these close-knit South Siders call Beverly and its sister community Morgan Park "the Ridge." The somewhat integrated neighborhood occupies the highest ground in Chicago, 30 to 60 feet above the rest of the city atop Blue Island Ridge.

Although the Ridge is just 15 miles from the Loop, most North Siders never venture south of Cermak Road except to invade Beverly on St. Patrick's Day weekend to see the parade and guzzle green beer at pubs lining Western Avenue. Chicago playwright Mike Houlihan called the strip the "South Side Irish Death March."

But there are more than a six-pack of reasons to visit Beverly. The Ridge Historic District is one of the country's largest urban areas on the National Register of Historic Places. Surprised, huh?

Architecture

Sadly, many Chicagoans are unaware of the rich architectural legacy on the city's far South Side. Beverly and Morgan Park encompass four landmark districts including the Ridge Historic District, three Chicago Landmark Districts, and over 30 Prairie Style structures.

Within approximately a nine-mile radius, from 87th Street to 115th Street and Prospect Avenue to Hoyne Avenue, one can view a vast collection of homes and public buildings representing American architectural styles developed between 1844 and World War II.

The 109th block of Prospect Avenue, every inch of Longwood Drive, and Victorian train stations at 91st Street, 95th Street, 99th Street, 107th Street, 111th Street, and 115th Street are all great Chicago landmarks. Walter Burley Griffin Place on W 104th Street has Chicago's largest concentration of Prairie School houses built between 1909 and 1913 by Griffin, a student of Frank Lloyd Wright and designer of the city of Canberra in Australia.

Beverly Area Planning Association (BAPA) (10233 S Wood St, 773-233-3100; www.bapa.org) provides a good architectural site map, plus events and shopping information for the district. History buffs might want to visit the Ridge Historical Society and museum, open Sundays and Thursdays from 2 pm to 5 pm (10621 S Seeley Ave, 773-881-1675; www.ridgehistoricalsociety.org).

Culture & Events

The new Beverly Art Center is the epicenter of Ridge culture. The $8 million facility provides visual and performance art classes for all ages and hosts Chicago's only contemporary Irish film festival during the first week of March (2407 W 111th St, 773-445-3838; www.beverlyartcenter.org).

Historic Ridge homes open their doors to the public on the third Sunday of May for the annual Home Tour, Chicago's oldest such tour. Sites are chosen for their diverse architectural styles and historical significance. Tour hours are from 11 am to 5 pm and tickets can be purchased through BAPA or the Beverly Art Center for $25 in advance or $30 the day of the event. Guided trolley tours are also offered for an additional $3.

A Chicago must-see, the justly famous South Side Irish Parade marches down Western Avenue from 103rd to 112th Streets on the Sunday nearest St. Patrick's Day. Contact BAPA at 773-233-3100 for more details.

Where to Eat

- **Café Luna**, 1742 W 99th St, 773-239-8990. Eclectic. Sink your teeth into their heart-healthy sandwiches and sinful desserts.
- **Franconello's**, 10222 S Western Ave, 773-881-4100. Italian. Perhaps the only pure Italians in Beverly making pasta dishes at this authentic Roma restaurant.
- **Janson's Drive-In**, 9900 S Western Ave, 773-238-3612. No indoor seating at this classic drive-thru.
- **Rainbow Cone**, 9233 S Western Ave, 773-238-7075. Ice cream. On summer nights more than 50 folks line up for sweet treats at this 76-year old soda fountain.
- **Top Notch Beefburger**, 2116 W 95th St, 773-445-7218. Burgers really are top notch at this '50s-style grill.

Where to Drink

- **Lanigan's Irish Pub**, 3119 W 111th St, 773-233-4004. Anyone know where you can find a pint in Beverly? I've got quite a mean thirst.
- **Dubliner**, 10910 S Western Ave, 773-238-0784. One of the many Irish pubs lining Western Avenue.

Where to Shop

- **Bev Art Brewer and Winemaker Supply**, 10033 S Western Ave, 773-233-7579. Everything you need to brew and bottle it yourself.
- **Calabria Imports**, 1905 W 103rd St, 773-396-5800. Imported Italian gourmet foodstuffs.
- **Optimo Hat Co**, 10215 S Western Ave, 773-238-2999. Custom made men's hats.
- **World Folk Music Company**, 1808 W 103rd St, 773-779-7059. Instruments, sheet music, and lessons for budding Guthries and Baezs.

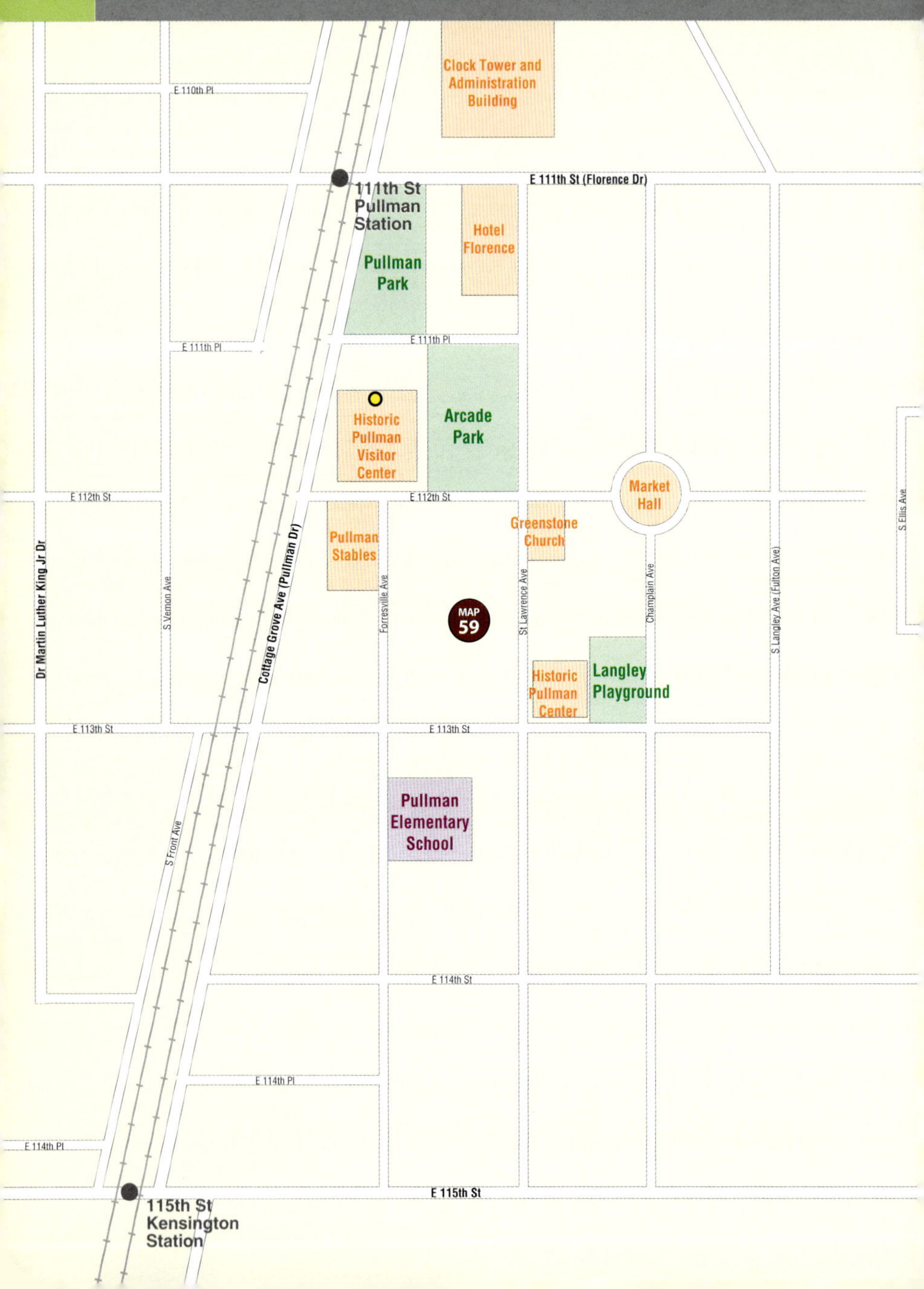
Clock Tower and Administration Building
E 110th Pl
E 111th St (Florence Dr)
111th St Pullman Station
Hotel Florence
Pullman Park
E 111th Pl
E 111th Pl
Historic Pullman Visitor Center
Arcade Park
Market Hall
E 112th St
E 112th St
Pullman Stables
Greenstone Church
S Ellis Ave
Dr Martin Luther King Jr Dr
S Vernon Ave
Cottage Grove Ave (Pullman Dr)
Forresville Ave
MAP 59
St Lawrence Ave
Champlain Ave
S Langley Ave (Fulton Ave)
Historic Pullman Center
Langley Playground
E 113th St
E 113th St
Pullman Elementary School
S Front Ave
E 114th St
E 114th Pl
E 114th Pl
E 115th St
115th St Kensington Station

Overview

Although railroad magnate George Pullman's utopian community went belly-up, the Town of Pullman he founded 14 miles south of the Loop survives as a National Landmark Historic District. Built between 1880 and 1885, Pullman is one of America's first planned, model industrial communities.

The "workers' paradise" earned Pullman humanitarian hoorahs, as well as a 6% return on his investment. Pullman believed that if laborers and their families lived in comfortable housing with gas, plumbing, and ventilation—in other words, livable conditions—their productivity would increase, as would his profits. Pullman was voted "the world's most perfect town" at the Prague International Hygienic and Pharmaceutical Exposition of 1896.

All was perfect on the plantation until a depression incited workers to strike in 1894 and the idealistic industrialist refused to negotiate with his ungrateful workers. While George Pullman's dream of a model community of indentured servitude died with him in 1897, hatred for him lived on. Pullman's tomb at Graceland Cemetery is more like a bomb shelter. To protect his corpse from irate labor leaders, Pullman was buried under a forest of railroad ties and concrete.

Architecture & Events

Architect Solon Beman and landscape architect Nathan Barrett based Pullman's design on French urban plans. Way back when, Pullman was made up of mostly brick rowhouses (95% still in use), several parks, shops, schools, churches, and a library, as well as various health, recreational, and cultural facilities.

Today, the compact community's borders are 111th Street (Florence Drive), 115th Street, Cottage Grove Avenue (Pullman Drive), and S Langley Avenue (Fulton Avenue). If you're interested in sightseeing within the historic district, we suggest you start at the Pullman Visitor Center (11141 S Cottage Grove Ave, 773-785-8901; www.pullmanil.org). There you can pick up free self-guided walking tour brochures and watch an informative 20-minute film on the town's history. Call the center for additional specialty tour information and lecture details.

The annual House Tour on the second weekend in October is a popular Pullman event where several private residences open their doors to the public from 11 am to 5 pm on Saturday and Sunday ($15 in advance, $18 on day of event). May through October, the center also offers a two-hour Guided Walking Tour every first Sunday of the month at 1:30 pm ($5). Key tour sites include Hotel Florence, Greenstone Church (interior), Market Square, the stables, and the fire station. Hotel Florence's interior is currently being restored, as well as the fire-damaged Clock Tower and Administration Building.

Where to Eat

• **Seven Seas Submarine**, 11216 S Michigan Ave, 773-785-0550. Dine in or take out at this tiny sandwich shop.

• **Cal Harbor Restaurant**, 546 E 115th St, 773-264-5435. Omelettes, burgers, etc. at family grill.

Where to Drink

• **Pullman's Pub**, 611 E 113th St, 773-568-0264. Suds in a pre-Prohibition watering hole.

How to Get There

By Car: Take I-94 S to the 111th Street exit. Go west to Cottage Grove Avenue and turn south, driving one block to 112th Street to the Visitor Center surrounded by a large, free parking lot.

By Train: Metra's Electric Main Line departs from Randolph Street Station (underground) at Michigan Avenue between S Water Street and Randolph Street. Ride 30 minutes to Pullman Station at 111th Street ($2.90 one-way). Walk east to Cottage Grove Avenue and head south one block to 112th and the Visitor Center.

By L: From the Loop, take the Red Line to the 95th Street station. Board CTA 111 Pullman bus going south ($2 with transfer).

By Bus: CTA 4 bus from the Randolph Street Station travels south to the 95th Street and Cottage Grove stop. Transfer to 111 Pullman bus heading south ($2 with transfer).

University of Illinois at Chicago

University of Illinois at Chicago

General Information

NFT Map: 26
Address: 1200 W Harrison St
Chicago, IL 60680
Phone: 312-996- 4350
Website: www.uic.edu

Overview

With over 25,000 students, the University of Illinois at Chicago (UIC) is the largest university in Chicago. Located on the city's Near West Side, UIC is ethnically diverse and urban to the core. It is a leading public research university and home to the nation's largest medical school.

However, its legacy as a builder in Chicago is a bit spotty. In the mid-1960s, the school leveled most of what was left of a vibrant Italian-American neighborhood to build its campus next to the Eisenhower. During current development of the South Campus, UIC continues to consume city blocks south of Roosevelt Road. UIC's expansion all but erased the colorful, landmark Maxwell Street flea market area. The saving grace of the school's construction craze is that many of the original, ugly, cement slab structures are kissing the wrecking ball and being replaced with more inspired buildings. But even with the multi-million dollar improvements, the campus still doesn't ignite any desire to visit. Other than going to class or the doctor, a lone trip to UIC to see the Jane Addams Hull-House Museum is sufficient.

Tuition

For the 2005-2006 academic year, an Illinois resident undergraduate student's tuition and fees will be $4,151; room and board will cost between $5,058 and $8,942 depending on the meal plan and type of housing one chooses. These figures do not include books, supplies, lab fees, or personal expenses.

Sports

Lately, the Division I Flames have been hot. The men's basketball team's first appearance in the NCAA Tournament was in 1997. They returned in 2002 after winning their first ever Horizon League Tournament and went on to win the title again in 2004. Additionally, the Flames women's gymnastics, tennis squad, and softball teams have all advanced to NCAA Tournament play in recent years.

Other Flames men's and women's teams are swimming & diving and cross-country/track & field. UIC also has men's tennis, gymnastics, baseball, and soccer, plus women's basketball and volleyball. Basketball games and women's volleyball matches are played at the recently renovated UIC Pavilion at the corner of S Racine Avenue and Harrison Street. For tickets, call 312-413-8421, or visit www.uicflames.com.

Too bad the NCAA doesn't have a bowling tournament, because UIC would be a strong contender. The campus has its own alley located at 750 S Halsted Street (312-413-5170), where the public is welcome to sling balls and swig beers with students.

Culture on Campus

Jane Addams Hull-House (800 S Halsted St, 312-413-5353) www.uic.edu/jaddams/hull, was America's first settlement house, which opened in 1889. The free museum documents the pioneering organization's social welfare programs supporting the community's destitute immigrant workers. Museum hours are 10 am to 4 pm Tuesday through Friday and noon to 4 pm on Sunday, closed on Mondays and Saturdays.

Department Contact Information

All area codes are 312 unless otherwise noted.

Admissions and Records 996-4350
Graduate College 413-2550
College of Architecture & the Arts 996-5611
College of Applied Health Sciences 996-6695
College of Dentistry 996-1020
College of Business Administration 996-2700
College of Education 996-5641
College of Engineering 996-2400
College of Liberal Arts and Sciences 996-3366
College of Medicine 996-3500
College of Nursing 996-7800
College of Pharmacy 996-2497
School of Public Health 996-6620
College of Social Work 996-7096
College of Urban Planning and Public Affairs. 413-8088
Office of Continuing Education 996-8025
University of Illinois Medical Center 355-4000

1. Laboratory for Astrophysics and Space Research
2. Astronomy and Astrophysics Center
3. Research Institutes
4. Biopsychological Research Center
5. Disciples Divinity House
6. Kovler Viral Oncology Laboratories
7. Ingleside Hall
8. Searle Chemical Laboratory
9. Jones Laboratory
10. Zoology
11. Hutchinson Commons
12. Reynolds Club
13. Statistics and Mathematics
14. Development Office-5733 S University
15 Calvert House
16. Student Counseling and Resource Service
17. Human Development
18. Development Office-5736 S Woodlawn
19. Nursery School-5740 S Woodlawn
20. Nursery School-5750 S Woodlawn
21. Abbott Memorial Hall
22. Goldblatt Pavillion
23. Armour Clincial Research
24. Goldblatt Memorial Building
25. McElwee Building
26. Gates-Blake Hall
27. Goodspeed Hall
28. Wieboldt Hall
29. Harper Memorial Library
30. Beecher Hall
31. Green Hall
32. Kelly Hall
33. Foster Hall
34. University High School
35. Orthogenic School
E 54th Pl
S Greenwood Ave
E Garfield Blvd
E 55th
E 56
E 57
E 58th St
E 59th St
Midway Plaisance
E 60th St
S Cottage Grove Ave
S Maryland Ave
S Drexel Ave
S Ingleside Ave
S Ellis Ave
S University Ave
S Woodlawn Ave
S Kimbark Ave
S Kenwood Ave
S Dorchester Ave
S Blackstone Ave
Stagg Field
Ratner Athletic Center
Housing Services
Young Memorial Building
Court Theatre
Pierce Hall
Cochrane-Woods Art Center
Smart Museum
Henry Crown Field House
Lutheran Campus Ministry
Brent House
Alumni House
Max Palevsky Residential Commons
Hyde Park Union Church
High Energy Physics
Jules Knapp Research Center
Biological Sciences Learning Center
Low Temperature Laboratory
Henry Moore's Nuclear Energy
Joseph Regenstein Library
Barlett Dinning Commons
Fenn House
University Church
Unitarian Campus Ministry
Snell and Hitchcock Hall
Anatomy Building
Interdivisional Research Building (under construction)
Kersten Physics Teaching Center
Mitchell Tower
Quadrangle Club
Special Events
Meadville/Lombard
MAP 19
Center for Advanced Medicine
Crerar Library
Culver Hall
Erman Biology Center
Mandel Hall
Hillel Center
Hinds Laboratory
Kent Chemical Laboratory
Comer Children's Hospital
Ronald McDonald House
Cummings Life Science Center
Ryerson Physical Laboratory
Eckhart Hall
Chapel House
Robie House
Blackstone Hall
Bookstore
Administration Building
Lillie House
Mitchell Hospital
Peck Pavillion
Surgery-Brain Research
Swift Hall
Walker Museum
Oriental Institute
Graduate School of Business
Wilder House
Children's Hospital
Emergency Room
Cobb Lecture Hall
Bond Chapel
Rosenwald Hall
Pick Hall
Rockefeller Memorial Chapel
Belfield Hall
Sunny Gymnasium
Gilman Smith Building
McLean Institute
Judd Hall
Middle School
Chicago Lying-In Building
Billings Hospital
Fulton Hall
Haskell Hall
Stuart Hall
Ida Noyes Hall
Kovler Gymnasium
International House
Classics Building
President's House
Blaine Hall
Bob Roberts Memorial Building
Hicks Building
Social Science Research
Midway Skating Rink
School of Social Service Administration Building
Midway Studios
Faculty Apartments
Burton-Judson Courts
1155 Building
Charles Stewart Mott Building
New Graduate Residence Hall
Chapin Hall
Hyde Park Day School
University Press
Edelstone Center
Laird Bell Law Quadrangle
Bulletin of Atomic Scientists
Center for Research Libraries
Steam Plant
Social Services Center

General Information

NFT Map:	19
Mailing Address:	University of Chicago Administration Building 5801 S Ellis Ave Chicago, IL 60637
Phone:	773-702-1234
Website:	www.uchicago.edu
Visitors Center:	Ida Noyes Hall, 1st Fl 1212 E 59th St
Phone:	773-702-9739
Guest Parking:	Lot located off Woodlawn Ave b/w 58th St and 59th St. Metered parking is available north of Ida Noyes Hall.

Overview

University of Chicago is a world-renowned research institution with a winning tradition in Nobel Prizes. 73 Nobel laureates have been associated with the university as faculty, students, or researchers. (Seven of the laureates are current faculty members.) More importantly (for some people), is the fact that University of Chicago helped found the Big Ten Conference and created "the world's first controlled release of nuclear energy"—uh, for us regular folks, that's the atomic bomb.

Besides producing hordes of brainy gurus of economics, business, law, and medicine, University of Chicago graduates include artists, writers, politicians, film directors, and actors. To name a few: Studs Terkel, Sara Paretsky, Carol Mosely-Braun, Kurt Vonnegut, Susan Sontag, John Ashcroft, Ed Asner, Saul Bellow, Katharine Graham, Philip Glass, Sherry Lansing, Martin Marty, and co-creators of Chicago's Second City comedy troupe, Bernard Sahlins and Mike Nichols.

Established in 1890, University of Chicago was founded and funded by John D. Rockefeller. Built on 200 acres donated by Marshall Field and designed by architect Henry Ives Cobb, the university's English Gothic buildings of ivy-clad limestone ooze old money and intellectual achievements. Rockefeller described the university as "the best investment I ever made." We just hope parents footing the bill for their kids' education feel the same.

Tuition

The University of Chicago operates on a trimester schedule, rather than the more common two-semester academic year. In the 2003-2004 academic year, an undergraduate student paid approximately $30,123 for tuition and fees, with an additional $9,624 for room and board. Most students spend another $2,560 on books, lab fees, and personal expenses, which all adds up to a grand total of $43,570 per year! Costs for graduate students vary based on the school. Chicago has 13,000 students, 4,400 of them undergraduate students. About 2,000 of the graduate students attend classes at the downtown riverfront campus' Gleacher Center (450 N Cityfront Plaza Dr, 312-464-8787, www.gleachercenter.com), where the popular Graham School of General Studies holds most of its continuing education classes.

Sports

There was a time when the University of Chicago racked up football trophies as well as Nobel Prizes. In 1935, the first Heisman Trophy winner was senior Jay Berwanger. The Maroons won seven Big Ten football championships between 1899 and 1924, followed by a steady losing streak. In 1946, the university threw in the proverbial towel, resigning from the Big Ten in favor of developing students' brains rather than brawn.

But the school hasn't totally abandoned sports. A member of the University Athletic Association, Chicago has women's volleyball, softball, swimming, tennis, soccer, basketball, cross-country, and track & field teams and men's baseball, basketball, cross-country, soccer, swimming, tennis, football, track & field teams, and a wrestling squad.

Culture on Campus

Located at 5757 S Woodlawn Avenue is Frank Lloyd Wright's Prairie style residential masterpiece Robie House (708-848-1976). The one-time private home is considered one of the most important buildings in the history of American architecture, and it will be even more impressive once the ten-year, $8-million-dollar renovation plans are complete. (Adults tickets cost $9, students and seniors pay $7.) Two must-see, but often overlooked, free museums on campus are the Oriental Institute Museum (1155 E 58th St, 773-702-9514; www.oi.uchicago.edu) and Smart Museum of Art (5550 S Greenwood Ave, 773-702-0200; www.smartmuseum.uchicago.edu). Showcasing archeological finds from university digs since the 1900s, the Oriental Institute has treasures from the ancient Near East dating from 9000 BC to 900 AD. The Smart Museum displays 8,000 fine arts items, with strong collections in painting and sculpture spanning centuries and continents.

The university's professional Court Theatre, which recently celebrated its 50th anniversary, presents fresh interpretations of classic dramas (5535 S Ellis Ave, 773-753-4472; www.courttheatre.org). Previous seasons have included critically acclaimed productions of Albee's *Who's Afraid of Virginia Woolf?*, Wilde's *The Importance of Being Earnest*, Beckett's *Endgame*, and Stoppard's *Travesties*.

Department Contact Information

Log onto www.uchicago.edu/uchi/directories/ for a university directory and links to division and department web pages.

Undergraduate Student Admissions	773-702-8650
Biological Sciences	773-702-8650
Humanities	773-702-8512
Physical Sciences	773-702-7950
Social Sciences	773-702-1234
Divinity School	773-702-8200
Graduate School of Business	773-702-7743
Graduate Affairs	773-702-7813
Graham School of General Studies	773-702-1722
Harris Graduate School of Public Policy Studies	773-702-8400
Law School	773-702-9494
Pritzker School of Medicine	773-702-1939
School of Social Service Administration	773-702-1250

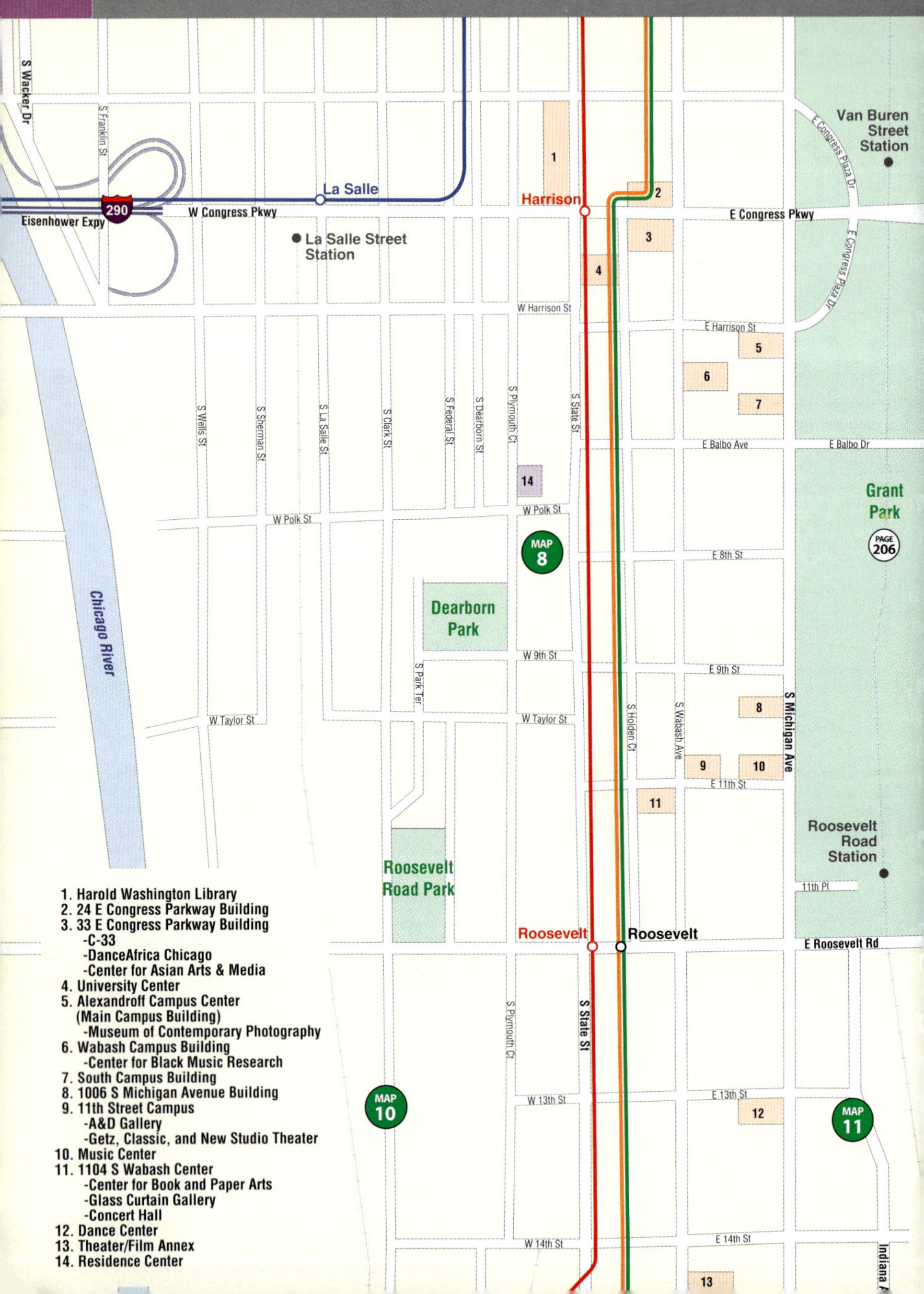

1. Harold Washington Library
2. 24 E Congress Parkway Building
3. 33 E Congress Parkway Building
   - C-33
   - DanceAfrica Chicago
   - Center for Asian Arts & Media
4. University Center
5. Alexandroff Campus Center (Main Campus Building)
   - Museum of Contemporary Photography
6. Wabash Campus Building
   - Center for Black Music Research
7. South Campus Building
8. 1006 S Michigan Avenue Building
9. 11th Street Campus
   - A&D Gallery
   - Getz, Classic, and New Studio Theater
10. Music Center
11. 1104 S Wabash Center
    - Center for Book and Paper Arts
    - Glass Curtain Gallery
    - Concert Hall
12. Dance Center
13. Theater/Film Annex
14. Residence Center

Name: Chester Gregory

Current profession: Actor in *Hairspray*, singer/songwriter

I am most proud of: My ancestors who have paved the way for who I have become today

Most recent accomplishment: Working with established producers in the recording industry

Most satiating read was: *The Alchemist*

Most vivid fantasy: To be the world's greatest entertainer

I am most influenced by: Lessons I received from my parents

My most satisfying creative experience has been: Every time people say that they are inspired by my music and/or work

My idea of success is: Fulfilling my personal goals and being kind to others

My personal "tribe" includes: My son, C3, (Chester III)

My launching pad: Columbia College Chicago

create... change

PHOTO BY WALTER SMITH

WWW.COLUM.EDU

General Information

NFT Maps: 8, 11
Address: 600 S Michigan Ave
Chicago, IL 60605
Phone: 312-663-1600
Website: www.colum.edu

Overview

Named after the Columbia Exposition World Fair, Columbia College began in 1890 as a women's college of speech. Over the years, the private college has evolved into the nation's largest Media Arts school, although psychologically staff and students grin and bear second fiddle status to the more highly acclaimed Art Institute of Chicago. Columbia's image is looking up, however, thanks in part to the successes of alumni from their reputable film and fiction departments, which have sprouted, in recent years, a bountiful harvest of novels and feature films (including the successful films *Barbershop* and *Real Women Have Curves* and the critically acclaimed novels of alums Joe Meno and Don DeGrazia, both now Fiction Department faculty). Other academic specialties include Entertainment Marketing and ASL Interpretation.

Tuition

The 2004-2005 school year has full-time students shelling out $14,880 per year. Room and board add another $7,000 to the tab. That's not including various lab, activity, and amenity fees.

Culture

The Dance Center of Columbia brings the DanceAfrica! exposition to Chicago every fall. The Museum of Contemporary Photography at the main campus building is one of only two fully accredited photography museums in the United States. The theater department's Getz Theater and New Studio Theater mount productions regularly. Story Week, a festival of writers and writing, occurs every spring in conjunction with the Printers Row Book Fair. In addition, several on-campus galleries and theaters feature the work of both students and international touring artists.

- **Center for Book and Paper Arts**
  1104 S Wabash Ave, 2nd Fl
  312-344-6630
  www.colum.edu/centers/bpa/
- **Museum of Contemporary Photography**
  600 S Michigan Ave
  312-344-7104
  www.mocp.org
- **A&D Gallery**
  72 E 11th St
  312-344-6156
- **Glass Curtain Gallery**
  1104 S Wabash Ave
  312-344-6650
- **C-33**
  33 E Congress Pkwy
  312-344-7696
- **Dance Center**
  1306 S Michigan Ave
  312-344-8300
  www.dancecenter.org
- **Getz, Classic, and New Studio Theaters**
  72 E 11th St
  312-344-6126
- **Concert Hall**
  1014 S Michigan Ave
  312-344-6179
- **DanceAfrica Chicago**
  33 E Congress Pkwy
  312-344-7070
  www.danceafricachicago.com
- **Center for Asian Arts & Media**
  33 E Congress Pkwy
  312-344-8213
  www.asianartsandmedia.org
- **Center for Black Music Research**
  623 S Wabash Ave
  312-344-7559
  www.cbmr.org

Department Contact Information

Undergraduate Admissions 312-344-7131
Graduate Admissions 312-344-7260
Alumni Office............................312-344-7420
Continuing Education.................. 312-344-8190
Art & Design 312-344-7380
Dance 312-344-8300
Educational Studies..................... 312-344-8140
Film and Video.......................... 312-344-6700
Journalism..............................312-344-7672
ASL – English Interpretation............ 312-344-7837
Marketing Communication............. 312-344-7600
Television.............................. 312-344-7410
Library................................. 312-344-7900

Quintessential Columbia College Chicago

1,300,000+
Square feet of classroom, office and living space in Chicago's South Loop

300,000+
Visitors per year take advantage of campus exhibitions, performances and special events

10,000+
Students in 2004-2005 school year . . . up from 125 students in 1963

2,500
Faculty and staff – 100 percent of faculty are working professionals in touch with the latest developments in their fields

225
National and international dance companies presented at our Dance Center in the last 30 years

11
2004 Emmy nominations among six alumni

1
Semester in LA – the only academic program permanently located on a working studio lot

1
The first undergraduate poetry major in the country

0
Other institutions like Columbia College Chicago

create... change

WWW.COLUM.EDU

Illinois Institute of Technology

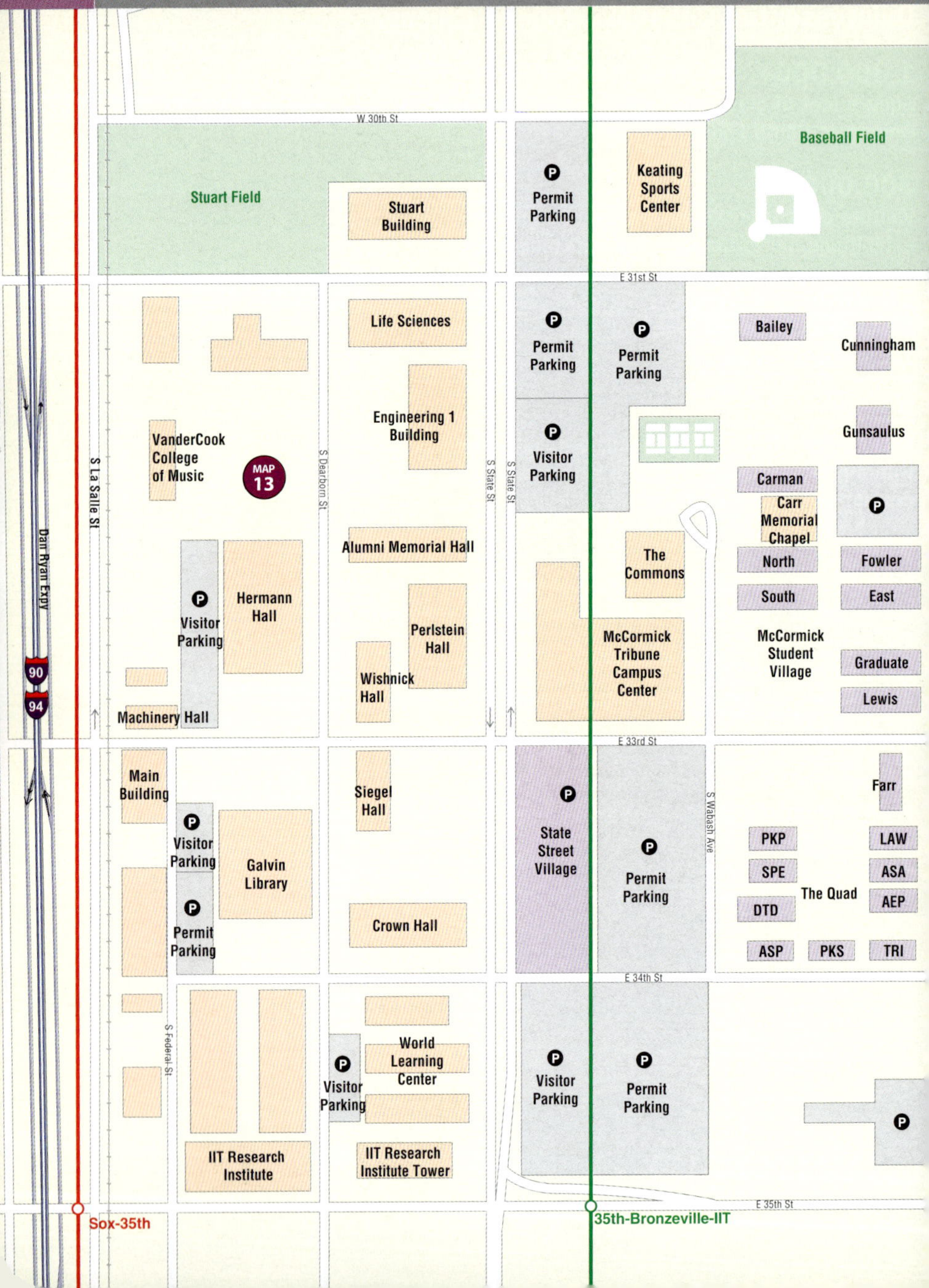

General Information

NFT Map: 13
Main Campus: 3300 S Federal St
Chicago, IL 60616
Phone: 312-567-3000
Website: www.iit.edu

Overview

In the 19th century, when higher education was reserved for society's upper crust, meat magnate Philip Danforth Armour put his money to good use and funded an institution dedicated to students from lower financial brackets. The Armour Institute carried his name until a merger with the engineering school in 1940 changed the name to Illinois Institute of Technology. Over the next 40 years, the college continued to merge with other small technical colleges, resulting in the IIT we know today. The school is as notable for its Mies Van Der Rohe-designed campus as for its groundbreaking work in aeronautics research. The new student center, designed by Dutch architect Rem Koolhaas, will include a space-aged metallic tube through which the local L train will travel.

IIT grants PhDs in a vast array of areas including science, mathematics, engineering, architecture, psychology, design, business, and law. The interprofessional, technology-focused curriculum is designed to prepare the 6,400 students to become leaders and groundbreakers in an increasingly complex global workplace. If that doesn't convince you to enroll, IIT was recently named a "College of Distinction" by a new college guide honoring some of America's top educational institutions. The title supports the university's claim that it provides "engaged students, great teaching, vibrant communities, and successful outcomes."

In June 2004, IIT's Research Institute Life Sciences Group was awarded $28 million in research funding. The prestigious award is among the largest ever received by IITRI for drug development.

Tuition

In the 2004-2005 academic year, undergraduate tuition cost $20,764. Room and board costs vary by residence, but generally run between $7,000 and $10,000.

Sports

The IIT Scarlet Hawks are affiliated with the National Association of Intercollegiate Athletics. Students can compete with other schools in baseball, basketball, cross-country, diving, soccer, swimming, and volleyball.

The 2004 swim season saw Scarlet Hawks' third year head coach, Rob Bond, named NAIA Men's Swimming and Diving National Coach of the Year.

New Developments on Campus

The newest student residency, completed in 2003, is State Street Village. Located at State and 33rd Streets, the hall was designed by well-known Chicago-based architect Helmut Jahn. The German-born designer was named one of the Ten Most Influential Living American Architects by the American Institute of Architects (AIA) in 1991. Jahn, a graduate of IIT himself, created the six-building complex across the street from Mies' masterful historical landmark, the S.R. Crown Hall. Jahn's new building brings student housing to a new level with the poured-in-place concrete, and glass-clad and corrugated stainless steel panels. Noise and vibrations from passing trains are reduced, while simultaneously exhibiting a cutting-edge aesthetic through its design.

Department Contact Information

Undergraduate Admissions 312-567-3025
Graduate Admissions 312-567-3020
Alumni Office 312-567-5040
Armour College of Engineering 312-567-3009
Center for Law and Financial Markets 312-906-6506
Center for Professional Development 630-682-6000
Chicago-Kent College of Law 312-906-5000
College of Architecture............. 312-567-3230
College of Science & Letters 312-567-3000
Institute of Business and 312-567-3947
Interprofessional Studies
Institute of Design 312-595-4900
Institute of Psychology............. 312-567-3500
Stuart Graduate School of Business . . 312-906-6500

General Information

Lincoln Park Campus:	Schmitt Academic Center 2320 N Kenmore Ave Chicago, IL 60614-3298 Phone: 773-325-7000 ext 5700
Loop Campus:	1 E Jackson Blvd Chicago, IL 60604 Phone: 312-362-8000
Website:	www.depaul.edu
Suburban Campuses:	
Barat	847-234-3000
Naperville	312-476-4500/630-548-9378
Oak Forest	312-476-3000/708-633-9091
O'Hare	312-476-3600/847-296-5348
Rolling Meadows	312-476-4800/847-437-9522

Overview

Established in 1898 by the Vincentian Fathers as a school for immigrants, DePaul has become the country's largest Catholic university (with over 23,000 students) and biggest private educational institution in Chicago. The university offers 150 undergraduate and graduate programs of study. According to The Princeton Review's recent survey of college students nationwide, DePaul students rated as some of the happiest college students in the country. It must be all the bars near campus on Halsted Street and Lincoln Avenue.

Of the university's seven campuses in the Chicago area, the Lincoln Park and Loop campuses serve as the core locations. The highly-acclaimed Theatre School, College of Liberal Arts and Sciences, School of Music, and School of Education hold down the 36-acre Lincoln Park campus amidst renovated, vintage homes on tree-lined streets.

DePaul's Loop Campus at Jackson Boulevard and State Street is where you'll find the College of Commerce, College of Law, and School of Computer Science, Telecommunications, and Information Systems. Nationally respected Kellstadt Graduate School of Business and DePaul's thriving continuing education program, the "School of New Learning," can also be found on the Loop Campus. The heart of the Loop campus is DePaul Center, located in the old Goldblatt Brothers Department Store. Prominent DePaul alumni include Chicago father-son mayors Richard M. Daley and his dad, the late Richard J. Daley; McDonald's Corporation's former CEO Jack Greenberg; Pulitzer Prize-winning composer George Perle; and actress Gillian Anderson.

Tuition

Each college has its own tuition; room and board costs depend on the residence facility and meal plan chosen. In the 2004-2005 academic year, undergraduate tuition for the College of Arts & Sciences was $19,700. Tuition for the School of Music and for the Theatre School cost about $23,500. Room and board cost between $6,000 and $8,500. Add on the cost of books, lab fees, and personal expenses.

Sports

DePaul's Blue Demons men's basketball team teased Chicago with an NCAA Division I Championship in 2000 when the team appeared in its first tournament since 1992. Coach Dave Leitao, who took over in '02, planned to reinstate the Demons' winning record, and almost succeeded in 2003. Almost. The team lost their chance at the title in the second round of the tournament, and hasn't been making headlines since. The Blue Demons play at United Center (1901 W Madison St, 312-455-4500; www.unitedcenter.com) and Allstate Arena (6920 N Mannheim Rd in Rosemont; www.allstatearena.com). For tickets, call Ticketmaster at 312-559-1212, visit www.ticketmaster.com, go to the stadiums' box offices, or visit the DePaul Athletic Center box office (2323 N Sheffield Ave, 773-325-7526; www.depaulblu edemons.com).

Blue Demons men's and women's teams include basketball, cross-country, soccer, tennis, and track & field. DePaul also has a men's golf team, as well as women's softball and volleyball squads. For stats and schedules, visit the Blue Demons' website.

Culture on Campus

DePaul's vibrant Theatre School is the oldest in the Midwest. Founded in 1925 as the Goodman School of Drama, the respected school stages over 200 performances during its Showcase, Chicago Playworks, New Directors Series, and School Workshop seasons. The Theatre School Showcase performs contemporary and classic plays at its 1,325-seat Merle Reskin Theatre located at 60 E Balbo Drive in South Loop. The Chicago Playworks for Families and Young Audiences and the School of Music's annual opera are also performed at the Merle Reskin Theatre, a French Renaissance-style theater built in 1910. For tickets ($8-$12), directions, and parking garage locations, call 312-922-1999, or go to theatreschool.depaul.edu. Take the Red Line to the Harrison Street or Jackson Street stops just southwest of the theater. CTA buses 29, 36, 151, and 146 also stop near the theater. Check the Theatre School website for New Directors Series and School Workshop productions, theater locations, and ticket prices.

DePaul University Art Gallery is located in the John T. Richardson Library at 2350 N Kenmore Avenue (773-325-7862). Permanent collections of sculpture and oils from local and international artists adorn the free gallery. A pay parking lot is located one block east of the library on N

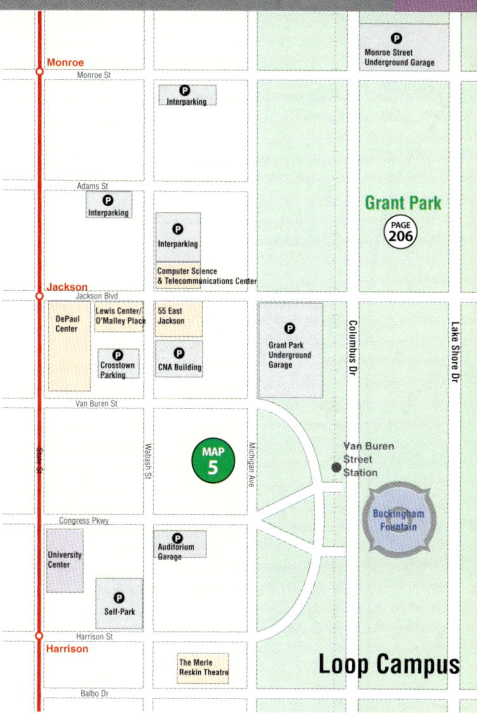

Sheffield Avenue. DePaul's John T. Richardson Library and Loop campus library in DePaul Center are open to the public year-round. But take plenty of change for the copy machines, as check-out privileges are reserved for students and faculty.

Department Contact Information

Log onto directory.depaul.edu/index/index.asp for a full university directory.

Lincoln Park Campus Admissions Office..... 773-325-7500
Loop Campus Admissions Office.............312-362-8300
College of Commerce.......................312-362-6783
College of Law............................312-362-8701
Undergraduate College of Arts & Sciences .. 773-325-7310
Graduate College of Arts & Sciences 773-325-7315
John T Richardson Library.................. 773-325-7862
Kellstadt Graduate School of Business 312-362-8810
Loop Campus Library 312-362-8433
School for New Learning 312-362-8001
School of Computer Science, Telecommunications and Information Systems...................312-362-8381
School of Music.............................773-325-7260
Theatre School..............................773-325-7917

Northwestern University (Evanston Campus)

Northwestern University (Evanston Campus)

General Information

Evanston Campus: 633 Clark St
Evanston, IL 60208
Phone: 847-491-3741

Chicago Campus: Abbot Hall
710 N Lake Shore Dr
Chicago, IL 60611
Phone: 312-503-8649

Website: www.northwestern.edu

Overview

Northwestern University, along with the University of Chicago, likes to think of itself as part of the "Ivy League of the Midwest." Almost 18,000 full- and part-time students attend Northwestern's 11 schools, located in Evanston and downtown Chicago.

Founded in 1851, Northwestern University was established in Evanston by many of the same Methodist founding fathers of the town itself. The 240-acre lakefront campus is bordered roughly by Lincoln Street to the north, and extends south to Clark Street, and west to Sheridan Road. The Evanston campus houses the Weinberg College of Arts and Sciences; McCormick School of Engineering and Applied Science; the Schools of Music, Communication, Education and Social Policy; the Graduate School; Medill School of Journalism; and J.L. Kellogg School of Management.

The university did a bit of branching out when it purchased land for the Chicago campus in 1920. Located between the lake and Michigan Avenue in the Streeterville neighborhood, the Chicago campus houses the Schools of Law, Medicine, and Continuing Studies. Graduate school and Kellogg courses are also offered at the Chicago campus. Several excellent hospitals and medical research institutions affiliated with the university dominate the northern edge of Streeterville. The Robert H. Lurie Medical Research Center at Fairbanks Court and Superior Street, completed in 2004, has expanded the university's research abilities with nine floors of laboratory space. The new women's hospital across from it will be finished in 2007.

Tuition

In the 2004-2005 academic year, undergraduate tuition and fees cost $29,940, and room and board cost $9,393.

Sports

Like all Big Ten Conference schools, Northwestern has football and basketball teams—but that's all we can really say of the Wildcats lately. There was more to talk about in the 1990s with back-to-back bowl appearances in the 1996 Rose Bowl (their first bowl appearance since winning in 1949) and the1997 Citrus Bowl. After Nebraska de-clawed, skinned, and gutted the Wildcats at the 2000 Alamo Bowl, it seems the team has been licking its wounds. They made an appearance in, and lost, the 2003 Motor City Bowl against Bowling Green.

The Wildcats' home field is Ryan Field at 1501 Central Avenue, about three blocks east of the Central Avenue stop on the Purple L Line. Basketball games are held at the Welsh-Ryan Arena behind the stadium. For tickets, call 847-491-2287. All sporting events are listed at www.nusports.com, where you can also purchase tickets online. Northwestern students can obtain free tickets to any game with the presentation of their WILDCARD ID.

Northwestern also has men's wrestling and baseball teams, plus men's and women's basketball, golf, soccer, tennis, and swimming and diving teams. Additionally, Wildcat women compete in cross-country, fencing, softball, field hockey, and volleyball, with a lacrosse team that's ranked number one in the country, as well as a tennis team ranked second.

Culture on Campus

The Mary and Leigh Block Museum of Art on the Evanston campus (40 Arts Circle Dr; 847-491-4000; www.blockmuseum.northwestern.edu) has 4,000 items in its permanent collection, including Old Masters' prints, architectural drawings, contemporary photographic images, and modern sculpture. The Block is also home to the state-of-the-art Pick-Laudati Auditorium that hosts film festivals and contemporary classics, as well as different cinema series' and lectures throughout the year. Hours: Tues: 10 am to 5 pm; Wed-Fri: 10 am to 8 pm; weekends: noon-5 pm. Admission is always free.

The Pick-Staiger Concert Hall (50 Arts Circle Dr, 847-491-5441; www.pickstaiger.com), is not only the main stage for the university's musical performances, but it is also home to several professional performance organizations such as the Chicago Chamber Musicians, Symphony of the Shores, Chicago String Ensemble, Performing Arts Chicago, and others. Each year, Pick-Staiger Concert Hall also hosts the Segovia Classical Guitar Series and the Keyboard Conversations Series. Call 847-467-4000 to purchase tickets.

Department Contact Information

Undergraduate Admissions 847-491-7271
Graduate School 847-491-7264
Weinberg College of Arts and Sciences 847-491-7561
Feinberg School of Medicine 312-503-8649
Kellogg School of Management 847-491-3300
Medill School of Journalism 847-467-1882
School of Communication................... 847-491-7530
School of Continuing Studies (Chicago)...... 312-503-6950
School of Continuing Studies (Evanston)..... 847-491-5611
School of Education and Social Policy........ 847-491-8193
McCormick School of Engineering
and Applied Science 847-491-5220
School of Law.......................... 312-503-3100
School of Music......................... 847-491-7575

Loyola University (Lake Shore Campus)

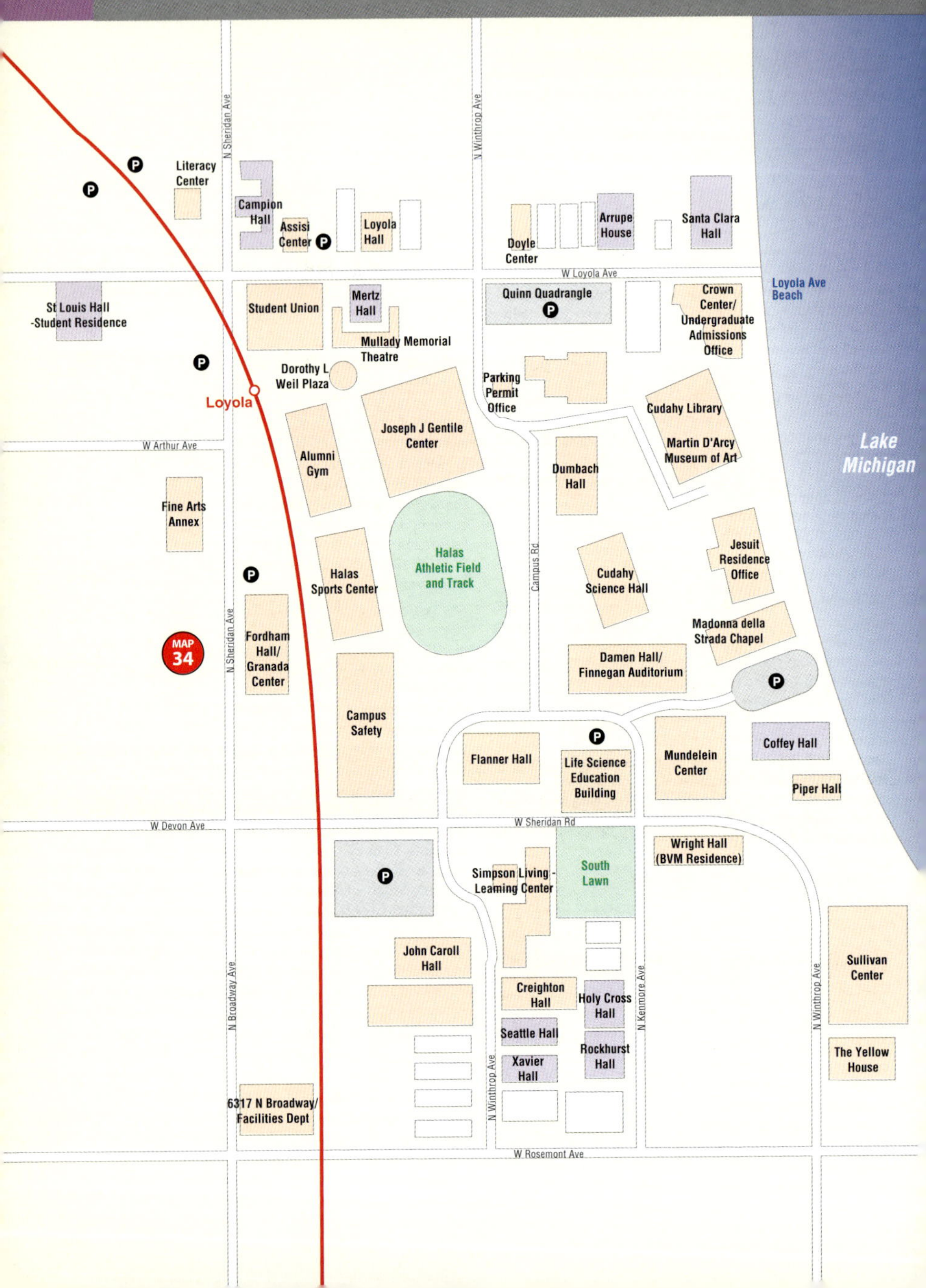

Loyola University (Lake Shore Campus)

General Information

Lake Shore:	6525 N Sheridan Rd Chicago, IL 60626 Phone: 773-274-3000
Water Tower/Lewis Towers Campus:	820 N Michigan Ave Chicago 60611 Phone: 312-915-6000
Medical Center:	2160 S First Ave Maywood, IL 60153 Phone: 708-216-9000
Website:	www.luc.edu

Overview

Loyola University, one of the largest Jesuit universities in the United States, is known throughout the Midwest for its first-rate schools of business and law, as well as for its Medical Center (a well-respected research institution). Approximately 13,000 students attend the university.

Lake Shore Campus, the largest campus of Loyola's four campuses, is on the lake in Rogers Park and houses the College of Arts & Sciences, the Graduate School, Niehoff School of Nursing, Mundelein College Adult Education Program, and Cudahy Library. The university's Water Tower campus downtown on Michigan Avenue is home to the Schools of Business, Education, Law, and Social Work and some College of Arts & Sciences courses. Loyola operates the Stritch School of Medicine and the Master's degree programs through the Niehoff School of Nursing at its suburban Maywood campus. The university also has a campus in Rome, one of the largest American campuses in Western Europe.

Tuition

In the 2004-2005 academic year, undergraduate tuition cost $22,060. Room and board prices ranged from $5,974 to $9,924. Add on books, lab fees, and personal expenses. Graduate student tuition, fees, and expenses vary by college. It seems like a hefty sum, but Loyola University was ranked by *U.S. News & World Report* as one of the "best values" for a college education.

Sports

Loyola is the only school in Illinois to win a Division I National Championship basketball tournament, with the Loyola Ramblers taking the NCAA men's basketball championship in 1963. The Ramblers' most recent tournament appearance was in 1985. If they keep winning every 22 years, the Ramblers should be making headlines any year now. Catch them at the Joseph J. Gentile Center on the Lake Shore Campus. For tickets, visit the box office, call 773-508-2569, or go to www.ramblermania.com.

Loyola University has men's and women's basketball, cross-country, track, soccer, and volleyball teams. The women also have a softball squad. The men's volleyball team is ranked as one of the top ten in the nation.

Culture on Campus

Scheduled to open in October 2005, the new Loyola University Museum of Art (LUMA) will become the new home of the famous Martin D'Arcy collection of Medieval, Renaissance, and Baroque art. Paintings by masters Tintoretto, Guercino, Bassano, and Stomer, plus sculpture, furniture, jewelry, decorative arts, and liturgical vessels, are part of the over 500-piece collection dating from 1150 to 1750. The museum, located at 920 N Michigan Avenue, charges $6 general admission and $5 for seniors. (Entry is free if you can pass for 18 or under.) Hours: Tues: 10 am-8 pm; Wed-Sun: 10 am-5 pm. For more information, call 312-915-7600. The university's Cudahy Library, Lewis Library at the Water Tower Campus, Science Library, Health Sciences Library, and Graduate Business School Library are all open to the public. Checkout privileges, however, are reserved for the university's students and faculty.

The Loyola University Theatre performs four classic dramas per year at the Kathleen Mullady Theatre (1134 W Loyola Ave, 773-508-3847) in the Centennial Forum/Mertz Hall building on the Lake Shore campus. Tickets cost $15 for the general public, $7 for seniors and students at other universities, and $5 for Loyola students. You can purchase tickets through the box office, which is open Monday through Friday, 3 pm to 7 pm.

Department Contact Information

Undergraduate Admissions	773-508-3075
Adult Education	312-915-6501
College of Arts & Sciences	773-508-3500
School of Business Administration	312-915-6113
School of Education	312-916-6800
School of Law	312-915-7120
Stritch School of Medicine	708-216-3223
Niehoff School of Nursing	773-508-3249
Rome Center of Liberal Arts	773-508-2760
School of Social Work	312-915-7005
Graduate School of Business	312-915-6120
The Graduate School	773-508-3396
University Libraries	773-508-2632

General Information

Chicago Park District:	www.chicagoparkdistrict.com 312-742-PLAY (7528)
Chicagoland Bicycle Federation:	www.chibikefed.org 312-427-3325
Chicago Area Runner's Association:	www.cararuns.org 312-666-9836

Overview

Greater Chicago offers dozens of recreational off-road paths that allow bikers, skaters, walkers, and joggers to exercise without worrying about vehicular traffic—now if only we could get dogs off the paths! In addition to recreational paths in the city's parks, designated off-street trails line the Lakefront, North Shore Channel, the North Branch Trail along the Chicago River, Burnham Greenway, and the Major Taylor Trail.

Lakefront Trail

Chicago has one of the prettiest and most accessible shorelines of any city in the US (if you survive the treacherous crossing of Lake Shore Drive to get there). Use one of Lake Shore Drive's over/underpasses and you'll discover 15 miles of bathing beaches and over 20 miles of bike paths—just don't anticipate being able to train for the Tour de France during summer weekends, when the sheer number of people makes it impossible to bike along the path at faster than a snail's pace. But thanks to Burnham's and Bennett's 1909 "Plan for Chicago," at least we can count on the shoreline remaining non-commercial, with great cycling, jogging, blading, skating, and swimming opportunities for all.

Major Taylor Trail

If you've ever wanted to take in a slice of Chicago's southwestern-most corner (and let's face it, who hasn't?), try the six-mile bike route that begins at Dawes Park at 81st and Hamilton Streets, near Western Avenue. The route incorporates an abandoned railroad right-of-way and runs to the southeast through Beverly and Morgan Park, ending up at the Cook County Forest Preserve near 130th and Halsted Streets. The trail was named in honor of cycling legend Marshall "Major" Taylor, one of the first African-American cyclists, who lived out the final years of his life in a YMCA in Chicago.

North Branch Trail

To access the northern end of the trail, take Lake Cook Road to the Chicago Botanic Garden, located east of I-94. You can also start from any of the forest preserves, as the path winds southward. To access the southern end of the trail in Chicago, take Milwaukee Avenue to Devon Avenue and head a short way east to the Caldwell Woods Preserve. The North Branch winds along the Chicago River and the Skokie Lagoons but, unlike most of the other trails, this one crosses streets, so be careful and look out for cars as you approach.

Burnham Greenway

The following information was dug up from a Trust For Public Land report on the state of the proposed route of the Burnham Greenway Trail before it was paved:

> Site History: Five-mile Conrail right-of-way between Chicago and the south suburbs, running through both industrial and natural areas.
> Contamination: Phase II indicated pollution from adjacent uses, including fly dumping, railroad pollutants, and some unnatural coloration in adjacent water. Assessment determined no risk as long as the soil remains undisturbed.
> REMEDIATION: Corridor will be paved.

So, as long as you stick to the paved trail and don't go digging around off the path, you should remain in good health! The path is suitable for riding, skating, rollerblading, and pedestrian activity.

North Shore Channel Trail

This trail follows North Shore Channel of the Chicago River from Lawrence Avenue through Lincolnwood, Skokie, and Evanston to Green Bay Road at McCormick Boulevard. Not all of the seven miles of the trail are paved bike paths, and you'll have to switch back and forth between path and street. Skokie recently paved the trail segment between Oakton and Howard Streets, but there are still many missing links in the route, much to the chagrin of Friends of the Chicago River (FOCR), who are trying to extend and improve the Channel Trail.

Chicago Park District

Many of the parks under the jurisdiction of the Chicago Park District have paths dedicated to cycling, jogging, walking, rollerblading, and skating. The Chicago Area Runner's Association is so committed to lobbying for runners' rights that it successfully petitioned to have the Lincoln Park running paths plowed through the winter so they could continue their running activities. This calls into question the sanity of such masochistic dedication, but we can only assume that the entire year is needed to prepare for the Chicago Marathon, held annually in October. Check out the chart on the facing page to determine Chicago Parks that designate jogging/walking and cycling/skating paths.

Park District—North Region	*Address*	*Phone*	*Jog/Walk*	*Bike/Skate*	*Map*
Brooks Park	7100 N Harlem Ave	773-631-4401	■		45
Emmerson Park	1820 W Granville Ave	773-761-0433	■		36
Eugene Field Park	5100 N Ridgeway Ave	773-478-9744		■	48
Oz Park	2021 N Burling St	312-742-7898	■		30
Peterson Park	5801 N Pulaski Ave	312-742-7584	■		46
Portage Park	4100 N Long Ave	773-685-7235	■		48
River Park	5100 N Francisco Ave	312-742-7516		■	38
Shabbona Park	6935 W Addison St	773-685-6205	■		47
Warren Park	6601 N Western Ave	773-262-6314	■	■	33
Frank J Wilson Park	4630 N Milwaukee Ave	773-685-6454	■		48
Winnemac Park	5100 N Leavitt St	312-742-5101	■		39

Park District—Central Region	*Address*	*Phone*	*Jog/Walk*	*Bike/Skate*	*Map*
Columbus Park	500 S Central Ave	312-746-5046	■	■	49
Douglas Park	1401 S Sacramento Ave	312-747-7670	■	■	50
Dvorak Park	1119 W Cullerton St	312-746-5083	■		26
Humboldt Park	1400 N Sacramento Ave	312-742-7549	■	■	50
Riis Park	6100 W Fullerton Ave	312-746-5363	■	■	49
Rutherford Sayre Park	6871 W Belden Ave	312-746-5368	■		47
Union Park	1501 W Randolph St	312-746-5494	■		24

Park District—Southwest Region	*Address*	*Phone*	*Jog/Walk*	*Bike/Skate*	*Map*
Bogan Park	3939 W 79th St	773-284-6456	■		53
Cornell Square Park	1809 W 50th St	312-747-6097	■		54
Hayes Park	2936 W 85th St	312-747-6177	■		54
LeClaire Courts/Hearst Community	5120 W 44th St	312-747-6438	■		53
Mt Greenwood Park	3724 W 111th St	312-747-6564	■		55
Rainey Park	4350 W 79th St	773-284-0696	■		53
Senka Park	5656 S St Louis Ave	312-747-7632	■		54
Sherman Park	1301 W 52nd St	312-747-6672	■		54
Avalon Park	1215 E 83rd St	312-747-6015	■		57
Bradley Park	9729 S Yates Ave	312-747-6022	■		60
Gately Park	810 E 103rd St	312-747-6155	■		59
Hamilton Park	513 W 72nd St	312-747-6174	■		57
Lake Meadows Park	3117 S Rhodes Ave	312-747-6287	■	■	14
Meyering Playground Park	7140 S Martin Luther King Dr	312-747-6545	■		57
Palmer Park	201 E 111th St	312-747-6576	■		59
Rosenblum Park	8050 S. Chapel	312-747-6649	■		60
Washington Park	5531 S Martin Luther King Dr	773-256-1248	■	■	57

Park District—Lakefront Region	*Address*	*Phone*	*Jog/Walk*	*Bike/Skate*	*Map*
Calumet Park	9801 S Ave G	312-747-6039	■		60
Jackson Park	6401 S Stony Island Ave	773-256-0903	■	■	58
Lincoln Park	2045 Lincoln Park West	312-742-7726	■	■	30
Loyola Park	1230 W Greenleaf Ave	773-262=8605	■	■	34
Rainbow Park & Beach	3111 E 77th St	312-745-1479		■	58

General Information

Chicagoland Bicycle Federation:	650 S Clark St, #300, 312-427-3325; www.biketraffic.org
Chicago Park District:	www.chicagoparkdistrict.com; 312-742-PLAY
Chicago Cycling Club:	www.chicagocyclingclub.org; 773-509-8093 (Organized weekend rides April through October)
Chicago Transit Authority:	www.transitchicago.com
DOT Bikes Website:	www.chicagobikes.org

Overview

Despite the environmental and physical benefits, and Mayor Daley's efforts to make Chicago streets more hospitable to pedallers, bike riders are still seen by most drivers as a road nuisance, and the designated bike lanes on streets such as Milwaukee, King Drive, and Elston are a joke—illegal passing lanes are more like it. Furthermore, designated lakefront bike paths are more often than not crowded with headphone-wearing roller bladers, leashless dogs, and shoulder-to-shoulder stroller pushers. Nonetheless, every year thousands of Chicagoans choose to take their lives into their hands by taking it to the street in a demonstration of the type of urban perseverance by which great cities were built. Or is it simple foolhardiness?

If you are a cyclist in Chicago, bear in mind that bicycles, like other vehicles of the roads, are subject to the same laws and rights as drivers—but good luck enforcing them. This includes the right to take a lane and the obligation to hand signal for turns. Helmets are still optional, but you'd have to have a pretty thick head to tempt fate without one. The same goes for an adequate assortment of chains and u-locks. Bike thievery is rampant in every neighborhood in the city.

Bikes Onboard Mass Transit

Bicycles are permitted (free) on all L trains at all times except 7 am-9 am and 4 pm-6 pm on weekdays. Use the accessible turnstile or ask an attendant to open an access gate. Don't try to take your bike through the tall steel gates—it will get stuck! Only two bikes per carriage are allowed, so check for other bikes before you get on. Bikes are only permitted on CTA buses equipped with front exterior bike racks, such as the 63rd Street, 72 North Avenue, 75th Street, and 65 Grand buses. If your bike is the first to be loaded, lower the rack and place it in position with the front wheel facing the curb. If there is already a bike on the rack, place your bike's rear wheel toward the curb. If two bikes are already loaded, wait for the next bus. Plan on taking the Metra? Leave your bike at home! Items larger than a briefcase are not permitted on Metra trains.

Bike Shops	*Address*	*Phone*	*Map*
Kozy Cyclery	219 W Erie St	312-266-1700	2
Sports Authority	620 N La Salle Dr	312-337-6151	2
Bike Chicago	600 E Grand Ave	800-915-BIKE	3
Mission Bay Multi Sports	738 W Randolph St	312-466-9111	4
Kozy Cyclery	601 S La Salle St	312-360-0020	8
Recycle Bike Shop	1465 S Michigan Ave	312-987-1080	11
Wheels & Things	5210 S Harper Ave	773-493-4326	19
Art's Cycle	1646 E 55th St	773-363-7524	20
Rapid Transit Cycle Shop	1900 W North Ave	773-227-2288	21
Quick Release Bike Shop	1527 N Ashland Ave	773-871-3110	22
Upgrade Cycle Works	1130 W Chicago Ave	312-226-8650	24
Irv's Bike Shop	1725 S Racine Ave	312-226-6330	26
Oscar Wastyn Cycles	2634 W Fullerton Ave	773-384-8999	27
Kozy Cyclery	1451 W Webster Ave	773-528-2700	29
Cycle Smithy	2468 1/2 N Clark St	773-281-0444	30
Performance Bicycle Shop	2720 N Halsted St	773-248-0107	30
Village Cycle Center	1337 N Wells St	312-726-2453	31
Roberts Cycle	7054 N Clark St	773-274-9281	34
Uptown Bikes	4653 N Broadway St	773-728-5212	40
Urban Bikes	4653 N Broadway St	773-728-5212	40
On The Route Bicycles	3146 N Lincoln Ave	773-477-5066	43
Johnny Sprocket's	3001 N Broadway	773-244-1079	44
Kozy Cyclery	3712 N Halstead St	773-281-2263	44
Sports Authority	3134 N Clark St	773-871-8500	44
Edgebrook Cycle & Sport	6450 N Central Ave	773-792-1669	46
Chicagoland Bicycle	10355 S Kedzie Ave	773-445-0811	56

General Information

Chicago Park District: 312-742-PLAY (7529); www.chicagoparkdistrict.com

Overview

Due to the temperature extremes that Chicago experiences, its residents can enjoy both ice skating and inline skating at various times of the year. Ice skating can be a fun, free winter activity if you have your own skates, and if you don't, many rinks rent them. Skateboarding is also a popular pastime and a number of parks throughout the city are equipped with skating facilities.

Inline Skating

Similar to bike riding, inline skating in Chicago serves dual purposes. If you plan on strapping on the blades to get from A to B, be super-careful navigating the streets. As it is, Chicago drivers tend to have difficulty seeing cyclers and, chances are, they won't notice you until you've slammed into their open car door. Wear protective gear whenever possible, especially a helmet, and learn to shout loudly so that people can anticipate your approach. If recreational skating is more your speed, check out the Recreational Paths page for cool places to skate. If you'd like to join the hundreds of summer skaters out there and you don't have your own gear, the following places offer skate rental: Londo Mondo, 1100 N Dearborn Street at W Maple Street, 312-751-2794; Bike Chicago at Navy Pier, 800-915-BIKE. Hourly rates range from $7 to $10, while daily rates are from $20 to $35.

Skate Parks

If what you're after is a phat jam session, grab your blades or board and a couple of buddies and head down to the magnificent Burnham Skate Park (east of Lake Shore Drive at 31st Street). With amazing grinding walls and rails, vert walls, and banks, Burnham Park presents hours of fun and falls. Less intense, but equally fun, are the two skate parks with ramps, quarter pipes, and grind rails. One can be found at West Lawn Park (4233 W 65th St, 773-284-2803) the other at Oriole Park (5430 N Olcott Ave, 773-631-6197).

Ice Skating

The long-running and popular Skate on State was canceled due to the opening of two new ice rinks: the McCormick Tribune Ice Rink at Millennium Park and the Midway Plaisance ice rink.

The rink at Millennium Park is a beautiful place to skate during the day or evening, with Chicago's glorious skyline in the background. And after the ice melts, the area plays host to al fresco dining and entertainment in the summer months. Located at 55 N Michigan Avenue, enter on the east side of Michigan Avenue between Monroe Drive and Randolph Street. Parking is available for $10 at the Grant Park North Garage. (Enter from Michigan Avenue median at Washington or Madison Streets.) Entry is free, skate rental is $7, and if you have your own and want them sharpened, it's a $5 fee (312-742-5222).

The Olympic-sized skating rink and warming house complex at Midway Plaisance is the alternative to Millennium Park. Located at 59th and Woodlawn Avenue, entry is free and skate rentals cost $3. During the summer, the facility is used for roller-skating and other entertainment (312-745-2470).

Other ice skating rinks are located seasonally at:

McFetridge Sports Complex (year-round) • 3843 N California Ave, 773-478-2609 (admission is $4 for kids under 12 years, $5 for adults + $3 skate rental)

Daley Bicentennial Plaza Rink • 337 E Randolph St, 312-742-7650 (free admission + $4 rental)

McKinley Park • 2210 W Pershing Rd, 312-747-5992 ($3-$5 rental)

Mt. Greenwood Park • 3721 W 111th St, 312-747-3690 ($2-$3 rental)

Navy Pier Ice Rink • 600 E Grand Ave, 312-595-5100 ($12 admission + rental)

Riis Park • 6100 W Fullerton Ave, 312-746-5735 ($2-$3 rental)

The Rink (roller skating) • 1122 E 87th St, 773-221-2600 ($1)

Rowan Park • 11546 S Avenue L, 773-646-1967 ($2-$3 rental)

Warren Park • 6601 N Western Ave, 773-262-6314 ($4 admission + $4 rental)

West Lawn Park • 4233 W 65th St, 773-284-2803 (free admission + $5 rental)

Gear

If you're after skateboard gear, check out Air Time Skate Boards at 3317 N Clark Street, 773-248-4970; and Uprise Skateboard Shop at 1820 N Milwaukee Avenue, 773-342-7763.

For skating equipment, Air Time (above) also does inline skates, as does Londo Mondo which has two locations: 1100 N Dearborn Street at W Maple Street, 312-751-2794; and 2148 N Halstead Street, 773-327-2218.

For all your ice skating needs, try the Skater's Edge store in the McFetridge Sports Complex (3843 N California Avenue, 773-463-1505). They deal in hockey skates and other equipment, as well as inline skates and accessories such as sequined dresses!

Chicago is blessed with a number of golf courses within the city limits. Most courses offer resident and seniors discounts, so be sure to ask. We couldn't possibly list all the great links in the surrounding suburbs, so we picked a few close to NFT's coverage area. Our Chicago favorites includes: Jackson Park, for being the closest 18 holes to the Loop; Sydney R. Marovitz executive course, for beautiful lake views; Harborside International, for a challenging Scottish-links experience; and Family Golf Center, for a lunchtime 9.

Golf Courses

Golf Courses	*Address*	*Phone*	*Map*	*weekdays*	*weekends*
Columbus Park Golf Course	5700 W Jackson Blvd	312-245-0909	49	$12	$13.50
Edgebrook Golf Course	6100 N Central Ave	773-763-8320	45	$24-44	$28-49
The Glen Club	2901 West Lake Ave, Glenview	847-724-7272	n/a	$105-140	$117-155
Glencoe Park District Course	621 Westley Rd, Glencoe	847-835-0250	n/a	$26	$30-45
Harborside International Golf Center	10959 S Doty Ave E	312-782-7837	59	$80	$92
Indian Boundary Golf Course	8600 W Forest Preserve Ave	773-625-9630	n/a	$25-44	$28-49
Jackson Park Golf Course	63rd St & Lake Shore Dr	312-245-0909	57	$22	$25
Marquette Park Golf Course	6700 S Kedzie Ave	312-747-2761	54	$17	$18
Peter N Jans Community Golf Course	1031 Central St, Evanston	847-475-9173	n/a	$17	$22
Riverside Golf Club	2320 Desplaines Ave	708-447-1049	10	$65	$75
Robert A Black Golf Course	2045 West Pratt Blvd	312-742-7931	34	$11.50	$13
South Shore Country Club	7059 South Shore Dr	312-245-0909	58	$10	$11.50
Sydney R Marovitz Golf Course	3600 N Recreation Dr	312-742-7930	43	$19	$22
Winnetka Park District Course	1300 Oak St, Winnetka	847-501-2050	n/a	$40	$46

Driving Ranges

Driving Ranges	*Address*	*Phone*	*Map*	*Fees*
Diversey Driving Range	141 W Diversey Dr	312-742-7929	3	$11/100 balls, $2 clubs
Harborside International Golf Center	11001 S Doty Ave	312-782-7837	59	$10/100 balls, $3 clubs
Jackson Park Golf Course	63rd St & Lake Shore Dr	312-245-0909	57	$6/50-65 balls, $2 clubs

Volleyball Courts

Hoops The Gym • 312-850-4667
Two locations: 1380 W Randolph St; 1001 W Washington Blvd
State-of-the-art court rentals. 24/7.

Lincoln Park/North Avenue Beach • 312-742-3224 (reservations and price information)
101 courts—12 are always open to the public. Much league play and reserved courts.
Office hours: Mon-Fri: 1 pm-9 pm; Weekends: 8 am-5 pm.

Lincoln Park/Montrose Beach • 312-742-5121
45 courts allotted on a first-come-first-served basis. League play in the evening.

Jackson Park/63rd Street Beach • 312-742-4838
Four free courts—first-come-first-served.

312-742-PLAY (general park info); 312-742-5121 (Department of Beaches and Pools). All outdoor pools are free for the summer (Memorial Day-Labor Day). During the year, all lap swim fees for indoor pools are for 10-week sessions ($20 before 9 am; $10 after 9 am).

Outdoor Pools	*Address*	*Phone*	*Map*
Avondale Park	3516 W School St	773-478-1410	48
Chase Park	4701 N Ashland Ave	312-742-7518	40
Douglas Park Cultural & Community Center	1401 S Sacramento Blvd	773-762-2842	50
Dvorak Park	1119 W Cullerton St	312-746-5083	26
Franklin Park	4320 W 15th St	312-747-7676	49
Gompers Park	4222 W Foster Ave	773-685-3270	48
Hamlin Park	3035 N Hoyne Ave	312-742-7785	42
Humbolt Park	1400 N Sacramento Ave	312-742-7549	50
Jefferson Park	4822 N Long Ave	773-685-3316	48
McFetridge Sports Center (California Park)	3843 N California Ave	773-478-2609	41
Piotrowski Park	4247 W 31st St	312-747-6608	51
Pulaski Park	1419 W Blackhawk St	312-742-7559	22
River Park	5100 N Francisco Ave	312-742-7516	38
Sherman Park	1301 W 52nd St	312-747-6672	54
Smith (Joseph Higgins) Park	2526 W Grand Ave	312-742-7534	50
Taylor Park	39 W 47th St	312-747-6728	15
Union Park	1501 W Randolph St	312-746-5494	24
Washington Park	5531 S Martin Luther King Dr	773-256-1248	18
Wentworth Gardens Park	3770 S Wentworth Ave	312-747-6996	13
Wrightwood Park	2534 N Greenview Ave	312-742-7816	29

Indoor Pools	*Address*	*Phone*	*Map*
Altgeld Park	515 S Washtenaw Ave	312-746-5001	50
Carver Park	939 E 132nd St	312-747-6348	59
Clemente Park	2334 W Division St	312-742-7466	21
Curie Park	4949 S Archer Ave	773-535-2020	51
Dyett Recreational Center	513 E 51st St	312-745-1211	16
Eckhart Park	1330 W Chicago Ave	312-746-5553	24
Fernwood Park	10436 S Wallace St	312-747-6164	59
Foster Park	1440 W 84th St	312-747-7612	54
Gill Park	833 W Sheridan Rd	312-742-5807	43
Harrison Park	1824 S Wood St	312-746-9490	25
Hayes Park	2936 W 85th St	312-745-2200	54
Independence Park	3945 N Springfield Ave	773-478-3538	48
Kelly Park	4136 S California Ave	773-535-4905	52
Kosciuszko Park	2732 N Avers Ave	312-742-7556	48
LaFollette Park	1333 N Laramie Ave	773-287-0541	49
Mather Park	5941 N Richmond St	773-534-2412	35
McGuane Park	2901 S Poplar Ave	312-747-7463	12
Nash Community Center	1833 E 71st St	773-256-0906	57
Orr Park	730 N Pulaski Rd	312-746-5354	49
Portage Park	4100 N Long Ave	773-685-7189	48
Ridge Park	9625 S Longwood Dr	312-747-0402	56
Sheridan Park	910 S Aberdeen St	312-746-5370	26
Stanton Park	618 W Scott St	312-742-9553	31
Welles Park	2333 W Sunnyside Ave	312-742-7515	39
Wentworth Park	5625 S Mobile Ave	312-747-6993	53

Bowling Alleys	*Address*	*Phone*	*Rate*	*Map*
Diversey-River Bowl	2211 W Diversey Pkwy	773-227-5800	Mon-Thurs: $19/hr per lane; Fri-Sat: $26/hr per lane, after 6 pm: $32/hr per lane; Sun $26/hr per lane, $3 for shoes	42
Habetler Bowl	5250 N Northwest Hwy	773-774-0500	$4 per game for adults, $2.50 for kids; $1 per game Tuesdays after 9:30 pm and Thursdays from 9 am-4 pm, $3.50 for shoes	46
Lucky Strike	2747 N Lincoln Ave	773-549-2695	$20/hr per lane, $2 for shoes	29
Southport Lanes & Billiards	3325 N Southport Ave	773-472-6600	Mon-Thurs: $15/hr per lane; Fri-Sat: $20/hr per lane; Sun: $10/hr per lane, $2 for shoes	43
Timber Lanes	1851 W Irving Park Rd	773-549-9770	$2.50 per game, $2 for shoes	39
Waveland Bowl	3700 N Western Ave	773-472-5900	Mon-Fri after 9:30 pm: $4 per game; weekends vary, $4 for shoes	42

312-742-7529 (general info); 773-256-0949 (Lake Front Region Office). All tennis courts (except Daley Bicentennial Plaza in Grant Park, Diversey Park, and Waveland Park) are free and open to the public on a first-come-first-served basis. Courts are open daily—check each park for individual hours.

Tennis Courts	Address	Phone	Map
Abbot Park	49 E 95th St	312-747-6001	58
Ada Park	11250 S Ada St	312-747-6002	56
Archer Park	4901 S Kilbourn Ave	773-284-7029	49
Armour Square Park	3309 S Shields Ave	312-747-6012	13
Ashe Beach Park	2701 E 74th St	312-745-1479	58
Athletic Field Park	3546 W Addison St	773-478-2889	48
Avalon Park	1215 E 83rd St	312-747-6015	57
Bell Park	302 N Oak Park Ave	312-746-5008	47
Bessemer Park	8930 S Muskegon Ave	312-747-6023	58
Beverly Park	2460 W 102nd St	312-747-6024	56
Blackhawk Park	2318 N Lavergne Ave	312-746-5014	48
Bogan Park	3939 W 79th St	773-284-6456	54
Bradley Park	9729 S Yates Ave	312-747-6022	60
Brainerd Park	1246 W 92nd St	312-747-6027	56
Brands Park	3259 N Elston Ave	773-478-2414	41
Brooks Park	7100 N Harlem Ave	773-631-4401	53
Brown Memorial Park	634 E 86th St	312-747-6063	57
California Park	3843 N California Ave	312-742-7585	41
Calumet Park	9801 S Ave G	312-747-6039	60
Chase Park	4701 N Ashland Ave	312-742-7518	40
Chopin Park	3420 N Long Ave	773-685-3247	48
Clemente Park	2334 W Division St	312-742-7538	21
Columbus Park	500 S Central Ave	312-746-5046	49
Cooper Park	11712 S Ada St	312-747-6096	56
Cornell Square Park	1809 W 50th St	312-747-6097	52
Daley Bicentennial Plaza	337 E Randolph St	312-742-7648	6
[$7/hr; reservations must be made in person; 7 am-10 pm]			
David Square Park	4430 S Marshfield Ave	312-747-6107	52
Douglas Park Cultural & Community Center	1401 S Sacramento Ave	312-747-7670	52
Dunham Park	4638 N Melvina Ave	773-685-3257	47
Ellis Park	707 E 37th St	312-747-0231	14
Emmerson Playground Park	1820 W Granville Ave	773-761-0433	36
Euclid Park	9800 S Parnell Ave	312-747-6124	55
Eugene Field Park	5100 N Ridgeway Ave	773-478-9744	48
Frank J Wilson Park	4630 N Milwaukee Ave	773-685-6454	48
Fuller Park	331 W 45th St	312-747-6144	15
Gompers Park	4222 W Foster Ave	773-685-3270	48
Grant Park	331 E Randolph St	312-742-7648	6
Green Briar Park	2650 W Peterson Ave	773-761-0582	35
Hamilton Park	513 W 72nd St	312-747-6174	57
Hamlin Park	3035 N Hoyne Ave	312-742-7785	42
Harrison Park	1824 S Wood St	312-746-5491	25
Hollywood Park	3312 W Thorndale Ave	773-478-3482	46
Horner Park	2741 W Montrose Ave	773-478-3499	38
Humboldt Park	1400 N Sacramento Ave	312-742-7549	50
Independence Park	3945 N Springfield Ave	773-478-3538	48
Indian Boundary Park	2500 W Lunt Ave	773-764-0338	33

Tennis Courts	*Address*	*Phone*	*Map*
Jackson Park	6401 S Stony Island Ave	773-256-0903	58
Jefferson Park	4822 N Long Ave	773-685-3316	48
Jensen Park	4600 N Lawndale Ave	312-742-7580	48
Jonquil Park	1023 W Wrightwood Ave		29
Kenwood Community Park	1330 E 50th St	312-747-6285	17
Kosciuszko Park	2732 N Avers Ave	312-742-7546	48
Lake Shore Park	808 N Lake Shore Dr	312-742-7891	32
Legion Park at the Chicago River	W Peterson Ave to W Foster Ave		35
Lerner Park	7000 N Sacramento Ave		33
Lincoln Park-Diversey Tennis Center [$12/hr; reservations must be made in person. Clay courts.]	141 W Diversey Ave	312-742-7821	44
Lincoln Park-Waveland Tennis Center [$12/hr; reservations must be made in person; 7:30 am-8 pm]	3650 N Lake Shore Dr	312-742-7674	44
Loyola Park	1230 W Greenleaf Ave	773-262-8605	34
Mandrake Park	900 E Pershing Rd	312-747-7661	12
Mather Park	5941 N Richmond St	312-742-7501	35
McFetridge Sports Center (California Park)	3843 N California Ave	773-478-2609	41
McGuane Park	2901 S Poplar Ave	312-747-6497	12
McKinley Park	2210 W Pershing Rd	312-747-6527	52
Metcalfe Park	4134 S State St		16
Nichols Park	1300 E 55th St	312-747-2703	19
Oz Park	2021 N Burling St	312-742-7898	30
Piotrowski Park	4247 W 31st St	312-747-6608	51
Pottawattomie Park	7340 N Rogers Ave	773-262-5835	34
Rainbow Park & Beach	3111 E 77th St	312-745-1479	58
Revere Park	2509 W Irving Park Rd	773-478-1220	38
River Park	5100 N Francisco Ave	312-742-7516	38
Rogers Park	7345 N Washtenaw Ave	773-262-1482	33
Roosevelt Park	62 W Roosevelt Rd	312-742-7648	8
Senn Park	1550 W Thorndale Ave		37
Sheridan Park	910 S Aberdeen St	312-746-5369	26
Sherman Park	1301 W 52nd St	312-747-6672	54
Smith (Joseph Higgins) Park	2526 W Grand Ave	312-742-7534	50
South Shore Culture Center	7059 S South Shore Dr	773-256-0149	57
Taylor Park	41 W 47th St	312-747-6728	15
Touhy Park	7348 N Paulina St	773-262-6737	34
Union Park	1501 W Randolph St	312-746-5494	24
Warren Park	6601 N Western Ave	773-262-6314	33
Washington Park	5531 S Martin Luther King Dr	773-256-1248	57
Welles Park	2333 W Sunnyside Ave	312-742-7511	39

General Information

NFT Map: 11
Address: 1410 S Museum Campus Dr
Chicago, IL 60605
Phone: 312-235-7000
Lost & Found: 312-235-7202
Website: www.soldierfield.net
Bears Box Office: 847-615-BEAR (2327)
Bears Website: www.chicagobears.com
Ticketmaster: 312-559-1212; www.ticketmaster.com

Overview

Like many Bears fans, the "new" Soldier Field is big, burly, and visually abrasive. The field was a key installment in the multi-million dollar Lakefront Improvement Plan for the Chicago shoreline between Navy Pier and McCormick Place. An estimated $365 million went towards the 63,000-seat stadium, which opened in time for the 2003-2004 NFL Season and debuted on ABC's *Monday Night Football*. Improved Solider Field amenities include 60% more seats on the sidelines, twice as many bathrooms (with 1,000 fixtures), three times as many concessions stands (400), several cozy meeting nooks throughout the stadium, two 82 x 23-foot video screens, and a 100,000-square-foot lounge/entertainment facility. Critics debate whether the expanded structure resembles a giant toilet-bowl or a spaceship. (Voters Decide: Toilet Bowl Wins in a Landslide!) But the fact remains that the Bears have yet to experience a winning season in the new facility. After the disappointing 2004-2005, all eyes are on Bears Head Coach Lovie Smith as he and his staff recruit, rework, and rebuild this historic franchise.

How to Get Tickets

Contact Ticketmaster to purchase individual game tickets. Season tickets should be easier to come by for the 2005-2006 season, because it is a rebuilding year for the Bears. The best way to get great seats (other than by having them left to you in a will) is to work with a licensed ticket broker. Fans marked their territory early in 2004 by purchasing a one-time Permanent Seat License (PSL) and, in exchange for paying big premiums to help cover construction expenses, PSL holders are promised first choice of ticket seating each year. Of the stadium's 63,000 seats, 27,500 are PSL zones and the remaining 33,500 are non-licensed seats in the stadium's higher altitudes. Call the Bears sales office to get on the season ticket waiting list.

How to Get There

By Car: From the north or south, take Lake Shore Drive; follow the signs to Soldier Field. For parking lots, exit at E McFetridge, E Waldron, E 14th Boulevard, and E 18th Drive. From the west, take I-55 E to Lake Shore Drive, turn north and follow the signs. Travel east on I-290, then south on I-90/94 to I-55; get on I-55 E to Lake Shore Drive.

Parking lots surrounding Soldier Field cost between $7 and $12, including the new underground North Parking Garage. Two parking and game-day tailgating lots are located south of Waldron Drive. There are also lots on the Museum Campus off McFetridge Drive and near McCormick Place off 31st Street and E 18th Street.

By Train: On game days, CTA Soldier Field Express bus 128 runs non-stop between the Ogilvie Transportation Center and Union Station to Soldier Field. Service starts two hours before the game, runs up to 45 minutes before kickoff, and up to 45 minutes post-game.

By L: Take the Red, Orange, or Green Lines to the Roosevelt station stop. Either board eastbound CTA bus 12 or the free Green Trolley to the Museum Campus, then walk south to Soldier Field.

By Bus: CTA buses 12, 127, and 146 stop on McFetridge Drive near Soldier Field. Contact the RTA Information Center for routes and schedules at 312-836-7000 or online at www.rtachicago.com.

By Trolley: The Green Trolley travels along Michigan Avenue, Washington Street, Canal Street, and Adams Street to the Museum Campus. From there, you can walk south to the field. For routes and schedules, visit www.cityofchicago.org/transportation/trolleys.

General Information

NFT Map:	43
Address:	1060 W Addison St Chicago, IL 60613
Cubs Box Office Phone:	773-404-2827
Tickets.com:	800-THE-CUBS (843-2827)
Lost & Found:	773-404-4185
Website:	www.cubs.com

Overview

North Chi-town's baseball masses descend upon Wrigley Field like faithful Catholics to St. Peter's in Rome. Built in 1914, and home to the Chicago Cubs since 1916, Wrigley Field is the second-oldest ball park in Major League Baseball (Boston's Fenway Park—1912) and is a refreshing throwback to simpler times. Wrigley Field's ivy-strewn walls, classic grass field, and hand-turned scoreboard transcend both time and technology during this age of artificial playing surfaces and high-tech super stadiums. The glow from night game lights warms the hearts of most North Chicago locals who aren't game attendees. On the other side of the fence, Wrigleyville activists have lobbied to limit the amount of time the lights are burning, in an attempt to preserve the otherwise tranquil neighborhood surrounding Wrigley Field.

Wrigley Field has been the site of some of baseball's most historic moments: Ernie Banks' 500th career home run in 1970, Kerry Wood's twenty strikeouts in 1998, and Sammy Sosa's sixty home runs in 1998, 1999, and 2001. The Cubs haven't won a World Series title since their back-to-back wins over Detroit in 1907 and 1908, yet this loveable losing team has one of the most impressive attendance records in Major League Baseball. Perhaps in 2006, the Cubs' 91st season at Wrigley Field, the prayers of faithful fans will finally be answered. Regardless of whether the Cubs win or lose, they still get to call Wrigley Field home. Nostalgia for the "old school" landmark ballpark has many fans challenging recent proposals to expand Wrigley Field.

How to Get Tickets

Individual game tickets can be purchased from the Cubs' website, by calling 800-843-2827, or in person at some Chicagoland Sears and Sears Hardware stores. You can also buy tickets at the Wrigley Field Box Office, open weekdays from 8 am to 6 pm and weekends from 9 am to 4 pm. You can usually score discount tickets to afternoon games Monday through Thursday in April, May, and September. Children aged two and up require tickets.

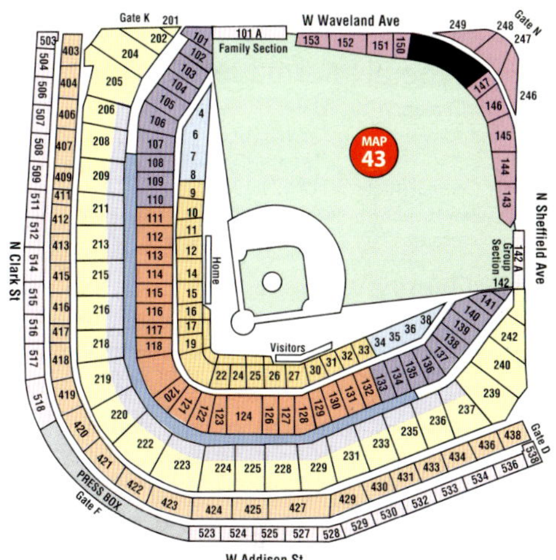

How to Get There

By Car: If you must... Traffic on game days is horrendous and parking prices are sky-high. Post-game spill-out from local bars freezes traffic as police do their best to prevent drunken revelers from stumbling into the streets. From the Loop or south, take Lake Shore Drive north; exit at Irving Park Road and head west to Clark Street; turn south on Clark Street to Wrigley Field. From the north, take Lake Shore Drive to Irving Park Road; head west to Clark Street and turn south. From Chicago's West Side, take I-290 E or I-55 N to Lake Shore Drive, then follow directions above. From the northwest, take I-90 E and exit at Addison Street; travel east three miles. From the southwest side, take I-55 N to I-90/94 N. Exit at Addison Street; head east to the park.

Street parking around Wrigley Field is heavily restricted. The Cubs operate a garage at 1126 W Grace Street. Purchase parking passes through the mail or at the Wrigley Field Box Office. On game nights, tow trucks cruise Wrigleyville's streets nabbing cars without a resident permit sticker. Park smart at the DeVry Institute and catch CTA bus 154/Wrigley Express to and from the park. ($6 covers parking and roundtrip shuttle per carload.)

By L: Riding the Howard/Dan Ryan Red Line is the fastest and easiest way to get to Wrigley Field ($1.75 one-way). Get off at the Addison Street stop one block east of the field.

By Bus: CTA buses 22, 8, and 152 stop closest to Wrigley Field ($1.75 one-way). For routes and schedules, visit www.rtachicago.com.

General Information

NFT Map: 13
Address: 333 W 35th St
Chicago, IL 60616
General Info: 312-674-1000
Ticket Sales: 866-SOX-GAME
Website: www.whitesox.com

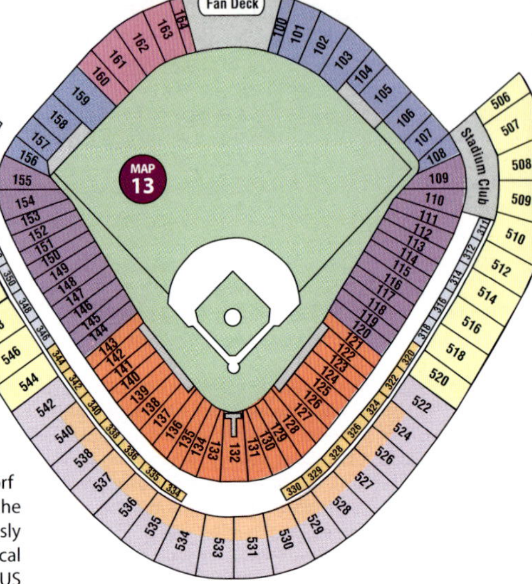

Overview

Whoever came up with the phrase "new and improved" hasn't attended a game in what was once the parking lot of South-Side Chicago's iconic Comiskey Park. Some Chicagoans have nicknamed the monstrosity that is US Cellular Field "The Joan" (after Joan Cusack; celeb, local resident, and spokesperson for US Cellular).

In 1988, Chicago White Sox owner Jerry Reinsdorf threatened movement of the White Sox to Florida if he didn't get a new stadium. Not only did the notoriously cheap Reinsdorf get his wish, he got taxpayers (both local and tourists) to pick up the tab for the $167 million US Cellular Field. The park opened in 1991 to mixed reviews and was renovated as recently as 2003 to accommodate the MLB All-Star Game. Where Wrigley Field is intimate, "The Joan" is boorish and somewhat whorish. The oft-Bohemic White Sox fans shout creative strings of curse words (between beer guzzles and finger flip-offs) and no one is spared from their gritty offensiveness. This is the ballpark where rowdy fans rush the field to pummel umpires into submission and assault off-duty Chicago Police Officers (and their wives!) when asked to curtail their expletive-laden jeering. But under all the crass commentary burns a fierce love for a tough ball club that has given their passionate fans plenty to cheer about since their last World Series win in 1917.

How to Get Tickets

Purchase tickets through the team's website or at the US Cellular Field Box Office (weekdays: 10 am-6 pm, weekends: 10 am-4 pm). Children shorter than the park's turnstile arm (approximately 36 inches) are admitted free, but must share your seat. Ballpark bargains include Half-Price Mondays for all regular seats, Pepsi Two-for-One Tuesdays (an empty Pepsi product plus the purchase of one Upper Level ticket earns you another seat for free), and Willy Wonka's Kids Days on select Sundays when children 13 and under get in for $1. All discounted tickets must be purchased at park ticket windows on game day. Check the website for Value Days schedules.

How to Get There

By Car: US Cellular Field is located at the 35th Street exit off the Dan Ryan Expressway. Take I-90/94, stay in the local lanes and exit at 35th Street. If you possess a prepaid green parking coupon or plan on paying cash for parking ($17), exit at 35th Street. Follow signs to "Sox Parking" at lots E, F, and L on the stadium's south side. Fans with red, prepaid season parking coupons exit at 31st Street and follow signs for "Red Coupons" to lots A, B, and C just north of the stadium. If the 35th Street exit is closed due to heavy traffic, which is often the case on game days, proceed to the 39th Street exit; turn right for "Sox Parking" and left for "Red Coupons." The handicapped parking and stadium drop-off area is in Lot D, west of the field and accessible via 37th Street.

By Bus: CTA buses 24 and 35 stop closest to the park. Others stopping in the vicinity are the 29, 44, and 39. Armies of cops surround the venue on game days because the neighborhood is rough, especially at night.

By L: Ride the Red Line to the Sox-35th Street stop just west of the ballpark. Get off the Green Line at the 35th-Bronzeville-IIT Station.

General Information

NFT Map: 23
Address: 1901 W Madison St
Chicago, IL 60612
Phone: 312-455-4500
Website: www.unitedcenter.com
Ticketmaster: 312-559-1212; www.ticketmaster.com
Chicago Bulls: 312-455-4000
Bulls Website: www.bulls.com
Chicago Blackhawks: 312-943-7000
Blackhawks Website: www.chicagoblackhawks.com

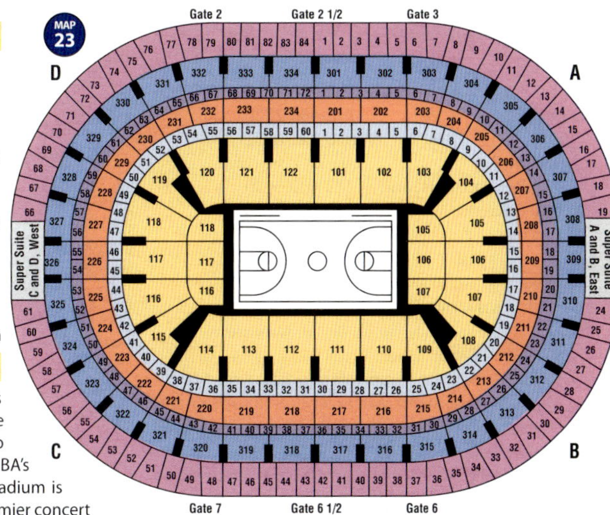

Overview

The commanding crown in Chicago's developing West Town/Near West Side District, the United Center is home to both the NHL's Blackhawks and the NBA's Chicago Bulls. This super high-tech stadium is also a theater, convention hall, and premier concert arena. Opened in 1994, the $175 million stadium was privately funded by deep-pocketed Blackhawks owner William Wirtz and penny-pinching Bulls majority owner Jerry Reinsdorf (a privately funded and owned stadium—what a concept!), and built to replace the beloved but aging Chicago Stadium. The Bulls have had trouble recapturing both the winning record and popularity they experienced during the Michael Jordan era; however, they still manage to sell out most of their home games. Local hopes are placed squarely on the shoulders of current head coach Scott Skiles. With the Bulls gaining momentum in the standings with each passing season, Skiles' efforts seem to be paying off. But just in case you forget whose house this is, the impressive Jordan statue located in front of the main entrance to the United Center is there to remind you.

Although it's been some time since the Blackhawks won the Stanley Cup (1961), the team enjoys unwavering support from its boisterous fans who relish games against their long-standing rivals, the St. Louis Blues. The Blackhawks made it to the playoffs of the 2001-2002 season, only to fall short of the big dance. Coach Brian Sutter hoped to heat things up again in 2004-2005, but the cancelled hockey season due to labor disputes put the kibosh on that. Loyal Chicago fans know the Blackhawks will show up for 2005-2006 in full battle gear and nothing short of bringing home the Stanley Cup will do.

How to Get Tickets

Book tickets over the phone or online with Ticketmaster, by United Center mail order, or visit the United Center box office at Gate 4. Box office hours are Monday to Saturday, 11 am to 6 pm. For Bulls and Blackhawks season tickets and group bookings call the phone numbers above.

How to Get There

By Car: From the Loop, drive west on Madison Street to United Center. From the north, take I-90/94 and exit at Madison Street; head west to the stadium. From the southwest, take I-55 N to the Damen/Ashland exit; head north to Madison Street. From the west, take I-290 E to the Damen Avenue exit; go north to Madison Street.

Parking lots surround United Center, as do countless cops. General public parking is in Lot B on Warren Boulevard (cars, $15-31; limo, RV, and bus parking, $25). Lot H on Wood Street is closest to the stadium and is reserved for VIPs. Disabled parking is in Lots G and H on Damen Avenue.

By L: Take the Forest Park Branch of the Blue Line to the Medical Center-Damen Avenue Station. Walk two blocks north to United Center.

By Bus: CTA bus 19 United Center Express is the most intelligent and safest choice. In service only on event and game days, this express bus travels from Chicago Avenue south down Michigan Avenue, then west along Madison Street to the United Center. Michigan Avenue stops are at Chicago Avenue, Illinois Street, and Randolph Street. On Madison Street, stops are at State Street, Wells Street, and Clinton Street ($1.75 one-way). Service starts two hours before events and continues for 45 minutes after events. CTA bus 20 also travels Madison Street beginning at Wabash Avenue and has "owl service."

General Information

Address:	10000 W O'Hare Chicago, IL 60666
Phone:	773-686-2200; 800-832-6352
Website:	www.ohare.com
Ground Transportation:	773-686-8040
Lost & Found:	773-894-8760
Parking:	773-686-7530
Traveler's Aid:	773-894-2427
Police:	773-686-2385
Customs Information:	773-894-2900

Overview

O'Delay might be a more fitting name for O'Hare, although Beck might take exception to such a name change. What else can we say about the world's busiest airport? To its credit, O'Hare, located in one of the country's most unpredictable weather zones, serves more than 190,000 travelers daily. While the airport is located just 17 miles northwest of the Loop, it's wise to leave the better part of a day to locate and arrive at your departure gate. Commuter traffic, airline snafus, parking, security checks, snowstorms, airport construction, and roadwork can make traveling from O'Hare as pleasurable as a migraine. And yet, O'Hare has been voted the "Best Airport in North America" by readers of the U.S. edition of *Business Traveler Magazine* for the last seven years running. Go figure.

Expansion spells relief, according to Mayor Daley and Governor Ryan, who have joined forces to push a controversial $6.6-billion plan designed to double O'Hare's capacity and secure its "busiest" title for the rest of the 21st century. The plan calls for building another runway, reconfiguring the other seven, building an additional entrance on the airport's west side, and spending millions in soundproofing area homes and schools. Recently, political opposition has thrown up hefty lawsuits to block legislation that would cement the Daley-Ryan deal into federal law.

Meanwhile, the rest of us are stuck in traffic, in line, on the runway, etc…

How to Get There

By Car: If you must drive, pack aspirin in your glove compartment along with your favorite CDs, because the crawl down the Kennedy will probably be the most grueling part of your entire trip. To be on the safe side, allow over an hour just for the drive (more during rush hours). From the Loop to O'Hare, take I-90 W. From the north suburbs, take I-294 S. From the south suburbs, take I-294 N. From the west suburbs, take I-88 E to I-294 N. Get off all of the above highways at I-190, which leads you directly to the airport. All of the major routes have clear signage, easily legible when you're moving at a snail's pace.

Parking: O'Hare Airport's parking garage reflects its hometown's passion for sports. All levels of the Main Parking Garage are "helpfully" labeled with Chicago sports teams' colors and larger-than-life logos (Wolves, Bulls, Blackhawks, White Sox, Bears, and Cubs). Annoying elevator muzak whines each team's fight song. If this isn't enough to guide you to your car, we can't help you, because the garage's numbering-alphabetical system is more aggravating than the tinny elevator tunes.

If you're parking for less than three hours, go to Level 1. Parking costs $3 for the first 3 hours, $21 for up to 4 hours, and a deterring $50 per day. Overnight parking close to Terminals 1, 2, and 3 on Levels 2 through 6 of the garage or in outside lots B and C costs $25 a day. For flyers with cash to burn, valet parking is available on Level 1 of the garage for $10 per hour or $32 per day (8-24 hours). Parking in the International Terminal 5's designated Lot D costs $3 per hour for the first two hours and $2 per hour thereafter; the daily rate is $30. Incoming international passengers always disembark in Terminal 5 (even if the airline departs from another terminal), because passengers must clear customs.

Long-term parking lots are Economy Lots E and G, which cost $13 per day. From Lot E, walk or take the free shuttle to the free Airport Transit System (ATS) train station servicing all terminals. From Lot G, the shuttle will take you to the ATS stop in Lot E. Budget-conscious frequent flyers may want to purchase a prepaid Lot E "ExpressLane Parking" windshield tag for hassle-free, speedy departure from the airport. Lot F is currently closed until further notice.

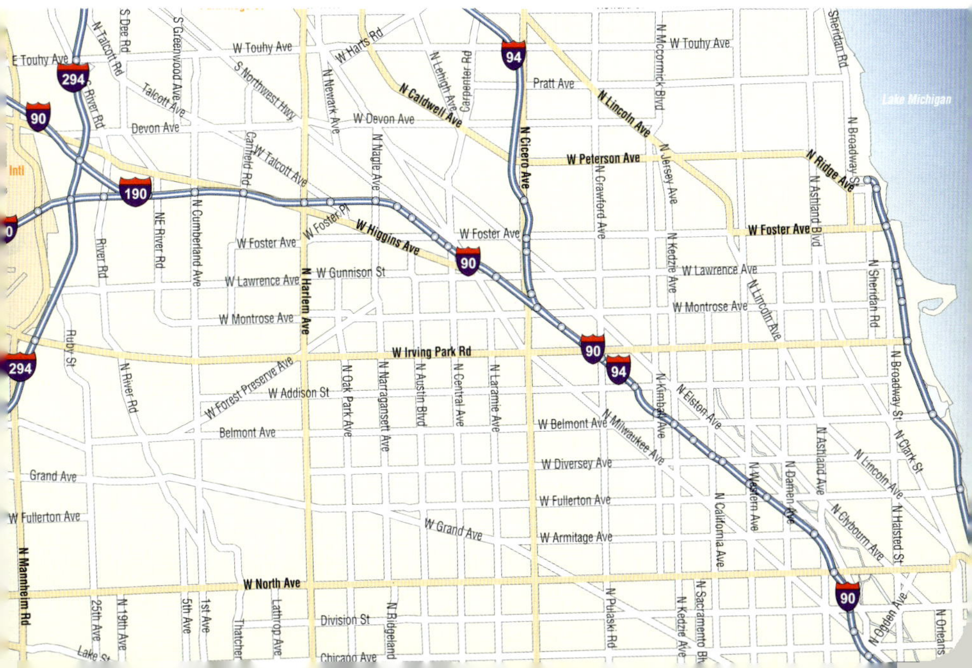

How to Get There—*continued*

By Bus: CTA buses 220 and 330 stop at the airport. If you're not near either of those bus lines, your best bet is to take your nearest bus line north or south to one of the O'Hare Blue Line train stations. The CTA also offers a special door-to-door service to and from the airport for Chicago-area residents and out-of-towners needing extra assistance. Call 312-663-4357 for additional information.

By Train: The odds of the Metra's schedule conveniently coinciding with your flight time are only slightly better than those of the Bulls winning the championship this year. The Wisconsin North Central Line departs Union Station for Antioch with a stop at the O'Hare Transfer station five times a day, starting in the afternoons on weekdays only ($3.15 one-way). Travel time is 30 minutes.

By L: We recommend the Blue Line as the best transportation method if you don't have several large bags or dependents in tow. The train runs between downtown Chicago and O'Hare 24 hours a day every 8 to 10 minutes ($1.75 one-way). Travel time from the Loop is 45 minutes. The train station is on the lowest level of the airport's main parking garage. Walk through the underground pedestrian tunnels to Terminals 1, 2, and 3. If you're headed for the International Terminal 5, walk to Terminal 3 and board the free Airport Transit System (ATS) train.

By Cab: Join the cab queue at the lower level curb-front of all terminals. There are no flat rates, as all of the cabs run on meters, but you probably won't have to spend more than $40. Some cab companies servicing O'Hare include American United, 773-327-6161; Flash Cab Co., 773-878-8500; Jiffy Cab Co., 773-487-9000; Yellow Cab, 312-225-7440; and Dispatch, 312-829-4222.

By Kiss & Fly: The Kiss & Fly is a convenient drop-off and pick-up point for "chauffeurs" who want to avoid the inevitable chaos at the terminal curb-side. But flyers should leave enough time for the ATS transfer to their terminals. The Kiss & Fly zone is off Bessie Coleman Drive. Take I-190 to the International Terminal exit to Bessie Coleman Drive. Turn left at the light and follow Bessie Coleman Drive north to the Kiss & Fly entrance and ATS stop.

By Shuttle: Continental Airport Express (312-454-7800 or 800-654-7871) provides a daily shuttle service between O'Hare and downtown Chicago from 6 am until 11:30 pm with departures approximately every 10-15 minutes. Shuttles stop at all major downtown hotels. Tickets cost $23 one-way ($42 return) for individuals, $16 per person ($30 return) for pairs going to the same destination and returning together, and $12 per person ($23 return) for three or more going to the same downtown destination and returning together. Shuttle ticket counters are located in the baggage claim areas of Terminal 1 by Door 1E and Terminal 3 at Door 3E; however, shuttles pick up passengers at Terminals 1, 2, 3, and 5. If you haven't pre-purchased a ticket at a counter, have cash ready for the driver.

Omega Airport Shuttle offers hourly service between O'Hare and Midway beginning around 7 am each day 'til about 11:45 pm, and between Hyde Park and O'Hare from 5 am to 11:45 pm. The shuttle leaves from the International Terminal's outside curb by Door 5E and from the airport's Bus Shuttle Center in front of the O'Hare Hilton Hotel by Door 4. Allow at least an hour for travel time between the airports and expect to pay $17 for a one-way fare. Omega also has over 20 pickup and drop-off locations on the South Side serving O'Hare and Midway Airports. (773-483-6634; www.omegashuttle.com).

By Limousine: Sounds pricey, but depending on where you're going and how many people you are traveling with, it may be cheaper to travel by limo than by cab or shuttle. Advance reservations recommended. Limo services include O'Hare-Midway Limousine Service, 312-558-1111 (or 800-468-8989 for airport pick-up), www.ohare-midway.com; My Chauffeur/American Limo, 630-920-8888, www.americanlimousine.com; and Sundling Limousine, 800-999-7552, www.limousineservicecorp.com (at least four hours notice required).

Airlines

Airline	*Terminal*	*Phone*
Aer Lingus	5	888-474-7424
Aeromexico	5	800-237-6639
Air Canada	2	888-247-2262
Air France	5	800-237-2747
Air India	5	800-621-8231
Air Jamaica	5	800-523-5585
Alaska Airlines	3	800-426-0333
Alitalia	5	800-223-5730
America West Airlines	2	800-235-9292
American Airlines:		800-443-7300
Domestic	3	
International	3 dep/5 arr	
American Eagle	3	800-433-7300
Aviacsa	5	888-528-4227
British Airways	5	800-247-9297
BMI British Midland	5	800-788-0555
Cayman Airways	5	800-422-9626
Continental Airlines	2	800-525-0280
Delta Airlines	3	800-221-1212
El Al	5	800-223-6700
Iberia Airlines	3 dep/5 arr	800-772-4642
Independence Air	2	800-359-3594
JJapan Airlines	5	800-525-3663
KLM Royal Dutch Airlines	5	800-374-7747
Korean Air	5	800-438-5000
Kuwait Airways	5	800-458-9248
LOT Polish Airlines	5	
Lufthansa	1 dep/5 arr	800-645-3880
Mexicana Airlines	5	800-531-7921
Northwest KLM Airlines	2	800-225-2525
Pakistan International Airlines	5	800-578-6786
Royal Jordanian	5	800-223-0470
Ryan Air	3 dep/5 arr	800-942-6735
Scandinavian Airlines SAS	5	800-221-2350
Spirit Airlines	3	800-772-7117
Swiss International Airlines	5	800-221-4750
TACA Airlines	5	888-337-8466
Ted Airlines	1	800-225-5833
Turkish Airlines	5	800-874-8875
United Airlines	1	800-241-6522
International arrivals	5	
United Express	1	800-241-6522
US Airways	2	800-428-4322
USA 3000	5	877-872-3000

Car Rental

Alamo • O'Hare Intl Arpt, 800-327-9633
Avis • 10000 Bessie Coleman Dr, 800-331-1212/ 773-825-4600
Budget • 580 Bessie Coleman Dr, 800-527-0700
Dollar • O'Hare Intl Arpt, 800-800-4000/773-471-3450
Enterprise • 4025 Mannheim Rd, 847-928-3320
Hertz • 10000 Bessie Coleman Dr, 800-654-3131
National • 560 Bessie Coleman Dr, 800-227-7368
Thrifty • 3901 N Mannheim Rd, 847-928-2000

Hotels

All shuttles to airport hotels depart from the Bus Shuttle Center in front of the O'Hare Hilton Hotel in the center of the airport.

Best Western • 10300 W Higgins Rd, 847-296-4471
Clarion • 5615 N Cumberland Ave, 877-424-6423
Courtyard • 2950 S River Rd, 847-824-7000
Crown Plaza • 5440 N River Rd, 847-671-6350
Days Inn • 1920 E Higgins Rd, 847-437-1650
Days Inn • 2175 E Touhy Ave, 847-635-1300
DoubleTree • 5460 N River Rd, 847-292-9100
Embassy Suites • 5500 N River Rd, 847-678-4000
Four Points Sheraton • 10249 W Irving Park Rd, 847-671-6000
Hampton Inn • 3939 N Mannheim Rd, 847-671-1700
Hampton Inns Suites • 5201 Old Orchard Rd, 847-583-1111
Hawthorn Suites • 1251 American Ln, 847-706-9007
Hilton • O'Hare Intl Arprt, 773-686-8000
Holiday Inn, 8201 W Higgins Rd, 773-693-2323
Hotel Sofitel • 5550 N River Rd, 847-678-4488
Hyatt Regency • 9300 W Bryn Mawr Ave, 847-696-1234
Hyatt Rosemont • 6350 N River Rd, 847-518-1234
La Quinta Inn • 1900 E Oakton St, 847-439-6767
Marriott • 8101 W Higgins Rd, 773-867-0000
Marriott Suites • 6155 N River Rd, 847-696-4400
Marriott Hotel • 8535 W Higgins Rd, 773-693-4444
Ramada Plaza • 6600 N Mannheim Rd, 847-827-5131
Residence Inn • 7101 Chestnut St, 847-375-9000
Sheraton Suites • 6501 N Mannheim Rd, 847-699-6300
InTown Suites • 2411 Landmeier Rd, 847-228-5500
Super 8 • 2951 Touhy Ave, 847-827-3133
Travelodge • 3003 Mannheim Rd, 847-296-5541
Westin • 6100 N River Rd , 847-698-6000
Wyndham • 6810 N Mannheim Rd, 847-297-1234

General Information

Address:	5757 S Cicero Ave Chicago, IL 60638
Phone:	773-838-0600
Website:	www.midwayairport.org
Police:	773-838-3003
Parking:	773-838-0756

Overview

Located just ten miles southwest of downtown Chicago is Midway—one of the fastest-growing airports in the country, serving 47,000 passengers daily. Considered the city's outlet mall of airports, Midway primarily provides service from budget carriers, such as Southwest Airlines and ATA.

However, expect Midway to gain altitude in national airport rankings with the recent completion of its $793 million terminal development. After ten years of planning and construction, the new features include a swank new terminal building, new concourses, a 3,000-space parking facility, food court, retail corridor, and a customs facility to facilitate international flights. In 2003, Concourses G and H were demolished to allow for the expansion of Concourse B. All the changes have upped Midway's jet gate count from 29 to 41.

How To Get There

By Car: From downtown, take I-55 S. From the northern suburbs, take I-290 S to I-55 N. From the southern suburbs, take I-294 N to I-55 N. From the western suburbs, take I-88 E to I-294 S to I-55 N. Whether you're traveling north or south along I-55, look for the Cicero Avenue/South/Midway Airport exit.

By Bus: CTA buses 55, 59, and 63 all run from points east to the airport. Take the Green Line or the Red Line to the Garfield Station and transfer to bus 55 heading west ($1.75 one-way including transfer). If you're coming from the south on the Red Line, get off at the 63rd Street stop and take bus 63 westbound ($1.80 one-way). Other buses that terminate at the airport include 54B, 379, 382, 383, 384, 385, 386, 831, and 63W.

By L: A 30-minute train ride on the Orange Line is the most convenient and cost-effective method for travel between the Loop and Midway Airport ($1.75 one-way). The Orange Line's first train departs from Midway Station (last stop on the line's southern end) for the Loop at 3:55 am daily and 5:35 am on Sundays and holidays. The first train of the day from the Loop's Adams/Wabash Station at 4:29 am arrives at Midway at 4:54 am, well in advance of the airport's first early bird flight. The last train from Midway to the Loop departs at 12:56 am and arrives at 1:23 am. The final Midway-bound owl train departs from the Adams/Wabash stop around 1:29 am, arriving at Midway by 1:53 am. Trains run every 5 to 7 minutes during rush hours, ten minutes most other times, and 15 minutes late evenings. We recommend that wee hours travelers stay alert at all times.

By Cab: Cabs depart from the lower level of the main terminal and are available on a first-come-first-served basis. There are no flat rates (all cabs run on meters), but you can plan on paying around $25 to get to the Loop. Some cab companies servicing Midway include American United, 773-327-6161; Flash Cab Co., 773-561-4444; Flash Dispatch, 773-561-1444; King Cab Co., 773-487-9000; and Yellow Cab, 312-808-9130.

By Shuttle: Continental Airport Express (312-454-7800 or 800-654-7871) travels between Midway and downtown and some northern suburban locations from 6 am until 10:30 pm. Shuttles depart every 15 minutes and make stops at all major downtown hotels. Tickets cost $18 one-way ($32 roundtrip) for individuals, $24 per person for pairs going to the same destination ($40 roundtrip), and $10 per person for three or more going to the same downtown destination ($18 roundtrip). The ticket counter and loading zone are in the terminal's lower level across from the baggage claim area by door LL3. To calculate a shuttle fare to north suburb locations, use the online fare calculator at www.airportexpress.com.

By Shuttle: Omega Airport Shuttle (773-483-6634; www.omegashuttle.com) offers service leaving every 45 minutes or so between Midway and O'Hare beginning around 7 am each day with the final shuttle departing around 10 pm. Allow at least an hour for travel time between the airports, and expect to pay $15 one-way. Contact Omega for information on more than 20 pickup locations on the South Side, to confirm schedules, to make reservations, and to prearrange home pickups.

By Limousine: Sounds pricey, but depending on where you're going and how many people you are traveling with, it may be cheaper to travel by limo than by cab or shuttle. Advance reservations recommended. Limo services include O'Hare-Midway Limousine Service, 847-948-8050 (or 800-468-8989 for airport pick-up), www.ohare-midway.com; My Chauffeur/American Limo, 630-920-8888, www.americanlimousine.com; and Sundling Limousine, 800-999-7552, www.limousineservicecorp.com (at least four hours notice required).

Parking

Short-term parking is on the third floor. Parking is free for the first half-hour, $3 for 30 minutes to an hour, and $2 for every hour thereafter, up to $50 for 24 hours. Levels 1, 4, 5, and 6 have the same rates for short-term parking, but the prices level off after four hours so that it only costs $23 per day. If you're planning on parking for a while, the best option is the economy lot for $10 a day on Cicero Avenue at 55th Street, a quarter-mile away. Allow extra time to take the free shuttle between the lot and the terminal.

Airlines

Concourse A

ATA	800-225-2995
ATA Connections/Chicago Express	800-225-2995
Southwest	800-435-9792
Ted	800-225-5833
US Airways	800-428-4322

Concourse B		**Concourse C**	
Southwest	800-435-9792	American	800-433-7300
AirTran	800-825-8538	Continental	800-525-0280
ComAir	800-927-0927	Frontier	800-432-1359
ATA	800-225-2995		
Northwest	800-225-2525		
Delta	800-221-1212		

Car Rental

Alamo	800-327-9633	Enterprise	800-566-9249
Avis	800-831-2847	Hertz	800-654-3131
Budget	800-517-0700	National	800-227-7368
Dollar	800-800-4000	Thrifty	800-527-7075

Hotels

Best Western • 8220 S Cicero Ave, 708-497-3000
Fairfield Inn • 6630 S Cicero Ave, 708-594-0090
Hampton Inn • 6540 S Cicero Ave, 708-496-1900
Hampton Inn • 13330 S Cicero Ave, 708-597-3330
Hilton • 9333 S Cicero Ave, 708-425-7800
Holiday Inn Express • 6500 S Cicero Ave, 708-458-0202
Howard Johnson • 4140 W 95th St, 708-425-7900
Holiday Inn Select • 6520 S Cicero Ave, 708-594-5500
Courtyard Midway • 6610 S Cicero Ave, 708-563-0200
Sleep Inn • 6650 S Cicero Ave, 708-594-0001

General Information

RTA Mailing Address: Regional Transportation Authority
175 W Jackson Blvd, Ste 1550
Chicago, IL 60604

Phone: 312-913-3200

RTA Information Center & Trip Planning by Phone: 312-836-7000

RTA Website:	www.rtachicago.com
CTA Phone:	888- 968-7282
CTA Website:	www.transitchicago.com
Pace Phone:	847-364-7223
Pace Website:	www.pacebus.com
Greyhound Phone:	800-229-9424
Greyhound Website:	www.greyhound.com

Overview

Chicago's rail system is complemented by three major bus networks: Chicago Transit Authority (CTA), Pace, and Greyhound. The Regional Transportation Authority (RTA) oversees CTA and Pace, the suburban bus service. To find the fastest point-to-point routes, check out RTA's website at tripsweb.rtachicago.com.

CTA Buses

CTA's buses cart about one million sweaty, crabby passengers around Chicago and its surrounding suburbs everyday. The CTA bus fleet constitutes the nation's second largest public transportation system. (New York's subway system is number one.) CTA's 152 bus routes mirror Chicago's efficient grid system. The majority of CTA routes run north-south or east-west and, in areas where the streets are numbered, the bus route is usually the same as the street.

Bus Stops: CTA stops are clearly marked with blue and white signs displaying the name and number of the route, as well as the final destination. Most routes operate from the early morning until 10:30 pm. Night routes, called "Night Owls," are identified on bus stop signage by an owl picture. Owl service runs approximately every half-hour through the night.

Fares: Buses accept exact fare only for individual rides. A regular one-way fare is $1.75. A transfer slip, good for two additional rides on either different CTA buses or CTA L/subway trains within two hours of issuance, costs an additional 25¢, for a grand total of $2 for a three-leg journey. Transfers must be purchased with the base fare on the first leg of your journey. An "express surcharge" of 25¢ is required (in addition to a valid transfer card) when you board buses 2, 14, 16, and 147 downtown in designated pickup zones.

Reduced fares of 85¢ per individual trip and 15¢ for a transfer are available for children ages 7-11, seniors age 65+ with an RTA Reduced Fare Riding Permit, and riders with disabilities. Elementary and high school students with a CTA Student Riding Permit ($5 per semester, $2 summer school) pay reduced fares on weekdays from 5:30 am to 8 pm. Children ages six and under ride free with a fare-paying traveler, as do "uniformed or ID-bearing categories authorized by the Chicago Transit Board."

The CTA offers a number of different fare packages:

- For the convenience of not having to fish for exact change, purchase ten packs of one-way tickets for $17.50.
- Unlimited Ride Passes: one-day ($5), two-day ($9), three-day ($12), and five-day ($18).

Frequent CTA riders prefer to buy Monthly Passes (unlimited rides) for $75, or Transit Cards, available in various incremements up to $100, sold through vending machines at all CTA rail stations. For every $10 you put on your card, the CTA gives you an extra dollar. Customers can also order a CTA Chicago Card Plus online at www.chicago-card.com. The card loads value from your credit card, swipes like a smart card, and can be used on CTA buses, Pace buses, and aboard the L.

Bicycles Onboard: Designated CTA buses are equipped with bike racks mounted on front grills to carry up to two bikes. Generally speaking, CTA bike buses are those that travel to lakefront beaches, like the 63rd Street and 72 North Avenue buses. Additional buses with bike racks are often added during summer months or for special events.

Loading your bike onto a CTA bus:

- If your bike is the first to be loaded, lower the rack and place it in position with the front wheel facing the curb.
- If there is already a bike on the rack, place your bike's rear wheel toward the curb.
- If two bikes are already loaded and the rack is full; wait for the next bus.

PACE Suburban – Chicago Buses

Pace buses serve over 35 million passengers in the Chicago suburbs and some parts of the city. With 240 routes covering 3,446 square miles, Pace provides a vital transportation service to commuters traveling between suburbs, within suburbs, to Metra train stations, and into the city. Buses usually run every 20-30 minutes, and service stops by mid-evening. Special express service is offered to Chicago-area entertainment and cultural venues. Contact Pace for specific bus route and schedule information.

Park-n-Ride Stations: Pace has 11 Park-n-Ride stations located throughout Pace's six-county coverage area (check the Pace website for locations).

Fares: Pace fares cost $1.25 for local service and $1.50 for express or expanded service. The one-way fare on express routes 210, 355, 855, and 1018 costs $3. CTA Transit Cards may be used on Pace buses. Pace offers discounts for students, children, seniors, and disabled riders, as well as several bus pass package purchase options. Pass options include the Pace 30-Day Commuter Club Cards (CCC), which allows unlimited Pace rides for $50. A combined Pace/CTA 30-day unlimited pass costs $75 and can be used on all Pace buses and CTA trains and buses. The PlusBus Sticker (sold by Metra with a Metra Monthly Train Pass) costs $30 and allows unlimited Pace bus use.

Greyhound Buses

Greyhound is the rock-bottom traveler's best friend. The bus line offers dirt-cheap fares, the flexibility drifters prefer, basic station amenities (i.e. dirty toilets and vending machines that steal your money), and the gritty, butt-busting experience of traveling America's scenic blue-line highways and rural byways with some colorful characters.

Tips on riding "the Dog" out of town:

- Pack your own toilet paper and Wet Ones.
- Air freshener, deodorant, a pillow, and earplugs make being bused more bearable.
- Pack a cooler. Then padlock it.
- Wear padded bicycle shorts or bring a cushion.
- Get your shots.

Stations: Greyhound's main train station is south of Union Station at 630 W Harrison Street in West Loop (312-408-5800). CTA buses 60, 125, 156, and 157 make stops near the terminal. The closest L stop is on the Blue Line's Forest Park Branch at the Clinton Street Station on Congress Parkway. Additional Chicago-area Greyhound stations are located within L train stations: 14 W 95th Street in the Red Line's 95th Street/Dan Ryan Station (312-408-5999), and 5800 N Cumberland Avenue on the Blue Line's O'Hare Branch in the Cumberland Station (773-693-2474). The general aura of the Chicago Greyhound Station is one of seediness and squalor. Keep your belongings with you at all times.

Shipping Services: Greyhound Package Xpress offers commercial and personal shipping services and is available at all three Chicago bus stations. Packages are held at the station for pick-up. The main terminal in South Loop also houses a UPS shipping office that provides door-to-door package delivery.

Fares: Tickets can be purchased on the phone or online with a credit card, or at a station with cash, travelers' checks, or credit cards.

Regular fare pricing applies for both individual advance ticket sales and minutes-before-departure sales. Tickets can be used for travel to the designated destination on any day or at any departure time. Because Greyhound does not reserve seats, boarding occurs on a first-come-first-served basis, so get in line at the boarding zone for a choice seat. However, Greyhound's bark is bigger than its bite—if a significant number of passengers turn out for the same bus, Greyhound rolls another bus, or two, or three out on the spot. Good dog.

Children under 12 receive 40% discounts off of regular fares, seniors 62 and older receive 5% discounts, military members receive 10% discounts, and patients of Veteran's Administration Hospitals receive a 25% discount. Other discounts are available online. The cost for an individual return ticket is always deeply discounted if it is purchased at the same time as a departure ticket.

Tickets purchased three days in advance earn a half-price companion ticket (no age restrictions). Passengers accompanying someone with a disability always ride at a reduced rate.

Super Friendly Fares offer the greatest savings for travelers who can purchase seven days in advance of travel. For example, a regular one-way ticket from Chicago to New York City costs $90 and a regular fare round-trip ticket costs $159. But booking a round-trip Super Friendly Fare costs $89. You do the math.

Transit • Metra Train Lines

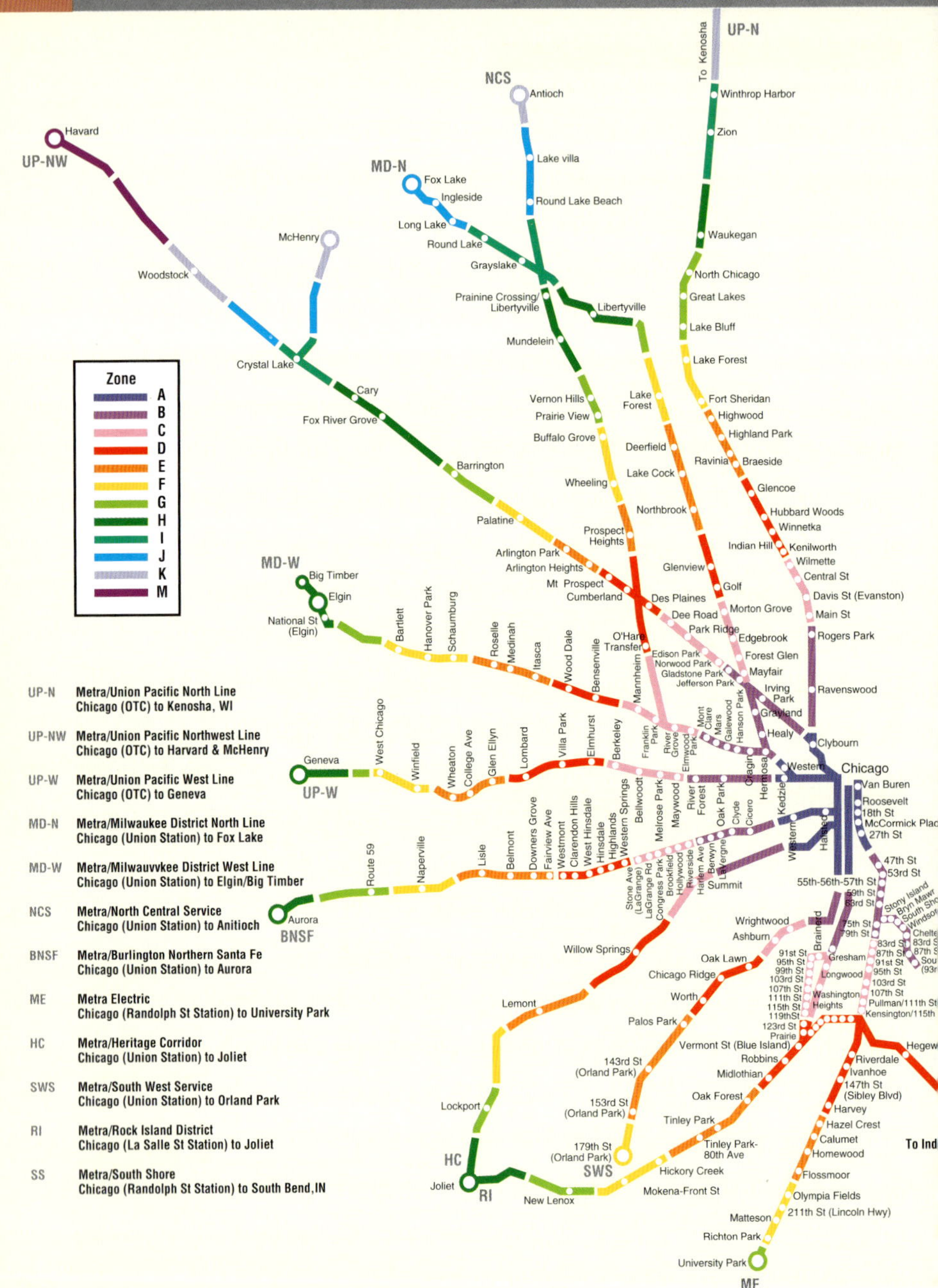

General Information

Metra Address:	Metra Passenger Services 547 W Jackson Blvd Chicago, IL 60661
Phone:	312-322-6777
Website:	www.metrarail.com
Metra Passenger Service:	312-322-6777
South Shore Metra Lines:	800-356-2079
RTA Information Center:	312-836-7000; www.rtachicago.com

Overview

With a dozen lines and roughly 495 miles of track overseen by the RTA, Metra does its best to service Cook, DuPage, Lake, Will, McHenry, and Kane counties with 230 stations scattered throughout the city and 'burbs. The rails emanating from four major downtown stations are lifelines for commuters traveling to and from the Loop.

The good news for Metra is that ridership is strong. The bad news for riders is that parking is difficult. In an attempt to resolve its parking issues, Metra is purchasing land surrounding many suburban stations and constructing new parking facilities. Check out Metra's website for updates on development plans.

Loop Stations

There are four major Metra train stations in the Loop from which 12 train lines emanate. Here's a chart to help clear up any possible confusion:

Station	**Line**
Richard B. Ogilvie T.C.	Union Pacific Lines
Union Station	Milwaukee District Lines North Central Service Southwest Service Burlington Northern Heritage Corridor Amtrak
La Salle Street Station	Rock Island Line
Randolph Street Station	South Shore Railroad Metra Electric—Three Branches: Main Line, South Chicago, Blue Island

Fares

Depending on the number of Metra zones you traverse, one-way, full-fare tickets cost between $1.85 and $6.95. To calculate a base one-way fare, visit www.metrarail.com/Data/farechk.html. Tickets may be purchased through a ticket agent or onboard the train (with a $2 surcharge if the ticket windows were open at the time you boarded the train). There is no reserved seating.

Metra offers a number of reasonably-priced ticket packages, including a Ten-Ride Ticket (which saves riders 15% off of one-way fares) and a Monthly Unlimited Ride Ticket (the most economical choice for commuters who use Metra service daily). If your commute includes CTA and/or Pace bus services, consider purchasing the Link-Up Sticker ($36) for unlimited connecting travel on CTA and Pace buses. Metra's Weekend Pass costs $5 and includes unlimited rides on Saturday and Sunday, with the exception of the South Shore route. You can buy all the aforementioned tickets in person, through the mail, or online at www.metrarail.com/TBI/index.html.

Children under 7 ride free. Children ages 7-11 ride for half-price on weekdays and for free on the weekends. Children ages 12-17 ride for half-price on weekends. Full-time grade school or high school students are eligibile to receive 50% off the cost of regular one-way fares. Senior citizens/disability fares are approximately half of the regular fare. US Military Personnel in uniform also ride Metra for half-price. Anyone wearing capri pants after Labor Day will be charged double.

Wendella RiverBuses

Spring through fall, commuters can get to North Michigan Avenue quickly on a Wendella RiverBus plying the Chicago River during rush hours, leaving from Transportation Center at the dock on the northwest corner of Madison Street. RiverBuses run daily from April 1 through November 29. The trip takes nine minutes one-way. The first boat leaves the train station dock at 7 am; the last boat departs from the dock at 400 N Michigan Avenue, at the base of the Wrigley Building, at 7 pm. The fare is $2 one-way. Discounted Monthly and Ten-Ride fares are also available (312-337-1446; www.wendellariverbus.com).

Baggage & Pets

While Metra may be "the way to really fly," Metra's restrictions on baggage are more stringent than those of most airlines. Bicycles, skis, golf clubs, non-folding carts, water buffaloes, and other large luggage items can never be transported on trains. This is one more reason, besides the limited schedules, not to take Metra to O'Hare. Pets, with the exception of service animals, are also prohibited aboard trains.

General Information

Loop Station Address:	Randolph Street Station 151 E Randolph St Underground at N Michigan Ave & E Randolph St Chicago, IL 60601
Phone:	312-782-0676
Lost & Found:	219-874-4221 x205
Website:	www.nictd.com

Overview

Although the historic South Shore train lines were built in 1903, they still get you from the Loop to Indiana's South Bend Airport in just 2.5 hours. The Northern Indiana Commuter Transportation District (NICTD) oversees the line and its modern electric trains, which serve as a vital transportation link for many northwest Indiana residents working in the Loop.

The South Shore's commuter service reflects its Indiana ridership. Outbound heading from the Loop, there are limited stops before the Hegewisch station, close to the Indiana state line. When traveling by train to Chicago's South Side, you're better off on an outbound Metra Electric Line train departing from the Randolph Street Station (see Metra page).

Fares

Regular one-way fares can be purchased at the stations (with cash or personal check) or on the train (cash only). Ticket prices vary with distance traveled. Tickets purchased onboard the train cost $1 more if the station's ticket windows were open at the time of departure.

Special South Shore fares and packages include commuter favorites: 10-Ride and 25-Ride Tickets and the Monthly Pass, which is good for unlimited travel. These can be purchased in person at stations staffed with ticket agents, station vending machines, and via the mail. Senior citizens/disability fares offer savings for persons aged 65 and older with valid identification and for disabled passengers. Students with school identification qualify for student fares, including reduced one-way tickets and discounted 25-Ride Tickets good for travel during weekdays. Youth fares range from free passage for infants under two years (who must sit in a paying passenger's lap) and half off a regular fare for children aged two to 13 years. Family fares are available on weekends and holidays, as well as off-peak times on weekdays. Each fare-paying adult (minimum age 21) may take up to two children (age 13 and under) with them free of charge. Additional children will be charged the reduced youth fare. There are no published fare discounts for military personnel.

Baggage & Pets

Any accompanying baggage must be placed in the overhead racks. No bicycles are permitted onboard. Apart from small animals in carry-on cages, the only pets allowed onboard are service dogs accompanied by handlers or passengers with disabilities. Animals must not occupy seats.

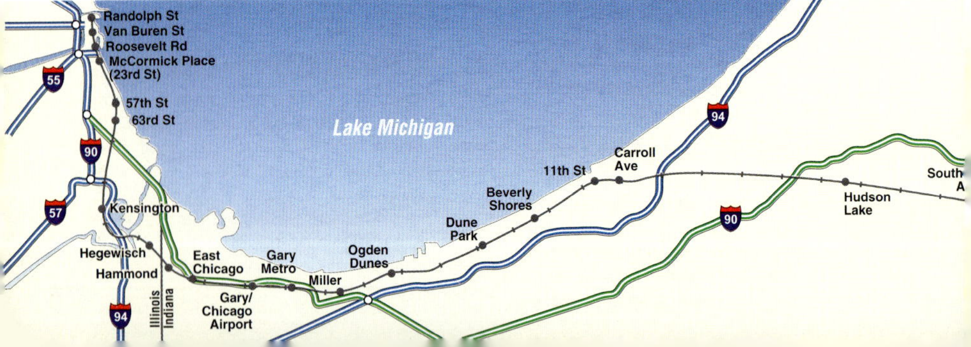

General Information

Amtrak Reservations:	1-800-USA-RAIL (872-7245)
Website:	www.amtrak.com
Union Station:	225 S Canal St, Chicago, IL 60606
Phone:	312-322-6900

Overview

Chicago is the nucleus for Amtrak's 500-station national rail network, which covers 46 states (every state but Alaska, Hawaii, South Dakota, and Wyoming). Departing from Chicago's Union Station, Amtrak trains head west to Seattle and Portland, east to New York City and Boston, north to Ontario, and south to New Orleans, San Francisco, and San Antonio.

Fares

Amtrak offers affordable fares for regional travel, but their prices can't compete with airfares on longer hauls. But, just as airlines offer deeply discounted fares, so does Amtrak. Ask Amtrak's sales agents about special fares and search Amtrak's website for the best deals. (Booking in advance does present some savings.) We recommend the website route, as callers run the risk of being on on hold longer than it takes to ride a train from Chicago to Los Angeles.

Amtrak offers special promotional fares year-round targeting seniors, veterans, students, children under 16, and groups of two or more persons traveling together. The "Rail SALE" page on Amtrak's website lists discounted fares between certain city pairs. Amtrak has hooked its sleeper cars up with plenty of travel partners to create interesting packages. The Air-Rail deals, whereby you rail it one way and fly back the other, are attractive for long distance travel. Call 877-937-7245 and surf the "Amtrak Partners" webpage for partner promotional fares.

Service

Those who can claim to have arrived on-time traveling Amtrak are few and far between, so tell whoever is picking you up you'll call them on your cell phone when you're close. Pack food on your ride, as dining car fare is mediocre and pricey. On the upside, Amtrak's seats are comfortable and roomy, some have electric sockets for computer hookups, bathrooms are in every car, and the train is almost always clean. Just be wary of strangers wanting to "switch" murders.

Within Illinois: Four main Amtrak lines travel south through Illinois on a daily basis: the "State House" travels to St. Louis, MO; the "Illinois Zephyr" travels to Quincy, IL; the "Illini Service" travels between Chicago and Carbondale, IL; and the "Ann Rutledge" travels to Kansas City, MO. The prices listed here are only quotes and are subject to change. Check Amtrak's website for updates.

Going to New York City or Boston: If you're heading east, the "Lake Shore Limited" breaks off at Albany and goes to New York (21 hours) and Boston (24 hours). One-way tickets cost between $72 and $133.

Going to Seattle or Portland: The "Empire Builder" takes passengers to Seattle and Portland and everywhere in between. With the journey to Seattle taking around 44 hours, we definitely recommend dropping some additional dollars on a sleeper car. A one-way fare costs between $118 and $229.

Going to San Francisco: You'll spend two solid days and then some riding the rails during the 52-hour journey on the "California Zephyr" to San Francisco (Emeryville). The fare costs approximately $122 to $238 one-way. "Zephyr" passes through Lincoln, Denver, and Salt Lake City and makes a whole host of small town America stops along the way.

Going to New Orleans: The "City of New Orleans" line runs from Chicago via Memphis to New Orleans in roughly 20 hours. The fare is approximately $91 to $174 one-way.

Going to San Antonio: The mighty "Texas Eagle" glides across the Alamo and stops at 40 cities on its way from the Midwest to the South. The 32-hour trip will cost approximately $98 to $191 each way (look at it this way: you're paying less than six bucks an hour!) However, why anyone would want to go to San Antonio is unclear.

Going to Milwaukee: "Hiawatha Service" runs seven times daily to Milwaukee, leaving Chicago approximately every two hours. The 90-minute trip costs $20 each way (a good alternative to driving from Chicago on busy weekends and rush hours).

Going to Kansas City: The "Missouri Routes" line terminates in Kansas City while the "Southwest Chief" passes through it on the way to Los Angeles. "Missouri" departs daily at 8:25 am and travels via St. Louis to Kansas City in just over 12 hours. The fare is about $38 one-way. "Southwest Chief" departs daily at 3:15 pm and reaches Kansas City in just over seven hours.

Going to Los Angeles: The "Southwest Chief" departs for Los Angeles, travels via Albuquerque, takes almost 42 hours, and costs $122-$150 one-way.

Union Station

210 S Canal St at E Adams St and E Jackson Blvd • 312-322-4269

An innovation for both design and travel, Chicago's Union Station is the "Grand Dame" of a rail service in a city once considered to be the undisputed rail center of the United States. Designed by the architects Graham, Anderson, Probst, and White and built during 1913-1925, Union Station is a terminus for six Metra lines and a major hub for Amtrak's long-distance services. In its peak (1940s), this local transportation treasure handled as many as 300 trains and 100,000 passengers on a daily basis. While today's volume is just half that, this monumental station stands as the last remaining grand station still in use in the City of Chicago, and was given landmark status in 2002. Most commuters don't take the time to gaze skyward when rushing through the Great Hall of Union Station (who really has the time to stop and assess their surroundings beyond that of their intended use?), but by not doing so, they are missing something special. Take the time to look up at the magnificent light-swathed ceiling and maybe then it will become clear why Union Station's ornate "Great Hall" is considered one of the United States' great interior public spaces. Union Station is also a premier location for formal functions, as it annually plays host to a multitude of private affairs and black-tie gatherings.

Both Metra's and Amtrak's train services are on the Concourse Level (ground floor) of the station. This level is then further divided into the North Concourse and South Concourse. Although not always adequately staffed, there is an information desk located between the concourses on this level. And while there is signage throughout Union Station, the many escalators, stairways, and multiple entrances/exits can make navigating the block-long building somewhat of a challenge.

Ticket Windows: The easiest way to get to Metra ticket agents is to enter Union Station at the Clinton Street entrance near East Jackson Boulevard and go down into and through the Grand Hall. Metra's ticket agents will be on your left in the North Concourse. Metra's ticket office is open weekdays 6 am-11:30 pm, Saturday 6:30 am-11:30 pm, and Sunday 7 am-11:30 pm. Metra Lines that terminate at Union Station are Milwaukee District East and West Lines, North Central Service, Burlington Northern Santa Fe, Heritage Corridor, and South West Service.

To get to the Amtrak action, enter Union Station off Canal Street, take the escalator down into the Grand Hall, and turn left. Amtrak's attractive, vintage ticket agent desk straddles the two concourses and is open daily 6:30 am-9 pm. Amtrak's waiting rooms and baggage claim are in the South Concourse. For more detail on Amtrak service, call 1-800-872-7245 or visit www.amtrak.com

Services: On the Mezzanine/Street Level, there is a plethora of convenience stores, newsstands, and eateries. ATMs are located in both concourses on this level.

Public Transportation: The closest L stop to Union Station is Clinton Street on the Blue Line, which stops two blocks south of the station. The Orange, Brown, and Purple Lines stop three blocks east of the station at the Quincy stop on Wells Street. CTA buses 1, 151, 157, and 125 all stop at Union Station. Most commuters heading to work in the Loop enter and exit the station from the Madison Street, Adams Street, and Jackson Boulevard doorways where cabs line up.

Richard B. Ogilvie Transportation Center

500 W Madison St at S Canal St • 312-496-4777

Built in 1911 and known locally as the North Western or Madison Street Station, the Metra's Union Pacific Lines originate from the Richard B. Ogilvie Transportation Center. Where Union Station is about form and function, Ogilvie focuses solely on function. Overtly stark and sterile, the tall, smoky-glass-and-green-steel-girder building replaced what was once a classic grand train station similar to the ornate, Beaux-Arts-inspired Union Station. Though most of the historic fixtures have been removed, some of the original clocks remain and serve as a reminder of earlier days. Even though promised renovations of the unused historic sub-level areas have yet to come to fruition (it is hoped that the empty space under the tracks can be turned into 120,000 square feet of shops and restaurants), this highly trafficked station remains quite active. Roughly 40,000 passengers pass through the Richard B. Ogilvie Transportation Center on a daily basis.

Ticket Windows: Metra's ticket office is on the Upper Level, across from the entrance to the train platform, and is open 5:30 am-12:40 am Monday-Saturday, and 7 am-12:40 am on Sundays. ATMs can be found on the Upper Level at Citibank and next to the currency exchange. Public phones are also by the currency exchange in the Southeast corner of the Upper Level. Trains depart from this level, and the smoking waiting room looks out onto the platform.

Services: Loads of junk food options are available on the Street Level food court, which also serves as a make-shift waiting room for commuters. If you want healthier fare, try the Rice Market and Boudin Sourdough Bakery on the east side of the building. There is available shopping about if you're killing time or wanting to pick up a last-minute gift. An interesting and annoying amenity footnote: the only restrooms in the station are on the Street Level, which is a LONG escalator ride from the train platform. There are no plans for this to change until the proposed renovations are completed. So it's best to "go before you go."

Public Transportation: The closest L station is the Green Line's Clinton Street stop at Lake Street, several blocks north of the station. CTA buses 20, 56, and 157 board at Washington and Canal Streets and travel to North Michigan Avenue and the Loop. Coming from the Loop, take the same bus lines west across Madison Street. If you're after a cab, you'll find other like-minded commuters lining up in front of the main entrance on Madison Street between Canal and Clinton Streets.

Randolph Street Station

151 E Randolph St at N Michigan Ave • 312-322-7819

Nicknamed the "Triple S" (South "Start" Station), the Randolph Street Station serves Metra's three electric commuter rail lines in Chicago (Main Line, South Chicago Branch, Blue Island Branch), in addition to several diesel lines. The underground station, centrally located in the Loop, services up to 100,000 commuters daily. This is also the station from which the South Shore Line to South Bend, Indiana originates. Schedules for all are somewhat sporadic except during weekday rush hour commutes. The Van Buren Street Station also serves both the Metra Electric and South Shore lines and is located at East Jackson Boulevard and Van Buren Street (312-322-6777). When planning train travel from the Randolph Street and Van Buren Street Stations, it's best to verify schedules and stops with the RTA Information Center (312-836-7000; www.rtachicago.com) before committing to a travel plan.

Ticket Windows: Enter the Randolph Street Station at East Randolph Street and North Michigan Avenue. The ticket office is immediately visible upon descending the steps off Michigan Avenue or entering via the Pedway which tunnels around the Loop and east under Michigan Avenue, ending at the station. Ticket office hours are 6 am-10:20 pm daily. The waiting room is open 5 am-12:50 am daily.

Services: The continuing Randolph Street Station renovation efforts have thrown a kink in the otherwise generous amenity offerings usually in place at this pinnacle station. Until the updates are completed, the best way to describe the amenities at the Randolph Street Station is "self-serve."

Public Transportation: Randolph Street Station is served by CTA buses 56, 151, 157 and, on days when there are events at the United Center, Express bus 19 becomes available. A little over one block west of the train station in the Loop is the Randolph Street L station, which the Orange, Green, Purple, and Brown Lines service.

La Salle Street Station

414 S La Salle St at E Congress Pkwy • 312-322-6509

The La Salle Street Station, located underneath the Chicago Stock Exchange, serves the Metra Rock Island District Line's passengers. This former behemoth of a station has been greatly reduced in both size and stature, handling roughly 15,000 commuters daily. The service has 11 main line stops and 10 south suburban stops on its way to Joliet.

Ticket Windows: Enter the station off La Salle Street, take the escalator one floor up, walk through the lobby past the bar to an open area where there are tracks and the ticket office. Agents are on duty 7 am-8 pm weekdays, 10:30 am-6:30 pm on Saturday, and closed on Sunday.

Services: There are no shops to speak of at the La Salle Street Station, but there IS a bar! During the week, the small waiting room is less crowded than the bar (go figure), especially after the markets close. Footnote: the worst time to be in or around the Chicago Stock Exchange is after the market closes, so the best advice is to avoid this area until later in the day. The waiting room is open 6 am-12 am daily.

Public Transportation: The Blue Line's La Salle Street stop at Congress Parkway and the Orange, Purple, and Brown Lines' La Salle Street stop at Van Buren Street drop L riders right in front of the train station. CTA buses 6 and 146 stop near the station as well.

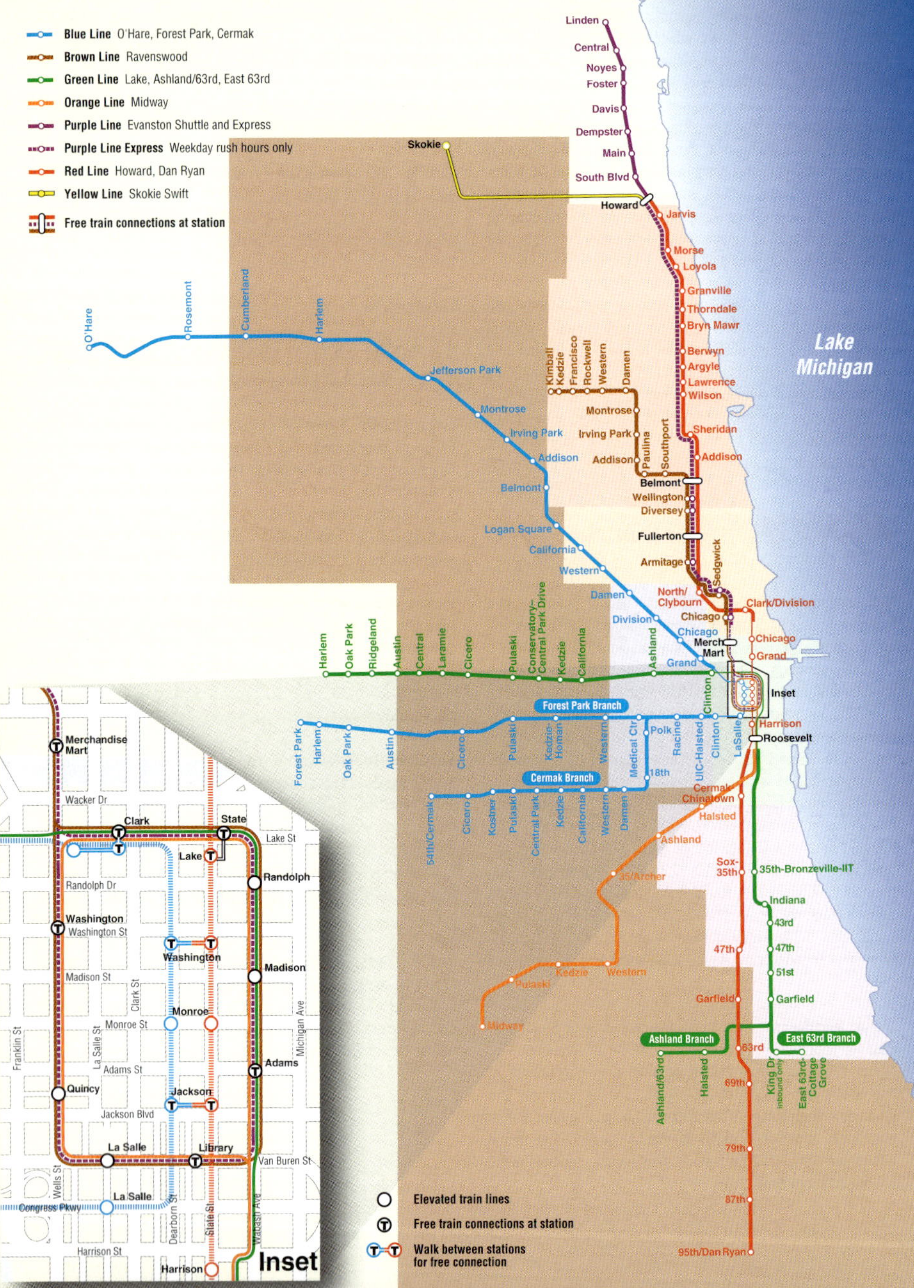
Blue Line O'Hare, Forest Park, Cermak
Brown Line Ravenswood
Green Line Lake, Ashland/63rd, East 63rd
Orange Line Midway
Purple Line Evanston Shuttle and Express
Purple Line Express Weekday rush hours only
Red Line Howard, Dan Ryan
Yellow Line Skokie Swift
Free train connections at station
Lake Michigan
Linden
Central
Noyes
Foster
Davis
Dempster
Main
South Blvd
Skokie
Howard
Jarvis
Morse
Loyola
Granville
Thorndale
Bryn Mawr
Berwyn
Argyle
Lawrence
Wilson
Sheridan
Addison
O'Hare
Rosemont
Cumberland
Harlem
Jefferson Park
Montrose
Irving Park
Addison
Belmont
Logan Square
California
Western
Damen
Division
Chicago
Grand
Kimball
Kedzie
Francisco
Rockwell
Western
Damen
Montrose
Irving Park
Addison
Paulina
Southport
Belmont
Wellington
Diversey
Fullerton
Armitage
Sedgwick
North/ Clybourn
Chicago
Merch Mart
Clark/Division
Chicago
Grand
Harlem
Oak Park
Ridgeland
Austin
Central
Laramie
Cicero
Pulaski
Conservatory–Central Park Drive
Kedzie
California
Ashland
Clinton
Inset
Forest Park Branch
Forest Park
Harlem
Oak Park
Austin
Cicero
Pulaski
Kedzie-Homan
Western
Medical Ctr
Polk
Racine
UIC-Halsted
Clinton
LaSalle
Harrison
Roosevelt
18th
Cermak Branch
54th/Cermak
Cicero
Kostner
Pulaski
Central Park
Kedzie
California
Western
Damen
Cermak Chinatown
Halsted
Ashland
35/Archer
Sox-35th
35th-Bronzeville-IIT
Indiana
43rd
47th
47th
51st
Garfield
Garfield
Western
Kedzie
Pulaski
Midway
Ashland Branch
East 63rd Branch
63rd
Ashland/63rd
Halsted
69th
King Dr inbound only
East 63rd-Cottage Grove
79th
87th
95th/Dan Ryan
Merchandise Mart
Wacker Dr
Clark
State
Lake St
Lake
Randolph
Randolph Dr
Washington
Washington St
Washington
Madison
Madison St
Clark St
Monroe
Monroe St
La Salle St
Michigan Ave
Franklin St
Adams St
Adams
Quincy
Jackson
Jackson Blvd
La Salle
Library
Van Buren St
Wells St
La Salle
Congress Pkwy
Dearborn St
State St
Wabash Ave
Harrison St
Harrison
Inset
Elevated train lines
Free train connections at station
Walk between stations for free connection

General Information

CTA Mailing Address: Chicago Transit Authority
Merchandise Mart Plaza, 7th Fl
PO Box 3555, Chicago, IL 60654
Phone: 312-664-7200
CTA Information: 888-YOUR-CTA (968-7282)
Website: www.transitchicago.com

Overview

Whether traveling underground, on street level, or above the sidewalk, Chicagoans refer to their elevated rapid transit system as the "L." (Though some prefer to call it the "Smell.") No matter which one you choose, either name says Chicago as loud and clear as the high-pitched whine, guttural grumble, and steely grind of the train itself. L tracks lasso Chicago's heart, creating The Loop, where six of the seven L lines ride side-by-side above the pulsating business and financial district.

L trains make 1,452 trips each day and serve 143 stations in the Chicago Metropolitan Area. The numerous track delays and stalls in service are a burden to thousands of daily commuters. Nonetheless, due to the general directness of the L routes, easy station-to-station transfers, and the difficulties of parking (especially near popular destinations such as Grant Park and Wrigley Field), the benefits of L transportation usually outweigh the discomforts and inconveniences.

Fares

The standard full fare on CTA trains is $1.75. A 25¢ transfer allows two additional rides within two hours of issuance and can be used for transferring from rail to bus (or vice versa), and also between buses. Transfer rates are automatically deducted from your farecard when reused within the time limit. On buses, when paying with cash, transfers must be purchased with the base fare on the first leg of the journey. Transferring within the rail network is free at determined, connected transfer stations.

To ride the L, you need a farecard. Farecards come in three shapes. There's the standard farecard that you can purchase at machines in every subway station. Note: These machines do not give change. Insert the amount of money you want to put on the card and push the "vend" button. Farecards can be used and reused as long as there is money on them, and can be reloaded with extra money as needed. When passing through turnstiles, insert the card in the slot, wait for the green light, retrieve the card, and you're on your way. A plus to the standard farecard is that you can buy it on the spot for whatever amount you need at the time. Some shortcomings are that if you lose the card, you're out of luck, and there is no longer a 10% bonus offered. That bonus is now reserved for the Chicago Card and the Chicago Card Plus.

The Chicago Card is another class of farecard. A Chicago Card is a plastic card, requiring a $5 fee (and another $5 for replacements, should that card get lost or stolen). Chicago Cards have the convenience of online reloading, and offer a 10% bonus for every increment of $10 that you reload (reload $10, get a $1 bonus, $20 = $2, $30 = $3, and so on). The Chicago Card also gives you the option of registering the card, protecting your money in the event that the card is lost or stolen. To use the card, simply touch it to the sensor at the CTA turnstile, or the fare box on the bus. Chicago Cards can be ordered online at www.chicago-card.com, by phone at 1-888-YOURCTA, or at the CTA main sales office located at 567 W Lake Street.

Finally, there is the Chicago Card Plus, which offers all the benefits of the Chicago Card, PLUS you can choose between a "Pay-Per-Use" program or an unlimited 30-Day Pass for $75 a month (automatically deducted from your credit card). All Chicago Farecards offer "passback" privileges, allowing you to share your card with up to six other people traveling with you, by—get this—passing the card back. The full fare for each rider will be deducted from your card, with the exception of the 30-Day Pass, in which the card holder gets the unlimited ride, while each additional fare is considered Pay-Per-Use, and so, deducted from your account and charged to your credit card.

Reduced fares (85¢) are available for children ages 7-11, seniors aged 65+ with an RTA Reduced Fare Riding Permit, and riders with disabilities (with an RTA permit) and their companion. Grade school students with CTA Student Riding Permits ($5 per semester; $2 summer school) pay reduced fares on weekdays from 5:30 am to 8 pm. Chicago Card and Chicago Card Plus do not accommodate the reduced fare structure. Free rides are reserved for children aged six and under. Riders that are in "other uniformed or ID-bearing categories authorized by the Chicago Transit Board" (whatever that means) also enjoy free rides. You might want that stinking badge after all…

Frequency of Service

CTA publishes schedules that say trains run every 3 to 12 minutes during weekday rush hours and every 6 to 20 minutes all other times. But service can be irregular, especially during non-rush hours, after-hours, and in bad weather. While the system is relatively safe late at night, stick to stations in populated areas as much as possible. Buses with Owl Service may be better options in the wee hours.

L Lines

Blue Line: Comprising the O'Hare, Forest Park, and Cermak branches traveling west, O'Hare and Forest Park run 24-hours, while Cermak is operational only on weekdays.

Red Line: Runs north-south from the Howard Street station down to the 95th Street/Dan Ryan station; operates 24-hours.

Brown Line: Starts from the Kimball Street station and heads south with service to the Loop and sometimes just to Belmont Avenue. On weekdays and Saturdays, the first Loop-bound train leaves Kimball Street at 4:01 am; the last train to leave the Loop is at 12:18 am. Sunday service begins at 6:46 am and ends at 11:40 pm. After that, take the Red Line to Belmont Avenue and transfer to the Brown Line where the last train leaves at 2:25 am (12:55 am on Sundays). The Brown Line also runs between Kimball Street and Belmont Avenue from 4 am to 2:04 am weekdays and Saturdays; and from 5:01 am to 2:04 am on Sundays. Note that at the time of this printing, the Brown Line is about to undertake a massive renovation project that will interrupt service at many stops. Repairs are scheduled to take place over the coming year, so you should check the CTA website before heading out to make sure that the stop you need is open.

Orange Line: Travels from Midway Airport to the Loop and back. Trains depart from Midway beginning at 3:55 am weekdays and Saturdays, and at 7 am on Sundays; the last train leaves the Loop for the airport at 1:29 am daily.

Green Line: Covers portions of west and south Chicago. The Harlem/Lake Street branch travels straight west. The Ashland Avenue/63rd Street and E 63rd Street/Cottage Grove branches go south and split east and west. Depending on the branch, service begins around 4 am weekdays with the last trains running around 1 am. Weekend schedules vary.

Purple Line: Shuttles north-south between Linden Place in suburban Evanston and Howard Street, Chicago's northernmost station. Service starts at 4:35 am and ends at 12:55 am weeknights, 1:45 am on weekends, and 12:55 am Sundays. Weekdays, an express train runs between Linden Place and the Loop between 6:25 am and 10:10 am and then again between 2:55 pm and 6:15 pm. At all other times, take the **Purple Line Express** to the Howard Street station and transfer to the Red Line to reach the Loop.

Yellow Line: Runs between the north suburban Skokie station and Chicago's Howard Street station on weekdays from 4:50 am to 10:18 pm. On weekends, take CTA bus 97 from Skokie station to Howard Street and catch the Red Line to the Loop.

Bicycles

Bicycles ride free and are permitted onboard at all times except weekdays from 7 am to 9 am and 4 pm to 6 pm. Only two bikes are allowed per car, so survey the platform for other bikes and check out the cars as they pull into the station for two-wheelers already onboard. When entering a station, either use the turnstile or ask an attendant to open the gate. Don't try to take your bike through the tall steel gates—it WILL get stuck!

Downtown's Pedway keeps Chicagoans moving throughout the central business district. An over 40-block network of tunnels and overhead bridges connects important public, government, and private sector buildings with retail stores, major hotels, rapid transit stations, and commuter rail stations. A subterranean city with shops, restaurants, services, and public art works, the Pedway is a welcome alternative to navigating trafficked intersections on foot and walking outdoors in Chicago's frigid winters. The underground walkway system is open 24-hours; however, access to a number of the buildings is limited after standard business hours. The first Pedway links were built in 1951 to connect the State Street and Dearborn Street subways at Washington Street and Jackson Boulevard. Today, Chicago's Pedway continues to grow as city government and the private sector cooperate to expand it.

General Information

City of Chicago Department of Transportation (DOT)
Non-Emergency/
24-Hour Road Conditions Phone: 311
Street Closings Hotline: 312-787-3387
Website: www.cityofchicago.org

Illinois Department of Transportation (IDOT)
Phone: 217-782-7820
IDOT Traffic Hotline: 312-368-4636
Website: www.dot.state.il.us/news.html

Chicago Skyway Bridge: 312-747-8383
Road Conditions: 800-452-4368
WBBM-AM 780: Traffic updates every eight minutes

Orientation

Driving in Chicago has the potential to skyrocket your blood pressure as high as the Sears Tower. We highly recommend taking public transportation whenever possible, especially since Chicago has such strong bus and rail systems. But if you must drive in the city, Chicago's grid system makes it relatively easy to navigate.

The intersection of State and Madison Streets in the Loop serves as the base line for both Chicago's street and house numbering system. Running north and south is State Street—the city's east/west dividing line. Madison Street runs east and west and divides the city into north and south. Street and building numbers begin at "1" at the State and Madison Streets intersection, and numerically increase going north, south, east, and west to the city limits. Street signs will let you know in what direction you're heading. The city is divided into one-mile sections, or eight square blocks, each with a consecutively higher series of "100" numbers. This explains why Chicagoans numerically refer to street locations, such as Irving Park Boulevard, as "40 hundred north" rather than "four thousand north."

Buildings with even number addresses are on the north and west sides of streets; odd numbers sit on the south and east sides. Chicago's diagonal streets also follow the grid numbering system. Generally, the South Side's north-south streets have names and the east-west streets mostly go by numbers, such as 30th Street located at 3000 or 30 hundred south. In many cases, the grid system's numbering extends into the surrounding suburbs.

Bridge Lift Season

While bridges spanning the Chicago River contribute to the city's architectural fame, they also serve as a major source of traffic congestion. Boating season demands that bridges lower and raise, so as to allow sailboats access to Lake Michigan. Chicago's bridge lift season runs from early April until June. Each month has designated lift days. Lifts generally begin at 9:30 am and affect the entire downtown area between 11:30 am and 1 pm. During May, more lifts are scheduled on Saturdays between 2 pm and 4 pm. The schedule intensifies on holiday weekends to include evening rush hours. Check out the DOT's website for detailed schedules.

Snow Routes

Failure to efficiently handle city snow removal seals the re-election fate of Chicago's mayors. The Department of Streets and Sanitation manages the ice and snow removal on Chicago's streets. Over 280 salt spreaders/plows cruise 607 miles of arterial streets divided into 245 designated snow routes. Parking is automatically restricted on these routes when snow is piled at least two inches on the pavement. Priority arteries also restrict parking daily from 3 am until 7 am between December 1 and April 1, whether or not snow is present (but it usually is).

Major Expressways and Tollways

While the city's grid system is logical, the interstate highway system feeding into the city is confusing for those who don't travel it often. Chicago has free expressways and tollways, which require paying a fee. Roads often transition from one to the other. The I-PASS (a local version of E-ZPass) speeds up the life of frequent tollway users, and can be purchased through the Illinois State Toll Highway Authority located in Downers Grove (800-824-7277).

DMVs

The Illinois Department of Motor Vehicles (DMV) is, and has always been, one of life's unavoidable hassles. But you'd be pleasantly surprised to see how many of your car-related responsibilities (like renewing your driver's license, getting vehicle registrations, etc.) can be completed online (www.dmv.org). Visit the website, or call 312-793-1010 for more information.

Chicago DMVs	*Map*	*Hours*
100 W Randolph St	5	Mon-Fri: 8 am-5 pm
69 W Washington St, Concourse Level	5	Mon-Fri: 8 am-5 pm
17 N State St, Ste 1000	5	Mon-Fri: 8 am-4:30 pm
5401 N Elston Ave	46	Mon-Tues: 8:30 am-5 pm; Wed: 10 am-7 pm; Thurs-Fri: 8:30 am-5 pm
9901 S Martin Luther King Dr	59	Mon-Tues: 8:30 am-5 pm; Wed: 10 am-7 pm; Thurs-Fri: 8:30 am-5 pm
5301 W Lexington Ave	49	Mon: 8:30 am-5 pm; Tues: 9 am-7 pm; Wed-Fri: 8 am -5:30 pm; Sat: 8 am-12 pm

General Information

Office of the City Clerk—Parking Permits

Mailing Address: City Hall
121 N La Salle St, Rm 107
Chicago, IL 60602
Phone: 312-744-6861
Hours: Weekdays, 8 am-5 pm
Website: www.chicityclerk.com

**Department of Revenue (DOR)—
Parking Ticket Payments**

Mailing Address: PO Box 88292
Chicago, IL 60680-1292
Phone: 312-744-6146
Website: www.cityofchicago.org/revenue
Parking Ticket Assistance & "Boot" Inquiries:
312-744-PARK (7275)
Auto Pound Headquarters: 312-744-4444
(for towed vehicles)
City Non-Emergency Phone: 311

City Stickers

Residents of Chicago who own motor vehicles must have an annually renewed city sticker for their cars. All classes of city vehicle stickers can be purchased from the Office of the City Clerk through the mail (by returning the renewal application you've received in the mail), in person at one of their offices, or online. New residents are required to purchase their sticker in person with a proof of residency at one of the offices within 30 days of their move-in date. A four-passenger vehicle sticker for long-time residents costs $75, while new residents get a price cut at $37. Senior citizens are also eligible for discounts. After March 1st of each year, half-year stickers are available at half-price for new city residents or current residents who've recently purchased a car. For more information on office locations and pricing, call 312-742-9200 or visit the City Clerk's website.

Residential Zone Permit Parking

Chicago's Residential Parking Permit program reserves street parking during peak parking hours for neighborhood residents and those who provide a service to the residents. Cars in violation of this ordinance will be ticketed. Permits cost $17.50 annually, and are available through the Office of the City Clerk via mail, online, and in person. Applicants must have a valid Chicago City Sticker and an Illinois State license plate. One-day guest passes may also be purchased and distributed by qualified residents. Fifteen 24-hour passes cost $3 per pack, at a two-pack limit, so choose your guests wisely and frugally. Check out the City Clerk website or call 312-744-5346 for more information.

Parking Tickets

The Department of Revenue (DOR) handles the payment of parking tickets. You can pay parking tickets by mail, online, or in person. For the addresses and hours of payment processing and hearing facilities, see the DOR website.

Your car gets fitted with the boot when you accrue three or more unpaid tickets. Ten or more tickets and the entire car is encased in molybdenum steel. If the violations are not paid within 24 hours of booting, your vehicle will be towed. In addition to the boot fee, towing and storage fees must be paid to retrieve your car from a City Auto Pound. If your car is towed due to a boot, contact the City of Chicago's Ticket Help Line (312-744-7275). All payments for outstanding parking ticket debt must be made to a DOR Payment Center, NOT at the pound. The city has two payment plans available for motorists with large ticket fines. The General Payment Plan requires either a deposit of $500 or 25% of your parking debt (whichever is greater), in addition to all outstanding boot, towing, and storage fees. If you qualify for the Hardship Parking Payment Plan, you can make a deposit of $250 or 25% of your debt, whichever is lower. Visit the DOR website for further requirements.

Auto Pounds

To locate your towed vehicle, contact the City of Chicago Auto Pound Headquarters (312-744-4444). There are six auto pounds in addition to the City's Central Auto Pound (400 E Wacker Dr, 312-744-7550) and the O'Hare Auto Pound (10000 W O'Hare at Remote Lot E, 773-694-0990).

For a standard vehicle, the towing fee is a hefty $150 plus a $10 per day storage fee for the first five days, then $35 per day thereafter. Fees are paid at the pound where they accept cash, VISA, MasterCard, Discover, American Express, and first-born children.

Failure to claim vehicles or request a hearing within 21 days of notification can result in your convenient mode of transportation being sold or destroyed and, even then, you still owe the city for the outstanding fines. In that case, see the rest of the Transit section for alternate ways of navigating your way through Chicago.

Transit • **Free Trolleys**

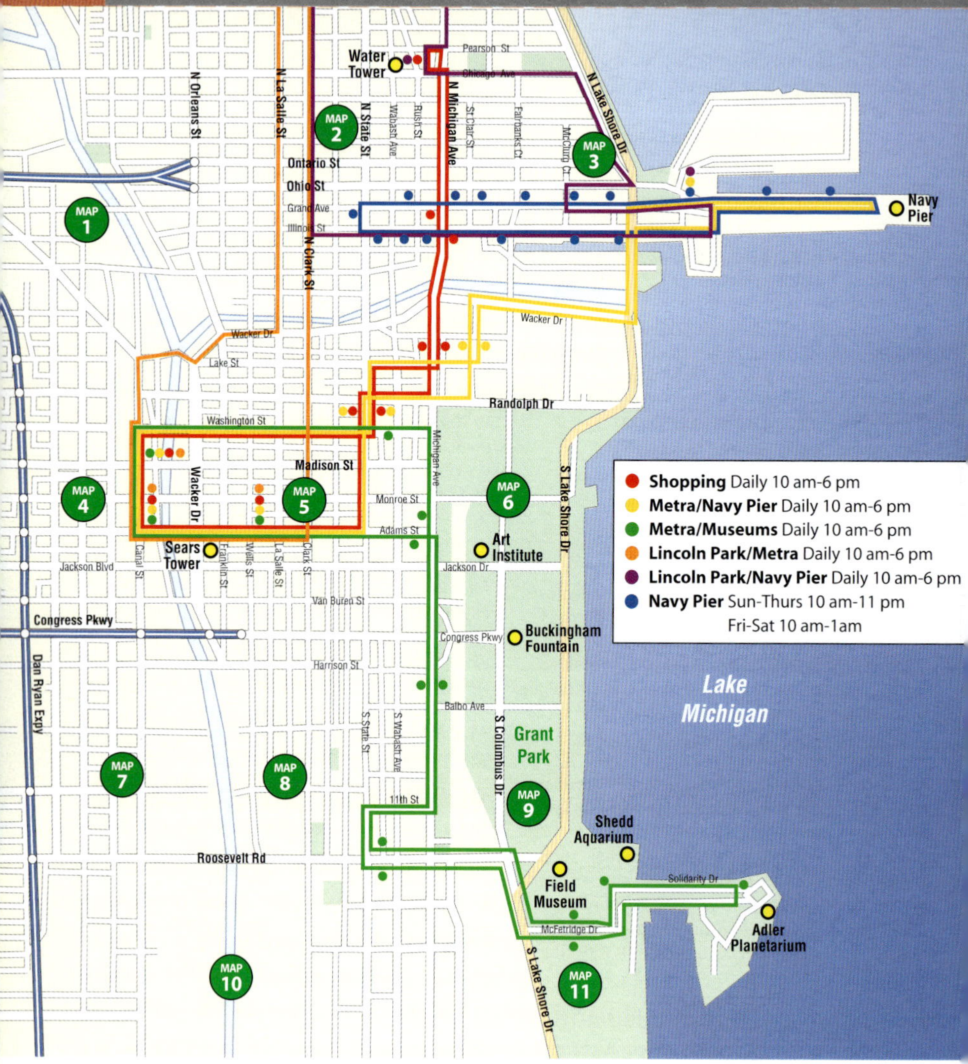

The city of Chicago runs a free trolley service from Memorial Day through Labor Day every year. Most trolleys run every 20-30 minutes 10 am-6 pm daily (check map for specific line hours). The six color-coded trolley routes dovetail with CTA bus routes, make stops at major Loop L stations and Metra stations, and travel to and from Chicago's most popular attractions. Trolley stops are identifiable by graphic, color-coded signage. Because fare-based trolley companies also roam the streets, be sure to look for the "Free Trolley" sign in the front window. You don't need a ticket to ride; just hop on and off as you please.

For more information contact: 877-244-2246; www.cityofchicago.org/Transportation/

Lake Michigan
Diversey Harbor
North Pond
Lincoln Park
Lincoln Park Lagoon
South Pond
South Pond
41
MAP 29
MAP 30
MAP 22
MAP 31
MAP 32
W Diversey Pkwy
W Diversey Ave
W Schubert Ave
W Drummond Pl
W Wrightwood Ave
W Deming Pl
W St James Pl
W Roslyn Pl
W Arlington Pl
W Fullerton Pkwy
W Kemper Pl
W Belden Ave
W Grant Pl
W Webster Ave
W Dickens Ave
W Armitage Ave
W Wisconsin St
W Menomonee St
W Willow St
W St Paul Ave
W Eugenie St
W Concord Pl
W Concord Ln
W Lutz Pl
W Weed St
W Blackhawk St
W Eastman St
W Schiller St
W North Ave
E North Ave
W Germania Pl
W Burton Pl
E Burton Pl
E Schiller St
N Halsted St
N Clark St
N Lincoln Ave
N La Salle St
N State Pkwy
N Lake Shore Dr
N Cannon Dr
N Ridge Dr
N Stockton Dr
N Lincoln Park W
N Sheridan Rd
N Lakeview Ave
N Commonwealth Ave
N Orleans St
N Sedgwick St
N Hudson Ave
N Mohawk St
N Fremont St
N Dayton St
N Wilton Ave
N Mildred Ave
N Burling St
N Orchard St
N Geneva Ter
N Edward Ct
N Pearl Ct
N Howe St
N Bissell St
N Cleveland Ave
N Fern Ct
N Crilly Ct
N Vine St
N Frontier Ave
N Meyer Ct
N St Michaels Ct
N North Park Ave
N Wieland St
N Larrabee St
N Sandburg Ter
N Dearborn Pkwy
N Astor St
N Hampden Ct
N Lehmann Ct
N Pine Grove Ave

Useful Phone Numbers

City Board of Elections	312-269-7900
State Board of Elections	312-814-6440
ComEd	800-334-7661
Peoples Gas Billing	866-566-6001
Peoples Gas Emergencies	866-566-6002
Drivers Licensing Facilities	312-793-1010
Office of Richard Daley	312-744-5000
Governor's Office	217-782-6830
General Aldermanic Information	312-269-7900

Helpful Websites

Angie's List • www.angieslist.com
Membership-driven list rating local contractors and other services. Great for home repair, caterers, etc.

Metromix • www.metromix.com
City guide put out by the Trib.

Citysearch Chicago • www.chicago.citysearch.com
Restaurants, clubs, etc.

City of Chicago • www.ci.chi.il.us
Helpful all-purpose guide to city services.

Spacefinder • www.chireader.com/spacefinder
The source for apartment rentals.

Pay parking tickets • www.parkingtickets.cityofchicago.org
Avoid the Denver boot!

Taxi Cabs

Checker	312-243-2537
American United	773-248-7600
Flash Cab (south)	312-467-1072
Flash Cab (north)	773-529-6137
Yellow Cab	800-829-4222

We're Number One!!!

World's Busiest Airport: O'Hare International
World's Largest Public Library: Harold Washington Library
World's Largest Aquarium: Shedd Aquarium
World's Largest Free Public Zoo: Lincoln Park Zoo
World's Largest Modern Art Museum: Museum of Contemporary Art
Worlds Largest Commercial Office Building: Merchandise Mart, 222 Merchandise Mart Plaza
World's Longest Street: Western Avenue
World's Busiest Roadway: The Dan Ryan Expressway
World's Largest Food Festival: Taste of Chicago

Chicago Timeline

1779: Jean-Baptiste Point du Sable establishes Chicago's first permanent settlement.
1803: U.S. Army constructs Fort Dearborn. It is destroyed during conflicts with Native Americans in 1812, and rebuilt in 1816.
1818: Illinois is admitted into the union.
1833: Chicago incorporates as a town of 350 people, bordered by Kinzie, Des Plaines, Madison, and the lakefront.
1837: Chicago incorporates as a city. The population is 4,170. Ogden becomes the city's first mayor.
1851: Northwestern University is founded.
1856: Fort Dearborn is demolished.
1860: Republican Party nominates Abraham Lincoln for President at Chicago's first political convention.
1865: Merry Christmas! Union stockyards open on Christmas Day.
1869: Water tower is completed.
1871: Great Chicago Fire!
1885: World's first "skyscraper," the 9-story Home Insurance building, goes up on La Salle Street.
1886: Haymarket Riots. 8 Chicago policemen are killed.
1889: Jane Addams opens Hull House.
1892: World's first elevated trains begin operation.
1893: Columbia Exposition celebrates 400th anniversary of Columbus' discovery of America.
1907: Chicago physicist Abraham Michelson is first American to win Nobel Prize.
1910: Original Comiskey Park opens.
1914: Wrigley Field opens.
1927: $750,000 donated to city to build fountain in honor of Clarence Buckingham.
1929: John G. Shedd presents Shedd Aquarium as a "gift to the Chicago People."
1930: Adler Planetarium opens through a gift from Max Adler.
1930: Merchandise Mart built by Marshall Field.
1931: Chicagoan Jane Addams becomes first woman to win Nobel Peace Prize.
1931: Al Capone sent to prison for 11 years for evading taxes.
1934: John Dillinger shot by FBI outside of Biograph theatre.
1955: O'Hare International Airport opens.
1958: End of the line: Last streetcar in Chicago stops operating.
1968: Democratic National Convention Riots.
1971: Chicago Union Stock Yards are closed.
1974: Sears Tower is completed.
1983: Harold Washington elected first black mayor.
1995: A heat wave contributed to the death of over 700 Chicagoans.
1997: City Council absolves Mrs. O'Leary's cow of blame for Great Chicago Fire.
1998: Six-peat! Chicago Bulls win their sixth world championship in eight years.
2003: Four-peat! Richard M. Daley re-elected for historic fourth term!

12 Essential Chicago Movies

Northside 777 (1948)
Man with the Golden Arm (1955)
Raisin in the Sun (1961)
Medium Cool (1969)
Blues Brothers (1980)
Risky Business (1983)
Ferris Bueller's Day Off (1986)
The Untouchables (1987)
Hoop Dreams (1994)
My Best Friend's Wedding (1997)
High Fidelity (2000)
Barbershop (2002)

Overview

WGN is the classic Chicago TV station. Its radio affiliate at 720 AM *is* Chicago talk radio. **WXRT** is the city's independent rock station—one of the few remaining stations still free from the smothering embrace of Clear Channel Communications. Their Sunday morning Beatles Brunch with host Terri Hemmert (a Chicago institution in her own right), is heaven for fans of the Fab Four. In general, the station is a little heavy on the white-boy blues (think Clapton and Stevie Ray Vaughan) and crunchy rock ala Dave Matthews and Hootie—if that's your thing. Midway down the dial, alt-music station **Q101's** morning host Mancow Muller is a more immature version of Howard Stern—less sex, more body secretions. In terms of print media, we'll put it this way: the **Tribune** appeals to Cubs fans, while the **Sun-Times** is favored by White Sox fans. **Time Out** is the latest alt entertainment weekly to come to Chicago, and the **Reader** is the essential paper for slacker job seekers and apartment hunters.

Television

	CLTV	(Cable)
2	WBBM	(CBS)
5	WMAQ	(NBC)
7	WLS	(ABC)
9	WGN	(WB)
11	WTTW	(PBS)
20	WYCC	(PBS)
23	WFBT	(Brokered—ethnic)
26	WCIU	(Independent)
32	WFLD	(Fox)
38	WCPX	(PAX)
44	WSNS	(Telemundo)
50	WPWR	(UPN)
60	WEHS	(Home shopping)
66	WGBO	(Univision)

Radio

AM

560	WIND	Spanish
620	WTMJ	News/Talk
670	WMAQ	Sports
720	WGN	Talk
780	WBBM	Talk
820	WCSN	Sports
850	WAIT	Standards
890	WLS	News/Talk
1000	WLUP	Sports
1110	WMBI	Religious
1200	WLXX	Spanish
1280	WBIG	Talk
1390	WGCI	Gospel
1450	WVON	Talk (Black-oriented)
1490	WPNA	Polish
1510	WWHN	Gospel
1570	WBEE	Jazz

FM

88.1	WCRX	Columbia College
88.5	WHPK	U of Chicago
88.7	WLUW	Loyola U
89.3	WNUR	Northwestern
90.1	WMBI	Christian
90.0	WDCB	Jazz
91.5	WBEZ	National Public Radio
93.1	WXRT	Rock
93.5	WJTW	Adult Contemporary
93.9	WLIT	Adult Contemporary
94.7	WZZN	Modern Rock
95.1	WIIL	Rock
95.5	WNUA	New Age
95.9	WKKD	Oldies
96.3	WBBM	Dance
97.9	WLUP	Rock
98.7	WFMT	Classical
99.5	WUSN	Country
100.3	WNND	Adult Contemporary
101.1	WKQX	Modern Rock
101.9	WTMX	Adult Contemporary
102.7	WVAZ	Urban Contemporary
103.1	WXXY	Latin Pop
103.5	WKSC	Top 40
104.3	WJMK	Oldies
105.1	WOJO	Spanish
105.9	WCKG	Rock
106.7	WYLL	Christian
107.5	WGCI	Urban Contemporary

Print

Chicago Defender	2400 S Michigan Ave	312-225-2400	Black community newspaper.
Chicago Free Press	3714 N Broadway St	773-325-0005	Gay community news.
Chicago Magazine	500 N Dearborn St	312-222-8999	Upscale glossy mag.
Chicago Reader	11 E Illinois St	312-828-0350	Free weekly with listings.
Chicago Reporter	332 S Michigan Ave	312-427-4830	Investigative reporting on issues of race, poverty, and social justice.
Chicago Sun-Times	401 N Wabash Ave	312-321-3000	One of the big dailies.
Chicago Tribune	435 N Michigan Ave	312-222-3232	The other big daily.
Crain's Chicago Business	740 N Rush St	312-649-5200	Business news.
Daily Herald	PO Box 280, Arlington Hts	847-427-4300	Suburban news.
Daily Southtown	6901 W 159th St, Tinley Pk	708-633-6700	News for southsiders.
Ebony	820 S Michigan Ave	312-322-9200	National glossy about African Americans.
Hyde Park Herald	5240 S Harper Ave	773-643-8533	Local for Hyde Parkers.
Korea Times	4447 N Kedzie Ave	773-463-1050	Daily Korean-language newspaper.
La Raza	3909 N Ashland Ave	773-525-9400	Hispanic community paper.
Lerner-Booster-Skyline	7331 N Lincoln Ave, Lincolnwood	847-329-2000	Conglomeration of neighborhood papers.
N'Digo	401 N Wabash Ave	312-822-0202	Black community weekly.
New City	770 N Halsted Ave	312-243-8786	Alternative free weekly.
The Onion	47 W Division St	312-751-0503	Local listings in AV Club insert.
Red Eye	435 N Michigan Ave	312-222-4970	Commuter-deigned offshoot of the Trib for 20 and 30-somethings.
Red Streak	401 N Wabash Ave	773-890-7333	Where goest the Tribune, there goest the Sun-Times.
Time Out Chicago	247 S State St	312-924-9555	Glossy arts and entertainment weekly.
Today's Chicago Woman	233 E Ontario St	312-951-7600	Weekly for working women.
Windy City Times	1940 W Irving Park Rd	773-871 7610	Gay-targeted news weekly.

15 Essential Chicago Books

Native Son, by Richard Wright. Gripping novel about a young black man on the South Side in the '30s.

Neon Wilderness, by Nelson Algren. Short story collection set in Ukrainian Village and Wicker Park.

One More Time, by Mike Royko. Collection of Royko's Tribune columns.

The Boss: Richard M. Daley, by Mike Royko. Biography of the former Mayor.

The Jungle, by Upton Sinclair. Gritty look at the life in the meat-packing plants.

Adventures of Augie March, by Saul Bellow. More Chicago in the '30s.

V.I. Warshawsky mystery series, by Sara Paretsky. Series firmly rooted in Chicago landscape.

50 Years at Hull House, by Jane Addams. Story of the Near West Side.

Secret Chicago, by Sam Weller. Off-the-beaten path guidebook.

Ethnic Chicago, by Melvin Holli & Peter D'A. Jones. Insider's guide to Chicago's ethnic neighborhoods.

House on Mango Street, by Sandra Cisneros. Short story collection about a Latina childhood in Chicago.

Our America: Life and Death on the South Side of Chicago, by Lealan Jones, et al. Life in the Chicago Projects as told by two schoolchildren.

The Coast of Chicago, by Stuart Dybek. Short stories of Chicago denizens.

Hairstyles of the Damned, by Joe Meno. Teen angst and punk rock in '80s Chicago.

Never a City So Real: A Walk in Chicago, by Alex Kotlowitz. Modern reflection on the city of big shoulders.

From May to June, every corner of the city is hopping with all manner of block parties, church carnivals, neighborhood festivals, and all-out hootenanny. Contact the Mayor's Office of Special Events for a complete list of the city's 100+ festivals.

Event	When & Where	Description
Chinese New Year	Sunday after the Chinese New Year (mid-February), Chinatown	2006 is the year of the Wood Rooster. Celebrate!
South Side St Patrick's Day Parade	Sunday closest to March 17, Western Ave, 103rd to 113th Sts	The "real deal," with oversized leprechauns and green beer flowing.
Women in the Director's Chair Festival	Two weeks in March, Chicago Cultural Center	Femme films. www.widc.org
Chicago Flower Show	Mid-March, Navy Pier	Escape from winter.
Chicago Latino Film Festival	Early-April, various venues	20+-year-old festival screens the best in local and international Latino film. www.latinoculturalcenter.org/Filmfest/
Printers Row Book Fair	Second weekend in June, Dearborn St, b/w Harrison St & Balbo Dr	Watch for *Booksellers Gone Wild* coming soon to pay-per-view.
Andersonville Midsommarfest	Second weekend in June, Clark St, b/w Foster & Balmoral Aves	Ain't it Swede?
Old Town Art Fair	Mid-June, 1800 N Orleans St, Menominee St, Lincoln Ave	Arts and crafts.
Taste of Chicago	Last week in June, first week in July, Grant Park	Why go to a restaurant when you can eat standing up in the hot sun in a crowd?
Country Music Fest	Last weekend in June, Grant Park	Annual Lakeside hoe-down. www.egov.cityofchicago.org
Gay Pride Parade	Last Sunday in June, Halsted/Broadway Sts b/w Halsted & Grace Sts	200,000 of the city's gay community and their fans take it to the streets. www.chicagopridecalendar.org
43rd Street BluesFest	Mid-June, Oakwood & Cottage Grove	The warm-up for the Grant Park Blues fest.
Beverly Arts Fair	Third week in June, Beverly Arts Center, 2407 W 111th St	Family fun in Beverly.
Juneteenth Celebration	Third Saturday in June, 79th & Stony Island	African American Pride celebration includes parade, music, and lots of barbeque at Rainbow Beach.
57th Street Art Fair	First week in June, 57th & Kimbark	Oldest juried art fair in the Midwest. www.57thstreetartfair.org
Jeff Fest	Late June, Jefferson Park	Neighborhood festival of guys named Jeff. We kid you not.
Bronzeville House Tours	Late June, 3402 S King Dr	The best way to peek into Chicago's African-American history.
Gospel Music Festival	First weekend in June, Grant Park	As much about the soul food as the music.
Chicago Blues Festival	Second weekend in June, Grant Park	Drawing the top names in blues for 21 years.
Old Town Art Fair	Mid-June, 1800 N Orleans St, Menominee St, Lincoln Ave	Arts and crafts.
Independence Eve Fireworks	July 3, Grant Park	Real fireworks occur when a million spectators try to leave Grant Park.
Venetian Night	Third weekend in July, Monroe Harbor	Wow! Decked out boats!

Event	When & Where	Description
Outdoor Film Festival	Tuesdays, Mid-July to mid-August, Grant Park	Classic movies, a carafe of vino, and KFC. Life is good.
Rock Around the Block	Second weekend in July	Lots of street-festival quality live music. Expect Bumpus and Underwater People.
Taste of Logan Square	Mid-July, Fullerton & Kedzie	It tastes cement-y.
Korean Street Festival	Mid-July, 3200-3400 W Bryn Mawr	One-stop shopping for your bibimbap, juk, and kimbap.
Fiesta Del Sol	Last weekend in July, Cermak Rd, b/w Throop & Morgan Sts	One of the most festive of the fests.
Bud Billiken Parade	Second Saturday in August, King Dr	World's biggest African-American parade. www.budbillikenparade.com
North Halsted Market Days	Second weekend in August, Halsted St b/w Belmont Ave & Addison St	See Gay Pride Parade. Add beer and live music.
Air and Water Show	Third weekend in August, lakefront	The Stealth Bombers never fail to thrill.
Viva Chicago Latin Music Fest	Last weekend in August, Grant Park	Salsa under the stars.
Taste of Polonia	Last weekend in August, 5200 W Lawrence Ave	Polka and keilbasa! Heaven! Pierogis! Paradise!
Gold Coast Art Fair	Early August, Wells St	Fine arts in a fancy neighborhood.
Summer Dance	August, Grant Park	Kick up your heels under the stars. Free lessons, and free DJs on Wednesday nights.
Celtic Fest	Second weekend in September, Grant Park	Clog dance in the bonny heath.
German-American Fest	Early September, Lincoln & Leland	Octoberfest in Lincoln Square. Bring your own leiderhosen.
World Music Festival	Late September, Grant Park	Music acts from around the world, plus beer.
57th St Children's Book Fair	Late September, b/w Kimbark & Dorchester Aves	Lots of kids. Lots of books.
Chicago International Film Festival	October, various locations	Worthy display of the best in international cinema. www.chicagofilmfestival.org
Halloween Parade	Halloween day, Halsted b/w Belmont & Addison	Flamboyant Boystown costume extravaganza.
Tree Lighting	Day after Thanksgiving, Daley Plaza	Decking the halls by City Hall.
Mag Mile Lights Festival	Saturday evening before Thanksgiving, Michican Ave	Festive celebration of obligatory consumption.
Thanksgiving Parade	Thanksgiving Day morning, 8:30 am, State St	8:30 am? Yeah, as if.

*All dates subject to change. For more up to date information and a schedule of neighborhood festivals, contact the Mayor's Office of Special Events at www.cityofchicago.org/specialevents.

General Information • **Police**

With 13,705 sworn-in police officers, Chicago's crime incidence keeps dropping. Index crime numbers are the lowest in every category since 1984.

Statistics	*2004*	*2003*	*2002*	*2001*
Murders	448	599	651	665
Criminal Sexual Assault	1,678	1,836	2,024	1,933
Robbery	15,914	17,328	18,530	18,450
Aggravated Assault and Battery	18,746	19,812	22,905	25,544
Burglary	24,425	25,151	25,613	26,009
Theft	93,245	97,921	97,468	97,939
Motor Vehicle Theft	22,803	22,729	25,098	27,689
Arson	782	947	1,016	1,004

Departments	*Address*	*Phone*	*Map*
1st District (Central)	1718 S State St	312-745-4290	11
9th District (Deering)	3501 S Lowe Ave	312-747-8227	13
21st District (Prairie)	300 E 29th St	312-747-8340	14
2nd District (Wentworth)	5101 S Wentworth Ave	312-747-8366	15
13th District (Wood)	937 N Wood St	312-746-8357	21
12th District (Monroe)	100 S Racine Ave	312-746-8309	24
14th District (Shakespeare)	2150 N California Ave	312-744-8290	27
18th District (Near North)	1160 N Larrabee St	312-742-5870	31
24th District (Rogers Park)	6464 N Clark St	312-744-5907	34
20th District (Foster)	5400 N Lincoln Ave	312-742-8714	35
19th District (Belmont)	2452 W Belmont Ave	312-744-5983	42
23rd District (Town Hall)	3600 N Halsted St	312-744-8320	44

Chicago hospitals are as varied and interesting as the citizens they serve. For one who isn't in the know, it would be easy to end up in a hospital where the only redeeming quality is that it is close to a bus line to a better hospital. That being said, you don't have to go far to find medical facilities in this city. Finding quality medical care is another story.

Chicago is home to a large and bustling "medical campus" on the near southwest side. Here you will find the brand-new **Stroger** hospital (basically the infamous Cook County Hospital with a facelift), which is actually several hospitals in one and home to the nation's first and oldest trauma unit. It is by far the busiest hospital in the area and serves a large and mostly indigent population. Unless you are in danger of certain demise, avoid Stroger's emergency department, since waits of up to 12 hours for a non-life-threatening reason may bore you to death. The medical campus is also home to the **University of Illinois Medical Center**, **Rush University Medical Center**, **Mt. Sinai Medical Center**, as well as several smaller hospitals.

On the north side, your best bet is to go to **Illinois Masonic Medical Center** for anything serious. **Northwestern Memorial Hospital** is also a good choice if you are closer to downtown and/or if you have really good insurance. They also house several hospitals in the same campus, and if you break your neck craning to look up at all the pretty skyscrapers in the Streeterville 'hood, they have a first-rate spinal cord unit.

On the south side, the **University of Chicago** hospitals are second to none. A large and imposing set of buildings set in a somewhat dubious neighborhood, the hospital has a first-rate children's emergency department, world-renowned staff, and an excellent reputation. Park on the street at your own risk—the garage may be expensive, but so is replacing your car stereo.

Hospital	*Address*	*Phone*	*Map*
Advocate Illinois Masonic Medical Ctr	836 W Wellington Ave	773-975-1600	43
Children's Memorial	707 W Fullerton Ave	773-880-4000	30
John H Stroger	1901 W Harrison	312-864-6000	25
Lincoln Park	550 W Webster Ave	773-883-2000	30
Louis A Weiss Memorial	4646 N Marine Dr	773-878-8700	40
Mercy	2525 S Michigan Ave	312-567-2000	11
Methodist Hospital of Chicago	5025 N Paulina St	773-271-9040	39
Michael Reese	2929 S Ellis Ave	312-791-2000	14
Mt Sinai	California Ave & 15th St	773-542-2000	50
Northwestern Memorial	251 E Huron St	312-926-2000	3
Provident	500 E 51st St	312-572-2000	16
Rush-Presbyterian St Luke's	1725 W Harrison St	312-942-5000	25
St Anthony's	2875 W 19th St	773-484-1000	25
St Elizabeth's	1431 N Claremont Ave	773-278-2000	21
St Joseph's	2900 N Lake Shore Dr	773-665-3000	44
St Mary of Nazareth	2233 W Division St	312-770-2000	21
Swedish Covenant	5145 N California Ave	773-878-8200	38
Thorek	850 W Irving Park Rd	773-525-6780	40
University of Chicago	5841 S Maryland Ave	773-702-1000	19
University of Chicago Children's Hospital	5721 S Maryland Ave	773-702-1000	19
University of Illinois at Chicago	1740 W Taylor St	312-996-1600	25
VA Lakeside Medical Center	333 E Huron St	312-569-8387	3
VA Medical Center	820 S Damen Ave	312-569-8387	25

The Chicago Public Library System has 75 branches serving Chicago citizens. Much to the delight of many Windy City book-borrowers, the city has recently constructed several new branches and renovated over 55 existing neighborhood branches with the help of a huge capital improvement program.

With the **Harold Washington Library** as their anchor, two regional libraries, **Sulzer Regional Library** in Lincoln Square and the Southwest side's **Woodson Library,** serve as backup reference and research collections. Neighborhood branches are geared towards the communities they serve: **Chinatown** has an impressive collection of Asian studies material and literature, the **Roger's Park** branch features a significant Russian Language selection, and Boystown's **John Merlo** collection houses a considerable offering of gay literature and studies. Many of the smaller branches have a decent selection of juvenile materials, as well as career guidance and adult popular literature (and Internet access). Architecturally, some of the more interesting branches include the **Chicago Bee** branch, the former newspaper headquarters that serves as a neighborhood landmark for Bronzeville, and the historic **Pullman** branch, which specializes in the history of the Pullman district. Chicago's first library branch, the neo-classical **Blackstone** library, is named after the Stockyards magnate. Families and schools should take advantage of the Chicago Public Library System's "Great Kids Museum Passports" available only to adult Chicago residents with a valid library card. You can check out any of their free passports using your library card, just like you would any other item, and the loan is good for one week. The pass entitles entry for up to 8 people to any one of the eleven participating cultural institutions in the city. For more information, call your local library or visit the general website at www.chipublib.org.

Chicago also has many excellent research libraries and university libraries, one of which is the independent **Newberry Library**, established in 1887. It shelves rare books, manuscripts, and maps, and hosts the raucous annual Bughouse Square debates in late July. Generally, Chicago's universities and colleges welcome the public to their libraries during specified hours, but it's best to call first and check.

Library	*Address*	*Phone*	*Map*
Albany Park Public Library	5150 N Kimball Ave	312-744-1933	38
Asher Library-Spertus Institute	618 S Michigan Ave	312-322-1749	9
Bessie Coleman Public Library	731 E 63rd St	312-747-7760	18
Bezazian Public Library	1226 W Ainslie St	312-744-0019	40
Blackstone Public Library	4904 S Lake Park Ave	312-747-0511	17
Budlong Woods Public Library	5630 N Lincoln Ave	312-742-9590	35
Canaryville Public Library	642 W 43rd St	312-747-0644	15
Chicago Bee Public Library	3647 S State St	312-747-6872	14
Chinatown Public Library	2353 S Wentworth Ave	312-747-8013	10
Daley Public Library	3400 S Halsted St	312-747-8990	13
Damen Avenue Library	2056 N Damen Ave	312-744-6022	28
Edgewater Public Library	1210 W Elmdale Ave	312-744-0718	37
Hall Public Library	4801 S Michigan Ave	312-747-2541	16
Harold Washington Public Library (Chicago Public Library Central Branch)	400 S State St	312-747-4300	5
Humboldt Park Public Library	1605 N Troy St	312-744-2244	27
Jefferson Park Public Library	5363 W Lawrence Ave	312-744-1998	48
John Merlo Public Library	644 W Belmont Ave	312-744-1139	44
Kelly Public Library	6151 S Normal Blvd	312-747-8418	57
King Public Library	3436 S Dr Martin L King Jr Dr	312-747-7543	14
Library of Columbia College	624 S Michigan Ave	312-344-7906	9
Lincoln Park Public Library	1150 W Fullerton Ave	312-744-1926	29
Lincoln-Belmont Public Library	1659 W Melrose St	312-744-0166	42
Logan Square Public Library	3255 W Altgeld St	312-744-5295	48
Lozano Public Library	1805 S Loomis St	312-746-4329	26
Mabel Manning Public Library	6 S Hoyne Ave	312-746-6800	23
Malcolm X College Library	1900 W Van Buren St	312-850-7244	23
Midwest Public Library	2335 W Chicago Ave	312-744-7788	23
Near North Public Library	310 W Division St	312-744-0992	31
Newberry Library	60 W Walton St	312-943-9090	32
Northtown Public Library	6435 N California Ave	312-744-2292	33
Rogers Park Public Library	6907 N Clark St	312-744-0156	34
Roosevelt Public Library	1101 W Taylor St	312-746-5656	26
Sullzer Public Library	4455 N Lincoln Ave	312-744-7616	39
University of Chicago Harper Memorial Library	1116 E 59th St	773-702-7959	19
University of Illinois at Chicago Library	801 S Morgan St	312-996-2726	26
Uptown Public Library	929 W Buena Ave	312-744-8400	40
US Library	77 W Jackson Blvd	312-353-2022	5

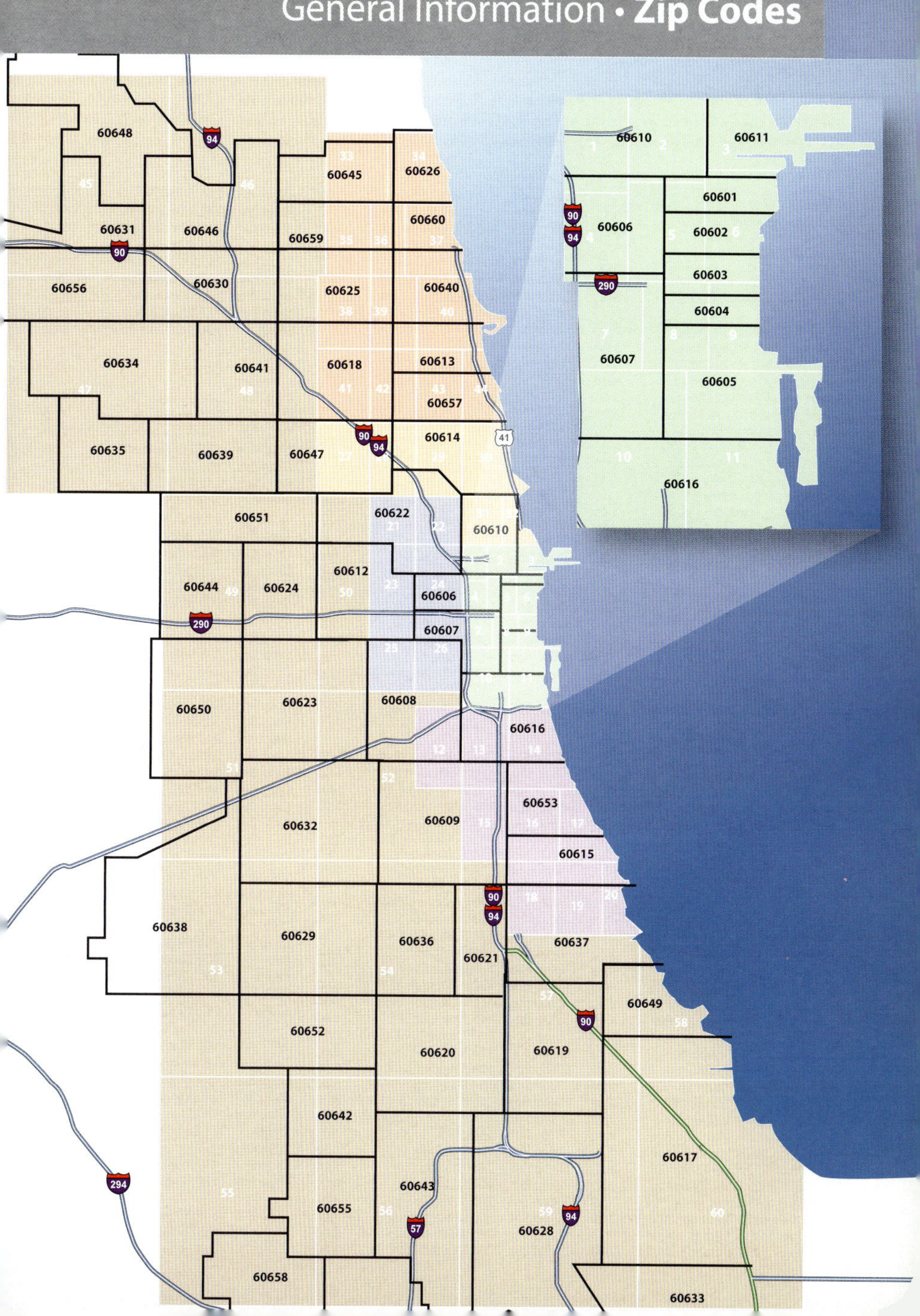
60648
94
60645
60626
60631
60646
60659
60660
90
60656
60630
60625
60640
60634
60641
60618
60613
60657
60635
60639
60647
90
94
60614
41
60651
60622
60610
60644
60624
60612
60606
290
60607
60650
60623
60608
60616
60632
60609
60653
60615
60638
60629
60636
60621
90
94
60637
60649
90
60652
60620
60619
60642
60617
294
60643
60655
57
60628
94
60658
60633
60610
60611
60601
90
94
60606
60602
60603
290
60604
60607
60605
60616

General Information • FedEx

The last FedEx drop in Chicago is at 10 pm at O'Hare Airport. Get off the Kennedy at Manheim Road South. Go to Irving Park Road and head west to the first light. Make a right on O'Hare Cargo Area Road. FedEx's address is Building 611, O'Hare Cargo Area Road (800-463-3339; www.fedex.com).

**=Pick-up time, pm; WSC=World Service Center*

Map 1

		*
Drop Box	400 W Erie St	7:30
Drop Box	430 W Erie St	7:30
Drop Box	600 W Chicago Ave	7:30
Drop Box	401 W Superior St	7:00
Drop Box	445 W Erie St	7:00
Drop Box	770 N Halsted St	7:00

Map 2

		*
WSC	222 Merch Mart Plz	9:00
WSC	350 N Clark St	9:00
Drop Box	205 W Wacker Dr	8:00
Drop Box	330 N Wabash Ave	8:00
Drop Box	420 N Wabash Ave	8:00
Drop Box	54 W Hubbard St	8:00
Drop Box	56 W Illinois St	8:00
Drop Box	77 W Wacker Dr	8:00
FedEx Kinko's	444 N Wells St	8:00
Drop Box	223 W Erie St	7:45
Drop Box	225 W Wacker Dr	7:30
Drop Box	308 W Erie St	7:30
Drop Box	311 W Superior St	7:30
Drop Box	343 W Erie St	7:30
Drop Box	401 N Wabash Ave	7:30
Drop Box	405 N Wabash Ave	7:30
Drop Box	414 N Orleans St	7:30
Drop Box	515 N State St	7:30
Drop Box	730 N Franklin St	7:30
Drop Box	1 E Wacker Dr	7:15
Drop Box	1 E Erie St	7:00
Drop Box	1 W Superior St	7:00
Drop Box	20 W Kinzie St	7:00
Drop Box	215 W Superior St	7:00
Drop Box	300 N State St	7:00
Drop Box	320 W Ohio St	7:00
Drop Box	444 N Wabash Ave	7:00
Drop Box	55 W Wacker Dr	7:00
Post Office	540 N Dearborn St	6:30
CompUsa	101 E Chicago Ave	6:00
Drop Box	325 N Wells St	6:00
Image Direct	211 W Wacker Dr	4:30

Map 3

		*
WSC	500 N Michigan Ave	9:00
Drop Box	233 E Erie St	8:00
Drop Box	303 E Ohio St	8:00
Drop Box	401 N Michigan Ave	8:00
Drop Box	680 N Lake Shore Dr	8:00
Drop Box	737 N Michigan Ave	8:00
Drop Box	150 E Huron St	7:30
Drop Box	211 E Ontario St	7:30
Drop Box	240 E Ontario St	7:30
Drop Box	251 E Huron St	7:30
Drop Box	333 E Ontario St	7:30
Drop Box	400 N McClurg Ct	7:30
Drop Box	400 N Michigan Ave	7:30
Drop Box	444 N Michigan Ave	7:30
Drop Box	505 N Lake Shore Dr	7:30
Drop Box	625 N Michigan Ave	7:30
Drop Box	633 N St Clair St	7:30
Drop Box	645 N Michigan Ave	7:30
Drop Box	430 N Michigan Ave	7:15
Drop Box	142 E Ontario St	7:00
Drop Box	211 E Chicago Ave	7:00
Drop Box	360 N Michigan Ave	7:00
Drop Box	401 E Illinois St	7:00
Drop Box	440 N McClurg Ct	7:00
Drop Box	455 E Illinois St	7:00
Drop Box	474 N Lake Shore Dr	7:00
Drop Box	676 N Michigan Ave	7:00
Drop Box	676 N St Clair St	7:00
FedEx Kinko's	540 N Michigan Ave	5:30

Map 4

		*
WSC	500 W Madison St	9:00
Drop Box	300 S Riverside Plz	8:30
Drop Box	550 W Washington Blvd	8:00
Drop Box	555 W Madison St	8:00
FedEx Kinko's	843 W Van Buren St	7:45
Drop Box	833 W Jackson Blvd	7:30
Drop Box	10 S Riverside Plz	7:00
Drop Box	100 N Riverside Plz	7:00
Drop Box	120 S Riverside Plz	7:00
Drop Box	2 N Riverside Plz	7:00
Drop Box	222 S Riverside Plz	7:00
Drop Box	322 S Green St	7:00
Drop Box	500 W Monroe St	7:00
Drop Box	547 W Jackson Blvd	7:00
Drop Box	550 W Jackson Blvd	7:00
Drop Box	641 W Lake St	7:00
Drop Box	651 W Washington Blvd	7:00
Drop Box	820 W Jackson Blvd	7:00
Drop Box	850 W Jackson Blvd	7:00
FedEx Kinko's	127 S Clinton St	7:00
Drop Box	600 W Jackson Blvd	6:30
Drop Box	130 S Jefferson St	6:00
Drop Box	730 W Randolph St	6:00
Drop Box	216 S Jefferson St	5:30

Map 5

		*
Drop Box	333 W Wacker Dr	9:00
WSC	111 W Washington	9:00
WSC	2 N La Salle St	9:00
WSC	200 W Jackson Blvd	9:00
WSC	227 W Monroe St	9:00
Drop Box	233 S Wacker Dr	8:30
Drop Box	1 N Franklin St	8:00
Drop Box	1 S Wacker Dr	8:00
Drop Box	100 W Monroe St	8:00
Drop Box	111 W Jackson Blvd	8:00
Drop Box	115 S La Salle St	8:00
Drop Box	120 N La Salle St	8:00
Drop Box	123 N Wacker Dr	8:00
Drop Box	125 S Wacker Dr	8:00
Drop Box	134 N La Salle St	8:00
Drop Box	150 S Wacker Dr	8:00
Drop Box	175 W Jackson Blvd	8:00
Drop Box	188 W Randolph St	8:00
Drop Box	190 S La Salle St	8:00
Drop Box	20 N Wacker Dr	8:00
Drop Box	200 N La Salle St	8:00
Drop Box	200 S Wacker Dr	8:00
Drop Box	200 W Madison St	8:00
Drop Box	205 W Randolph St	8:00
Drop Box	208 S La Salle St	8:00
Drop Box	210 S Clark St	8:00
Drop Box	222 N La Salle St	8:00
Drop Box	225 W Washington St	8:00
Drop Box	230 W Monroe St	8:00
Drop Box	250 S Wacker Dr	8:00
Drop Box	30 N La Salle St	8:00
Drop Box	30 S Wacker Dr	8:00
Drop Box	71 S Wacker Dr	8:00
FedEx Kinko's	203 N La Salle St	8:00
FedEx Kinko's	6 W Lake St	8:00
Drop Box	311 S Wacker Dr	7:45
Drop Box	10 S Wacker Dr	7:30
Drop Box	105 W Madison St	7:30
Drop Box	135 S La Salle St	7:30
Drop Box	150 N Wacker Dr	7:30
Drop Box	155 N Wacker Dr	7:30
Drop Box	180 N Wabash Ave	7:30
Drop Box	2 S Dearborn St	7:30
Drop Box	36 S Wabash Ave	7:30
Drop Box	407 S Dearborn St	7:30
Drop Box	1 N State St	7:00
Drop Box	100 N La Salle St	7:00
Drop Box	100 W Randolph St	7:00
Drop Box	11 E Adams St	7:00
Drop Box	171 N Clark St	7:00
Drop Box	191 N Wacker Dr	7:00
Drop Box	20 S Clark St	7:00
Drop Box	200 W Adams St	7:00
Drop Box	200 W Monroe St	7:00
Drop Box	203 N Wabash Ave	7:00
Drop Box	247 S State St	7:00
Drop Box	25 E Washington St	7:00
Drop Box	29 E Madison St	7:00
Drop Box	29 N Wacker Dr	7:00
Drop Box	30 W Monroe St	7:00
Drop Box	300 S Wacker Dr	7:00
Drop Box	303 W Madison St	7:00
Drop Box	309 W Washington St	7:00
Drop Box	33 N Dearborn St	7:00
Drop Box	401 S State St	7:00
Drop Box	53 W Jackson Blvd	7:00
Drop Box	55 E Jackson Blvd	7:00
Drop Box	55 W Monroe St	7:00
Drop Box	70 E Lake St	7:00
FedEx Kinko's	101 N Wacker Dr	7:00
FedEx Kinko's	29 S La Salle St	7:00
WSC	400 S La Salle	7:00
Drop Box	1 E Jackson Blvd	6:30
Drop Box	65 E Wacker Dr	6:30
Drop Box	209 S La Salle St	6:00
Drop Box	140 S Dearborn St	6:00
FedEx Kinko's	55 E Monroe St	6:00
Drop Box	230 S Dearborn St	5:45
Drop Box	219 S Dearborn St	5:30

Drop Box	844 N Rush St	6:00
Global	1151 N State St	6:00

Map 6		*
WSC	130 E Randolph St	9:00
WSC	225 N Michigan Ave	9:00
WSC	34 S Michigan Ave	9:00
Drop Box	150 N Michigan Ave	8:00
Drop Box	200 S Michigan Ave	8:00
Drop Box	224 S Michigan Ave	8:00
Drop Box	30 N Michigan Ave	8:00
Drop Box	300 E Randolph St	8:00
Drop Box	332 S Michigan Ave	8:00
Drop Box	333 N Michigan Ave	8:00
Post Office	200 E Randolph St	8:00
Drop Box	155 N Michigan Ave	7:30
Drop Box	8 S Michigan Ave	7:30
Drop Box	20 N Michigan Ave	7:00
Drop Box	307 N Michigan Ave	7:00
Drop Box	310 S Michigan Ave	7:00
Drop Box	35 E Wacker Dr	7:00
Drop Box	430 S Michigan Ave	7:00
Drop Box	233 N Michigan Ave	6:00
FedEx Kinko's	111 E Wacker Dr	6:00

Map 8		*
Drop Box	47 W Polk St	8:00
Drop Box	536 S Clark St	7:30
Drop Box	800 S Wells St	7:30
Drop Box	542 S Dearborn St	7:00
Drop Box	600 S Federal St	7:00
Drop Box	640 N La Salle St	7:00
FedEx Kinko's	700 S Wabash Ave	7:00
Drop Box	819 S Wabash Ave	5:00

Map 9		*
Drop Box	1000 N Lake Shore Dr	6:30

Map 10		*
FedEx Kinko's	1242 S Canal St	8:00
Drop Box	329 W 18th St	7:30

Map 11		*
Drop Box	1211 S Michigan Ave	7:00
Post Office	2035 S State St	5:00

Map 12		*
Drop Box	970 W Pershing Rd	6:00

Map 13		*
Business Services	3201 S Halsted St	6:00
Drop Box	3300 S Federal St	6:00
Drop Box	710 W 31st St	6:00

Map 14		*
Drop Box	10 W 35th St	6:00
PostNet	120 E 35th St	6:00

Map 19		*
Drop Box	1155 E 60th St	7:00
Drop Box	1525 E 53rd St	7:00
Drop Box	1554 E 55th St	7:00
Drop Box	5801 S Ellis Ave	7:00
FedEx Kinko's	1315 E 57th St	7:00
Drop Box	5841 S Maryland Ave	6:45
Drop Box	1126 E 59th St	6:30
Drop Box	59th & Kimbark	6:30
Drop Box	956 E 58th St	6:30

Map 20		*
Post Link	1634 E 53rd St	5:30

Map 21		*
Drop Box	1608 N Milwaukee Ave	8:00
FedEx Kinko's	1800 W North Ave	8:00
CopyMax	1573 N Milwaukee Ave	6:00

Map 22		*
WSC	875 W Division St	9:45
Drop Box	935 W Chestnut St	7:30
Drop Box	939 W North Ave	7:00
Drop Box	848 W Eastman St	6:45

Map 23		*
Drop Box	1700 W Van Buren	7:00
Packaging & Shipping Specialists	2002 W Chicago Ave	6:00
Drop Box	2023 W Carroll Ave	5:30

Map 24		*
WSC	1260 W Madison St	9:00
Drop Box	400 N Noble St	7:00
Drop Box	1550 W Carroll Ave	6:30
Drop Box	1030 W Chicago Ave	5:00

Map 25		*
Drop Box	1725 W Harrison St	6:30
Drop Box	820 S Damen Ave	6:00
Drop Box	715 S Wood St	4:00

Map 26		*
Drop Box	1100 W Cermak Rd	7:00
Drop Box	1201 W Harrison St	6:30
Drop Box	851 S Morgan St	5:30
University Village	1258 S Halsted St	5:00

Map 28		*
Drop Box	2525 N Elston Ave	7:30
CopyMax	1829 W Fullerton Ave	7:00
Drop Box	2355 N Damen Ave	7:00
Drop Box	1965 N Milwaukee Ave	4:00

Map 29		*
FedEx Kinko's	2300 N Clybourn Ave	8:00
Drop Box	990 W Fullerton Ave	7:15
Drop Box	2000 N Racine Ave	7:00
Drop Box	2323 N Seminary Ave	7:00

Map 30		*
Drop Box	802 W Belden Ave	7:15
Drop Box	1749 N Wells St	7:00
Drop Box	2500 N Clark St	7:00

Map 31		*
Drop Box	900 N Franklin St	8:00
Drop Box	213 W Institute Pl	7:30
Drop Box	820 N Orleans St	7:30
Drop Box	1333 N Kingsbury St	7:00
Drop Box	1350 N Wells St	7:00
Drop Box	900 N Kingsbury St	5:30

Map 32		*
WSC	875 N Michigan Ave	9:00
FedEx Kinko's	1201 N Dearborn St	8:00
Drop Box	1 E Delaware Pl	7:30
Drop Box	100 E Walton St	7:30
Drop Box	900 N Michigan Ave	7:00
Drop Box	919 N Michigan Ave	7:00
Drop Box	980 N Michigan Ave	7:00
Drop Box	1165 N Clark St	6:30
Drop Box	844 N Rush St	6:00
Global	1151 N State St	6:00

Map 33		*
Drop Box	7555 N California Ave	7:15
Unik Business	2337 W Devon Ave	7:00

Map 34		*
Post Office	1723 W Devon Ave	7:00
Post Office	7056 N Clark St	6:00

Map 36		*
Drop Box	5215 N Ravenswood Ave	6:00

Map 37		*
Drop Box	5419 N Sheridan Rd	7:30
Bedmar Courier	5655 N Clark St	6:30
Drop Box	6335 N Broadway St	6:30
Postal Mart	5250 N Broadway St	5:00

Map 38		*
Post Office	2522 W Lawrence Ave	7:00

Map 39		*
Drop Box	1807 W Sunnyside	7:30
Drop Box	4619 N Ravenswood Ave	7:00
Drop Box	1700 W Irving Park Rd	6:30
Drop Box	4001 N Ravenswood Ave	6:30
Remesas	1924 W Montrose Ave	6:00

Map 40		*
Drop Box	4753 N Broadway St	7:00
Post Office	4850 Broadway St	6:30
Mailstop	1338 W Irving Park Rd	5:30
Dcii	4539 N Sheridan Rd	5:00

Map 41		*
Drop Box	2704 W Roscoe St	7:00
Drop Box	3401 N California Ave	7:00
Drop Box	3611 N Kedzie Ave	7:00
Drop Box	2630 W Bradley Pl	6:30

Map 42		*
FedEx Kinko's	3435 N Western Ave	7:45
Drop Box	1800 W Larchmont Ave	7:30
Drop Box	3717 N Ravenswood Ave	7:00
Mailbox Plus	2154 W Addison St	6:00

Map 43		*
Drop Box	1300 W Belmont Ave	7:30
FedEx Kinko's	3524 N Southport	7:30
Post Office	3024 N Ashland Ave	6:00

Map 44		*
FedEx Kinko's	3001 N Clark St	8:00
Drop Box	3660 N Lake Shore Dr	7:30
Drop Box	2800 N Sheridan Rd	7:00
Postal Place	3304 N Broadway	6:30
Postal Plus	559 W Diversey Pkwy	6:00
PostNet	636 W Diversey Pkwy	6:00

Chicago's lesbian and gay communities are a diverse, politically influential presence within the city. Just look to the pride pylons lining North Halsted Street, the city's officially recognized gay ghetto, as well as the numerous city politicians who vie for a prime spot in the city's annual gay pride parade, which attracts over 200,000 spectators and participants on the last Sunday in June.

Gay life in Chicago is not just limited to Halsted, though, nor is it relegated to the last week in June. From Edgewater to South Shore to Humbolt Park, gays and lesbians have become visible entities in many of Chicago's far-reaching 'hoods, notwithstanding the hundreds who live quietly in domestic bliss from Edison Park to Pullman.

With such a diverse array of lesbigay life thriving in the city, it's no wonder that the city's lesbigay offerings are equally diverse. Whether your interests are activism or acupuncture, draperies or drag kings, literature, liturgies, or leather bars, or some combination of the above, you can find your niche in Chicago.

Note: This listing was compiled with the help of the *OUT! Guide* and *Windy City Media Group*, publishers of the *OUT! Guide*, *Windy City Times*, *Nightspots*, *Identity*, and producers of Windy City Radio, www.windycitymedia.com

Publications/Media

Pick up a copy of the following publications, log onto a website, or tune in to find out what's happening around town, from the current political headlines to the hottest clubs. Gay rags can be found in gay-friendly bookstores, cafés, bars, and various shops.

Windy City Times • www.wctimes.com
Gay and Lesbian news weekly—check this site for a calendar of events.

Identity • A cross-cultural GLBT monthly, focusing on race, gender, and culture published by Windy City Media Group.

Nightspots • www.outlineschicago.com/nightlines.html • Columns, astrology, and happenings around town. Sassy!

OUT! Guide • Comprehensive GLBT resource guide with listings for services including therapists, carpenters, real estate brokers, accounting services, social services, restaurants, and much, much more. Indispensable!

Chicago Free Press • www.chicagofreepress.com
Weekly publication with features on political issues, arts, culture, spiritual life, entertainment, and resource lists.

Gay Chicago • www.gaychicagomag.com • One of the city's oldest gay publications, with events listings, columns, news, astrology, and reviews. Male-focused.

Boi • Heavily advertising-based guide to the club scene for circuit boys.

Dyke Diva • www.dykediva.com • An online guide, for gals, of Chicago events and happenings.

Windy City Radio • Tune in Sunday nights, 11 pm–midnight, on WCKG, 105.9 FM, or tune in online at www.WindyCityRadio.com anytime.

Arts & Culture

Women & Children First Books • 5233 N Clark St
773-769-9299 • This 20-year-old lesbian resource in Andersonville is the largest feminist bookstore in the world. Hosts events and discussions regularly.

Unabridged Books • 3251 N Broadway St
773-883-9119 • Largest gay selection in the city, located in the heart of the Boys Town. You will find a well-annotated book selection, as well as calendars and magazines.

Gerber/Hart Gay and Lesbian Library and Archives • 1127 W Granville St • 773-381-8030
This amazing library houses more than 10,000 books, magazines, newspapers, and videos. Regularly hosts both gay and lesbian book discussion groups. For special events including readings and screenings, check the website at www.gerberhart.org.

Barbara's Bookstore • 1110 N Lake St, Oak Park
Gay-friendly bookstore with a large selection of gay and lesbian fiction and non-fiction titles.

Seminary Cooperative Bookstore
5757 University Ave • 773-752-4381
Located in Hyde Park, this bookstore has sections on GLBT studies.

57th Street Books • 1301 E 57th St • 773-684-1300
Another Hyde Park bookstore with a strong GLBT section.

Specialty Video • 3221 N Broadway St • 773-248-3434; 5307 N Clark • 773-878-3434
Huge selection of gay and lesbian videos and DVDs. Dirty movies in the back.

Chicago Filmmakers • 5243 N Clark St • 773-293-1447 • Sponsors of the Chicago Lesbian and Gay International Film Festival.

Chicago Lesbian & Gay International Film Festival • www.chicagofilmmakers.org/reeling • Movies by and about LGBT.

Facets Multimedia • 1517 W Fullerton Ave 773-281-9075 • Large selection of gay arthouse films.

About Face Theatre • 773-784-8565 Roving gay & lesbian theatre company.

Bailiwick Repertory Theatre • 1229 W Belmont Ave • 773-883-1090 • Sponsors annual Gay Pride theatre festival.

Theatre Building • 1225 W Belmont Ave • 773-327-5252 • Many gay theatre productions are mounted here.

Aldo Castillo Gallery • 230 W Huron St 312-337-2536 • Fine arts gallery with lesbigay latino/a bent.

Woman Made Gallery • 2418 W Bloomingdale 773-489-8900 • www.womanmade.org Regularly features lesbian artists.

Las Manos Gallery • 5220 N Clark St • 773-728-8910 • Lesbian-owned and -operated, regularly features gay and lesbian artists.

Mountain Moving Coffeehouse for Women & Children • 1650 W Foster Ave • 312-409-0276 Alcohol- and smoke-free woman-only performance venue, with events most Saturdays.

Literary Exchange • PO Box 238583, 60643 773-509-6881 • Black lesbian writers' group publishes the 'zine *Literary Express*.

Blithe House Quarterly • www.blithe.com • Online gay & les literary journal published from Chicago.

Artemis Singers • PO Box 578296, 60657 773-764-4465 • Lesbian-feminist chorus.

Chicago Gay Men's Chorus • 3540 N Southport Ave, PO Box 333, 60657 • 773-773-296-0541 www.cgmc.org • The name says it all. Mounts fun, campy annual Christmas concert.

Windy City Gay Chorus • 3023 N Clark St 773-404-WCGC• Sponsers four different gay choruses, including UNISON and The Slickers.

Lakeside Pride Freedom Band www.lakesidepride.org • 773-381-6693 Chicago's gay & lesbian marching band. Doesn't every city have one?

The Finger @ Early to Bed • 5232 N Sheridan Rd 773-271-1219 • Queer open mike every third Sunday, hosted by the inimitable Nomy Lamm.

Homelatte • www.scottfree.net • Weekly queer reading series with writers and musicians.

Chicago Kings • www.chicagokings.com Chicago's premier female-to-male drag troupe. Hosts monthly party, Kingdom Come, every last Friday at Circuit nightclub.

Sports & Recreation

Chi-Town Squares • PO Box 269149 • 773-339-6743 • Gay and lesbian square dancing—what else?

Chicago Metropolitan Sports Association www.ChicagoMSA.com • 312-409-7932 Organizes all variety of gay and lesbian competitive athletics: bowling, softball, etc.

Chicago Smelts • 3712 N Broadway St • 312-409-7932 • Gay & lesbian swim club.

Frontrunners/Frontwalkers • www.frfwchicago.org • 312-409-2790 Weekly LBG running and walking group sponsers annual "Proud to Run" race.

Gay Games Chicago • www.gaygameschicago.org Gay Games Chicago 2006 Official Website. Start signing up for events now!

Windy City Rodeo• 312-409-3835 • Rope 'em up, rough riders.

Leaping Lesbians • www.leapinglesbians.org Recreational Sapphic skydiving.

Team Chicago Athletics • PO Box 13470, 60613 312-409-5155 • Chicago's Gay Games team.

Thousand Waves Spa • 1212 W Belmont 773-549-0700 • Women-only spa offers herb wraps and massages, along with jacuzzi, steam room, and sauna.

Windy City Athletic Association • www.wcaa.net 773-327-WCAA • Also organizes gay and lesbian competitive sports.

Social Groups/Organizations

Men of All Colors Together (MACT) • PO Box 408922, 60640 • 312-409-6916

Amigas Latinas Lesbianas/Bisexuales www.AmigasLatinas.org • 312-409-5697

Association of Latin Men for Action (ALMA) info@almachicago.org • 773-929-7688

Asians & Friends, Chicago • www.afchicago.org 312-409-1573

P-FLAG • Parents & Friends of Lesbians and Gays www.pflag.org

Chicagoland Bisexual Network www.bisexual.org/chicagoland

Chicago Gender Society • PO Box 578005, 60657 708-863-7714

Political Groups/Activism

Equality Illinois • 3712 N Broadway St, #125, 60613 773-477-7173

Human Rights Campaign Chicago • 312-409-9129

Illinois G&L Political Action Network 847-856-0064

Oak Park Area Lesbians/Gays • 708-848-0273

Stonewall Democrats • 3712 N Broadway • 312-683-5232

Religious Services

AIDS Pastoral Care Network • APCN@aol.com 4753 N Broadway St, #400, 60640 • 773-334-5333

Archdiocesan Gay and Lesbian Outreach (AGLO) 711 Belmont Ave, #106, 60657 • 773-525-3872 Roman Catholic

Broadway United Methodist Church 3344 N Broadway St • 773-348-2679 • Reconciling

Church of the Open Door • 5954 S Albany Ave, 60629 • 773-778-3030 • Black LBGT church

Congregation Or Chadash • 656 W Barry Ave, 60657 • 773-248-9456 • LBGT synagogue

Dignity Chicago • www.dignitychicago.org 312-458-9438 • LBGT Catholic

Good Shepherd Parish and Christ the Redeemer MCC • 7045 N Western Ave, 60645 • 773-275-7776 Non-denominational

Integrity/Chicago • PO Box 3232, Oak Park, 60303 773-348-6362 • Episcopal, meets 3rd Friday for Eucharist/reception

Lake Street Church of Evanston • 607 Lake St, Evanston • 847-864-2181 • Inside/Out GL group

Pilgrim Congregational Church • 460 Lake St, Oak Park • 708-848-5860 • Actively inclusive

Resurrection MCC • 5757 S University Ave, 60637 773-288-1535 • Non-demominational

Vajrayana Buddhist Center • 3534 N Hoyne Ave, 60618 • 773-529-1862

Health Center & Support Organizations

Horizons Community Services www.horizonsonline.org • The Midwest's largest lesbian, gay, bisexual, and transgendered social service agency.

- **Lesbian and Gay Help Line** • 773-929-HELP (6 pm until 10 pm)
- **The Crisis Hotline/Anti-Violence Project** 773-871-CARE
- **Legal Services** • 773-929-HELP legal@horizonsonline.org
- **Mature Adult Program** • 773-472-6469 x245 perryw@horizonsonline.org
- **Psychotherapy Services** • 773-472-6469 x261 sarag@horizonsonline.org
- **Youth Services** • 773-472-6469, ext 252 premp@horizonsonline.org

Illinois State HIV/AIDS/STD Hotline 772-AID-AIDS

AIDS Foundation of Chicago • 411 Wells St, Ste 300, Chicago, IL 60607 • 312-922-2322 A charitable foundation, not a direct service provider.

AIDSCARE • 315 W Barry Ave, Chicago, IL 60657 773-935-4663

GLAAD Chicago • PO Box 46343, Chicago, IL 60614 773-871-7633

PFLAG Chicago • PO Box 11023, Chicago, IL 60611 773-472-3079

Howard Brown Health Center • 4025 N Sheridan Rd • 773-388-8882 • General counseling as well as anonymous, free AIDS-testing and GLBT Domestic Violence Counseling and Prevention Program. Also provides general practitioner care for men and women, on a sliding fee scale.

Lesbian Community Cancer Project • Howard Brown Health Center • Support and resources for lesbians with cancer. Free quit-smoking clinics.

AA – New Town Alano Club • 909 W Belmont Ave, 2nd Fl • 773-529-0321 • Gay and lesbian AA , CA, OA, ACOA, Coda, etc.

Support Groups • Many support groups exist for men, women, and families in Chicago. Call Howard Brown or Horizons for referrals.

Bars & Clubs

Gay

- **Anvil** • 1137 W Granville St • 773-973-0006 Leather/Levis old-school joint.
- **Bucks Saloon** • 3439 N Halsted St • 773-525-1125 Typical gay watering hole.
- **Cell Block** • 3702 N Halsted St • 773-665-8064 Leather bar.
- **Charlie's** • 3726 N Broadway St • 773-871-8887 Country & Western.
- **Chicago Eagle** • 5015 N Clark St • 773-728-0050 Leather bar with back room.
- **Hunter's** • 1932 E Higgins Rd, Elk Grove Village 847-439-8840 • Dance/video bar in the 'burbs.
- **Little Jims** • 3501 N Halsted St • 773-871-6116 Neighborhood bar, 4 am license.
- **Lucky Horseshoe** • 3169 N Halsted St • 773-404-3169 Male dancers.
- **Madrigals** • 5316 N Clark St • 773-334-3033 Women welcome, male dancers.
- **Manhandler** • 1948 N Halsted St • 773-871-3339 Country & Western.
- **North End** • 3733 N Halsted St • 773-477-7999 Another bar on the strip.
- **Nutbush** • 7201 W Franklin St, Forest Park 708-366-5117 • Video bar in the 'burbs.
- **Second Story Bar** • 157 E Ohio St • 312-923-9536 • Streeterville hideout.
- **Sidetrack** • 3349 N Halsted St • 773-477-9189 • Huge video bar, women welcome.
- **Touché** • 6412 N Clark St • 773-465-7400 • Far North leather bar.
- **Annex** • 3160 N Clark St • 773-327-5969 • Video bar.

Lesbian

- **The Closet** • 3325 N Broadway St • 773-477-8533 4 am license, men welcome.
- **Club Intimus** • 312 W Randolph St • 312-901-1703 Roving women's dance party. Call for info.
- **Lost & Found** • 3058 W Irving Park Rd 773-463-7599 • Old-school women's bar with door buzzer and billiards.
- **The Patch** • 201 155th St, Calumet City 708-891-3980 • 4 am license, entertainment sometimes.
- **StarGaze** •5419 N Clark St • 773-561-7363 • Restaurant, dancing, Salsa nights.
- **Temptations** • 10235 W Grand Ave, Franklin Park 847-455-0008 • Entertainment and dancing in the land of the big hair.
- **Chix Mix** • www.chixmixproductions.com Roving women's dance parties.

Both

- **Berlin** • 54 W Belmont Ave • 773-348-4975 • Mixed dance clubs. Women-only nights every first and third Wednesday.
- **Big Chicks** • 5024 N Sheridan Rd • 773-728-5511 Mostly men. Very crowded on weekends.

Charmers 1507 W Jarvis Ave • 773-465-2811 • Art Deco neighborhood bar.

- **Circuit/Rehab** • 3641 N Halsted St 773-325-2233 • Big nightclub. Women's nights on some Fridays.
- **Clark's on Clark** • 5001 N Clark St • 773-728-2373 4 am license, mostly men.
- **Club Escape** • 1530 E 75th St • 773-667-6454 Mixed dance venue, some entertainment.
- **Cocktail** • 3359 N Halsted St • 773-477-1420 Dancing plus male dancers.
- **Gentry on Halsted** • 3320 N Halsted St 773-348-1053 • Cabaret shows, piano bar.
- **Gentry on State** • 440 N State St • 312-836-0933 Cabaret shows, piano bar.
- **Jeffery Pub** • 7041 S Jeffery St • 773-363-8555 4 am, Southside institution, dancing.
- **Roscoe's** • 3356 N Halsted St • 773-281-3355 Mostly men, cavernous, dancing, videos, café.
- **Scot's** • 1829 W Montrose Ave • 773-528-3253 Mostly men, friendly neighborhood bar.
- **Spin Nightclub** • Halsted St & Belmont Ave 773-327-7711 • Mostly men, dancing.
- **T's Bar & Restaurant** • 5025 N Clark St 773-784-6000 • Not gay-exclusive, *very* gay-friendly. Bar food.
- **Pour House** • 103 155th St, Calumet City 708-891-3980 • 4 am, dancing.
- **Atmosphere** • 5355 N Clark St • 773-784-1100 Neighborhood bar, dancing.
- **Escapades** • 6301 S Harlem Ave • 773-229-0886 4 am license, dancing, videos.
- **Hydrate** • 3458 N Halsted St • Former Manhole, now a mixed fern bar.
- **Lola's** • 1005 N Western Ave • 773-862-7208 Mixed drag-friendly bar in Ukranian Village.

Forget **Wrigley Field,** the **Water Tower**, and **Buckingham Fountain**. Alright, maybe we didn't forget those emblems of the city in the listings below. Nonetheless, some of the city's landmarks nearest to locals' hearts are those obscure sites only known by insiders. Whose instructions for anything in Uptown don't include its proximity to the **Uptown Theatre**? Who doesn't look for the **Morton Salt Girl** when traversing Elston? For years Chicago lesbians have used the **totem pole** at Waveland and the lake as a rallying point for weekend softball games, and **St. Ben's Church** has become an anchor for an entire neighborhood.

The **Pacific Garden Mission** (which recently announced plans to relocate to a plot at 14th Place and Canal Street…in two years) keeps trying to lure unwitting audiences with free tickets to the long-running radio drama *UNSHACKLED!* Eventually everyone ends up sopping up the booze in their stomach with a late-night or early morning omelette, flaming saganaki, and giant piece of cake at 24-hour **Zorba's** in Greektown. The **Marina Towers** reach for the sky like two heaven-bound corn cobs. The **Union Stockyard Gates**, and the memory of bubbly creek, where all the butchered remains were disposed of, remind us of our less than savory industrial past. A reminder of another kind comes with the moving **Monument to the Great Northern Migration** located at 26th and King Drive, celebrating the historic migration of African Americans, who traveled from the south looking for opportunities.

The giant, neon-lit hot dog sweethearts on top of the Northwest Side's **Superdawg** have been winking at passersby for decades. On the Southwest Side, the not-quite-p.c. dime-store Indian atop **Capital Cigar Store** has been enticing would-be smokers for at least as long.

Map 1 • River North / Fulton Market District

The Blommer Chocolate Co	600 W Kinzie St • 312-226-7700	Opened in 1939. Eventually became largest commercial chocolate manufacturer in the US.

Map 2 • Near North / River North

Courthouse Place	54 W Hubbard St	This Romanesque-style former courthouse has witnessed many legendary trials.
House of Blues	329 N Dearborn St • 312-923-2000	Concert venue, hotel, and bowling alley.
Marina Towers	300 N State St	Bertrand Goldberg's riverside masterwork. Love the parking.
Merchandise Mart	222 Merchandise Mart Plz • 312-527-7600	Houses furniture showrooms and a small mall.
Sotheby's	215 W Ohio St • 312-396-9599	Renowned auction house.

Map 3 • Streeterville / Mag Mile

Navy Pier	600 E Grand Ave • 312-595-5300	A bastion of Chicago tourism.
Tribune Tower	435 N Michigan Ave • 312-222-2116	Check out the stones from famous buildings around the world—including a real-life rock from the moon!

Map 4 • West Loop Gate / Greek Town

Dugan's Drinking Emporium	128 S Halsted St • 312-421-7191	Sports bar in Greektown. Fantastic beer garden and favorite cop hangout.
Union Station	200 S Canal St • 312-322-4269	Built in 1925, the architecture is not to be missed!
Zorba's House Restaurant	301 S Halsted St • 312-454-1397	24-hour Greek food—hangout for cops and hospital workers; everybody ends up here sooner or later.

Map 5 • The Loop

Chicago Board of Trade	141 W Jackson Blvd • 312-435-3590	The goddess Ceres tops this deco monolith.
Chicago Board Options Exchange	400 S La Salle St • 312-786-5600	The world's largest options market.
Chicago Cultural Center	78 E Washington St • 312-744-FINEART	The spot for free lectures, exhibits, concerts and movies.
Chicago Mercantile Exchange	20 S Wacker Dr • 312-930-1000	Economics at work in polyester jackets.
Chicago Stock Exchange	440 S La Salle St • 312-663-2222	The second largest stock exchange in the country.
Daley Civic Plaza	50 W Washington St • 312-443-5500	Home of Picasso sculpture, Christmas tree ceremony, and alfresco lunches.
Harold Washington Library Center	400 S State St • 312-747-4300	The world's largest public library building; nearly 100 works of art on every floor.
Sears Tower	233 S Wacker Dr • 312-875-9696	Tallest building in the US with a cool skydeck.

Map 6 • The Loop / Grant Park

Art Institute of Chicago	111 S Michigan Ave • 312-443-3600	World-class art museum.
Auditorium Building	430 S Michigan Ave • 312-431-2354	Designed by Louis Sullivan; on National Register of Historic Places.
Fine Arts Building	410 S Michigan Ave • 312-427-7602	Frank Lloyd Wright had an office here.
Symphony Center	22 S Michigan Ave • 312-294-3000	Classical music headquarters.

Map 7 • South Loop / River City

Old Post Office	404 W Harrison St	Straddling I-90/94 and I-290 as they enter downtown, this massive, vacant edifice is a benchmark for traffic reports.
River City	800 S Wells St	A fluid cement design experiment built by architect Bertrand Goldberg in the '80s; considered a flop, but actually brilliant.
US Postal Distribution Center	433 W Harrison St • 312-983-8391	The city's main mail routing center, employing over 6,000 people and operating 24 hours a day.

Map 8 • South Loop / Printers Row / Dearborn Park

Columbia College Center for Book & Paper Arts	1104 S Wabash Ave, 2nd Fl • 312-344-6630	Two galleries feature changing exhibits of handmade books, paper, letterpress, and other related objects.
Former Elliot Ness Building	618 S Dearborn St	Former headquarters of Elliot Ness. Now an insurance agency.
Old Dearborn Train Station	47 W Polk St	Turn-of-the-century train station with a lighted clocktower visible for several blocks. Al Capone took a train to prison from here.

Map 9 • South Loop / South Michigan Ave

Buckingham Fountain	Columbus Dr & E Congress Pkwy	Built of pink marble; inspired by Versailles.
Chicago Hilton and Towers	720 S Michigan Ave • 312-922-4400	Check out the frescoes in the lobby; sneak a kiss in the palatial ballroom.
Julian and Doris Wineberg Sculpture Garden	681 S Michigan Ave	A tranquil spot to ponder traffic on Michigan Avenue.
Shedd Aquarium	1200 S Lake Shore Dr • 312-939-2435	Marine and freshwater creatures from around the world are on view in this 1929 Classical Greek-inspired Beaux Arts structure.

Map 10 • East Pilsen / Chinatown

Chinatown Gate	S Wentworth Ave & W Cermak Rd	Built in 1976. The characters on the gate read "The world belongs to the people."
Chinatown Square	S Archer Ave	Near S Wentworth in the Chinatown Square Plaza.
On Leong Merchants Association Building	2216 S Wentworth Ave • 312-328-1188	1926 Oriental-style building inspired by architecture of the Kwangtung district of China. Now the home of the Pui Tak Center.
Ping Tom Memorial Park	300 W 19th St • 312-747-7661	Park with Chinese landscape elements.

Map 11 • South Loop / McCormick Place

America's Courtyard	South of Adler Planetarium on the lakefront	A spiral of stones that echoes both the milky way and ancient structures. Designed by Denise Milan and Ary R. Perez.
The Chicago Daily Defender	2400 S Michigan Ave • 312-225-5656	Founded in 1905, it was the country's most influential black newspaper through the '50s. Still in operation, but much-diminished.
Clarke House	1827 S Indiana Ave	Built in 1836 by an unknown architect, this Greek Revival-style home has been relocated twice and is now an official Chicago landmark.
Field Museum	1400 S Lake Shore Dr • 312-922-9410	Go see Sue, the largest, most complete, and best preserved T. rex ever found.
Hillary Rodham Clinton Women's Park and Gardens of Chicago	S Prairie Ave, b/w 18th & 19th Sts	A garden from a former first lady.
Hyatt Regency McCormick Place	2233 S Dr Martin L King Jr Dr • 312-567-1234	The only hotel attached to the city's main convention center.
McCormick Place	2301 S Lake Shore Dr • 312-791-7000	Hard to miss.
Merrill C Meigs Field	Waterfront	Airport bulldozed by Mayor Daley in the Midnight Meigs Massacre.
National Vietnam Veterans Art Museum	1801 S Indiana Ave • 312-326-0270	Features art about the war created by Vietnam veterans from all sides of the conflict.
Quinn Chapel, African Methodist Episcopal Church	2401 S Wabash Ave • 312-791-1846	Built in 1892, this Victorian Gothic-style church houses Chicago's oldest African American congregation. Martin Luther King, Jr was here.
Raymond Hilliard Homes	2030 S State St	Designed by Bertrand Goldberg (of the River City apartments). There are plans to rehab the public housing complex into upscale rentals.
Second Presbyterian Church	1936 S Michigan Ave • 312-225-4951	This Gothic Revival-style church was built in 1874 by James Renwirk, then reconstructed in 1900 by Howard Van Doren Shaw.
Soldier Field	425 E McFetridge Dr • 312-747-1285	A once-antiquated arena is now a world-class stadium for Da Bears and concert events.
The Wheeler Mansion	2020 S Calumet Ave • 312-945-2020	This Second Empire-style mansion now houses a boutique hotel for high-end travelers.
Willie Dixon's Blues Heaven Foundation	2120 S Michigan Ave • 312-808-1286	Former Chess Records studio where many influential '60s blues & rock albums were recorded. Tours, exhibits, workshops, and performances.

Map 12 • Bridgeport (West)

Library Fountain	W 34th St & Halsted St	Pretty water.
Monastery of the Holy Cross	3111 S Aberdeen St • 773-927-7424	Have your breakfast served by monks in this bed & breakfast monastery.
Wilson Park	S May St & W 34th Pl	A nice respite in the middle of the city.

Map 13 • Bridgeport (East)

McGuane Park	W 29th St & S Halsted St	A park for playing.
Old Neighborhood Italian American Club	3031 S Shields Ave • 312-326-6420	Founded by Angelo LaPietra, a former high-ranking Chicago mobster, after his release from Leavenworth.
Richard J Daley House	3536 S Lowe Ave	Childhood home of Mayor Richard J. Daley.

Map 14 • Prairie Shores / Lake Meadows

Chicago Bee Building	3647-55 S State	Formerly the HQ of the Chicago Bee Newspaper; now offices.
Douglas Tomb	E 35th St & Lake Park	Entrance on East side of Lake.
Dunbar Park	S Indiana Ave & E 31st St	Dunbar High's girl's softball team plays here.
Ida B Wells / Barsnett home	3624 S King Dr	Former home of the journalism and civil rights pioneer.
Interesting Benches	S Dr Martin L King Jr Dr b/w E 33rd St & E 35th St	13 artists created these 24 unique bench sculptures. Sit on it.
Monument to the Great Northern Migration	S Dr Martin L King Jr Dr & E 26th St	Statue by Alison Sarr depicts a man in a shoe suit atop a pile of old shoes. Represents the journey of African Americans from the south.

Map 15 • Canaryville / Fuller Park

Union Stockyard Gate	Exchange Ave & Peoria St	This limestone gate marks the place that made Chicago the "Hog Butcher to the World."

Map 16 • Bronzeville

Bronzeville Walk of Fame	Martin Luther King Jr. Blvd from 25th St to 47th St	Features 91 bronze plaques laid upon 1.5 miles of sidewalk honoring significant African Americans who lived there, such as Joe Louis and Sammy Davis, Jr.
Metcalf Park	4130-4300 S State St	It's a park!
Mural	3947 S Michigan Ave	Painted in 1979, *Another Time's Voice Remembers My Passion's Humanity* by Mitchell Caton and Calvin Jones, is on an outside wall of the Donnelley Youth Center.
Mural	49th St & S Wabash Ave	Painted by William Walker in 1974 entitled *History of the Packinghouse Worker*. Located on an exterior wall of the abandoned United Packinghouse Workers.

Map 17 • Kenwood

Louis Farrakhan Home	4855 S Woodlawn	Well-guarded home of the leader of the Nation of Islam.
South Kenwood Mansions	b/w S Dorchester Ave (east), S Ellis Ave (west), S Hyde Park Blvd (south), & E 47th St (north)	Built in the early 1900s by wealthy businessmen looking to flee the cramped North Side. Once in a state of disrepair, the mansions have (mostly) been rehabbed, and are still the Jewels of the South Side.

Map 18 • Washington Park

Aquatic Center & Refectory	5531 S Martin Luther King Jr Dr • 773-256-1248	Designed by Daniel Burnham's firm, the Refectory now holds locker rooms for the Aquatic Center and its 36-foot waterslide.
DuSable Museum of African-American History	740 E 56th Pl • 773-947-0600	Founded in 1961 and dedicated to preserving and honoring African-American culture. The oldest non-profit institution of its kind.
Former Home of Black Panther Jesse Binga	5922 S Dr Martin L King Jr Dr	Home of nation's first African-American banker.
Washington Park	E 60th St thru E 51st St, from S Cottage Grove Ave to S Dr Martin L King Jr Dr	A sprawling 367-acre park with beautiful lagoons and fields. Check out the "Fountain of Time" sculpture.

Map 19 • Hyde Park

Frederick C Robie House	5757 S Woodlawn Ave	Designed by Frank Lloyd Wright; renovations procceding.
Midway Plaisance Park & Skating Rink	S Ellis Ave & S University Ave, from E 59th to E 60th Sts • 312-747-0233	Olympic-sized outdoor skating rink.
Nichol's Park	1300 E 55th St	Home of the Parrots of Hyde Park.
Nuclear Energy Sculpture	5600 Block S Ellis	Birthplace of the Atomic Age.
Rockefeller Memorial Chapel	5850 S Woodlawn Ave • 773-702-2100	Authentic English cathedral built in 1928.

Map 20 • East Hyde Park / Jackson Park

Osaka Garden/Wooded Island	just south of the Museum of Science and Industry, b/w the West and East Lagoons	A Japanese garden in the middle of Jackson Park—why not?
Promontory Point Park	5491 S Shore Dr	Picnic with a view.

Map 21 • Wicker Park / Ukrainian Village

Coyote Building	1600 N Milwaukee Ave	This 12-story Art Deco building was constructed in 1929.
Crumbling Bucktown	1579 N Milwaukee Ave	Structural icon seen from miles away; nucleus of Around the Coyote Arts Festival.

Division Street Russian Bath	1916 W Division St • 773-384-9671	Treat yourself to an old-school day at the spa, complete with Swedish massages and a granite heating room.
Flat Iron Building	1579 N Milwaukee Ave	This distinct triangular-shaped building is a part of the Chicago Coalition of Community Cultural Centers and houses artist studios.
Holy Trinity Orthodox Cathedral and Rectory	1121 N Leavitt St • 773-486-6064	Designed by Louis Sullivan to look like a Russian cathedral.
Wicker Park	Pierce & Hoyne Sts	The homes in this district reflect the style of Old Chicago.

Map 22 • Noble Square / Goose Island

House of Crosses	1544 W Chestnut St	Eccentric owners have coverer the property with hundreds of wooden crosses.
Morton Salt Elston Facility	Elston Ave & Blackhawk St	Has a painting of the famous salt girl.
Nelson Algren Fountain	Division St & Ashland Blvd	Has a recent controversial addition.
North Avenue Bridge	W North Ave	Wretched traffic jams; river view.
Polish Museum of America	984 N Milwaukee Ave • 773-384-3352	Right-to-life painting on the side.
Pulaski Park/Pulaski Fieldhouse	Blackhawk St & Cleaver St	Has an outdoor swimming pool.
St Stanislaus Kostka Church	1351 W Evergreen Ave • 773-278-2470	One of the oldest in Chicago.
Weed Street District	b/w Chicago River & Halsted St	Several bars and clubs in one area.

Map 23 • West Town / Near West Side

First Baptist Congregational Church	1613 W Washington Blvd • 312-243-8047	Official Chicago landmark.
Metropolitan Missionary Baptist Church	2151 W Washington Blvd • 312-738-0053	Official Chicago landmark.
Ukrainian Cultural Center	2247 W Chicago Ave • 773-384-6400	A gathering place to share and celebrate Ukrainian culture. Yeah!
Ukrainian National Museum	721 N Oakley Blvd • 312-421-8020	Museum, library, and archives detail the heritage, culture, and people of Ukraine.
United Center	1901 W Madison St • 312-455-4500	Statue of His Airness still draws tourists.

Map 24 • River West / West Town

Eckhart Park/ Ida Crown Natatorium	Noble St & Chicago Ave • 312-746-5553	One of two swimming pools in the area.
Goldblatt Bros Department Store	1613-35 W Chicago Ave	Official Chicago Landmark.
Harpo Studios	1058 W Washington Blvd • 312-591-9222	Home of the Oprah Winfrey Show.

Map 26 • University Village / Little Italy / Pilsen

National Italian American Sports Hall of Fame	1431 W Taylor St	How many Italian American sports stars do you know? DiMaggio is right out front.

Map 27 • Logan Square

Illinois Centennial Monument	3100 W Logan Blvd	Every city needs an obelisk or two…
Logan House	2656 W Logan Blvd	Reknowned for over-the-top Holiday décor.

Map 28 • Bucktown

Margie's Candies	1960 N Western Ave • 773-384-1035	The Beatles ate here.

Map 29 • DePaul / Wrightwood / Sheffield

Biograph Theater	2433 N Lincoln Ave • 773-348-4123	Site of the gangster John Dillinger's infamous death in 1934. Still a movie theater.
Courtland Street Drawbridge	1440 W Cortland St	Built in 1902 by John Ernst Erickson, this innovative leaf-lift bridge changed the way the world built bridges.
McCormick Row House District	W Chalmers Pl, W Belden Ave, & W Fullerton Pkwy	Quaint example of late 19th-century urban planning and architecture.
Pumpkin House	1052 W Wrightwood Ave	A Halloween spectacle of lighted pumpkins.

Map 30 • Lincoln Park

Dewes Mansion	503 N Wrightwood Ave • 773-477-3075	Ornate historic home done in the German baroque style and built in 1896.
Kauffman Store and Flats	2312 N Lincoln Ave	One of the oldest existing buildings designed by Adler and Sullivan. It's amazing that its characteristic features have survived.
Lincoln Park Boat Club	N Cannon Dr & Fullerton Pkwy • 773-549-2628	Paddling, rowing, and sculling since 1910.
Lincoln Park Conservatory	2391 N Stockton Dr • 312-742-7736	Sister to Garfield Park Conservatory. Built in 1891.
Lincoln Park Cultural Center	2045 N Lincoln Park W • 312-742-7726	Programming in visual arts for all ages.
Lincoln Park Zoo	Cannon Dr & Fullerton Pkwy • 312-742-2000	Oldest free zoo in the US.
Peggy Notebaert Nature Museum	2430 N Cannon Dr • 773-755-5100	An oasis for adults and kids to reconnect with nature by playing with wildflowers and butterflies.

Map 30 • Lincoln Park—*continued*

Theurer-Wrigley House	2466 N Lakeview Ave	Early Richard E. Schmidt (and maybe Hugh H.G. Garden) based on late-Italian Renaissance architecture.
Willis Building	3221 W Larence	1924 Renaissance Revival building designed by Jens Jenson.

Map 32 • Gold Coast / Mag Mile

Water Tower Place and Park	845 N Michigan Ave • 312-440-3165	Huge shopping—6 floors—Marshall Field's.

Map 33 • West Rogers Park

Bernard Horwich JCC	3003 W Touhy Ave • 773-761-9100	Community center with programming for kids/adults, pool/ fitness center, senior center, and sports leagues.
Croatian Cultural Center	2845 W Devon Ave • 773-338-3839	A place where families can relax, socialize and congregate. Intended to benefit the Croatian community in Chicago (duh).
High Ridge YMCA	2430 W Touhy Ave • 773-262-8300	Community center with programming for kids/adults, summer activities, child care programs, sport teams, and a pool.
India Town	W Devon St, near N Washtenaw Ave	Features Indian and Pakistani shops, grocery stores, restaurants, and more.
Indian Boundary Park	2500 W Lunt Ave • 773-742-7887	Petting zoo, tennis courts, chess tables, ice rink, skate park, batting cages, spray pool, with seasonal community center classes.
Rogers Park/ West Ridge Historical Society	7344 N Western Ave • 773-764-4078	Photos/memorabilia/historical documents of the community's history detailing its ethnic diversity.
Thillen's Stadium	Devon & Kedzie Aves	Chicago landmark. 16 softball fields. Features little league baseball and various other games and benefits.
Warren Park	6601 N Western Ave • 312-742-7888	Seasonal free entertainment, pony rides, ethnic food festivals, amusement park rides, arts & crafts, winter sledding hill, baseball diamond, picnic pavilions, and dog play areas.

Map 34 • East Rogers Park

Angel Guardian Croatian Catholic Church	6346 N Ridge Ave • 773-262-0535	1905 red-brick Romanesque church. Turn-of-the-century German stained glass windows by Franz Mayer and F.X. Zettler.
Robert A Black Golf Course	2045 W Pratt Blvd • 773-764-4045	The newest Chicago Park District course. 2,300-yard, par 33 layout for all skill levels.

Map 36 • Bryn Mawr

Rosehill Cemetery & Mausoleum	5800 N Ravenswood Ave	Chicago's historical glitterati entombed among unsurpassed sculpture and architecture.

Map 37 • Edgewater / Andersonville

Ann Sather's Restaurant	5207 N Clark St • 773-271-6677	More than a restaurant; a cultural field trip.
The Belle Shore Hotel Building	1062 W Bryn Mawr Ave	Former homes of roaring 1920s nightlife, now historic landmarks, restored to their former glory as apartments.
Edgewater Beach Apartments	5555 N Sheridan Rd	The big pink building symbolizing the end of the lakeshore bike path.
Philadelphia Church	5437 N Clark St • 773-728-5106	Complete with can't-miss neon sign.
Swedish American Museum	5211 N Clark St • 773-728-8111	Everything you want to know about Swedish culture, which is more than you thought.
Swedish Bakery	5348 N Clark St • 773-561-8919	Famous Tasty Pastries and Cakes.

Map 38 • Ravenswood / Albany Park

Albany Park Community Center	5101 N Kimball Ave • 773-509-5650	Local community center at SW corner of Ainslie & Kimball.
Fish Furniture Co Building	3322 W Lawrence Ave	Striking 1931 Art Moderne building with fish motif, currently houses Interstate Blood Bank.
North Branch Pumping Station	Lawrence Ave & the Chicago River	With its 1930s Art Deco facade, it seems like something prettier should be happening than North Side sewage pumping…
Paradise	2916 W Montrose Ave • 773-588-1989	It's a sushi restaurant. It's a beauty shop. It's a sauna ($12, unlimited time). It's paradise. Of course, it's a neighborhood landmark.
Ravenswood Manor Park	4626 N Manor Ave	It's just a tiny triangle wedged between the non-elevated El and several streets, but it's ground zero for garden sales, neighborhood associations, dogs, kids & community activity.
River Park	5100 N Francisco Ave	More than 30 acres of park, including one of the few city canoe launches.
Ronan Park Walking Trail	3000 W Argyle St	
Willis Building	3221 W Lawrence Ave	1924 Renaissance Revival building designed by Jens Jensen.

Map 39 • Ravenswood / North Center

Old Town School of Folk Music	4544 N Lincoln Ave	Northern expansion of beloved Chicago institution. Classes and concert venue.
St Benedict's Church	2215 W Irving Park Rd • 773-588-6484	The namesake of the St. Ben's neighborhood.

Map 40 • Uptown

Graceland Cemetery	4001 N Clark St • 773-525-1105	Chicago famous buried in masterpiece of landscape architecture.
Green Mill Pub	4802 N Broadway St • 773-878-5552	Live jazz seven nights a week. Dillinger drank here.
Lakeview Lounge	5110 N Broadway St • 773-769-0994	Old school bar with live music on weekends. John Dillinger used to drink here too—shot and a beer type of joint.
Tattoo Factory	4408 N Broadway St • 773-989-4077	Tattoos for famous and infamous.
Uptown Theatre	4707 N Broadway St • 773-561-5700	An acre of seats in a magic city.

Map 41 • Avondale / Old Irving

Com-Ed Plant	N California Ave & W Roscoe St	What's that humming sound in Avondale? Must be this ginormous electrical plant.

Map 43 • Wrigleyville / East Lakeview

Southport Lanes	3325 N Southport Ave • 773-472-6600	Four hand-set lanes. Eat a Honeymooner while you wait.
Vic Theatre	3145 N Sheffield Ave • 773-472-0449	Drink, watch films, and take in an occasional band at this old theatre.
Wrigley Field	1060 W Addison St • 773-404-CUBS	Legendary neighborhood ballpark claims full houses whether the team wins or loses.

Map 44 • East Lakeview

Belmont Rocks	W Briar Pl at the lake	Popular lakefront hangout.
Dog Beach	Northern tip of Belmont Harbor	Fun and frolic with your pup.
The Giraffes	N Elaine Pl & W Roscoe Ave	Iconic public art.
Totem Pole	W Waveland Ave & N Belmont Harbor Dr	Where did it come from? Why is it there? Nobody knows.

Outer Areas • Northwest

The Admiral Theater	3940 W Lawrence Ave	Built in 1928, this former vaudevile theater is now a well-known gentleman's club.
Copernicus Center	5216 W Lawrence Ave • 773-777-9184	Jefferson Park's cultural hub.
Eugene Field Park	5100 N Ridgeway Ave • 773-478-9744	Features a 1928 Tudor Revival fieldhouse, the Eugene Field Cultural Center (home of the Albany Park Theater Project).
Gompers Park	4222 W Foster Ave	Large riverfront park.
Hanson Park Fieldhouse	5501 W Fullerton Ave	Very old fieldhouse with WW2 Barracks.
Harlem CTA Station	N Harlem Ave & Kennedy Expy	One of the more "L"egant stations.
Logan Square Column	3100 W Logan Blvd	It's just like Paris, yet different.
Superdawg Drive-In	6363 N Milwaukee Ave	Everyone knows the Superdog and his sexy girlfriend.
Walt Disney House	2156 N Tripp Ave	Where old Walt learned to ride his bike.

Outer Areas • West

Austin Town Hall	5610 W Lake St	115 year-old former town hall; now a public recreation building.
Bison Statues at Humboldt Park	1400 N Sacramento Ave	Meet up by the Bison.
Columbus Park Refectory	500 S Central Ave	Historic refectory now available for weddings and other fetes.
Delta Fish Market	228 S Kedzie Ave	Defunct fish fry-up features live blues in its parking lot.
Engine 44 Firehouse Mural	412 N Kedzie Ave	When kids do it, it's called graffiti.
Garfield Park Conservatory	300 N Central Park Ave	Tropical oasis in the midst of the urban jungle.
Our Lady of Sorrows School	3121 W Jackson	Unsung treasure built in the late 19th century.
Refectory	Columbus Park, 500 S Central Ave	

Outer Areas • Southwest

Capital Cigar Store	6258 S Pulaski Rd	World's most conspicous cigar-store Indian.
Givens Irish Castle	10244 S Longwood Dr	Hilltop beacon of Beverly.
Graffiti Mural	W 59th St & S Damen Ave	An example of when it's public "art" not public "nuisance."
Midway Airport	5700 S Cicero Ave	We fly—cheaply.
Original Rainbow Cone	9233 S Western Ave	People line up day and night in the summer.

Outer Areas • South

Chicago Skyway	8801 S Anthony St • 312-747-8383	Soar 125 feet over the southside on this thrilling overpass!
New Regal Theater	1645 E 79th St	80-year-old former movie-house.
Oak Woods Cemetery	1035 E 67th St	Former Mayor Washington and civil rights activist Ida B. Wells rest here.
Pullman Clock Tower	11141 S Cottage Grove Ave • 773-785-8901	This beacon of Pullman can be seen from far and wide.
South Shore Cultural Center	7059 South Shore Dr • 773-747-2536	A glittering pearl on the south lakefront.

Make no bones about it, Chicago is a dog's kind of town. More than 750,000 canines live and play in the Windy City. Dogs socialize and exercise their owners daily at designated Dog-Friendly Areas (DFAs), shady parks, and sprawling beaches.

Dog-Friendly Areas

DFAs are off-leash areas reserved just for canines. Amenities vary by park, but often include: doggie drinking fountains; agility equipment; wood chips, pea pebble, and asphalt surfaces; "time out" fenced-in areas for shy or overexcited dogs; trash receptacles and doggie bags for, well, not take-out; and bulletin boards and information kiosks to post animal lovers' announcements.

DFAs are managed jointly by the neighborhoods' dog owners' councils and the Chicago Park District. These spaces are essential to the happiness of Chicago dogs and their owners, as police are notorious for dealing out hefty fines and even arresting dog owners who fail to clean up after, or leash, their dogs. But at the DFA, canines run free and poop where they please. Just remember to clean up after your pooch, ensure that your dog is fully immunized, de-wormed, licensed, and wearing ID tags. There are limits on how many pups one person can bring at once and, please, no puppies under four months, dogs in heat, dogs with the name "killer," or children under 12.

- **Challenger Park**, 1100 W Irving Park Rd (Map 40)
  Nestled next to a cemetery and under the El tracks, this relatively new DFA has plenty of amenities and neighborhood action. Avoid at all costs during Cubs games.
- **Churchill Field Park**, 1825 N Damen Ave (Map 28)
  This triangular space next to the train tracks is covered with pea gravel and asphalt and many abandoned tennis balls (Golden Retrievers can't get enough).
- **Coliseum Park,** 1466 S Wabash Ave (Map 11)
  Long, narrow, and fenced-in park where dogs race the overhead trains. Nothing to write home about, but, hey, it's legal.
- **Hamlin Park**, 3035 N Hoyne Ave at Wellington Ave (Map 42)
  Located in the shady southwest corner, this active L-shaped park appeals to tennis-ball chasers and fetching owners.
- **Margate Park**, 4921 N Marine Dr (Map 40)
  Called "Puptown" by the Uptown canine-loving community, this beloved DFA is usually packed with doggone fun. Locals are diligent about keeping the pea gravel picked up.
- **Noethling (Grace) Park,** 2645 N Sheffield Ave (Map 29)
  Dogs and owners from the Lincoln Park area love to hang out at the "Wiggley Field" dog run—Chicago's pilot pooch park. Wiggley's got a doggy obstacle course, an asphalt surface, drinking fountain, "time out" area, and info kiosk.
- **Ohio Place Park,** N Orleans St and W Ohio St (Map 2)
  Next to the I-90/94 exit ramp, this fenced-in strip of concrete flanked by bushes isn't pretty, but a dog can play fetch here without a leash. Careful: as the lot is not a Chicago Park District facility, it is not double-gated.
- **River Park**, 5100 N Francisco Ave (Map 38) The city's newest DFA.
- **Walsh Playground Park,** 1722 N Ashland Ave (Map 29
  A 4,500-square-foot park with a small off-leash area for fetching, with pea gravel and shade.
- **Wicker Park**, 1425 N Damen Ave (Map 21)
  Popular pooch as well as dog owner pick-up park. Often packed with dog-walkers wrangling fleets of frisky canines.

Creating a DFA takes a serious grass-roots effort spearheaded by the neighborhood's dog owners. They must organize themselves to get the community to bow to their desires through site surveys and three community meetings, and raise one-half of the funds needed to build the DFA. Most importantly, they must unleash the support of their alderman, police precinct, and park district. For information on DFAs, call the Park District at 312-742- 7529. Chicago's Dog Advisory Work Group, DAWG, (312-409-2169) also assists neighborhood groups in establishing DFAs

Top Dog Parks and Beaches

Leashed dogs and well-behaved owners are welcome in most of Chicago's parks and on its beaches, except during the height of swimming season, when the sands are off-limits. Here are some local canines' top picks.

- **Calumet Park and Beach (9800 South)**
  A 200-acre beach and park getaway in the city with tennis courts, baseball fields, basketball courts, water fun, and plenty of parking.
- **Dog Beach (3200 N Lake Shore Dr)**
  This crescent of sand at the north corner of Belmont Harbor is separated from the bike path by a fence, which has made it an unofficial dog sand box. But the water is dirty and the police do ticket, so it's not the most ideal dog-frolicking area.
- **Horner Park (2741 W Montrose Ave)**
  Dog heaven with lots of trees, grass, squirrels to chase, and other pups to meet, particularly after work.
- **Lincoln Park (2045 Lincoln Park W)**
  Paws down, the best dog park in town for romping, fetch, and Frisbee. Unofficial "Bark Park" where pet lovers congregate is a grassy area between Lake Shore Dr and Marine Dr.
- **Montrose/Wilson Avenue Beach (MonDog) (4400 North)**
  The city's only legal off-leash beach, MonDog is perfect for pooches to practice dogpaddling. Lake water is shallow, and the beachfront is wide.
- **Ohio Street Beach and Olive Park (400 N Lake Shore Dr)**
  The perfect combo for cross-training canines: Olive Park's fenced-in grassy areas for running and neighboring Ohio Street Beach's calm waters for swimming.
- **Promontory Point (5401 South Shore Dr)**
  Radical run for daring, buff dogs that dive off the scenic picnic area's rocks into the deep water below.
- **Sherman Park (1301 W 52nd St)**
  The best place in the city for a Victorian-style stroll over picturesque bridges and through lagoons.

More Doggie Information

Chicago's canine community keeps up to sniff on doggie doings through *Chicagoland Tails Magazine*, www.chicagolandtails.com and the Chicago Canine website, www.chicagocanine.com. The definitive local resource for all things dog is Margaret Littman's book *The Dog Lover's Companion to Chicago* (Avalon Travel Publishing).

In a city with the nation's busiest convention center, it's no wonder that Chicago hotels are designed for the business traveler, with expense account prices to boot. Really, the price of even an average downtown room can be outrageous. For a special urban splurge, book a suite at one of Chicago's premier palace hotels—the **Ritz-Carlton**, **Four Seasons**, **Le Meridien**, or **Peninsula**. Hip hoteliers will want to stay at one of downtown's two "**W**" hotels, **Hotel 71**, the **Sofitel,** or the (relatively) new kid, **The Hard Rock Hotel**—located in the vintage Union Carbide building on Michigan Avenue. For out-of-town guests on a budget, try the **Chicago Travelodge Downtown**. It's not much, but the location between Millennium Park and the Museum Campus can't be beat for the price.

Around the corner at the **Congress Plaza Hotel**, picketers have been marching with placards for what seems like forever—the Hotel Workers Union is on strike with the management, and it seems unlikely that their dispute will be settled anytime soon. The strike has hurt business, so some good deals can be had—let your conscience be your judge, and brace yourself for heckling strikers should you take the plunge (and remember that Upton Sinclair would *not* approve).

Good values can be had away from downtown. **City Suites** on Belmont, and the **Days Inn** on Diversey offer relatively cheap deals in fun neighborhoods. If that's still too rich for your blood, **Heart o' Chicago Motel** is skipping distance from the Edgewater White Castle—and a short walk to the life-affirming Andersonville community. **Sheffield House**, once a transient hotel, offers spare, cheap rooms, appealing to the backpacking European traveler, and a stone's throw from Wrigley Field. Finally, if even that's too much, there are three youth hostels in Chicago open to the public with rates as low as $15 a night for card-carrying international youth hostel members. For deals, **Hot Rooms** is a Chicago-based reservation service offering low-rates on undersold rooms: www.hotrooms.com.

Map 2 • Near North / River North

			Pricing	*Rating*
Amalfi Hotel	20 W Kinzie St	312-395-9000	353	★★★★
Best Western Inn	125 W Ohio St	312-467-0800	124	★★★
Cass Hotel	640 N Wabash Ave	312-787-4031	89	★
Club Quarters	75 E Wacker Dr	312-357-6400	94	
Comfort Inn & Suites--Downtown	15 E Ohio St	312-894-0900	177	★★★
Courtyard by Marriott	30 E Hubbard St	312-329-2500	189	★★★
Embassy Suites Hotel	600 N State St	312-943-3800	225	★★★
Hampton Inn	33 W Illinois St	312-832-0330	157	★★★
Hilton Garden Inn	10 E Grand Ave	312-595-0000	199	★★★
Holiday Inn	350 N Orleans St	312-836-5000	135	★★★
Homewood Suites	40 E Grand Ave	312-644-2222	172	★★★
Hotel 71	71 E Wacker Dr	312-346-7100	185	★★★★
House of Blues Hotel Loews	333 N Dearborn St	312-245-0333	175	★★★★
Le Meridien	521 N Rush St	312-645-1500	219	★★★★
Lenox House Suites	616 N Rush St	312-337-1000	134	★★★
Ohio House Motel	600 N La Salle Dr	312-943-6000	85	
Peninsula Chicago Hotel	108 E Superior St	312-337-2888	451	★★★★★
Westin River North Chicago	320 N Dearborn St	312-744-1900	247	

Map 3 • Streeterville / Mag Mile

			Pricing	*Rating*
Allerton Crowne Plaza	701 N Michigan Ave	312-440-1500	259	★★★★
Best Western Inn	162 E Ohio St	312-787-3100	159	★★★
Embassy Suites Lakefront	511 N Columbus Dr	312-836-5900	218	★★★
Fairfield Inn	216 E Ontario St	312-787-3777	193	★★
Fitzpatrick Chicago Hotel	166 E Superior St	312-787-6000	295	★★★★
Holiday Inn	300 E Ohio St	312-787-6100	189	★★★★
Hotel Inter-Continental	505 N Michigan Ave	312-944-4100	236	★★★★
Marriott Chicago Downtown	540 N Michigan Ave	312-836-0100	220	★★★
Omni Chicago Hotel	676 N Michigan Ave	312-944-6664	310	★★★★
Park Hyatt Hotel	800 N Michigan Ave	312-335-1234	377	★★★★★
Radisson Hotel	160 E Huron St	312-787-2900	189	★★★
Red Roof Inn Chicago	162 E Ontario St	312-787-3580	95	

Map 3 • Streeterville / Mag Mile—*continued*

			Pricing	*Rating*
Sheraton Hotel & Towers	301 E North Water St	312-464-1000	139	★★★★
W Chicago Lakeshore	644 N Lake Shore Dr	312-943-9200	234	★★★★
Wyndham Chicago	633 N St Clair St	312-573-0300	206	★★★★

Map 4 • West Loop Gate / Greektown

			Pricing	*Rating*
Crowne Plaza Mid City Plaza	1 S Halsted St	312-829-5000	114	★★

Map 5 • The Loop

			Pricing	*Rating*
Buckingham Athletic Club	440 S La Salle St	312-663-8910	217	★★★★
Club Quarters Central Loop	111 W Adams St	312-214-6400	129	
Crowne Plaza Silversmith	10 S Wabash Ave	312-372-7696	163	★★★★
Hilton Palmer House	17 E Monroe St	312-726-7500	151	★★★★
Hotel Allegro	171 W Randolph St	312-236-0123	179	★★★★
Hotel Burnham	1 W Washington St	312-782-1111	185	★★★★
Hotel Monaco	225 N Wabash Ave	312-960-8500	195	★★★★
Palmer House Hilton	17 E Monroe St	312-726-7500	186	★★★
Renaissance Chicago Hotel	1 W Wacker Dr	312-372-7200	299	★★★★
W Chicago City Center	172 W Adams St	312-332-1200	195	★★★★

Map 6 • The Loop / Grant Park

			Pricing	*Rating*
Fairmont Hotel	200 N Columbus Dr	312-565-8000	344	★★★★
Hard Rock Hotel	230 N Michigan Ave	312-345-1000	383	★★★★
Hyatt Regency Chicago Hotel	151 E Wacker Dr	312-565-1234	243	★★★★
Swissotel Chicago	323 E Wacker Dr	312-565-0565	276	★★★★

Map 7 • South Loop / River City

			Pricing	*Rating*
Holiday Inn	506 W Harrison St	312-957-9100	131	★★★

Map 8 • South Loop / Printers Row / Dearborn Park

			Pricing	*Rating*
Chicago Travelodge Downtown	65 E Harrison St	312-427-8000	114	★★★★
Ho Jo Inn	720 N La Salle St	312-664-8100	106	★★
Hostelling International	24 E Congress Pkwy	312-692-1560	35	
Hotel Blake	500 S Dearborn St	312-986-1234	180	★★★

Map 9 • South Loop / South Michigan Ave

			Pricing	*Rating*
Best Western Grant Park Hotel	1100 S Michigan Ave	312-922-2900	112	★★
Congress Plaza Hotel	520 S Michigan Ave	312-427-3800	142	★★★
Essex Inn	800 S Michigan Ave	312-939-2800	85	★★
Hilton & Towers Chicago	720 S Michigan Ave	312-922-4400	186	★★★★

Map 11 • South Loop / McCormick Place

			Pricing	*Rating*
Hyatt Regency at McCormick Place	2233 S Dr Martin L King Jr Dr	312-567-1234	197	★★★
Wheeler Mansion	2020 S Calumet Ave	312-945-2020	297	★★★★

Map 14 • Prairie Shores / Lake Meadows

			Pricing	*Rating*
Amber Inn	3901 S Michigan Ave	773-285-1000	110	
Bronzeville's First Bed & Breakfast	3911 S Dr Martin L King Dr	773-373-8081	187	

Map 17 • Kenwood

			Pricing	*Rating*
Ramada Inn Lake Shore	4900 S Lake Shore Dr	773-288-5800	99	★★

Map 20 • East Hyde Park / Jackson Park

			Pricing	*Rating*
Wooded Isle Suites	5750 S Stony Island Ave	773-288-5578	151	

Map 21 • Wicker Park / Ukrainian Village

			Pricing	*Rating*
Wicker Park Inn B&B	1329 N Wicker Park Ave	773-486-2743	131	

Map 26 • University Village / Little Italy / Pilsen

			Pricing	Rating
Marriott Chicago Downtown Medical District/UIC	625 S Ashland Ave	312-491-1234	170	★★★

Map 30 • Lincoln Park

			Pricing	Rating
Belden Stratford Hotel	2300 N Lincoln Park West	773-281-2900	193	
Days Inn	1816 N Clark St	312-664-3040	109	

Map 32 • Gold Coast / Mag Mile

			Pricing	Rating
Ambassador West	1300 N State St	312-787-3700	125	★★★
Doubletree Guest Suites	198 E Delaware Pl	312-664-1100	206	★★★
Drake Hotel	140 E Walton St	312-787-2200	295	
Four Seasons Hotel Chicago	120 E Delaware Pl	312-280-8800	383	★★★★★
Millenium Knickerbocker	163 E Walton St	312-751-8100	214	★★★★
Omni Ambassador East Hotel	1301 N State Pkwy	312-787-7200	202	★★★★
Raphael Hotel	201 E Delaware Pl	312-943-5000	193	★★★
Residence Inn	201 E Walton St	312-943-9800	228	★★★
Ritz Carlton Hotel	160 E Pearson St	312-266-2343	363	★★★★★
Seneca Hotel	200 E Chestnut St	312-787-8900	169	★★★
Sofitel Water Tower	20 E Chestnut St	312-324-4000	245	★★★★
Sutton Place Hotel	21 E Bellevue Pl	312-266-2100	257	★★★★
Talbot Hotel	20 E Delaware Pl	312-943-0161	301	★★★★
Tremont	100 E Chestnut St	312-751-1900	177	★★★
Westin MIchigan Avenue	909 N Michigan Ave	312-943-7200	285	★★★★
Whitehall Hotel	105 E Delaware Pl	312-944-6300	226	★★★★

Map 34 • West Rogers Park

			Pricing	Rating
Super 8 Motel	7300 N Sheridan Rd	773-973-7440	99	

Map 35 • East Rogers Park

			Pricing	Rating
Apache Motel	5535 N Lincoln Ave	773-728-9400	54	
Lincoln Inn	5952 N Lincoln Ave	773-784-1118	49	
Lincoln Motel	5900 N Lincoln Ave	773-561-3170	47	
O' Mi Motel	5611 N Lincoln Ave	773-561-6488	55	
Summit Motel	5308 N Lincoln Ave	773-561-3762	50-55	
Tip Top Motel	6060 N Lincoln Ave	773-539-4800	55	

Map 37 • Edgewater / Andersonville

			Pricing	Rating
Chicago Lodge	920 W Foster Ave	773-334-5600	80	
Heart O' Chicago Motel	5990 N Ridge Ave	773-271-9181	64	
Lakeside Motel	5440 N Sheridan Rd	773-275-2700	58	

Map 43 • Wrigleyville / East Lakeview

			Pricing	Rating
City Suites Hotel Chicago	933 W Belmont Ave	773-404-3400	181	★★★

Map 44 • East Lakeview

			Pricing	Rating
Best Western Hawthorne Terrace	3434 N Broadway St	773-244-3434	169	★★★
Days Inn	644 W Diversey Pkwy	773-525-7010	187	
Hotel Majestic	528 W Brompton Ave	773-404-3499	175	★★★
Inn at Lincoln Park	601 W Diversey Pkwy	773-348-2810	100	★★
Willows	555 W Surf St	773-528-8400	173	★★★1/2

Chicago is a kid's kind of town. From sandy beaches and leafy parks to diverse downtown museums, concerts and suburban attractions, Chicago's options for family fun are non-stop—just like your kids.

The Best of the Best

The best part about Chicago family-style is that lots of stuff is *free*…or practically free. Great entertainment and educational venues keep cash in parents' pockets for school supplies, groceries, gas, and an occasional adult night out.

★ **Neatest Time-Honored Tradition:** Marshall Field's Christmas Windows (111 N State St, 312-781-1000; http://target.com/state_street/index.jhtml). Generations of Chicagoans kick off the holiday season on State Street by viewing the over-150 year-old retailer's imaginative, animated window displays telling a different Christmas tale every year. Line up to see authentic, jolly Santa Claus and dine at the oh-so-refined Walnut Room where the decadent green Frango mint pie is a must.

★ **Top Park:** Lincoln Park (Lake Shore Dr & North Ave, 312-742-7529; www.chicagoparkdistrict.com). From an expansive sandy beach, baseball diamonds, basketball courts, and bike paths to grassy meadows, fishing lagoons, museums, and the nation's oldest free zoo, Lincoln Park promises a full day of outdoor activity.

★ **Generations of Amusement:** Kiddieland (8400 W North Ave, Melrose Park, 708-343-3000; www.kiddieland.com). Before Disney and Six Flags there was Kiddieland, one of the nation's oldest family-owned and run amusement parks. Many of the over 30 rides and attractions are original to this wholesome, 77-year-old icon of fun, including the jelly-bean-colored bumper cars, carousel, swirling tea cups, and "Little Dipper" rollercoaster. Thrill-seeking tweens scream on the "Log Jammer" and high-flying "Galleon." Kids need more steam? Free Pepsi served all day. Unlimited rides for $20 admission fee (ages six and up); $17 (ages 3-5, seniors); free under age 2; discounted admission after 5 pm. Open April-October. Call for seasonal schedule.

★ **Spellbinding Story Time:** Lincoln Park Zoo (2200 N Cannon Dr, 312-742-2000; www.lpzoo.com). Donning safari khakis and pith helmet, Professor Bonnie spins adventurous tales and sings for preschoolers at the *Farm-in-the-Zoo* on Mondays and Wednesdays at 9:15 am and 10 am. Wildly popular, this story hour is the toughest ticket in town. Arrive early to secure admission (donation suggested). At the free "Second Sunday Stories," children's book authors read their works about life on the farm followed by activities and tours of the *Farm-in-the-Zoo*. Call for schedule.

★ **Slickest Sledding Hill:** Soldier Field Lakefront Park (312-742-7529; www.chicagoparkdistrict.com). The best part of the Soldier Field's pretty 17-acre park is the free, giant sledding hill with frozen lake views. BYO ride and bundle up for frigid lakefront winds. In warmer months, check out the Children's Garden.

★ **Coolest Ice Rink:** McCormick Tribune Ice Rink in Millennium Park (55 N Michigan Ave, 312-742-7529; www.chicagoparkdistrict.com). Skate hand-in-hand in the shadow of architectural landmark buildings lining the Mag Mile. Open daily, admission is free to the 16,000-square-foot rink; skate rental available and warming room on-site.

★ **Best Kept Secret:** Chicago Public Library's "Great Kids Museum Passport" (Main Branch at 400 S State St, 312-747-4090 and branches city-wide; www.chipublib.org). Families can't afford not to know about the passports on loan for one week that gets family members free admission to over a dozen of Chicago's premier cultural institutions including the biggies at the Museum Campus plus the Art Institute, Peggy Notebaert Museum, and Chicago Historical Society. Available only to Chicago Public Library card-carrying adult Chicago residents. See website for participating institutions and details.

★ **Railroad Shop That Rocks:** Berwyn's Toy Trains & Models (7025 Ogden Ave, Berwyn, 708-484-4384). A roundhouse of activity, this hobby shop is the best reason to go to Berwyn, besides all the dollar stores. Engineers of all ages play at the many display train tables. Don't miss the charming, 7-by-14-foot tooting train layout in the backroom.

★ **WOW Waterparks:** (312-742-7529; www.chicagoparkdistrict.com). The Chicago Park District operates over 20 free waterparks with arching jets, umbrella sprays, pipe falls, and bubble jets in Chicago's neighborhood parks and beaches. All facilities open daily in summer 11 am to 8 pm.

★ **Best Beach:** North Avenue Beach (1600 North Ave, 312-742-7529; www.chicagoparkdistrict.com). From swimming, spiking volleyballs, and kickboxing to sunbathing and sipping sun-downers, this expansive beach on Lake Michigan rivals any on the California coast. The tug-boat shaped beach house has locker facilities, rents volleyball equipment, roller blades, and bikes. On the upper deck is Castaways restaurant and ice cream parlor. There's also a full outdoor fitness center with weights and spin cycles plus a roller blade rink for pick up hockey under the summer sun.

★ **Sensational Soda Fountain:** Margie's Candies (1960 N Western Ave, 773-384-1035). Celebrating 85 years of scoop, this old-fashioned ice cream parlor serves yummy frozen treats like soda fountains of yesteryear. Kids who flash report cards with an A get a free ice cream cone.

★ **A Child's Choice Bakery:** Sweet Mandy B's (1208 W Webster Ave, 773-244-1174). Trendy and tasty, this cheery bakery's kid convections include awesome cupcakes, chunky whoopee pies, and whimsical cut-out frosted cookies. Signature sweet: "Dirt Cups"—a cake, crushed Oreo cookie, and whipped cream combo crawling with psychedelic gummy worms.

★ **Teen Scene:** Jive Monkey (854 W Belmont Ave, 773-404-8000, ext. 229). Hipsters come from across the urban jungle to buy, sell, and swap all things cool including fashionable vintage T-shirts, jewelry, Mod Squad mushroom hats, and the latest Levi's. Best buys are used T-shirts, $3 each.

★ **Coolest Family Concerts:** Joe Segal's Jazz Showcase (59 W Grand Ave, 312-670-2473; www.jazzshowcase.com). Hipster kids and jiving parents and grandparents hang out at this swank, serious jazz club's Sunday 4 pm matinee performances where top musicians jam. Non-alcoholic beverages and snacks served. Discount adult admission; children under 12 free. All Ages Blue Chicago Show (736 N Clark St, 312-661-1003; www.bluechicago.com) on Saturday nights from 8 pm to midnight where families rock to the Gloria Shannon Blues Band in the basement of the Blue Chicago store. Adult admission $5; kids under age 11 free. No alcohol or smoking allowed.

★ **Flying High:** Mayor Daley's Kids and Kites Festival (Alternating lakefront locations, 312-744-3869; www.cityofchicago.org/specialevents). Every spring and fall, the Windy City lives up to its blow-hard reputation lifting kids' spirits and kites to new heights along the lakefront. Kite flying professionals and instructors help enthusiasts of all ages construct kites and fly them for free. Complimentary kite kits provided, or bring your own. Free family entertainment, crafts, and storytelling on-site.

★ **Not So Little League:** Chicago White Sox FUNdamentals Field (U.S. Cellular Field, 333 W 35th St, 312-674-1000; www.whitesox.com). Little sluggers age 3 and up play ball in a 15,000 square-foot field of their own within the White Sox's home park. While junior trains, parents spy the pro game going on below from the new, kid-friendly interactive baseball diamond and skills area perched above the left-field concourse. Budding all-stars hone their pitching, batting, and base-running techniques under the sharp eyes of college and pro coach-instructors from the year-round Chicago White Sox Training Academy in Lisle. Batter yet, it's all free with ball-park admission.

★ **Masterpiece Portraits:** Classic Kids (917 W Armitage Ave, 773-296-2607; 566 Chestnut St, Winnetka, 847-446-2064). Pricey but priceless photos from this studio capture your kid at his or her model best. Pay a $300 sitting fee, plus cost for handcrafted prints, and treasure your tyke forever.

★ **Weirdest City Sight:** Chicago River runs green (Chicago River downtown along Wacker Dr). No, it's not algae or bile, but bio-degradable green dye. Every St. Patrick's Day the city turns the Chicago River emerald green like the Incredible Hulk.

★ **Parents' Parking Dream:** Little Parkers Program, Standard Parking Garages (888-700-7275; www.standardparking.com). Select garages downtown specially equip families for road trips home with puzzles, crayons, and coloring books. Family-friendly garage amenities include spacious bathrooms with diaper-changing stations. Some rent family videos to monthly parkers. Participating garages: Grant Park North Garage, 25 N Michigan Ave; East Monroe Garage, 350 E Monroe St; Chicago Historical Society Garage, 1730 N Stockton Dr; Huron-St. Claire Self Park near Northwestern Memorial Hospital; Erie-Ontario Self Park in Streeterville neighborhood; and 680 N Lake Shore Dr Self Park.

★ **Finest Family Festivals:** Tall Ships (312-744-3370; www.cityofchicago.org/specialevents). Ahoy there, matey! In early August, over 25 old-world sailing vessels drop anchor along the lakeshore at Navy Pier, DuSable Harbor, and the Chicago River filling the skyline with billowing sails. There are daily deck tours ($10 boarding fee) as well as free entertainment and fireworks.

★ **Kudos Kids' Theatre:** Marriott Theatre for Young Audiences (Marriott Lincolnshire Resort, 10 Marriott Dr, Lincolnshire, 847-634-0200; www.marriottheatre.com). Not a bad seat in the house at this intimate arena theatre where actors welcome pint-sized audience participation and roam the isles interacting with kids. Post-performance, the actors conduct Q&A answering kids' theatrical questions. Family productions run year-round. Tickets $10 per person; free parking.

★ **Oscar Performances:** Children's International Film Festival (city-wide, 773-281-9075; www.cicff.org). For over two weeks each fall, Chicago's theater venues feature hundreds of witty, ingenious long- and short-form children's movies from around the world, some created by kids. Filmmakers, directors, and animators teach seminars for movie-lovers of all ages.

★ **Hippest Halloween Happening:** Chicago Symphony Orchestra's Hallowed Haunts Concert (220 S Michigan Ave, 312-294-3000; www.cso.org). Skeletons rattle and ghosts boogie to classical morbid music at the Chicago Symphony Orchestra's creepy family concert featuring hair-raising Romantic Era pieces and medieval chants. Come in costume to the concert and ghoulish pre-performance party. Tickets: $7-$45.

★ **Perfect Pumpkin Patch:** Sonny Acres Farm (29 W 310 North Ave, West Chicago, 630-321-9515; www.sonnyacres.com). During October, the Feltes family homestead has it all for fall: jack-o-lanterns for carving, homemade pies, decorative Thanksgiving and Halloween displays, and a killer costume shop. Kids love the mountains of pumpkins, crunchy caramel apples, scary hay rides, youngster carnival rides, and haunted barns (one for tiny tikes and another for blood-thirsty teens). Free farm admission and parking; purchase tickets for attractions.

★ **Fields of Dreams:** Of course Wrigley Field, but a family outing at the venerable ballpark amounts to a month's down payment on a mini van. For $10 or less per ticket, take the family to the burbs' farm league games at pristine ballparks complete with entertainment, eats, and fireworks: Kane County Cougars (34W002 Cherry Ln, Geneva, 630-232-8811; www.kccougars.com) and Shaumburg Flyers (1999 S Springinsguth Rd, Schaumburg, 847-891-2255; www.flyersbaseball.com).

★ **No-Flab Family Workout:** Tri-Star Gymnastics' "Family Fun Night" (1401 Circle Ave, Forest Park, 708-771-7827; www.tri-star.com). Families bounce on trampolines, swing on bars, tumble across mats, and climb ropes together at Tri-Star's warehouse-sized gymnastic training facility. Held from 4:30 to 5:30 pm on Saturday nights during the school year, admission is $5 per child and parents get in free. Parental supervision (no more than two kids per adult) and signed waiver required.

★ **Musical Marathon Encounter:** Chicago Symphony Orchestra's "Day of Music" (220 S Michigan Ave, 312-294-3000; www.cso.org). A free live music marathon lasting eight hours held each fall. In addition to the world-renowned Chicago Symphony Orchestra, hear the city's top musicians perform classical, jazz, blues, world music, plus lively family entertainment. For year-round family concert performances, check out the orchestra's Kraft Matinee Series.

★ **Horse'n Around:** Arlington Park Race Track's "Family Day" (2200 W Euclid Ave, Arlington Heights, 847-385-7500; www.arlingtonpark.com). From mid-May through mid-September, it's a sure bet you'll win big with the kids on a Sunday afternoon at the horse races. Wild West, luau, and circus-themed family activities surround the seriously fun thoroughbred racing action at this swank, clean track. Pony rides, face painters, and petting zoo on-site. From noon to 1 pm, attend the free Junior Jockey Club events (847-385-7796) including educational equine care talks and behind-the scenes track tours (children 12 and under).

★ **Brightest Christmas Lights:** Cuneo Museum and Gardens' "Winter Wonderland Holiday Light Festival" (1350 N Milwaukee Ave, Vernon Hills, 847-362-3042; www.lake-online.com/cuneo). The largest drive-through Christmas display in Northern Illinois twinkles with millions of lights creating dazzling holiday scenes. Superhero and storybook light sculptures dance in the woods. Festival runs first Friday after Thanksgiving through New Year's weekend from 6 pm to 10 pm. Admission per car is $10 on weekends, $5 weekdays.

★ **Winter Blahs Buster:** Fantasy Kingdom (1422 N Kingsbury St at Evergreen St, 312-642-5437). When Chicago's plunging temps prevent playground play, take tikes to this warehouse-turned-play-space magic kingdom to blow off steam. Kids clamor through a giant castle fitted with slides and tunnels (socks required) while donning Camelot costumes for dress-up fun. $12 per child.

Rainy Day Activities

Art Institute of Chicago, 111 S Michigan Ave, 312-443-3600; www.artic.edu. While kids find the doll house-sized Thorne Miniature Rooms and shiny medieval armor very cool, they also discover artistic expression from around the world at the Kraft Education Center. Interactive exhibitions introduce children to art from other cultures, time periods, and world-wide geographic regions. "Edutaining" art books and masterpiece puzzles in the children's library reinforce visual learning. Free kids' programs and drawing workshops are also held throughout museum galleries. Admission is free on Tuesdays (however, donation strongly suggested); children under 5 always free.

Cernan Earth and Space Center, Triton College Campus, 2000 Fifth Ave, River Grove, 708-456-0300, ext. 3372; www.triton.edu/cernan). Named after Apollo astronaut Eugene Cernan, a native Chicagoan and the last man on the moon, this cozy planetarium's intimate dome theater features kids' star programs ($5), earth and sky shows, and laser light shows. Monthly sky watch and lectures hosted. Mini space-related museum (free admission) and great celestial gift shop.

Chicago's Museum Campus, 1200-1400 S Lake Shore Dr. The closest you'll come to an educational amusement park. Dinosaurs, live sharks, giant mechanical insects, ancient mummies, and exploding stars are just a handful of adventures your kids will encounter on the lakefront's brainy peninsula home to the Field Museum (312-922-9410; www.fieldmuseum.org), Adler Planetarium & Astronomy Museum (312-922-7827; www.adlerplanetarium.org), and John G. Shedd Aquarium (312-939-2438; www.shedd.org). Check with each institution for its free admission days and special family programs.

Diversey River Bowl, 2211 W Diversey Pkwy, 773-227-5800. Families, couples, and serious bowlers mix it up at this upbeat city alley. Decent grilled food served and full bar on-site. Wednesday through Sunday nights at 8 pm, glow-in-the-dark bowling known as *Rock'in Bowl* goes well past the little one's bedtime, but is fun for teens with chaperones.

DuPage Children's Museum, 301 N Washington St, Naperville, 630-637-8000; www.dupagechildrensm useum.org. The 45,000-square-foot museum loaded with hands-on, action-packed exhibits keeps pre-schoolers with nano-second attention spans exploring until exhaustion.

Exploritorium, 4701 Oakton St, Skokie, 847-674-1500, ext. 2700; www.skokieparkdistrict.org. From finger paints and water games to costumes and a multi-storied jungle gym, this facility tuckers tykes out. The climbing gym outfitted with twisting ropes, tubes, and tunnels even brings out the Tarzan in parents. Miniscule admission fee; free for Skokie adult residents and kids under 3.

Federal Reserve Bank of Chicago Visitors' Center, 230 S LaSalle St, 312-322-5111; www.chicagofed.org. The buck stops here where kids learn the power of pocket change through hands-on and computerized exhibits explaining the Fed's role in managing the nation's money. Kids love the rotating, million-dollar cube of cash and $50,800 coin pit. Sneak a peak into the vault stocked with $9 million, trace our country's currency history, and learn how to identify fake bills. Free admission. Open weekdays 9 am-1 pm; free guided tours on Mondays at 1 pm.

Garfield Park Conservatory, 300 N Central Park Ave, 312-746-5100; www.garfield-conservatory.org. Kids really dig *Plants Alive!*, the free, landmark Conservatory's 5,000-square-foot greenhouse blooming with child-friendly vegetation. Kids climb a two-story twisting daisy stem that doubles as a slide and come nose-to-stinger with a Jurassic-sized bumble bee. Attend story-telling, plant seeds, and dig in the soil pool.

Kohl Children's Museum of Greater Chicago, 165 Green Bay Rd, Wilmette, 847-256-6056; www.kohlchildrensmuseum.org. Kids climb the rigging of a pirate ship, "ride" an L train, meander through mazes, and push mini carts through a fully stocked grocery store.

Milano Model & Toy Museum, 116 Park Ave, Elmhurst, 630-279-4422; www.toys-n-cars.com. Magical place for motor heads and rail buffs of all ages featuring hundreds of rail-related toys and models. Adults, $4; kids under 10, free.

Mitchell Museum of the American Indian, 2600 Central Park Ave on Kendall College Campus, Evanston, 847-475-1030; www.mitchellmuseum.org. From real teepees and dug-out canoes to bow-and-arrows and tom-toms, this compact sensory museum's engaging hands-on exhibits and crafts sessions teach kids about the rich Native American life and culture. During the school year, sessions are offered semi-monthly on Saturdays, and on Tuesdays, Wednesdays, and Thursdays in summer. All programs held from 10:30 am to noon.

Museum of Science and Industry, 57th St at S Lake Shore Dr, 773-684-1414; www.msichicago.org. The ultimate hands-on learning experience for families, this massive museum is a tsunami of scientific exploration. Favorite kid exhibits are the 3,500 square-foot *The Great Train Story* model railroad, the United Airlines jet, a walk-through human heart, a working Coal Mine, and the Idea Factory workshop packed with gears, cranks, and water toys. OMNIMAX Theater on-site. Call for free day schedule.

Navy Pier, 600 E Grand Ave, 312-595-7437; www.navypier.com. A mega-sized free entertainment emporium jettisoning into Lake Michigan, Navy Pier has an IMAX Theater and tons of carnival-like attractions. The renowned Shakespeare Theater performs kid-friendly shorts of Willy's works. The 57,000-square-foot Chicago Children's Museum has 15 permanent engaging exhibits for toddlers to pre-teens (312-527-1000; www.chichildrensmuseum.org). Museum admission free on Thursday nights from 5 pm to 8 pm.

Oak Brook Family Aquatic Center, 1450 Forest Gate Rd, Oak Brook, 630-990-4233; www.obparks.org. Wet, wild fun for the whole family at this splashy indoor aquatic facility. They've got a zero-depth pool and slide for tadpoles as well as an Olympic-sized pool for bigger fish. Special swim events include watery holiday-themed parties, arts and crafts, water sports days, and dive-in movie nights where you can watch a family flick from your inflatable raft.

Peggy Notebaert Nature Museum, 2430 N Cannon Dr, 773-755-5100; www.naturemuseum.org. Kids delight in *Butterfly Haven*, a soaring tropical greenhouse habitat, which is home to hundreds of exotic winged beauties from around the world. The Children's Gallery replicates prairie and wetland habitats. Hands-on, free scientific activities and animal feedings always scheduled. Chicago residents enjoy a $1 discount on admission fee. On Thursdays, admission is free, however donations are strongly suggested.

Pelican Harbor Indoor/Outdoor Aquatic Park, 200 S Lindsay Ln, Bolingbrook, 630-759-2727; www.bolingbrookparks.org. Chicago area's only indoor/outdoor waterpark open year-round. Kids zip down six thrilling water slides (one 75-foot tall), float on inner tubes, and plunge into the diving well. There is a large zero-depth pool for little swimmers, lap pool, sand volleyball, whirlpool, and concessions.

Shops at Northbridge, 520 N Michigan Ave, 312-327-2300; www.northbridgechicago.com. The entire third floor is not only lined with child apparel, toy, and accessory stores, but has The LEGO Store with play stations and a spacious LEGO building zone. Best part is parents don't have to clean up those blasted colored blocks!

Spertus Museum of Judaica, 618 S Michigan Ave, 312-922-9012; www.spertus.edu/museum. The Children's ARTiFACT Center recreates an impressive archeological site where kids dig up artifacts from ancient Middle East civilizations and experiment with writing in Cuneiform. Free admission on Fridays; all-inclusive, $10 family pass sold the rest of the week.

Outdoor *and* Educational

Fresh air family fun venues that work your kids' muscles and minds pack the city and suburbs. Here are some of the best:

Brookfield Zoo, First Ave & 31st St, Brookfield, 708-485-0263; www.brookfieldzoo.org. Chicago's largest zoo spanning 216 wooded acres is home to over 2,500 animal residents from around the world. Hamill Family Play Zoo and the Children's Zoo offer interactive programs on animal antics and opportunities to pet kid-friendly creatures babysat by helpful docents. Several dolphin shows daily. Family and child educational classes offered, plus summer camps and special holiday events. Explore the woodsy Indian Lake district where a life-sized dinosaur "lives." Open daily. Admission is free October through March on Tuesdays and Thursdays.

Cantigny Park, 1 S 151 Winfield Rd, Wheaton, 630-668-5161; www.rrmtf.org/cantigny. The 15-acre complex named after a World War I battle is home to the First Division Museum showcasing the history of the famed U.S. Army's 1st Infantry Division, and *Chicago Tribune* founder's Robert R. McCormick Mansion Museum. After clamoring over the cannons, kids can stop to smell the flowers blooming in the manicured gardens. Family programs and concerts scheduled year-round. Park opens Tuesday through Sunday 9 am to sunset; museum is open 9 am-4 pm. Park and museum admission free; car parking fee, $7. Nearby is the top-rated, public Cantigny Golf Course (630-260-8197) offering junior golf instruction and a 9-hole Youth Links Course (630-260-8270).

Chicago Botanic Garden, 1000 Lake Cook Rd, Glencoe, 847-835-5440; www.chicagobotanic.org. Open daily, admission is free to this 385-acre living preserve with more than 1.2 million plants rooted in 23 gardens, three tropical greenhouses, three natural habitats, eight lagoons, and bike paths. Kids love the winding, willow-branch tunnel in the Children's Garden where they can dig for worms and plant seeds. On Monday nights in summer, picnickers listen to the resonating chimes of carillon bell concerts on Evening Island. Late May through October, come for the Jr. Railroad where model trains puff through a garden of America's best loved landmarks (exhibit admission charged).

Cuneo Museum and Gardens, 1350 Milwaukee Ave, Vernon Hills, 847-362-3042; www.lake-online.com/cuneo. Kids romp through the 75-acre wooded estate's formal gardens, animal sanctuaries, and deer park surrounding a palatial Italianate mansion. Open Tuesday-Sunday 10 am-5 pm; $5 grounds admission fee; mansion tours cost $10 for adults, $5 for children.

Fermi National Accelerator Laboratory, Kirk Rd & Pine St, Batavia, 630-840-8258; www.fnal.gov. Release energy outdoors biking, hiking, and rollerblading the nature trails at the nuclear plant's 680-acre campus. Rare species of butterflies, plants, birds, and baby buffalos live on the rural grounds. Guided prairie tours offered in summer. Picnickers welcome and lake fishing available. Open daily; admission free. Kids power up their nuclear knowledge at the Leon M. Lederman Science Education Center learning about nature's secrets and how the universe began. Admission free; open weekdays. Fermilab physicists conduct behind-the-scenes lab tours and Q&A with guests the first weekend of every month.

Graceland Cemetery, Clark St & Irving Park Blvd, 312-922-3432; www.architecture.org. Eerie and educational, the famous 119-acre necropolis built in 1860 is a national architectural landmark filled with palatial mausoleums, haunting headstones, and reportedly disappearing angelic statues marking the graves of Chicago's rich, famous, and infamous. The

Chicago Architecture Foundation's (312-922-3432; www.architecture.org) spine-chilling cemetery tour is a drop-dead Halloween family favorite.

Grosse Pointe Lighthouse, Sheridan Rd & Central St, Evanston, 847-328-6961; www.grossepointelighthouse.org. The pretty grounds surrounding the charming, white, tapering lighthouse built in 1873 and fairy-tale stone cottage are open year-round. Tours of both structures are offered weekends June through September for children aged 8 and up. A wooded trail twists down a grassy slope to the isolated Lighthouse Landing Beach.

Tempel Lipizzans Farm, Wadsworth Rd & Hunt Club Rd, Wadsworth, 847-623-7272; www.tempelfarms.com. Trained in the centuries-old tradition of the Spanish Riding School in Vienna, dancing, white Lipizzaner stallions fly through the air performing fancy four-footed feats. Performances are Wednesdays and Sundays, June through August. Tours of the historic stables offered year-round.

Lambs Farm, 14245 W Rockland Rd, Libertyville, 847-362-4636; www.lambsfarm.org. Over 40 years old, this is Chicagoland's favorite farmyard, a non-profit residential farm for persons with developmental disabilities. Animal petting zoo, mini-golf, and vintage carousel open in season. Year-round feel-good family events include an old-fashioned Breakfast with Santa, Easter Brunch, fall festival, and more. Shops and kid-friendly country restaurant open Tuesday through Sunday.

Lincoln Park Zoo, 2200 N Cannon Dr, 312-742-2000; www.lpzoo.com. The nation's oldest free zoo recently opened the new Ape House and Regenstein African Journey habitat and North American animal exhibit at the Pritzker Family Children's Zoo. Kids love the graceful giraffes, lumbering elephants, and giant hissing Madagascar cockroaches. Additional family favorites are the *Farm-in-the-Zoo*, lion house, sea lion pool, and old-fashioned carousel (summer). Call for information on family programs including the ever popular *Night Watch* where families sleep over at the zoo!

Morton Arboretum, 4100 Illinois Rte 53, Lisle, 630-968-0074; www.mortonarb.org. Forests, meadows, gardens and wetlands cover 1,700 acres of this outdoor tree and plant museum with paved roads and 14 miles of trails for hiking and biking. Kids dig the new Children's Adventure Garden and Maze. Overall, a great place to tromp around and picnic. Food service on-site. Guided tours and kid/family nature classes offered year-round. Favorite family fall activities include leaf collecting and the "Scarecrow Trail." Open daily. Discounted admission on Wednesdays.

Naper Settlement, 523 S Webster St, Naperville, 630-420-6010; www.naper.settlement.museum. Kids experience life on the Midwestern prairie of the past at this re-creation of a 19th-century agrarian community. Working blacksmith shop, post office, and school house manned by costumed interpreters. The living history village's seasonal programs cater to kids with games, pony rides, and entertainment.

North Park Village Nature Center, 5801 N Pulaski Rd, 312-744-5472; www.cityofchicago.org/environment. You'll think you're a hundred miles west of the city at this 46-acre rolling woods and wetlands where deer roam and owls screech. Nature paths throughout. Admission free; open year-round. Popular week-long EcoExplorers summer camps for kids aged 5 to 14 years also offered.

Sears Tower Skydeck, 233 S Wacker Dr, 312-875-9696; www.theskydeck.com. OK, so only a pane of glass separates your baby from the sky blue. But the "Knee-High Chicago" kids' exhibit is worth the parental panic. Interactive displays tell tales of Chicago from a bird's eye view. A touch-and-talk computer explains city landmarks.

Classes

Many of the city's fine cultural institutions have stellar, kid-focused curricula and host popular summer camps. Chicago and suburban park districts offer solid sports instruction, dance, and crafts classes. But private specialty schools also instruct many pint-sized prodigies. Here are some of the most popular and pedigreed organizations:

Academy of Movement and Music, 605 Lake St, Oak Park, 708-848-2329. This 33-year-old school offers popular dance and movement classes. The cool, creative Boys Production class for guys ages 5 to 9 focuses on high-energy body movement practically applied to mini-manly visual arts projects, including mazes, puzzles, murals, sculptures, and machinery.

Alliance Francaise, 810 N Dearborn St, 312-337-1070; www.afchicago.com. Cultivating everything French in Chicagoans of all ages since 1897, this institution breeds petite Francophiles through intense language classes, camps, and cultural programs.

Bubbles Academy, 1504 N Fremont St, 312-944-7677. Yoga for youngsters taught with a creative twist in an open, airy studio.

Dennehy School of Irish Dance, 2555 W 111th St, 773-881-3990; www.dennehydancers.com. A South Side Irish institution, Dennehy has churned out high-stepping Irish dancers for over forty years. Its most-famous pupil so far is egomaniac, foot-pounding Michael Flatley of stage hits *River Dance* and *Lord of the Dance.*

Flavour Cooking School, 7401 W Madison St, Forest Park, 708-488-0808; www.flavourcookingschool.com. Kids learn to really stir it up from scrambled eggs and lasagna to stir-fry and California cuisine at this cozy cooking school and culinary cookware shop. Class content determined by chefs' ages: Kitchen Helpers (age 4-6); Young Chefs (age 7-11); Sous Chefs (age 12+). Kids' summer cooking camps are also offered.

Gallery 37, 66 E Randolph St, 312-744-8925; www.gallery37.org. Spearheaded by Maggie Daley, as in Mayor Richie's wife, Gallery 37's creative curriculum provides 14- to 21-year-old Chicago residents with educational on-the-job training in the visual, literary, media, culinary, and performing arts. Under the direction of professional artists, apprentices are paid while creating art projects throughout the city such as bench-painting, sculpture, play-writing, and multicultural dance. Eight-week summer program and limited programming during school year. Applications required.

Illinois Rhythmic Gymnastics Center, 491 Lake Cook Rd, Deerfield, 847-498-9888; www.multiplexclubs.com. This top flexible factory turns out more national and Olympic gymnastic team members than any other in the country.

Language Stars, locations city-wide, 866-557-8277; www.languagestars.com. Children aged 1 through 10 are instructed in foreign language through play-based immersion.

Lou Conte Dance Studio, 1147 W Jackson Blvd, 312-850-9766; www.hubbardstreetdance.org. The dance studio of esteemed Hubbard Street Dance Chicago offers killer classes for teens (aged 11 to 14) in hip-hop, tap, jazz, ballet, African, modern, and more. Also teaches children and teen dance classes through the new, thriving Beverly Arts Center (2407 W 111th St, 773-445-3838; beverlyartcenter.org).

Merit School of Music, 47 W Polk St, 312-786-9428; www.meritmusic.org. This tuition-free conservatory provides economically disadvantaged youth with excellent instruction in playing classical and jazz instruments. An answer to the public school system's sad arts education cuts.

Music Institute of Chicago, 1490 Chicago Ave, Evanston, 847-905-1500; www.musicinst.com. Students of all ages flock to this esteemed school specializing in the Suzuki Method for many instruments. Group and private instruction in string, wind, brass, and percussion instruments offered.

Old Town School of Folk Music, 4544 N Lincoln Ave & 909 W Armitage Ave, 773-728-6000; www.oldtownschool.org. Opened in 1957, this is Chicago's premier all-American music center specializing in lessons on twangy instruments. The school is best known for its Wiggleworms music movement program catering to the under-5 folk. Engaging teen curriculum in music, theater, dance, and art is also offered. Kids' concerts, actually all concerts, rock.

Ruth Page Center for the Arts, 1016 N Dearborn St, 312-337-6543; www.ruthpage.com. Prima ballerina classes for beginners to advanced students offered at this fine school whose graduates dance for the American Ballet Theatre, the New York City Ballet, and professional companies world-wide.

Second City Training Center, 1616 N Wells St, 312-664-3959; www.secondcity.com. Sign up your bucket of laughs for famed Second City's improvisational classes. Hilarious kids ages 4-12 attend hour-long sessions on Saturdays. Teen improv program is also offered.

Sherwood Conservatory of Music, 1312 S Michigan Ave, 312-427-6267; www.sherwoodmusic.org. Over-a-century-old Sherwood Conservatory specializes in the Suzuki Method for children ages 3 to 12 in cello, violin, viola, flute, piano, harp, and guitar. Also teaches classes at the South Side's Beverly Arts Center (2407 W 111th St, 773-445-3838; beverlyartcenter.org).

The Chopping Block, 4747 N Lincoln Ave, 773-472-6700; www.thechoppingblock.net. The Lincoln Square neighborhood store and kitchen complex of this sophisticated culinary store hosts cooking classes for kids ages 7-12 two times a week. Four-day cooking camp for two hours a day held in summers.

Tri-Star Gymnastics, 1401 Circle Ave, Forest Park, 708-771-7827; www.tri-star.com. This women-run gym pumps out gymnastic champs ages 18 months through teens. Flexing its muscle since 1987, the not-for-profit center offers caring instruction for boys and girls in gymnastics, tumbling, and trampoline. The center is home to a GIJO Team (Junior Olympics) and USGA Teams.

Shopping Essentials

Designer duds, high-style child furniture, imaginative toys, and kids' tunes. Chicago stores have it all for newborns to teens. Here's just a sampling of the top shops:

- **Active Kids** • 838 W Armitage Ave • 773-281-2002 • Child sportswear.
- **Alamo Shoes** • 5321 N Clark St • 773-334-6100; 6548 W Cermak Rd, Berwyn • 708-795-818 • Experienced staff for toddler shoe fittings.
- **American Girl Place** • 111 E Chicago Ave • 312-943-9400 • Dolls and books.
- **The Baby's Room** • 640 N LaSalle St • 312-642-1520 • Every furniture need fulfilled.
- **Bearly Used** • 401 Linden Ave, Wilmette • 847-256-8700 • Fab deals on duds and furniture.
- **Bellini** • 2100 N Southport Ave • 773-880-5840 (stores also in Highland Park and Oak Brook) • High-end, custom bedding, furniture, and clothes.
- **Building Blocks Toy Store** • 3306 N Lincoln Ave • 773-525-6200 • Old-fashioned, brain-building toys.
- **Carrara Children's Shoes** • 2505 1/2 N Clark St • 773-529-9955 • Tot soles from Italy.
- **Children in Paradise** • 909 N Rush St • 312-951-5437 • Personable kids' bookseller.
- **Cut Rate Toys** • 5409 W Devon Ave • 773-763-5740 • Discounted favorites.
- **Disney Store** • 717 N Michigan Ave • 312-654-9208 • Princess paraphernalia and Mouse gear.
- **Forest Bootery** • 492 Central Ave, Highland Park • 847-433-1911; 284 E Market Sq, Lake Forest • 847-234-0201 • Great but pricey shoe store.
- **Galt Toys + Galt Baby** • 900 N Michigan Ave • 312-440-9550; Northbrook Court, Northbrook • 847-498-4660 • High-end toy store and baby supplies.
- **Gymboree** • 835 N Michigan Ave • 312-649-9074 • Designer preemie and kids' clothes.
- **Kozy's Bike Shop** • 601 S LaSalle St • 312-360-0020 • Everything for biking families.
- **LMNOP** • 2572 N Lincoln Ave • 773-975-4055 • Hip, fun kids' clothes.
- **Land of Nod** • 900 W North Ave • 312-475-9903 (stores also in Oak Brook Center and Northbrook Court) • Cute kids' furniture.
- **Lazar's Juvenile Furniture** • 6557 N Lincoln Ave, Lincolnwood • 847-679-6146 • Tried-and-true children's furniture store.
- **Little Strummer** • 909 W Armitage Ave • 773-751-3410 • Kids' tunes.
- **Madison and Friends** • 940 N Rush St • 312-642-6403 • Designer clothes.
- **Mini Me** • 900 N Michigan Ave • 312-988-4011 • European designer clothes.
- **Oilily** • 520 N Michigan Ave • 312-527-5747 • Colorful patterned kids' clothes.
- **Pottery Barn Kids** • 2111 N Clybourn Ave• 773-525-8349 (stores also in Oak Brook Center, Old Orchard Center and Deer Park Town Center) • Furnishings for the completely coordinated kid's boudoir.
- **POSH Skate Shop** • 628 Church St, Evanston • 847-424-8605 • www.skateboardingchicago.com • Cool skateboarders' shop.
- **Psycho Baby** • 1630 N Damen Ave • 773-772-2815 • Funky kids' clothes.
- **Pumpkin Moon** • 1028 North Blvd, Oak Park • 708-524-8144 • Funky, vintage toys.
- **Red Balloon Company** • 2060 Damen Ave • 773-489-9800 • Toys, clothes, furniture.
- **The Right Start** • 2121 N Clybourn Ave • 773-296-4420 • Baby equipment galore.
- **Uncle Fun** • 1338 W Belmont Ave • 773-477-8223 • Hilarious novelties and vintage tin wind-up toys.
- **Shops at Northbridge** • 520 N Michigan Ave • 312-327-2300 • Entire third floor is kids' clothing, toys, and accessories, including Nordstrom.
- **Saturday's Child** • 2146 N Halsted St • 773-525-8697 • Creative toys.
- **The Second Child** • 954 W Armitage Ave • 773-883-0880 • Gently used designer clothes.
- **Timeless Toys** • 4749 N Lincoln Ave • 773-334-4445 • Old-fashioned, hand-crafted toys.
- **Toyscape** • 2911 N Broadway St • 773-665-7400 • Toys galore.
- **U.S. Toy–Constructive Playthings** • 5314 W Lincoln Ave, Skokie • 847-675-5900 • Educational toys favored by teachers.
- **Zany Brainy** • 2163 N Clybourn Ave • 773-281-2371 • Imagination-igniting toys.

Where to go for more information

Chicago Parent Magazine • www.chicagoparent.com
Oaklee's Guide for Chicagoland Kids • www.OakleesGuide.com

Veterinarian

Veterinarian	Address	Phone	Map
Chicago Veterinary Emergency Services	3123 N Clybourn Ave	773-281-7710	42

Pharmacies

Pharmacies	Phone	Map
Walgreens:		
641 N Clark St	312-587-1416	2
757 N Michigan Ave	312-664-8686	3
111 S Halsted St	312-463-9142	4
501 W Roosevelt St	312-492-8559	7
3405 S Dr M L King Jr Dr	312-326-4058	14
1554 E 55th St	773-667-1177	19
1931 W Cermak Rd	773-847-5781	25
1520 W Fullerton Ave	773-929-6968	29
1601 N Wells St	312-642-4008	31
1200 N Dearborn St	312-943-0973	32
7510 N Western St	773-764-1765	33
5625 N Ridge Ave	773-989-7546	37
3302 W Belmont Ave	773-267-2328	41
3046 N Halsted St	773-325-0413	44
Broadway St & Belmont Ave	773-327-3591	44
6310 N Nagle Ave	773-774-2225	45
4343 N Central Ave	773-427-9456	48
4040 N Cicero Ave	773-283-5321	48
5600 W Fullerton Ave	773-745-1640	48
4748 W North Ave	773-745-6642	49
5435 S Kedzie Ave	773-436-7396	54
11 E 75th St	773-224-1211	57
1633 W 95th St	773-445-9277	56
7109 S Jeffery Blvd	773-324-1880	57
8628 S Cottage Grove Ave	773-651-8500	57
2924 E 92nd St	773-721-6603	58
CVS:		
3944 N Western Ave	773-279-7600	39
2815 N Western Ave	773-486-4102	41
8639 S Cicero Ave	773-284-6332	53
7855 S Western Ave	773-436-6000	54
3951 W 103rd St	773-881-3323	56
Osco Drug:		
1224 S Wabash Ave	312-663-4646	11
5532 N Clark St	773-784-7348	37
3572 N Elston Ave	773-583-9858	41
2941 N Ashland Ave	773-348-4155	43
6426 W Irving Park Rd	773-725-2900	47
5324 S Pulaski Rd	773-284-7402	53

Delivery & Messengers

Delivery & Messengers	Address	Phone	Map
Deadline Express	449 N Union Ave	312-850-1200	1
On The Fly Courier	131 N Green St	312-738-2154	4

Gyms

Gyms	Address	Phone	Map
XSport Fitness	230 W North Ave	312-932-9100	31
Chicago Fitness Center	3131 N Lincoln Ave	773-549-8181	43
XSport Fitness	3240 N Ashland Ave	773-529-1461	43

Copy Shops

Copy Shops	Address	Phone	Map
Kinko's	444 N Wells St	312-670-4460	2
Kinko's	127 S Clinton St	312-258-8833	4
24 Seven Copies	222 N La Salle St	312-704-0247	5
Kinko's	29 S La Salle St	312-578-8520	5
24 Seven Copies	200 E Randolph St	312-616-1847	6
Kinko's	1242 S Canal St	312-455-0920	10
Kinko's	1800 W North Ave	773-395-4639	21
Kinko's	2300 N Clybourn Ave	773-665-7500	29
Kinko's	3524 N Southport Ave	773-975-5031	43
Kinko's	3001 N Clark St	773-528-0500	44

Plumbers

Plumbers	Phone
A Metro Plumbing & Sewer Service	877-872-3060
A-AAAA Plumbing & Sewer	773-282-2878
A Better Man Plumbing & Sewer	773-286-9351
Roto-Rooter	800-438-7686
Sears HomeCentral	773-737-3580
Emergency Response	773-736-3247
O'Bannon Plumbing & Sewer (Northside)	773-486-5748
O'Bannon Plumbing & Sewer (Southside)	773-862-5112
Top Quality Plumbing & Sewer	773-523-1160
Sunrise Plumbing & Sewer	773-960-6462
Apex Plumbing & Sewer	773-477-7714
FPS	773-268-4604
Action Plumbing & Sewer	773-376-6666

Locksmiths

Locksmiths	Phone
Gateway Locksmith	800-964-8282
A-AAround the Clock	800-281-5445
Safemasters	312-627-8209
Always Available	773-478-1960
Five Star Lock & Key	773-778-2066
Aabbitt	312-719-8200
A-ABC 24-hour Locksmith	773-772-3930

The impeccably restored **Music Box Theatre**, built in 1929, features fantastic Moorish architecture, floating clouds on the ceilings, and live organ music at many weekend screenings. Specialties include the latest art house and international releases, as well as restored classics and weekend matinee double-features that follow monthly themes. Holiday season sing-alongs of *White Christmas* are huge hits that sell out in advance. The Music Box is also the major screening ground for International Film Festival and Gay and Lesbian Film Festival releases.

Other worthy art-house screening rooms include the **Landmark Century Centre Cinema** at the Century Mall and **Lowes Piper's Alley Theater** in Old Town. For even more esoteric options, pick up a schedule for the **Gene Siskel Film Center** of the Art Institute or **Facets Multimedia** on Fullerton in the DePaul neighborhood.

The latest action features should be seen at **Leows** at Webster Place which offers ample theaters and show times. Cheap seats on relatively new releases can be had at the **3 Penny Cinema** on Lincoln and Lincoln Square's **Davis Cinema**.

One of Chicago's most notorious places to catch a flick is **The Vic's** "Brew and View" where the drunken frat boy audiences are almost as annoying as the movies that they show.

Theater	*Address*	*Phone*	*Map*
AMC	2600 N Western Ave	773-394-1601	28
AMC River East	322 E Illinois St	312-596-0333	3
Chicago Filmmakers	5243 N Clark St	773-293-1447	37
Davis Cinema	4614 N Lincoln Ave	773-784-0894	39
Facets Multimedia Theatre	1517 W Fullerton Ave	773-281-9075	29
Gene Siskel Film Center	164 N State St	312-846-2800	5
Landmark Century Centre Cinema	2828 N Clark St	773-509-4949	44
Loews	1471 W Webster Ave	773-327-3100	29
Loews	600 N Michigan Ave	312-255-9347	3
Logan Theater	2646 N Milwaukee Ave	773-252-0627	27
Lowes Esquire	58 E Oak St	312-280-1205	32
Lowes Lincoln Village	6341 N McCormick Rd	773-604-4072	46
Lowes Piper Alley Theater	1608 N Wells St	312-642-6275	31
Museum of Contemporary Art	220 E Chicago Ave	312-397-4010	3
Music Box Theatre	3733 N Southport Ave	773-871-6604	43
Navy Pier IMAX Theatre	700 E Grand Ave	312-595-5629	3
Omnimax Theatre	Museum of Science & Industry, E 57th St & Lake Shore Dr	773-684-1414	20
Three Penny Cinema	2424 N Lincoln Ave	773-935-5744	30
University of Chicago Doc Films	1212 E 59th St	773-702-8575	19
Vic Theatre Brew & View	3145 N Sheffield Ave	773-929-6713	43
Village North Theaters	6746 N Sheridan Rd	773-764-9100	34
Village Theater	1548 N Clark St	312-642-2403	32
Village Theatres Burnham Plaza	826 S Wabash Ave	312-554-9100	8

This past year has been an interesting one for the burgeoning art scene in Chicago—newer galleries and local art fairs have pumped fresh energy into the city's art scene. The perception of Chicago as an exciting incubator city for emerging start-ups has become well-deserved—there are more alternative spaces than ever before.

As for where all this is happening, there continues to be a shift in the art districts in the city. New York's SoHo-to-Chelsea migration mirrored a similar change in the traditional River North gallery area. In search of larger, cheaper, and more contemporary gallery spaces, River North galleries flocked to the West Loop. The West Loop has solidly positioned itself as the center for more cutting edge contemporary spaces and now has a large enough number of them to make the trip to the neighborhood well worth your time. (Public transportation in the area is not great, but certainly do-able.) Though there are still some impressive hold-outs in River North, namely **Zolla-Lieberman Gallery**, **Zg Gallery**, and the newly expanded **Catherine Edelman Gallery** for photography, most of the scene can be found about a mile-and-a-half southwest.
The intersection of Peoria and Washington Streets serves as the axis for the West Loop Galleries. **Carrie Secrist Gallery** and **Kavi Gupta Gallery** at 835 W Washington are good starting points for the emerging and established variety, while a half-block north, buildings on either side of the street are home to a gaggle of smaller spaces such as **Aaron Packer Gallery**, **Peter Miller Gallery**, **ThreeWalls, Bodybuilder & Sportsman Gallery**, and **Bucket Rider** to name a few standouts. Get ambitious and walk several more blocks northwest to find **Lisa Boyle Gallery** and **Western Exhibitions** and you will be rewarded with quality work by emerging artists in the ever-expanding movement to the Fulton Street Market District.

Finally, for the most adventurous, be sure to try and feel out some of the many alternative part-time gallery spaces in the city. Though they are a little dicier as far as the exhibition scheduling and location, they often pay off with some of the most unusual and thought-provoking stuff Chicago has to offer. **Suitable**, **Deadtech**, **Polvo Art**, **Dogmatic**, and **Heaven Gallery** are a few examples—check www.chicagoart.net for more info on galleries in the city.

1 • River North / Fulton Market District

Northeastern Illinois University Fine Arts Center Gallery	5500 N St Louis Ave	773-442-4944

2 • Near North / River North

Akainyah Gallery	357 W Erie St	312-654-0333
Alan Koppel Gallery	210 W Chicago Ave	312-640-0730
Aldo Castillo Gallery	233 W Huron St	312-337-2536
Andrew Bae Gallery	300 W Superior St	312-335-8601
Ann Nathan Gallery	212 W Superior St	312-664-6622
Byron Roche Gallery	750 N Franklin St, Ste 105	312-654-0144
Carl Hammer Gallery	740 N Wells St	312-266-8512
Carrie Secrist Gallery	835 W Washington Blvd	312-491-0917
Catherine Edelman Gallery	300 W Superior St	312-266-2350
Galeria Gala	708 N Wells St	312-640-0517
Gwenda Jay/ Addington Gallery	704 N Wells St	312-664-3406
Habatat Galleries	222 W Superior St	312-440-0288
Hildt Galleries	617 N State St	312-255-0005
I Space	230 W Superior St	312-587-9976
Jean Albano Gallery	215 W Superior St	312-440-0770
Judy A Saslow Gallery	300 W Superior St	312-943-0530
Kass Meridian Gallery	325 W Huron St	312-266-5999
Kenneth Probst Galleries	46 E Superior St	312-440-1991
Lydon Fine Art	309 W Superior St	312-943-1133
Marx-Saunders Gallery	230 W Superior St	312-573-1400
Mary Bell Gallery	740 N Franklin St	312-642-0202
Maya Polsky Gallery	215 W Superior St	312-440-0055
Melanee Cooper Gallery	740 N Franklin St	312-202-9305
Mongerson Gallery	704 N Wells St	312-943-2354
Nicole Gallery	230 W Huron St	312-787-7716
NIU Art Gallery	215 W Superior St	312-642-6010
Northern Illinois University Art Gallery	215 W Superior St	312-642-6010
Oskar Friedl Gallery	1020 W 35th St	312-493-4330
Perimeter Gallery	210 W Superior St	312-266-9473
Peter Bartlow Gallery	44 E Superior St	312-337-1782
Portals	742 N Wells St	312-642-1066
Primitive Art Works	706 N Wells St	312-943-3770
Printworks	311 W Superior St	312-664-9407
RH Love Galleries	645 N Michigan Ave	312-640-1300
Richard Norton Gallery	612 Merchandise Mart Plz	312-644-8855
Rita Bucheit Fine Art & Antiques	449 N Wells St	312-527-4080
Robert Henry Adams Fine Art	715 N Franklin St	312-642-8700
Rosenthal Fine Art, Inc	3 E Huron St	312-475-0700
Roy Boyd Gallery	739 N Wells St	312-642-1606
Russell Bowman Art Advisory	311 W Superior St, Ste 115	312-751-9500
S2 Art Gallery	300 W Superior St #203	312-943-8500
Schneider Gallery	230 W Superior St	312-988-4033
Sonia Zaks Gallery	311 W Superior St, Ste 207	312-943-8440
Stephen Daiter Gallery	311 W Superior St	312-787-3350
TBA Exhibition Space	230 W Huron St	312-587-3300
Trowbridge Gallery	703 N Wells St	312-587-9575
Vale Craft Gallery	230 W Superior St	312-337-3525
Zg Gallery	300 W Superior St	312-654-9900
Zolla-Lieberman Gallery	325 W Huron St	312-944-1990
Zygman Voss Gallery	222 W Superior St	312-787-3300

3 • Streeterville / Mag Mile

City Gallery	806 N Michigan Ave	312-742-0808
Inspire Fine Art	435 E Illinois, Ste 131	312-595-9475
Joel Oppenheimer Gallery	410 N Michigan Ave	312-642-5300
Lora D Art Gallery	435 E Illinois St	312-245-9005
Ogilvie/Pertl Gallery	435 E Illinois, Ste 151	312-321-0750
RS Johnson Fine Art	645 N Michigan Ave, Ste 234	312-943-1661
The Arts Club of Chicago	201 E Ontario St	312-787-3997

4 • West Loop Gate / Greektown

Gallery 2	847 W Jackson Blvd	312-563-5162
Thomas McCormick Gallery	835 W Washington Blvd	312-226-6800

5 • The Loop

Donald Young Gallery	933 W Washington St	312-455-0100
Illinois State Museum Chicago Gallery	100 W Randolph St, 2nd Fl	312-814-5322

6 • The Loop / Grant Park

Cliff Dwellers Gallery	200 S Michigan Ave	312-922-8080
Fine Arts Building Gallery	410 S Michigan Ave	312-913-0537
Hilligoss Gallery	520 N Michigan Ave	312-755-0300

8 • South Loop / Printers Row

Art House Gallery	43 W Harrison St	708-763-9533
Bella Vista Fine Art Gallery	746 N La Salle St	312-274-1490

11 • South Loop / McCormick Place

Woman Made Gallery	2418 W Bloomingdale Ave	773-489-8900

13 • Bridgeport (East)

MN Gallery	3524 S Halsted St	773-847-0573

19 • Hyde Park

Artisans 21	5225 S Harper Ave	773-288-7450

20 • East Hyde Park / Jackson Park

Hyde Park Art Center	5307 S Hyde Park Blvd	773-324-5520

21 • Wicker Park / Ukrainian Village

Carlos E Jimenez Gallery	2301 W North Ave	773-235-5328
David Leonardis Gallery	1352 N Paulina St	773-278-3058
Gallery 203	1579 N Milwaukee Ave	773-252-1952
Heaven Gallery	1550 N Milwaukee Ave	773-342-4597

22 • Noble Square / Goose Island

1112 Gallery	1112 N Milwaukee Ave	773-486-9612
Madrone LLC	1000 W North Ave, 3rd Fl	312-640-1302

23 • West Town / Near West Side

Gallery 406	406 N Wood St	773-255-4546
Open-End Art Gallery	2000 W Fulton Market	312-738-2140

24 • River West / West Town

Aaron Packer Gallery	118 N Peoria St	312-226-8984
ARC Gallery	734 N Milwaukee Ave	312-733-2787
Bodybuilder and Sportsman Gallery	119 N Peoria St, #2C	312-492-7261
Bucket Rider Gallery	119 N Peoria St #3D	312-421-6993
Douglas Dawson Gallery	400 N Morgan St	312-226-7975
Flatfile Galleries	217 N Carpenter	312-491-1190
Frederick Baker Gallery	1230 W Jackson Blvd	312-243-2980
Function + Art	1046 W Fulton Market	312-243-2780
Gallery 312	845 W Fulton	312-850-1234
Gescheidle	118 N Peoria St	312-654-0600
GR N'Namdi Gallery	110 N Peoria St	312-563-9240
Kavi Gupta Gallery	835 W Washington Blvd	312-432-0708
Klein Art Works	400 N Morgan St	312-243-0400
Linda Warren Gallery	1052 W Fulton Market	312-432-9500
Lisa Boyle Gallery	1648 W Kinzie St	773-655-5475
Monique Meloche Gallery	118 N Peoria St	312-455-0299
Peter Miller Gallery	118 N Peoria St	312-226-5291
Rhona Hoffman Gallery	118 N Peoria St	312-455-1990
Richard Milliman Fine Art	1364 W Grand Ave	312-432-9900
Rogeramsay Gallery	711 N Milwaukee Ave	312-491-1400
Schopf Gallery	942 W Lake St	312-432-1630
Stolen Buick Studio	1303 W Chicago Ave	312-226-5902
Walsh Gallery	118 N Peoria St, 2nd Fl	312-829-3312
Western Exhibitions	1648 W Kinzie St	312-307-4685

26 • University Village / Little Italy

Colibri Gallery	2032 W 18th St	312-733-8431
Gallery 400	1240 W Harrison St	312-996-6114
Polvo Art Studio	1458 W 18th St	773-344-1940

27 • Logan Square

Deadtech	3321 W Fullerton Ave	773-395-2844

28 • Bucktown

Art Gallery Kafe	1907 N Milwaukee Ave	773-235-2351
Gallery 1633	1633 N Damen Ave	773-384-4441
Idao Gallery	1616 N Damen Ave	708-386-3884
Morlen Sinoway-Atelier	1052 W Fulton Market	312-432-0100

29 • DePaul / Wrightwood / Sheffield

Chicago Center for the Print	1509 W Fullerton Ave	773-477-1585
DePaul University Art Museum	2350 N Kenmore Ave	773-325-7506
Havana Gallery	1139 W Webster Ave	773-549-2492
La Llorona Gallery	1474 W Webster Ave	773-281-8460

30 • Lincoln Park

Contemporary Art Workshop	542 W Grant Pl	773-472-4004
Old Town Triangle	1763 N North Park Ave	312-337-1938

31 • Old Town / Near North

Thomas Masters Gallery	245 W North Ave	312-440-2322

32 • Gold Coast / Mag Mile

Aaron Gallery	50 E Oak St	312-943-0660
Armstrong Fine Arts	200 E Walton St	312-664-9312
Billy Hork Galleries	109 E Oak St	312-337-1199
Colletti Gallery	67 E Oak St	312-664-6767
FL Braswell Fine Art	73 E Elm St	312-636-4399
Galleries Maurice Sternberg	875 N Michigan Ave	312-642-1700
The Hart Gallery	64 E Walton St	312-932-9646
Richard Gray Gallery	875 N Michigan Ave, Ste 2503	312-642-8877
Valerie Carberry Gallery	875 N Michigan Ave, Ste 2510	312-397-9990

37 • Edgewater / Andersonville

Las Manos Gallery	5220 N Clark St	773-728-8910

39 • Ravenswood / North Center

Peter Jones Gallery	1806 W Cuyler Ave	773-472-6725

40 • Uptown

Beacon Street Gallery	4131 N Broadway St	773-525-7579

42 • North Center / Roscoe Village

August House Studio	2113 W Roscoe St	773-327-5644

43 • Wrigleyville/ East Lakeview

Bell Studio	3428 N Southport Ave	773-281-2172
Fourth World Artisans	3727 N Southport Ave	773-404-5200

44 • East Lakeview

Leigh Gallery	3306 N Halsted St	773-472-1865

57 • South Chicago

The Renaissance Society	5811 S Ellis Ave	773-702-8670

Bar trends come and go, and far be it from us to spotlight the latest "in" spots—Tuesday's passion is Wednesday's pariah. All the same, let's not discount the few Chicago institutions that have managed, for better or for worse, to stand the test of time.

Appealing mostly to tourists and suburban punters is the rowdy-young-drunk behemoth known as **Mother's**. A cornerstone of the Rush/Division scene (glorified in John Hughes' movie *Class*), Mother's is the big bad grandma of the hijinks bars of the area. Get your neon-shots, your Red Bull-and-something, and your blurry phone numbers on matchbooks here. For the same flavor, but not as much spice, head further north to Lincoln Park's **Gamekeepers**. Gamekeepers has been a local sports bar/watering hole/pick-up spot for twenty-something jocks, Lincoln Parkers, and yuppie-wannabes seemingly forever, and its popularity hasn't wavered. For the slightly more trend-conscious members of the scene, look no further than Bucktown's **Danny's**. Once a little-known arty hangout, Danny's renown has spread, making it one of the most enduring of the yuppy-hipster hangouts that dominate the 'hood. Another is the late-night **Borderline,** packed every weekend with last-chance partiers after the local 2 am bars close.

The best places in town to play the struggling artist, or meet one, are Wicker Park's **Gold Star** and **Rainbo Club**, or Roscoe Village's **Hungry Brain**. And speaking of Roscoe Village, where a tavern seems to pop up every two steps, **The Village Tap** is a longtime local favorite. Also on the Northside, **Ginger Man Tavern** in Wrigleyville is a nice place to meet friends, unless the Cubs are in town, in which case, it's filled to the brim with sports fans. On the Southside, U of C students and faculty have been juicing up at **Woodlawn Tap** and **The Cove** for ages. If dive is more your style, **Old Town Ale House** was recently voted one of the nation's best dive bars. Dive-with-a-rock-star-attitude is the temperature at **Delilah's**, a long-lasting rock venue with eclectic DJ's and the best rock jukebox in the city. **Exit** is another local rock bar legend, leaning heavily towards the punk and goth end of the spectrum.

If you want to down a nice Irish pint and be entertained with spine-tingling folklore at the same time, belly-up at Lincoln Avenue's **Red Lion Pub**. This classic Irish pub is widely rumored to be haunted. For a banshee-free pub experience, head northwest to **Chief O'Neill's** on North Elston Avenue. Here you can get a well-drawn pint, served with a brogue, along with traditional pub fare and live Celtic music—it's enough to get anyone's Irish up.

A few other Chicago stalwarts worth mentioning: North Chicagoans cozy up at **Hopleaf**—a very popular (read: usually packed) neighborhood bar with a jazz jukebox and amazing selection of Belgian beers. **Big Chicks** has been a mixed-gay fave since the mid-eighties. Other gay bars of note include **Roscoe's**, **Sidetrack,** and **The Closet**.

Clubs & Cabarets

Chicago is a live music town. In summer it seems to be streaming from street fairs at nearly every corner in the city (see the Calendar of Events for more information). Year round, world-class music venues spread as far as the L tracks from one side of the city to the other. Whether it's hot jazz, Chicago-style electric blues, the latest as-of-yet-unknown Smashing Pumpkins, Liz Phair, or Tortoise, or the pulsing beats of celebrity DJ's like Derrick Carter and DJ Psychobitch that gets you hot and sweaty, Chicago is a great place to get your groove on.

For blues, Chicagoans know to drive past the tourist-friendly Northside blues joints and head either down south to **Lee's Unleaded**, or due west to **Rosa's Lounge**. For jazz, **The Green Mill** was the home bar of acclaimed Blue Note artists Patricia Barber and Kurt Elling and is well known for its late-night jam sessions and Sunday night poetry slams. **Andy's** in Streeterville draws an upscale jazz crowd. World music fans should check out international acts at **HotHouse** or catch traditional Celtic music at **Chief O'Neill's**.

For Chicagoans who like their music and their venue raw and gritty, Chicago's rock-n-roll upstarts can be found at **Bottom Lounge**. More successful rock groups, both local and touring, play at the smelly **Empty Bottle**, which also has avant-garde jazz nights. The highest rung on the local ladder for indie groups are **Metro** and **Doubledoor**—headlining at either of these two places is the golden ring for local rock groups. Many local bands get their first gig at the rock dump, **The Mutiny**—caveat emptor.

For ambient grooves, check out **Darkroom**, **Sonotheque,** or the hip but welcoming **Rodan**. **Berlin** is a long-established and legendary gay club with a mixed clientele and tiny, packed dance floor. **Circuit** also draws homos and heteros alike with dancing and special theme nights. For downtown clubbing, **Sound Bar** is the latest craze (at least as we write this). Meanwhile, the platinum card set slinks at **Le Passage** and folks from outside the city boundaries stand in long lines at **Crobar** and **Excalibur**. If goth is your groove and you haven't moved beyond the eighties, the retro vibe at **Neo** may be for you.

Finally, a word on smoking—as of this writing the anti-smoking frenzy that's captured the coasts has not yet bled into the second city—although suburbs Oak Park and Wilmette are leading the pack in the race to "butt out." All the same, considering that we're talking about a demographic that refuses to see the health risks in a diet of hot links and Italian beefs, let alone rooting for any of the local sports teams, we have a hard time believing that a ban on smoking would ever pass muster here—no matter what those milquetoasts think in LA or NY.

Map 1 • River North / Fulton Market District

Emmit's Irish Pub & Eatery	495 N Milwaukee Ave	312-563-9631	An old-school Chicago establishment.
Funky Buddha Lounge	728 W Grand Ave	312-666-1695	See and be seen at this trendy live music lounge.
Motel	600 W Chicago	312-822-2900	It's a hotel bar without the hotel!
Rednofive & Fifth Floor	440 N Halsted St	312-733-6699	Two levels of existence; downstairs=dancing, upstairs=posing.
Rive Gauche	306 N Halsted	312-738-9971	Late night dancing in lavish setting.

Map 2 • Near North / River North

Andy's	11 E Hubbard St	312-642-6805	Laid-back jazz club for old bones.
Bin 36	339 N Dearborn St	312-755-9463	Wine bar with everything that entails.
Blue Chicago	736 N Clark St	312-642-6261	Touristy blues bar.
Blue Frog Bar & Grill	676 N La Salle Dr	312-943-8900	Board games and karoake.
Brehon Pub	731 N Wells St	312-642-1071	Irish Pub, lots of TVs for sports.
Cyrano's Bistrot & Wine Bar	546 N Wells St	312-467-0546	Charming.
Excalibur	632 N Dearborn St	312-266-1944	Touristy club in a historic castle building that survived the Chicago Fire.
Frankie's Blue Room	16 W Chicago Ave	630-416-4898	Rock/Pop.
Gentry	440 N State St	312-836-0933	Piano bar one of the many features of this multi-themed gay club.
Green Door Tavern	678 N Orleans St	312-664-5496	A Chicago landmark; old-school classic.
House of Blues	329 N Dearborn St	312-923-2000	Swampy Bayou concert hall transplanted into the heart of Chicago.
Howl at the Moon	26 W Hubbard St	312-863-7427	Late night dinner and pianists who encourage patrons to sing.
Martini Ranch	311 W Chicago Ave	312-335-9500	Tightly packed hipster haven.
Minx	111 W Hubbard St	312-828-9000	Nibble upstairs on Pan-Asian food, and recline downstairs to lounge.
Mother Hubbard's	5 W Hubbard St	312-828-0007	Another Rush Street nightmare.
Narcisse	710 N Clark St	312-787-2675	Posh champagne and caviar club.
Redhead Piano Bar	16 W Ontario St	312-640-1000	Snug piano bar favorite of the area.
Rock Bottom Restaurants & Brewery	1 W Grand Ave	312-755-9339	Great micro-brews, decent pub grub.
Spy Bar	646 N Franklin St	312-587-8779	Basement club, house music, fashionable crowd, pricy drinks.
Uncommon Ground Café	388 N Clark St	773-929-3680	Local acts play while sipping a latte.
Vision	640 N Dearborn St	312-266-1944	Attached to Excalibur, the venue offers a modern alternative—i.e. the oxygen bar.

Map 3 • Streeterville / Mag Mile

Billy Goat Tavern	430 N Michigan Ave	312-222-1525	Home of infamous cheezeboigas.
Dick's Last Resort	435 E Illinois St	312-836-7870	Between Mardi Gras & Hell.
O'Neill's Bar & Grill	152 E Ontario St	312-787-5269	A touristy joint with pub food.
Timothy O'Toole's Pub	622 N Fairbanks Ct	312-642-0700	A touristy joint with pub food.

Map 4 • West Loop Gate / Greek Town

Reserve	858 W Lake St	312-455-1111	The latest trendy concept lounge.
Reunion	811 W Lake St	312-491-9600	Mainly a fashionable black crowd, but Thursday and Saturday's it's rainbow (gay).
Snuggery Saloon & Dining Room	Union Station, Canal & Adams	312-441-9334	Eclectic.

Map 5 • The Loop

Cal's	400 S Wells St	312-922-6392	Dictionary definition of dump draws grungy rockers, and neighborhood drunks. (Often both are the same!)
Exchequer Pub	226 S Wabash Ave	312-939-5633	Art institute where students drink.
Govnor's Pub	207 N State St	312-236-3696	The place to get sauced after work.
Manhattans	415 S Dearborn St	312-957-0460	Tired of martini bars? Try small but fun Manhattans.
Miller's Pub	134 S Wabash Ave	312-263-4988	A Loop tradition.

Map 6 • The Loop / Grant Park

Alumni Club	150 N Michigan Ave	312-345-1400	Desperados and Dingbats love this place.
Houlihan's	111 E Wacker Dr	312-616-FOOD	Rowdy meeting place.

Map 7 • South Loop / River City

Scarlett's Gentleman's	750 S Clinton St	312-986-1300	Strip club.

Map 8 • South Loop / Printers Row / Dearborn Park

Buddy Guy's Legends	754 S Wabash Ave	312-427-0333	One of the oldest blues clubs in Chicago, and the hardest to get a drink in.

Map 8 • South Loop / Printers Row / Dearborn Park—*continued*

George's Cocktail Lounge	646 S Wabash Ave	312-427-3964	Columbia students and faculty quaff in this dive between classes.
HotHouse	31 E Balbo Ave	312-362-9707	Funky world music and jazz venue.
Kasey's Tavern	701 S Dearborn St	312-427-7992	108-year-old neighborhood oasis.
South Loop Club	701 S State St	312-427-2787	There's something creepy about this place.
Tantrum	1023 S State St	312-939-9160	Tucked away, nicely appointed bar that attracts a lively South Loop following.

Map 9 • South Loop / South Michigan Ave

Kitty O'Shea's	720 S Michigan Ave	312-294-6860	Guinness Fish and Chips with your Guinness?
Savoy Bar and Grill	800 S Michigan Ave	312-939-1464	Serious drinking in a kooky '50s hotel; early morning breakfast.

Map 11 • South Loop / McCormick Place

Chicago Legends	2109 S Wabash Ave	312-326-0300	25-and-over cocktail lounge/nightclub.
The Cotton Club	1710 S Michigan Ave	312-341-9787	Zoot suit or not, it's a hip place for you and daddy.
Velvet Lounge	2128 1/2 S Indiana Ave	312-791-9050	Raw, gritty jazz haven.
Wabash Tap	1233 S Wabash Ave	312-360-9488	Casual neighborhood oasis.

Map 13 • Bridgeport (East)

Jimbo's Lounge	3258 S Princeton Ave	312-326-3253	Close to Sox park.
Puffer's Bar	3356 S Halsted St	773-927-6073	A Southside standby.
Schaller's	3714 S Halsted St	773-376-6332	Neighborhood Sox bar with grub.

Map 14 • Prairie Shores / Lake Meadows

Cobblestone's Bar and Grill	514 E Pershing Rd	773-624-3630	A quiet neighborhood bar. Closes early.
Darryl's Den	2600 S State St	312-842-1984	You won't see the light of day.
Mr T's Lounge	3528 S Indiana Ave	312-326-4046	Welcome to the basement.

Map 15 • Canaryville / Fuller Park

Kelley's Tavern	4403 S Wallace St	773-924-0796	A neighborhood place.

Map 19 • Hyde Park

Lucky Strike	1055 E 55th St	773-347-2695	1920s decor in Hyde Park haven.
Woodlawn Tap	1172 E 55th St	773-643-5516	Popular with students.

Map 20 • East Hyde Park / Jackson Park

Bar Louie	5500 S South Shore Dr	773-363-5300	Martini madness.
The Cove	1750 E 55th St	773-684-1013	Popular Hyde Park watering hole.

Map 21 • Wicker Park / Ukrainian Village

Bar Thirteen	1944 W Division St	773-394-1313	Restaurant by day, trendy bar at night.
Borderline	1954 W North Ave	773-278-5138	When you really shouldn't have one more, but you do anyway, you have it here.
Club Foot	1824 W Augusta Blvd	773-489-0379	Play Tetris and listen to Prince.
D'Vine	1950 W North Ave	773-235-5700	Restaurant turns into over-priced bar at night.
Davenport's	1383 N Milwaukee Ave	773-278-1830	Once legendary skanker bar, now yuppy fern bar. Whattya gonna do?
Double Door	1572 N Milwaukee Ave	773-489-3160	Top local and national alt-rock acts..
Empty Bottle	1035 N Western Ave	773-276-3600	Avant-garde jazz and indie rock. Smells like cat.
Estelle's Café & Lounge	2013 W North Ave	773-782-0450	Weird, dark, and sticky.
Gold Star Bar	1755 W Division St	773-227-8700	Hear the Cars and Cash in under an hour.
Iggy's	1840 W North Ave	773-227-4449	Martini bars and lounge. Sunday movie-night with vintage horror flicks.
Inner Town Pub	1935 W Thomas St	773-235-9795	Wicker dump.
Innjoy	2051 W Division St	773-394-2066	WP Scene-ster place for drinking and local acts.
Lava Lounge	859 N Damen Ave	773-772-3355	DJs spin amidst a heavy crowd of heavy drinkers.
The Note	1565 N Milwaukee Ave	773-489-0011	Eclectic jazz-type fare.
Phyllis' Musical Inn	1800 W Division St	773-486-9862	Affordable drinking hole with bands playing original songs.
Pontiac Café	1531 N Damen Ave	773-252-7767	Summertime hangout for WP peeps and wintertime weeps.
Rainbo Club	1150 N Damen Ave	773-489-5999	Cool-kid mecca and favorite hang of local celeb John Cusack. Enough said.
Rodan	1530 N Milwaukee Ave	773-276-7036	Ultra modern lounge—video mirrors in the bathrooms.
Small Bar	2049 W Division St	773-772-2727	Small is the New big at this hipster-cool, cozy hang.
Subterranean Cabaret & Lounge	2011 W North Ave	773-278-6600	Performances by musicians in the heart of Wicker Park.

Ten 56	1056 N Damen Ave	773-227-4906	Small, music-based hipster bar. DJs spin nightly. Glows "red" at night.
Vintage Wine Bar	1942 W Division St	773-772-3400	Way-cool retro-look wine bar with solid wine list.

Map 22 • Noble Square / Goose Island

Biology Bar	1520 N Fremont St	312-397-0580	Latin beat music in a science lab environment—a chemistry of its own.
Crobar	1543 N Kingsbury St	312-266-1900	Club creatures come for the music, tourists come for the creatures.
Exit	1315 W North Ave	773-395-2700	Ooohh. Dark and scary. Eighties punk/goth throwback.
Four	1551 W Division St	773-235-9100	Formally Big Wig—got a facelift and four rooms to play in.
Hot Shots	1440 N Dayton St	312-654-8204	Romanian music.
Joe's	940 W Weed St	312-337-3486	Huge sports bar and music venue for national bands and drunk people.
Slow Down, Life's Too Short	1177 N Elston Ave	773-384-1040	Lounge around and get drunk on two floors.
Zentra	923 W Weed St	312-787-0400	Image is everything. National DJ acts, fashionable crowd, and hookahs.

Map 23 • West Town / Near West Side

Darkroom	2210 W Chicago Ave	773-276-1411	No flash is necessary; artsy crowd, electro music, and industry parties.
Sak's Ukrainian Village Restaurant	2301 W Chicago Ave	773-278-4445	One of the few bastions of the old country remaining in the Village.
Tuman's	2159 W Chicago Ave	773-782-1400	Revived local legend. Cheap beer and comfort food.

Map 24 • River West / West Town

Babalu	1645 W Jackson Blvd	312-733-3512	Live Latin bands and djs on the weekends.
Betty's Blue Star Lounge	1600 W Grand Ave	312-243-1699	Where hipsters get drunk and f*ck.
Café Fresco	1202 W Grand Ave	312-733-6378	Comfy, local environs.
Chromium	817 W Lake St	312-666-7230	Is just how it sounds—chromy.
Dante's	1200 W Hubbard St	312-243-9350	Red-illuminated lounge atmosphere, guest djs, weekly drink specials.
Estate	1111 W Lake St	312-850-3740	Hip Hop and House danceclub that gets rough and rowdy.
Fulton Lounge	955 W Fulton Market	312-942-9500	Hip but laid back, cool music, outside seating .
Guess Bar	820 W Lake St	312-226-4500	Likes to keep its patrons guessing what events will happen next.
J Patrick's	1367 W Erie St	312-243-0990	Irish flags, beers, and accents.
Jack's Tap	901 W Jackson Blvd	312-666-1700	From the good folks who brought us the Village Tap.
Matchbox	679 N Milwaukee Ave	312-666-9292	Goes way beyond intimate.
Sonotheque	1444 W Chicago Ave	312-226-7600	Super sleek: the design, the crowd, the music.
Tasting Room	1415 W Randolph St	312-942-1313	Swank, low-key wine bar.
Transit	1431 W Lake St	312-491-8600	It'll keep you moving.
Twisted Spoke	501 N Ogden Ave	312-666-1500	$2 Jim Beams served by suicide girls and free porn on Saturday nights.

Map 25 • Illinois Medical District

White Horse Lounge	2059 W 19th St	312-432-9754	Spanish-speaking neighborhood place.

Map 26 • University Village / Little Italy / Pilsen

Bar Louie	1321 W Taylor St	312-633-9393	Generally good music and decent entrees.
Bevi Amo Wine Bar	1358 W Taylor St	312-455-8255	Good selection, if a bit pricey.
Hawkeye's Bar & Grill	1458 W Taylor St	312-226-3951	Quality bar food (including the healthy side).
The Illinois Bar & Grill	1421 W Taylor St	312-666-6666	Great greasy food and burgers.
Skylark	2149 S Halsted St	312-948-5275	Hip hangout for Pilsen arty crowd.

Map 27 • Logan Square

3030	3030 W Cortland St	773-862-3616	Experimental art and jazz music in a church—no cover.
Fireside Bowl	2648 W Fullerton Ave	773-486-2700	No longer a punk rock venue, it's just bowling now.
Streetside Café	3201 W Armitage Ave	773-252-9700	Micro-brews, DJs spin smooth house, ample ambiance.
The Winds Café	2657 N Kedzie Blvd	773-489-7478	Neighborhood bar smack dab in the middle of the 'hood.

Map 28 • Bucktown

Artful Dodger Pub	1734 W Wabansia Ave	773-227-6859	For patrons who prefer loud and crowded good times.
Bar Louie	1704 N Damen Ave	773-645-7500	Beer, wine, mammoth sandwiches.
Cans	1640 N Damen Ave	773-227-2277	Canned beers galore! Loud crowd, loud music, great hot wings!
Charleston Tavern	2076 N Hoyne Ave	773-489-4757	Yuppie dive.
Danny's	1951 W Dickens Ave	773-489-6457	Bohemian scene-ster bar includes a muffin lady and tamale man.

Map 28 • Bucktown—*continued*

Danny's	2222 N Western Ave	773-489-3622	Once was a quirky hipster place.
Gallery Cabaret	2020 N Oakley Ave	773-489-5471	Hip dive bar with local acts, attracts plenty of wannabe barflies.
Lemmings	1850 N Damen Ave	773-862-1688	Another yuppie hot spot.
The Liar's Club	1665 W Fullerton	773-665-1110	Only sometimes overly hipster, otherwise rad music & good times.
Lincoln Tavern	1858 W Wabansia Ave	773-342-7778	Neighborhood bar.
The Map Room	1949 N Hoyne Ave	773-252-7636	International travel theme.
Marie's Rip Tide Lounge	1745 W Armitage Ave	773-278-7317	Drunk wannabes welcome here.
The Mutiny	2428 N Western Ave	773-486-7774	Fledgling local rock bands get their start here.
Northside Café	1635 N Damen Ave	773-384-3555	Popular Wicker Park pick-up bar.
Quenchers Saloon	2401 N Western Ave	773-276-9730	Crowded on the weekends, but ultra comfy couches and free popcorn.

Map 29 • DePaul / Wrightwood / Sheffield

Big House	2354 N Clybourn Ave	773-435-0130	A Tiger Woods type of place: martinis and a Golden Tee course.
Charlie's Ale House	1224 W Webster Ave	773-871-1440	Shivers.
Delilah's	2771 N Lincoln Ave	773-472-2771	Punk rock dive.
Gin Mill	2462 N Lincoln Ave	773-549-3232	College bar.
Green Dolphin Street	2200 N Ashland Ave	773-395-0066	Big band and jazz venue that serves late-night dinner and vibrations.
The Hideout	1354 W Wabansia Ave	773-227-4433	Haven for alt-country and other quirky live tune-age.
Hog Head McDunna's	1505 W Fullerton Ave	773-929-0944	Sports bar with all American bar food and people.
Irish Eyes	2519 N Lincoln Ave	773-348-9548	Small Irish pub.
Jack Sullivan's	2142 N Clybourn Ave	773-549-9009	Sports bar.
Kincade's	950 W Armitage Ave	773-348-0010	Happy hour sports bar.
Local Option	1102 W Webster Ave	773-348-2008	Neighborhood hole-in-the-wall and proud of it.
Nic and Dino's Tripoli Tavern	1147 W Armitage Ave	773-477-4400	Quality bar food.
The (Prop) House	1675 N Elston Ave	773-486-2086	In the middle of the industrial area, house beats resonate.
Red Lion Pub	2446 N Lincoln Ave	773-348-2645	It's haunted!
Webster Wine Bar	1480 Webster Ave	773-868-0608	Perfect place for "getting to know you" while enjoying flights and pairings.
Wrightwood Tap	1059 W Wrightwood Ave	773-549-4949	Neighborhood tavern.
Zella	1983 N Clybourn Ave	773-549-2910	Great summer seating.

Map 30 • Lincoln Park

B.L.U.E.S.	2519 N Halsted St	773-528-1012	Smaller but notorious blues bar with an older African-American crowd.
Bacchus	2242 N Lincoln Ave	773-477-5238	Yup-to-be dance club.
Bar Louie	1800 N Lincoln Ave	312-337-9800	Another outpost of the chain.
Blu	2247 N Lincoln Ave	773-549-5884	Lincoln Park nightclub.
Corner Pocket	2610 N Halsted St	773-281-0050	Student-y billiards bar.
Gamekeepers	345 W Armitage Ave	773-549-0400	Where young singles mingle.
Glascott's	2158 N Halsted St	773-281-1205	The pub that beckons on sunny afternoons.
GoodBar	2512 N Halsted St	773-296-9700	Candles, DJ, wine bar.
Griffin's Public House	2710 N Halsted St	773-525-7313	Sports bar for the loyal Michiganians rehashing the ol' days.
Hidden Shamrock	2723 N Halsted St	773-883-0304	Halsted Street staple.
Katacomb	1909 N Lincoln Ave	312-337-4040	Late night lounge with private nooks resembling… catacombs!
Kingston Mines	2548 N Halsted St	773-477-4646	Name-dropping North Side blues club.
Lion Head Pub & The Apartment	2251 N Lincoln Ave	773-348-5100	DJ, etc.
Neo	2350 N Clark St	773-528-2622	Popular eighties retro night. Gag me with a spoon.
Park West	322 W Armitage Ave	773-929-1322	Costs extra to reserve a table.
Sauce	1750 N Clark St	312-932-1750	Sleek, chic place to drink.
Second City	1616 N Wells St	312-664-4032	Drama and food in front of you.
Tequila Roadhouse	1653 N Wells St	312-440-0535	Nightmarish.
Wise Fools Pub	2270 N Lincoln Ave	773-929-1300	Vibes are high for live local legends and jam sessions.

Map 31 • Old Town / Near North

Burton Place	1447 N Wells St	312-664-4699	Great late night; good bar food.
Dragon Room	809 W Evergreen Ave	312-751-2900	Asian inspired dance club, sushi served, young yuppyish crowd.
North Park Tap	313 W North Ave	312-943-5228	Laid-back crowd.
Old Town Ale House	219 W North Ave	312-944-7020	Local flare.
Spoon	1240 N Wells St	312-642-5522	Trendy young crowd.

Weeds	1555 N Dayton St	312-943-7815	Pinball, bras, shoes, poetry, and free tequila: anything but ordinary.
Zanies Comedy Club	1548 N Wells St	312-337-4027	After a few drinks, everything is funny. Well, almost.

Map 32 • Gold Coast / Mag Mile

Backroom	1007 N Rush St	312-751-2433	Old jazz club w/ lots of baby boomers.
Bar Chicago	9 W Division St	312-654-1120	Dancing of sorts.
Butch McGuire's	20 W Division St	312-337-9080	Wet T-shirt contests anyone?
Cru Wine Bar	888 N Wabash Ave	312-337-4078	Another little wine bar.
Dublin's	1050 N State St	312-266-6340	Gold Coast pub.
The Hunt Club	1100 N State St	312-988-7887	The ultimate yuppy sports bar.
Jilly's Retro Club	1007 N Rush St	312-664-1001	Not all that glitters is gold. Gold digger's heaven.
Le Passage	937 N Rush St	312-255-0022	Super chic.
Leg Room	7 W Division St	312-337-2583	Bar food and funky music.
Mothers	26 W Division St	312-642-7251	The mother of frat-boy shenanigans.
She-nanigans	16 W Division St	312-642-2344	Another Rush vicinity hellhole.
Signature Lounge	875 N Michigan Ave	312-787-9596	Unbelievable view from the women's room.
Underground Wonder Bar	10 E Walton St	312-266-7761	Mostly jazz.
Zebra Lounge	1220 N State St	312-642-5140	Garish, cramped piano bar—in other words, it's a hit.
The Whisky	1015 N Rush St	312-475-0300	Sutton Place Hotel.

Map 33 • West Rogers Park

Cary's Lounge	2251 W Devon Ave	773-743-5737	Locals place to go for a nightcap.
Mark II Chicago	7436 N Western Ave	773-465-9675	Pool tables & dart boards.
McKellin's	2800 W Touhy Ave	773-973-2428	Cozy neighborhood Irish bar.
Mullen's Sports Bar and Grill	7301 N Western Ave	773-465-2113	Food until 1 am (10 pm on Sundays).

Map 34 • East Rogers Park

Charmers	1502 W Jarvis Ave	773-465-2811	Vintage neighborhood gay bar circa 1929.
Heartland Café	7000 N Glenwood Ave	773-465-8005	Crunchy folk music venue.
No Exit	6970 N Glenwood Ave	773-743-3355	Standard coffee house.

Map 35 • Arcadia Terrace / Peterson Park

Hidden Cove	5338 N Lincoln Ave	773-275-6711	Sports bar with trivia, darts, and karaoke.

Map 36 • Bryn Mawr

Claddagh Ring	2306 W Foster Ave	773-271-4794	Traditional Irish-American bar with plentiful pub fare.
Leadway Bar & Café	5233 N Damen Ave	773-728-2663	Pool hustlers and artistes mingle in Bryn Mawr's latest addition.

Map 37 • Edgewater / Andersonville

Atmosphere	5355 N Clark St	773-784-1100	See and be seen in Andersonville.
Charlie's Ale House	5308 N Clark St	773-751-0140	Andersonville's newest yuppie gathering spot.
Edgewater Lounge	5600 N Ashland Ave	773-878-3343	Alehouse with open-mike on Tuesdays for singers.
Farraguts Tavern	5240 N Clark St	773-728-4903	Neighborhood dive, less yuppy than Simon's.
Granville Anvil	1137 Granville Ave	773-973-0006	Gay old-timers drink here.
Joie de Vine	1744 W Balmoral Ave	773-989-6846	Wine & wide screen TV.
Madrigals	5316 N Clark St	773-334-3033	A gay bar for everyone.
Moody's Pub	5910 N Broadway St	773-275-2696	Beer, beer and beer garden.
Ollie's	1064 W Berwyn Ave	773-784-5712	A rare quiet neighborhood joint.
Simon's	5210 N Clark St	773-878-0894	Loads of cool locals with an interesting mix of local restaurant-goers as well as the best ever-changing jukebox in Chicago.
StarGaze	5419 N Clark St	773-561-7363	Lesbian bar with salsa on Friday nights.

Map 38 • Ravenswood / Albany Park

Brisku's Bistro	4100 N Kedzie Ave	773-279-9141	Croation bar food & pool.
Candlestick Maker	4432 N Kedzie Ave	773-463-0158	Jazz.
Lincoln Square Lanes	4874 N Lincoln Ave	773-561-8191	Brews and bowling above a hardware store. Cheap date.
Montrose Saloon	2933 W Montrose Ave	773-463-7663	Classic Chicago "Old Style." No cell phones, please.
Peek Inn	2825 W Irving Park Rd	773-267-5197	Neighborhood joint.

Map 39 • Ravenswood / North Center

Chicago Brauhaus	4732 N Lincoln Ave	773-784-4444	Oktoberfest year round.
Daily Bar & Grill	4560 N Lincoln Ave	773-561-6198	Bar food in retro ambiance.
The Long Room	1612 W Irving Park Rd	773-665-4500	Friendly and loooooonnnnggg.
Lyon's Den	1934 W Irving Park Rd	773-871-3757	Live music & comedy.
Resi's Bierstube	2034 W Irving Park Rd	773-472-1749	Wear your leiderhosen.

Map 40 • Uptown

Big Chicks	5024 N Sheridan Rd	773-728-5511	Neighborhood gay bar.
Carol's Pub	4659 N Clark St	773-334-2402	Late night country dancin' dive bar.
Crew Bar & Grill	4804 N Broadway St	773-784-CREW	Chicago's only gay sports bar. We only need one.
Green Mill Pub	4802 N Broadway St	773-878-5552	Famous poetry slam and live jazz.
Hopleaf	5148 N Clark St	773-334-9851	Crowded neighborhood tavern with lots of imported beers.
Joy-Blue	3998 N Southport Ave	773-477-3330	Traditional bar for young professionals.
Lakeview Lounge	5110 N Broadway St	773-769-0994	A shot and a beer, please.
Riveria	4746 N Racine Ave	773-275-6800	Rock out and revel at the old architecture.
T's	5025 N Clark St	773-784-6000	Eclectic sofa spot with food.
The Uptown Lounge	1136 W Lawrence Ave	773-878-1136	Former dump becomes trendy lounge in up and coming neighborhood.

Map 41 • Avondale / Old Irving

Chief O'Neill's	3471 N Elston Ave	773-473-5263	Celtic music and top-of-the-line pub food.
Christina's Place	3759 N Kedzie Ave	773-463-1768	$2 Guiness/4 am/karaoke/dive.
N	2977 N Elston Ave	773-866-9898	Argentinian flair with electro grooves.

Map 42 • North Center / Roscoe Village / West Lakeview

Art of Sports	2444 W Diversey Ave	773-276-7298	More sports than art.
Beat Kitchen	2100 W Belmont Ave	773-281-4444	Live music and decent bar food.
Black Rock	3614 N Damen Ave	773-348-4044	Pub with lots of scotch.
Cabo Grill	3407 N Paulina St	773-871-1200	Excellent drink specials, neighborhood feel, friendly staff, best burritos.
Cody's Public House	1658 W Barry Ave	773-528-4050	Friendly neighborhood pub.
Four Moon Tavern	1847 W Roscoe St	773-929-6666	Neighborhood tavern.
Four Treys	3333 N Damen Ave	773-549-8845	One of 5,000 drinking options in this area.
G&L Fire Escape	2157 W Grace St	773-472-1138	Neighborhood tavern.
Hungry Brain	2319 W Belmont Ave	773-935-2118	Eclectic to say the least.
Martyrs'	3855 N Lincoln Ave	773-404-9494	Drink to Kurt Cobain and other dead musicians. Brunch on Sundays.
Mulligan's Public House	2000 W Roscoe St	773-549-4225	Villagers do not go thirsty.
Riverview Tavern & Restaurant	1958 W Roscoe St	773-248-9523	Another Roscoe Village watering hole.
Seanchai	2345 W Belmont Ave	773-549-4444	DJ in back room, drunk locals in front room.
Tiny Lounge	1814 W Addison St	773-296-9620	Intimate bar with low lighting and an occasional local act.
The Village Tap	2055 W Roscoe St	773-883-0817	Fave neighborhood spot.
Xippo	3759 N Damen Ave	773-529-9135	Martini lounge in unlikely 'hood.

Map 43 • Wrigleyville / East Lakeview

Berlin	954 W Belmont Ave	773-348-4975	Tiny classic "pansexual" dance club.
Bottom Lounge	3206 N Wilton St	773-975-0505	Local acts and some touring gigs.
Bungalow Bar and Lounge	1622 W Belmont Ave	773-244-0400	Swank little neighborhood spot.
Cherry Red	2833 N Sheffield Ave	773-477-3661	Red lighting, huge dance floor and space, red-hot.
Cubby Bear	1059 W Addison St	773-327-1662	Home of the "bar band."
Elbo Room	2871 N Lincoln Ave	773-549-5549	Chill music venue of live national acts and sweaty swingers.
Fizz Bar and Grill	3220 N Lincoln Ave	773-348-6000	Micro-brews, live sets, a perfect man place.
Fly Me to the Moon	3400 N Clark St	773-528-4033	Swanky piano bar turns nightclub.
Ginger Man Tavern	3740 N Clark St	773-549-2050	Not bad when there's no Cubs game.
Goose Island Brewery	3535 N Clark St	773-832-9040	Micro-brew enthusiasts spot.
Gunther Murphy's	1638 W Belmont Ave	773-472-5139	German beers, German cheers.
Guthrie's Tavern	1300 W Addison St	773-477-2900	Comfortable atmosphere, good drinks, a range of board games to play with.
Higgin's Tavern	3259 N Racine Ave	773-281-7637	Yuppies and drunks.
Improv Olympic	3541 N Clark	773-880-0199	Get laughs and drunk.
Jack's Bar & Grill	2856 N Southport Ave	773-404-8400	Classy wine bar.
John Barleycorn	3524 N Clark St	773-549-6000	Lots of TVs and beer to forget your troubles.
Justin's	3358 N Southport Ave	773-929-4844	Great bar for Sunday football.
Lincoln Tap Room	3010 N Lincoln Ave	773-868-0060	Great mix of people, comfortable couches.
Metro	3730 N Clark St	773-549-0203	Internationally renowned venue for top local and touring rock music.
Murphy's Bleachers	3655 N Sheffield Ave	773-281-5356	Another Cubbie beer fest.
Pops for Champagne	2934 N Sheffield Ave	773-472-1000	Jazz and champers.
Raw Bar	3720 N Clark St	773-348-7291	Post-Metro rock star hangout.
Schuba's	3159 N Southport Ave	773-525-2508	Rock/pop/fok/country. Decent restaurant.
Sheffield's	3258 N Sheffield Ave	773-281-4989	Outdoor area attracts afternoon revelers.
Slugger's	3540 N Clark St	773-248-0055	Batting cages—some people's heaven, others' hell.
Smart Bar	3730 N Clark St	773-549-4140	Underground dance.
Ten Cat Tavern	3931 N Ashland Ave	773-935-5377	Cute neighborhood spot.

Trace	3714 N Clark St	773-477-3400	Laid back two-floor lounge. A hideout from the sports bars.
Underground Lounge	952 W Newport Ave	773-327-2739	A place for everyone.
Wild Hare	3530 N Clark St	773-327-4273	Attire: Dreads, beads, and beanies.
Y*k-zies-Clark	3710 N Clark St	773-525-9200	Loud post-Cubs hangout.

Map 44 • East Lakeview

Charlie's Chicago	3726 N Broadway St	773-871-8887	Gay country & western bar. That's right.
Circuit	3641 N Halsted St	773-325-2233	Huge boys town dance club—recently remodeled.
The Closet	3325 N Broadway St	773-477-8533	Boy-friendly lesbian bar, 4 am license.
Cocktail	3359 N Halsted St	773-477-1420	Small dance floor, occasional male strippers.
Crush	2843 N Halsted St	773-528-7569	Adult playground: TVs, lounge, and dance floor.
Duke of Perth	2913 N Clark St	773-477-1741	Great Irish pub with fish & chips.
Gentry on Halsted	3320 N Halsted St	773-348-1053	A upscale gay piano bar that boasts "classy."
Hydrate	3458 N Halsted St	773-975-9244	Just what Boys Town needs —a gay-friendly fern bar!
Kit Kat Lounge	3700 N Halsted St	773-525-1111	Live drag queen shows.
Little Jim's	3501 N Halsted St	773-871-6116	Gay dive.
Monsignor Murphy's	3019 N Broadway St	773-348-7285	Irish pub.
Roscoe's	3354 N Halsted St	773-281-3355	Cavernous mingling for the gay sweater set.
Sidetrack	3349 N Halsted St	773-477-9189	Popular showtune sing-a-longs!
Spin	800 W Belmont Ave	773-327-7711	Lots of theme days throughout the week.
Town Hall Pub	3340 N Halsted St	773-472-4405	Unassuming, mixed clientele, live music.

Maps 45-48 • Northwest Chicago

5th Province Pub (Irish-American Heritage Center)	4626 N Knox Ave	773-282-7035	Authentic pub located in the Heritage Center.
Abbey Pub	3420 W Grace St	773-478-4408	Reputable live music venue.
Emerald Isle	6686 N Northwest Hwy	773-775-2848	The brothers and sisters of Kerry gather here.
Fischman Liquors	4780 N Milwaukee Ave	773-545-0123	We call beer "piwo" 'round here.
Hollywood Lounge	3301 W Bryn Mawr Ave	773-588-9707	Friendly neighborhood bar with extensive beer selection.
Little Rascals	4356 W Belmont Ave	773-545-1416	Neighborhood dump with a grill and a colorful cast of regulars.
Moretti's	6727 N Olmsted Ave	773-631-1223	Sports-guy type of hangout.
New Polonia Club	6103 W Belmont Ave	773-237-0571	A Polish bar on the NW side? Go figure.
Old Irving Park Sports Bar & Grill	4217 W Irving Park Blvd	773-725-5595	Hole-in-the-wall sports bar.
Rosa's Lounge	3420 W Armitage Ave	773-342-0452	Friendly blues haven.
Vaughan's Pub	5485 N Northwest Hwy	773-631-9206	Cozy neighborhood joint with nice beer selection and Irish food.

Maps 49-52 • West Chicago

The 5105 Club	5105 W North Ave	773-237-9490	Neighborhood bar with occasional live R&B and blues.
Black Beetle	2532 W Chicago Ave	773-384-0701	Nice bright bar with decent food.
California Clipper	1002 N California Ave	773-384-2547	Retro bar for hipsters honering for granny's era.
La Justicia	3901 W 26th St	773-522-0041	Live rock en espanol on Friday nights only!

Maps 53-56 • Southwest Chicago

Cork & Kerry	10614 S Western Ave	773-445-2675	Black-and-tans on the South Western Pub strip.
Dubliner	10910 S Western Ave	773-238-0784	Quaint, cozy pub.
Groucho's	8355 S Pulaski Rd	773-767-4838	Mainstream and big-hair live rock venue.
Inn Exile	5758 W 65th St	773-582-3510	Gay video bar near Midway.
Jeremy Lanigan's Irish Pub	3119 W 111th St	773-233-4004	Live celtic music from time-to-time.
Keegan's Pub	10618 S Western Ave	773-233-6829	Anyone know where you can find a pint of Guinness around here?
Murphy's Law	9247 S Cicero Ave, Oak Lawn	708-636-1555	As great as its name.
TC's Pub	9700 S Cicero Ave, Oak Lawn	708-425-4252	Neighborhood bar with karaoke & sports aplenty.

Maps 57-60 • South Chicago

Jeffrey Pub	7041 S Jeffery Blvd	773-363-8555	Gay men & lesbians mingle at this southside dance club.
Lee's Unleaded Blues	7401 S Jeffrey Blvd	773-493-3477	Dress sharp at this Southside blues institution.
New Apartment Lounge	504 E 75th St	773-483-7728	Where Von Freeman jams every Tuesday night.
Pullman's Pub	611 E 113th St	773-568-0264	Pre-Prohibition watering hole.
Reds	6926 S Stony Island Ave	773-643-5100	Popular place to mack on the opposite sex.

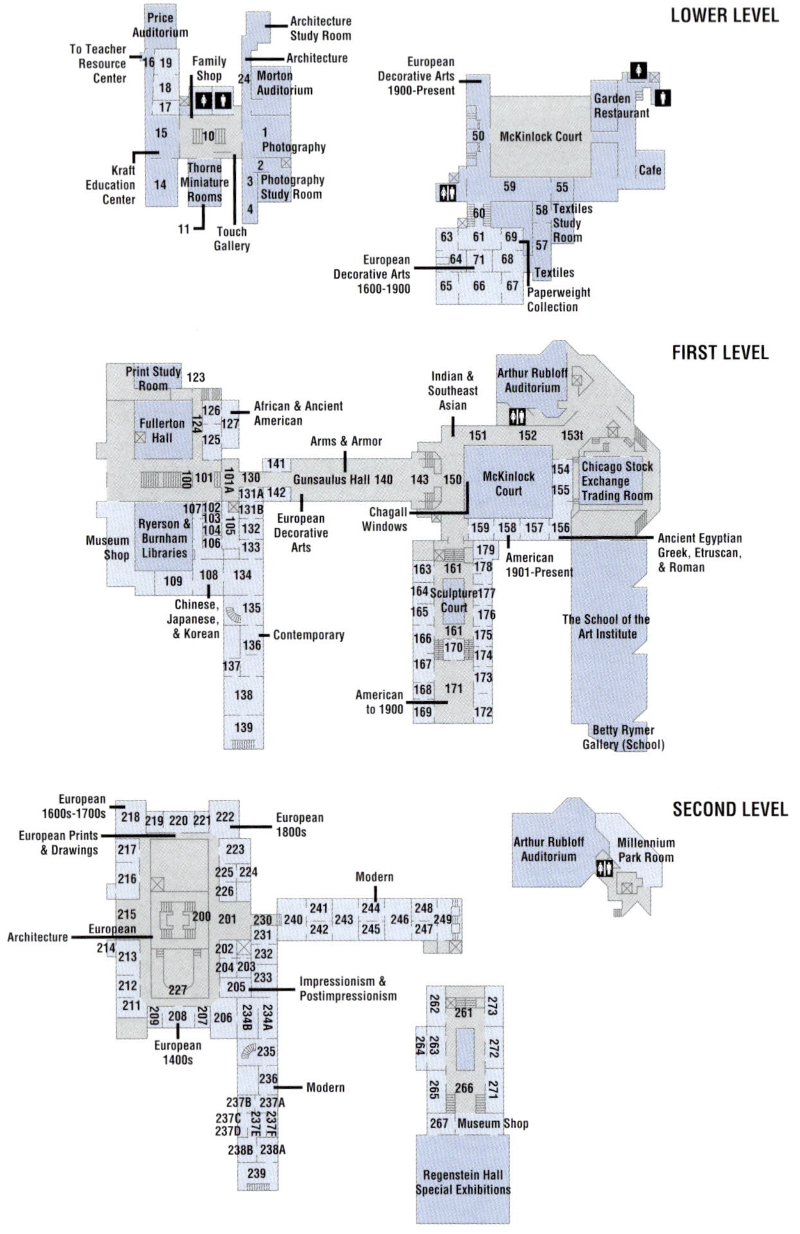

LOWER LEVEL
Price Auditorium
To Teacher Resource Center
16 19
18
17
Family Shop
Architecture Study Room
Architecture
24 Morton Auditorium
15
10
1 Photography
2
3 Photography Study Room
4
Kraft Education Center
14
Thorne Miniature Rooms
11
Touch Gallery
European Decorative Arts 1900-Present
Garden Restaurant
50
McKinlock Court
Cafe
59
55
60
58 Textiles Study Room
63 61 69
57
European Decorative Arts 1600-1900
64 71 68
Textiles
65 66 67
Paperweight Collection
FIRST LEVEL
Print Study Room
123
Fullerton Hall
124
126
127
125
African & Ancient American
Indian & Southeast Asian
Arthur Rubloff Auditorium
151 152 153t
Arms & Armor
141
100 101 101A 130
Gunsaulus Hall 140
143 150
McKinlock Court
154
155
Chicago Stock Exchange Trading Room
131A 142
107 102 131B
103 104 106
105
132
133
Ryerson & Burnham Libraries
Museum Shop
European Decorative Arts
Chagall Windows
159 158 157 156
Ancient Egyptian Greek, Etruscan, & Roman
179
American 1901-Present
163 161 178
109 108 134
Chinese, Japanese, & Korean
135
136
Contemporary
164 Sculpture Court 177
165 176
166 161 175
170 174
167
137
138
139
173
American to 1900
168 171
169 172
The School of the Art Institute
Betty Rymer Gallery (School)
SECOND LEVEL
European 1600s-1700s
218 219 220 221 222
European 1800s
European Prints & Drawings
217
223
216
225 224
226
Modern
Arthur Rubloff Auditorium
Millennium Park Room
215
200 201
230 240 241 242 243 244 245 246 248 247 249
231
Architecture
European
214 213
202 232
204 203
233
212
227
205
Impressionism & Postimpressionism
211
209 208 207 206
234B 234A
European 1400s
235
236
Modern
237B 237A
237C 237D 237E 237F
238B 238A
239
262 261 273
264 263 272
265 266 271
267 Museum Shop
Regenstein Hall Special Exhibitions

General Information

Address: 111 S Michigan Ave
Chicago, IL 60603
Phone: 312-443-3600
Website: www.artic.edu
Hours: Mon-Wed & Fri: 10:30 am-4:30 pm; Thurs: 10:30 am-8 pm; Sat & Sun: 10 am-5 pm; Thanksgiving & Christmas: closed
Admission: $12 for adults, $7 for students/children/seniors, free for kids under 5, free for all on Tuesdays

Overview

Built in 1892 as the only permanent structure of the '93 Columbian Exposition, the Classical Revival Allerton Wing of the Art Institute of Chicago began life as the "Palace of Culture" for the World's Fair. (The lions were added 2 years later.) Today the Art Institute is one of the preeminent art museums in the country, housing the largest collection of 19th-century French art outside of Paris (and its modern art collection isn't anything to sneeze at, either). There are also impressive exhibitions such as the Japanese wood block prints, the Touch Gallery designed specifically for the visually impaired, as well as really, really old vases and things, but who are we kidding? Everyone comes here for an up-close and personal look at such celebrated paintings as Caillebotte's *Paris Street; Rainy Day*, Seurat's *Grand Jatte*, Grant Wood's *American Gothic*, and Hopper's *Nighthawks*, along with their impressive collection of Monets, Manets, Van Goghs, and Picassos.

Construction of the new $198 million Renzo Piano wing is well underway. The modern addition, as well as its surrounding gardens, has been designed to harmonize with the adjoining Millennium Park. Construction is slated to be finished in 2007. If the new addition has anything more than just its backyard in common with the Millennium Park project, we'll put off buying our gown for the opening until closer to 2010. Fortunately, Piano's work will probably be worth the wait…

Restaurants and Services

The Cafe, on the lower-level of the Rubloff Building, offers self-service dining with burgers, pizza, and deli sandwiches at reasonable prices 11 am-4 pm daily. For a more elegant lunch, dine next door at the Garden Restaurant. Now open year-round 11:30 am-3 pm daily, the restaurant features patio dining with seasonal cuisine and a full bar. The museum also offers free jazz concerts for Garden diners with their Jazz in the Garden program on Thursday evenings from July to September.

While postcards, books, and magnets may be purchased at kiosks throughout the museum, the Museum Shop, just off the main lobby, offers an extensive collection of art-oriented gifts and souvenirs (and you don't have to pay admission to shop there!). The lower-level Woman's Board Family Shop, adjacent to the Kraft Education Center and the Touch Gallery, hawks kid-oriented goodies.

School of the Art Institute of Chicago

Boasting such illustrious alumni as Georgia O'Keefe, Claes Oldenburg, Laurie Anderson, and David Sedaris, the School of the Art Institute of Chicago (SAIC) offers a fine-art higher education for tomorrow's budding Renoirs for just $13,575 per semester.

Gene Siskel Film Center

160 N State St, 312-846-2600;
www.siskelfilmcenter.org
The film branch of the Art Institute offers art house, foreign films, and revivals, with frequent lectures by academics and industry professionals.

How to Get There

By Car: The Art Institute is located on Michigan Avenue between Monroe and Jackson. From I-90/94 N (the Dan Ryan), exit to Congress East (Loop exit). From I-90/94 S (Kennedy Expressway), exit Monroe Steet East. Affordable parking is located underground at Millennium Park garages (enter at Columbus and Monroe) and Grant Park garages (enter on Michigan, either between Madison and Randolph, or between Van Buren and Adams).

By Metra: Nearest stops are the Randolph and Van Buren stations served by the Metra Electric and South Shore Lines. For other Metra lines, transfer to the 151 Sheridan Avenue bus at Union Station .

By Bus: Numerous lines serve this strip of Michigan Avenue. Important buses include (from the south) the 3 King Drive, the 4 Collage Grove, and the 6 Jackson Park Express, (from the west) the 126 Jackson and 20 Madison, and (from the north) the 151 Sheridan, the 145 Wilson-Michigan Express, and the 146 Inner Drive/Michigan Express.

By L: From the Red and Blue lines, exit at Monroe. Brown, Orange, Purple and Green exit at Adams and Wabash.

The Grande Dames of Chicago's museum scene, **The Art Institute of Chicago**, the **Museum of Science and Industry**, and the Museum Campus' **Adler Planetarium**, **The Field Museum**, and **Shedd Aquarium**, may offer a lifetime worth of wonder, speculation, and enrichment, but, impressive though they are, these cultural epicenters are only the tip of the iceberg when it comes to our city's museum offerings.

Art Museums

Although the Art Institute's collection *is* undeniably impressive (see the preceding page), Chicago's true art lovers know to look past the lions to some of Chicago's less celebrated arty treasures.

Columbia College's **Museum of Contemporary Photography** is one of two accredited photography museums in the nation. Other campus-linked art museums include University of Chicago's **David and Alfred Smart Museum**, where the collection spans some 5,000 years, and Loyola University's **Martin D'Arcy Museum of Art**, a free museum specializing in Medieval, Renaissance, and Baroque art. The **Terra Museum of American Art** has closed and their considerable collection of works by Whistler, Cassat, Winslow Homer, Georgia O'Keefe, and more has been moved to the Art Institute. Artwork created by and commemorating veterans (from both sides) of the Vietnam War hangs on the walls of the **National Vietnam Veterans Art Museum**.

One of the country's largest collections of art post-1945 is housed at the always eye-opening **Museum of Contemporary Art**. The first Friday of the month, twenty-something singles converge here for cocktails, live entertainment, and friendly flirtation.

History

The **Chicago Historical Society** is a tremendous archive of the city's past and present. African-American history is celebrated at the nation's oldest museum focusing on the black experience, the **DuSable Museum of African-American History.** The **Oriental Institute** specializes in artifacts from the ancient Near-East, including Persia, Mesopotamia, and Egypt. Nobel Prize-winning sociologist **Jane Addams' Hull-House** examines Chicago's history of immigration, ethnic relations, and social work. "Artifacts" such as a John Lennon guitar and song lyrics by Bono are highlights of the collection at **The Peace Museum**. No word yet on what role Mother Theresa's coffee mug, Martin Luther King Jr.'s toothbrush, or Nelson Mandela's sunglasses will play.

Science and Technology

As if the aforementioned **Adler Planetarium**, **Shedd Aquarium**, and **The Field Museum** (all of which get special treatment within the Parks & Places listings under "Museum Campus") and the **Museum of Science and Industry** (listed with "Jackson Park") weren't enough to keep your head spinning, Chicago is also home to a handful of quirky, smaller science museums. The **International Museum of Surgical Science** offers a window to the world of questionable surgical practices of yore. **The Museum of Holography** examines the art and technology of making things appear 3-D. For kids, the **Children's Museum** presents a hands-on approach to learning about science and geography. Conservation and the environment are the focus of the **Peggy Notebaert Nature Museum**, which also features a butterfly haven, delighting the child in us all.

Architecture

The city itself is perhaps one of the best architecture museums in the world. Examine it yourself by embarking on one of the tours offered by the **Chicago Architecture Foundation**. Frank Lloyd Wright's influence on Chicago architecture can be examined at the **Robie House** in Hyde Park and the **Frank Lloyd Wright Home and Studio** in Oak Park. Chicago's Prairie Avenue District offers an architectural glimpse at Chicago's Victorian Golden Age. Joint tours of the oldest house in Chicago, the **Clarke House** (c. 1836), and the neighboring **Glessner House** offer the curious an interesting inside peek.

Ethnic Museums

The **Swedish American Museum Center** looks at the impact of Swedish immigration on Chicago. The **Hellenic Museum and Cultural Center** is a celebration of all things Greek. The **Mexican Fine Arts Center** is the largest such museum in the country, and examines the Mexican experience through art and culture. The **Spertus Museum** specializes in Jewish history and heritage. Its hands-on reproduction of an archeological dig is eternally popular with kids.

Miscellaneous

Housed in the former home of the legendary, influential blues label, Chess Records, **Willie Dixon's Blues Heaven Foundation** offers tours of where Chuck Berry, Muddy Waters, and even the Rolling Stones once recorded. (The site is memorialized in the Stones' song "2120 South Michigan.")

For the darker side of sightseeing, the **Leather Archives and Museum** exhibits a small but conversation-starting collection of fetish, bondage, and S&M artifacts, viewable by appointment only.

Museum	Address	Phone	Map
ABA Museum of Law	321 N Clark St	312-988-6222	32
Adler Planetarium and Astronomy Museum	1300 S Lake Shore Dr	312-922-STAR	11
The Art Institute of Chicago	111 S Michigan Ave	312-443-3600	6
Chicago Architecture Foundation	224 S Michigan Ave	312-922-3432	6
Chicago Children's Museum	700 E Grand Ave	312-527-1000	3
Chicago Historical Society	1601 N Clark St	312-642-4600	32
Chicago Maritime Society	310 S Racine Ave	312-421-9096	24
Clarke House Museum	1827 S Indiana Ave	312-745-0040	11
Columbia College for the Book and Paper Arts	1104 S Wabash Ave	312-344-6630	8
David and Alfred Smart Museum	5550 S Greenwood Ave	773-702-0200	19
DL Moody Museum	820 N La Salle Dr	312-329-4404	32
DuSable Museum of African-American History	740 E 56th Pl	773-947-0600	18
The Field Museum	1400 S Lake Shore Dr	312-922-9410	11
Glessner House Museum	1800 S Prairie Ave	312-326-1480	11
Hellenic Museum and Cultural Center	801 W Adams St	312-655-1234	6
International Museum of Surgical Science	1524 N Lake Shore Dr	312-642-6502	32
Intuit: Center for Intuitive and Outsider Art	756 N Milwaukee Ave	312-243-9088	24
Jane Addams Hull-House Museum	800 S Halsted St	312-413-5353	26
Jazz Institute of Chicago	410 S Michigan Ave	312-427-1676	6
Leather Archives & Museum	6418 N Greenview Ave	773-761-9200	34
Martin D'Arcy Museum of Art	6525 N Sheridan Rd- Loyola University	773-508-2679	34
Mexican Fine Arts Center	1852 W 19th St	312-738-1503	25
The Museum of Broadcast Communications	400 N State St	312-245-8200	2
Museum of Contemporary Art	220 E Chicago Ave	312-280-2660	3
Museum of Contemporary Photography	600 S Michigan Ave Columbia College	312-344-7104	9
Museum of Holography-Chicago	1134 W Washington Blvd	312-226-1007	24
Museum of Science and Industry	5700 S Lake Shore Dr	773-684-1414	20
National Vietnam Veterans Art Museum	1801 S Indiana Ave	312-326-0270	11
The Newberry Library	60 W Walton St	312-943-9090	32
Oriental Institute Museum	1155 E 58th St University of Chicago	773-702-9514	19
Peggy Notebaert Nature Museum	2430 N Cannon Dr	773-755-5100	30
Polish Museum of America	984 N Milwaukee Ave	773-384-3352	22
Robie House	5757 S Woodlawn Ave	773-834-1847	19
Rogers Park/West Ridge Historical Society	7344 N Western	773-764-4078	33
Shedd Aquarium, John G	1200 S Lake Shore Dr	312-939-2438	9
Smart Museum of Art	5550 S Greenwood Ave University of Chicago	773-702-0200	19
Smith Museum of Stained Glass	700 E Grand Ave (Navy Pier)	312-595-5024	3
Spertus Museum	618 S Michigan Ave	312-922-9012	9
Swedish American Museum	5211 N Clark St	773-728-8111	37
Ukrainian Institute of Modern Art	2320 W Chicago Ave	773-227-5522	23
Ukrainian National Museum of Chicago	721 N Oakley Blvd	312-421-8020	23
Willie Dixon's Blues Heaven Foundation	2120 S Michigan Ave	312-808-1286	11

Is the "city of big shoulders" also the city of big readers? Oprah and Da Mare would have you think so, what with their "Chicago Reads" and "Oprah's Book Club" campaigns. To be sure, there's no lack of bookshops in the city, and Chicago's multitude of quirky, independent stores stand defiantly side-by-side with the bookselling super chains that continue to pop up every day.

For general, all-purpose bookshops, **Barbara's** flagship store on North Wells is an institution, as is 25-year-old **Unabridged Books**, with its specialties in kids' books, travel, and gay and lesbian literary selections. Down by the University of Chicago campus, **57th Street Books** and **Seminary Co-op Bookstore** both appeal to the brainiac set, whereas **Beck's Book Store** specializes in textbooks for Chicago's community colleges.

Specialty stores abound in the city. **Women & Children First** may have the largest selection of feminist and woman-focused books in the country. **Afrocentric Bookstore** specializes in black literature and culture. Heal thyself at **Transitions Bookplace**—a peaceful, feng shui enclave in the chaotic Clybourn corridor shopping district. **Soliloquy** will appeal to your inner thespian with their fine selection of scripts and monologues, while the **Occult Bookstore** on Milwaukee Avenue offers everything a budding witch or warlock could desire.

Quimby's in Wicker Park specializes in esoteric small-press books and 'zines with a marked counter-culture feel. **Printer's Row Fine & Rare Books** specializes in architecture. Travelers would be wise to pay a visit to **Savvy Traveler** before setting sail.

Shuffle through the used stacks at **Bookworks** on North Clark or **Myopic** in Wicker Park. **Selected Works** on Broadway sells used books and sheet music. **Powell's** has made a name for themselves for their great selection of remaindered and off-price lit. **Rain Dog Books** on Michigan Avenue has a cozy café where you can enjoy an espresso as you paw through the gently used selection.

If you must chain it, the **Barnes & Noble** near the Webster Place cinema has a convenient parking lot. **Borders** on North Michigan is accessible for Mag Mile shoppers, ditto the address at 150 North State for State Street excursions.

Map 1 • River North / Fulton Market District

N Fagin Books	459 N Milwaukee Ave	312-829-5252	Social sciences.

Map 2 • Near North / River North

Abraham Lincoln Book Shop	357 W Chicago Ave	312-944-3085	History and military specialty store.
After-Words	23 E Illinois St	312-464-1110	New & used.
B Dalton	222 Merchandise Mart Plz	312-329-1881	Chain.
Beck's Book Store	50 E Chicago Ave	312-944-7685	Where there's a Beck's, there's a campus.

Map 3 • Streeterville / Mag Mile

Abbott Hall Book Center	710 N Lake Shore Dr	312-503-8486	Textbooks.
Barbara's Bestsellers	201 E Huron St	312-926-2665	Branch of local chain.
Barbara's Bestsellers	Navy Pier	312-222-0890	Branch of local chain.
University of Chicago Bookstore	450 N Cityfront Plz Dr	312-464-8650	Textbooks.

Map 4 • West Loop Gate / Greek Town

Waldenbooks	500 W Madison St	312-627-8334	Chain.

Map 5 • The Loop

Barbara's Bestsellers	Sears Tower, 233 S Wacker Dr	312-466-0223	Branch of local chain.
Barbara's Bestsellers	111 N State St	312-781-3033	Branch of local chain.
Beck's Book Store	209 N Wabash Ave	312-630-9113	Where there's a Beck's, there's a campus.
Beck's Book Store	315 S Plymouth Ct	312-913-0650	Where there's a Beck's, there's a campus.
Books-a-Million	144 S Clark St	312-857-0613	Chain.
Borders Books & Music	150 N State St	312-606-0750	State Street books.
Brent Books & Cards	309 W Washington St	312-364-0126	General.
Culture Bookstore	100 W Randolph St	312-263-4514	
Graham Crackers Comics	69 E Madison St	312-629-1810	Comics.
Prairie Avenue Bookshop	418 S Wabash Ave	312-922-8311	Specialty in architecture.
Tower Records Video Books	214 S Wabash Ave	312-663-0660	Chain.

Map 6 • The Loop / Grant Park

Business Savvy	310 S Michigan Ave	312-408-0667	Business books.
Chicago Architecture Foundation	224 S Michigan Ave	312-922-3432	Lots of pretty pictures.
Phillips & Fort Booksellers	410 S Michigan Ave	312-697-0700	Rare books.
Rain Dog Books	408 S Michigan Ave	312-922-1200	Small selection of used books plus a cozy café.
Savvy Traveller	310 S Michigan Ave	312-913-9800	Travel books, maps, money belts.

Map 8 • South Loop / Printers Row / Dearborn Park

Powell's Book Store	828 S Wabash Ave	312-341-0748	Used and remainders.
Printers Row Fine & Rare Books	715 S Dearborn St	312-583-1800	The name says it all.
Sandmeyer's Bookstore	714 S Dearborn St	312-922-2104	General.

Map 9 • South Loop / South Michigan Ave

Columbia College Bookstore	624 S Michigan Ave	312-344-7406	Some general books, mostly textbooks.
L Wiley Book Store	816 S Michigan Ave	312-583-0640	Textbooks.

Map 10 • East Pilsen / Chinatown

Chinese Champion Book & Gift	2167 S China Pl	312-326-3577	Chinese books.
World Journal Bookstore	2116 S Archer Ave	312-842-8005	A world of Chinese books.

Map 11 • South Loop / McCormick Place

Paragon Book Gallery	1507 S Michigan Ave	312-663-5155	Asian arts.

Map 16 • Bronzeville

Afrocentric Book Store	4655 S King Dr	773-924-3966	Celebrates the African-American literary tradition.

Map 19 • Hyde Park

57th Street Books	1301 E 57th St	773-684-1300	Frequented by U of C brainiacs.
Borders Books & Music	1539 E 53rd St	773-752-8663	General/chain.
O'Gara & Wilson	1448 E 57th St	773-363-0993	Used books.
Powell's Book Store	1501 E 57th St	773-955-7780	Remainders and off-price books. Mostly scholarly.
Seminary Co-op Bookstore	5757 S University Ave	773-752-4381	University press books.
University of Chicago Bookstore	970 E 58th St	773-702-8729	Textbooks.

Map 21 • Wicker Park / Ukrainian Village

Occult Book Store	1579 N Milwaukee Ave	773-292-0995	I put a spell on you.
Quimby's Bookstore	1854 W North Ave	773-342-0910	Edgy, counter-culture bookshop.

Map 22 • Noble Square / Goose Island

Brainstorm	1648 W North Ave	773-384-8721	Comic books.
Revolution Books	1103 N Ashland Ave	773-489-0930	Radical and revolutionary books.
Transitions Book Place	1000 W North Ave	312-951-7323	Heal thyself.

Map 23 • West Town / Near West Side

CNW Book Store	1900 W Van Buren St	312-829-6482	Get your Malcolm X College textbooks here.

Map 24 • River West / West Town

Joyce & Company	400 N Racine Ave	312-738-1933	Out of print books.

Map 25 • Illinois Medical District

Logan Medical Bookstore	600 S Paulina St	312-733-4544	Medical books.
UIC Medical Bookstore	828 S Wolcott Ave	312-413-5550	Reading material for when you're laid up.

Map 26 • University Village / Little Italy / Pilsen

Chicago Textbook	1076 W Taylor St	312-733-8398	Textbooks.

Map 28 • Bucktown

Libreria Nsra De Lourves	1907 N Milwaukee Ave	773-342-8890	Spanish books.

Map 29 • DePaul / Wrightwood / Sheffield

Barnes & Noble	1441 W Webster Ave	773-871-3610	Convenient for the run-in-and-grab-something shopper.

Map 30 • Lincoln Park

Books in the City	2428 N Lincoln Ave	773-472-2665	Textbooks.
Graham Crackers Comics	2562 N Clark St	773-665-2010	Where good and evil meet.
Tower Records	2301 N Clark St	773-477-5994	Chain.

Map 31 • Old Town / Near North

Borders Books & Music	755 W North Ave	312-266-8060	General/chain.

Map 32 • Gold Coast / Mag Mile

Barnes & Noble	1130 N State St	312-280-8155	Chain.
Borders Books & Music	830 N Michigan Ave	312-573-0564	Mag Mile books.
Children In Paradise	909 N Rush St	312-951-5437	Kids' books.
Europa Books	832 N State St	312-335-9677	Foreign language books.
Newberry Bookstore	60 W Walton St	312-255-3520	Connected to the cultural library.
Waldenbooks	900 N Michigan Ave	312-337-0330	Chain.

Map 33 • West Rogers Park

India Book House & Journals	2551 W Devon Ave	773-764-6567	Spiritual/cultural.
Iqra Book Center	2751 W Devon Ave	773-274-2665	Islamic books.
Russian American Book Store	2746 W Devon Ave	773-761-3233	Russian books.
U Arbat-Cobecedhnk	2810 W Devon Ave	773-262-1846	Russian books

Map 34 • East Rogers Park

Armadillos Pillow	6753 N Sheridan Rd	773-761-2558	General used.
Beck's Book Store	6550 N Sheridan Rd	773-743-2281	Where there's a Beck's, there's a campus.
Under the Table Books	1443 West Jarvis Ave	773-743-3728	General used.

Map 35 • Arcadia Terrace / Peterson Park

Korean Books	5773 N Lincoln Ave	773-769-1010	Korean books.

Map 37 • Edgewater / Andersonville

Ginkgo Leaf Books	1759 W Rosehill Dr	773-989-2200	Rare and collectable books.
Heritage Books	1135 W Granville Ave	773-262-1566	Books of African-American interest.
Left of Center Book Store	1043 West Granville Ave	773-338-1513	
Women & Children First	5233 N Clark St	773-769-9299	Spacious feminist bookshop.

Map 38 • Ravenswood / Albany Park

Kurt Gippert Bookseller	2910 W Eastwood Ave	773-583-7613	Out-of-print and antiquarian books.

Map 39 • Ravenswood / North Center

Book Cellar	4736 N Lincoln Ave	773-293-2665	General books and café.
Variety Comic Book Store	4602 N Western Ave	773-334-2550	

Map 40 • Uptown

Book Box - Shake, Rattle and Read	4812 N Broadway St	773-334-5311	Weird little store. Mostly used, some new.
Borders Books & Music	4718 N Broadway St	773-334-7338	General/chain.
Libreria de Hable Hispana	4441 N Broadway St	773-878-2117	Spanish-language bookstore.

Map 42 • North Center / Roscoe Village / West Lakeview

Galaxy Comic Zone	3804 N Western Ave	773-267-1043	Comic books.
Soliloquy	1724 W Belmont Ave	773-348-6757	Oh, the drama!
Stern's Psychology Book Store	2004 W Roscoe St	773-883-5100	Psychology books.

Map 43 • Wrigleyville / East Lakeview

Bookworks	3444 N Clark St	773-871-5318	Used and rare books.
Chicago Comics	3244 N Clark St	773-528-1983	Fun! Not geeky, really…
Gallery Bookstore	923 W Belmont Ave	773-975-8200	Used books.
Hanley's Bookstore	923 W Belmont Ave	773-281-9999	General used books.
Healing Earth Resources	3111 N Ashland Ave	773-327-8459	New Age books.
Powell's Book Store	2850 N Lincoln Ave	773-248-1444	Remainders and off-price books. Large art, architecture, photography and rare departments.

Map 44 • East Lakeview

Barnes & Noble	659 W Diversey Pkwy	773-871-9004	Chain.
Bookman's Corner	2959 N Clark St	773-929-8298	Used non-fiction.
Borders Books & Music	2817 N Clark St	773-935-3909	Bohemoth on Clark & Broadway.
Selected Works Bookstore	3510 N Broadway St	773-975-0002	Quirky, junky used book store.
Unabridged Books	3251 N Broadway St	773-883-9119	Great literary bookshop, best gay selection in town.

Overview

The Chicago restaurant scene has exploded in recent years. After a pretty staid decade or so, lately it seems that trendy new hotspots are popping up by the minute. Lincoln Square, the South Loop, and West Town, in particular, are seeing a head-spinning amount of action. The onslaught has given the dining scene a much-needed injection of energy and innovation, albeit at the price of an over-abundance of pan-something fusion and gimmicky themes.

What follows is a breakdown of some of our favorite spots, old and new. Of course, with so many openings, there are nearly as many closings. At this writing, some of the notable closings include Andersonville's Atlantique, Ixcapazulco, The Outpost, and Saiko. More are always on the way. Therefore, we offer this caveat: phone first.

That's Chicago

Some restaurants are more than just places to grab a bite. They are defining institutions for the city. The (original) **Billy Goat Tavern**, for example. Although branches have been popping up near sporting arenas all over town, only the original, below-Michigan Avenue branch has the authentic Chicago aura. Other Chicago institutions include **Pizzeria Uno**, **Superdawg**, **Wiener's Circle**, **Manny's Coffeeshop**, **Rosebud**, **Charlie Trotter'**s, and **Frontera Grill**.

Auspicious Starts

High-drama dining has been on the rise in Chicago. If it's the combination of high-concept food and over-the-top ambiance you are looking for, head right to **Moto**, where each dish is treated like a scientific experiment. Other high concept–high theater spots include Indian-Latin fusion at **Vermillion**, elegant, upscale, Franco-Japanese at **Japonais,** and the veggie-friendly offerings at Shawn McClain's new **Green Zebra**. Other dramatic dining can be found at **Opera**, and its theatrical forebear, **Marché**.

Little Bites

Chicago is bursting at the seams with new sushi and tapas spots. For trendy sushi, head to **Mirai Sushi** on Division, **Oysy** in the South Loop, **Bluefin**, **Starfish**, or Brazillion-sushi fusion at **Sushisamba Rio**. Other newish sushi spots: **Bob San**, **Kaze Sushi**, **Matsu Yama**, **Usugi Ya**, **Tanoshii**, **Sushi X**... **Andalucia** in North Center is cooking up inexpensive, authentic tapas, while **Sangria Restaurant & Tapas Bar** gives it a contemporary spin. At the time this is being written**, X/O** is the latest in small plate dining, and, it had to happen**, Tsuki** offers both sushi *and* tapas. Our favorite tapas joint is Lakeview's **Arco de Cuchilleros**, where the casual, intimate dining room and comfy traditional tapas seem just right.

Budget Busters

Have a white-hot expense account? Feel like burning through your kid's college tuition? Choosing your last meal? Just remember—it's not only the food you're paying for, it's the *experience*. To find out for yourself what meal could possibly be worth all that money, empty your wallet at one of these high-priced haunts: **Charlie Trotter's**, **Tru, Spiaggia,** the **Ritz-Carlton Dining Room, Les Nomades,** or **Everest**.

Here's the Beef

We're a meat-and-potato town and Chicagoans like their steak and chops. Out of all of them, **Morton's** has been doing it the best for years. Meanwhile, no carnivore will turn down your invite to **Smith & Wollensky** or **Gene & Georgetti** either, although really there are more high-quality (and high-priced) steak and chop houses in the city than we could possibly mention without breaking into a chant (or starting to drool). For ground-steak served on a bun, you can't do better than **Moody's Pub** in Edgewater or Beverly's **Top Notch Beefburger**. And, if you like your meat with tangy sauce, head to **Gale Street Inn** in Jefferson Park, street-festival mainstay **Robinson's**, **Smoke Daddy**, **Carson's**, or the Southside stalwart **Leon's Barbeque**. For encased meats, Chicago has no lack of options. Try encased exotic meats such as ostrich or wild boar at **Hot Doug's,** or try one of their named specials, such as the "Mighty Mighty Hot" Jennifer Garner (formerly The Britney Spears). On weekends they feature french fries cooked in duck fat.

Fishy Business

Bob Chinn's and the former **Shaw's Crab House** (now just called "Crab House") are the grand poobah's of the lobster-bib scene, although **McCormick & Schmick's** and **Joe's Seafood** have been giving them a run for their money. **Scylla** in Bucktown is one of the new-ish fish in the Chicago pond. For ethnic seafood, head down to **Emperor's Choice** in Chinatown or Pilsen's **Playa Azul**.

Speaking of Ethnic Cuisine...

Here's a quick-pick sampling of Chicago's numerous options that are cheaper than an international flight.

Mexican: **Nuevo Leon, Abril Mexican Restaurant, Tecalitlan Restaurant, Frontera Grill**
Nuevo Latino: **May Street Café, Mas, Nacional 27, De Cero**
Cuban: **Café 28, Café Laguardia**
Caribbean: **Calypso Café, Toucan**
Puerto Rican: **La Palma**
African: **Mama Desta's Red Sea, Ethiopian Diamond, Ras Dashen**
North African: **Tizi Melloul**
Korean: **Jin Ju, San Soo Gap San, Hama Matsu**
Chinese: **Phoenix Café, Evergreen, Furama**
Japanese: **Matsuya, Shiroi Hana, Kamehachi, Tanoshii**
Thai: **Amarind's, Opart Thai House, Arun's**
Middle Eastern: **Andie's, Cousin's, Aladdin's Eatery, Old Jerusalem, Noon O Kabab,** and so on...
Greek: **Costa's, Athena, Santorini**
Eastern European: **Paprikash, Red Apple, Sayat Nova**
German: **Mirabell, Glunz Bavarian Haus, Chicago Brauhaus**
Swedish: **Tre Kroner, Svea, Ann Sather**
Indian: **Monsoon, Mysore Woodlands, Udupi Palace, Arya Bhavan**
English/Irish: **Red Lion Pub, Chief O'Neill's, Abbey Pub & Restaurant**
French: **Avec, Café Matou, Bistro Campagne, Ambria, Tournesol, Brasserie Jo, La Petite Folie, Cyrano's Bistrot**

Speaking of Ethnic Cuisine—*continued*

& Wine Bar, Bistrot Zinc, and so on and so on and so on…
Italian: **Osteria Via Stato, Ignotz, Bacchanalia Ristorante, Tuscany, La Vita, Trattoria No 10, Vivere, Rosebud on Rush, Spiaggia, Angelina Ristorante, Via Emilia Ristorante**, and so on and so on and so on and so on, into infinity.

Soul Food/Southern Cooking

Perhaps the most American of all American cuisines, Chicago has lots of real good, down home soul food places. On the Southside, you can't go wrong with **Army & Lou's**—it's a Chicago legend. Other Southside soul food institutions include **Barbara's**, **Helen's,** and **Gladys' Luncheonette**. On the Westside, head out to **Edna's** on Madison. They'll take real good care of you. For Cajun, try Chicago breakfast staple **Wishbone**, or **Heaven on Seven**. The **Negro League Café**, in Bronzeville, offers soul food with a Cajun twist.

Vegetarian Chicago

Vegetarian food in Chicago may seem oxymoronic. Actually, there's a surprising amount of tasty options. Of course, all vegetarians know to check out veg-friendly ethnic cuisines like Middle-Eastern, Asian, and Indian. Some ethnic spots in the city are veg-only. There are the North-Indian **Arya Bhavan** and Southern-Indian **Mysore Woodlands** and **Udupi Palace**. For vegan Thai food, go northwest to **Amitabul**. Other vegetarian options include **Chicago Diner** and the **Heartland Café**. **Karyn's** offers raw vegan fare, and chef Karyn turns on the heat with her newest venture, **Karyn's Cooked**. For upscale veg, try Shawn McClain's new **Green Zebra** or choose the vegetarian tasting menus at **Arun's** and **Charlie Trotter's**. **Victory's Banner** is a quirky Roscoe Village veg where you're served by either monks, or Hare Krishnas, or some other people in robes. And you can dig into 100% vegetarian soul food at **Soul Vegetarian East**.

Breakfast

If you are one of those annoying people who manage to be up and dressed before dinner time, you may enjoy one of these places: **Sweet Maple Café**, **Orange, Room 12, Ina's, Ann Sather, The Bongo Room**, **Flo**, **Hot Spot,** or **Mamma Kitty's**.

Diners

Sometimes you just want a cup of joe and a patty melt. When that's the case, any of the following are good bets: **Jim's Grill**, **Salt & Pepper Diner**, **Ramova Grill**, **Salonica Grill**, **Hollywood Grill**, **Nookies**, **Clarke's Pancake House**, **Clara's, Manny's Coffee Shop**, **Windy City Café, Huddle House**, or the **Blue Angel.**

Honorable Mention…

For fine dining in a clubby atmosphere, we adore **Narcisse**. Other honorable mentions are funky **Leo's Lunchroom** and **Tweet**, **Taco & Burrito House** (both on Broadway and on Fullerton), chicken burritos at **El Famous Burrito**, tacos al pastor at **Taqueria Trespazada**, cheap-eats French-style at **La Creperie**, and dining late at the swanky **Pepper Lounge.**

*Key: $: Under $10 / $$: $10-$20 / $$$: $20-$30 / $$$$: $30+ * : Does not accept credit cards. / † : Accepts only American Express.*

Map 1 • River North / Fulton Market District

Chilpancingo	358 W Ontario St	312-266-9525	$$$	Gourmet Mexican madness.
Iguana Café	517 N Halsted St	312-432-0663	$	Internet cafe with bagels and such.
Japonais	600 W Chicago Ave	312-822-9600	$$$	Elegant, way-upscale Asian.
La Scarola	721 W Grand Ave	312-243-1740	$$	Authentic Italian in a super-close atmosphere.
Reza's	432 W Ontario St	312-664-4500	$$$	Wide variety of Persian food, large portions.
Scoozi!	410 W Huron St	312-943-5900	$$	Typical Italian.
Thyme	46a4 N Halsted St	312-226-4300	$$$	Eclectic eating in funky atmosphere.
Zealous	419 W Superior St	312-475-9112	$$$	Over-the-top gourmet from Trotter protégé.

Map 2 • Near North / River North

1492 Tapas Bar	42 E Superior St	312-867-1492	$$	Tasty tapas in River North graystone.
Allen's New American Café	217 W Huron St	312-587-9600	$$$	Innovative new-American cuisine.
Avenues	108 E Superior St	312-573-6754	$$$$	Sophisticated menu with a view.
Ben Pao	52 W Illinois St	312-222-1888	$$	Chinese spot.
Bijan's Bistro	663 N State St	312-202-1904	$$	Light, contemporary American fare.
Bin 36	339 N Dearborn St	312-755-9463	$$$	Wine tastings and pairings.
Bob Chinn's Crab House	315 N La Salle Dr	312-822-0100	$$$	Worth the wait.
Brasserie Jo	59 W Hubbard St	312-595-0800	$$$	Swanky French.
Brett's Kitchen	233 W Superior St	312-664-6354	$	Charming breakfast and sandwich stop.
Café Iberico	739 N La Salle Blvd	312-573-1510	$	Shoulder-to-shoulder tapas joint.
Carson's Ribs	612 N Wells St	312-280-9200	$$	Immense barbecue pork chops that lasts for days!
Cerise	Le Meridien Hotel, 521 N Rush St	312-645-1500	$$$	Precious, pretty food.
Chicago Chop House	60 W Ontario St	312-787-7100	$$$$	You want chops? They got chops.
Club Lago	331 W Superior St	312-951-2849	$$	Generous servings of basic Italian.
Coco Pazzo	300 W Hubbard St	312-836-0900	$$$$	Hearty, high-end Italian.
Crofton on Wells	535 Wells St	312-755-1790	$$$	Pushing the envelope with some top regional cuisine.
Cyrano's Bistrot & Wine Bar	546 N Wells St	312-467-0546	$$	Steak frites!
Fogo De Chao	661 N La Salle St	312-932-9330	$$$$	The meatiest place on earth!

Frontera Grill	445 N Clark St	312-661-1434	$$	Rick Bayless's famous cantina—expect to wait awhile.
Gaylord India	678 N Clark St	312-664-1700	$	Indian buffet.
Gene & Georgetti	500 N Franklin St	312-527-3718	$$$$	Big steaks.
Harray Caray's	33 W Kinzie St	312-828-0966	$$	Tourist trap for suburban punters.
House of Blues	329 N Dearborn St	312-923-2007	$$	Sunday gospel brunch buffet.
Joe's Seafood, Prime Steak & Stone Crab	60 E Grand Ave	312-379-5637	$$$	Part of popular Miami beach chain.
Karyn's Cooked	738 N Wells	312-587-1050	$$	Hot food by the queen of raw food.
Keefer's	20 W Kinzie St	312-467-9525	$$$	French-influenced steakhouse.
Kevin	9 W Hubbard St	312-595-0055	$$$	Promising new fusion.
Kinzie Chophouse	400 N Wells St	312-822-0191	$$$	Neighborhood steak house.
Klay Oven	414 N Orleans St	312-527-3999	$$	Upscale Indian buffet.
L8	222 W Ontario	312-266-0616	$$$	Small plate cuisine in River North.
Lawry's The Prime Rib	100 E Ontario St	312-787-5000	$$$	Carnivore's delight.
Linos	222 W Ontario St	312-266-6159	$$$	Old school service at this classic Italian. Closed on Sundays.
Lou Malnati's Pizzeria	439 N Wells St	312-828-9800	$	Famous in a city famous for pizza.
Maggiano's Little Italy	516 N Clark St	312-644-7700	$$	Gut-busting family-style Italian.
Mr Beef	666 N Orleans St	312-337-8500	$	Get your Italian beef fix at this tried-and-true Chicago classic.
Nacional 27	325 W Huron St	312-664-2727	$$$	Pan-Latin supper club with dance floor. Babaloo!
Naha	500 N Clark St	312-321-6242	$$$$	Mediterranean-inspired luxury.
Narcisse	710 N Clark St	312-787-2675	$$$$	Dripping in luxury in a champagne, foie gras way.
Original Gino's East	633 N Wells St	312-943-1124	$	Great for teenagers.
Osteria Via Stato	620 N State	312-642-8450	$$$$	Menu-oriented Italian. Fancy, but reasonably priced.
Pizzeria Due	619 N Wabash Ave	312-943-2400	$	Sister to Pizzeria Uno.
Pizzeria Uno	29 E Ohio St	312-321-1000	$	Legendary Chicago pizza.
Redfish	400 N State St	312-467-1600	$$	Fun Cajun; free beads and good drinks.
Rosebud on Rush	720 N Rush St	312-266-6444	$$	A branch of Chicago's legendary, old school Italian.
Roy's	720 N State St	312-787-7599	$$$	Pretty Hawaiian contemporary cuisine.
Rumba	351 W Hubbard St	312-222-1226	$$	Burgers, fries, the regular.
Ruth's Chris Steak House	431 N Dearborn St	312-321-2725	$$	Consistent steak chain.
Shanghai Terrace	Peninsula Hotel, 108 E Superior St	312-573-6744	$$$$	The city's most extravagant Chinese restaurant.
Shaw's Crab House & Blue Crab Lounge	21 E Hubbard St	312-527-2722	$$$$	A seafood destination.
Smith & Wollensky	318 N State St	312-670-9900	$$$$	Chicago branch of New York steak emporium.
Sorriso	321 N Clark St	312-644-0283	$$$	Italian in lovely environs.
Star of Siam	11 E Illinois St	312-670-0100	$	Thai—heard the quality's gone down.
Sugar: A Dessert Bar	108 W Kinzie St	312-822-9999	$$$	Decadent desserts and cocktails.
Sullivan's Steakhouse	415 N Dearborn St	312-527-3510	$$$$	Another upscale steakhouse.
Sushi Naniwa	607 N Wells St	312-255-8555	$$	Quality sushi. Great outdoor.
Sushisamba Rio	504 N Wells St	312-595-2300	$$$	Riding the Brazilian sushi craze.
SWK	710 N Wells St	312-274-9500	$$$	Sophisticated new American.
Thai Star Café	660 N State St	312-951-1196	$	Scrappy Thai—good food overcomes décor.
Tizi Melloul	531 N Wells St	312-670-4338	$$$	Exotic setting for Moroccan tangines.
Topolobampo	445 N Clark St	312-661-1434	$$$$	Standard bearer for upscale Mexican.
Vermillion	10 W Hubbard St	312-527-4060	$$$	Indian-Latin fusion—what next?
Vong's Thai Kitchen	6 W Hubbard St	312-644-8664	$$	Thai with a satisfying kick.
Weber Grill	Hilton Garden Inn, 539 N State St	312-467-9696	$$	Weird Weber Grill-themed concept place.
Wildfire	159 W Erie St	312-787-9000	$$	Fun, trendy American.

Map 3 • Streeterville / Mag Mile

Bandera	535 N Michigan Ave	312-644-3524	$$	Lunch above Mag Mile.
Benihana of Tokyo	166 E Superior St	312-664-9643	$$	Tepanyaki chain.
Billy Goat Tavern	430 N Michigan Ave	312-222-1525	$*	Cheezboiga; no fries, chips; pepsi, no coke.
Bubba Gump Shrimp Co	Navy Pier, 700 E Grand Ave	312-252-4867	$$	Navy Pier tourist trap.
Cambridge House Grill	167 E Ohio St	312-828-0600	$	Diner; open late.
Capital Grille	633 N St Clair St	312-337-9400	$$$$	Macho steak & zin.
Cite	Lake Point Tower, 70th Fl 505 N Lake Shore Dr	312-644-4050	$$$$	Contemporary with a view.
Dick's Last Resort	435 E Illinois St	312-836-7870	$$	Tourist's last memory of the night.
Eli's the Place for Steaks	215 E Chicago Ave	312-642-1393	$$	The place for cheesecake.
Emilio's Tapas Sol y Nieve	215 E Ohio St	312-467-7177	$$$	One of the nicest branches of the local tapas chain.
Heaven on Seven	600 N Michigan Ave	312-280-7774	$$	Cajun grub and cocktails.
Hot Diggity Dogs	251 E Ohio St	312-943-5598	$*	Walk-up chicawga dawgs.
Indian Garden	247 E Ontario St	312-280-4910	$$	Good veggie options.

*Key: $: Under $10 / $$: $10-$20 / $$$: $20-$30 / $$$$: $30+ * : Does not accept credit cards. / † : Accepts only American Express.*

Map 3 • Streeterville / Mag Mile—*continued*

Kamehachi	240 E Ontario St	312-587-0600	$$	One of Chicago's top sushi spots.
Les Nomades	222 E Ontario St	312-649-9010	$$$$	Deluxe haute cuisine.
Nomi	Park Hyatt Chicago Ave, 800 N Michigan Ave	312-239-4030	$$$$	Deluxe French fusion.
Riva	Navy Pier, 700 E Grand Ave	312-644-7482	$$$	Touristic fine dining on the Pier.
Ron of Japan	230 E Ontario St	312-644-6500	$$$	Guilty pleasure teppanyaki.
Sayat Nova	157 E Ohio St	312-644-9159	$$	Armenian.
Tru	676 N St Clair St	312-202-0001	$$$$	Dazzling contemporary cuisine.
Volare	201 E Grand Ave	312-410-9900	$$$	Casual Italian.
Wave	644 N Lake Shore Dr	312-255-4460	$$$	Trendy W Hotel gruberie is making a…you guessed it.

Map 4 • West Loop Gate / Greek Town

Artopolis Bakery & Café	306 S Halsted St	312-559-9000	$$	Frappes to Mediterranean pizza.
Athena	212 S Halsted St	312-655-0000	$$$	Goddess Athena-inspired outdoor and indoor.
Avec	615 W Randolph St	312-377-2002	$$	Rustic French. Homemade sausages!
Azure	832 W Randolph St	773-455-1400	$$$	Cal-Ital.
Blackbird	619 W Randolph St	312-715-0708	$$$$	Chic les plus ultra.
Bluepoint Oyster Bar	741 W Randolph St	312-207-1222	$$$	Trendy gulpers.
Byzantium	232 S Halsted St	312-454-1227	$$	Tapas Greek piano bar.
Costa's	340 S Halsted St	312-263-9700	$$$	Greece at its warmest. Have the octopus.
Gold Coast Dogs	Union Station, 225 S Canal St	312-258-8585	$*	Gotta have the dogs.
Greek Islands	200 S Halsted St	312-782-9855	$$$	Greek Heaven—not to be missed.
J&C Inn	558 W Van Buren St	312-663-4114	$$$	Dingy outside—best sandwiches in town inside.
Lou Mitchell's	565 W Jackson Blvd	312-939-3111	$*	Rub shoulders with local pols at this legendary grill.
Nine	440 W Randolph St	312-575-9900	$$$	Toast marshmallows at the table at this ultra trendy contemporary spot.
Nine Muses	315 S Halsted St	312-902-9922	$$$	Brick bars and backgammon.
Parthenon	314 S Halsted St	312-726-2407	$$$	Creaters of flaming saganaki!
Pegasus Restaurant & Taverna	130 S Halsted St	312-226-3377	$$$	Rooftop garden—Chicago secret!
Red Light	820 W Randolph St	312-733-8880	$$$$	Fusion of Asian dishes in a oriental atmosphere.
Robinson's No 1 Ribs	225 S Canal St	312-258-8477	$*	Dress down and dig in.
Rodity's	222 S Halsted St	312-454-0800	$$$	Greek lamb since 1972.
Santorini	800 W Adams St	312-829-8820	$$$	Fish, shellfish, and roasted chicken. Yum.
Starfish	804 W Randolph St	312-997-2433	$$	Flamboyant sushi place.
Sushi Wabi	842 W Randolph St	312-563-1224	$$$	Self-consciously chic sushi.

Map 5 • The Loop

Atwood Café	1 W Washington St	312-368-1900	$$$	High tea with contemporary flair.
Barro Cantina	73 E Lake St	312-346-8457	$$	South American tapas.
Berghoff Restaurant	17 W Adams St	312-427-3170	$$	Chicago icon with hearty German fare.
Billy Goat Tavern	330 S Wells St	312-554-0297	$*	Chain of cheezboiga joint made famous by John Belushi.
Everest	440 S La Salle St	312-663-8920	$$$$	High fallutin' food. Cute sommelier.
French Quarter/ Palmer House Hilton	17 E Monroe St	312-621-7363	$$$	Festive Chicago tradition.
Gold Coast Dogs	159 N Wabash Ave	312-917-1677	$*	Classic dog joint.
Gold Coast Dogs	17 S Wabash Ave	312-578-1133	$*	Onion peppers, pickle spear, tomato, celery salt, mustard.
Heaven on Seven	111 N Wabash Ave	312-263-6443	$$	Cajun Chicago classic. Closed for dinner.
Italian Village	71 W Monroe St	312-332-4040	$$$	Theater dining tradition.
La Cantina Enoteca	71 W Monroe St	312-332-7005	$$	Pre-show fave.
La Rosetta	70 W Madison St	312-332-9500	$$	Family-style Italian.
Miller's Pub	134 S Wabash Ave	312-263-4988	$$	Down-to-earth grub in a pub.
Mrs Levy's Delicatessen	233 S Wacker Dr	312-993-0530	$	No surprises here.
Nick's Fishmarket & Grill	Bank One Plz, 51 S Clark St	312-621-0200	$$$	Power lunch.
Oasis Café	21 N Wabash Ave	312-558-1058	$$*	Middle Eastern hideout inside of a jewelry store.
Rhapsody	Symphony Ctr, 65 E Adams St	312-786-9911	$$$	Upscale pre-symphony grub.
Russian Tea Time	77 E Adams St	312-360-0000	$$$	Elegant Russian cuisine.
Trader Vic's	Palmer House Hilton, 17 E Monroe St	312-917-7317	$$	Polynesian fare, tropical drinks.
Trattoria No 10	10 N Dearborn St	312-984-1718	$$$	Authentic Italian.
The Village	71 W Monroe St	312-332-7005	$$	Quaint, casual Italian looks like a village.
Vivere	71 W Monroe St	312-332-4040	$$$	Stylish Italian, packed before shows.

Map 6 • The Loop / Grant Park

Aria	200 N Columbus Dr	312-444-9494	$$$$	Artistic, creative pan-global grub.
Art Institute Restaurant on the Park	111 S Michigan Ave	312-443-3600	$$	Lovely, scenic lunch-time dining. Closes at 2:30 pm.
Artist's Café	412 S Michigan Ave	312-939-7855	$$*	Sit at the counter. They've got the chattiest waiters in town.
Bennigan's	150 S Michigan Ave	312-427-0577	$$	The busiest Bennigan's in the world!
China Grill	230 N Michigan	312-334-6700	$$$	Les So Very Tres.
Park Grill	11 N Michigan Ave	312-521-7275	$$$	Contemporary American cooking in Millenium Park.
Rain Dog Books & Café	408 S Michigan Ave	312-922-1200	$	Killer smoothies keep you from being a starving writer.

Map 7 • South Loop / River City

Bake for Me	608 W Roosevelt Rd	312-957-1994	$	Good coffee and pastries.
Manny's Coffee Shop	1141 S Jefferson St	312-939-2855	$	Famous deli—popular with politicians.
White Palace Grill	1159 S Canal St	312-939-7167	$	Greasy cabbie chow.

Map 8 • South Loop / Printers Row / Dearborn Park

Blackie's	755 S Clark St	312-786-1161	$*	A famous burger, lesser-known best breakfast in South Loop on Fri, Sat, Sun.
Hackney's	733 S Dearborn St	312-939-3870	$$	A specialty burger and onion loaf, a northshore legend since 1939, now has a little known outlet in downtown.
Room 12	1152 S Wabash Ave	312-427-9972	$$	Ecclectic, fun breakfast & lunch.
South Loop Club	701 S State St	312-427-2787	$	Very casual bar resturant with surprisingly good kitchen.
SRO	610 S Dearborn St	312-360-1776	$$*	Great kitchen boasting Chicago's #1 Turkey Burger.
Trattoria Caterina	616 S Dearborn St	312-939-7606	$$	A little touch of Italy, and a great value for Italian cuisine.

Map 9 • South Loop / South Michigan Ave

Oysy	888 S Michigan Ave	312-922-1127	$$$	Chic, industrial sushi setting.

Map 10 • East Pilsen / Chinatown

Emperor's Choice	2238 S Wentworth Ave	312-225-8800	$	Start with seafood; finish with tea.
Evergreen	2411 S Wentworth Ave	312-225-8898	$$	More upscale than most Chinatown grub.
Happy Chef Dim Sum House	2164 S Archer Ave	312-808-3869	$	Entrees priced to try several dishes.
Joy Yee's Noodle Shop	2159 Chinatown Sq	312-328-0001	$	Huge portions of Korean & Chinese, plus bubble tea.
Lao Sze Chuan Spice City	2172 S Archer Ave	312-326-5040	$	Authentic Chinese dishes plus great evening karaoke.
Penang	2201 S Wentworth Ave	312-326-6888	$	Malaysian favorites.
Phoenix Café	2131 S Archer Ave	312-328-0848	$	The best Chinese breakfast in town.
Three Happiness	209 W Cermak Rd	312-842-1964	$	So good it has a junior restaurant nearby. Long waits for dim sum.
Won Kow	2237 S Wentworth Ave	312-842-7500	$	Cheap, tasty dim sum.

Map 11 • South Loop / McCormick Place

Chef Luciano	49 E Cermak Rd	312-326-0062	$	Walk-in restaurant with eclectic entrees; Italian/African/Cajun influences.
Chicago Firehouse Resturant	1401 S Michigan Ave	312-786-1401	$$$$	Transformed Chicago firehouse complete with pole and fine dining.
Gioco	1312 S Wabash Ave	312-939-3870	$$$	Great Italian dining.
NetWorks	Hyatt Regency, 2231 S Dr Martin L King Dr	312-567-1234	$$	Contemporary American with a focus on Chicago specialties.
Opera	1301 S Wabash Ave	312-461-0161	$$$	Theatrical Asian grub.
Triad	1933 S Indiana Ave	312-225-8833	$$$	Guess what? Another sleek sushi lounge.

Map 13 • Bridgeport (East)

August Moon Restaurant	225 W 26th St	312-842-2951	$$*	Super Indonesian.
Franco's Ristorante	300 W 31st St	312-225-9566	$$	Family-style Italian near Sox park.
Furama	2828 S Wentworth Ave	312-225-6888	$$	Great dim sum and karaoke to boot!
Healthy Foods Restaurants	3236 S Halsted St	312-326-2724	$$*	listed in restos. Add to neighborhood map list.
Kevin's Hamburger Heaven	554 W 39th St	773-924-5771	$*	Hamburgers and milkshakes.
Offshore Steak House	480 W 26th St	312-842-1362	$$	Great deals, simple setting.
Phil's Pizza	3551 S Halsted St	773-523-0947	$*	Pizza-rific.
Ramova Grill	3510 S Halsted St	773-847-9058	$*	Old-school diner.
Scumaci's Italian Sandwiches	220 W 31st St	312-328-0502	$*	Bridgeport subs.
Wing Yip Chop Suey	537 W 26th St	312-326-2822	$*	Nader bumper sticker on window.

*Key: $: Under $10 / $$: $10-$20 / $$$: $20-$30 / $$$$: $30+   * : Does not accept credit cards. / † : Accepts only American Express.*

Map 14 • Prairie Shores / Lake Meadows—*continued*

Blue Sea Drive Inn	427 E Pershing Rd	773-285-3325	$*	Fast food and carry out.
Bronzeville Market & Deli	339 E 35th St	312-225-2988	$	Simple, convenient, easy, and old-fashioned.
Chicago Rib House	3851 S Michigan Ave	773-268-8750	$*	It is named like that for a reason. All day lunch.
Hong Kong Delight	327 E 35th St	312-842-2929	$$*	Not quite like being there, but close enough.

Map 16 • Bronzeville

Barbara's	353 E 51st St	773-624-0087	$*	Soul breakfast & lunch.
Gladys' Luncheonette	4527 S Indiana Ave	773-548-4566	$*	Soul food legend.
Harold's Chicken Shack	307 E 51st St	773-373-9016	$*	Fries, bread, and chicken.
Harold's Chicken Shack	364 E 47th St	773-285-8362	$*	It may say #7 but it is #1 around here.

Map 17 • Kenwood

Fung's Chop Suey	1400 E 47th Dr	773-924-2328	$*	When you're thinking delivery.
Kenny's Ribs & Chicken	1461 E Hyde Park Blvd	773-241-5550	$	Cheap and good to go.
Lake Shore Café	4900 S Lake Shore Dr	773-288-5800	$$	Basic Hotel Food.
The Original Pancake House	1517 E Hyde Park Blvd	773-288-2322	$*	A pancake style for every person.

Map 18 • Washington Park

Ms Lee's Good Food	205 E Garfield Blvd	773-752-5253	$*	It is good.
Rose's BBQ Chicken	5426 S State St	773-268-3401	$*	Don't mind the floor, it's the sauce.

Map 19 • Hyde Park

Bonjour Café Bakery	1550 E 55th St	773-241-5300	$	Have a pastry and be seen.
C'Est Si Bon	5225-F S Harper	773-363-4123	$$	Go for Sunday Brunch.
Calypso Café	5211 S Harper Ave	773-955-0229	$$	Good Caribbean. Great drinks.
Cedars Mediterranean Kitchen	1206 E 53rd St	773-324-6227	$$	Great food, horrible service.
Daley's Restaurant	809 E 63rd St	773-643-6670	$$*	The mayor ought to try this place.
Dixie Kitchen and Bait Shop	5225 S Harper Ave	773-363-4943	$$	A little taste of the South.
Hyde Park Gyros	1368 E 53rd St	773-947-8229	$*	Gyros and Fried Mushrooms—yum!
Kikuya Japanese Restaurant	1601 E 55th St	773-667-3727	$$	Best sushi in the neighborhood.
La Petite Folie	1504 E 55th St	773-493-1394	$$	The only haute cuisine in the neighborhood. The most expensive in the area—worth it.
Maravilla's Mexican Restaurant	5211 S Harper Ave	773-643-3155	$	Cheap, good Mexican. Stinging salsa. Open real late.
Medici on 57th	1327 E 57th St	773-667-7394	$	The essence of life at U of C.
Mellow Yellow	1508-10 E 53rd St	773-667-2000	$	Comfort food for morning and night.
Nathan's	1372 E 53rd St	773-288-5353	$	A Taste of Jamaica.
Noodles Etc	1333 E 57th St	773-947-8787	$	More collegiate than the original.
Rajun Cajun	1459 E 53rd St	773-955-1145	$	Cheap, good Indian and vegetarian.
Ribs N Bibs	5300 S Dorchester Ave	773-493-0400	$	Finger lickin'. Wear the bib.
Salonica	1440 E 57th St	773-752-3899	$	Where to go the morning after.
Thai 55 Restaurant	1607 E 55th St	773-363-7119	$	Good Americanized Thai.
Valois	1518 E 53rd St	773-667-0647	$*	See Your Food.

Map 20 • East Hyde Park / Jackson Park

Café Corea	1603 E 55th St	773-288-1795	$*	Cozy Café.
Marina Café	6401 S Coast Guard Dr	773-947-0400	$$$	Boaters order dockside. Live jazz on weekends.
Morry's Deli	5500 S Cornell Ave	773-363-3800	$	Good on the go.
Nile Restaurant	1611 E 55th St	773-324-9499	$	Varied Middle Eastern.
Orly's Café	1660 E 55th St	773-643-5500	$	Stick to the Mexican. Have a margarita.
Piccolo Mondo	1642 E 56th St	773-643-1106	$$	Best Italian in the area.
Siam Thai Cuisine	1639 E 55th St	773-324-9296	$	More Thai in Hyde Park.
Snail's Thai Cuisine	1649 E 55th St	773-667-5423	$	Great Hyde Park Thai.

Map 21 • Wicker Park / Ukrainian Village

Adobo Grill	2005 W Division St	773- 252-9990	$$$$	Upscale Mexican for yuppies.
Blue Line Club Car	1548 N Damen Ave	773-395-3700	$$	Mix a diner with a Martini club and here you go.
Bluefin	1952 W North Ave	773-394-7373	$$$	Upscale, trendy sushi bar.
Bob San	1805 W Division St	773-235-8888	$$$$	Youthful sushi joint.
The Bongo Room	1470 N Milwaukee Ave	773-489-0690	$	Great breakfast spot, expect to wait on weekends.
Cleo's	1935 W Chicago Ave	312-243-5600	$	Off the beaten Wicker Park/East Village path. Polished with local attitude.
Cold Comfort Café & Deli	2211 W North Ave	773-772-4552	$$	Freshly made deli sandwiches; groceries.
D'Vine Restaurant & Wine Bar	1950 W North Ave	773-235-5700	$$$$	Another place to be seen and blow your paycheck.
Earwax	1561 N Milwaukee Ave	773-772-4019	$	Wicker Park staple and eclectic health food mecca.

Feast	1616 N Damen Ave	773-772-7100	$$$	Popular for Sunday brunch.
Green Ginger	2050 W Division St	773- 486-6700	$$$	Asian-fusion as hip as it is tasty.
Half & Half	1560 N Damen Ave	773-489-6220	$$	Breakfast "cuisine."
Iggy's	1840 W North Ave	773-227-IGGY	$$$	Old bar, new location. Old world bordello meets New world metal and neon.
Las Palmas	1835 W North Ave	773-289-4991	$	Great al fresco dining and atrium seating.
Leo's Lunchroom	1809 W Division St	773-276-6509	$*	Tiny BYOB—great for breakfast, lunch or dinner.
Leona's	1936 W Augusta Blvd	773-292-4300	$	Local chain restaurant. Sub-par food, even worse service.
Lulu's Hot Dogs	1000 S Leavitt St	312-243-3444	$*	Hot dawg!
Mas	1670 W Division St	773-276-8700	$$	Stylish Latin cooking, dinner only.
Milk & Honey	1920 W Division St	773-395-9434	$	Heaven for breakfast.
Mirai Sushi	2020 W Division St	773-862-8500	$$	Chic dining and good sushi.
MOD	1520 N Damen Ave	773-252-1500	$$	Contemporary American hipster destination.
Moonshine	1824 W Division St	773-862-8686	$$	Auto repair garage turned vintage barn with neon lights and televisions!
Pacific Café	1619 N Damen Ave	773-862-1988	$$	Inexpensive sushi/Japanese.
Parlor	1745 W North Ave	773-782-9000	$$$	Pseudo-swank, contemporary-classic, American eater with mostly American wine list.
Picante	2016 W Division St	773- 328-8800	$*	Very very very very very small taqueria.
Piece	1927 W North Ave	773-772-4422	$$	"Designer" pizza joint.
Settimana Café	2056 W Division St	773-394-1629	$$	Thai the summer patio.
Sigara Hookah Café & Lounge	2013 W Division St	773-292-9190	$	Middle Eastern coffee, smokes, and eats.
Smoke Daddy	1804 W Division St	773-772-6656	$	Barbecue and blues.
Souk	1552 N Milwaukee Ave	773-227-1818	$$	Middle Eastern fare with belly dancers and hookhas.
Spring	2039 W North Ave	773-395-7100	$$$$	Vogue, overpriced Asian.
Sultan's Market	2057 W North Ave	773-235-3072	$	Cheap Middle Eastern, groceries.
Thai Lagoon	2223 W North Ave	773-489-5747	$$	Great Thai, funky atmosphere.
Thai Village	2053 W Division St	773- 384-5352	$	Cheap, tasty, and great outdoor seating.
Tre Via	1575 N Milwaukee Ave	773-227-7990	$$$	Ambitious Italian with many comfort-food options.

Map 22 • Noble Square / Goose Island

Corosh	1072 N Milwaukee Ave	773-235-0600	$$	Italian and pub fare, great patio.
El Barco Mariscos Seafood	1035 N Ashland Blvd	773-486-6850	$$	Outdoor seating, terrific ceviche.
Hilary's Urban Eatery	1500 W Division St	773-235-4327	$$	Salmon cakes to die for.
Luc Thang	1524 N Ashland Blvd	773-395-3907	$	Thai with Chinese and Vietnamese touches.
NYC Bagel	1001 W North Ave	312-274-1278	$	NY-style deli, best egg salad in the city.
Sangria Restaurant and Tapas Bar	901 W Weed St	312-266-1200	$$	Specialty sangria & contemporary tapas in bright, lively room.

Map 23 • West Town / Near West Side

A Tavola	2148 W Chicago Ave	773-276-7567	$$$	Upscale Italian charm in an intimate setting.
China Dragon Restaurant	2008 W Madison St	312-666-3766	$$*	Dependably fantastic Chinese.
Il Jack's Italian Restaurant	1758 W Grand Ave	312-421-7565	$$	Neighborhood Italian with *Sopranos* feel.
Munch	1800 W Grand Ave	312-997-2400	$	Laid-back, funky brunch place.
Old Lviv	2228 W Chicago Ave	773-772-7250	$*	Eastern European buffet.
Tecalitlan Restaurant	1814 W Chicago Ave	773-384-4285	$	Popular family-style, Mexican restaurant.

Map 24 • River West / West Town

160 Blue	160 N Loomis St	312-850-0303	$$$	Ameri-French owned by Michael Jordan.
Amelia's Mexican Grille	1235 W Grand Ave	312-421-2000	$$	OK food, outside seating can get quite noisy.
Amore Ristorante	1330 W Madison St	312-829-3333	$$$	Eat Italian cuisine while listening to live music.
Aroma	941 W Randolph St	312-492-7889	$	Busy Thai restaurants serving up the yummies. They do delivery.
Bella Notte	1374 W Grand Ave	312-733-5136	$$$$	Romantic, Italian, and schmoozy.
Billy Goat Tavern	1535 W Madison St	312-733-9132	$*	Cheezeboiga chain.
Blyss	1061 W Madison St	312-433-0013	$$$	East-coast style seafood experience.
Breakfast Club	1381 W Hubbard St	312-666-3166	$$	Brunch and then some.
Buongiorno Café	1123 W Grand Ave	312-829-7433	$	A new, yet another Italian café to choose your paninis from your ponzeros.
Burger Baron	1381 W Grand Ave	312-733-3285	$	Burgers and beer for the everyman.
Cannella's on Grand	1132 W Grand Ave	312-433-9400	$$$$	Long standing fine-dining favorite.
D'Agostino's Pizzeria	752 N Ogden Ave	312-850-3247	$	Cheezey take on the Italian family Restaurants.
D'Amotos Italian Bakery	1124 W Grand Ave	312-733-5456	$*	Old Italy's finest baked goods to go, amazing focaccia bread.
De Cero	814 W Randolph St	312-455-8114	$$$	Made-to-order tacos, fresh fruit cocktail, Mexican heaven.

*Key: $: Under $10 / $$: $10-$20 / $$$: $20-$30 / $$$$: $30+ * : Does not accept credit cards. / † : Accepts only American Express.*

Map 24 • River West / West Town—*continued*

Dragonfly Mandarin Restaurants	832 W Randolph St	312-787-7600	$$$	This place can't seem to land anywhere; more dance club than anything.
Flo	1434 W Chicago Ave	312-243-0477	$$	Mexican-influenced breakfast in a relaxed atmosphere.
Follia	953 W Fulton St	312-243-2888	$$$	Swanky, upscale Italian.
Green Zebra	1460 W Chicago Ave	312-243-7100	$$$$	Innovative and mostly vegetarian, by Spring's Shawn McClain.
Hacienda Tecalitlan	820 N Ashland Blvd	312-243-1166	$$	Beautiful, authentic interior with amazing margaritas.
Ina's	1235 W Randolph St	312-226-8227	$$$	Special occasion breakfasts. Try the scrapple—it's better than it sounds.
Jerry's Sandwiches	1045 W Madison St	312-563-1008	$	Fresh and slightly gourmet concoctions.
La Borsa	375 N Morgan St	312-563-1414	$$$	Not-too-traditional Italian.
La Sardine	111 N Carpenter St	312-421-2800	$$	Tuesdays fixed price for $20!
Le Peep Grill	1000 W Washington Blvd	312-563-9990	$	Flurry of brunch options, sunny color scheme, outdoor seating .
Marche	833 W Randolph St	312-226-8399	$$$	Theatrical French brasserie dining.
Misto	1118 W Grand Ave	312-226-5989	$$$$	Contemporary Italian cuisine, but more popular bar.
Moretti's	1645 W Jackson Blvd	312-850-0208	$	Pizzeria with garden patio.
Moto	945 W Fulton Market	312-491-0058	$$$$	Conceptual laboratory food creations.
Oggi Trattoria Café	1378 W Grand Ave	312-733-0442	$$	One of the godfathers of the neighborhood.
Rushmore	1023 W Lake St	312-421-8845	$$$$	Sophisticated comfort.
Salerno's Pizza and Pasta	1201 W Grand Ave	312-666-3444	$	Tony Soprano would be proud, and full.
Silver Palm	768 N Milwaukee Ave	312-666-9322	$$$	Dine in a 1940s train car on upscale American food.
Sushi X	1136 W Chicago Ave	312-491-9232	$$	Speakeasy sushi bar with fish so fresh they swim to your plate. BYOB.
Twisted Spoke	501 N Ogden Ave	312-666-1500	$	Famous for serving smut movies and eggs simultaneously.
Union Park	228 S Racine Ave	312-243-9002	$	Clubby groove with bar food.
Vinnie's Sandwich Shop	1204 W Grand Ave	312-738-2985	$	No frills, handy for construction workers.
Vivo	838 W Randolph St	312-733-3379	$$$$	One Restaurants Row's first resident of Italian dining.
West Town Tavern	1329 W Chicago Ave	312-666-6175	$$$	Home cooking if you're fancy and have a lot of time on your hands.
Windy City Café	1062 W Chicago Ave	312-492-8010	$	Small town diner feel and menu, grab a booth.
Wishbone	1001 W Washington Blvd	312-850-2663	$$	Comfort food, comfort folks.

Map 25 • Illinois Medical District

Carnitas Uruapan Restaurant	1725 W 18th St	312-226-2654	$*	Carnitas muy necesitas.
El Charco Verde	2253 W Taylor St	312-738-1686	$	A Mexican favorite.
TJ's Family Restaurant	1928 W Cermak Rd	773-927-3349	$*	Neighborhood diner.

Map 26 • University Village / Little Italy / Pilsen

Al's Number 1 Italian Beef	1079 W Taylor St	312-226-4017	$*	Where's the beef? Right here.
Café Viaggio	1435 W Taylor St	312-226-9009	$$	A variety of pasta, chicken and veal.
Caffe La Scala	626 S Racine Ave	312-421-7262	$$$	Upscale Italian near United Center.
Carm's Beef and Snack Shop	1057 W Polk St	312-738-1046	$*	Italian subs and sausages.
Chez Joel	1119 W Taylor St	312-226-6479	$$$	Delicious French cuisine in Little Italy.
Couscous	1445 W Taylor St	312-226-2408	$$	Middle Eastern & Maghrebin Cuisine. Unique falafel.
De Pasada	1519 W Taylor St	312-243-6441	$	Inexpensive, good quality Mexican—friendly staff.
Francesca's	1400 W Taylor St	312-829-2828	$$	Loud, bustling dining room.
Gennaro's	1352 W Taylor St	312-733-8790	$	Standard fare served in generous portions.
Golden Thai	1509 W Taylor St	312-733-0760	$	Always busy, but there's better Thai out there.
La Vita	1359 W Taylor St	312-491-1414	$$$	Date-spot for northern Italian.
Little China	1520 W Taylor St	312-455-0667	$	A bit salty, but if that's what you're looking for…
May Street Café	1136 W Cermak	312-421-4442	$	Inexpensive, super casual pan-Latin.
New Rosebud Café	1500 W Taylor St	312-942-1117	$	Popular with the United Center crowd.
Nuevo Leon	1515 W 18th St	312-421-1517	$	Real-deal Mexican grub in Pilsen.
Playa Azul	1514 W 18th St	312-421-2552	$$	Seafood ala Mexicaine.
Siam Pot	1509 Taylor St	312-733-0760	$	Reasonable Thai in large amounts.
Sweet Maple Café	1339 W Taylor St	312-243-8908	$	Super-homey breakfast, homemade biscuits.
Taj Mahal	1512 W Taylor St	312-226-6546	$$	Affordable Indian.
Taylor Street Taco Grill	1412 W Taylor St	312-850-9717	$	On the cheaper end, but not bad.
Tuscany	1014 W Taylor St	312-829-1990	$$	Elegant Taylor Street Italian.

Map 27 • Logan Square

Abril Mexican Restaurant	2607 N Milwaukee Ave	773-227-7252	$$	Tacos and tequila.
Buona Terra Ristorante	2535 N California Ave	773-289-3800	$$	Logan Square shmoozy Italian.
Café Bolero	2252 N Western Ave	773-227-9000	$$	Tasty Cuban fare.
Choi's Chinese Restaurant	2638 N Milwaukee Ave	773-486-8496	$$	Good, fresh Chinese food.
Dunlay's on the Square	3137 W Logan Blvd	773-227-2400	$$	American food and sports viewing.
El Cid	2116 N Milwaukee Ave	773-252-4747	$	Authentic Mexican for the masses.
El Nandu	2731 N Fullerton Ave	773-278-0900	$$	Argentinian delicacies mixed with music.
Hot Spot	2824 W Armitage Ave	773-770-3838	$	Sunny hipster brunch spot.
Johnny's Grill	2545 N Kedzie Blvd	773-278-2215	$*	Diner food for the grunge crowd.
Lula Café	2537 N Kedzie Blvd	773-489-9554	$$*	Pan-ethnic nouveau for hipsters.
Mama Kitty's	1616 N Kedzie Ave	773-235-4889	$*	Diner fare. No dinner.

Map 28 • Bucktown

Café De Luca	1721 N Damen Ave	773-342-6000	$$	Café and Italian sandwiches.
Café Laguardia	2111 W Armitage Ave	773- 862-5996	$$	Cuban food like you wouldn't believe.
Café Matou	1846 N Milwaukee Ave	773-384-8911	$$$	Fantastic French food, dodgy locale.
Club Lucky	1824 W Wabansia Ave	773-227-2300	$$	Age-old Italian joint.
Darwin's	1935 N Damen Ave	773-772-3719	$$	Grown-up bar food.
Hollywood Grill	1601 W North Ave	773-395-1818	$	24-hour Wicker Park dive.
Hot Chocolate	1747 N Damen	773-489-1747	$$	Much more than just hot chocolate.
Jane's	1655 W Cortland St	773-862-5263	$$$	Good-for-you gourmet.
Le Bouchon	1958 N Damen Ave	773-862-6600	$$	Affordable, crowded French.
Margie's Candies	1960 N Western Ave	773-384-1035	$	Immense ice cream concoctions.
Meritage	2118 N Damen Ave	773-235-6434	$$$$	Great food, great domestic wine list. A real neighborhood eatery.
My Pie Pizza	2010 N Damen Ave	773-394-6900	$	A.Y.C.E. pizza & salad bar.
Northside Bar & Grill	1635 N Damen Ave	773-384-3555	$$	Bucktown institution; outdoor seating.
Rinconcito Sudamericano	1954 W Armitage Ave	773-489-3126	$$	Yummy South American food.
Roong Thai Restaurant	1633 N Milwaukee Ave	773-252-3488	$$	Tasty Thai.
Scylla	1952 N Damen	773-227-2995	$$$	Seafood in Bucktown.
Silver Cloud Club & Grill	1700 N Damen Ave	773-489-6212	$$	Comfort food and drinks.
Think	2235 N Western	773-394-0537	$$$	Gourmet Italian—reasonable prices.
Toast	2046 N Damen Ave	773-772-5600	$	Simple but Chic breakfast. Killer food.

Map 29 • DePaul / Wrightwood / Sheffield

Buffalo Wild Wings	2464 N Lincoln Ave	773-868-9453	$	Sports bar with wings.
Charlie's Ale House	1224 W Webster Ave	773-871-1440	$	Yuppies eat and drink here.
Clarke's Pancake House & Restaurant	2441 N Lincoln Ave	773-472-3505	$	Great pancake and omelette spot.
Demon Dogs	944 W Fullerton Ave	773-281-2001	$*	Classic Chicago Dogs.
Good Island Brewing Company	1800 N Clybourn Ave	312-915-0071	$	Pub grub at its best.
Green Dolphin Street	2200 N Ashland Ave	773-395-0066	$$$$	Live jazz club and contemporary American.
John's Place	1200 W Webster Ave	773-525-6670	$	Healthy comfort food.
Lindo Mexico	2642 N Lincoln Ave	773-871-4832	$	Sunny Mexican.
Red Lion Pub	2446 N Lincoln Ave	773-348-2695	$	It's haunted!
Sai Café	2010 N Sheffield	773-472-8080	$$$	Traditional sushi place.
Salt & Pepper Diner	2575 N Lincoln Ave	773-525-8788	$*	Retro burger joint.
Shine & Morida	901 W Armitage Ave	773-296-0101	$$	Chinese and Japanese all-in-one.
Taco & Burrito House	1548 W Fullerton Ave	773-665-8389	$*	Super-cheap burrito shack, open very late.
Tsuki	1441 W Fullerton Ave	773-883-8722	$$	It was bound to happen: tapas and sushi.
Twisted Lizard	1964 N Sheffield Ave	773-929-1414	$$	Yuppie Mexican.

Map 30 • Lincoln Park

Aladdin Café	2269 N Lincoln Ave	773-871-7327	$	Dine-in or take-out hummos hut.
Ambria	2300 N Lincoln Park W	773-472-5959	$$$$	Luxe French with impeccable service.
Asiana	2546 N Clark St	773-296-9189	$$$$	Veggie vietnamese noodles.
Athenian Room	807 W Webster Ave	773-348-5155	$	Casual Greek cuisine.
Boka	1729 N Halsted St	312-337-6070	$$$	Ambitious menu, swank decor.
Café Ba-Ba-Reeba!	2024 N Halsted St	773-935-5000	$$$	Noisy, bustling tapas joint.
Café Bernard	2100 N Halsted St	773-871-2100	$$	Charming French.
Carmichaels Chicago Steakhouse	1052 W Monroe St	312-433-0025	$$$$	Great steaks in a vintage-style dining room.
Charlie Trotter's	816 W Armitage Ave	773-248-6228	$$$$	World-famous nouvelle cuisine.
Dunlays	2600 N Clark St	773-883-6000	$$$	Upscale American.
Emilio's Tapas	444 Fullerton Pkwy	773-327-5100	$$$	Cavernous branch of local tapas chain.
Fattoush	2652 N Halsted St	773-327-2652	$$	Nicely priced Middle-East nosh.
Frances' Deli	2552 N Clark St	773-248-4580	$	Inventive deli.
Geja's Café	340 W Armitage Ave	773-281-9101	$$$	Romantic fondue with live flamenco.
Itto Sushi	2616 N Halsted St	773-871-1800	$$	Your typical sushi spot.
Karyn's	1901 N Halsted Ave	312-255-1590	$$	The queen of raw food.
King Crab	1816 N Halsted St	312-280-8990	$$$	Reliable fish and seafood.

*Key: $: Under $10 / $$: $10-$20 / $$$: $20-$30 / $$$$: $30+   * : Does not accept credit cards. / † : Accepts only American Express.*

Map 30 • Lincoln Park—*continued*

Mon Ami Gabi	2300 N Lincoln Park W	773-348-8886	$$$	Ambria's more casual neighbor.
My Pie Pizza	2417 N Clark St	773-929-3380	$	A.Y.C.E. pizza & salad bar.
Nookies	1746 N Wells St	312-337-2454	$*	24-hour diner. Cleaner than most.
Nookies, Too	2114 N Halsted St	773-327-1400	$*	24-hour grill.
North Pond	2610 N Cannon Dr	773-477-5845	$$$$	Earthy contemporary American.
O'Fame	750 W Webster Ave	773-929-5111	$$	Nice, neighborhood casual Italian.
Original Pancake House	2020 N Lincoln Park W	773-929-8130	$$*	Breakfast-y grill.
PS Bangkok	2521 N Halsted St	773-348-0072	$	Popular Thai with delivery.
Piattini	934 W Webster Ave	773-281-3898	$$	Italian tapas.
Ranalli's	1925 N Lincoln Ave	312-642-4700	$	Huge patio for summertime quaffing.
Ranalli's	2301 N Clark St	312-440-7000	$	Local chain with 100+ beers.
RJ Grunt's	2056 N Lincoln Park W	773-929-5363	$$	Great grub.
Robinson's No 1 Ribs	655 W Armitage Ave	312-337-1399	$*	Down home ribs in Lincoln Park.
Salvatore's Ristorante	525 W Arlington Pl	773-528-1200	$$$	Cute neighborhood Italian.
Sushi O Sushi	346 W Armitage Ave	773-871-4777	$$	Newly remodeled fresh seafood.
Taco Burrito Palace #2	2441 N Halsted St	773-248-0740	$*	Speedy Mexican.
Tilli's	1952 N Halsted St	773-325-0044	$$	Cute staff and good food.
Twin Anchors	1655 N Sedgwick St	312-266-1616	$$	Regulars will vouch for the ribs.
Via Emilia Ristorante	2119 N Clark St	773-248-6283	$$	Elegant Italian, nice wine list.
Vinci	1732 N Halsted St	312-266-1199	$$$	Homemade pasta raises the bar.
Wiener's Circle	2622 N Clark St	773-477-7444	$*	Classic dogs served with a generous helping of sass.

Map 31 • Old Town / Near North

Bistrot Margot	1437 N Wells St	312-587-3660	$$$$	Great date place.
Chic Café	361 W Chestnut St	312-873-2032	$$	Gourmet prix fixe by culinary students.
Cucina Bella Osteria & Wine Bar	1612 N Sedgwick St	312-274-1119	$$*	Solid Italian; wine bar.
Fireplace Inn	1448 N Wells St	312-664-5264	$$$	Popular spot to watch sports.
Flat Top Grill	319 W North Ave	312-787-7676	$$	Choose yer own adventure or stir-fry, as it were.
Fresh Choice	1534 N Wells St	312-664-7065	$*	Sandwich and smoothie king.
Kamehachi	1400 N Wells St	312-664-3663	$$$	Sushi favorite with upstairs lounge.
Kiki's Bistro	900 N Franklin St	312-335-5454	$$$$	Stylish French.
Las Pinatas	1552 N Wells St	312-664-8277	$$	Festive atmosphere, fantastic food.
Mitchell's	101 W North Ave	312-642-5246	$	Classic diner, great sundaes.
MK	868 N Franklin St	312-482-9179	$$$$	Very stylish.
O'Brien's	1528 N Wells St	312-787-3131	$$$	Best outdoor in Old Town.
Old Jerusalem	1411 N Wells St	312-944-0459	$$	Cheap, good food.
Pluton	873 N Orleans St	312-266-1440	$$$$	Super chi-chi "it" place.
Salpicon	1252 N Wells St	312-988-7811	$$	Colorful Mexican with tequila tastings.
Topo Gigio Ristorante	1516 N Wells St	312-266-9355	$$$	Crowded reliable Italian. Big outdoor.

Map 32 • Gold Coast / Mag Mile

Ashkenaz	12 E Cedar St	312-944-5006	$	Chicago's true Jewish deli.
Bistro 110	110 E Pearson St	312-266-3110	$$$	Popular Sunday jazz brunch.
Bistrot Zinc	1131 N State St	312-337-1131	$$	Quiet elegance.
Café des Architectes	20 E Chestnut St	312-324-4000	$$$	French Mediterranean with late kitchen.
Café Spiaggia	980 N Michigan Ave	312-280-2750	$$	More casual and less pricey than its Spiaggia forebear.
Cape Cod Room	140 E Walton St	312-787-2200	$$$$	Over-the-top nautical decor.
Cheesecake Factory	875 N Michigan Ave	312-337-1101	$$	40+ kinds of cheesecake.
Cru Wine Bar & Café	888 N Wabash Ave	312-337-4001	$$$	Cool, funky wine and cheese.
Dave & Buster's	1030 N Clark St	312-943-5151	$$	Chuck E. Cheese for grown-ups.
Foodlife	835 N Michigan Ave	312-335-3663	$$$	Le food court deluxe.
Gibson's Steakhouse	1028 N Rush St	312-266-8999	$$$$	If you love steak, get a reservation.
Hugo's Frog Bar	1024 N Rush St	312-640-0999	$$$	Hearty seafood.
Johnny Rockets	901 N Rush St	312-337-3900	$	Jukebox and malts—outdoor seating, late night eating.
Le Colonial	937 N Rush St	312-255-0088	$$$	Vietnamese/French fare.
McCormick & Schmick's	41 E Chestnut St	312-397-9500	$$$$	Seafood chain that outdoes itself on portions and taste.
Mike Ditka's	100 E Chestnut St	312-587-8989	$$$	The place for Ditka, Chicago sports, and meat.
Morton's of Chicago	1050 N State St	312-266-4820	$$$$	The steakhouse standard.
Original Pancake House	22 E Bellevue Pl	312-642-7917	$$*	The apple waffle/pancake is right!
Pane Caldo	72 E Walton St	312-649-0055	$$$$	Tucked-away genius Italian trattoria.
Pump Room	Omni Ambassador East Hotel, 1301 N State Pkwy	312-266-0360	$$$$	Chicago old-school tradition. Dress code.
Ra Sushi	1139 N State St	312-274-0011	$$$	Rock-n-roll sushi bar.
Ritz-Carlton Dining Room	Ritz Carlton Hotel, 160 E Pearson St	312-573-5223	$$$$	Hotel dining deluxe.

Signature Room at the 95th	875 N Michigan Ave	312-787-9596	$$$$	It's the view. Proposal hot spot.
Spiaggia	980 N Michigan Ave	312-280-2750	$$$$	One of Chicago's best—gorgeous lake view and Italian cuisine.
Tavern on Rush	1031 N Rush St	312-664-9600	$$$$	Summer mainstay, American menu.
Tempo	6 E Chestnut St	312-943-4373	$$*	24/7 patio seating and huge menu.
Tsunami	1160 N Dearborn St	312-642-9911	$$$	Sushi and sake in a club-like atmosphere.
Whiskey Bar and Grill	1015 N Rush St	312-475-0300	$$	Great summer place where hip and trendy folks abound.

Map 33 • West Rogers Park

Arya Bhavan	2508 W Devon Ave	773-274-5000	$$	Northern Indian all-vegentarian.
Café Montenegro	6954 N Western Ave	773-761-2233	$*	Greek-accented coffeeshop.
Delhi Darbar Kabab House	6403 N California Ave	773-338-1818	$	Open 24-hours everyday. Indian/Pakistani.
Desi Island	2401 W Devon Ave	773-465-2489	$	Think corner diner, but spicy.
Fluky's	6821 N Western Ave	773-274-3652	$*	"Famous" hot dog joint. Breakfast, lunch, and dinner, outdoor seating.
Ghandi India Restaurant	2601 W Devon Ave	773-761-8714	$$	Family-style North and South Indian fare.
Good Morgan Kosher Fish Market	2948 W Devon Ave	773-764-8115	$$*	Fish market/restaurant in the Devon kosher strip.
Hashalom	2905 W Devon Ave	773-465-5675	$*	Israeli/Moroccan, kosher, BYOB, closed Sat/Sun.
Hema's Kitchen	6406 N Oakley	773-338-1627	$$	Indian comfort food.
Mysore Woodland's	2548 W Devon Ave	773-338-8166	$$	Yummy Indian.
Tiffin	2536 W Devon Ave	773-338-2143	$$	Most upscale Indian restaurant on Devon, yet moderately priced.
Udupi Palace	2543 W Devon Ave	773-338-2152	$	Pure vegetarian Indian food, low-fat, not too spicy.
Viceroy of India	2520 W Devon Ave	773-743-4100	$$	Popular Indian restaurant, vegetarian options.

Map 34 • East Rogers Park

Deluxe Diner	6349 N Clark St	773-743-8244	$*	Retro-styled greasy spoon.
El Famous Burrito	7047 N Clark St	773-465-0377	$*	Mexican treats for the college crowd.
Ennui Café	6981 N Sheridan Rd	773-973-2233	$*	Tasty tidbits.
Heartland Café	7000 N Glenwood Ave	773-465-8005	$$	Eclectic health food.
Morseland	1218 W Morse Ave	773-764-8900	$$$	Rogers Park café with ambitious fare.
Panini Panini	6764 N Sheridan Rd	773-761-4110	$$*	Italian flavor for the North Side.
Speakeasy Supperclub	1401 W Devon Ave	773-338-0600	$$	Tasty neighborhood BYOB.

Map 35 • Arcadia Terrace / Peterson Park

Aztecas Mexican Taqueria	5421 N Lincoln Ave	773-506-2052	$	Standerd Mexican fare.
Charcoal Delights	3139 W Foster Ave	773-583-0056	$*	The name says it all.
Fondue Stube	2717 W Peterson Ave	773-784-2200	$$	Fun fondue!
Garden Buffet	5347 N Lincoln Ave	773-728-1249	$*	Korean/Japanese with huge buffet and sushi bar.
Katsu	2651 W Peterson Ave	773-784-3383	$$$	familiar, family sushi place.
Pueblito Viejo	5429 N Lincoln Ave	773-784-9135	$$	Adorable Columbian village-theme with live music on weekends.
Woo Chon	5744 N California Ave	773-728-8001	$	Authentic Korean BBQ. Brusque but oddly fun service.

Map 36 • Bryn Mawr

El Tipico	1836 W Foster Ave	773-878-0839	$	Neighborhood hangout with semi-authentic Mexican food.
Fireside Restaurant & Lounge	5739 N Ravenswood Ave	773-878-5942	$$	Diverse crowd and eclectic menu from ribs to pizza.
Max's Italian Beef	5754 N Western Ave	773-989-8200	$$	Chicago institution; home of the pepper-and-egg sandwich.
San Soo Gap San Korean Restaurant and Sushi House	5247 N Western Ave	773-334-1589	$$	Do-it-yourself Korean barbeque at 4 am.

Map 37 • Edgewater / Andersonville

Andie's	5253 N Clark St	773-784-8616	$$	Fresh Middle Eastern in airy atmosphere.
Ann Sather	5207 N Clark St	773-271-6677	$	Andersonville landmark with Swedish-inspired food.
Carson's Ribs	5970 N Ridge Ave	773-271-4000	$	They say ribs, but it's really the pork chops.
Corner Grille	5200 N Clark St	773-271-3663	$	Breakfast & lunch spot.
Francesca's Bryn Mawr	1039 W Bryn Mawr Ave	773-506-9261	$$	Dined in an SRO before?
Indie Café	5951 N Broadway St	773-561-5577	$$	Thai and sushi. Yummy and cheap.
Jin Ju	5203 N Clark St	773-334-6377	$$$	Upscale Korean.
La Fonda Latino	5350 N Broadway St	773-271-3935	$$	Real tasty pan-Latin.
La Tache	1475 W Balmoral Ave	773-334-7168	$$	Neighborhood French bistro.
M Henry	5707 N Clark St	773-561-1600	$$	Stylish brunch option in Andersonville.
Moody's Pub	5910 N Broadway St	773-275-2696	$*	Burgers only, but the best.

*Key: $: Under $10 / $$: $10-$20 / $$$: $20-$30 / $$$$: $30+ *: Does not accept credit cards. / †: Accepts only American Express.*

Map 37 • Edgewater / Andersonville—*continued*

Pasteur	5525 N Broadway St	773-878-1061	$$$$	Easy to imagine you're in Vietnam 50 years ago.
Pauline's	1754 W Balmoral Ave	773-561-8573	$*	Weekend breakfast hotspot; try the famous five-egg omelette.
Reza's	5255 N Clark St	773-561-1898	$$	Many Persian options, leftovers for lunch the next day.
South	5900 N Broadway St	773-989-7666	$$$	Southern new orleans fare.
Sushi Luxe	5204 N Clark St	773-334-0770	$$	Sushi & bar.
Svea	5236 N Clark St	773-275-7738	$*	Adorable, tiny swedish diner.
Swedish Bakery	5348 N Clark St	773-561-8919	$*	Famous tasty pastries and cakes.
Tanoshii	5547 N Clark St	773-878-6886	$$	Sit at the bar and put yourself in Sushi Mike's competant hands.
Taste of Lebanon	1509 W Foster Ave	773-334-1600	$*	Lebanese casual.
Tomboy	5402 N Clark St	773-907-0636	$$$	Loud, hip and fun, BYOB.
Urban Epicure	1512 W Berwyn Ave	773-293-3663	$$*	Great gourmet salads, sandwiches, and foods.

Map 38 • Ravenswood / Albany Park

Arun's	4156 N Kedzie Ave	773-539-1909	$$$$	Worldwide rep for four-star prix fixe Thai.
Cousin's Turkish Restaurants	3038 W Irving Park Rd	773-478-6868	$$$	Well-regarded Turkish restaurants.
Great Sea Chinese Restaurants	3254 W Lawrence Ave	773-478-9129	$$	Otherwise basic Chinese Restaurants locally famous for its hot wings.
Han Bat	2723 W Lawrence Ave	773-271-8640	$$$	Very traditional Korean. The seollongtang is reportedly sublime.
Huddle House	4748 N Kimball	773-588-5363	$*	This cozy diner open 24 hours.
Kang Nam	4849 N Kedzie Ave	773-539-2524	$$	Could be the best Korean BBQ in town. Crazy excellent.
Korean Restaurants	2659 W Lawrence Ave	773-878-2095	$$	Excellent Korean eats with pleasant service whenever you want it.
Lutz Continental Café	2458 W Montrose Ave	773-478-7785	$$	If Grandma was German, she would serve these pastries.
Manzo's Ristorante	3210 W Irving Park Rd	773-478-3070	$$	Do not miss the Sunday buffet. Tasty, plentiful and cheap Italian.
Noon O Kabab	4661 N Kedzie Ave	773-279-8899	$	Bring doggie bag for day-after lunch.
Penguin	2723 W Lawrence Ave	773-271-4924	$*	High-fat, authentic Argentine ice cream (empanadas and pizza, too, but go straight for dessert).
Rockwell's Neighborhood Grill	4632 N Rockwell St	773-509-1871	$	Familiar bar food and brunchtime favorites in a friendly atmosphere.
Santa Rita Taqueria	2752 W Lawrence Ave	773-784-1522	$*	Inexpensive tasty fare open late. Weekend pastor is fantastic.
Shelly's Freez	5119 N Lincoln Ave	773-271-2783	$*	Classic Italian beef and dipped soft-serve.
Thai Little Home Café	4747 N Kedzie Ave	773-478-3944	$	Two rooms + one lunch buffet = less than $10.

Map 39 • Ravenswood / North Center

Andalucia	1820 W Montrose Ave	773-334-6900	$	Inexpensive, authentic tapas.
Bistro Campagne	4518 N Lincoln Ave	773-271-6100	$$	Organic French fare in a cozy room.
Café 28	1800 W Irving Park Rd	773-528-2883	$$	Trendy Cuban.
Café Selmarie	4729 N Lincoln Ave	773-989-5595	$$	Bakery/café.
Chicago Brauhaus	4732 N Lincoln Ave	773-784-4444	$$	Live German band!
Daily Bar & Grill	4560 N Lincoln Ave	773-561-6198	$	Bar food in retro ambiance.
Garcia's	4749 N Western Ave	773-769-5600	$	Mexican/Tex-Mex with great shakes.
Glunz Bavarian Haus	4128 N Lincoln Ave	773-472-4287	$$	Weiner schnitzel and beer.
Jury's Food & Drink	4337 N Lincoln Ave	773-935-2255	$	Neighborhood pub.
La Boca della Verita	4618 N Lincoln Ave	773-784-6222	$$	Cozy Italian café.
O'Donovan's	2100 W Irving Park Rd	773-478-2100	$	Three words: Dollar Burger Night.
Opart Thai House	4658 N Western Ave	773-989-8517	$*	Cheap, tasty Thai BYOB.
Pizza DOC	2251 W Lawrence Ave	773-784-8777	$$	European-style, wood-oven pizza.
Roong Petch	1828 W Montrose Ave	773-989-0818	$	One of many Thai options in Lincoln Square.
She She	4539 N Lincoln Ave	773-293-3690	$$$$	Upscale/eclectic American.
Smokin' Woody's	4160 N Lincoln Ave	773-880-1100	$$	Ribs 'n' wings 'n' other sticky eats.
Tank Sushi	4515 N Lincoln Ave	773-769-2600	$$	Bright BYOB sushi spot.
Thai Oscar	4638 N Lincoln Ave	773-878-6220	$	BYOB Thai & Sushi including some wacky named maki.
Toucan	4603 N Lincoln Ave	773-989-9000	$$	Caribbean.
Tournesol	4343 N Lincoln Ave	773-477-8820	$$	Sunny French Provencal.

Map 40 • Uptown

Andie's	1467 W Montrose Ave	773-348-0654	$$	Middle Eastern food in Babylonian surroundings.
Atlantique	5101 N Clark St	773-275-9191	$$$	Fancy neighborhood seafood.
Bale French Bakery	5018 N Broadway St	773-561-4424	$	French/Asian bakery and sandwiches.
Deleece	4004 N Southport Ave	773-325-1710	$$	Ambitious global fare in cute storefront.
Don Quijote	4761 N Clark St	773-769-5930	$*	Burritos as big as your head.
Frankie J's, An American Theatre and Grill	4437 N Broadway St	773-769-2959	$$$	Laugh and eat.
Furama	4936 N Broadway St	773-271-1161	$$	Dim sum with karaoke.
Golden House Restaurant	4744 N Broadway St	773-334-0406	$	Pancakes and ambience next to the river.
Hama Matsu	5143 N Clark	773-506-2978	$$$	Japanese & Korean fare.
Holiday Club	4000 N Sheridan Rd	773-348-9600	$$*	The Rat Pack is back! With food.
Jim's Grill	1429 W Irving Pk	773-525-4050	$*	Korean/American Grill with counter service.
La Donna	5146 N Clark St	773-561-9400	$$	Friendly, tasty Italian.
Magnolia Café	1224 W Wilson Ave	773-728-8785	$$	Magnolias in an American bistro.
Pho Xe Tang	1007 W Argyle	773-878-2253	$	Cheap Asian noodles.
Riques	5004 N Sheridan Rd	773-728-6200	$	Inexpensive & creative Mexican BYOB.
Siam Noodle & Rice	4654 N Sheridan Rd	773-769-6694	$*	Damn fine Thai food.
Silver Seafood	4829 N Broadway St	773-784-0668	$	Asian delights from the sea.
Smoke Country House	1465 W Irving Park Rd	773-327-0600	$$	Great barbecue on the north side (huh… imagine that!).
Thai Pastry and Restaurants	4925 N Broadway St	773-784-5399	$	Free pastry with every order!
Tokyo Marina	5058 N Clark St	773-878-2900	$	Sushi in a pinch.
Tweet	5020 N Sheridan Rd	773-728-5576	$$*	Gourmet food without pretension.

Map 41 • Avondale / Old Irving

Chief O'Neill's	3471 N Elston Ave	773-583-3066	$	Excellent traditional pub fare.
Clara's	3159 N California Ave	773-539-3020	$*	Ultimate cheap greasy spoon.
Hot Doug's	3324 N California Ave	773-279-9550	$*	Get your weird game dogs at this campy encased meat emporium.
IHOP	2818 W Diversey Ave	773-342-8901	$	Open 24-hours.
La Finca	3361 N Elston Ave	773-478-4006	$	Servicable Mexican, margaritas.
Taqueria Trespazada	3144 N California Ave	773-539-4533	$*	Tasty, cheap tacos & salsas—no atmoshpere.

Map 42 • North Center / Roscoe Village / West Lakeview

Brett's Café Americain	2011 W Roscoe St	773-248-0999	$$$	Go for brunch or dessert. Great bread basket.
Costello Sandwich & Sides	2015 W Roscoe St	773-929-2323	$	Yummy baked sandwiches.
El Tinajon	2054 W Roscoe St	773-525-8455	$$	Good, cheap Guatemalan. Great mango margaritas.
Four Moon Tavern	1847 W Roscoe St	773-929-6666	$	Neighborhood tavern. Cozy back room. Thespian crowd.
Kaze Sushi	2032 W Roscoe St	773-327-4860	$$	Innovative, gourmet sushi.
Kitsch'n on Roscoe	2005 W Roscoe St	773-248-7372	$$	Clever retro food and tiki bar. Friendly staff.
La Mora	2132 W Roscoe St	773-404-4555	$$	Neighborhood Mediterranean-influenced Italian fare.
Lee's Chop Suey	2415 W Diversey Ave	773-342-7050	$*	Chop suey and booze.
Piazza Bella Trattoria	2116 W Roscoe St	773-477-7330	$$$	Neighborhood Italian.
Riverview Tavern & Grill	1958 W Roscoe St	773-248-9523	$$	Frat food and beer.
Thai Linda Café	2022 W Roscoe St	773-868-0075	$$	Standard-issue neighborhood Thai.
Victory's Banner	2100 W Roscoe St	773-665-0227	$	Best vegetarian in the city complete with toga-clad waitstaff.
The Village Tap	2055 W Roscoe St	773-883-0817	$	Beer garden and good bar food.
Wishbone	3300 N Lincoln Ave	773-549-2663	$$	Southern and soul food paradise. Go early for brunch.

Map 43 • Wrigleyville / East Lakeview

Ann Sather	929 W Belmont Ave	773-348-2378	$	Warm, family friendly ambience, Swedish comfort food.
Blue Bayou	3734 N Southport Ave	773-871-3300	$$	New Orleans-themed, in case you couldn't guess.
Bolat	3346 N Clark St	773-665-1100	$$	West African cuisine—try the okra with rice.
Clarke's Diner	930 W Belmont	773-348-5988	$$	All night, alright and helluv kitschy diner fun.
Coobah	3423 N Southport Ave	773-528-2220	$$	Trendy Latin spot near Music Box.
Cy's Crab House	3819 N Ashland Ave	773-883-8900	$$	Persian-tinged seafood emporium.
Heaven on Seven	3478 N Clark St	773-477-7818	$$	An epicurean jaunt to N'awlins. Yum.
Mama Desta's Red Sea	3216 N Clark St	773-935-7561	$$	No forks at this authentic Ethiopian restaurant.
Matsu Yama	1059 W Belmont	773-327-8838	$$	Lovely, fresh sushi.
Matsuya	3469 N Clark St	773-248-2677	$$	One of the best on Sushi Row.
Menagerie	1232 W Belmont Ave	773-404-8333	$$$	Styish fusion.

*Key: $: Under $10 / $$: $10-$20 / $$$: $20-$30 / $$$$: $30+   * : Does not accept credit cards. / † : Accepts only American Express.*

Map 43 • Wrigleyville / East Lakeview—*continued*

Mia Francesca	3311 N Clark St	773-281-3310	$$	Contemporary Italian date place.
Moti Mahal	1031-35 W Belmont Ave	773-348-4392	$	So-so Indian buffet in shabby environment. Popular all the same.
Orange	3231 N Clark St	773-549-4400	$$	Super stylish brunches.
Original Gino's East	2801 N Lincoln Ave	773-327-3737	$$	Family-style sit-in pizza joint.
Outpost	3438 N Clark St	773-244-1166	$$	Hey mate, dining from Down Under.
Penny's Noodle Shop	3400 N Sheffield Ave	773-281-8222	$$	Pad thai, pad see ew, popular place for a lite lunch.
Penny's Noodle Shop	950 W Diversy Ave	773-281-8448	$$	Pad thai, pad see ew, popular place for a lite lunch.
Pepper Lounge	3441 N Sheffield Ave	773-665-7377	$$	Loungey late-night dining. Smoker friendly.
Platiyo	3313 N Clark St	773-477-6700	$$	Festive & contemporary Mexican.
PS Bangkok	3345 N Clark St	773-871-7777	$	Popular neighborhood Thai that delivers.
Rise	3401 N Southport Ave	773-525-3535	$$	Sushi nightspot.
Salt & Pepper Diner	3537 N Clark St	773-883-9800	$*	Old-school greasy-spoon diner.
Shiroi Hana	3242 N Clark St	773-477-1652	$$	Tastiest sushi ever.
Socca	3301 N Clark St	773-248-1155	$$	Tasty, satisfying Mediterannean.
Standard India	917 W Belmont Ave	773-929-1123	$	Yet another Indian buffet.
Strega Nona	3747 N Southport Ave	773-244-0990	$$	Casual Italian near the Music Box.
Tango Sur	3763 N Southport Ave	773-477-5466	$$	Argentinian steakhouse.
Tombo Kitchen	3244 N Lincoln Ave	773-244-9885	$$	Modern, very good sushi. Try the eel.
Wrigleyville Dog	3737 N Clark St	773-296-1500	$*	Hot dog heaven.

Map 44 • East Lakeview

Aladdin's Eatery	614 W Diversey Pkwy	773-327-6300	$	Fresh Middle-Eastern.
Angelina Ristorante	3561 N Broadway St	773-935-5933	$$$	Casual, romantic Italian.
Ann Sather	3411 N Broadway St	773-305-0024	$	Airy branch of local comfort food chain.
Arco de Cuchilleros	3445 N Halsted St	773-296-6046	$$$	Intimate tapas; great sangria.
The Bagel	3107 N Broadway St	773-477-0300	$	Great deli fare.
Café Bordeaux and Crepes	2932 N Broadway St	773-327-6898	$	Like your neighborhood Paris café. BYOB.
Chicago Diner	3411 N Halsted St	773-935-6696	$$	A vegetarian institution.
Clark Street Dog	3040 N Clark St	773-281-6690	$*	24-hour hot dogs and cheese fries.
Cornelia's Restaurant	750 W Cornelia Ave	773-248-8333	$$	Neighborhood casual dining institution.
Cousin's	2833 N Broadway St	773-880-0063	$$	Veggie-friendly Turkish food.
Duck Walk	919 W Belmont Ave	773-665-0455	$	Your basic Thai restaurant, cheap but good.
Duke of Perth	2913 N Clark St	773-477-1741	$	Fish and chips.
Erwin, An American Café & Bar	2925 N Halsted St	773-528-7200	$$$$	Elegant.
Firefly	3335 N Halsted St	773-525-2505	$$	Upscale neighborhood joint.
Half Shell	676 W Diversey Pkwy	773-549-1773	$$$*	Casual raw bar.
Jack's on Halsted	3201 N Halsted St	773-244-9191	$$$$	Great wine list.
Kit Kit Lounge & Supper Club	3700 N Halsted St	773-525-1111	$$	Drag shows while you dine.
Koryo	2936 N Broadway St	773-477-8510	$$	Upscale Korean.
La Creperie	2845 N Clark St	773-528-9050	$$	Live French music. Shabby, but cute.
Las Mananitas	3523 N Halsted St	773-528-2109	$$	Lethal margaritas.
Mark's Chop Suey	3343 N Halsted St	773-281-9090	$	The BEST eggrolls.
Mars	3124 N Broadway St	773-404-1600	$$	White tablecloth Chinese.
Melrose	3233 N Broadway St	773-327-2060	$$	24-hour diner.
Monsoon	2813 N Broadway St	773-665-9463	$$	Pan-Asian fusion.
Nancy's Original Stuffed Pizza	2930 N Broadway St	773-883-1977	$	Seedy pizza parlor.
Nookie's Tree	3334 N Halsted St	773-248-9888	$*	24-hour diner.
Sinbad's	921 W Belmont Ave	773-477-6020	$	Falafel, hummus and the like, fast and inexpensive.
X/O	3441 N Halsted	773-348-9696	$$	Small plate cuisine in Boy's Town.
Yoshi's Café	3257 N Halsted St	773-248-6160	$$$	Franco-Japanese fusion.

Maps 45-48 • Northwest Chicago

Amitabul	6207 N Milwaukee Ave	773-774-0276	$$	Buddha-inspired Korean Vegan.
Basta Pasta	6733 N Olmstead Ave	773-763-0667	$$	Friendly, family-style Italian
Blue Angel	5310 N Milwaukee Ave	773-631-8700	$	Chicago's only stunt flier-themed 24-hour diner.
Don Juan	6730 N Northwest Hwy	773-775-6438	$$	Popular Mexican spot.
Gale Street Inn	4914 N Milwaukee Ave	773-725-1517	$$$	Classy ribs 'n' jazz joint.
Grota Smorgasborg	3112 N Central Ave	773-6224677	$$	All-you-can-eat chow in medieval-feeling banquet hall.
Halina's Polish Delights	5914 W Lawrence Ave	773-205-0256	$*	Tiny authentic Polish diner.
Hiromi's	3609 W Lawrence Ave	773-588-6764	$	Phillipine and Japanese food. Tagalong karaoke (English on request).

Mario's Café	5241 N Harlem Ave	773-594-9742	$	Need a quick Bulgarian fix? Mario's is the place.
Mayan Sol	3830 W Lawrence Ave	773-539-4398	$$	Upscale Central American and South American cuisine.
Mirabell Restaurant	3454 W Addison Ave	773-463-1962	$$	Adorable German tavern.
Montasero's Ristorante	3935 W Devon Ave	773-588-2515	$$	Don't be surprised to find an envelope full of unmarked bills in the toilet tank.
Noodles	5956 W Higgins Ave	773-775-7525	$$	Come for the Italian, stay for the dancing old folks.
Paprikash	5210 W Diversey Ave	773-736-4949	$$	Heavy, Hungarian comfort food.
Red Apple	3121 N Milwaukee Ave	773-588-5781	$*	Polish comfort food. Is there any other kind?
Ristorante Agostino	2817 N Harlem Ave	773-745-6464	$$	Elegant date place for impeccable Italian.
Sabatino's	4441 W Irving Park Blvd	773-283-8331	$$	Romantic date place.
Seo Hae	3534 W Lawrence Ave	773-539-2444	$$	Korean.
Taqueria La Oaxaquena	6113 W Diversey Ave	773-637-8709	$$	Fancy and innovative Mexican comfort food.
Teresa II Polish Restaurants & Lounge	4751 N Milwaukee Ave	773-283-0184	$$*	Clean your plate or Teresa will scold you.
Trattoria Pasta D'Arte	6311 N Milwaukee Ave	773-763-1181	$$	Upscale, creative Italian.
Tre Kronor	3258 W Foster Ave	773-267-9888	$$	Scandinavian diner.

Maps 49-52 • West Chicago

Amarind's	6822 W North Ave	773-889-9999	$$	People drive from all over for awesome Thai food.
Atomic Sub	6353 S Cottage Grove Ave	773-684-2602	$*	Watch out the bomb has hit!
Bacchanalia Ristorante	2413 S Oakley Ave	773-254-6555	$$*	Cozy Italian spot.
Bruna's	2424 S Oakley Ave	773-254-5550	$$	Cozy old-school Italian.
Edna's Restaurant	3175 W Madison St	773-638-7079	$	Best soul food on the west side.
Falco's Pizza	2806 W 40th St	773-523-7996	$*	Popular casual Italian spot.
Flying Saucer	1123 N California Ave	773-342-9076	$$*	Creative diner fare at hipster hangout.
Ignotz	2421 S Oakley Ave	773-579-0300	$$*	Northern Italian in cozy setting.
La Palma	1340 N Homan Ave	773-862-0886	$*	Authentic Puerto Rican grub at no-frills cafeteria.
Lalo's	3515 W 26th St	773-522-0345	$$	Local chain popular for their margaritas.
Lindy's and Gertie's	3685 S Archer Ave	773-927-7807	$*	Local chili & ice-cream chain.Try the chili-ice cream sundae.
Taquerias Atotonilco	3916 W 26th St	773-762-3380	$*	Quick, friendly eat-in or take-out hangover cure-all.
Tommy's Rock-n-Roll Café	2500 W Chicago	773-486-6768	$	Homemade donuts, sandwiches, and guitars.

Maps 53-56 • Southwest Chicago

Franconello's Italian Restaurant	10222 S Western Ave	773-881-4100	$$	Peek-a-boo with the chefs in the exhibition kitchen as they crank out old-world class.
Hoe China Tea	4020 W 55th St	773-284-2463	$	Come for the fruity cocktails.
Janson's Drive-In / Snyder's Red Hots	9900 S Western Ave	773-238-3612	$*	No indoor seating at this classic drive-thru.
Leon's Bar-B-Que	1206 W 59th St	773-778-7828	$*	One of the most lip-smacking BBQ joints in Chicago. Take-out only.
Lume's	11601 S Western	773-233-2323	$	Pancakes from around the world.
Tatra Inn	6040 S Pulaski Rd	773-582-8313	$	Eastern European smorgasbord.
Top Notch Beefburger	2116 W 95th St	773-445-7218	$*	Burgers and fries in '50s environment—very *Happy Days*.

Maps 57-60 • South Chicago

Army & Lou's	422 E 75th St	773-483-3100	$$	Southside soul food.
Atomic Sub	6353 S Cottage Grove Ave	773-684-2602	$*	Watch out, the bomb has hit!
Chatham Pancake House	700 E 87th	773-874-0010	$	Cheap, hearty breakfast.
Captain Hard Times	436 E 79th St	773-487-2900	$$$	Southside date destination.
Dat's Donuts	8251 S Cottage Grove Ave	773-723-1002	$*	Krispy Kreme, eat your heart out.
Helen's Restaurant	1732 E 79th St	773-933-9871	$*	Even James Brown goes to Helen's when he wants down-home cooking.
Leon's Bar-B-Que	8249 S Cottage Grove Ave	773-488-4556	$*	Southside BBQ fixture.
Phil's Kastle	9232 S Commercial Ave	773-734-9591	$*	'50s soda shop with prices to match.
Soul Queen	9031 S Stony Island Ave	773-731-3366	$*	Inexpensive comfort food.
Soul Vegetarian East	205 E 75th St	773-224-0104	$$	Vegetarian soul food? SVE pleases even the skeptics.
Tropic Island Jerk Chicken	1922 E 79th St	773-978-5375	$*	Caribbean carry-out.

Chicago is comprised of several small shopping districts (and a few rather huge ones), each with its own distinct character. North Michigan Avenue, a.k.a the Mag Mile, features superstore after superstore, from the **Virgin Megastore** to **Niketown** to the **Apple Computer** store (iPod central) to **The Disney Store,** as well as the gamut of high-end powerhouses (**Gucci**, **Tiffany**, **Hermes**...). Tucked on a side street off Michigan, a two-block strip of Oak Street houses some of the city's most chi-chi boutiques, including **Prada**, **Nicole Miller, Ultimo**, and **BCBG.** Most of Chicago's department stores also appear on the Michigan strip. **Bloomingdale's**, **Neiman-Marcus**, and **Lord & Taylor** can all be found here. The old State Street district still features the gorgeous **Marshall Field's** flagship building and **Carson Pirie Scott**, but pricier retailers have cleared out and given way to such staunchly proletariat meccas as **Sears**.

Armitage Street in Lincoln Park is home to exclusive boutiques a-plenty. People flock from all corners to shop at **Lori's Designer Shoes** or browse the racks at **Cynthia Rowley**. Chic upstarts, such as the French housewares shop **Porte Rouge** and the hip women's clothing shop **Penelope's,** flank Division Street in Wicker Park. Meanwhile, the Lincoln Square and Beverly/Morgan Park areas each have their own vibe. Lincoln Square's feel is crunchy and hippie/boho, as characterized by the international instrument collection at **Nbahari Rhythms** and the gourmet cheese emporium **The Cheese Stands Alone**. Beverly's is more arty-crafty. Here you can gear up to make your own green brew at **Bev Art Brewer and Winemaker Supply**. East Lakeview's shopping has long appealed to the young alterna-set, with its plethora of vintage and used clothing and record shops, as well as funky retail spots like the **Alley** complex and **Hollywood Mirror**.

With a **Whole Foods**, **Best Buy**, **Cost Plus World Market**, **Old Navy**, and much more, it seems that everyone in the city converges on the Clybourn Corridor shopping district, especially on weekends, when navigating its labyrinthine streets and parking lots is enough to drive one to therapy. Thankfully, self-help bookshop **Transitions,** with its gurgling fountains and new-age soundtrack, is an oasis of calm amid the chaos. If that doesn't work, hit the free samples of wine down the street at **Sam's Wine and Liquor Warehouse**.

Some of Chicago's best shopping treasures are the unique little stores that anchor every neighborhood. From housewares shops in Chinatown, to Sari palaces on Devon, from academic bookshops in Hyde Park, to the West Side's **Harlem Irving Plaza**, Chicago offers the willing consumer plenty of opportunities to burn through their credit limits.

Map 1 • River North / Fulton Market District

Doolin's	511 N Halsted St	312-243-9424	Party decorations galore, closed Sundays.

Map 2 • Near North / River North

Jazz Record Mart	25 E Illinois St	312-222-1468	Jazz-lover's emporium.
Mary Wolf Gallery	705 Dearborn St	312-588-1478	Unusual oils, including lots of Chicago scenes.
Mig and Tig Furniture	540 N Wells St	312-644-8277	Classic well made furniture.
Montauk	401 N Wells St	312-951-5688	The most comfortable sofas.
Paper Source	232 W Chicago Ave	312-337-0798	Great paper and invitations.

Map 3 • Streeterville / Mag Mile

Apple Store	679 N Michigan Ave	312-981-4104	All of their newest and shiniest offerings, plus classes and seminars.
Chicago Place	700 N Michigan Ave	312-266-7710	Upscale mall.
Disney Store	717 N Michigan Ave	312-654-9208	M-I-C-K-E-Why?
Garrett Popcorn Shop	670 N Michigan Ave	312-944-4730	Everything you could possibly think of related to popcorn...
Neiman-Marcus	737 N Michigan Ave	312-642-5900	Affectionately known as "Needless Mark-up."
Niketown	669 N Michigan Ave	312-642-6363	Nike label sports clothing.
Tiffany & Co	730 N Michigan Ave	312-944-7500	Deluxe jeweler.
Virgin Megastore	540 N Michigan Ave	312-645-9300	Music, books, videos, DVDs.

Map 4 • West Loop Gate / Greek Town

Athenian Candle Co	300 S Halsted St	312-332-6988	Candles, curse-breakers, Greek trinkets and much more.
Greek Town Music	330 S Halsted St	312-263-6342	Music, T-shirts, hats—everything Greek!

Map 5 • The Loop

American Music World	111 N State St	312-786-9600	The place to go if you're looking to buy an instrument.
Carson Pirie Scott	1 S State St	312-641-7000	Department store.
Gallery 37 Store	66 E Randolph St	312-744-7274	Speciality gifts.
Jeweler's Mall	7 S Wabash Ave	312-460-9117	Jewelry that sparkles.
Marshall Field's	111 N State St	312-781-1000	Department store.
Rock Records	175 W Washington St	312-346-3489	Good CD store.
Sears	2 N State St	312-373-6000	Blue-collar stalwart.

Map 6 • The Loop / Grant Park

Art & Artisans	108 S Michigan Ave	312-641-0088	Art gallery.
Museum Shop of the Art Institute	111 S Michigan Ave	888-301-9612	Art Institute gift shop.
Poster Plus	200 S Michigan Ave	800-659-1905	Vintage posters and custom framing.
Precious Possessions	28 N Michigan Ave	312-726-8118	Mineral shop.
Rain Dog Books and Café	408 S Michigan Ave	312-922-1200	Awesome used books and geek-chic clientele.
The Savvy Traveller	310 S Michigan Ave	312-913-9800	Travel goods.

Map 7 • South Loop / River City

Fishman's Fabrics	1101 S Des Plaines St	312-922-7250	Huge fabric wholesaler.
Joseph Adam's Hats	544 W Roosevelt Rd	312-913-1855	Haberdashery and menswear.
Lee's Foreign Car Service	727 S Jefferson St	312-663-0823	Import parts and service.
Morris & Sons	555 W Roosevelt Rd	312-243-5635	Mostly men, off-price Italian designers.

Map 8 • South Loop / Printers Row / Dearborn Park

Kozy's Bike Shop	601 S La Salle St	312-360-0020	Bikes and accessories in a fun loft setting.
Printer's Row Fine and Rare Books	715 S Dearborn St	312-583-1800	Fine and rare books.
Sandmeyer's Book Store	714 S Dearborn St	312-922-2104	Dream come true if you love books and atmosphere.

Map 9 • South Loop / South Michigan Ave

Bariff Shop	618 S Michigan Ave	312-322-1740	Unique Hanukkah gifts.

Map 10 • East Pilsen / Chinatown

Chinatown Bazaar	2221 S Wentworth Ave	312-225-1088	Part clothing store, part knick-knack shop.
Pacific Imports	2200 S Wentworth Ave	312-808-0456	Mostly home furnishings.
Sun Sun Tong	2260 S Wentworth Ave	312-842-6398	Stock up on Chinese herbs and teas.
Ten Ren Tea & Ginseng Co	2247 S Wentworth Ave	312-842-1171	The only place to buy ginseng.
Woks 'n' Things	2234 S Wentworth Ave	312-842-0701	Stir-fry utensils and cookware.

Map 11 • South Loop / McCormick Place

Blossoms of Hawaii	1631 S Michigan Ave	312-922-0281	Florist.
Blue Star Auto Stores	2001 S State St	312-225-0717	All your auto needs.
Cycle Bicycle shop	1465 S Michigan Ave	312-987-1080	Bike shop, obviously.
Waterware	1829 S State St	312-225-4549	Designer plumbing fixtures.
Y'lonn Salon	1802 S Wabash Ave	312-225-9247	Beauty salon.

Map 12 • Bridgeport (West)

Bridgeport Antiques	2963 S Archer Ave	773-927-9070	Old stuff.

Map 13 • Bridgeport (East)

Accutek Printing & Graphics	260 W 26th St	312-808-9903	Printing and copying needs.
Ace Bakery	3200 S Halsted St	312-225-4973	Excellent breads and pastries.
Augustine's Spiritual Goods	3323 S Halsted St	773-843-1933	Mystical and religious knick-knacks.
Bridgeport News Travel & Tours	3252 S Halsted St	312-225-6311	Travel store.
Health King Enterprises Chinese Medicinals	238 W 31st St	312-567-9978	Natural remedies.
Let's Boogie Records & Tapes	3321 S Halsted St	773-254-0139	Music.

Map 14 • Prairie Shores / Lake Meadows

Ashley Stewart	3455 S Dr Martin L King Jr Dr	312-567-0405	Women's clothing.
Avenue	3409 S Dr Martin L King Jr Dr	312-808-1492	Modern plus-size clothes.

Map 16 • Bronzeville

Afrocentric Bookstore	4655 S King Dr	773-924-3966	The authority on Afrocentic literature.
Issues Barber & Beauty Salon	3958 S Cottage	773-924-4247	Beauty salon.
Parker House Sausage Co	4601 S State St	773-538-1112	All types of sausages.

Map 17 • Kenwood

Coop's Records	1350 E 47th St	773-538-5277	Music.
South Shore Decor	1328 E 47th St	773-373-3116	Wall coverings, paint, blinds, and window treatments galore.

Map 19 • Hyde Park

57th Street Books	1301 E 57th St	773-684-1300	Brainy, independent bookstore.
Akente Express II	5210 S Harper Ave	773-288-7130	Afrocentric gift shop.
The Baby PhD Store	5225-I S Harper Ave	773-684-8920	For the smart kid.
Border's Books and Music	1539 E 53rd St	773-752-8663	Check out the outside patio.
Coconuts	1506 E 53rd St	773-667-2455	Mainstream music anyone?
Cohn & Stern For Men	1500 E 55th St	773-752-8100	Men's accessories.
Dr Wax Records and Tapes	5225-D S Harper Ave	773-493-8696	Old-style vinyl.
Futons N More	1370 E 53rd St	773-324-7083	Futons 'n more.
House of Africa	1352 E 53rd St	773-324-6858	Afrocentric everything.
Hyde Park Records	1377 E 53rd St	773-288-6588	Buy/sell vintage LPs.
O'Gara and Wilson	1448 E 57th St	773-363-0993	Rare and out-of-print books.
Powell's Bookstore	1501 E 57th St	773-955-7780	Famous bookstore.
Toys Et Cetera	5211-A S Harper Ave	773-324-6039	Just for fun.
Wesley's Shoe Corral	1506 E 55th St	773-667-7463	Shoes.
Wheels and Things	5210-E S Harper Ave	773-493-4326	Bike sales and repairs.

Map 20 • East Hyde Park / Jackson Park

Art's Cycle Sales & Service	1636 E 55th St	773-363-7524	Bike sales and repairs.

Map 21 • Wicker Park / Ukrainian Village

American Apparel	1563 N Milwaukee Ave	773- 235-6778	Sweatshop-free clothes Wicker Park boutique.
Asian Essence	2121 W Division St	773-782-9500	Homewares with an Asian flavor.
Asrai Garden	1935 W North Ave	773-782-0680	Flowers and garden.
Casa de Soul	1919 W Division St	773-252-2520	Asian/African-inspired global lifestyle boutique for men and women.
Cattails	1935 W Division St	773-486-1621	A unique flower market.
City Soles/Niche	2001 W North Ave	773-489-2001	Up to $600 a pop for the latest European soles.
DeciBel Audio	1407 N Milwaukee Ave	773-862-6700	New and used stereo equipment.
House of Monsters	1579 N Milwaukee Ave, Gallery 218	773-292-0980	A ghoulish gallery and morbid merchandise shop of doom.
Lille	1923 W North Ave	773-342-0563	Great little things for the home.
Modern Times	1538 N Milwaukee Ave	773- 772-8871	Vintage mid-century modern funishings.
Myopic Bookstore	1564 N Milwaukee Ave	773-862-4882	A Wicker Park brainy-hipster institution.
Nina	1655 W Division St	773-486-8996	Yarn shop includes delicate, frayed thread from old saris.
Noir	1726 W Division St	773-290-6919	Upscale/modern clothing for women.
Noir-Men	1740 W Division St	773-489-1957	Upscale/modern clothing for men.
Orange Skin	1429 N Milwaukee Ave	773- 394-4500	Objects of desire and high design.
Paper Doll	1747 W Division St	773-227-6950	Paper and cards.
Penelope's	1913 W Division St	773-395-2351	Casual, stylish women's clothes.
Porte Rouge	1911 W Division St	773-269-2800	Fancy French housewares & free tea.
Quimby's Bookstore	1854 W North Ave	773-342-0910	Books and music.
Ragstock	1433 N Milwaukee Ave	773-486-1783	Funky vintage clothes and trendy irregulars.
Reckless Records	1532 N Milwaukee Ave	773-235-3727	Mostly indie music—new and used.

The Silver Room	1410 N Milwaukee Ave	773-278-7130	Clothing and accessories.
Stinkerbelle	1951 W Division St	773-252-4120	chichi beauty boutique for the ladies.
Symmetry	1925 W Division St	773-645-0502	Upscale/modern furniture and décor featuring Tibetan rugs.
Una Mae's Freak Boutique	1422 N Milwaukee Ave	773.276.7002	A Wicker Park staple—vintage and New clothing.
Untitled	1941 W North Ave	773- 342-0500	Uber-hipster clothing.
Wag Artworks	2121 W Division St	773-772-2922	Gallery featuring wall art, jewelry, and various other forms of artwork.

Map 22 • Noble Square / Goose Island

Best Buy	1000 W North Ave	312-988-4067	Electronics & home appliances monolith.
Cost Plus World Market	1623 N Sheffield Ave	312-587-8037	Like Pier One, but with food & wine.
Dusty Groove Records	1120 N Ashland Ave	773-342-5800	Vinyl and CDs. Specializes in funk, soul, rare groove, now sound, and world music.
Expo Design Center	1500 N Dayton St	312-694-2400	Big furniture and home-design place.
Irv's Luggage Warehouse	820 W North Ave	312-787-4787	Carries some discounted luggage and briefcases.
Nocturnal Dominion	913 N Ashland Ave	773-782-9097	One stop Goth shopping.
Old Navy	1569 N Kingsbury	312-397-0485	Inexpensive, semi-trendy fashion chain.
Olga's Flower Shop	1041 N Ashland Ave	773-645-9160	Flowers for all occasions.
Restoration Hardware	938 W North Ave	312-475-9116	Fancy housewares.
Right-On Futon	1184 N Milwaukee Ave	773-235-2533	Need a new bed? Check this place out!
Transitions Bookplace	1000 W North Ave	312-951-7323	Books on spirituality, health, etc. Has a café.
Wax Addict Records	1014 N Ashland Ave	773-772-9930	Popular with deejays and other wax addicts.

Map 23 • West Town / Near West Side

Alcala's	1733 W Chicago Ave	312-226-0152	Western-wear emporium sells boots, jeans and cowboy hats.
Decoro Studio	2000 W Carroll St	312-850-9260	Lot filled with Asian antiques and furniture.
Donofrio's Double Corona Cigars	2058 W Chicago Ave	773-342-7820	Brian Donofrio sells very fine imported cigars.
H&R Sports	1741 W Chicago Ave	312-226-8737	Soccer gear.
Rotofugi	1953 W Chicago Ave	312- 491-9501	Really cool toy store with urban vinyl figures.
Salvage One Architectural Artifacts	1840 W Hubbard St	312-733-0098	Warehouse of antique, vintage and salvaged architectural pieces for home/loft restoration.
Sprout Home	745 N Damen Ave	312-226-5950	Plants and gardening supplies meet modernism.
Tomato Tattoo	1855 W Chicago Ave	312-226-6660	Every hip strip needs a tattoo parlor.

Map 24 • River West / West Town

3 Design Three	1431 W Chicago Ave	312-738-0333	Funky furniture with style, open by appointment.
Aesthetic Eye	1520 W Chicago Ave	312-243-1520	Art gallery, irregular hours.
Casati	949 W Fulton Market	312-421-9905	Mid-century Italian furniture and accessories.
Design Inc	1359 W Grand Ave	312-243-4333	Architecturally centered home design.
Douglas Dawson Gallery	400 N Morgan St	312-226-7975	Fancy artifacts from around the world.
Jan's Antiques	225 N Racine Ave	312-563-0275	Mind-boggling antinque emporium.
PakMail	1461 W Chicago Ave	312-664-2866	Packing supplies, FedEx, UPS.
Pet Care Plus	1212 W Grand Ave	312-397-9077	For the pet-obsessed.
The Realm	1430 W Chicago Ave	312-491-0999	Exotic furniture from far-away places.
Roots	1140 W Grand Ave	312-666-6466	Trendy hair salon.
RR#1 Chicago Apothecary	814 N Ashland Blvd	312-421-9079	Old school pharmacy.
Snap	470 N Ogden Ave	312-226-5110	Hair and nail salon.
Spiced	1162 W Grand	312-850-1940	Health spa, spray tan.
Upgrade Cycle Works	1130 W Chicago Ave	312-226-8650	Bikes, accessories and servicing.
X/S Salon	1433a W Chicago Ave	312-492-8490	Cozy hair salon.
Xyloform	1423 W Chicago Ave	312-455-7949	Furniture store.

Map 26 • University Village / Little Italy / Pilsen

Scafuri Bakery	1337 W Taylor St	312-733-8881	The secret's in the bread.

Map 27 • Logan Square

MegaMall	2502 N Milwaukee Ave	773-489-2525	Tube socks, sunglasses, gold necklaces… one-stop shopping!
Threads, Etc	2327 N Milwaukee Ave	773-276-6411	Resale clothes and furniture.

Map 28 • Bucktown

Bleeker Street Antiques	1946 N Leavitt St	773-862-3185	Fine selection of antiques.
G Boutique	2131 N Damen Ave	773-235-1234	Lingerie and bedroom accessories.
Goddess and the Grocer	1646 N Damen	773-342-3200	Gourmet groceries and take-out.
Jean Alan	2134 N Damen Ave	773-278-2345	House and home.
Jolie Joli	1623 N Damen Ave	773-342-7272	Clothing and accessories.
Mark Shale Outlet	2593 N Elston Ave	773-772-9600	Great deals on grown-up clothes.
Pagoda Red	1714 N Damen Ave	773-235-1188	House and home.
Pavilion Antiques	2055 N Damen Ave	773-645-0924	Antique furniture.
Red Balloon Company	2060 N Damen Ave	773-489-9800	A unique store for children—toys, clothes and furniture.
T-Shirt Deli	1739 N Damen Ave	773-276-6266	Pricey—but quality—custom-made T-shirts.
Viva La Femme	2115 N Damen Ave	773-772-7429	Style beyond size.
Yardifacts	1864 N Damen Ave	773-342-9273	Flowers and garden.

Map 29 • DePaul / Wrightwood / Sheffield

Active Endeavors	853 W Armitage Ave	773-281-8100	Playing sports or heading into the great outdoors, this is your place for gear.
Isabella Fine Lingerie	1127 W Webster Ave	773-281-2352	Fine after-hours wear.
Jayson Home & Garden	1885 N Clybourn Ave	773-248-8180	Flowers and garden.
Sam's Wine and Liquor Warehouse	1720 N Marcey St	312-664-4394	Great selection, accessories, classes and free samples.
SOLEPassion	1745 N Clybourn Ave	312-202-9992	Shoes.
Tabula Tua	1015 W Armitage Ave	773-525-3500	Housewares.
Uncle Dan's	2440 N Lincoln Ave	773-477-1918	One-stop shopping for survivalists.
Vosges Haut Chocolat	951 W Armitage Ave	773-293-9866	Delicious exotic gourmet chocolates flavored with Indian spices, whiskey, etc.
Wine Discount Center	1826 1/2 N Elston Ave	773-489-3454	Wine warehouse—free tastings every Saturday.

Map 30 • Lincoln Park

Art & Science	1971 N Halsted St	312-787-4247	Beauty salon.
Cynthia Rowley	808 W Armitage Ave	773-528-6160	Apparel and accessories.
Ethan Allen	1700 N Halsted St	312-573-2500	Furniture store.
Gallery 1756	1756 N Sedgwick St	312-642-6900	Fine art.
GNC	2740 N Clark St	773-327-6585	General nutrition center.
Lori's Designer Shoes	824 W Armitage Ave	773-281-5655	Designer shoes.
Sally Beauty Supply	2727 N Clark St	773-477-6222	Wholesale for stylists. License ID needed.
Triangle Gallery of Old Town	1763 N North Park Ave	312-337-1938	Don't miss their openings.

Map 31 • Old Town / Near North

Crate & Barrel Outlet Store	1864 N Clybourn Ave	312-787-4775	Housewares.
Etre	1361 N Wells St	312-266-8101	Upscale boutique.
Fleet Feet Sports	210 W North Ave	312-587-3338	The staff watches you run to make sure the shoes fit.
Fudge Pot	1532 N Wells St	312-943-1777	A chocolate institution.
Jumbalia	1427 N Wells St	312-335-9082	Great gift store.
Old Town Gardens	1555 N Wells St	312-266-6300	Beautiful plants and flowers.
The Spice House	1512 N Wells St	312-274-0378	Spice up your cooking.
Village Cycle	1337 N Wells St	312-751-2488	Good urban cycling store.

Map 32 • Gold Coast / Mag Mile

Anthropologie	1120 N State St	312-255-1848	Hip clothing and knick-knacks.
Barney's New York	25 E Oak St	312-587-1700	Upscale boutique, clothing and accessories.
BCBG	55 E Oak St	312-787-7395	Apparel and accessories.

Bloomingdale's	900 N Michigan Ave	312-440-4460	Upscale department store.
Bravco Beauty Center	43 E Oak St	312-943-4305	For those who like to be pampered.
Chanel at the Drake Hotel	935 N Michigan Ave	312-787-5000	Classic, expensive clothing, accessories and fragrances.
Elements	102 E Oak St	312-642-6574	Cool housey stuff.
Europa Books	832 N State St	312-335-9677	International magazines.
Fitigues Surplus	939 N Rush St	312-943-8676	Outlet store of women's designer gear.
Frette	41 E Oak St	312-649-3744	European furniture and accessories.
G'bani	949 N State St	312-440-1718	Shoes.
Gucci	900 N Michigan Ave	312-664-5504	Tom Ford's alluring and provocative clothes and accessories.
H&M	840 N Michigan Ave	312-640-0060	European department store taking Chicago by storm.
Hermes	110 E Oak St	312-787-8175	Fancy scarves and more.
Lord & Taylor	835 N Michigan Ave	312-787-7400	You'd have to be a lord to shop here.
MAC	40 E Oak St	312-951-7310	Fabulous make-up.
Nicole Miller	63 E Oak St	312-664-3532	Female fashion.
Paul Stuart X/S	875 N Michigan Ave	312-640-2650	Located on the second floor, one of only two Paul Stuart outlets in the world. So far.
Portico	48 E Walton St	312-475-1307	Homewares.
Prada	30 E Oak St	312-951-1113	Expensive, but delightful clothing and accessories.
Pratesi	67 E Oak St	312-943-8422	Linens.
Tod's	121 E Oak St	312-943-0070	Clothing.
Ultimate Bride	106 E Oak St	312-337-6300	Bridal gear.
Ultimo	114 E Oak St	312-787-1171	Apparel and accessories.
Urban Outfitters	935 N Rush St	312-640-1919	Retro clothing, nifty gifts and cool accessories.
Water Tower	845 N Michigan Ave	312-440-3165	Marshall Fields.

Map 33 • West Rogers Park

Cheesecakes by JR	2841 W Howard St	773-465-6733	Over 20 flavors of cheesecakes.
Chicago Harley Davidson	6868 N Western Ave	773-338-6868	Hogs, gear, etc.
Dilshad	2645 W Devon Ave	773-761-5740	Eyebrow threading and henna tattoos.
Office Mart	2801 W Touhy Ave	773-262-3924	Combination office supply store and an Internet coffee shop.
Taj Sari Palace	2553 W Devon Ave	773-338-0177	Beautiful Indian clothing and accessories.

Map 34 • East Rogers Park

Mar-Jen Discount Furniture	1536 W Devon Ave	773-338-6636	Cheap futons, dorm furniture.

Map 37 • Edgewater / Andersonville

Alamo Shoes	5321 N Clark St	773-334-6100	Large selection for the soles from local retailer.
Atelier Asia	1477 W Balmoral Ave	773-275-3001	Antique asian furniture.
Bon Bon	5410 N Clark St	773-784-9882	Sweet handmade chocolate boutique.
Brown Elephant	5228 N Clark St	773-271-9382	Resale shop benefits local hiv clinic.
Cassona	5241 N Clark St	773-506-7882	Gorgeous home furnishings.
Early to Bed	5232 N Sheridan Rd	773-271-1219	Woman-oriented grown-up toys. Boy-friendly.
Elda de la Rosa	5407 N Clark St	773-769-3128	Custom gowns and dresses.
Erickson Jewelers	5304 N Clark St	773-275-2010	Large selection of jewelry.
Gethsemane Garden Center	5739 N Clark St	773-878-5915	Flowers and garden.
Johnny Sprocket's	1052 W Bryn Mawr	773-293-1695	Caters to all your bicycle needs.
Paper Trail	5309 N Clark St	773-275-2191	Paper and cards.
Presence	5216 N Clark St	773-989-4420	Cool boutique for young women.
Scout	5221 N Clark St	773-275-5700	Beautiful urban antiques.
Surrender	5225 N Clark St	773-784-4455	Health and beauty.
Toys & Treasures	5311 N Clark St	773-769-5311	Educational toys and quality books for kids.
White Attic	5408 N Clark St	773-907-9800	Clean home furnishings and art work.
Women & Children First	5233 N Clark St	773-769-9299	World's biggest feminist book and music store.

Map 38 • Ravenswood / Albany Park

Lincoln Antique Mall	3115 W Irving Park Rd	773-604-4700	Mid-sized antique mall.
The Music Store	3121 W Irving Park Rd	773-478-7400	Guitars and other musical instruments.

Map 38 • Ravenswood / Albany Park—*continued*

Odin Tatu	3313 W Irving Park Rd	773-442-8288	Get inked.
Rave Sports	3346 W Lawrence	773-588-7176	Athletic shoes and clothing.
Sassy Boutique	3210 W Lawrence	773-539-1738	Cute partywear for 20-somethings. (Sign on store inexplicably reads "Tomato.")
Scents & Sensibility	4654 N Rockwell St	773-267-3838	Cards. And things to put your cards and candles and flowers into.

Map 39 • Ravenswood / North Center

Architectural Artifacts	4325 N Ravenswood Ave	773-348-0622	Renovator's dream.
The Book Cellar	4736-37 N Lincoln Ave	773-293-2665	Book store/coffee shop/wine bar. Also has sandwiches.
The Cheese Stands Alone	4547 N Western Ave	773-293-3870	Artisinal cheeses from Europe and America in this delightfully stinky shop.
The Chopping Block	4747 N Lincoln Ave	773-472-6700	Gourmet cooking utensils and cooking classes.
Delicatessen Meyer	4750 N Lincoln Ave	773-561-3377	German delicatessen, excellent sausage, German wines & beers, etc.
Different Strummer	4544 N Lincoln Ave	773-751-3398	Guitars and such.
East Meets West	2118 W Lawrence Ave	773-275-1976	Asian Indian and Buddhist religious supplies.
European Import Center	4752 N Lincoln Ave	773-561-8281	Beer steins and other gifts from Bavaria.
Gallimaufry Gallery	4712 N Lincoln Ave	773-728-3600	Artisan crafts including instruments, incense, stone fountains.
Glass Art & Decorative Studio	4507 N Lincoln Ave	773-561-9008	Stained glass and gifts.
Griffins & Gargoyles Antiques	2140 W Lawrence Ave	773-769-1255	Pine furniture from Europe.
Laurie's Planet of Sound	4639 N Lincoln Ave	773-271-3569	Funky CD shop.
Martin's Big & Tall Store for Men	4745 N Lincoln Ave	773-784-5853	Store for big and tall men.
Merz Apothecary	4716 N Lincoln Ave	773-989-0900	German and other imported toiletries, herbal supplements, etc. The original; there is a branch on the first floor of the State Street Field's.
Nbahri Rhythms	4726 N Lincoln Ave	773-878-2575	Musical instruments from Africa and the Middle East.
Play It Again Sports	2102 W Irving Park Rd	773-463-9900	Sporting goods.
Quake Collectables	4628 N Lincoln Ave	773-878-4288	Vintage toys and fun!
Timeless Toys	4749 N Lincoln Ave	773-334-4445	Old fashioned toys.

Map 40 • Uptown

Arcadia Knitting	1613 W Lawrence Ave	773-293-1211	Knitting store.
Eagle Leathers	5005 N Clark St	773-728-7228	Come to daddy.
Shake Rattle and Read Book Box	4812 N Broadway St	773-334-5311	Funky used bookstore, great finds, but cluttered.
Tai Nam Market Center	4925 N Broadway St	773-275-5666	Vietnamese. Very good.
Wilson Broadway Mall	1114 W Wilson Ave	773-561-0300	Socks, shoes, ethnic shopping, music, luggage—it's all here.

Map 42 • North Center / Roscoe Village / West Lakeview

Antique Resources	1741 W Belmont Ave	773-871-4242	Large inventory of antique furniture.
Father Time Antiques	2108 W Belmont Ave	773-880-5599	Antiques store.
Glam to Go	2002 W Roscoe St	773-525-7004	Girly-girls get pampered.
Good Old Days Antiques	2138 W Belmont Ave	773-472-8837	Antiques and treasures.
Lynn's Hallmark	3353 N Lincoln Ave	773-281-8108	Cards, stationary, and gift wrap.
My Closet	3350 N Paulina St	773-388-9851	Marked-down designer wear from Bloomingdale's and Macy's.
Sam & Willy's	3405 N Paulina St	773-404-0400	Pet store.

Map 43 • Wrigleyville/ East Lakeview

Alley	3228 N Clark	773-883-1800	Skulls, tattoos, big boots.
Bookworks	3444 N Clark St	773-871-5318	Friendly, well-organized used books.
Hollywood Mirror	812 W Belmont	773-404-2044	Vintage clothes and kitschy doo-dads.
Midwest Pro Stereo	1613 W Belmont Ave	773-975-4250	DJ equipment, fog machines, strobe lights.
Namascar	3946 N Southport Ave	773-472-0930	Yoga accessories.

Ragstock	Belmont Ave & Dayton St, 2nd Fl	773-868-9263	Vintage resale and trendy off-price clothes.
Strange Cargo	3448 N Clark St	773-327-8090	Hip affordable threads for the 20-somethings.
Uncle Fun	1338 W Belmont Ave	773-477-8223	Cramped and crazy retro toys and novelties.

Map 44 • East Lakeview

The Brown Elephant Resale	3651 N Halsted St	773-549-5943	Resale boutique benefits Howard Brown Health Clinic.
Century Mall	2828 N Clark St	773-929-8100	Most notable occupants include the cinema and Bally's Fitness.
Equinox	3401 N Broadway St	773-281-9151	Gifts and glassware—great X-mas ornament selection.
GayMart	3457 N Halsted St	773-929-4272	Gay Barbie and other homo kitsch and gifts.
The Pleasure Chest	3155 N Broadway St	773-525-7151	Sextastic adult store.
Unabridged Bookstore	3251 N Broadway St	773-883-9119	Helpful bookstore with great travel, kids and gay sections.

Maps 45-48 • Northwest Chicago

Albany Office Supply	3419 W Lawrence Ave	773-267-6000	A substantial portion of the store is devoted to Hello Kitty. Some other stuff too, but who cares about that?
American Science & Surplus	5316 N Milwaukee Ave	773-763-0313	Your one-stop obscure gizmo shop.
Chicago Produce	3500 W Lawrence Ave	773-478-4325	Fresh produce stand with a full service butcher shop and deli.
El Mundo del Dulce (Candy World)	4806 N Drake Ave	773-866-0659	Candy for children, pinatas, party supplies.
Harlem Irving Plaza	N Harlem Ave & W Irving Park Blvd	773-625-3036	Every tacky, low-end, wholesale-to-public you could ever want.
NY Shoes Imports	3546 W Lawrence Ave	773-509-9903	Has slightly fetishistic edge, interesting lingerie in back.
Perfumes 'R' Us	3608 W Lawrence Ave	773-463-9575	Well-known name brand perfumes including Nina Ricci, Chanel, DKNY, etc., discounted and wholesale.
Rolling Stone Records	7300 W Irving Park Rd	708-456-0861	The place to rock, with lots of big-haired in-store appearances.
Srpska Tradicija	3615 W Lawrence Ave	773-588-7372	Music, books, religious icons and gifts from Serbia and Montenegro.
Sweden Shop	3304 W Foster Ave	773-478-0327	Gifts from Scandinavia.

Maps 53-56 • Southwest Chicago

African American Images Bookstore	1909 W 95th St	773-445-0322	Books, art, & jewelry with an African American theme.
Bev Art Brewer and Winemaker Supply	10033 S Western Ave	773-233-7579	One stop source for bootleggers.
Beverly Records	11612 S Western Ave	773-779-0066	Flip through actual vinyl here. Remember that stuff?
Calabria Imports	1905 W 103rd St	773-396-5800	Italian deli foodstuffs.
Ford City Shopping Center	7601 S Cicero Ave	773-725-8248	One-stop shopping for everyone on the Southwest Side and Suburbs. Multiplex cinema shows all their blockbusters.
Grich Antiques	10857 S Western Ave	773-233-8734	Furniture, housewares, and vintage electronics.
Izzy Rizzy's House of Tricks	6356 S Pulaski Rd	773-735-7370	Where to get your whoopie cushions, hand-buzzers, and fake puke.
Ms Priss	9915 S Walden Pkwy	773-233-7747	Clubby young woman's fashion haven.
Optimo Hat	10215 S Western Ave	773-238-2999	Custom-made men's hats.
Reading on Walden	9913 S Walden Pkwy	773-233-7633	Hidden neighborhood bookstore right off the Metro Rock Island line.
World Folk Music	1808 W 103rd St	773-779-7059	Weird instruments and lessons on such for kids and adults.

Maps 57-60 • South Chicago

Underground Afrocentric Bookstore	1727 E 87th St	773-768-8869	New and used books of African-American interest.

If you live in Chicago, you know a few things for sure: hot dogs should have sweet relish, pickles, tomato, onion, sport peppers, and yellow mustard; the Cubs always lose; deep-dish is the best kind of pizza; and Chicago is a *theater* town. You can't swing Mrs. O'Leary's cow without hitting a tiny, struggling off-Loop storefront theater. The storefront theaters are so prevalent here that the city's Department of Cultural Affairs, in its effort to bring smaller productions to the newly revitalized "theater district" (more on that later), named its new downtown venue after them (**Storefront Theater**).

A recent count of theaters at Chicago's theater newspaper, *PerformInk*, listed nearly 200 theaters on its links page, in addition to 30 or so improvisational theater troupes. Large theaters producing traveling shows, off-Loop theaters producing original plays of all stripes, improvisational shows at all hours of the night—you name it, Chicago has it.

General Tips

The Theater section of the *Chicago Reader*, a free weekly available citywide in bookstores, cafés, bars, and in boxes on street corners (or online at www.chicagoreader.com) is the best friend of the Chicago theatergoer-in-the-know. Turn to the Short List, look for "Highly Recommended" status, or search for Critic's Choices to ferret out your best bets. Another source is the *New City*'s "Top Five Shows to See Now" list. Look for free copies of *New City* in the same places as the *Reader*. Hottix (www.hottix.org), a program of the League of Chicago Theaters, offers half-price tickets to same-day shows on a first-come-first-served basis. Also, if you are new in town and want to break into the biz, drop by any theater in your 'hood and pick up a copy of *PerformInk*, the Chicago trade paper for theater and the performing arts, or check 'em out online at www.performink.com.

Let's get this out of the way. If you want to see a big, traveling Broadway show, check out www.broadwayinc hicago.com. There you can find the listings for **Cadillac Palace Theatre**, **Ford Center for the Performing Arts/ Oriental Theatre**, the **LaSalle Bank Theatre**, or the beautiful and historic **Auditorium Theatre** (designed by Louis Sullivan). But Chicago, my friends, offers so much more than just second runs…

Downtown Theaters aka "The Downtown Theater District"

There are many large theaters producing quality work in downtown Chicago. One of the oldest theaters in Chicago, **The Goodman Theatre** is a stalwart of the downtown theater scene. Now in its new location at 170 North Dearborn, the Goodman is a professional theater featuring high quality plays by well-known and lesser-known playwrights. One of the classic Chicago theaters, **Steppenwolf Theatre Co.** produces wonderful ensemble productions with notable Chicago actors. Among their famous ensemble members are John Mahoney, John Malkovitch, Laurie Metcalf, Martha Plimpton, and Gary Sinise. Similarly, **Lookingglass Theatre** (known for ensemble member David Schwimmer of *Friends* fame) creates productions with an artistic ensemble. Their new location (in Chicago's Water Tower Water Works building, one of the few structures to survive the famous 1871 Chicago fire) is well worth a trip downtown. Known as a playwright's theater, **Victory Gardens Theater** produces original works by contemporary, living playwrights. Also worth mentioning in this category, though they run at neighborhood theaters, are the Chicago production of the *Blue Man Group* (**Briar Street Theatre**); **Chicago Shakespeare Theater** on Navy Pier, offering pricey but elegant productions of the Bard's classics; and *Tony n' Tina's Wedding* (www.tonyntina.com). The latter offers up a live dinner theater event at Piper's Alley, replete with a re-enactment of the wedding reception of a loud, dysfunctional Italian family.

Medium-Sized Neighborhood Theaters

Really amazing productions can be found at medium-sized neighborhood theaters. Some of the best picks include the longest running show in Chicago today, *Too Much Light Makes the Baby Go Blind* (at **The Neo-Futurarium**). Proclaiming to perform thirty plays in sixty minutes, the show ends when one or the other is over. Other good bets include **Stage Left Theatre** (political plays), **Live Bait Theater** (first-run plays), **About Face Theatre** (high-quality gay/lesbian/bisexual works), theater company Famous Door Theatre (original and "seldom-produced" works), **Redmoon Theater** (highly unique large-scale puppetry productions), and **Teatro Luna** (Chicago's only all-Latina performance troupe).

Improv

Chicago is also well known for its improv scene. The original, **The Second City** (the famed training ground for most of *Saturday Night Live*'s original cast) keeps on going with its many shows at four venues in Chicago. Check out www.secondcity.com for show times. Other improv venues include **The Playground Theater**, **ImprovOlympic Theater** (with its free Friday and Saturday midnight "Cage Match"), **Annoyance Theatre**, **Comedy Sportz,** and theater company WNEP Theater. Most of these venues feature improv teams battling against one another for audience approval. Information about all venues can be found on www.improvchicago.com.

Fringe/Performance Art/Other

Two very different organizations are solely devoted to the presentation of large performance art events in Chicago. They are the (rather large) **Museum of Contemporary Art** (www.mcachicago.org) and the (much smaller) **Performing Arts Chicago** (www.pachicago.org). Performing Arts Chicago presents the PAC/Edge Festival of performance every March, representing some of Chicago's quirkiest talent. Both organizations present some of the finest in local, national, and international performance art.

But if you don't catch the bigger shows (read: more expensive) at the MCA or PAC, some of Chicago's best productions occur in alternative spaces. They are created by smaller companies who don't have a venue (whether by choice or by size). These are the tiny, glittering gems of the Chicago "theater" scene. Find these productions in the Performance Listings in the *Reader*. Don't shy away from a theater company you've never heard of producing at a rented venue. This is very common in Chicago and these productions are often worth the trip. We can't list them all here (for they are too numerous), but here are some of our favorites.

For girl-on-girl combat action, check out *Babes with Blades* (www.babeswithblades.com) in semi-regular productions at various venues. 500 Clown (www.500clown.com) produces loose adaptations of classic tales (Frankenstein, MacBeth) in original, dangerous clown theater that the authors wouldn't recognize. *Defiant Theatre* (www.defianttheatre.org) subverts the social, moral, and aesthetic expectations of the theater with edgy productions at varied venues. Roadworks Productions (www.roadworks.org) is an outpost for gripping plays by new and overlooked playwrights. Collaboraction (known mainly for its *Sketchbook* series) is a collective comprising cross-disciplinary artists presenting short unique works in all media. Drawing from diverse sources, Goat Island Performance Ensemble (www.goatislandperformance.org) offers up heady movement-based performance created in a lengthy ensemble process. *Plasticene* (www.plasticene.com) confronts audiences with rare physical theater. In the summer, look for remounts of favorite local productions at **Theater on the Lake** (www.chicagoparkdistrict.com), a screened-in theater venue situated near Fullerton Avenue on Chicago's lakefront. Curious Theater Branch (curioustheaterbranch.org) has presented original, engaging theater for the last eleven years. **Bailiwick Repertory Theatre** offers up the hit *Naked Boys Singing*, which is pretty much what it sounds like. And finally, the truly horrifying **American Girl Place** offers up *Circle of Friends: An American Girl Doll Musical* inside the American Girl Doll Store. This is not a recommendation for the discerning theatergoer; however if you want to witness the indoctrination of small girls in American capitalist culture, look no further.

Theater	*Address*	*Phone*	*Map*
A Red Orchid Theatre	1531 N Wells St	312-943-8722	31
About Face Theatre	1222 W Wilson Ave	773-784-8565	44
The Actor's Workshop Theater	1044 W Bryn Mawr Ave	773-728-7529	37
American Girl Place	111 E Chicago Ave	877-247-5223	2
Angel Island Theater	731 W Sheridan Rd	773-871-0442	44
Annoyance Theatre	4840 N Broadway St	773-929-6200	43
Apollo Theater Chicago	2540 N Lincoln Ave	773-935-6100	29
Arie Crown Theatre	2301 S Lake Shore Dr	312-791-6190	11
Athenaeum Theatre	2936 N Southport Ave	773-935-6860	43
Auditorium Theatre	50 E Congress Pkwy	312-922-2110 x0	5
Bailiwick Repertory Theatre	1229 W Belmont Ave	773-883-1090	43
Beverly Arts Center of Chicago	2407 W 111th St	773-445-3838	56
Billy Goat Experiment Theatre Company	5917 N Broadway St	773-250-3331	37
Boxer Rebellion Theater	1257 W Loyola Ave	773-465-7325	34
Breadline Theatre	1802 W Berenice Ave	773-327-6096	42
Briar Street Theatre	3133 N Halsted St	773-348-4000	44
Cadillac Palace Theatre	151 W Randolph St	312-977-1700	5
Casa Aztlan	1831 S Racine Ave	312-666-5508	26
Chase Park Theater	4701 N Ashland Ave	312-742-7518	40
Chicago Center for the Performing Arts	777 N Green St	312-327-2000	1
Chicago Dramatists	1105 W Chicago Ave	312-633-0630	24
Chicago Shakespeare Theater	800 E Grand Ave	312-595-5600	3
The Chicago Theatre	175 N State St	312-462-6300	5
Chicago Theater Co (Parkway Community House)	500 E 67th St	773-493-5360	57
Chopin Theater	1543 W Division St	773-278-1500	22
City Lit Theater Co	1020 W Bryn Mawr Ave	773-293-3682	37
Civic Opera House	20 N Wacker Dr	312-332-2244	5

Theater	*Address*	*Phone*	*Map*
Comedy Sportz	2851 N Halsted St	773-549-8080	44
Cornservatory	4210 N Lincoln Ave	312-409-6435	39
Court Theatre	5535 S Ellis Ave	773-753-4472	19
Dance Center of Columbia College	1306 S Michigan Ave	312-344-8300	11
Drury Lane Theatre at Water Tower Place	175 E Chestnut St	312-642-2000	32
Duncan YMCA Chernin Center for the Arts	1001 W Roosevelt Rd	312-738-5887	26
Ford Center for the Performing Arts/ Oriental Theatre	24 W Randolph St	312-782-2004	5
Free Street Theater	1419 W Blackhawk St	773-772-7248	22
Getz Theater (Columbia College)	62 E 11th St	312-663-1124	8
Greenview Arts Center	6418 N Greenview Ave	773-508-0085	34
The Goodman Theatre	170 N Dearborn St	312-443-3800	5
Griffin Theatre Co	5404 N Clark St	773-769-2228	37
Harris Theater for Music and Dance	205 E Randolph St	312-334-7777	5
His Way Theatre (NBC Tower)	454 N Columbus Dr	312-222-1188	3
ImprovOlympic Theater	3541 N Clark St	773-880-0199	43
Ivanhoe Theater	750 W Wellington Ave	312-335-8499	44
Kathleen Mullady Memorial Theatre	1125 W Loyola Ave	773-508-3847	34
Lakeshore Theatre	3175 N Broadway St	773-472-3492	44
Lifeline Theatre	6912 N Glenwood Ave	773-761-4477	34
Links Hall Studio	3435 N Sheffield Ave	773-281-0824	43
Live Bait Theater	3914 N Clark St	773-871-1212	43
Lookingglass Theatre	821 N Michigan Ave	312-337-0665	43
Loop Theater	8 E Randolph St	312-744-5667	5
Lunar Cabaret	2827 N Lincoln Ave	773-327-6666	43
Mercury Theater	3745 N Southport Ave	773-325-1700	43
Merle Reskin Theatre	60 E Balbo Ave	312-922-1999	8
Methadome Theatre	4437 N Broadway St	773-769-2959	40
Museum of Contemporary Art	220 E Chicago Ave	312-280-2660	3
National Pastime Theater	4139 N Broadway St	773-327-7077	40
The Neo-Futurarium	5153 N Ashland Ave	773-275-5255	37
Northeastern Illinois University Auditorium	5500 N St Louis Ave	773-794-6652	46
O'Malley Theater-Roosevelt University	430 S Michigan Ave	312-341-3719	6
O'Rourke Center for the Performing Arts	1145 W Wilson Ave	773-878-9761	40
Pegasus Players	1145 W Wilson Ave	773-878-9761	40
The Playground Theater	3209 N Halsted St	773-871-3793	42
Profiles Theatre	4147 N Broadway St	773-549-1815	40
Prop Theatre	3504 N Elston Ave	773-539-7838	39
Puppet Parlor	1922 W Montrose Ave	773-774-2919	39
Raven Theatre	6157 N Clark St	773-338-2177	33
Red Hen Productions	5123 N Clark St	773-728-0599	40
Redmoon Theater Co	1438 W Kinzie St	312-850-8440	43
Royal George Theatre Center	1641 N Halsted St	312-988-9000	30
Ruth Page Center Theater	1016 N Dearborn St	312-337-6543	32
Second City	1616 N Wells St	312-337-3992	31
Second City etc/Second City Skybox	1608 N Wells St	312-337-3992	31
The Side Studio	1520 W Jarvis Ave	773-973-2105	34
Stage Left Theatre	3408 N Sheffield Ave	773-883-8830	43
Steep Theatre	3902 N Sheridan Rd	312-458-0722	43
Steppenwolf Theatre Co	1650 N Halsted St	312-335-1650	30
Storefront Theater	66 E Randolph St	312-742-8497	5
Strawdog Theatre	3829 N Broadway St	773-528-9696	44
Teatro Luna	556 W 18th St	312-829-7552	10
Theater on the Lake	2400 N Lake Shore Dr	312-742-7994	30
Theatre Building	1225 W Belmont Ave	773-327-5252	43
TimeLine Theatre Co	615 W Wellington Ave	773-281-8463	44
TinFish Theatre	4247 N Lincoln Ave	773-549-1888	39
Trap Door Productions	1655 W Cortland St	773-384-0494	28
UIC Theatre	1044 W Harrison St	312-996-2939	26
Viaduct Theater	3111 N Western Ave	773-296-6024	42
Vittum Theater	1012 N Noble St	773-871-3000	22
Wing & Groove Theatre	1935 W North Ave	773-782-9416	21

Essential Numbers

General

All emergencies **911**
AIDS Hotline 800-342-AIDS
Animal Anti-Cruelty Society.......... 312-644-8338
Chicago Dental Referral Service 312-836-7305
Chicago Department of Housing.......... 773-285-5800
City of Chicago Board of Elections.......... 312-269-7900
Dog License (City Clerk).......... 312-744-6875
Driver's Licenses.......... 312-793-1010
Emergency Services 312-747-7247
Employment Discrimination 312-744-7584
Gas Leaks 312-240-7000
Income Tax (Illinois).......... 800-732-8866
Income Tax (Federal).......... 800-829-3676
Legal Assistance.......... 312-332-1624
Mayor's Office 312-744-4000
Parking (City Stickers).......... 312-742-9200
Parking Ticket Inquiries 312-744-7275
Report Crime in Your Neighborhood 312-372-0101
Passports.......... 312-341-6020
Police Assistance (non-emergency) 311
Social Security.......... 773-890-2492
Streets and Sanitation 312-744-5000
Telephone Repair Service 888-611-4466
Voter Information 312-269-7900
Water Main Leaks.......... 312-744-7038

Helplines

Alcoholics Anonymous 312-346-1475
Alcohol, Drug and Abuse Helpline 800-234-0420
Alcoholism and Substance Abuse 312-988-7900
Domestic Violence Hotline.......... 800-799-7233
Drug Care, St. Elizabeth's.......... 773-278-5015
Gamblers Anonymous.......... 312-346-1588
Illinois Child Abuse Hotline 800-252-2873
Narcotics Anonymous 708-848-4884
Parental Stress Services.......... 312-372-7368
Runaway Switchboard.......... 800-621-4000
Sexual Assault Hotline 888-293-2080
United Way Community Information
and Referral 312-876-0010
Violence – Anti-Violence Project.......... 773-871-CARE

Complaints

Better Business Bureau of Chicago 312-832-0500
Consumer Fraud Division (Attorney General's Office).......... 312-814-3000
Chicago Department of Consumer Services 312-744-9400
Citizen's Utility Board 800-669-5556
Department of Housing Inspection Complaints.......... 312-747-9000
Mayor's Office 312-744-4000
Postal Service Complaints.......... 312-983-8400

darkroom

2210 west chicago avenue 773•276•1411

www.darkroombar.com

HOT PROPERTY®
RESIDENTIAL BROKERAGE

IS NOW EVEN HOTTER

BE HOT! WHY NOT?

IF IT'S EXPOSURE you're looking for, turn to the most highly regarded real estate agent agency in Chicago — **HOT PROPERTY.**® Hot Property's® willingness to expose your property every week until it's sold will make your **PROPERTY HOT!** Call Hot Property® for your free market analysis and get ready to be **HOT!** For current listings or more information about Hot Property® visit www.hotpropertyonline.com.

HOT PROPERTY®
RESIDENTIAL BROKERAGE

773.868.6700

Independently owned and operated by **CKS PARTNERS, LLC**

HOT PROPERTY® IS NOW OPEN AT **2754 NORTH CLYBOURN** IN CHICAGO!
WWW.HOTPROPERTYONLINE.COM

PALM PROPERTIES

REAL ESTATE BROKERAGE

Your Winning Team
in Real Estate

If you're looking to buy or sell real estate in Chicagoland, don't just hire an agent, **hire a team.**

1726 W. BELMONT AVE.
CHICAGO, IL 60657

Contact:
Sandra Palm or Nikki Rinkus
Phone: 773-472-PALM (7256)
Fax: 773-472-5202

Residential & Commericial Real Estate Sales

Apartment Leasing

Attorney Services

Mortgage Services

Appraisal Services

Relocation Services

TMD THE MORTGAGE DEPARTMENT INC.

Refinancing • Purchases • Cast-Out • Debt Consolidation
Bruised Credit • Jumbo Mortgages • Self-Employed
Can't Prove Income / No Doc Loans
Second Mortgages & Equity Lines
Investment Property • Commercial

FAST APPROVALS

Illinois Residential Mortgage Licensee

2720 S. River Rd., Suite 140 Des Plaines

THE MORTGAGE DEPARTMENT INC.

NOT FOR TOURISTS™ Guidebooks

Your ad here

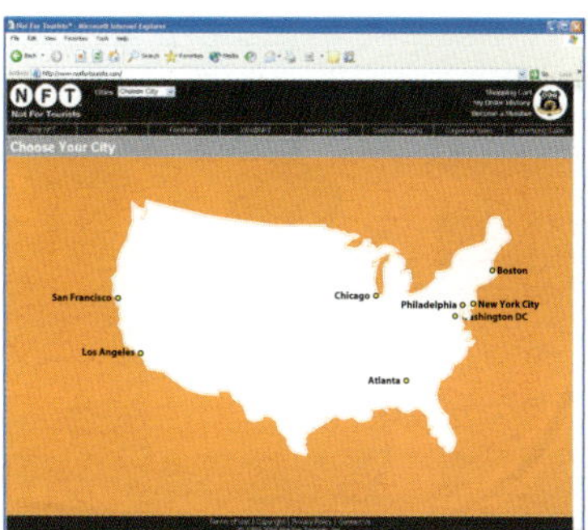

or here.

We offer half- and full-page advertising options inside each of the **Not For Tourists™** Guidebooks, including multi-city packages for national companies and organizations, as well as space on our website. Advertising in **NFT™** means that the city dwellers who rely on our indispensable guidebooks everyday will literally have your business information right at their fingertips wherever they go. Come on. Everybody's doing it.

For a media kit and space rates, call 212 965 8650 x223 or email us at advertising@notfortourists.com

RELOAD
BAGGAGE
custom handmade
MESSENGER BAGS
+
ACCESSORIES
+
rare
BIKES
PARTS
+
CLOTHING
608 N 2ND STREET
PHILADELPHIA
215. 922. 2018
RELOADBAGS.COM
RE
LOAD

Street Index

Some of the townships and communities immediately adjoining Chicago proper thought it would be a fun joke to restart street numbering at their borders—or name a street exactly the same name as an entirely unrelated Chicago street. These cases are designated with an asterisk.*

Street Index

Street Index

A

Street Index

B

C

Street Index

D

E

H

I

L

N

O

P

S

T

U

V

Y

NOT FOR TOURISTS™ Custom Books

Customize your NFT.

We can put your organization's logo or message on **NFT** using custom foil stamps of your (or our) design. **Not For Tourists Guidebooks** make great gifts for employees, clients, and promotional events.

For more informaion, call us at 212 965 8650, or visit www.notfortourists.com/corporate

Not For Tourists™ **www.notfortourists.com**

New York City • Brooklyn • Los Angeles • Chicago • San Francisco • Boston • Washington DC • Atlanta • Philadelphia